D1453236

OLD TESTAMENT STUDIES

Edited by

David J. Reimer

OLD TESTAMENT STUDIES

The mid-twentieth century was a period of great confidence in the study of the Hebrew Bible: many historical and literary questions appeared to be settled, and a constructive theological programme was well underway. Now, at the beginning of a new century, the picture is very different. Conflicting positions are taken on historical issues; scholars disagree not only on how to pose the questions, but also on what to admit as evidence. Sharply divergent methods are used in ever more popular literary studies of the Bible. Theological ferment persists, but is the Bible's theological vision coherent, or otherwise?

The Old Testament Studies series provides an outlet for thoughtful debate in the fundamental areas of biblical history, theology and literature. Cyril Rodd's comprehensive study of Old Testament ethics probes especially the problematic relationship in relating these three facets to modern moral questions. Given that the Old Testament is often invoked in contemporary ethical debate, Rodd attempts to identify more closely the nature of the bible's contribution on a wide range of issues. Rodd's many years of writing on and teaching Old Testament ethics inform this substantial study.

GLIMPSES OF A STRANGE LAND

GLIMPSES OF A STRANGE LAND

Studies in Old Testament Ethics

Cyril S. Rodd

T&T CLARK
EDINBURGH

T&T CLARK
A Continuum imprint
The Tower Building
11 York Road
London
SE1 7NX
www.tandtclark.co.uk
www.continuumbooks.com

First published 2001

ISBN 0 567 08753 0

British Library Cataloguing-in-Publication Data
A catalogue record for this book is available from the British Library

Printed and bound in Great Britain by Bookcraft Ltd, Avon

CONTENTS

PREFACE

This book has taken a life-time to write. I first had an interest in Old Testament ethics when I was appointed lecturer in Old Testament Language and Literature at the Methodist Handsworth College in Birmingham in 1956. At that time ethics was a non-subject, and Norman Snaith warned me off it, saying that there was no future in it. I wrote an article on motivation in the prophets, which two journals rejected – and I became despondent. My interest remained, nevertheless, and in 1971 Leslie C. Mitton accepted an article on Genesis 18.25 for *The Expository Times*. It was only when I was given a free hand to introduce the subject into the curriculum at Roehampton Institute in the 1980s that I was able to pick up the interest again. By then, of course, Old Testament scholars had rediscovered ethics and my concern with the subject did not seem so odd. Nevertheless, my early experiences made me hesitant about working up my lectures into a book, and it was only the repeated urging of my students that made me begin to think of doing so. For this nudging, and the keen interest in what they complained was the most difficult of all the modules they had to do in their degree course, I remain grateful. My gratitude to two Old Testament scholars can never be adequately expressed. First, Richard Coggins tried to convince me that what I was doing was worthwhile. To him I also owe the further immense debt for working meticulously over my draft manuscript and making many most valuable suggestions. Secondly, David Reimer not only suggested that my book might be included in the series he was editing, but also gave the encouragement of showing considerable enthusiasm for it. Finally, I cannot possibly omit expressing my deep thanks to a friend from my Cambridge days, G. W. S. Knowles, who worked through the draft, pointing out infelicities of expression and asking for greater clarity on many pages. He has also acted as a reader of the proofs and checked the Index.

To my wife I owe more than I can ever tell. Despite her firm conviction that too many books are written (which is probably true), she has borne with my adding to their number without complaint.

A Note on the Biblical Quotations.

I spent a considerable time thinking about which translation to use in the quotations. My preference would have been for the RV, since it is closest to the Hebrew, and, although archaic, enables singular and plural second person forms to be identified. In the end I decided that this might seem hopelessly old-fashioned, especially as the version is no longer in print, so I chose the RSV. Many will raise objections to what is commonly now rejected as a patriarchal or androcentric translation, preferring the more inclusive language of the NRSV, REB, or NJB. My choice, therefore, needs to be defended.

What is overlooked in favouring an inclusive language translation is the fact that if masculine forms of verbs and possessives in English foster a patriarchal attitude (as they almost certainly do), precisely the same thing operated in ancient Israel. It is therefore an error to remove masculine forms where we suppose they should include women as well as men.[1] To recover something of the feel which the Hebrew must have had, it is necessary to go back at least fifty years – to the period before the rise of the modern feminist movement, when it was accepted that 'the masculine embraces the feminine' and married women were designated by the 'Christian' name of their husbands.[2] The right conclusion to be drawn from this is that, if using masculine forms promotes strong support for patriarchal attitudes in English, this also prevailed in the Old Testament – even more so, since second person verbs, pronouns and suffixes possess masculine and feminine forms.

The difficulty with adopting a translation which does not use inclusive language and reproduces the genders of the Hebrew is that in our modern culture, where 'man' no longer possesses the meaning of 'human being' as well as male man that it once had, the patriarchal aspect comes across in an exaggerated way. Nevertheless, I believe that to retain the masculine forms introduces less distortion than to follow the inclusive language versions.

The biblical references follow the Hebrew verses, and where the English numbering differs this is added in brackets.

---

[1] I am fully aware that my 'should' is ambiguous. On the one hand it refers to the fact that sometimes in the Hebrew Old Testament, masculine forms refer to both men and women, while on the other it points to a modern understanding of the equality of women and men. One of the most extreme examples of the second is the NJB translation of the commandment: 'You shall not set your heart on your neighbour's spouse', where the context shows that only men are being addressed. The same version attempts to make the sages in Proverbs address both sons and daughters, where again the context shows that the advice only makes sense when given to sons.

[2] This was actually required in making nominations in my own church!

Additional Note

Two important books and a new series reached me only after the present study was in proof. I have been unable, therefore, to incorporate their insights into the text, although I have added a few footnote references. The books are: *Double Standards in Isaiah: Reevaluating Prophetic Ethics and Divine Justice* by Andrew Davies (E. J. Brill, 2000), and *The Material Culture of the Bible: An Introduction* by Ferdinand E. Deist, edited with a preface by Robert P. Carroll (Sheffield Academic Press, 2000). I have reviewed both books in *ET* 112, 2000–01, 73–77.

The first two volumes in the series The Earth Bible are: Norman C. Habel, ed., *Readings*, and Norman C. Habel and Shirley Wurst, eds., *Earth Story*. It is noteworthy that the aim is to discuss 'how the Bible has played, and may continue to play, a role in the current ecological crisis' (*Readings*, 9), and to 'read the Bible from the perspective of Earth' (*Earth Story*, 9). The editors note the 'tendency among ecotheologians and ecoexegetes, willy-nilly, to find a way to retrieve a positive message about Earth in the text', and they accept that the Bible is 'likely to be anthropocentric'. The intention in the series is to explore whether particular ecological principles are affirmed or negated. Keith Carley's 'Psalm 8' may be singled out as an example of negation. Note also Habel's comments on 'ruling' in Genesis 1.26–28 and Ps 72.8.

ABBREVIATIONS

AB	The Anchor Bible (Doubleday).
ABD	*The Anchor Bible Dictionary*, eds. Freedman, David Noel, Herion, Gary A., Graf, David F. and Pleins, John David (Doubleday, 1992).
ANET	*Ancient Near Eastern Texts Relating to the Old Testament*, ed. Pritchard, James B. (Princeton University Press, 1950, 1969).
BA	*Biblical Archeologist.*
BDB	*A Hebrew and English Lexicon of the Old Testament with an Appendix Containing the Biblical Aramaic*, eds. Brown, Francis, Driver, S. R. and Briggs, Charles A., (Clarendon Press, corrected impression 1952).
BJRULM	*Bulletin of the John Rylands University Library Manchester*, formerly *Bulletin of the John Rylands Library [BJRL].*
BRev	*Bible Review.*
BTB	*Biblical Theology Bulletin.*
BWANT	Beiträge zur Wissenschaft vom Alten und Neuen Testament.
BZAW	*Beihefte zur Zeitschrift für die alttestamentliche Wissenschaft.*
CB	*Coniectanea Biblica.*
CBC	The Cambridge Bible Commentary on the New English Bible.
CBQ	*Catholic Biblical Quarterly.*
DBI	*A Dictionary of Biblical Interpretation*, eds. Coggins, Richard J. and Houlden, J. L. (SCM Press, 1990).
DBI, A–J	*Dictionary of Biblical Interpretation*, ed. Hayes, John H., Vol. 1 (Abingdon Press, 1999).
DBI, K–Z	*Dictionary of Biblical Interpretation*, ed. Hayes, John H., Vol. 2 (Abingdon Press, 1999).
DCE	*A Dictionary of Christian Ethics*, ed. Macquarrie, John (SCM Press, 1967).
DCH	*The Dictionary of Classical Hebrew*, ed. Clines, David J. A., exec. ed. Elwolde, John (Sheffield Academic Press, 1993–).

ET	*Expository Times.*
EvQ	*Evangelical Quarterly: An International Review of Bible and Theology.*
EvT	*Evangelische Theologie*
FOTL	The Forms of the Old Testament Literature.
HALOT	*The Hebrew and Aramaic Lexicon of the Old Testament,* eds. Koehler, Ludwig and Baumgartner, Walter, revised by Baumgartner, Walter and Stamm, Johann Jakob, trans. and ed. under the supervision of Richardson, M. E. J. (4 vols., E. J. Brill, 1994–).
HAT	Handbuch zum Alten Testament.
HBT	*Horizons in Biblical Theology.*
HDB 1963	*Hastings' Dictionary of the Bible,* ed. Hastings, James, rev. edn. eds. Grant, Frederick C. and Rowley, H. H. (T&T Clark, 1963).
HTR	*Harvard Theological Review.*
HUCA	*Hebrew Union College Annual.*
ICC	The International Critical Commentary on the Holy Scriptures of the Old and New Testaments.
IDBSup	*The Interpreter's Dictionary of the Bible,* Supplementary Volume, ed. Crim, Keith (Abingdon Press, 1976).
JAAR	*Journal of the American Academy of Religion.*
JBL	*Journal of Biblical Literature.*
JETS	*Journal of the Evangelical Theological Society.*
JJS	*Journal of Jewish Studies.*
JLA	*Jewish Law Annual.*
JNES	*Journal of Near Eastern Studies.*
JRelEthics	*Journal of Religious Ethics.*
JSNTSup	Journal for the Study of the New Testament Supplement Series.
JSOT	*Journal for the Study of the Old Testament.*
JSOTSup	Journal for the Study of the Old Testament Supplement Series.
JTS	*Journal of Theological Studies.*
JTSoA	*Journal of Theology for Southern Africa.*
LTJ	*Lutheran Theological Journal.*
NCBC	The New Century Bible Commentary.
NDCE	*A New Dictionary of Christian Ethics,* eds. Macquarrie, John and Childress, James (SCM Press, 1986).
NDCEPT	*New Dictionary of Christian Ethics and Pastoral Theology,* eds. Atkinson, David J. and Field, David H. (IVP, 1995).

NDT	*New Dictionary of Theology*, eds. Ferguson, Sinclair B. and Wright, David F. (IVP, 1988).
NERT	*Near Eastern Religious Texts Relating to the Old Testament*, ed. Beyerlin, Walter (SCM Press, 1978).
NIB	*The New Interpreter's Bible*, eds. Keck, Leander E. *et al.* (12 vols., Abingdon Press, 1994–).
NIBC	New International Biblical Commentary.
NICOT	The New International Commentary on the Old Testament.
NRT	*Nouvelle Revue Theologique.*
OBC	*The Oxford Bible Commentary*, eds. Barton, John and Muddiman, John (OUP, 2001).
OBO	Orbis Biblicus et Orientalis.
OBT	Overtures to Biblical Theology.
OTE	*Old Testament Ethics*
OTL	Old Testament Library.
OTS	*Oudtestamentische Studien.*
PEQ	*Palestine Exploration Quarterly.*
PRS	*Perspectives in Religious Studies*
PSB	*Princeton Seminary Bulletin.*
RB	*Revue Biblique.*
RevExp	*Review and Expositor.*
SBLDiss	Society of Biblical Literature Dissertations Series.
SBT	Studies in Biblical Theology.
SJTh	*Scottish Journal of Theology*
SOTS	Society for Old Testament Study.
TBC	The Torch Bible Commentaries.
TDOT	*Theological Dictionary of the Old Testament*, eds. Botterweck, G. Johannes and Ringgren, Helmer, trans. Willis, John T. (Eerdmans, 1974–).
TS	*Theological Studies.*
TynB	*Tyndale Bulletin.*
USQR	*Union Seminary Quarterly Review.*
VT	*Vetus Testamentum.*
VTSup	*Supplements to Vetus Testamentum.*
WBC	Word Biblical Commentary.
ZAW	*Zeitschrift für die alttestamentliche Wissenschaft.*
ZEE	*Zeitschrift für Evangelische Ethik*

1

WHY ONLY GLIMPSES?

A major problem in writing about Old Testament ethics[1] is to know where to begin. An obvious place might seem to be the Ten Commandments. After all, they are the best known ethical statements in the whole Bible and are generally regarded as central to the Old Testament morality. They have also been accorded very great importance in later Christian thought. In many churches they used to be written in a prominent position, often alongside the Lord's Prayer. They were prominent in catechisms taught to the young. Even in our modern secular society it is common to hear politicians urging a return to the morality of the Ten Commandments. As we shall see, however, this pre-eminence is not fully justified.

An alternative to starting with what is thought by many today to be the heart of the Old Testament's own morality might be to pick up ethical issues which are seen as urgent in the modern world. Thus we might consider the place of women in society, or attitudes to war, or the way animals were treated, or ecological issues. This approach would have the advantage of being topical and arousing immediate interest. It might, also, throw up features of Old Testament ethics which are often overlooked. Whether it is fair to impose modern interests upon ancient Israel, however, is very doubtful. To select moral dilemmas which trouble us might well distort the ethical thought of the Old Testament itself.

In his study of Old Testament ethics[2] John Barton begins by noting features which present moral difficulties to us – laying down the death penalty for adultery (Lev. 20.10; Deut. 22.22), accepting mutilation as a punishment (Ex. 21.23–24; Lev. 24.19–20; Deut. 19.21), forbidding

---

[1] The term 'ethics' presents considerable problems, both grammatical and with regard to the meaning. I have tried to restrict the meaning of 'ethics' to the philosophical study of the principles of morality and to those principles themselves, using 'morals' for the actual practice of morality, and avoiding 'ethic' (in the singular) as being irretrievably ambiguous. Following Fowler-Gowers, I normally use a singular verb with 'ethics' where it refers to the science, but allow a plural in some of the more general uses, according to the context (*Modern English Usage*, 170–171, 260).

[2] John Barton, *Ethics*. The topics mentioned are found on pp. 1–3. Despite his disclaimer, Barton still has a tendency to concentrate on those features of Old Testament ethics of which we can approve today.

interest on loans (Deut. 23.19), the approval of the massacre of the inhabitants of whole cities during the conquest of Canaan (Josh. 6; 11). His aim is to stress the difficulty in establishing the relevance of Old Testament ethics for life today and to avoid the charge of explaining away the 'blemishes' in the Bible by limiting his discussion to the more attractive features. It is right that these difficulties should be recognized, but it is doubtful whether this is the best place to start. The difficulties are of different kinds and are best treated in their contexts. Moreover, those who accept the Old Testament as scripture usually hold that the offending ethical stances must be explained away, justified, or ignored, and this easily leads to a distortion of the Old Testament morality itself.

Most scholars who write monographs on Old Testament ethics attempt to discover a pattern lying behind the ethics and begin their studies by tracing this out. Three recent works show this clearly.

C. J. H. Wright divides his study between the Framework and Themes. In the first part he sets out the principles which lie behind the individual laws and exhortations, and he finds these in what he terms 'the ethical triangle', which has God, Israel and the Land at its vertices, or, as he expresses it in another way, the theological, social and economic angles.[3] This emphasizes Wright's conviction that theology and ethics are inseparable. Creation, election and covenant are the dominant features in this understanding of Old Testament ethics. Having set out the framework, Wright proceeds to examine six themes: economics and the land, politics and the world of nations, righteousness and justice, law and the legal system, society and culture, and the way of the individual. Using 'paradigm' in the way it is used in grammars, as a model which exemplifies the way other verbs or nouns of a similar type are formed, he suggests that ethics are not so much to be imitated as to be applied to similar situations in our own day.

Similarly Walter C. Kaiser, Jr. begins with a discussion of 'Definition and Method'.[4] He contrasts Old Testament ethics with philosophical ethics, describing its ethics as personal, theistic, internal, future oriented and universal, and then proposes a 'comprehensive' approach which combines synchronic, diachronic, and central theme approaches together with exegetical studies of particular texts. In the main body of the book he expounds the ethics

---

[3] Christopher J. H. Wright, *People of God*, see pp. 19–20. The ideas are developed in chs. 1–3.
[4] Walter C. Kaiser, Jr., *Ethics*. Although Kaiser initially recognizes the diversity of genres and times of writing of the various parts of the Old Testament he is so constrained by his conservative theological position that the diversity largely drops away in the later discussion The effect is to present an extremely 'flat' picture of the Old Testament.

first according to the various collections of laws (Decalogue, Book of the Covenant, Law of Holiness, and Law of Deuteronomy) and then by topics, concluding with a discussion of moral difficulties and New Testament applications.

Waldemar Janzen's primary purpose is to help Christians to appropriate the guidance provided by the Old Testament for their ethics and this to some extent controls his approach.[5] He argues that it is better to begin with the genre of story than with that of law, since this is the main way in which the biblical faith was transmitted. On the basis of what might appear as the somewhat unpromising stories in Genesis 13, Numbers 25, 1 Samuel 25, 1 Samuel 24 and 1 Kings 21, he uncovers five paradigms of the good life, which he terms the familial, priestly, wisdom, royal, and prophetic. The first of these is dominant, with the other four paradigms providing supporting models, while within the familial paradigm three 'dimensions' are found: life in community, the possessing of land, and the giving of hospitality. The great virtue of this work is that, in striking contrast to Kaiser, it keeps the liveliness of the Old Testament itself always before the reader. To start with the stories is an excellent way in. The ethical paradigms arise naturally from the stories. Moreover the qualifications to many of his assertions, which Janzen makes in the extensive notes at the end of each chapter, show that he is aware of the many facets that the ethics present. But he does not go far enough in giving place to the diversity of the material within the Old Testament.

Apart from the dominance of the attempt to show the relevance of Old Testament ethics for Christians in the modern world in most of these works, the presentation of the ethics within a systematic frame distorts the ethics themselves. All ethics, apart possibly from those deliberately formulated by philosophers, contain inconsistencies, illogical inferences, variations, and differences of emphasis and application. If, therefore, Old Testament ethics is to be viewed as a living reality these features must not be concealed under a general principle or abstract pattern. Aspects which chime in with modern sensitivities must not be allowed a prominence which they lacked in Israelite society.

Often when we visit a mediaeval castle we climb a spiral staircase to the top of the keep. For most of the time we are surrounded by blank walls, but as we clamber up we pass slit windows through which we obtain glimpses of the countryside that surrounds the castle. The view is narrowly restricted and we often find it difficult to imagine what the whole panorama looks like.

In the present study I have deliberately rejected an overall scheme, model, paradigm, dominant theme, underlying principle, or any other

[5] Waldemar Janzen, *Ethics*.

attempt to discover a unifying motif by means of which the ethics can be packaged. The chapters are distinct, and are best understood as the windows through which glimpses of occasional features of Old Testament ethics may be obtained.[6]

Even so, uncertainty remains. What is the country that we are viewing? Is it the 'real world' of Israelite society, or no more than pictures on the glass which fills the window? The doubt is profound, for all we possess are the texts that make up the Hebrew Bible and some remains discovered by archaeology, largely non-epigraphic. If, as many scholars now think, the texts were written in the Persian period (I hesitate to say after the Exile, since whether the Exile is historical fact or ideology is now very much a hotly debated question),[7] the relation between the writings and the life and history of ancient Israel is uncertain. As we peer out of the windows we shall never know whether the glimpses we obtain are of 'ancient Israel' or Israel as later priests and scribes wished us to think of it. Ideas, beliefs and morals are far more elusive than material culture, more obscure even than historical events, as we shall discover. While I refer to dates from time to time, and attempt to distinguish between the several different layers of ethics (actual practice in ancient Israel, the norms and values of the Israelites, and the morality and ethics revealed in the biblical texts, both in their final form and possible earlier stages of development), I accept that any such distinctions are highly dubious, and in general I have simply taken the 'final form' of the texts.[8]

I hope that what is lacking in systematic organization may be more than counterbalanced by liveliness and the odd moment of insight.

[6] It will be seen that I have made little attempt to deal systematically with the question of methodology. This is largely because I believe that discussing method in theoretical terms can impose blinkers on our view of the Old Testament itself. A central conviction running through the whole of this study is that the only valid approach is to look long and seriously at the Old Testament as it is. *Semeia* 66 contained four articles on methodology: John Barton, 'Basis', Bruce C. Birch, 'Moral Agency', Eryl W. Davies, 'Ethics', and Robert R. Wilson, 'Sources and Methods'.

[7] See Richard J. Coggins, 'The Exile', and Lester L. Grabbe, ed., *Captivity*. In his most recent work Grabbe insists that the Fall of Jerusalem, the destruction of the temple, the loss of statehood and the incorporation of Judah in the great empires marked a watershed (*Judaic Religion*, 5–6).

[8] This does not mean that I subscribe to Brevard S. Childs's 'canonical' approach, which appears to me highly questionable. But I am also very doubtful about attempts to present an account of the historical development of the laws and the ethics, such as that of Frank Crüsemann (see my review of *The Torah*, *ET* 108, 1996–97, 321–322).

2

ETHICS AND PURITY

I take Leviticus 19 as my point of entry. Although it is generally regarded as part of the 'Holiness Code', which itself lies within the priestly writings in the Pentateuch, it stands apart as a distinct collection of laws.[1] Two features strike the reader. There are similarities with the Ten Commandments, especially in the earlier part of the chapter,[2] and it contains a very mixed collection of laws, ethical and ritual, with no obvious logical arrangement.

Among the more plainly ethical laws are the prohibitions of stealing, dealing falsely, lying, robbery and oppression (vv. 11, 13). Other laws stress social justice: not being partial in judgment (v. 15), avoiding slander (v. 16), using accurate measures of length and weight (vv. 35–36), and probably the demand not to swear by Yahweh's name falsely, if the context is the assembly of elders in the gate, which acted as the local law court (v. 12). More broadly, but still within the ethical sphere, are reverence to parents, with mother unusually placed before father (v. 3), paying the wages of the hired labourer each evening (v. 13), leaving gleanings for the poor and resident alien at the time of harvest (vv. 9–10), not cursing the deaf or putting a stumbling block before the blind (v. 14), showing respect to the aged (v. 32) – all perhaps summed up (in our minds, though not

---

[1] Most commentators accept this, although some divide it into two separate collections, vv. 1–18, 19–37, e.g., Erhard S. Gerstenberger, *Leviticus*, and others propose further subdivisions: e.g., Philip J. Budd, *Leviticus*, divides the chapter into six sections, vv. 1–10, 11–18, 19–25, 26–31, 32–34, 35–37; G. J. Wenham, *Leviticus*, and Walter C. Kaiser, Jr., 'Leviticus', take 'I am the Lord' as marking out paragraphs or subsections, arranged in three main sections, vv. 3–8 (or 10), 9 (or 11)–18, 19–37. It may well have had a pre-history. Commentators note the alternations of singular and plural address, and possible evidence of redactional additions to an original text; some discern a set of ten laws. This, however, is irrelevant to the present purpose. Whatever components may be traced, the present completed text marks the intention of the final redactor.

[2] Wenham asserts that 'all ten commandments are quoted or alluded to, and sometimes expounded or developed in a new way' (*Leviticus*, 264), and Kaiser regards them as 'the formative principle' underlying the chapter, which is 'a further reinforcement and a practical illustration' of the Decalogue ('Leviticus', 1131). As will be shown later, verbal similarities are not close and there is little reason to suppose there is any direct connection between Lev. 19 and the Ten Commandments.

very obviously in the ordering of the chapter) in the call to love both one's neighbour and the foreigner who has settled in an Israelite village and who is not to be wronged but rather treated as a native Israelite (vv. 17–18, 33–34). All in all it presents a picture of a civilized society.

At the other extreme, however, is the prohibition of mixed breeding of animals,[3] the sowing of fields with two kinds of seed, and the wearing of clothes made of two different materials (v. 19). Further prohibitions which seem to have little ethical significance oppose certain types of cutting of the hair and the beard, and tattooing (vv. 27–28), and the treatment of newly planted fruit trees, where the term 'uncircumcision' ('foreskin') is used of the first three years when the fruit is not to be eaten, and the fruit in the fourth year is holy (vv. 23–25). Mediums and wizards are not to be consulted, for to do so causes defilement (v. 31), and augury and witchcraft are not to be practised (v. 26). Moreover, while to forbid forcing one's daughter into prostitution might be regarded as within the sphere of ethics, this is described as profaning her and the motivation is in order to avoid letting the land fall into harlotry (v. 29). Keeping the sabbath, referred to twice in the chapter (vv. 3, 30) and the rejection of idols (v. 4) are familiar to us because of the Decalogue, but are nevertheless hardly within the sphere of ethical requirements. Laws which are equally matters of cultic practice are the requirements concerning the destruction of the meat left over on the third day after communion sacrifices (vv. 5–8) and the prohibition against eating flesh with the blood in it (v. 26). Finally it should be observed that the call to Israel to be holy because Yahweh is holy, which is the basis for describing Leviticus 17–26 as the Holiness Code, stands at the beginning of the chapter and asserts the aim of all the varied laws as maintaining this holiness, a term which attracts ethical connotations but which is not primarily within the semantic field of ethics.

How then is this failure of the compiler of the chapter to make any distinction between the different kinds of law to be explained? For it is clear that he treats them all as of equal validity and importance. The highest ethical ideas sit alongside what we would regard as the triviality of wearing a coat made of linen and wool.

The popular answer is that at the time ethics in Israel had not developed sufficiently for the distinction to be made between ritual and moral requirements. All the things in the chapter which are

---

[3] The presence of mules in ancient Israel (e.g., 2 Sam. 13.29; 18.9; Ps. 32.9) is curious. Was the law disregarded with horses and donkeys, or is it an indication that the law is a utopian priestly construction? Or were horses and donkeys regarded as the same species, so that interbreeding was not treated as a 'mixture'?

condemned were regarded as equally displeasing to God and therefore to be avoided.

This is true, but it hardly provides a completely satisfying explanation. For a clue to the thought underlying the compilation of laws in this chapter it is necessary to fasten on the demand for holiness set at the beginning. Essential to understanding the chapter is the call to be holy because God is holy and to do nothing to impair the holiness of his land and his people. It is less a matter of keeping God's laws simply because he commanded them and will punish those who break them, than that both actions which break ethical precepts and those which infringe cultic and ritual purity equally affect Israel's holiness.

There have been many important studies of holiness,[4] and it is not the intention here to add to these. No more than an outline of the central features that relate to the ethics of the Old Testament will be given before turning more directly to the question of purity.

Holiness in ancient Israel was not what it is to us, goodness with a veneer of piety. As we have seen, holiness was primarily linked to God. Indeed, it might almost be regarded as the 'godness' of God. Dominant in the concept was the idea which Rudolf Otto termed the *numinous* – that sense of terrifying mystery which at the same time attracts with an uncanny fascination.[5] In these days we have learnt to be cautious about filling out gaps in our knowledge of ancient Israel from anthropology,[6] and hesitate to transfer ideas of *mana* and *taboo* from Polynesian religion directly to ancient Israel. Yet it is fairly clear that holiness was more than a subjective feeling to the Israelite. The most helpful analogy today, perhaps, is atomic radiation, a physical force which is unseen yet powerful and potentially destructive. In the same way it was regarded as dangerous for the Israelite to come too close to the holy God. The high priest had to take special precautions when he entered the holy of holies on the day of atonement (Lev. 16.2–5, 12–13, 23–24). The destructive power of God's holiness is seen in the story of David's first attempt to bring the ark into Jerusalem. The oxen stumbled and Uzzah put out his hand to steady it. Because he touched holy things, even with a good intention, contact with its holiness killed him (2 Sam. 6.1–11).[7]

Underlying the laws in Leviticus 19 is the idea of God's holiness. Israel has to maintain its own holiness in order to live safely with the

---

[4] As well as the main Old Testament theologies, see John G. Gammie, *Holiness*.

[5] Rudolf Otto, *The Holy*.

[6] See John Rogerson, *Anthropology*.

[7] While holiness is a major concern of the priestly writings, it is not limited to these, and Gammie's study (n. 4) extends to the prophetic, wisdom, and apocalyptic writings.

holy God. To go against God's laws will bring upon the transgressor the destructive force of that holiness. Securing holiness in Israel requires both obedience to the ethical norms and upholding ritual purity. It might seem to us that impurity was treated as a 'sin', but the reverse is probably the case: to break ethical norms is a form of impurity and impairs the holiness of Israel before the holy God.

Closely linked with the idea of holiness is that of purity and pollution.[8] Two forms are found in the Old Testament: the natural uncleanness of certain animals, and the temporary impurity of certain physical conditions, such as following bodily emissions, skin diseases, and moulds on materials or buildings. Wenham notes that temporary uncleanness is regarded as more serious than that which is permanent.[9] Unclean animals do not pass on their uncleanness to others: they simply cannot be eaten. Temporary uncleanness, on the other hand, is contagious and requires cleansing rites.[10] There are various degrees of temporary uncleanness, persisting for differing lengths of time and requiring their own type of cleansing rites.

The lists of clean and unclean animals in Leviticus 11 and Deuteronomy 14 have puzzled readers from early times. Mary Douglas and Walter Houston discuss most of the explanations that have been offered.[11] Mary Douglas argues that the critical distinction is between what are 'proper' members of their class of animals and those creatures that seem to slip between the classes, since holiness contains the sense of wholeness. Houston classifies the theories under four heads: moral-symbolic, cultic, aesthetic, and hygienic, and offers some critical comment on most of them. In particular he rejects Mary Douglas's idea of the anomaly that does not fit into the distinct classes of animals. His own proposal is that the systematic classification of animals as clean and unclean for food developed at the sanctuaries and was based on those animals which were acceptable for sacrifice. The deeper roots of the distinction lay in the customs of an economy that was strongly pastoral. Only in our present texts was the distinction made absolute by becoming a demand for total abstinence from 'unclean' food as a mark of dedication to God.

---

[8] L. William Countryman, makes a sharp distinction between the two collections of purity law in Lev. 11–16 and 17–26, seeing the first as concerned primarily with those aspects of uncleanness that call for some rite of purification, and the second as calling on the people as a whole to cleanse itself by removing offenders (*Dirt*, 22–23).

[9] G. J. Wenham, *Leviticus*, 21. His whole discussion of 'Holiness' and 'Sacrifice' (pp. 18–29) is valuable.

[10] For its seriousness cf. Num. 19.11–13, where the failure to carry out the cleansing rite after touching a dead body defiles the tabernacle. Such a person is to be 'cut off from Israel' (a phrase denoting 'excommunication' or even execution).

[11] Mary Douglas, *Purity and Danger*, esp. 29–57 (she has modified this somewhat in *Leviticus*); Walter Houston, *Purity and Monotheism*, 68–123.

Whatever the origins and rationale of the laws concerning clean and unclean animals, the idea of lack of wholeness has been widely adopted to explain many of the temporary forms of uncleanness, such as the uncleanness of women when menstruating and after childbirth, and 'leprosy'.[12] In a similar way, although they are not 'unclean', the animals offered in most of the sacrifices must be 'whole', 'without blemish', as must men who become priests. The idea of lack of wholeness may be the reason why men who have tasks uncompleted are excused or disqualified from war.[13]

Mary Douglas has argued that in many societies a purity system exists alongside the system of ethics.[14] Pollution rules do not correspond closely with moral ones: some behaviour is clearly wrong and yet is not polluting, whereas some actions which are not very reprehensible cause pollution. She suggests four ways in which pollution can uphold a moral code: (1) when a situation is morally ill-defined, a pollution belief can provide a rule for determining whether an infraction has taken place; (2) in cases of conflicts between moral principles, pollution can provide a simple focus of concern; (3) when an action that is held to be morally wrong fails to provoke indignation, belief in the harmful consequences of pollution can increase its seriousness and so marshal public opinion on the side of right; and (4) when moral indignation is not reinforced by sanctions, belief in pollution can provide a deterrent to wrongdoers. She also points out that because pollution can be fairly easily cleansed through special rites, pollution beliefs can make reconciliation and forgiveness easier, especially when the cleansing rite includes confession. Besides stressing that the moral and purity systems are often poorly integrated, Mary Douglas provides evidence of the way pollution rules can take on a cultural life of their own, and once established may even provide grounds for breaking the moral code.

In the Old Testament there are few examples of the direct and explicit linking of ethics and purity. With regard to the moral laws of

---

[12] I use this term for ṣāraʿaṯ simply because no other adequate alternative has been suggested; cf. the vain attempts of modern translations: 'a contagious skin-disease' (NJB), 'an infectious skin disease' (NIV), 'a malignant skin-disease' (NEB), 'a virulent skin disease' (REB), 'a dreaded skin disease' (GNB). GNB is perhaps the best paraphrase, but it fails to convey the sense of uncleanness and ostracism from both God and human beings connoted by the biblical term and which the word 'leper' conveys to modern ears. The Hebrew noun does not refer to Hansen's disease. It is important to notice that it is not the fact of having the disease but the piebald appearance of the skin which marks the uncleanness. Someone whose skin is completely covered with the disease is *not* unclean (Lev. 13.13).

[13] Deut. 20.5–7; cf. 24.5, and see the discussion in Chapter 15 below.

[14] *Purity and Danger*, ch. 8. Her main examples are taken from the Nuer and Bemba people.

Leviticus 19.18, 35, Countryman states: 'These are not purity rules themselves, but are set in this context so that they will be reinforced by association with purity rules, taking advantage of the apparently automatic distaste or even disgust that dirt evokes.'[15] This is hardly a correct application of the insights that Mary Douglas has provided, for no direct link between morals and purity is made in the chapter. He is, however, on firmer ground when he points out that in Deuteronomy 25.13–16 those who act dishonestly by using unequal weights and measures are an 'abomination' (*tōʿēḇāh*) to Yahweh. Further, he notes that purity language is applied by Jeremiah, Ezekiel, and in Proverbs to ethical offences.[16]

Helmer Ringgren makes some useful distinctions.[17] He states: 'both sin and uncleanness can be viewed as expressions of the hostile reality that permeates life, attempting again and again to penetrate the sphere of what is divine and good. There is, so to speak, a sphere of evil and death that continually threatens man's life: it is called uncleanness, sin, chaos.' Thus there are two different concepts of sin, which he terms 'mechanistic', in which both deliberate and accidental violations of God's commandments create a 'sphere of evil' that results in punishment and suffering, and 'personal', when the individual knows that he or she has broken the law and accepts responsibility for it. This is helpful, providing that it is recognized that 'sin' is not limited to ethical wrongdoing. Nevertheless it is confusing to use the concept of responsibility as the means of distinguishing between mechanistic and personal 'sin'.

K. van der Toorn, on the other hand, describes the distinction between moral and cultic laws as between ethics and etiquette, 'the seemingly arbitrary rules of conduct to be observed in the intercourse with the gods'.[18] Although they appear to be irrational, the cultic laws set out what is pleasing to God, and since there is no higher standard than the pleasure of the gods, moral precepts are ultimately validated by the same idea. Some things that please God correspond to the human sense of justice, while others are to be respected simply out of consideration for the personal likes and dislikes of the gods.[19] This,

---

[15] Countryman, *Dirt*, 28.

[16] *Ibid.*; no references are given.

[17] Helmer Ringgren, *Israelite Religion*, 142–143. Ringgren repeats this in his article on *ṭāmē'* ('unclean', *TDOT* V, 332). In the same article G. André discusses idolatry and sin under 'Metaphorical Usage', listing a number of passages where uncleanness 'is equated explicitly with sin, transgression, and iniquity' (e.g., Lev. 16.16, 19; 22.9; Isa. 6.5; 64.5[6]; Lam. 1.8f.; 4.15; Ezek. 14.11; 18.6, 11, 15; 37.23; Zech. 13.1–2). The land is polluted by murder (Num. 35.33–34), while Gen. 34.27 speaks of 'defilement through unchastity' (*ibid.*, 338–340).

[18] K. van der Toorn, *Sin and Sanction*, 12.

[19] *Ibid.*, 27. Van der Toorn finds little difference in ethics between Israel and the countries of Mesopotamia, though huge differences in religion (p. 39).

however, does not greatly assist the attempt to determine the relation between the two systems.

To return to the term 'Abomination' (*tō'ēḇāh*). The word is applied in Leviticus to homosexuality (18.22; 20.13), but elsewhere is used generally of the offences (mainly sexual) which the writer ascribes to the previous inhabitants of the land (18.26, 27, 29, 30), and which are also said to pollute the land so that it vomited out its inhabitants. Deuteronomy equally speaks of the abominations of the nations (Deut. 18.9, 12; 20.18), but also uses the term of image worship and serving other gods (7.25, 26; 13.15 [14], 17.4; 27.15), Canaanite religious practices, especially burning their children to their gods (12.31), unclean animals (14.3), offering blemished animals in sacrifice (17.1), using the hire of a harlot to pay a vow (23.19[18]), transvestites (22.5), remarrying a wife who has been divorced (24.4), and dishonesty in weights and measures (25.16). Only the last is clearly ethical.

The usage in Jeremiah and Ezekiel is similar, as might be expected from their close links with deuteronomistic and priestly thought. The only specific moral references in Jeremiah are to stealing, murder, adultery, false swearing (as well as burning incense to Baal and going after other gods, Jer. 7.9–10), though some of the general references may possibly include ethical offences.[20] In Ezekiel the only example of what may be regarded as a moral fault is adultery (Ezek. 33.26), the other uses of the term being mainly general or related to uncleanness.[21]

Proverbs is quite distinct in using the term for a wide range of ethical wrongs, including false balances (Prov. 11.1; 20.10, 23), lying lips (12.22), 'perversity' (3.32; 11.20), acquitting the wicked and convicting the innocent (17.18); general wickedness (8.7; 13.19; 15.8, 9, 26; 16.12; 21.27; 29.27), the arrogant and scoffers (16.5; 24.9), and turning away from the law (28.9). In 6.16–19 a list of seven things which Yahweh hates and which are an abomination to him are haughty eyes, a lying tongue, hands that shed innocent blood, a heart that devises wicked plans, feet that make haste to run to evil, a false witness and a man who sows discord among brothers, while the man who has seven abominations in his heart is described as possessing hatred, dissembling with his lips and harbouring deceit in his heart, and the warning is against his false words (26.24–26). Although several of these proverbs speak of God's rejection of prayer and

[20] The other references are Jer. 2.7; 6.15; 8.12; 16.18; 32.34, 35; 44.4, 22.
[21] Ezek. 5.9, 11; 6.9, 11; 7.4, 8, 9, 20; 8.17; 9.4; 11.21; 14.6; 16.22, 36, 43, 47, 51; 18.24 (although the wider context includes such sins as robbery, murder, adultery, oppression, and righteous actions such as giving bread to the hungry); 33.26, 29; 36.31; 43.8; 44.6, 7, 13.

sacrifice by those who commit these abominations the underlying disposition is ethical rather than within the sphere of purity, and it seems probable that the sense of 'abomination' has changed. Perhaps overtones of uncleanness remain, but in the setting of Proverbs these hardly represent a living belief.[22]

All this makes it doubtful whether there was any conscious attempt to relate a distinct purity system to an independent ethical system. Purity language is occasionally applied to matters which we would regard as ethical, and some offences which we would treat as moral lapses are seen as breaches of purity. Moreover, despite Countryman's claims, sexual offences are generally viewed as matters of purity.[23] It is difficult not to conclude that by speaking of purity and ethical systems we are separating concepts which had not yet crystallized out in Israelite thought.[24]

The discussion, however, needs to be broadened to take into account other phrases and terms.

Leviticus and Ezekiel speak of profaning the name of Yahweh. In the first it is usually the result of uncleanness – unclean priests (Lev. 21.6; 22.2), and the result of giving children to Moloch (20.3). Perhaps naturally, swearing by Yahweh's name falsely profanes his name (19.12), and although it immediately refers to keeping Yahweh's commandments in 22.32, this comes at the end of a section of ritual laws. Every example in Ezekiel refers to idols (Ezek. 20.39; 36.20–23), but on two occasions there is mention of Yahweh being profaned (without 'the name', 13.19; 22.26), where a wider range of offences are included. Amos speaks of profaning Yahweh's name in 2.7. If this is limited to the nearer wrongs it is caused by 'father and son [going] in to the same girl',[25] which may refer to sacred

---

[22] None of the other references to 'abomination' in the other Old Testament books is related to ethics.

[23] Countryman distinguishes between sexual purity and sexual property.

[24] For completeness it may be added that the other Hebrew word translated 'abomination' in many English versions (√ *šqṣ*) is never used in an ethical setting. The noun *šiqqūṣ* is predominantly used of idols and the gods of other peoples (e.g., 1 Kgs. 11.5, 7; 2 Kgs. 23.13). Hosea says that Israel became 'detestable' (*šiqqūṣīm*) by consecrating themselves to Baal. Leviticus uses *šeqeṣ* in 7.21; 11.10–12, 13, 20, 23, 41–42, referring to water creatures lacking fins and scales, birds which may not be eaten, winged insects apart from locusts and grasshoppers, and 'swarming things'. The word *šeqeṣ* is rare outside Leviticus (only Ezek. 8.10; Isa. 66.17). Mary Douglas suggests that it is used idiosyncratically in Leviticus to avoid the pejorative associations of *šiqqūṣ*. She argues that it should be rendered 'You shall absolutely shun everything that swarms', etc., and proposes that this means that God is 'telling his people to avoid certain things, keep out of their way, not harm, still less eat, them' (*Leviticus*, 167), adding that 'though contact with these creatures is not against purity, harming them is against holiness' (*ibid.*, 168). See a further discussion below, Ch. 16.

[25] There is no equivalent to 'same' in the Hebrew, and the meaning of the oracle is disputed and obscure. The 'girl' may be a temple prostitute or a household slave (cf.

prostitution. If the wider context is taken into account, social wrongs are included – trampling the head of the poor into the dust of the earth and turning aside the way of the afflicted. Jeremiah declares that taking back their slaves whom they had freed, apparently in obedience to the laws of Exodus 21.2 and Deuteronomy 15.12, profaned Yahweh's name. Occasionally, therefore, moral wrongs are said to pollute God's holiness, but usually this is ascribed to matters of ritual uncleanness.

A phrase found in Deuteronomy but never in the priestly law, and elsewhere only in Judges 20.13, is that translated 'you shall purge the evil from your midst' (*ūbiʿartā hārāʿ miqqirbekā*). It almost certainly belongs to the purity system, although the precise meaning is disputed.[26] Since in all cases apart from Deuteronomy 19.19 it is added to the imposition of the death penalty, it seems most probable that it refers to the removal of the uncleanness that attaches to the notorious sinner and so maintains the purity of the nation (or by some of those accepting the theory of the amphictyony, of the tribal confederation).[27] It occurs in the cases of prophets and dreamers who urge the following of other gods (13.6[5]), those worshipping other gods (17.7), those who refuse to accept the judgment of the 'higher court' of priests or judge (17.12), the malicious witness (19.19),[28] the rebellious son (21.21), the bride who was not a virgin when she was married (22.21), both the man found lying with the wife of another man and the woman (22.22), and the kidnapper (24.7). It is significant that in four of these (enticing to worship and the worshipping of other gods, the rebellious son, and the bride who is not a virgin) execution is by stoning, the punishment which keeps the unclean criminal at a distance from his executioners.[29] After noting that what he regards as the oldest section

---

Henry McKeating, *Amos*, 23; James L. Mays, *Amos*, 46; Francis I. Andersen and David Noel Freedman, *Amos*, 318–319). But *hālak* is not the usual verb for sexual intercourse, cf. Carolyn S. Leeb, who concludes that the young woman was 'working outside the home', away from the protection of the father, and was vulnerable (*Away from the Father's House*, 146–150).

[26] A. D. H. Mayes denies that it is a legal formula, since its direct address indicates instruction or teaching of the law (*Deuteronomy*, 233–234). He also rejects any cultic background, since there is no reference to Yahweh. This appears to limit the interpretation too narrowly to the form of the phrase.

[27] Helmer Ringgren, article *bʿr* in *TDOT* II, 203–204, compares the formula with 'that man shall be cut off from among his people' in the priestly writings (e.g., Lev. 17.4, 9, 14), and argues that while the latter refers to excommunication as a punishment, purging out the evil coming after the declaration of the penalty expresses the idea of purifying the community.

[28] This is the only instance where the penalty is not that of death but is the penalty which belongs to the crime of which the witness accuses his fellow Israelite.

[29] Cf. the stoning of the ox which gored a human being to death, even if that person was a slave (Ex. 21.28, 29, 32), and the command that human beings and animals who

of a group of casuistic laws in Deuteronomy (19.11–13; 21.18–21; 22.22; 24.7) have a counterpart in the phrase *mōt yūmāt* ('shall be put to death') in Exodus 21.12–17, Ringgren points out that the verb is used in the rite to cleanse the land when a murderer cannot be found, though with the object 'innocent blood' instead of 'the evil' (Deut. 21.1–9). This strongly supports the contention that the phrase belongs to the purity system, for the land would be polluted unless the rite were duly performed by the elders. The same idea is found in the incident of the Levite's concubine in Judges 19–20, where the other Israelite tribes demand the punishment of the evildoers in Gibeah in order to purge the evil.

In addition to the unique cleansing rite in Deuteronomy 21.1–9, the expiatory sacrifices in the priestly writings show that ethical wrongs were also regarded as pollutions.

We begin with the Day of Atonement (Lev. 16).[30] This ceremony comprises two main rites. In the first Aaron (signifying the later high priest) takes of the blood of the *ḥaṭṭā't* bull and of the *ḥaṭṭā't* goat[31] which had previously been chosen by lot, and sprinkles it on and in front of the 'mercy seat' (*kappōret*, the golden cover on the ark in the holy of holies), the 'tent of meeting', the main part of the temple, and the four horns of the altar. In the second rite Aaron places both hands[32] on the head of the other goat and confesses over it the sins of the people. This goat is then sent away into the desert. Underlying the various rites is the belief that the uncleannesses and sins of Israel during the previous year have polluted the temple, which has to be cleansed. The purpose of the manipulation of the blood of the *ḥaṭṭā't* bull and goat on and before the 'mercy seat' and on the horns of the

---

strayed on the holy mountain were to be stoned (Ex. 19.13). Achan, who kept back part of the goods subject to the 'ban' (Josh. 7:25), and Naboth, who was accused of cursing God and the king (1 Kgs. 21.10, 13), are also stoned; in both cases the issue is one of holiness. The priestly writer uses a different Hebrew word for stoning (*rāgam*, found once in Deuteronomy, in 21.21), but the connection with impurity is even stronger (cf. Lev. 20.2, 27; 24.14, 16, 23; Num. 15.35, 36).

[30] The previous history of the chapter is not of primary importance for the present purpose, although it impinges upon the precise way in which the rites are to be envisaged (see the commentaries by Budd, Wenham and Gerstenberger).

[31] The usual translation is 'sin offering' (RSV, NRSV, NIV, NEB, GNB). JB and NJB have 'sacrifice for sin'. Only REB's 'purification offering' avoids the false overtones which the word 'sin' introduces. The Hebrew name of the sacrifice, of course, is the same as one of the words for sin, but this must not be allowed to distort the meaning of the sacrifice.

[32] This is the only instance where both hands are placed on the animal, as opposed to the worshipper's placing of one hand on the head of the animal to be offered in sacrifice (e.g., Lev. 1.4), where it probably indicates the ownership of the victim or that it is dedicated or set apart for the sacrifice (see, Budd, *Leviticus*, 47–48; contrast Wenham, *Leviticus*, 61–62, who favours substitution ('the animal is taking the place of the worshipper') or the transference of sin).

altar is stated as 'to make atonement' for the holy place, the tent of meeting and the altar. In the second rite the sins of the people are then transferred to the live goat which removes them from the land and takes them into the desert.[33]

David P. Wright argues that the two parts of the atonement rituals remove different evils, the *ḥaṭṭā't* blood rites remove the *impurity* attached to the temple (Lev. 16.16, 19), while the scapegoat removes the *'transgressions'* (his word) of the people (vv. 21–22).[34] He recognizes, however, that these cannot be sharply distinguished, since verse 16 also refers to the removal of 'their transgressions, all their sins', a phrase almost exactly repeated in the account of the scapegoat ('all the iniquities of the people of Israel, and all their transgressions, all their sins', v. 21). He resolves the apparent contradiction by treating the phrase '(all) their transgressions, all their sins' as an addition to the original text. He accepts, however, that the two evils are intimately related, since sin in the priestly writings is the cause of the impurity of the sanctuary.[35] Thus he concludes: 'The two evils belong naturally together, and, consequently, the two parts of the rite belong together.'

It seems to me, however, that both rites concern the removal of pollution. Indeed, commentators frequently use ambiguous language in their accounts of the meaning. Even Wright can say: 'Sending the goat to the wilderness is only to remove the impurity from the sanctuary and habitation so that they might become and remain clean.'[36] It is true, of course, that if it were the sins that the goat was carrying these would also be polluting, and therefore uncleanness would also be removed. The crucial issue, however, is whether ethical wrongdoing can be transferred. This seems to be as impossible among the Israelites as it is among us. What is transferred through the confession of sins is the pollution that they carry, and it is that pollution which is removed. Both rites deal with pollution, the blood rites cleansing the temple, which has been polluted by the people's sins, and the scapegoat removing the pollution from the land and the people.[37]

---

[33] Azazel is probably the name of a demon.

[34] David P. Wright, *Disposal*, 15–21. He discusses the meaning of Azazel on pp. 21–25. In his study he compares biblical rites with those of the Hittites and in Mesopotamia, and argues that there is no evidence that in the priestly writings the impurities and sins were taken to the underworld, as in these other cultures. In addition he stresses that ideas of substitution and appeasement found in Hittite and Mesopotamian rites are absent from the biblical ones. The scapegoat 'merely receives the community's sins and bears them to a harmless locale' (pp. 73–74).

[35] He refers to Lev. 4.1–5.13; 15.31; 20.3; Num. 19.13, 20. He also notes the pollution of the man who took the scapegoat into the desert (Lev. 16.26).

[36] Wright, *Disposal*, 73.

[37] So Philip J. Budd, *Leviticus*, 232: 'Some kind of transference seems to be implied

With this ceremony may be compared the rite using live birds to carry away the impurity of 'leprosy' in both healed persons and restored buildings (Lev. 14.2–9, 48–53). Somewhat similarly to the Day of Atonement rites,[38] two birds are taken, one is killed 'in an earthenware vessel over running water'.[39] The other bird is then dipped into the blood and water, together with cedar wood, scarlet stuff and hyssop, and the liquid is sprinkled seven times on the person or the house. Finally the live bird is released into the open country. The blood removes the impurity from the person and the house. It has also been transferred to the live bird, which removes the impurity from the community generally (in v. 53 the priest sends the bird 'out of the city'). Washings on the seventh day complete the cleansing of the person.[40]

Wright sees a major difference between the release of the bird and the scapegoat. In the latter the blood rites remove impurity, the scapegoat removes the sin, whereas with 'leprosy' both blood and live bird remove impurity. He points out, however, that since impurity and sin are 'different sides of the same coin', the difference is less.[41] It seems more probable, as I have argued earlier, that it is impurity which is removed in all the rites: on the Day of Atonement the impurity caused by moral wrongs, in the 'leprosy' ceremony the

---

here, though this too is probably a purificatory rite. Just as the blood of the sin offerings carries away any defilements incurred by (or threatening) the sanctuary so the scapegoat carries away the iniquities of Israel (v. 22) – i.e., those she has incurred and which threaten her status as the holy people.' By contrast Wenham (*Leviticus*, 233–234) sees the rite as transferring *sins* to the goat; the ceremony removes the sins from the people and leaves them in an unclean place. In a recent article, 'Animal Sacrifice', J. W. Rogerson, apparently accepting the theory of Douglas Davies, 'Sacrifice in Leviticus', distinguishes between the cleansing of the holy place from 'the defilement of Israel's wrongdoings', and the symbolical removal of 'these wrongdoings' from among the people as the scapegoat 'proceeds from the holy place through the camp and out into the wilderness'. Rogerson suggests that if we wish to understand the scope of Old Testament sacrifice, 'it is probably best to operate with the distinction clean/unclean' ('Sacrifice', 53).

[38] Wright, *Disposal*, 79, finds three differences between the two. The third of these will be considered later.

[39] The Hebrew is difficult to understand. Literally it reads: 'and he shall slaughter the one bird to (*'el*) a vessel of earthenware over (*'al*) living water'. RSV, JB and NJB follow this closely, but what actually happened is not easy to visualize. Several translations offer intelligible actions, but the relation to the Hebrew is not clear. Most suppose that spring or river water is collected in a pot and the bird killed over this so that its blood falls into the water and is mixed with it (so NEB, REB, NIV, NRSV (apparently), and GNB). Gerstenberger offers: 'The priest shall command further that one bird be slaughtered over an earthen vessel alongside running water' (*Leviticus*, 173).

[40] Martin Noth describes the rite, with its 'very crude ideas of the effectiveness of magic', as aimed at the removal of all cultic uncleanness caused by the disease (*Leviticus*, 107).

[41] Wright, *ibid.*, 80, tentatively suggests that originally both goats removed impurity, and it was a later development which ascribed the removal of sins to the scapegoat.

residual impurity that remains after the 'disease' has been 'cured'. Sins are mentioned in the ceremonies of the Day of Atonement because it was the annual build-up of the impurity that these produced which had to be removed through the rites.

Since our purpose is not to give a full account of all the purification rites in ancient Israel, the *ḥaṭṭā'ṯ* and *'āšām*[42] sacrifices will not be discussed. The distinction between them is difficult to determine, but both are concerned with the removal of uncleanness, resulting either from an impure condition or an ethical wrong, and so restoring relations with God and avoiding the destructiveness of divine holiness.[43]

Finally, a few other texts which relate sin to pollution may be mentioned. In one of the accounts of the cities of refuge (Num. 35.9–34), the justification for executing deliberate murderers and the refusal of a ransom for their life is that the land should not be polluted, 'for blood pollutes the land, and no expiation can be made for the land, for the blood that is shed in it, except by the blood of him who shed it' (v. 33). The law declares: 'You shall not defile [make unclean] the land in which you live . . . for I the LORD dwell in the midst of the people of Israel' (v. 34). Bloodshed, of course, is a special type of crime, since the blood was regarded as the life, and as such belongs to God. Nevertheless, the passage as a whole is concerned with protecting those whose action was accidental.[44] Jeremiah sees sin as polluting the land (Jer. 2.7; 3.1, 9), while the late passage in Isaiah 24.5–6 declares that the land is polluted because the people have disobeyed God's laws and broken the covenant.

Ethics within the Old Testament cannot be divorced from the question of purity. It has been shown that sin always creates uncleanness, which has to be removed by means of sacrifice and cleansing rites, although uncleanness is also caused by non-ethical actions and states, such as touching dead bodies and menstruation. Essentially there is no difference between the two with regard to the dangers to which they give rise when faced with the holiness of God.

This does not mean that ethics are subsumed under impurity or that morality was treated less seriously. It does call into question, however, some of the rather imprecise language which is often used about sin and forgiveness by many writers. It also entails that care must be taken to differentiate between the two when actions which appear to

---

[42] Usually translated 'guilt offering' (RSV, NRSV, NIV, NEB). Some translations introduce the idea of reparation: 'sacrifice of reparation' (JB, NJB), 'reparation offering' (REB), 'repayment offering' (GNB).

[43] See, in addition to the Old Testament theologies and the commentaries, articles in *TDOT* by D. Kellermann (I, 429–437), and K. Koch (IV, 309–319). See also the discussion of 'confess' (*yāḏāh*, hithp.) in V, 439–442 by G. Mayer. In *NIDOTTE*, Richard E. Averbeck contributes two useful discussions (1, 557–566; 2, 93–103).

[44] Intention and responsibility will be discussed in Chapter 9 below.

us as being within the sphere of morals are considered. As has been seen, the reaction to murder by an unknown person is to remove the pollution that the crime has produced rather than devising ways of tracking down the murderer.

It will have been noticed that most of the examples that have been given are from the priestly writings, Deuteronomy,[45] and Ezekiel. Whether these writings also represent the views of the Israelite peasant, the court, or earlier periods in Israel's history is impossible to determine. Almost certainly there has been some modification of traditional practices by the priests in their own interests. Yet it is hard to believe that the attitudes to sin and impurity were invented by them. Impurity, after all, is a well-defined state, as Mary Douglas has shown, and is likely to have been accepted by all groups within Israel during most of its history. The priests may have refined the rites but it is more probable that they reflect common ideas than that the priests practised a secret set of ceremonies within a closed community. Hence it is probable that, allowing for some increased rigidity, formality and precision in the definition of uncleanness and purity rites, the priestly understanding of ethics and purity was that of ancient Israel in general.[46]

This discussion of ethics and purity has shown how far removed the Old Testament ways of thinking are from modern ethics.[47] In the next chapter we shall consider another feature of life in ancient Israel which should also make us hesitate about speaking too confidently about Old Testament ethics.

---

[45] Mary Douglas, however, draws a sharp distinction between Leviticus and Deuteronomy. She thinks Deuteronomy has a 'more political agenda', and follows Moshe Weinfeld in describing Leviticus as 'ritualist, sacrificial, formal' and Deuteronomy as 'rationalist, humanist, anti-ritualist' (*Leviticus*, 66, 89, see the whole chapter, 'The Totally Reformed Religion', 87–108, also 14, 29, 41).

[46] The writers of the wisdom books (especially Proverbs) may stand somewhat apart from this, though Job offers ʿōlōṭ (Job 1.5; the term strictly refers to the sacrifice which was wholly burnt on the altar) on behalf of his sons, lest they had sinned and cursed God in their hearts.

[47] It may be noted, however, that, far from regarding the purity system in the Old Testament as remote from the ethics of the present day, John Barton finds a concern for the natural order in the laws of clean and unclean animals (*Ethics*, 68–71). Mary Douglas goes further, declaring it 'frivolous' to suppose that the 'analogical thought system' of Leviticus excludes something we call 'ethics'. 'Any person raised in a closed and strongly positional society would know what is moral and what is immoral. Injunctions to be compassionate would not be necessary because kindness would be predicated in the rules of behaviour as well as exemplified in the narratives' (*Leviticus*, 44). Even if this is accepted (and the existence of 'ethical' laws within Leviticus raises questions), it shows that our conception of 'ethics' is very different from the culture of the biblical text.

3

ETHICS AND HONOUR

With much of the Old Testament we feel quite at home. We interpret the Ten Commandments as laws, and see the punishments set out in many of the other laws in the Pentateuch as similar to our own criminal law. For we are accustomed to the death penalty, even though it has been abolished in many countries. Even when we come upon the punishment of cutting off a hand (Deut. 25.11–12), our recent increased knowledge of traditional Islamic law makes it seem less outlandish, even if no less barbaric. But then suddenly we find this scenario:

> If brothers dwell together, and one of them dies and has no son, the wife of the dead shall not be married outside the family to a stranger; her husband's brother shall go in to her, and take her as his wife, and perform the duty of a husband's brother to her. And the first son whom she bears shall succeed to the name of his brother who is dead, that his name may not be blotted out of Israel. And if the man does not wish to take his brother's wife, then his brother's wife shall go up to the gate to the elders, and say, 'My husband's brother refuses to perpetuate his brother's name in Israel; he will not perform the duty of a husband's brother to me.' Then the elders of his city shall call him, and speak to him: and if he persists, saying, 'I do not wish to take her,' then his brother's wife shall go up to him in the presence of the elders, and pull his sandal off his foot, and spit in his face; and she shall answer and say, 'So shall it be done to the man who does not build up his brother's house.' And the name of his house shall be called in Israel, The house of him that had his sandal pulled off (Deut. 25.5–10).

The custom of taking the deceased brother's wife, though odd, is familiar to us because of the question the Sadducees put to Jesus in the Gospels,[1] but the action of the woman when her brother-in-law refuses to take her appears extremely curious. The passage begins exactly like any of the other casuistic laws, outlining the situation and setting out what is to be done when brothers are living together and one dies without having fathered a son.[2] Then, again in normal

---

[1] Mk. 12.18–23; Mt. 22.23–28; Lk. 20.27–33.
[2] The form-critical analysis of the Old Testament laws is usually traced back to Albrecht Alt, 'Origins'. For later discussions see Dale Patrick, *Old Testament Law*, Harry W.

casuistic fashion, the further situation in which the brother refuses to carry out the levirate is presented. The widow first takes her brother-in-law before the elders who try to persuade him to do his duty. If he persists in his refusal, the widow is to pull his sandal off his foot, spit in his face, and utter a formal statement that is almost a curse. Instead of punishment as a sanction, therefore, there is public shaming, reinforced by the mocking of the man's family as 'The house of him that had his sandal pulled off', its 'name' now being a matter of shame rather than of honour.

A large part of our sense of the strangeness of this legal passage springs from the fact that Christianity is obsessed with sin and guilt, forgiveness and punishment. Even though Christian influences are diminishing in modern secular society, crime, guilt and punishment dominate the culture. It makes it harder to move imaginatively into a society in which honour and shame were important, and shaming was not an alternative 'punishment' but belonged to a different way of thinking within the culture.[3]

In an important study Lyn M. Bechtel has argued that shaming was an important means of social control in ancient Israel.[4] Building on the work of David Daube on shame in the book of Deuteronomy,[5] she presents an analysis of 'shame' and offers evidence of three main types of shaming: formal judicial shaming, formal and informal political shaming in war and diplomacy, and informal shaming in everyday social life. The second of these is illustrated from the stripping of captives by victorious armies (cf. Isaiah's symbolic actions in Isa. 20.1–6 and Assyrian and other bas-reliefs) and the treatment of David's ambassadors by Hanun, the new Ammonite king (2 Sam. 10.1–5), while the individual

---

Gilmer, *If-You Form*. A distinction should be made between clauses in which a punishment is prescribed and those which declare what action is to be taken (as here).

[3] Social anthropologists formerly distinguished between a 'shame' culture and a 'guilt' culture, but it is now recognized that all cultures contain elements of both, even our own highly individualistic one where guilt is dominant (and 'anxiety' has increasing importance). Johs. Pedersen made an early study of honour and shame, somewhat distorted by his idiosyncratic view of 'soul' in *Israel I–II*, 213–244. Recently New Testament scholars have shown an interest in the culture of honour and shame in the Mediterranean world (see Jerome H. Neyrey, *Honor and Shame*, and the extensive bibliography which he has collected). For a further definition and analysis of 'honour' and 'shame' see also Bruce J. Malina and Jerome H. Neyrey, *Honour and Shame*, 25–65, and Saul M. Olyan, 'Honor, Shame'. Michael Herzfeld, 'Honour and Shame' points out that honour and shame always need to be understood in relation to the culture in which they are found.

[4] Lyn M. Bechtel, 'Shame as a Sanction'.

[5] David Daube, 'The Culture of Deuteronomy' and 'To Be Found Doing Wrong'. Daube stresses that he deliberately speaks of 'shame-cultural elements' in Deuteronomy, not 'shame culture', because Deuteronomy is 'a curious blend' of shame and guilt cultures, and he suggests that the guilt-culture predominates.

laments in the Psalter and the book of Job offer examples of informal social shaming. For 'judicial shaming', which is most pertinent to the present enquiry, Bechtel fastens on the levirate law (Deut. 25.5–10) and the attempt to avoid excessive shaming by limiting judicial beating to forty stripes (Deut. 25.1–3). She fails to notice, however, that the part played by the shaming is different in the two examples.

The threat of shaming by the widow was intended to put pressure on the reluctant brother-in-law to carry out his duty to the deceased. The significance of the 'name' underlies the actions, for not only was the purpose of the levirate to continue the dead brother's 'name'[6] – the main way in which life was held to continue after death – but the whole family of the brother who refused to take the widow is shamed by the 'name' by which it is to be known. The label now attached to the brother's family affected their status in the community; Bechtel thinks it may have 'threatened their very survival'.[7] Nevertheless, the isolation of this ordinance may be significant. Daube holds that it is the only law in the Pentateuch where 'the punishment consists in public degradation'.[8] The propriety of speaking of 'punishment' here is doubtful. In the sense that it brings dishonour upon the brother and his family and so affects their position within the community it may be so regarded, but the term 'punishment' is better restricted to situations where a crime has been committed and retribution is exacted. Here the intention is to secure compliance with custom. It is also questionable whether it is properly called 'judicial', since, although the elders are involved, they do not impose the sanction, and despite the quasi-legal formulation of the final verse of the passage, it is more the recognition of what happened within Israelite society than a formal legal sentence.[9]

There is a hint of a similar use of shaming in Numbers 12, to which Bechtel draws attention in her attempt to explain the symbolism of taking off the sandal and spitting. Embedded in the account of Miriam's leprosy, which God imposed as a punishment for her opposition to Moses, is the divine decree that Miriam is to be shut up outside the camp for seven days. This is justified by the comment: 'If her father had but spit in her face, should she not be shamed seven

[6] A. D. H. Mayes holds that the main purpose was to avoid the loss of property to the family (*Deuteronomy*, 328).
[7] 'Shame as a Sanction', 61.
[8] 'The Culture of Deuteronomy', 35, cf. 27.
[9] A. D. H. Mayes discerns 'a certain weakening in the institution' in that failure to fulfil the duty of the levirate 'is seen as a disgrace but not as a crime deserving of punishment' (*Deuteronomy*, 329). The practice may have been dying out (the limitation to brothers who are living together probably indicates this), but the implication that disgrace was of less weight than punishment is not to be accepted.

days?' (v. 14). This must refer to the shaming of a daughter for some misdemeanour, although the original context is now lost. It is possible that the daughter had spoken disrespectfully to her parents or had failed to preserve sexual modesty.[10]

Rightly Bechtel states that such shaming is an objective act, and is to be distinguished both from subjective feelings – 'being ashamed' – and from a sense of 'guilt'. The reluctant brother and the disobedient daughter suffer loss of status within the village hierarchy, the brother and his 'house' permanently, the daughter for a fixed period of time. Here are clear examples of shaming as a sanction of social control.

The forty stripes, on the other hand, is a punishment which follows the finding of the 'judge' – 'acquit', 'innocent', 'condemn' and 'guilty' are forensic terms – and the beating is carried out in his presence. It is only in the final motive clause that a word within the vocabulary of honour and shame is found: 'lest . . . your brother be degraded [*niqlāh*] in your sight'.[11] It is not clear whether the beating itself contains an element of shame. Bechtel points out that the text does not deal with the degree of shame the guilty person suffered by having his guilt revealed in public and suffering the humiliation of a public beating, though she believes that it did involve shame and this functioned as 'an important deterrent and means of control'. To this extent it was acceptable shame. Excessive beating, however, was degrading, and the law protects the dignity of the individual. What is central in public beating, however, is punishment, and is primarily retributive, though it also acts as a deterrent to others. The two systems of control are distinct, even though the one involves elements of the other.

Informal shaming may possibly have played a part in social control, though from the evidence of the book of Job it would appear that the shaming followed the punishment which the friends believed God had inflicted on Job. The belief against which the writer protests is that God punishes wrongdoing with misfortune and illness. Loss of his property and children, and the disease with which he is afflicted, destroy Job's honourable place within society, a fact that Job bitterly describes in his final speeches and elsewhere. Men younger than he is, men of much lower social status, mock him (Job 30.1). They spit at the sight of him (Job 30.10). His relatives, even his slaves, no longer show him respect or wish to be with him (Job 19.13–19). Job sets his humiliation in vivid contrast to the honour with which he had once been held (Job 29.7–12). But this destruction of Job's honour is the result of his misfortunes and is hardly a form of social control

---

[10] See Eryl W. Davies, *Numbers*, 125.

[11] Bechtel offers the translation 'it will dishonour your brother' and wrongly takes the verb as hiph'il. It does not affect her argument.

in itself. The shaming would not have happened had not disaster struck Job.

Shaming within the Psalter is to be understood in a similar way. The vocabulary of shaming clusters in a small number of psalms, notably in national and individual laments. Among the national laments Psalms 44 and 74 stand out. In the first of these the psalmist contrasts past victories, when God 'put to confusion those who hate us' (44.8[7]) with their present humiliation (44.14–17[13–16]), while in the second the attacks of the enemy are highlighted and their scoffing and mocking is stressed (74.4–11, 18, 21, 22). In Ps. 69 the psalmist, who is apparently seriously ill, repeatedly refers to the shaming to which he is subjected (vv. 8[7], 10–13[9–12], 20–21[19–20]). Other psalmists pray that God will not allow them to be shamed, and seek revenge on those who mock them (e.g., 25.1–3; 31.2[1], 18[17]; 71.1, 13, 24; 35.4, 26). How closely shaming is related to the judicial process is doubtful. If some of the psalms are prayers by the accused, the link may be close, although whether this is a correct interpretation has been questioned and it has to be noted that the psalms which can most convincingly be viewed in this way contain no references to shaming (Pss. 7, 26, 27).[12] It seems more probable that the shaming in the psalms is to be understood against the background of sin and its consequences,[13] as in the book of Job. Some psalmists assert with complete confidence that those who trust in Yahweh will never be shamed (Ps. 37.18–19). Those who are ill find their suffering increased because they are seen as bearing the consequences of wrongdoing and are mocked by their 'enemies'.

From the evidence on which she bases her claims, therefore, it would seem that Bechtel goes too far in claiming that shaming was 'a prevalent and important sanction of behavior'. While she seems to be correct in seeing its use as a means to 'manipulate status' and to 'dominate others', there is little evidence that it was used as a formal sanction by the elders to control deviant activity. Rather, if the psalmists correctly reflect what happened within the Israelite towns and villages, it was illness and misfortune which were interpreted as divine punishment. The mockery and shaming were a consequence of this.

Nevertheless, there is more to be said.

Although David Daube, as we have seen, regards the levirate law in Deuteronomy 25 as the only example of shaming as a sanction, he

---

[12] H. Schmidt made the claim for over thirty psalms in *Gebet*. Although criticisms of the theory have been made, many accept that it is a plausible interpretation at least for these three psalms. See also his commentary, *Die Psalmen*.

[13] Whether this should be correctly described as sin and punishment has been effectively questioned by Klaus Koch, 'Retribution', who argues that what is usually described as retribution should be seen as an automatic working out of the consequences of wrong-doing. For his discussion of Psalms see pp. 69–75.

finds elements of shame-culture in the book.[14] He believes that
disgrace awaits those who slip away from the army out of fear (Deut.
20.8, in the light of vv. 3–4). In the law concerning the straying ox or
sheep (Deut. 22.1–4) the Hebrew 'you shall not hide yourself' points
to shame – you must not try to escape without being noticed, for not
to help would be shameful.[15] The man who claims that his wife was
not a virgin when he married her 'brings an evil name upon her'
(Deut. 22.13, cf. vv. 17, 19) – and the law seeks to save her from
being unjustly shamed. In the law prohibiting remarriage of a
divorced wife to her first husband if she had been remarried and
divorced in the meantime, the cause of the initial divorce is stated as
the finding by her husband of 'some indecency' in her (Deut. 24.1).
Daube points out that the phrase occurs elsewhere only in
Deuteronomy 23.14, and reflects the shame aspect.[16] He sees the
prohibition of entering a neighbour's house to fetch his pledge (Deut.
24.10–11) as showing sensitivity to shame.[17] More generally Daube
finds evidence of elements of a shame culture in the deterrent 'that all
Israel hear and fear' (Deut. 13.12[13]; 17.13; 19.20; 21.21) and the
communal display of happiness (Deut. 12.7, 12, 18; 14.26; 16.11, 14,
15; 26.11). He holds that the demand to 'purge out the evil from the
midst of you' (Deut. 13.6[5] and twelve other times) reflects a
concern with the look of things and hence is related to shame, but it is
more probable that it is related to purity, as we have already seen.[18]
Equally uncertain are his claims that the use of the imperfect 'thou
canst not' (Deut. 12.17; 16.5; 17.15; 21.16; 22.3, 19; 24.4) is distinct
from 'thou shalt not'. Behind this unique form by which
Deuteronomy urges that the prohibited actions should be regarded as
impossible to a people conforming to this code (an important
observation in itself) Daube sees an appeal to shame. Finally, he
draws attention to the curious phrase 'if there be found' (Deut. 17.2;
21.1; 22.22; 24.7). He denies that it is the equivalent of 'if a man shall
. . . ', restricts the punishment to those caught in the act, or means 'if
found out' or 'discovered by chance'. Rather, he argues, the laws
stress the fearfulness of the appearance of the misdemeanour and the
expression is a further mark of the shame-cultural element in the

---

[14] In the two articles listed in n. 5 above.

[15] The EVV paraphrase and give a different sense: 'withhold your help' (RSV) 'do not
ignore it' (NIV, GNB, NRSV). RV retains 'hide thyself from them'.

[16] By contrast Mayes (who regards the clause as a later addition) suggests it implies
some state of impurity (*Deuteronomy*, 322).

[17] S. R. Driver interprets the motive as preserving the right of the borrower to select
the article offered as a pledge (*Deuteronomy*, 275). P. C. Craigie mentions both
interpretations but adds: 'It means that a man can borrow with honor' (*Deuteronomy*,
308).

[18] See above, pp. 13–14.

book. The construction is not identical in each of the four laws, however, and it is doubtful whether a single interpretation should be given to all of them.

Daube over-presses the evidence, but he has shown that shame must not be overlooked in any discussion of Old Testament ethics.

To take the matter further, it is to be noted that the Hebrew vocabulary for shame is extensive.[19] What is significant from the perspective of ethics, however, is that the main word for shame ($b\bar{o}\check{s}$) is found more frequently in the prophets than elsewhere in the Old Testament. Horst Seebass even claims that the root and its derivatives 'play practically no role at all before the great literary prophets of the 8th century B.C.'[20] Too much should not be made of this. While the prophets refer primarily to the shame which will come upon Israel and Judah through defeat by their enemies, several of the metaphors which they apply to Israel point to the practice of shaming in everyday life. The most striking of these images is the public stripping of women (Hos. 2.5[3], 12[10]; Ezek. 16.37–39; 23.10, 29; Isa. 47.2–3). Jeremiah's account of the treatment of Jerusalem in 13.22, 26, however, may refer to rape rather than shaming, while Isaiah 47.2–3 refers primarily to the treatment of captives in war, though here the dominant feature is the shame of nakedness (and loss of honour by being forced to do the work of slaves). In these examples, however, the metaphor is contaminated by features from conquest of the nation by an enemy, and it is not always certain which 'punishments' were actually inflicted on adulteresses. It is true that the law decreed that those committing adultery should be put to death (Lev. 20.10; Deut. 22.22), but as McKeating has pointed out, there is no recorded evidence of anyone actually being put to death for adultery in the Old Testament, the stories describing only the *threat* but not its being implemented (Gen. 38.24; Susanna 41, 45,[21] Jn. 7.53–8.11).[22]

What, then, can be concluded from this discussion? Bechtel has argued that shame was an important social sanction in the culture of ancient Israel. Daube offers examples of several different kinds and

---

[19] Bechtel points this out and lists eight main verbs and associated nouns, as well as actions that express shame, such as spitting and wagging the head ('Shame as a Sanction', 54). The place that shaming held within Israelite culture, however, cannot be proved from the width of the vocabulary and the contrast with the fewer number of words for sin and guilt. For useful discussions of the words connected with honour and shame see *TDOT*.

[20] Horst Seebass, '*bôsh*' (*TDOT* II, 50–60), 52.

[21] Note that Susanna's veil is stripped off (v. 32). The narrator says this is in order for the 'wicked men' to feast upon her beauty, but it is also shaming – and shaming before she is found guilty.

[22] H. McKeating, 'Sanctions against Adultery'. See the next chapter for a fuller discussion.

applications of shame, but in the end admits that all he has proved is the presence of shame-cultural elements in the book of Deuteronomy. Pedersen, one of the earliest scholars to analyse shame in the Old Testament, displays the significance of shame as clearly as any of the later scholars. He points out that the man who is rich in blessing, successful in all he undertakes, and wealthy, is held in honour, as the book of Job so clearly shows. Honour for a woman is primarily to bear a man's name and to provide him with children (cf. Isa. 4.1; Gen. 30.23).[23] Not to possess the strength to maintain one's honour leads to shame, as when an army is defeated and steals back into the city ashamed (2 Sam. 19.4[3], cf. national laments in the Psalter). To appear abandoned by God or under his judgment and displeasure, because of illness or misfortune, leads to shame and to being mocked, thence the anguished petitions of the psalmists. Shame causes acute distress in the one who is shamed. But whether there was a 'system' of shame, parallel to that of right and wrong, goodness and evil, in the same way that there was a purity system is doubtful. Shaming as a *sanction* appears to be limited to a very narrow range of wrongdoing. The main types of 'immorality' with which the sanction is linked are sexual, and shame may be experienced even when the person bearing the shame is the innocent victim, as in the case of Tamar (2 Sam. 13.13, 19). For the rest, however, the shame accompanies or follows various kinds of failure. Only very occasionally does the law attempt to ensure that no one is shamed for circumstances over which they have no control.

Despite this limited conclusion, the importance of shame must not be underestimated. The Israelites were extremely sensitive to honour and shame, and the shame that followed disasters that were regarded as divine punishment increased the bitterness of that punishment. Hence on the one hand the prophets could elaborate on the shame to which Israel would be brought as a powerful support for their demand for justice and obedience to God's will, while on the other hand the suffering of Job and the psalmists was increased by the shame which their plight entailed. Shaming Israel is part of God's reaction to Israel's sin, but equally the pleas of Job and the psalmists show that by mocking those who suffer, the 'friends' of Job and the 'enemies' of the psalmists have failed to understand the relation between

---

[23] Malina and Neyrey express it differently: 'for males, shame is the loss of honor; shame, then is a negative experience, as in being shamed: for females, shame is the sensitivity to and defense of honor: female shame (having shame), then is a positive value in a woman; a woman branded as "shameless" means for a female what being shamed means for a male' (*Honor and Shame*, 41f.). This accepts the difference in what constitutes 'honour' for the two sexes, but is an odd way of expressing it. The 'shameless' woman is one who has no sense of the difference between honour and shame.

suffering and wrong-doing. Shame can be a powerful sanction and a fearful consequence of a few types of sin. As powerfully and fearfully it can be misapplied and harm the innocent. It can season the eloquence of the prophet. Equally it enters into the plea of those who are ill. No study of Old Testament ethics can ignore it, but too great emphasis upon it risks exaggerating the importance of sexual sins, for it is to these that shame is mainly attached, and distorting the motivation for keeping the law.[24]

The glimpses of the biblical social landscape which we have obtained through these two windows have suggested that our understanding of ethics may be too narrow. Ethics, purity and honour are all visible. Moreover, while we make clear distinctions between them, it may well be that the Israelites failed to do so, indeed, were completely unaware that such differences existed. If this is right, our attempts to analyse the biblical scene and fasten on ethics may lead to false interpretations. We need to climb higher.

---

[24] See Ferdinand E. Deist, *Material Culture*, 293–294, 297. He sees shame and guilt as universal social control mechanisms. Importantly, he stresses that 'shame' is not a feeling but a social status, as guilt is a legal status: 'One can only be shamed *after* one has been "caught out".' Jacqueline E. Lapsley has a useful discussion of shame in *Moral Self*, 129–156 (this reached me too late to include a discussion).

4

ADULTERY

In the last chapter we noticed briefly that Henry McKeating pointed out that the Old Testament never records anyone actually being put to death for adultery, despite the laws which decree this as the penalty. It will advance our understanding of Old Testament ethics if we pursue this a little further.

The laws on adultery are few in number, short, and far from clear.

In the Decalogue just two Hebrew words issue the command: 'Thou shalt not commit adultery' (Ex. 20.14; Deut. 5.18). No definition of adultery is given, no punishment for offenders is laid down, no situations which might allow for extenuating circumstances are suggested. Anthony Phillips, however, argues that the Decalogue was Israel's criminal law and that the punishment for breaking the commandments was death.[1] It will be necessary to return to this later.

In Deuteronomy adultery carries the death penalty:

> If a man is found lying with the wife of another man, both of them shall die, the man who lay with the woman, and the woman; so you shall purge out the evil from Israel (Deut. 22.22).

Here the offence is more plainly defined. Adultery is committed when a man has sexual intercourse with a married woman. No more and no less, although a woman who is betrothed counts as married (Deut. 22.24).[2] There is no hint that the man has committed a wrong against his own wife, were he married. The offence is entirely against the woman's husband, and even if the man was not married he is still regarded as an adulterer. Nothing is said about having sexual intercourse with a woman who is not married. Laws regarding the seducing of unmarried women who are not betrothed are quite different. In that case the man has to pay the *mōhar* ('bride-price'), whether he is willing to marry the woman or not, since her value to her father is less because she is no longer a virgin (Ex. 22.15–16[16–17]; Deut. 22.28–29; note that the amount of the

---

[1] Anthony Phillips, *Israel's Criminal Law*.
[2] Although the reference in this law is to rape, the situation of the betrothed virgin seems to be the same, especially as it was assumed that the woman had given her consent if the rape occurred within a town.

payment is specified and the man is required to marry the woman, the marriage being indissoluble; whether the law refers to seduction or rape is not certain).

Several features in this adultery law, however, are ambiguous. Three suggestions have been offered as the grounds of the offence: (1) the woman is the husband's property, (2) the offence comes within the purity system, and (3) adultery disturbed the patriarchal system by introducing uncertainty about the father of any children who might result from the act.[3] The first may well have been part of the popular attitude towards adultery, but the much greater severity with which it was treated shows that this is not the main reason. Pollution was always involved, whatever the chief purpose may have been. Questions of the paternity of the children are never raised explicitly, though it may well have been one motive (see the law of the jealous husband, pp. 30f.).

Two further points of procedure should be noted. First, the law contains the phrase, 'if a man is found', which, as we have seen, Daube takes to imply the shame that adultery causes by emphasizing the fearfulness of the appearance of the misdemeanour.[4] Here, however, it is more natural to take the phrase to mean that the couple are caught in the act.[5] There is no law in Deuteronomy to meet the situation of a husband who entertains suspicions that his wife has had sexual relations with another man but has no firm evidence.[6] Second, the method of execution is not defined. If the case of the betrothed virgin can be taken as in some sense parallel, it was by stoning, which, as we have already seen, is the only form of execution where those carrying it out have no physical contact with the wrong-doer, and were this the punishment decreed for adultery here, it would support the view that the chief evil that the law found in adultery was impurity. This is supported by the further clause attached to the law: 'so you shall purge the evil from Israel', which we have had reason to link with the purity system.[7]

The final reference to adultery found in the law codes is included in the list of sexual offences in Leviticus 18, part of the Holiness Code:

> You shall not lie carnally with your neighbour's wife, and defile yourself with her (Lev. 18.20).

The wording is curious. A baldly literal rendering would be something

---

[3] See A. D. H. Mayes, *Deuteronomy*, 170, 311.

[4] See p. 24 above.

[5] Of the offences in the four laws in which the phrase occurs, adultery is the only one which can only be proved if the couple are caught in the act – hence the common resort to an ordeal (see n. 11 below).

[6] Num. 5.11–31 will be considered later (pp. 30f.).

[7] See above pp. 13–14.

like: 'And to the wife of your neighbour (companion[8]) you shall not give your lying for seed for (to) pollution in (with, by) her.' The main problem is in the phrase 'lying *for* seed', instead of the usual 'a lying *of* seed' (construct relation, Lev. 15.16, 18, 32; 22.4; Num. 5.13), which refers to the emission of semen. Westbrook suggests that the offence is not adultery in the strict legal sense. Rather the offender has agreed to sleep with his companion's wife with his consent in order to provide a child for the couple who were childless. If this is so, the offence is not conceived as being against the woman's husband, and there is no prospect of legal proceedings being undertaken. Indeed, Westbrook points out that the matter is not likely to come to light.[9] The Holiness Code says nothing about a legal punishment but states that it causes defilement.[10] In other words, it is interpreted unambiguously in terms of purity. Further, such defilement will cause the land to be defiled and it will 'vomit out' its inhabitants. To avoid this, whoever commits any of these 'abominations', 'shall be cut off from among their people' (Lev. 18.28–29). What is intended by this last phrase is not entirely certain. It might imply the death penalty, and this is decreed later in the code, in a law which is parallel to that in Deuteronomy 22.22:

> If a man commits adultery with the wife of his neighbour, both the adulterer and the adulteress shall be put to death (Lev. 20.10).

Or it might mean some form of 'excommunication' (the term is strictly anachronistic, since it applies only to the Christian church; it is used loosely to signify exclusion from the covenant community). The words may bear some relation to the Deuteronomic call to 'purge out' the evil. On the other hand, since verses 24–30 are expressed in non-legal terms, it is more probable that the Holiness Code is thinking in terms of divine retribution, maybe through a quasi-automatic evil consequence, though under the control of God.

To complete this survey of the legal evidence, the case of the jealous husband needs to be considered (Num. 5.11–31). This is the only example of trial by ordeal in the Old Testament, although ordeals were common in the ancient world, and, indeed, were practised in

---

[8] Apart from Zech. 13.7 the Hebrew word ('*āmît*) is found only in Leviticus, where it appears to refer to a male fellow Israelite. Sometimes it expresses reciprocal relations (Lev. 19.11). In 5.21[6.2] it seems to mean 'business associate'.

[9] Raymond Westbrook, 'Adultery', 568.

[10] N. H. Snaith, *Leviticus and Numbers*, 125, suggests that the defilement is due to contact with the husband's semen which it is assumed is present in the woman's vagina (cf. contact with menstrual blood in v. 19). This is possible, but it seems more probable that it is simply sexual contact with a woman who belongs to another that causes the uncleanness.

Britain up to modern times.[11] The passage is complex. Because of repetitions (the woman is brought twice before Yahweh (vv. 16, 18), takes an oath twice (vv. 19, 21), and drinks the water twice (vv. 24, 26–27)), some suppose that there were originally two separate forms of the ordeal. Possibly, however, there were two rites, one with holy water, the other with a cereal offering and a curse. It has been suggested that the ordeal had two purposes: to give a decision about the guilt of the woman where no evidence was available, and to assuage the husband's jealousy. If the consequences for the guilty wife are to be interpreted as a miscarriage (as REB makes explicit: 'by bringing upon you miscarriage and untimely birth'), the law would seem to be directed at a woman who has become pregnant and her husband suspects that he is not the father. On the other hand 'when the Lord makes your thigh fall away and your body swell' (v. 21, cf. v. 27) has been taken to mean that the woman will suffer a prolapsed uterus, which will put an end to her ability to bear children. Dating is difficult. The emphasis upon defilement and the central place played by the priest may reflect the interests of the post-exilic period. But ordeals may have been common in rural Israel before the exile, and it is possible that the author of Numbers was anxious to give a place for the ordeal for suspected adultery within the law. Possibly ordeals were going out of fashion among those who formulated the Israelite law codes, but were still favoured by ordinary Israelites, and as a consequence this one was retained here.

The stories of adultery that are recorded in Genesis are of doubtful interpretation. They are probably stories from the 'heroic' age, told (or retold) at a much later time, and so either preserving early traditions or showing how the narrators thought the patriarchs behaved. Their historicity is impossible to determine.

The precise situation in the story of Tamar (Gen. 38) is far from clear. Judah's demand that she should be put to death may show the authority of the male head of the family at a time before the Mosaic laws were established.[12] But he is not Tamar's father. She had

---

[11] River ordeals were widespread in the ancient Middle East. The Laws of Ur-Nammu decree a river ordeal for a wife accused of fornication (law 11), the Code of Hammurabi for sorcery (law 2) and adultery (law 132), and the Middle Assyrian Code for adultery (laws 17, 22, and 24). See P. Kyle McCarter, 'River Ordeal', who argues that although the legal material in the Old Testament provides no evidence for a river ordeal and it is impossible to determine whether Israel had any memory of a legal river ordeal, references in the Psalms reflect a *cosmic* river ordeal. De Vaux, *Ancient Israel*, 158, sensibly suggests that the absence of river ordeals in Israel may simply be because apart from the Jordan, the country has no river in which anyone could possibly be drowned. Eryl W. Davies provides a selection of literature (*Numbers*, 51).

[12] Execution by burning is found elsewhere only in Lev. 20.14 (marriage with mother and daughter) and 21.9 (the daughter of a priest who becomes a prostitute). Phillips compares two laws of Hammurabi (laws 110, 157) from which he supposes the penalty

remained a widow in her own father's house on Judah's instructions, waiting for the time when Shelah would be old enough to take her in levirate marriage. Possibly Judah is acting on behalf of his son, who is still a minor, but there is no indication of this in the narrative and no evidence of the practice elsewhere in the Old Testament. Moreover, the charge Judah brings against Tamar is not adultery but becoming a common prostitute.[13] The main theme of the narrative, however, is not adultery but Judah's unwillingness to allow his third son, Shelah, to carry out the duties of the levirate, and this gives greater significance to Judah's demand, for the narrator would have had no special reason to change what either he or the tradition regarded as the normal punishment. Who informed on Tamar is not stated, but the vagueness of 'it was told' supports its being the conventional penalty for prostitution by married or betrothed women.

Three narratives tell of the taking of Sarah and Rebekah into the harems of the Pharaoh or Abimelech (Gen. 12.10–20; 20.1–7; 26.6–11).[14] In all three accounts the patriarch not only connives in adultery but puts his wife in a position where it is virtually certain that another man will take her. The basis for the actions of Abraham and Isaac was probably the husband's complete authority over his wife. Abraham expects to gain materially from the Egyptians' interest in Sarah, and does so. God plays a central part in each story. In the first, he sends plagues on the whole household of Pharaoh, punishing him for his actions even though he acts entirely innocently.[15] God takes an even more immediate action in the second incident by appearing to Abimelech in a dream and issuing a warning (though the words are in the form of a declaration of punishment for wrongdoing). When Abimelech pleads his innocence God tells him to restore Sarah to Abraham, who will then pray for him so that the punishment will be removed. There are oddities in the story. God shows no awareness that Abimelech had not had sexual relations with Sarah, and later in the story we discover that God had already sent disease on Abimelech

---

was borrowed. He thinks the punishment was never inflicted, and suggests that Judah's order in Gen. 38.24 is a priestly gloss (*Israel's Criminal Law*, 129). De Vaux suggests that burning was the earlier form of execution, for which stoning was later substituted (*Ancient Israel*, 36).

[13] The narrative is ambiguous, since Tamar is referred to as a 'sacred prostitute' in vv. 21–22, although the word for an ordinary prostitute is used in vv. 15 and 24.

[14] The relation between these passages is immaterial for our present purpose. If they are variants of a 'stock' theme, this gives them increased significance.

[15] Claus Westermann sets the story within the larger narrative, with the heading: 'The Ancestral Mother in Danger' (*Genesis 12–36*, 159–168). He stresses the importance of the final words of the Pharaoh and Abraham's silence, which shows that he has been put to shame and had forgotten God. He also notes the 'old notion' that a crime inexorably demanded its fated punishment, which is accepted by the narrator alongside the later view of divine punishment.

and made his wife and his slave-wives barren. Further Abraham defends his actions by stressing his fear and pointing out that Sarah was his half-sister as well as his wife. Whether this shows a higher ethical sense on the part of the narrator, as is sometimes claimed, is doubtful. It smacks of sophistry and may simply be a part of the variant folk tradition.[16] Whether Abimelech's riposte to God in his dream and God's response (vv. 3–6) is a step on the road that leads to the recognition of the importance of motive will be taken up in Chapter 10.

The briefer Isaac incident is notable for the high moral stand which Abimelech takes. Once he discovers that Rebekah is Isaac's wife he immediately ensures that she is not violated and that Isaac is protected. God does not directly intervene. The terminology is worth examining. Abimelech comments: 'One of the people might easily have lain with your wife, and you would have brought guilt (*'āšām*) upon us' (Gen. 26.10). This is not a concept which belongs to the legal realm, but is religious. Despite the later developments of the term *'āšām* as a kind of sacrifice, the idea here appears to be guilt which will bring divine punishment.[17] 'Guilt' is probably interpreted within the general field of morality, but conceived as an action of which God (or the gods) disapproves. It has nothing of the modern subjective sense of feeling guilty. The adjective has similar connotations in the Joseph story where the brothers declare: 'In truth we are guilty concerning our brother . . . ' (Gen. 42.21).[18] Moreover, the fact that Abimelech is a non-Israelite implies that this view of adultery is a universal norm.

Joseph's response to Potiphar's wife, 'How then could I do this great wickedness, and sin against God?' (Gen. 39.9) is more specific, but it falls under the same general proviso. Joseph clearly regards having sexual intercourse with his master's wife as contrary to God's will as well as being 'wicked' in human terms because it would be an offence against his master. Presumably the writer of the story and his hearers interpreted the action as adultery. Joseph and the narrator regard God as the source of the ethics which Joseph feels bound to obey.

The story of David and Bathsheba (2 Sam. 11.1–12.25) is beset with problems. David is king, and it might be questioned whether he could

---

[16] The suggestion, championed by E. A. Speiser, *Genesis*, 91–94, that marriage with one's sister was highly esteemed on the basis of supposed Hurrian practice has now been largely abandoned.

[17] Note NEB 'you would have made us liable to retribution'.

[18] The different renderings of the EVV bring out the difficulty of determining the precise sense: 'we are paying the penalty' (NRSV), 'we deserve to be punished' (NEB), 'we are being punished' (REB, NJB); cf. 2 Sam. 14.13, where 'guilty' cannot have a legal sense, for the law requires the avenging of murder, though whether it has a 'purely moral sense' (so Kellermann, *TDOT* I, 437) is doubtful.

be brought to legal account. In Israel, however, the king seems not to be above the law, despite the high royal ideology found in the Psalms (e.g., Pss. 2; 101; 110; and cf. 2 Sam. 7; 23.1–7). God might be expected to condemn him and Bathsheba, but the punishment falls upon their child. Moreover, what the wrongs are of which Nathan accuses David is uncertain. One offence is murder (2 Sam. 12.9), but what is implied by 'you have taken his wife to be your wife' and 'you did it secretly' (2 Sam. 12.9, 12)? Nathan's parable might be taken as viewing the king's wrongdoing primarily as acting violently against Uriah and exerting his royal power against someone who is defenceless and without the support of a clan (he is a Hittite). An important feature of David's sin in Nathan's eyes seems to be his attempt to cover up his adultery. Whatever the exact nuances of the story, it is of first importance that Nathan makes no reference to any laws, and one of the punishments which he threatens is 'I will take your wives before your eyes, and give them to your neighbour, and he shall lie with your wives in the sight of this sun' (2 Sam. 12.11), which is fulfilled exactly by Absalom (2 Sam. 16.22). The divine punishment which immediately follows is the death of David's son. All this bears little relation to any of the laws in the Old Testament.

Other examples from the historical books are equally ambiguous. If Michal was held still to be David's wife, even though he had left her, fled from Saul and become an outlaw, she and Paltiel were guilty of adultery, but this is not suggested in the narrative (1 Sam. 25.44). The breaking up of the 'marriage' between Michal and Paltiel by David on his becoming king is one of the most pathetic little dramas in the whole Bible, but nothing is said about possible adultery in the whole sad story. The king can act as he pleases with regard to other men's wives, and this may reflect the norms which underlie the Bathsheba incident. In any case politics control the negotiations with Abner (2 Sam. 3.12–16).

Abner's taking of Saul's concubine Rizpah is yet more uncertain since it is not clear that she had become Ishbosheth's 'concubine' (*pīlegeš*). Having sexual relations with a concubine may not have been regarded as adultery. But the main point in the story is that Abner was aspiring to kingship (2 Sam. 3.7–11).

Further evidence is found in the books of the prophets and the wisdom writers.

The prophets refer to adultery both literally and as a metaphor. No penalty or sanctions are specified when actual adultery is condemned (Hos. 4.2, 13–14; Jer. 5.7–8; 7.9; 9.1[2]; 23.10, 14; 29.23; Mal. 3.5).[19]

---

[19] Hos. 4.2 and Jer. 7.9 have often been seen as referring to the Decalogue. On this see below, Chapter 8 .

In their metaphorical use of the term as an image for Israel's apostasy, Hosea and Ezekiel describe the stripping of the adulteress in public (Hos. 2.5[3], 12[10]; Ezek. 16.37–39; cf. Jer. 13.22, 26–27, which may, however, be rape rather than public shaming). Although this is metaphorical and symbolizes the devastation of the land by a foreign enemy, it can hardly be totally unrelated to the punishment inflicted on some wives. The intention of the action is uncertain. Some see it as constituting the punishment itself, submitting the woman to public shaming and humiliation, a punishment which is found in many societies and well documented for the ancient Middle East.[20] Others regard it as signifying divorce, the husband declaring that he will no longer clothe and feed his wife (at Nuzi an adulterous wife was stripped before being driven out of the house). It is possible, though somewhat unlikely, that it was a preliminary to the trial and stoning; Ezekiel 16 on which this claim is based is a highly metaphorical passage, where the historical facts have contaminated the description. Jeremiah 3.8, another metaphorical passage treating Israel's unfaithfulness as adultery or harlotry, seems to show that divorce was one possible option for the husband, even though the reality of Israel's exile under the Assyrians lies behind the image and may have influenced it. Ezekiel refers to cutting off the nose and ears of the adulteress and to stoning (Ezek. 16.40; 23.25).

Turning to the wisdom writings, Job contains a vivid picture of the adulterer waiting for the evening gloom to mask his activities, but the writer does no more than show disapproval (Job 24.15). In Proverbs the young man is warned against the enticements of other men's wives, and this is backed up with descriptions of the consequences of committing adultery (Prov. 6.24–35; cf. 7.5–27, which may be metaphorical, as 9.13–18 certainly is). The punishments are not entirely clear. There appear to be references to the loss of honour, the wrath of the jealous husband, and wounds (possibly inflicted by the husband). Even more uncertain is whether the death penalty is alluded to in such statements as: 'the wife of another stalks a man's very life' (Prov. 6.26); 'he who does it destroys himself' (Prov. 6.32); 'he goes like an ox to the slaughter, or bounds like a stag toward the trap until an arrow pierces its entrails. He is like a bird rushing into a snare, not knowing that it will cost him his life' (7.22–23); and the guests of the 'foolish woman' are 'in the depths of Sheol'. The references to dying may well be metaphorical, or refer to premature death rather than to a humanly inflicted punishment. If the woman is a prostitute, adultery has not been committed, but in Proverbs 7.19 she is plainly a married woman, for she declares that her husband is on a long journey from home so that the coast is clear for her lover. These pieces of

---

[20] A good survey is provided by R. Westbrook, 'Adultery'.

instruction, however, do not sound as if they contemplated the execution of the adulterer or the adulteress.

Nathan's threat that another man will lie with David's wives has already been noted. It might be described as a 'vicarious talion' and parallels can be found in several of the law codes from the ancient Middle East. For example, if a man strikes the daughter of a free man and she dies 'they shall put his daughter to death', and where a builder failed to make a house strong and it collapses and kills the owner, the builder is put to death, but if it were the owner's son who is killed, the builder's son is put to death'.[21] In the Middle Assyrian Code, law 55 decrees that, if a free man's virgin daughter is raped, her father takes the wife of the rapist and gives her to be raped. The same idea is found in Job's great oath of clearance, in which he says:

> If my heart has been enticed by a woman,
> and I have lain in wait at my neighbour's door;
> then let my wife grind for another,
> and let others bow down upon her.
> For that would be a heinous crime;[22]
> that would be an iniquity to be punished by the judges;[23]
> for that would be a fire which consumes unto Abaddon,
> and it would burn to the root all my increase. (Job 31.9–12)

He appears to expect the divine punishment for his adultery to be the sexual abuse of his own wife. The same form of retribution is found in the metaphorical oracle in Jeremiah 8.10.

This survey of the main passages relating to adultery leaves a very confused picture. It has led to a debate between Henry McKeating and Anthony Phillips, which A. A. Anderson has attempted to resolve, and also forms part of the evidence on which G. J. Wenham draws in his discussion of the gap between law and ethics in the Old Testament.

Phillips argues that Israel distinguished between 'crime' and 'tort'. The criminal law is grounded in the covenant, and the Ten Commandments are 'to be thought of neither as ethical norms nor as regulations for the good ordering of society, but as the stipulations whose observance maintained the covenant relationship'. Since breaking any of these laws threatened the covenant relationship the offence was treated as a crime and the offender was executed to propitiate Yahweh.[24] On the basis of the various laws recorded in the Old Testament he presents a history of the treatment of adultery. It

---

[21] CH 209–10, 229–230, *ANET*, 176. Cf. discussion in G. R. Driver and John C. Miles, *The Babylonian Laws*, I, 413–416; Westbrook, 'Adultery', 569.

[22] *zimmāh* is associated particularly with adultery, incest, and licentiousness (see S. Steingrimsson, '*zmm* etc.' in *TDOT* IV, 89–90).

[23] Westbrook, 'Adultery', interprets the Hebrew as meaning 'an offence solely my own'.

[24] Phillips, *Israel's Criminal Law*, 153.

was the Deuteronomic reform which brought women within the scope
of Israel's criminal law. Originally they were not equal members of
the covenant community with men. In this period the wife was
divorced and her lover executed. After the exile the crime of adultery
was reinterpreted to include all sexual offences and breach of any of
them was punished by excommunication, the priests relying on divine
punishment.[25]

In his first article[26] McKeating argued that the casuistic laws
prescribe the death penalty for adultery, but while there is evidence
that this penalty was known, there is no evidence that it was actually
applied. Instead public humiliation (and presumably also divorce) was
sometimes practised, while the wisdom writings imply that the main
sanctions were loss of reputation and the anger of the offended
husband. He concluded that there is no proof that the death penalty
was *never* resorted to, but it was certainly not *always* imposed. Further
there was always the possibility of direct divine punishment, implied
by the apodeictic laws, and such references as Joseph's mention of
'sin against God' (Gen. 39.9), God's punishment for David's adultery
with Bathsheba (2 Sam. 12.13), the guilt of Abraham and Isaac (Gen.
12; 20; 26, esp. 26.10), and the much later teaching of Wisdom
3.16–19; 4.6.

So far as the laws go, McKeating points out that adultery is not
mentioned in Deuteronomy 27 or the Book of the Covenant. He
argues that Deuteronomy and the Holiness Code appear to be
making what had earlier been a possible penalty mandatory, taking it
out of the realm of family law where the husband had discretion and
making it an offence against God or the community. The idea that
adultery was displeasing to God, however, appears quite early, and
these two collections of law built upon that idea, but did not
leave God to punish it. Despite this, alternative penalties are still
found in writings from the eighth to the sixth century, more or less
contemporary with Deuteronomy and the Holiness Code. Thus the
attempt to take adultery out of family law had only limited success.

McKeating concludes from this that society's ethical values cannot
be read off from the law. Before this can be done it is necessary to
know how readily resort was made to the law, how rigorously it was
applied, and whether the prescribed penalty was that normally
inflicted or merely a possible maximum permitted. The status of the
law codes also needs to be known – did they comprise rules that were
actually applied in the administration of justice, or were they
suggestions for reform, or even simply statements of principle or
ideals? While the laws may have value in revealing the ideals held by

[25] *Ibid.*, 110–129.
[26] McKeating, 'Sanctions against Adultery'.

members of Israelite society, even describing how people were supposed to behave, the study of ethics must begin with the actual behaviour recorded in the narratives. The sanction of law is rarely the only one available. Usually offences are discouraged by a battery of sanctions. Conscience, a sense of religious duty, ridicule or hostility by neighbours, losing respect within the community, ostracism – all these play a part in controlling behaviour. In the Old Testament adultery fell into different spheres, each with appropriate sanctions: moral and religious principles, prudence, and law. For most Israelites, McKeating believes, adultery was a private matter for the conscience of the offender and the decision of the offended husband. The laws show that it was felt that marriage was not a purely private concern, and they attempted to maintain marital fidelity, by forcefully asserting what was desirable, even if they were rarely resorted to. In practice, however, adultery fell not very far beyond the bounds of what was regarded as tolerable in Israelite society. He adds that the ethics of the Old Testament and the ethics of ancient Israelite society do not necessarily coincide.

This presented a direct challenge to Phillips, who took it up in an article in the same journal two years later.[27] In his opinion the ground of the distinction between the view that he and others, such as Moshe Greenberg and Shalom Paul, hold, and the approach of those like Bernard Jackson and Henry McKeating, is whether Old Testament law was regarded as distinctive or whether it was part of the general laws of the ancient Middle East. He finds McKeating guilty of two serious methodological errors: he assumes that because the death penalty for adultery first appears in Deuteronomy and the Holiness Code the attempt to make it mandatory dates from the time of these laws, and he does not consider the possibility that these two collections of laws may be the product of legal development rather than being new laws. The key factor, in Phillips's opinion, is the exclusion of women from liability under the criminal law of adultery before these two laws. Once this is accepted the earlier material falls into place: the adulterer would have been executed, the wife would have been dealt with by her husband, usually by divorce, for it is unlikely that he would have had the power to put her to death. To treat adultery as a crime was unique in the ancient Middle East, and once women were included in the covenant people the husband could not pardon the criminal, take private revenge, or settle for damages. This situation was due to the Decalogue.

In response,[28] McKeating pointed out that he did not challenge the *existence* of adultery as a 'sacral crime', but the fact remained that

---

[27] Phillips, 'Another Look at Adultery'.
[28] McKeating, 'Response'.

there is no recorded instance of its being punished by death in the whole Old Testament. Thus the principle was not universally acknowledged and remained religious theory rather than practical law. Further, he accepts that the law making death mandatory for adultery might have existed before Deuteronomy and the Holiness Code, but there is no evidence that it was. Thus it is *probable* that it was newly introduced at the end of the seventh century, or an attempt was made at that time to reassert it. The main issue, however, is methodological, Phillips, McKeating claims, takes it for granted that we know how law functioned in Israelite society. We do not. The law contains very little to indicate how it was applied, how seriously the laws were taken, and which laws were more than theoretical principles. To discover this the *narratives* have to be examined, together with the books of the prophets and the wisdom writings. When this is done it is found that there is no support for Phillips's view that Israel was governed by a unique sacral criminal law.

A useful assessment of the debate has been made by Arnold A. Anderson.[29] As he rightly observes, the difference between Phillips and McKeating concerns the sanctions against adultery and their implications. Phillips sees adultery not merely as a wrongful act against the woman's husband but above all as an absolute sin against God. To fail to carry out the death penalty would bring divine sanctions against Israel. McKeating, on the other hand, sees the law as a forceful statement of what is desirable. Its sanctions are very rarely brought into play, and for most Israelites adultery was a private matter to be settled by the unofficial action of the husband. The law is largely a matter of religious theory.

Anderson confesses himself not convinced by the arguments of Phillips. He finds no evidence that women were outside the scope of the criminal law before Deuteronomy, claims that David showed little consideration for Israel's criminal law and its sanctions, and notes that no legal action was taken against David. He thinks it probable that the Decalogue was addressed to the nation, telling the Israelites how they should live. It is also probable that in the early period husbands could take action against an adulterer just as the next of kin did with murder. From the references to adultery in the prophets Anderson infers that divorce was one option open to the husband if his wife committed adultery.

Anderson's conclusion is that wives were not executed for unfaithfulness in the pre-exilic period, otherwise adultery as a theological metaphor would exclude the possibility of repentance. For the adulterer, the *maximum* penalty was death, but this was probably not mandatory and other punitive measures were available, which,

[29] Arnold A. Anderson, 'Law'.

whether legal options or not, were commonly found in ancient Israel. Thus Anderson basically sides with McKeating.

Without reference to this earlier discussion, G. J. Wenham examines the relation between law and ethics in an article which considers worship of other gods, homicide, and 'sexual morality'.[30] Here I limit myself to a consideration of the last, together with Wenham's discussion of the principles involved. He argues that scholars have misrepresented biblical ethics by failing to distinguish between (1) the world of the writers themselves, (2) the world of law, and (3) the ethical world of the actors. The writers rarely make explicit moral comments. Laws imply an ethical stance, which may be 'elucidated by analysis and synthesis'. The actors behave in accordance with certain ethical principles which may not be congruent with those enshrined in the laws or held by the biblical writers.

Wenham's chief concern is with the ethical position of the biblical writers. Thus he asserts that while the writers seldom express moral approval or disapproval of the actors' actions, they expect their readers to share their moral outlook and to be shocked when the fathers of the nation behave in sinful ways. Equally the law sets a minimum standard of behaviour, which the writers frequently surpass. For example, because the law punished adulterers with death only where the woman was married, it does not mean that affairs by husbands with unattached girls or prostitutes were permissible. In most societies what the law enforces is not the same as what upright members of society feel is socially desirable, let alone ideal.

When he comes to deal specifically with sexual morality, Wenham writes: 'Although Abraham resorted to surrogate marriage to have a child through Hagar, an accepted practice in the ancient Near East, that does not mean that the narrator approved of it. On the contrary the subtle echoes of Genesis 3 in Genesis 16 suggest that Abraham and Sarah were making a mistake comparable to that of Adam and Eve in the Garden of Eden.' Coming more directly to the law of adultery, he points out that the 'double standard' found in ancient Israel meant that men had more sexual freedom than women, and the law discriminated harshly against women. But the writers hoped for a higher standard. In reality social custom curtailed men's freedom. Early arranged marriages meant that there were few unattached girls. We might wonder how Wenham knows this. As de Vaux points out, the historical books provide little information, and the legal texts provide evidence of the custom of engagement.[31] The laws concerning unbetrothed virgins show that not all young women were engaged. Intercourse with a single girl was liable to severe punishment, as in

---

[30] G. J. Wenham, 'Law and Ethics'.
[31] De Vaux, *Ancient Israel*, 32.

the case of Dinah. The size of the marriage present meant that few men apart from wealthy patriarchs and kings could marry more than one wife. And the 'dowry system' would have discouraged capricious divorce. Given this social situation, in which lifelong monogamy was the normal pattern of marriage, it is to be expected that the biblical writings reflect a positive attitude towards monogamy, as the prophets and wisdom writings do. Further, Genesis 29–50 is a graphic portrayal of the tensions and sorrows caused by bigamy. Legal texts allow for bigamy but reveal a dislike of it (cf. Lev. 18.18; Deut. 17.17; 21.15–17). So although the law does not require monogamy, the writers clearly 'hoped for better behaviour'.

In the same way 'though a married man may not face the charge of adultery for extramarital affairs, this does not mean that the Bible condones male infidelity'. The historical books never speak approvingly of prostitutes. Proverbs devotes nearly three chapters to warning young men against the folly of resorting to them. Job claims that he was completely loyal to his wife. Wenham holds that whether Job is 'exceptionally upright' in this depends upon the Israelite view of marriage, and we have no wedding rites from Bible times. On this two comments might be made: (1) Wenham certainly would not accept that the rape of a man's wife is fitting punishment for the man's adultery, yet this is the implication of Job's solemn oath; (2) the reason we have no wedding rites may have been that there were none. If it was regarded as a covenant mutual loyalty would have been a key element in it. That several prophets likened God's covenant with Israel to marriage suggests that husbands should be more than simply faithful but should care supremely for their wives' welfare.

In all the three spheres which he examines, Wenham holds that the 'ideals are most clearly set out in the opening chapters of Genesis and in the wisdom literature'. The law is only 'the floor below which human behaviour must not sink'. The ethical ceiling is 'as high as heaven itself' for the key principle of biblical ethics is 'the imitation of God'. He stresses that he is trying to elucidate the standpoint of the biblical writers. Many in Israel no doubt 'were simply happy just to do the minimum to escape punishment'. Finally, he draws three consequences from the immense gap between the ethical ideal and the lower standards of the law: (1) it suggests that the Bible 'expects understanding and toleration' of those who fall short of the ideal; (2) the narratives should be judged by the ideals expressed in Genesis 1–3, Psalms and the wisdom literature, and in assessing their ethics we should not just consider explicit statements in the text; and (3) on the level of ethics there is little to choose between the Old and New Testaments.

Wenham is right in drawing attention to the distinctions between the law, behaviour in Israelite society, and the views of the biblical writers. Where he is wrong is in assuming that a single ethic was held by all the different writers of the biblical books. He is even more in error in believing that any of the writers could so leap out of their own culture as to become supporters of a twentieth-century 'Christian' ethic. While the attention he gives to the gap between law and practice is valuable, his reading of the Old Testament is entirely 'flat' and lacking in any proper understanding of the all-pervasive influence of culture and social pressures. It is open to him to select a few ethical ideals from the Old Testament writings if he wishes, but he should not then suppose that these ideas controlled the ethics of the 'biblical writers', who were men of their times (the term 'men' is deliberate, since it provides yet another example of the way culture controlled so many parts of biblical life).

On the other hand, we cannot read off the 'biblical ethic', or even the ethic of the contemporary society, from what is written in the law. In terms of method and approach McKeating is right. The relation between law, social norms, and actual behaviour is difficult to determine, but unless the distinctions are made, all that will be achieved will be little more than a reiteration of the laws, if only because these are the fullest and most detailed source of ethical demands. The distinctions between the biblical writers, the laws, and the actors themselves, to which Wenham has drawn attention, are also important, and once his idealism is seen for what it is, useful insights can be derived from his study. Further distinctions, such as that between what the Israelite peasant regarded as 'right and proper' and the practice of kings and courtiers, who dominate the pages of the Old Testament, might be made as well.

This last point deserves to be emphasized. McKeating writes as if the biblical narratives provide a clear and panoramic snapshot of Israelite society. This is not so. Not only do they have a propagandist, theological purpose, but the world they inhabit and report is largely that of the court. Where peasants and merchants appear it is almost always due to their relation to the king.

The principles upon which the study of Old Testament ethics must be conducted are becoming plainer as a result of this debate over adultery. Nevertheless, it is less certain that any of the several 'systems of ethics' found in ancient Israelite society can be recovered. Was there a change from an early period when adultery was treated as a purely family matter, to be dealt with by the husband, to an attempt by the law-makers of Deuteronomy and the Holiness Code to make adultery a sacral offence? Does the fact that nowhere in the Old Testament narratives is found any instance of the death penalty for adultery being carried out in the Old Testament narratives show that the laws are late or that they were inventions by priests concerned with purity, and were disregarded by ordinary Israelites? What weight is to be given to the alternative punishments reflected in the oracles of the prophets, metaphorical as some of these are, and the wisdom writers? And has too much attention been paid to sanctions? Do not most people maintain an ethic because it is the accepted norm, internalized from an early age, rather than out of fear of punishment?

Simply to pose these questions reveals the extent of our ignorance and the unlikelihood of its being dissipated. We shall probably never know how the man who seduced his neighbour's wife was actually treated, or what precise punishment was meted out to the wife who welcomed another man into her bed. We possess the 'official' ethic, and can put alongside it occasional glimpses of the behaviour of kings and other members of the upper classes. We have been alerted to the danger of reading off behaviour directly from what is set out in the laws. We have also become aware that a large gap exists between law, ethical norms, and actual behaviour. To this extent our study of Old Testament ethics has been advanced by our examination of adultery.

5

'SUCH A THING IS NOT DONE IN ISRAEL'

The last chapter ended in a mood of considerable depression. It was seen that Israelite ethics cannot be read off from the legal enactments found in the Old Testament. The extent to which the laws were realistic or priestly ideals was deemed uncertain. There was no agreement on the distinctiveness of Israelite law. Whether it is possible to trace any change or development in the ethics of ancient Israel seemed doubtful. It appeared virtually impossible to discover what the Israelite peasant held to be right and wrong, though it was recognized that a considerable gap existed between this moral sensibility and what was actually done. Above all it was recognized that our only sources are the documents preserved in the Hebrew Bible, so that we can never be sure that we have recovered the living 'ancient Israel'. Is there any way forward?

Progress will have of necessity to be slow and piecemeal. We will first examine a phrase which has latent possibilities for unearthing something of the customary morality of ancient Israel.

In the story of David and his family Tamar begins her well-expressed and forceful appeal to Amnon not to rape her with: 'No, my brother, do not force me; for such a thing is not done ($l\bar{o}$-$y\bar{e}^c\bar{a}\acute{s}eh$) in Israel; do not do this wanton folly' (2 Sam. 13.12). The niph'al of $^c\bar{a}\acute{s}\bar{a}h$ bears this special connotation rarely in the Old Testament, but on each occasion it has considerable significance for our quest. Here Tamar appeals to her half-brother on the grounds that to rape her goes against what is customary in Israel. But custom has a stronger force than it would have today. For the ethics of the community are enshrined in such custom and bind that community together. As P. Kyle McCarter puts it: 'the expression refers to serious violations of custom (Gen. 20.9; 29.26) that threaten the fabric of society'.[1] So Tamar probably does not appeal to any law but fastens on something which she believes will have greater weight – tradition, custom, what is *comme il faut*. We do not know whether the laws concerning rape were written or known at this time, so that we cannot say that Tamar deliberately avoided mentioning the law.[2] What is clear is that she felt

[1] P. Kyle McCarter, *II Samuel*, 322.
[2] The situation is further confused by Tamar's later assertion that David would allow

certain of the force of a community ethic which was both recognized and followed. Were this not so the passion in her appeal would be lost. This is supported by her use of another fairly rare term, *n'bālāh*, translated here as 'wanton folly', for this too is grounded in community ethical norms. Phillips argues that it refers to a wider range of ethical wrongs than sexual crimes, and is 'a general expression for serious disorderly and unruly action resulting in the break-up of an existing relationship whether between tribes, within the family, in a business arrangement, in marriage, or with God. . . . It indicates the end of an existing order consequent upon breach of rules which maintained that order.'[3] Whether it should also be described as 'sacrilege', as Roth claims,[4] is doubtful. It belongs to the social mores rather than to religious faith and practice, in the same way that Tamar's 'shame' does (the other ground for her appeal to Amnon). Robert P. Carroll gets it right when he describes the phrase 'to commit folly in Israel' as 'an idiomatic phrase for some outrageous act contrary to the good order of the community'.[5] Whatever the law might decree, therefore, here is an ethic grounded in the community and not in any divine commandment.[6]

In Abimelech's complaint against Abraham for passing off Sarah as his sister (Gen. 20.9) the RSV translates 'things that are not done' by 'things that ought not to be done'. The slightly awkward Hebrew 'and thus it is not done' in Jacob's sons' angry reaction to the rape of Dinah (Gen. 34.7) is also rendered by 'for such a thing ought not to be done'. To western ears this bears definite ethical overtones which are certainly found in the original – but there they have a different basis. The actions are condemned, not because they offend against any law or innate sense of right and wrong, but because they are contrary to established custom, custom which carries strong moral force. The verse in the Dinah episode also contains the word *n'bālāh*, 'folly', which, as has been seen, has very strong ethical connotations. REB

Amnon to marry her. This is forbidden in Deut. 27.22 and Lev. 18.9, 11; 20.17. Various proposals have been made as to what the situation was at the time of David: the laws were not yet in effect, they were not recognized in Jerusalem, they were understood in Jerusalem as referring only to casual sexual intercourse between siblings, and David was expected to allow the marriage despite the law (see McCarter, *II Samuel*, 323–324).

[3] Anthony Phillips, 'NEBALAH', 241. See also W. M. W. Roth, '*NBL*' and G. Gerlemann, 'Der Nicht-Mensch'.

[4] Followed by McCarter, who describes the term as 'a violation of the sacred taboos, that define and maintain the social structure' (*II Samuel*, 327–328).

[5] Robert P. Carroll, *Jeremiah*, 554, on Jer. 29.23.

[6] H. Wheeler Robinson noted this early in the present century, but disparaged it as leading to the 'externalism of morality', opposing it to the attitude of the 'honourable man to-day, who is controlled by a sense of duty' (*Doctrine of Man*, 47–49).

gets closer to the sense with its 'Shechem had done what the Israelites hold to be an intolerable outrage', though it still misses the sense that it is part of the custom which everyone accepts.[7]

The only other example of the niph'al of *'āśāh* in precisely this sense is the incident where Laban passes off Leah for Rachel to Jacob. Laban defends his deceit with the words: 'It is not so done in our country, to give the younger before the first-born' (Gen. 29.26). Custom is more obvious here, as REB makes explicit with its 'It is against the custom of our country', but we tend not to be aware of the moral force behind the custom. The fact that the phrase is similar to that in Genesis 20.9 (with *kēn*) indicates that the power of tradition underlies both actions.[8]

The term *n'bālāh*, though still rare, is found rather more frequently than the niph'al of *'āśāh*. Its use in the stories of Tamar has already been noted. Beyond this it is prominent in the story of the rape of the Levite's concubine in Judges 19–20. Here the old man pleads with the men who beat on the door of the house and demand that the traveller be brought out to them 'that we may know him': 'No, my brethren, do not act so wickedly; seeing that this man has come into my house, do not do this vile thing' (*n'bālāh*, 19.23). He follows this with the offer of his own virgin daughter and the traveller's concubine: 'Ravish them and do with them what seems good to you; but against this man do not do so vile a thing' (*n'bālāh*, 19.24). Despite some uncertainty about the precise demand of the men of Gibeah, it seems that the chief offence of which they are guilty is breaking the customary rule of hospitality. John Gray thinks that the wrong was compounded because the Levite was a resident alien (19.1), whose only protection was the recognized sanctity of his status and the convention of hospitality and who was under the protection of God.[9] When the Levite tells the assembled Israelites what had happened to him and his concubine in Gibeah he declares that the men intended to kill him (20.5), describing their actions as 'abomination (*zimmāh*) and wantonness (*n'bālāh*)' (20.6), and in their response they also employ the word *n'bālāh* (20.10).[10] However intermixed the various crimes may be in this

---

[7] The colloquialism of CEV also manages to convey something of the feeling: 'Nothing is more disgraceful than rape, and it should not be tolerated in Israel.'

[8] Somewhat similar, however, is the reaction to the rape of the Levite's concubine at Gibeah: 'Such a thing has never happened or been seen from the day the people of Israel came up out of the land of Egypt until this day' (Jdg. 19.30), which is also a reaction to the violation of custom.

[9] J. Gray, *Joshua, Judges, Ruth*, 352.

[10] The LXX omits *zimmāh* in v. 6. Martin Noth regarded the action of Israel against the tribe of Benjamin as an example of the punishment of offences against the law of the amphictyony, and, indeed, describes 'folly wrought in Israel' as a technical term which 'apparently signified a violation of the divine law then in force in the tribal society' (*History*, 105), but the theory of the amphictyony has now gone out of favour.

narrative, it is certain that custom underlies the basic moral thrust of the story.

In Joshua 7.15 Achan's failure to carry out the *ḥērem* (the ban) at Jericho is described both as breaking the covenant and an act of *nᵉḇālāh*. As is well known, the *ḥērem* was practised outside of Israel, most famously by King Mesha of Moab, and although in this narrative it is set firmly within the commands of Yahweh, essentially it belongs to the customs of the region with regard to the waging of war.

Apart from the application of the term to speech (Isa. 9.16[17]; 32.6; Job 42.8) and Abigail's play on the name of her husband (1 Sam. 25.25), the only other example of *nᵉḇālāh* in the Old Testament is in the law of Deuteronomy 22.21, where it is used of a wife who is found not to be a virgin on marriage. Even here the elaboration of the casuistic law suggests that it is founded on custom.[11]

The obverse of *nᵉḇālāh* is *ṣedeq/ṣᵉdāqāh*, conventionally translated 'righteousness', although the word has virtually dropped out of current secular speech, and REB and GNB usually give alternative translations suited to the contexts. Although attempts have been made to distinguish between them, there appears to be little difference in meaning or usage between the masculine and feminine forms of the word, apart from the fact that only *ṣᵉdāqāh* is used in the plural, often referring to the 'saving acts', 'vindication', even 'victories' of God (e.g., Jdg. 5.11; 1 Sam. 12.7; Mic. 6.5).

Despite the efforts of biblical scholars to provide a rich meaning to the term, *ṣedeq/ṣᵉdāqāh* is as empty of concrete meaning as 'right' or 'good' in modern English.[12]

---

[11] A. D. H. Mayes points to the casuistic form, parallels in other codes, and the slight contact with anything specifically Israelite as indications of the antiquity of the laws in 22.13–30 (*Deuteronomy*, 309). Rather than ancient laws, I prefer to see here traditional customs.

[12] A few examples may be offered. W. Eichrodt sets 'righteousness' firmly within the covenant and judicial procedure, and declares that it 'exalts over all abstract ethical ideas a *loyalty manifested in the concrete relationships of community*' (*Theology*, I, 240–249, quotation 249, his italics). H. D. Preuss, however, points out that there is no Old Testament passage where 'righteousness' and 'covenant' occur together; he stresses that righteousness means 'less a general, normative behavior that, for instance, is oriented to the divine commandments and more a behavior that is specially related to the community (e.g., "to be found innocent of the accusations of others"; Deut. 25.1ff.)' (*Theology*, II, 167). G. von Rad denies that it is an 'absolute ideal ethical norm' and, following H. Cremer, finds its centre in the claims made on conduct by relationships, mutually between human beings and between human beings and God (*Theology*, I, 370–383). W. Zimmerli similarly claims that it is not 'blindfolded "justice"' but Yahweh's righteousness means 'the social bond existing between him and his people and Yahweh's actions based on that bond', with human justice as a reflection of Yahweh's justice, and is associated with keeping the commandments (*Theology*, 142–144). L. Koehler finds the origin of *ṣaddīq*, the adjective, in 'legal

In an article on justice in the prophets J. L. Mays glimpses this, though he does not carry through its implications because he rushes too quickly to expound the message of the prophets in their own society. Early in the article, however, he writes: 'They hurl the word out in their messages, as though it were self-evident what it means, never lingering to analyze, justify, or explain.' Mays goes on to declare that it 'connotes a complex of meanings like equal, fair, right, good, which, however modulated, constitute a focus of value that is understood to be essential to social well-being'.[13] All these words, however, are empty jars, waiting to be filled with meaning.

What is needed, then, is to ask not what *ṣedeq/ṣ'dāqāh* is but what it means for the king, the prophet, the wise man, the peasant farmer. And that is no easy task, made the more difficult because *ṣedeq* is completely absent from the historical books and *ṣ'dāqāh* occurs in them only ten times, three of these in poems.

The place to start is the phrase 'balances of *ṣedeq*, weights [lit. 'stones'] of *ṣedeq*, an ephah of *ṣedeq*' (Lev. 19.36; cf. Deut. 25.13–15). The number of shekels in the weights, the size of the ephah are not defined. The demand is simply that the balances weigh accurately, the weights and measures are 'true'. In Ezekiel 45.10, which REB translates as 'your scales must be honest, as must your ephah and your bath', the prophet specifies the standard relations between the various measures, though not the precise amounts. Here *ṣedeq* refers to the standard, a standard which has to be derived from

---

parlance' with the sense of 'innocent' (*Theology*, 166–167). H. Ringgren warns against treating it as 'exclusively [or] even primarily a juristic or moral concept' and sees it as a norm found within God's own nature, but also signifying human conduct that is in accord with the norms of society (though even these norms are based on the righteousness of God), and further having a cosmic aspect (*Israelite Religion*, 83). N. H. Snaith emphasizes the development of *ṣedeq/ṣ'dāqāh* into 'benevolence', 'almsgiving' in post-biblical Hebrew and the Aramaic of Dan. 4.24[27], and argues that it never meant blind justice, but depends entirely on the nature of God and has 'a persistent tendency to topple over into benevolence', a 'bias in favour of the helpless' (*Distinctive Ideas*, 68–78). For a recent comprehensive survey, with bibliography, see David J. Reimer, '*ṣdq*' (NIDOTTE 3, 744–769). Andrew Davies recognizes that the same is true of terms for evil: 'we are told plainly [by Isaiah] that it is bad to be evil, . . . but we are still none the wiser as to what these evil deeds and evil people are' (*Double Standards*, 37–38). The absence of an agreed meaning of 'justice' in modern English is beautifully illustrated in the underrated novel by Mrs Humphry Ward, *Marcella*, where Aldous Raeburn and Marcella Boyce take opposite sides over the killing of a gamekeeper by poachers. Both are of high integrity and support 'justice', but fill it out sufficiently differently for Marcella to break off her engagement to Raeburn.

[13] J. L. Mays, 'Justice', 6–7. Because he uses only the English words he can make such statements as, '[Justice] frequently appears in synonymous relation with "righteousness"', and then define 'righteousness' as 'a quality of intention and act, a characteristic of persons. It is present when a person tries to fulfil the possibilities of given or assumed relationships in a way that is fair and favorable to others.' (p. 8).

the norms of actual practice. The reference to 'sacrifices of righteousness' (Deut. 33.19; Ps. 4.6[5]; 51.21[19]; Mal. 3.3) is similar. They are sacrifices offered with the proper ritual, or, as REB has it in Psalm 51, 'the appointed sacrifices'. 'Paths of righteousness' (Ps. 23.3) are 'right paths'.

Two lines of meaning can then be traced further. In terms of the administering of justice in the law courts among the elders 'at the gate' or by the king in his position as vicegerent of Yahweh, 'righteousness' means giving a true judgment by acquitting the innocent and condemning the guilty, where the word translated innocent is itself *ṣaddīq*. Thus the lawgivers call on the judges to 'judge fairly' and not be 'partial in judgment' (Deut. 1.16; cf. 16.18–20, where the demand is reinforced by the rejection of bribery; Lev. 19.15, 'you are to administer justice . . . with strict fairness', REB). The king is expected to 'maintain law and justice' (1 Kgs. 10.9, REB) as David is said to have done (2 Sam. 8.15), and as Yahweh himself does (1 Kgs. 8.31–32). Although such fairness in justice is an ethical good, in itself it provides no content for the actions that make those brought before the judge 'innocent' or 'guilty'.

In terms of morality, righteousness in the first place is conformity to the prevailing norms of society. This is seen clearly in the story of Judah and Tamar, where Judah commends Tamar as being 'more righteous than I' (Gen. 38.26), even though she had acted as a prostitute and as such was guilty of an offence that merited the death penalty. She was 'in the right' (REB) because she had attempted in the only way open to her to conform to the social norms of the time in providing a son to maintain the name of her dead husband. Saul's comment when David spared him in the cave appears superficially similar, but in fact moves beyond what is required by social norms: 'You are more righteous than I' (REB 'the right is on your side, not mine', 1 Sam. 24.18[17]). Here, as Saul points out, ordinary practice would be to kill an enemy who is in one's power, but David has spared Saul and shown him mercy.

Whence does Saul derive his 'higher' ethic? Not from the law, for no laws require the sparing of an enemy. Hardly from custom, for Saul implies that custom allows the killing of an enemy (cf. v. 20[19]). David grounded his actions in the ideology which held the anointed king to be sacrosanct (vv. 7[6], 9[10]). The plot of the narrative, of course, is controlled by the belief that God has already determined that David shall be king on the death of Saul, and does not provide an analysis of the ethical actions of the participants, and it may be the writer who draws the ethic from the royal ideology, evidence of which is also found in the Psalms. The point to be made here is that *ṣedeq/ṣᵉdāqāh* always has to be filled out from the substantive ethic which the actors or writers hold.

If righteousness can go beyond the established standards of the time, how is it filled out? Mays seeks to discover this by asking what it was in society which provoked the prophets to cry for justice. What was the nature of the social crisis which they addressed? What criteria mark the good society for them? He finds his answer in the economic development of the times, when ownership of the land was passing from the small peasants to the large landowners (see Isa. 5.8–10; Mic. 2.1–2). This came about with the introduction of the monarchy, and through practices – enforcing creditors' rights, foreclosure on land and crops, selling Israelites into slavery for debt – which those who carried them out regarded as both 'legal' and desirable. The prophets opposed this, not out of hostility to private ownership, but rather from a traditional and theological belief in the rights of inheritance and the Exodus deliverance. The story of Naboth's vineyard reveals the first, and the Deuteronomic teaching that possession of land was a sign of salvation the second (1 Kgs. 21; Deut. 26.3, 10). Mays holds that the central political issue was the administration of justice. The monarchy overlaid the customary law, which was secular and simply what had been long accepted and established, with powers of taxation, the *corvée*, and the appropriation of land for the state and its officials. Alongside of this were the theological commandments, which Mays describes as 'rules of righteousness'. The prophets held that what was happening, although 'legal' was a travesty of 'justice'. Moreover, justice was being 'commercialized'. As the difference between rich and poor increased 'the rich could afford more "justice" than the others'.[14]

If this is one way in which it is possible to discern how the prophets fill in the content of *ṣedeq/ṣʿdāqāh*, a second way is to examine the places where they add definitions to the terms. A clear example is Ezekiel 18 where the background contrast is between the 'righteous' man, who 'does what is lawful and right', and the 'wicked' man, who sins. What it means to be 'righteous' is expounded in verses 6–9 and 14–17: 'he does not eat upon the mountains or lift up his eyes to the idols of the house of Israel, does not defile his neighbour's wife or approach a woman in her time of impurity, does not oppress any one, but restores to the debtor his pledge, commits no robbery, gives his bread to the hungry and covers the naked with a garment, does not lend at interest or take any increase, withholds his hand from iniquity, executes true justice between man and man', and obeys God's laws. It is a mixture of things that are forbidden in various laws, and actions, such as feeding the hungry, which go beyond the law and are found in

---

[14] *Ibid*, esp. 8–14. Ferdinand E. Deist sees the change as the superimposing of a 'redistribution' economy on a 'subsistence' economy (*Material Culture*, 255, cf. 178–181). The ethics of the prophets belong to a subsistence economy.

other prophetic writings (Isa. 58.7) and in the wisdom writings (e.g., Job 22.7; 31.17). Other passages where righteousness is filled out are Isaiah 33.15, Jeremiah 22.3, 15–16, and Psalm 72.4, 12–14. The first of these has similarities with the 'entrance liturgies' of Psalms 15 and 24, and may be derived from the cult. Jeremiah 22 and Psalm 72 are descriptions of the righteous king, and indicate the way the king is expected to maintain justice and protect those in the community who are powerless.

How far can *ṣedeq/ṣᵉdāqāh* be filled out from the legal material in the Torah? Zimmerli emphasizes the close association of 'righteousness' and keeping the commandments, quoting Ezekiel 18 to support this, but also draws attention to the entrance liturgies.[15] But Ezekiel's description goes beyond what can be found in the laws, though some of the actions to be avoided are prohibited in the Torah. The entrance liturgies are not necessarily dependent on the laws found in the Pentateuch. And Zimmerli himself shows that more than laws are implied, when, by comparing Psalms 111 and 112, he argues that human righteousness is essentially the imitation of God.[16]

The empty concept 'righteousness', then, is filled out in different ways. Originally, and perhaps predominantly, it represents the customary ethic of the peasant society. The cult emphasized types of actions which are required of those who approach God in the sanctuary, and also describe the kind of righteous rule expected of the king. The prophets are essentially traditionalists, opposing the social changes which they regard as unjust because they are detrimental to the wellbeing of society and press harshly on those who were traditionally weak and liable to be oppressed. Through much of this runs a juridical strain. Further, as has been seen, H. Schmidt argues that some psalms are the pleas of those who have been accused of crimes and have come to the sanctuary to secure a favourable verdict from God through the priests.[17] Ethics and 'justice in the gate' were closely related in Israel, which is why the prophets are so hostile to the bending of justice in the lawcourts of their day.

In a few places, however, the idea of what is right seems to go beyond relationships within Israelite society and the laws which have been collected in the Pentateuch, and we glimpse these through our next window.

[15] *Theology*, 142–144.
[16] But see further Chapter 7 below.
[17] *Gebet*, and *Die Psalmen*, e.g., 12–13, 47–48.

6

ABRAHAM'S QUESTION

In the course of his plea to God not to destroy Sodom, Abraham says this:

> Wilt thou indeed destroy the righteous with the wicked? Suppose there are fifty righteous within the city; wilt thou then destroy the place and not spare it for the fifty righteous who are in it? Far be it from thee to do such a thing, to slay the righteous with the wicked, so that the righteous fare as the wicked! Far be that from thee! Shall not the Judge of all the earth do right (*mišpāṭ*)? (Gen. 18.23–25)

Most scholars in the period between the two wars and for some years after were convinced that the great central feature of Old Testament theology was God's salvation of his people in the Exodus, and that the ethics which followed from this was obedience to God's commands. Norman Snaith sets out this view in his forthright manner:

> *Tsedeq*, with its kindred words, signifies that standard which God maintains in this world. It is the norm by which all must be judged. What this norm is, depends entirely upon the Nature of God. This is why *tsedeq-tsedaqah* meant sound ethical conduct to the eighth-century prophets. It is also why it meant more than sound ethical conduct, and shows a persistent tendency to topple over into benevolence, and easily to have a special reference to those who stand in dire need of a Helper. There is to the Hebrew no *Ananke* (Necessity) and no *Dike* (Justice) to which both gods and men must conform. God is His own necessity. Justice is what God wills because such is His Nature.[1]

Helmer Ringgren expresses the same idea more tersely: 'Ethical conduct is determined by divine commandments.'[2] It is an interpretation of ethics which has provoked the wrath of moral philosophers. To give just one example, W. G. Maclagan declares that to derive morality from God's commands turns the difference between right and wrong into the fiat of an arbitrary tyrant, who might equally well have decided otherwise from what he decreed.[3] It stands under the condemnation of Kant's 'heteronomy'. Moreover it is inadequate, because it is still morally possible to ask whether God's command is

---

[1] Norman H. Snaith, *Distinctive Ideas*, 77, cf. 74–77.
[2] Helmer Ringgren, *Israelite Religion*, 131, cf. 131–138.
[3] W. G. Maclagan, *Frontier of Ethics*.

52

good or not, and if the theory is supported by the claim that God's nature is by definition perfect in goodness, this statement in itself sets up an absolute standard by which God's character is judged.[4] An analysis of Abraham's question has more than local significance, therefore.

At least four interpretations seem possible.

(1) Abraham may be contrasting the action of an upright judge with one who is unjust. Normally in the Old Testament this contrast is expressed in terms of acquitting the innocent and condemning the guilty (e.g., Ex. 23.7; Deut. 25.1; 1 Kgs. 8.32; Isa. 5.23; Prov. 17.15). Here, however, the meaning would have to be widened, probably along the lines of von Rad, who finds the passage 'absolutely unique' in the Old Testament and comments, 'Basically, Abraham is wrestling, as his appeal to the righteous Judge of the world clearly shows, with a new interpretation of the concept of "the righteousness of God"', but then adds that righteous actions are always defined by communal relationships.[5] It seems that for von Rad human understanding of God's righteousness can evolve, but presumably this was God's nature all the time.

(2) The term *mišpāṭ* may retain something of its basic sense of precedents and past judicial decisions. If this is so, two possible interpretations are feasible. (a) Abraham may be saying that God's action in destroying Sodom would be out of accord with his past actions. This is almost equivalent to saying that it would be out of character. (b) The *mišpāṭ* may refer primarily to human justice. This would be to assert that God's proposed destruction of the entire population of Sodom falls short of the loftiest human moral insights, or even of the actual practice in the law courts in the gate.

(3) The term may be taken in a more abstract sense of 'what is just', as REB appears to do.

The first of these hardly seems adequate to the situation or to the force of Abraham's argument, and may be speedily put aside. The second (2a) would involve a kind of 'appeal to God against God', which some scholars have found in the book of Job (Job 16.18–21). Even this, however, would imply that Abraham has some standard by which he could discriminate between God's better and worse self, since if it is merely a matter of contrasting what God does most of the time with what he does occasionally, we may still ask whether his aberrations swerve toward the good or toward the evil.

---

[4] Maclagan seeks to avoid this conclusion by identifying morality with God.

[5] Gerhard von Rad, *Genesis*, 1961, 208, cf. *Theology*, I, 395. He finds it difficult to place it in the evolution of Israel's theology, but the new feature is its placing of 'something new in the place of collective thinking'. In *Genesis* he asserts that 'Righteousness in Old Testament thought does not consist in the perfection of action, in the sense of approximation to an ideal, absolute norm.'

In this passage Abraham appears to be setting his own moral standard against God's proposed action, whether he derives this standard from the traditional practice of human justice (2b) or some more abstract standard (3). If it is objected that this is a profoundly irreligious attitude, it may be pointed out that the writer of the narrative seems to sense this, for Abraham stresses his insignificance before the majesty of God. It is as though he is making Abraham say: 'I have no right to set my own insight over against your divine will, but nevertheless I must express my moral convictions and make a further plea for the few in Sodom who are innocent of the city's sin.'

How a decision between Abraham's own, human sense of what is right and some kind of Platonic form of the Good is to be made is difficult to determine. It is commonly asserted that the latter is too abstract and philosophical for ancient Israel, but whichever precise meaning is adopted, the striking feature of the narrative is that the writer depicts Abraham as setting up some standard over against God and by which he dares to judge God's proposed action.[6]

But is this story isolated in the ethical thought of the Old Testament? It appears not.

In the first place there are the wisdom writings, of large extent and uncertain origins.[7] At one time it was generally accepted that Proverbs, Job, and Qoheleth and a few Psalms[8] stand apart from much of the rest of the Old Testament. Recently this has been questioned. Attempts have been made to integrate wisdom more closely into the canon. Whether Job should be seen as a wisdom writing or a development of the lament has been debated.[9] Some have claimed that none of the Psalms should be classed as wisdom writings.[10]

The provenance of the wisdom writings is even more uncertain. Do they come from a class of advisers or professional sages at the court,[11] from within the family, in scribal schools, from a group of well-to-do thinkers,[12] or have they a popular origin similar to traditional African proverbs?[13] Was there an 'old wisdom', which had few religious features and was concerned simply with ways of achieving success, an early group of sayings which describe various forms of anti-social

---

[6] I have worked this out in rather more detail in '(Gen 18[25])'.

[7] For discussions see Gerhard von Rad, *Wisdom*, D. F. Morgan, *Wisdom*, and James L. Crenshaw, *Wisdom*, which contains an extensive bibliography.

[8] The number of wisdom Psalms is disputed. While some scholars include as many as thirteen, a conservative view accepts only 1; 37; 49; and possibly 73; 111 and 112 (details in J. Day, *Psalms*, 54–56).

[9] Claus Westermann, *Structure of Job*.

[10] For example, Erhard S. Gerstenberger, *Psalms: Part 1*, 19–21, places them firmly within the cult.

[11] So William McKane, *Prophets and Wise Men*, Crenshaw, *Wisdom*, 20–23.

[12] See R. N. Whybray, *Intellectual Tradition*.

[13] Friedemann W. Golka, *Leopard's Spots*.

behaviour that harm the community, and types of sentence that have been influenced by Yahwistic piety?[14]

Ben Sirach is usually regarded as differing from the wisdom writings in the Hebrew Bible in that he identifies Wisdom with the Torah, probably due to the growing authority of the Law in the developing Judaism of his time. John J. Collins questions this. After quoting E. P. Sanders: 'Sirach was intentionally defining the values of the well-established wisdom tradition in terms of the Mosaic covenant: that wisdom which is universally sought is in fact truly represented by and particularized in the Torah given by God through Moses'[15] as 'a fair representation of what is meant by the identification of wisdom and Torah in the rabbinic tradition', he points out that Ben Sirach does not cite biblical laws directly, draws on other sources of wisdom besides the Torah, and grounds all wisdom, including the Law, in the order of creation.[16] Rather Ben Sirach 'wanted to bring together the wisdom tradition inherited from Proverbs with the Torah-based wisdom of the Levitical teachers'.[17]

In the biblical wisdom books there is no mention of the Exodus, election and covenant, and it seems unlikely that their writers' ethics are derived from the law. Indeed, both the form and content of the works are closely similar to that of writings from Egypt and Mesopotamia, and this international aspect of the literature almost certainly means that the basis of their ethics is to be found in other places than Yahweh's commands.

In Job the friends base their teaching on their own experience of life and the instruction of earlier wisdom teachers. Thus Bildad admonishes Job:

> For inquire, I pray you, of bygone ages,
>   and consider what the fathers have found;
> for we are but of yesterday, and know nothing,
>   for our days on earth are a shadow.
> Will they not teach you, and tell you,
>   and utter words out of their understanding? (Job 8.8–10)

and Eliphaz says that he and his companions are 'grey-haired' and 'aged', older than Job's father, implying that they have greater experience of life (Job 15.10).

---

[14] See William McKane, *Proverbs*, 10–22.

[15] E. P. Sanders, *Paul and Palestinian Judaism*, 331.

[16] John J. Collins, *Jewish Wisdom*, 55; the whole discussion on pp. 46–61 is important. Collins recognizes that Ben Sirach associates wisdom with the commandments in several places although 24.23 is the only place where he asserts that wisdom *is* the book of the Law, but points out that this makes little impact on the way wisdom is described in the wisdom poems. Ben Sirach's view of wisdom is rooted in the tradition found in Proverbs.

[17] *Ibid.*, 61.

Although Zophar recognizes that God may speak to human beings, what he imparts is the 'secrets of wisdom' (Job 11.5–6). On the other hand Eliphaz's rhetorical question, 'Have you listened in the council of God?' (Job 15.8) implies that he believes that such direct revelation is impossible.[18]

Crenshaw sees Job 31 as an excellent passage to illustrate the character of wisdom ethics.[19] He points out that parallels to Job's oath are found in chapter 125 of the Egyptian Book of the Dead (but also in the Code of Hammurabi). Normally the result of committing the wrongs is omitted in such imprecations, but Job states the punishment four times (31.8,10, 22, 40). Job's code of ethics, Crenshaw holds, is grounded in his relation with all human beings regardless of social status. We may note in particular:

> If I have rejected the cause of my manservant or my maidservant,
>   when they brought a complaint against me;
> what then shall I do when God rises up?
>   When he makes inquiry, what shall I answer him?
> Did not he who made me in the womb make him?
>   And did not one fashion us in the womb? (Job 31.13–15)

The reference to God's rising up in judgment, reminds us that both Job and the friends argue from the assumption that God *maintains* the ethics, but is not its source. The difference between them is that they believe that God is actually punishing Job for his sin, while Job will not give up his conviction that he has committed no wrong that deserves so great a punishment. It is striking that, even where there are parallels with laws in the Torah, instead of drawing directly on these laws Job makes a simple declaration: 'I was eyes to the blind, and feet to the lame' (Job 29.15, cf. Deut. 27.18; Lev. 19.14). Job is presented as acting out his own understanding of justice, and everything he says could appear in a non-Israelite declaration of innocence.[20] There are, indeed, marked parallels to sayings in the prophets (cf. the words of Eliphaz in Job 22.6–7 with Isa. 58.7 and the Book of the Dead 125: 'I have given bread to the hungry and water to the thirsty, clothes to the naked and a ferry to one without a boat'), but it is impossible to decide which is the dependent source. The general view is that the prophets incorporated wisdom ideas.

---

[18] Nevertheless Eliphaz describes a revelation which came to him in 4.12–17. Gary V. Smith explains away the difficulty by arguing that Eliphaz is quoting a vision received by Job ('Eliphaz's Vision?'). The strength of his article lies in its ability to show that the message of the mysterious visitant suits Job's position better than that of Eliphaz. Whether or not Smith is right, what Eliphaz is denying in 15.8 is being present at God's council.

[19] Crenshaw, *Wisdom*, 7–9.

[20] Crenshaw notes that Westermann has denied that Job is a wisdom writing, and also suggests that chapter 31 does not exclusively reflect wisdom ethics.

Here is an ethics drawn from a common morality accepted across the ancient world, not an ethics derived from a revealed law. The reasons for maintaining it look to the common humanity shared by Job and those with whom he has dealings.

Similarly the sages in Proverbs rely almost entirely upon their knowledge of life for their teaching. Where 'commandments' are mentioned, as in 'the wise of heart will heed commandments' (Prov. 10.8, the same word as in Ex. 21.1), these are not divine laws but the admonitions of the wise men. There is little in the sentence literature to suggest that those who wrote these proverbs derived their ethics from divine revelation. The ethics are essentially humanistic. It is true that the name Yahweh occurs fairly often, but mainly this is in the stock phrase, 'the fear of Yahweh'. There is little to suggest that the sages looked to Yahweh's commands as the source of their ethics. Equally in the instruction sections of Proverbs the wise man gives advice to his 'son' with little reference to God, and the ethics are again essentially humanistic.

This is confirmed by the kinds of motives for obeying this teaching which are added. Unlike the motive clauses in the laws, these are similar to those in non-biblical wisdom writings. McKane comments that their function in the Instruction of Ptah-hotep and the Instruction of Meri-ka-re is to recommend the advice by showing that it is reasonable and effective, or to expand or explain the motivation. The imperatives 'do not have the character of naked or arbitrary commands'.[21] This might equally be said of Proverbs. Even where Yahweh is mentioned in the motive clauses, instead of referring back to his salvation in the past, the sages declare that he watches the actions of men and women (e.g., Prov. 5.21; 24.17–18). He protects those who 'walk in integrity' and 'keep sound wisdom' (e.g., Prov. 2.7–8; 3.21, 26). He pleads the cause of the poor and 'despoils of life' those who despoil them (Prov. 22.23). Wisdom declares that those who find her obtain favour from Yahweh (Prov. 8.35). The upright are admitted into the divine council (Prov. 3.32). For the most part, however, the motive clauses speak of the happy consequences which follow doing right as coming almost automatically and without suggesting that Yahweh is conferring reward or punishment.[22]

---

[21] McKane, *Proverbs*, 78. The whole discussion of the form of Ptah-hotep and Meri-ka-re is important, 75–82.

[22] The motive clauses may be analysed under six heads: (1) to follow the teaching of wisdom or the sages will give pleasure (e.g., Prov. 2.10; 3.13–18: 8.33–34); (2) various happy consequences will follow, such as a long and happy life (e.g., Prov. 3.2, 18; 4.10, 13, 22, 23; 8.35), or great prosperity (Prov. 3.10; 8.18–21); (3) wisdom will protect those who seek her (Prov. 2.11–12; 3.23: 4.6); (4) disaster will come to those who do not follow the teacher's advice (Prov. 5.9–11; 6.11, 26, 32–35; 23.3, 5, 8, 9, 21, 27–35), and 'death' will be the fate of the wicked (Prov. 1.32; 2.18–19; 5.4–6,

Koch, indeed, has questioned whether the wisdom writers in Proverbs accepted a theory of retribution or whether they envisaged a world in which disaster followed wickedness because that is how life is.[23] He claims that in the section Proverbs 25–29 there is but one solitary passage which mentions Yahweh as giving a reward for goodness, 25.21–22, and even here he interprets 'the LORD will reward you' as meaning 'will complete' the good action 'by means of the appropriate consequences which follow'. He facilitates the completion of something which the previous action has already set in motion.[24] Koch gives examples of the same relationship between human actions and their consequences in Proverbs 11.1, 3–6, 17–21, 27, 30–31, explaining the few exceptions where Yahweh is mentioned by stressing that what is expressed is not his imposition of reward or punishment but his delight or outrage (vv. 1, 20), and that there is no hint of juridical terminology. Koch concludes: 'there is not even a single convincing reference to suggest a retribution teaching' in the book of Proverbs. Time and again what is found is the view that 'human actions have a built-in consequence'. The part that Yahweh plays is to 'pay close attention to the connection between actions and destiny', to 'hurry it along', and to '"complete" it when necessary'.[25] This seems to go somewhat beyond the evidence, but it remains true that the overall impression given by the wisdom writings is that the wise men are convinced that this is how the world is. If you follow their advice you will be acting along the grain of the universe and will therefore succeed. And although they occasionally ascribe this course of affairs to the creator (Prov. 3.19; 8.22–36), more commonly they simply accept that it is so. We are presented, therefore, with an ethics which is not derived from direct divine commands, and even though God is ultimately its author since he made a world which functions in this way, a considerable distance is set between the creator and the actions of men and women. Indeed, one proverb appears to teach that God is the hidden, transcendent One, whose glory resides in mystery (Prov. 25.2).

This then is a second place in the Old Testament where the ethics does not derive from divine commands but is drawn from what is commonly accepted by human beings and has been built into the structure of the universe by God. Is it limited to the wisdom writings and an isolated incident in Genesis?

22–23; 7.26–27; 8.36; 9.18); (5) sometimes this reward or punishment is ascribed to God's intervention (e.g., Prov. 2.6–8; 3.12, 26; 5.21; 23.11; 24.12); and (6) more often the retribution is the natural consequence of some actions and follows automatically without any direct action by God (e.g., Prov. 1.26–27; 2.21–22; 6.15, 27–29; 22.25; 23.21; 24.16, 20).

[23] Klaus Koch, 'Retribution'.

[24] *Ibid.*, 60–61.

[25] *Ibid.*, 64.

In a series of articles and a short book John Barton has argued that alongside the ethics of divine will there is a 'natural law' ethics.[26] Leaving aside for the moment whether 'natural law' is the correct term to use, we examine first some of the evidence which Barton presents in support of the view that there were some in Israel (apart from the wisdom writers), who based their ethics on what most people would accept as right and just, or who thought that there was a morality woven into the fabric of the created world, available to everyone and not limited to what God had revealed to Israel.

In Genesis, after the flood, God blessed Noah and gave him the charge to 'be fruitful and multiply and fill the earth' (Gen. 9.1). This is followed by permission to eat flesh, but not with the blood, and continues: 'Whoever sheds the blood of man, by man shall his blood be shed' (Gen. 9.6). Although this is a command from God in the narrative, and so might be regarded as further evidence that Old Testament ethics are what God arbitrarily decrees, Barton, following Horst, argues that the meaning is that human beings have been so created in God's image that they are inherently sacrosanct. Since the writer of this section of Genesis includes all humanity within the covenant with Noah, it is not limited to Israel in the way that the Sinai laws are. God is ultimately the source of the ethics, but as creator, not as law-giver.[27] I am not completely convinced by this. Since the narrative presents God's words as a command (and its 'crime and punishment' form is the same as other commands within the legal sections of the Bible) God might have made a different law for the punishment of murder. Moreover, within the same blessing that is part of the Noachic covenant with all human beings God changed his original decree about what animals and human beings were permitted to eat,[28] and this perhaps tells against it as well. At most one could question its being entirely 'arbitrary'.

In the same article Barton alludes briefly to Amos 1–2, which he discusses more fully in his later book, and it will be convenient to deal with that next. The series of prophecies directed against the small states surrounding Israel comes to a climax in the condemnation of Israel's sins. The offences which these nations have committed are largely atrocities in war and include cruelty to non-Israelites and not just injuries inflicted on Israel. In particular Moab is threatened with destruction because 'he burned to lime the bones of the king of Edom' (Amos 2.1). Barton argues that Amos's hearers must be seen as agreeing with the prophet's accusations if his final thrust against them

---

[26] John Barton, 'Natural Law', 'Ethics in Isaiah', 'Approaches to Ethics', *Amos's Oracles*. See also 'Understanding'.
[27] Barton, 'Natural Law', 2–3.
[28] Gen. 9.3, contrast 1.29–30.

was to have its effect. This means that the people in these non-Israelite states were credited with knowing that what they had done was wrong, or at least they should have known it, even though they had not received Yahweh's laws. This could be explained either by supposing that their own gods, or 'whatever ultimate principle or force the nation in question recognizes' gave them this ethics, or by assuming the existence of universal moral norms, 'part of the common moral sense of all right-minded men'.[29] This interpretation depends upon the oracles being given on a single occasion, leading up to the accusation of Israel, a view commonly held, though it is not impossible that they were collected later by an editor. If this were so, it would mean that the idea of natural law came from the editor and not from the prophet himself. The question might also be asked whether sufficient weight has been given to the word which Amos uses for the sins of the non-Israelite states. It is *peša'*, 'rebellion', which may support the alternative interpretation that the nations had rebelled against Yahweh, even if they did not acknowledge him, since he is God of the whole earth. This might perhaps be linked with one interpretation of Psalm 82, that Yahweh is supreme God, but the gods of the nations are responsible for maintaining justice in their own lands.

In the book of Isaiah Barton finds two pointers to the existence of the idea of natural law.

First, although many of the sins the prophet condemns are forbidden in various collections of laws, others are not, and some could not be. Among the first kind are murder and theft (Isa. 1.21), oppression of widows and orphans (Isa. 1.17, 23; 3.15), bribery and corruption in the law courts (Isa. 1.23; 3.9; 5.23; 10.1–2), and dispossession of the poor in order to enlarge landed estates (Isa. 5.8–10). Alongside these wrongs, however, there is the denunciation of luxury (Isa. 3.16–4.1), drunkenness (Isa. 5.11–17, 22; 28.1–14), the overturning of moral values (Isa. 5.20), and, above all, pride (Isa. 5.21; 9.8–9[9–10]; 10.5–15; 22.15–19). It has been suggested that Isaiah may have been influenced by wisdom ideas in regarding these actions and attitudes as wrong. Whether this is so or not, here are clearly sins which cannot be regarded as breaking Yahweh's revealed law. Moreover while the oracle,

> The ox knows its owner,
>   and the ass its master's crib;
> but Israel does not know,
>   my people does not understand (Isa. 1.3)

implies a special relationship between Yahweh and Israel, the primary emphasis is upon the unnaturalness of Israel's rebellion, in contrast to

---

[29] Barton, *Amos's Oracles*, 42–45.

the natural response of the animals, rather than focusing on law-breaking.

The second feature of Isaiah's prophecies which indicates that he is not basing his ethics on what Yahweh expressly wills and commands through his law is the way punishment is viewed. Those who 'join house to house' and amass large estates will find that their beautiful houses will become desolate and the estates yield scanty crops (Isa. 5.8–10). Similarly the reason why the 'proud and lofty' cedars of Lebanon as well as the haughtiness and pride of men will be humbled is that God alone should occupy the highest place in the world he has created and sustains (Isa. 2.6–22, esp. 12–17). Here the stress is on the appropriateness of the punishment to the sin, 'poetic justice' in fact. Barton rejects Koch's theory of pre-rational automatic consequence ('the deed is the seed'), but argues that instead of attempting to discover how retribution was thought to work, we should consider instead what the passages imply for the nature of the moral norms. This would lead to a form of natural law. When human beings ignore the universal moral order they become foolish. Barton suggests that here is a theme which he terms 'cosmic nonsense', a reversal of a sane way of looking at the world, found in both Amos and Isaiah. The classic example of this is Amos's rhetorical questions:

> Do horses run upon rocks?
> Does one plough the sea with oxen? (Amos 6.12[30])

Israel's social sins, described as turning justice into poison, are wrong because they go against the natural ordering of the world instead of fitting one's life into the patterns that can be observed in the world that God has created.

On this we might comment that Isaiah's oracle that lofty trees will be brought low is curious, but need not imply natural law. The day of Yahweh is likened to a storm which brings down all tall trees, and too much should not be made of the imagery. Moreover, if the picture is drawn from mythological features in the pre-Yahwistic storm god, there is still less reason for finding natural law here.

Even with these hesitations, it is probable that it is too simplistic to suppose that the whole Old Testament, with the exception of the wisdom writings, understands Israel's ethics as Yahweh's revealed law, his direct command. Barton is willing to concede that possibly in the final form of the Old Testament, at the level of canon, obedience to God's law is 'the only normative model for understanding ethics', but distinguishes this from the thought of Amos, Isaiah and P.[31]

---

[30] Accepting the usual redivision and repointing of the Hebrew.
[31] Barton, 'Natural Law', 8.

In his study 'Ethics in Isaiah of Jerusalem', Barton expresses his understanding of the assumptions which underlie Isaiah's moral demands in this way:

> Isaiah, then, begins with a picture of the world in which God is the creator and preserver of all things, and occupies by right the supreme position over all that he has made. The essence of morality is cooperation in maintaining the ordered structure which prevails, under God's guidance, in the natural constitution of things, and the keynote of the whole system is order, a proper submission to one's assigned place in the scheme of things and the avoidance of any action that would challenge the supremacy of God or seek to subvert the orders he has established.[32]

He claims that Isaiah sees this hierarchically ordered universe as having a moral pattern that should be apparent to everyone, and holds that the prophet 'derives all particular moral offences from the one great sin, a disregard for natural law'.[33] Here, then, is a theological form of natural law which is a remote ancestor of such classic texts as Romans 1.19–25. To the objection that such a natural law ethics has left no mark on the Hebrew language (such as the Egyptian *ma'at*), he replies that the lack of abstract terms is a characteristic of Hebrew, and this does not prevent us from using categories from our own language to describe Israelite ideas. Against the claim that the prophets were not objecting even to particular sins but speaking to specific situations, and that it is unsound to fail to distinguish between different kinds of oracle (as he has done), he argues that his aim is not to suggest that Isaiah was constructing a system of ethics, but to examine the presuppositions upon which his oracles addressed to specific situations in eighth-century Judah were based.[34] We shall have to examine this in greater detail when we consider the ethics of the prophets. For the present we must be satisfied with finding evidence of an ethics that is not derived from the law or the direct commands of Yahweh in Isaiah.

A possible further passage that may be drawn from the prophets in support of a theory that natural law played a part in Israelite moral thinking is Ezekiel 18.25, 29; 33.17, 20: 'Yet you say, "The way of the Lord is not just".' The Hebrew uses the verb *tākan* Ni., which in 1 Samuel 2.3 is used of God's 'weighing' human actions. Here the people claim that God's way has not been 'weighed' or 'adjusted to standard'. REB translates: 'You say that the Lord acts without principle.'[35] If God's actions can be assessed in this way there must be

---

[32] Barton, 'Ethics in Isaiah', 11.
[33] *Ibid.*, 13.
[34] *Ibid.*, 13–18. Barton rejects the proposal of H. H. Schmid, that *sedeq / s^edāqāh* and *mišpāṭ* function as the equivalents of *ma'at*.
[35] My attention was drawn to this translation (in NEB) by John A. Newton in a private

a standard other than God by which they are judged, and the people as quoted by Ezekiel are close to the thought of Abraham in his plea for the sparing of Sodom. Moshe Greenberg, however, holds that the meaning is that the people complain that God's way is 'erratic, arbitrary', though his translation is 'does not conform to rule'.[36]

Even if natural law is found comparatively rarely outside of the wisdom writings, the significance of such references is important, for, as John Barton points out, it brings this type of ethics into the mainstream of Old Testament thought. It is present 'not just at the primitive or early stages of Israelite thought, not just in peripheral literature, not just in material influenced by foreign sources, but at the conscious level of the arguments presented by the prophets, and probably also in some parts of the Pentateuch.'[37]

But is it rightly termed 'natural law', a concept with a distinguished pedigree in moral philosophy, drawing its inspiration from the work of Augustine and Aquinas, and reaching back into classical philosophy? 'Natural law' is usually understood as the way of ethics which seeks to discover what ethical duties can be derived from a study of the nature of human beings. Such a philosophical approach would be far removed from anything which can be found in the Old Testament. The wisdom writers were not philosophers in the Greek and modern sense, even if Qoheleth were influenced by Greek thought. Barton begins his first *JTS* essay by referring to the article by V. J. Bourke on 'Natural Law'.[38] Bourke defines natural law as 'the view that there are certain precepts or norms of right conduct, discernible by all men', and suggests as sub-types, 'those rules of justice which may be found written in the hearts or consciences of men', and 'a set of ethical judgments obtained by reflecting on man's ordinary experience, as contrasted with the divine laws that may be supernaturally revealed'. From this Barton draws two meanings of natural law: in a weaker sense, moral principles supposed to be common to all men, and a stronger one, principles built into the structure of things. He finds evidence of the first in Job 31.13–15, Genesis 9.5–6, and Amos 1–2, and of the second in Abraham's question, some oracles by Isaiah, and Amos's rhetorical questions about horses charging up a crag and ploughing the sea with oxen.

---

communication.

[36] Moshe Greenberg, *Ezekiel, 1–20*, 326, 333. Most other commentators do not consider the exact meaning.

[37] Barton, 'Natural Law', 13–14.

[38] In *DCE*. The article was replaced by one by Gerard J. Hughes in *NDCE*, in which Hughes finds a common element in all natural law theories: 'they start from a view of human nature arrived at by scientific and/or philosophical reflection; and they assert that this view of human nature will provide the basis for an account of moral values and obligations'.

This interpretation of the biblical material is correct, but to describe it as 'natural law' is not fully in accord with the normal philosophical understanding of the term. It may be justified, however, because it points to groups or individuals within ancient Israel who moved outside the legal idea of ethics as what God commands by direct revelation. The wisdom writers almost certainly derived their ethics from their contacts with the international movement, and also drew largely on their experience and tradition. This had the effect of making the ethics largely a conventional one. The prophets glimpsed a wider ethics, though they do not seem to have explored its ground. But the writer of the story of Abraham, and perhaps the aggrieved men of Judah whose questioning Ezekiel recorded, were sufficiently bold to posit an ethics to which even God had to submit, for if he did not he would have been guilty of injustice.[39]

But if space must be given to purity, to honour and shame, and to custom, if the evidence of the historical books must be granted its proper place, and if there is found an ethics grounded in what may be described as 'natural law', where does this leave the commandments? Before we reach the window that enables us to look out on the Ten Commandments, however, we have to pass one that gives a glimpse of a different issue.

---

[39] Andrew Davies's important study of ethics in the Book of Isaiah (*Double Standards*), which is highly relevant to the discussion in this chapter and the next, reached me only after the present book was in proof. It has been impossible, therefore, to discuss it here. Davies concludes that the actions of Yahweh as depicted in the Book of Isaiah do not always accord with the ethical demands he lays on Israel. He finds a solution to this problem in the author's monotheism, which requires that God is the originator of everything that happens, whether good or evil. Isaiah's God '*cannot* be "ethical" and still be God'. This, however, does not permit the Israelites to act as God does, for this would be to put themselves on a level with the supreme God. Davies adds: 'Isaiah can only demonstrate that Yahweh is not bound to an ethical system by showing how he exceeds and contradicts it, which is precisely what the book does. This not only means that Yahweh permits and creates evil in Isaiah, but also that from the perspective of any of Isaiah's readers working out of an ethical system which happens to be contradicted by his actions, Yahweh occasionally *is* evil' (p. 193, his italics). I believe that Davies has drawn attention to an important feature of the presentation of Yahweh in the Book of Isaiah, but I have doubts about his explanation and am quite certain that it cannot be applied to the whole of the Old Testament. For a fuller discussion see my review in *ET* 112, 2000–01, 73–75.

7

THE IMITATION OF GOD

Walther Eichrodt called attention to the way the Holiness Code 'links submission to the unconditional will of God with conduct toward one's neighbour . . . by teaching men to understand the faultless regulation of life in accordance with God's commandment as a *forming of human nature after the pattern of the divine'*. He goes on to speak of God's will 'to see the immaculate purity of his own nature . . . reflected in a holy people'.[1] Earlier in his discussion of 'the nature of the covenant God' Eichrodt had spoken of the incorporation of moral perfection in the concept of holiness, and, quoting Leviticus 19.2, declared that this 'crucial text' and the commands which follow show that this holiness, which is required of the people because of the holy nature of God, implies moral purity.[2] Eichrodt's point, however, is that 'holiness' had a moral component, rather than that Leviticus expounded the idea of the imitation of God.

John Barton took this up in one of his early articles on Old Testament ethics. He raised the question of whether the imitation of God might be found alongside an ethics as obedience to God's revealed will and conformity to a pattern of natural order. 'It could indeed be argued that the element of grateful response to God which often accompanies obedience in the Old Testament (and arguably reduces its "irrationality") could more accurately be seen as an imitation of God', he writes, and points to Deuteronomy 5.15; 10.17–19; 15.15; 24.17–18.[3] Of these passages, 5.15 and 15.15 are simply motive clauses, which do not necessarily imply the imitation of the divine action described in them. Deuteronomy 24.17–18 which applies the Exodus motive clause to perverting justice and taking a widow's garment in pledge, can be regarded as imitating God's actions only by abstracting an ethical principle from the deliverance from Egypt and applying it to a different situation, as Barton does. 'Thus *to be kind* to strangers and the helpless because Yahweh *was kind* to the helpless Israelites, sojourning as aliens in Egypt, is an instance both of grateful response to the divine grace, issuing in

[1] Walther Eichrodt, *Theology* II, 373 (his italics).
[2] *Ibid.*, I, 277–278.
[3] John Barton, 'Understanding', 60–61.

obedience to God's laws, and also an attempt to be like God,
modelling one's own conduct on his as it is seen in Israel's history.'[4]
In a sense this can be regarded as the imitation of God, but at some
remove, and I wonder whether it is not a matter of approaching the
text with twentieth-century eyes. It is only the second passage (Deut.
10.17–19) that offers support for the idea. With bold anthropomorphic
language God is described as the one who 'is not partial and takes no
bribe. He executes justice for the fatherless and the widow, and loves
the sojourner, giving him food and clothing'. The Israelites are
therefore called to 'love the sojourner'. Yet apart from the fact that
this command is linked directly with the motive clause 'for you were
sojourners in the land of Egypt', it is difficult to know precisely what
the writer envisaged when he spoke of God as not taking bribes,
giving justice to orphans and widows, and providing resident aliens
with food. Mayes regards the passage as an assertion of Yahweh's
kingship, for being impartial, not taking bribes, and helping the poor
and oppressed were royal functions.[5] Does not this imply that an
ethics which was expected of human kings has been transferred to
God, and then echoed back to human beings generally? How far, then,
it is correct to describe this as the imitation of God is perhaps
doubtful. Craigie, however, refers to the hymnlike nature of v. 17 and
finds two reasons why the Israelites should love the resident aliens:
'First, the love of God extended not only to themselves, but also to the
aliens; whom God loved, therefore, they should also love. Second,
they were to remember that they too had been aliens in Egypt and
there, in the latter years, had not been treated with love and respect.
Having experienced God's love and care during their own time as
aliens, they were to express similar love and care to the aliens resident
in their midst.'[6] On this interpretation the writer has the idea that the
care of the fatherless, widows, and resident aliens is based on the
character and actions of God, and thus presents the idea of the
imitation of God.[7] Wright expresses the same thought using his
favourite image of paradigm, though his concern is with the
tension between the election of Israel and the universal lordship of
Yahweh (and hence the universality of the ethics): 'Once again we
find this remarkable balance-in-tension between the particularism of
Yahweh's action for Israel in redemption and covenant and the
universality of his character on which that behavior is based. His

---

[4] Barton, 'Understanding', 61 (my italics).

[5] A. D. H. Mayes, *Deuteronomy*, 210–211, citing Pss. 96.10, 13; 99.4, the Epilogue to
Hammurabi's law code, and referring to Aubrey R. Johnson, *Sacral Kingship*, 4–7.

[6] P. C. Craigie, *Deuteronomy*, 205–207, quotation on 207.

[7] Earlier S. R. Driver commented on 10.19: 'in your attitude towards the dependent
foreigner imitate Jehovah, by not only treating him with justice (1.16), but also
befriending him with the warmer affection of love' (*Deuteronomy*, 126).

action for Israel was paradigmatic *for them*, but it was also paradigmatic *of God*.'[8]

In a later article Barton developed this idea.[9] In this article he usefully examines obedience to God's declared will and natural law, before offering a major assessment of the theme of the imitation of God. The two texts where the 'model' is 'particularly visible' are Deuteronomy 10.17–19 and Leviticus 19.2. In the first 'the God who enjoins care for the needy cares for them also: Yahweh asks of human agents nothing that is not also self-imposed'.[10] The main importance of the article, however, lies in the way Barton attempts to trace the idea of the imitation of God in the Old Testament in spite of the fact that he confesses that he is 'not sure how many concrete examples of imitation-ethics can really be found'.[11]

He seeks to establish it with three arguments. First, although many texts assert that God does *not* act like human beings and the parallel between human beings and God is not exact, a central aspect of the biblical way of thinking is that 'God is bound by moral laws just as human actors are'. This is why God is upbraided for failure to do so in the Psalms, in Job, and in Abraham's insistence that the Judge of all the earth should 'do right'. Thus 'Yahweh is a *good* God, in some sense which at least is not incompatible with what people in Israel would have meant by good, and whom therefore it made sense for them to try to imitate.' One of the senses of being made 'in the image of God' is that 'Yahweh and humanity share a common ethical perception, so that God is not only the commander but also the paradigm of all moral conduct'.[12]

Secondly, Barton points out that while we expect the biblical ethics to be heavily deontological, close inspection reveals a strongly teleological element in much of the moral teaching. As examples he offers the fact that *tōrāh* is 'not exactly "law" – directives sent down from on high – but "teaching", advice on how to follow the path that will take the hearer or the reader to the goal God has in mind'. In the same way, the wisdom literature is strongly teleological (e.g., Prov. 3.1–2). It might be argued that the possibility of moral conduct with no goal in view was hardly envisaged before Job.[13]

---

[8] Christopher J. H. Wright, *Deuteronomy*, 150 (his italics). He stresses that God's election of Israel was not favouritism and does not conflict with Deut. 10.15. He sees God's giving food and clothing to the resident alien as echoing Deut. 8.3–4. What God did for Israel was 'typical of him' (*ibid.*, 149).

[9] John Barton, 'Basis'.

[10] *Ibid.*, 18, referring to Eckart Otto commenting on Johannes Hempel's *Ethos* in 'Forschungsgeschichte', 19–20.

[11] *Ibid.*, 18.

[12] *Ibid.*, 18–19 (his italics).

[13] *Ibid.*, 19.

Thirdly, Barton claims that the moral life is seen as 'a co-operative venture between God and people. Its commonest image is of a path, leading to the place where it will converge with the highway trodden by God.' Examples are the cases of those who 'walked with' God (e.g., Enoch, Gen. 5.22, 24). Further, while the idea of vocation, singling out individuals to be God's agents, can be interpreted on the 'obedience model', it also involves having an insight into the intentions and character of God. 'The mysteriously godlike character of those with such a vocation, as we see it, for example, in Moses, or Samuel, or other prophets, speaks of the possibility of the divine life and human life running in parallel; and this may be connected with the idea of the imitation of God.' Even though this is not the role of the ordinary person, 'it implies an affinity between the divine and the human; it implies that the human is *capax dei*. And thus it suggests that the imitation of God may indeed lie near the heart of what the Hebrew Bible has to say about human morality.'[14]

All this is highly suggestive, but it must be questioned. In the first place, if the idea of actively *imitating* God, and not just living a life which is *similar* in some respects to that of God underlies so much of the Old Testament, one might have expected it to be expressed more often, and not just in Deuteronomy 10.17–19 (for, as I shall argue, it is not found in Leviticus 19.2).

Secondly, I fail to see why the fact that God and human beings are both bound by some common ethics, or even that both share a common ethical perception, necessarily leads to the claim that this makes God 'the paradigm of all moral conduct'. Does not Abraham's pleading for Sodom and Gomorrah point in just the opposite direction? Far from accepting God's initial judgment, Abraham sets his own understanding of justice against it. The ethics move from humanity to God and not the other way round.

Much the same is true of the teleological element which Barton finds in the Old Testament (correctly, in my view). In one sense, to be given teaching which leads to the goal God has in mind is to become conformed to the character of God and to live according to his ethical practice. But this is not the same as being invited (or even commanded) to *imitate* him, and in any case the goal which God has in mind for human beings is not necessarily the same as the goal for himself (if one may speak with a gross anthropomorphism).

I leave over a discussion of 'walking with God' or 'in God's way' (two distinct ideas which need to be separated) until I have considered Eryl Davies's article, since he makes more of it than Barton. Here I simply point out that the fact that the divine life and the human life run parallel in no way implies that human beings imitate God.

[14] *Ibid.*, 20.

The most thorough argument for the place of the imitation of God in Old Testament ethics has been presented by Eryl W. Davies, though it must be said, without the circumspection that John Barton shows.[15]

He begins with Leviticus 19.2, which he accounts 'the most clear and explicit expression of the principle of *imitatio Dei* in the Old Testament', expounding its meaning as: 'the Israelites are commanded to comport themselves in a manner that reflects the very character of God himself'. He admits that at first sight this appears an 'abstract, utopian ideal', but he fills it out from the specific social obligations in verses 3, 9–10, 14, 15, 35–36, adding that these show that the holiness demanded was not limited to cultic or ceremonial duties but 'encompassed the kind of moral behaviour expected of the people in their day-to-day activities'. The Israelites are commanded 'to imitate a particular divine *attribute*; in other passages, however, they are enjoined to imitate a particular divine *action*'. This he then expands by pointing to the Exodus deliverance, the Sabbath rest because God rested on the seventh day, and 'divine partiality shown towards the poor and needy' (Deut. 10.18–19), and the experience of God's compassion imitated in the release of slaves (Deut. 15.13–15). In all these passages God's activity provided 'a blueprint or paradigm' for the ethical behaviour demanded of his people.

There are problems with this. Quite apart from the fact that Davies declares that the ethical behaviour is 'demanded' by God, and thus it seems that a command underlies the *imitatio Dei*, it is doubtful whether what is envisaged in Leviticus 19 is actually *imitating* God. Imitating involves copying an action, repeating it, reproducing it. This is not what is found in the chapter. Rather what is required of Israel is to be holy (in its own way) because God is holy (in his),[16] and although human holiness and divine holiness as purity may be thought to coincide, the moral actions which are called out by it need not be. None of the social obligations which Davies lists has an original in the divine activity.

Davies points to the Sabbath law in the Ten Commandments as an example of imitating God, but he is able to introduce the ethical giving rest to slaves and aliens only by conflating the two versions of the commandment. In the Exodus form, which alone contains the reference to Genesis 2.1–3, the stress lies on God, humans and animals 'sabbathing' (*šābaṯ*). It is in Deuteronomy that it is decreed that the peasant and his whole household shall 'rest' (*nūaḥ*). It is true

---

[15] Eryl W. Davies, 'Walking'. He notes in particular Barnabas Lindars's argument in 1973 that the idea did not become a factor in Jewish ethical thought until New Testament times and there it 'remains peripheral' ('Imitation' 401–402), the two articles by John Barton, and Eckhart Otto's suggestion that it may well lie 'at the core of Old Testament ethics' ('Entwürfe', 20).

[16] The phrase is '*because* (*kî*) I am holy', not 'according to my holiness'.

that in Exodus 20.11 God 'rested' from his work, and in Deuteronomy 5.15 the Israelites are to remember that they were slaves in Egypt and Yahweh delivered them. But the link between God's resting and the keeping Sabbath is not made in Exodus 20, while in Deuteronomy 5 the natural way of taking the motive clause is as it is found elsewhere: the Israelites know what it is like to be a slave, and the command is to be obeyed out of gratitude for God's deliverance, with possibly the overtones that they should sympathize with slaves.[17]

Returning to Leviticus 19, most of the cultic laws, such as sacrifice (Lev. 19.5–8), mixtures (Lev. 19.19), avoiding eating blood, witchcraft, and certain funeral customs (Lev. 19.26–28, 31) cannot be envisaged as imitating divine actions, yet the statement 'I am Yahweh' occurs with these as much as with the humanitarian laws. Moreover, when Davies asserts that 'it is in Israel's humanitarian, rather than cultic, obligations that the requirement to emulate God's activity comes most prominently to the fore',[18] this is entirely a modern interpretation, probably based on the common belief that Christianity superseded the ritual and cultic laws, though retaining the moral ones. The way the command to be holy as Yahweh is holy occurs in the Holiness Code should also be noted. The phrase is directly applied only to the laws against walking in the customs of the Canaanites and maintaining the distinction between clean and unclean animals (Lev. 20.22–26), the priests practising forbidden funeral customs and marrying a prostitute or a woman who has been defiled or divorced (Lev. 21.1–8). 'I am Yahweh' occurs more frequently and appears with moral laws as well as cultic ones. Outside the Holiness Code both phrases are attached to the prohibition of defilement with 'swarming things' (Lev. 11.44).

Davies's next claim that 'the command to imitate God is implied' in the exhortations to 'walk in the ways of the Lord' (Deut. 8.6; 10.12; 11.22; 26.17; 28.9)[19] seems based on a misunderstanding of the meaning of the phrase. What is demanded is not to follow in Yahweh's footsteps, like King Wenceslas's page,[20] but rather to be presented with a map on which the path is marked and being called to walk in it – to obey God's commandments. This is perfectly plain in

---

[17] Davies refers also to Ex. 31.12–17, but this offers contrary evidence rather than supporting the concept of *imitatio Dei*. There is no reference to 'resting' (we must not be misled by the English 'sabbath of solemn rest' (*šabbaṭ šabbāṭōn*, v. 15, cf. HALOT 4, 1412: 'a sabbath with special sabbath celebrations'), still less of giving rest to slaves and animals. Instead anyone who works on the Sabbath is to be put to death. Is this a feature of the divine character that is to be imitated?

[18] *Ibid.*, 102.

[19] He rightly distinguishes the phrase from walking *with* God (*ibid.*, 108).

[20] 'Such imagery implies that Israel was destined to travel on a journey in which God was to lead the way as a guide and example for the people to follow' (*ibid.*, 103).

Deuteronomy 5.32–33, where Israel is not to 'turn aside to the right hand or to the left' but to 'walk in the way which the LORD your God has commanded'.[21]

It is yet more difficult to discover the imitation of God in the words of the prophets. To say that 'justice, truth and compassion' were 'not simply abstract concepts but constituents of God's own character'[22] may well be true, but this does not prove that the prophets taught that the Israelites should imitate his actions. That the prophets entered into dialogue with Yahweh may have meant that they discerned his nature, but it lends no support to the claim that they urged their hearers to imitate him. The perversion of justice (Isa. 10.1–2) may be 'an affront to the very holiness of God himself', but this is very different from justice being presented as imitating God's actions. To say that 'to take up the cause of the widow and defend the fatherless (Isa. 1.17; Zech. 7.10) was merely to act as God had acted towards his people when they were defenceless slaves in Egypt' is to introduce a link which is not made by Isaiah (or any of the prophets), and to impose upon the biblical account of the Exodus overtones of modern liberation theology and the option for the poor.[23] The meaning of 'the knowledge of God' has long been debated.[24] It is doubtful, however, whether it was applied by Hosea or any of the prophets to imitating God's character. It is highly unlikely, therefore, that Davies is correct in his assertion that 'the message of the prophets was largely based on the presupposition that the manner in which the God of Israel had acted towards his people should be mirrored in the way they were to act in their dealings with each other'.[25] This is not at all to question Davies's observation that the prophets perceived that God was righteous (Jer. 9.23[24]). But to see Jeremiah's demand that the king should 'do justice and righteousness', delivering the oppressed, not wronging 'the alien, the fatherless and the widow' (Jer. 22.3), as imitating his righteousness ('if God demanded righteousness, it was because he himself was perceived as righteous; if God demanded mercy, it was because he himself was perceived as merciful') fails to take account of the fact that the actions which Jeremiah required of

---

[21] There is no space to consider in detail the rest of the paragraph, except to say that the emphasis in Deut. 4.5–8 rests on the 'statutes and ordinances' rather than 'mirroring the divine activity'. Cf. also David's final instructions to Solomon (1 Kgs. 2.3).

[22] *Ibid.*, 104.

[23] *Ibid.*, 105.

[24] Perhaps the most famous discussions are those of Hans Walter Wolff, 'Wissen um Gott' and 'Erkenntniss', cf. *Hosea*, 79, 120–121. In *Prophecy and Covenant* R. E. Clements suggested that the covenant tradition with its two themes of divine grace revealed in Israel's election and the law formed what Hosea described as the knowledge of God (pp. 55–56, 96).

[25] Davies, 'Walking', 105.

the king were those which were expected of kings across the whole
Middle East. In their ethics the prophets draw heavily on the cult.
Again, Davies misunderstands the significance of the references to
'Yahweh's activity in the arena of history'. Amos 2.10–11 leads into a
condemnation of the people's rejection of the Nazirites and prophets
whom God gave to them after he had saved them. Amos 9.7 is a
rejection of the covenant, but there was nothing in the covenant
relationship to suggest that Israel should 'imitate' God. Even if Micah
6.3–8 is a unity, the link between the historical events and the ethical
demand is that of gratitude rather than imitation. The first half of
Davies's concluding sentence, 'The significance of the prophets . . .
may be seen to lie in their penetrating insights into the nature of God'
expresses a true, if partial, interpretation; what has not been proved is
the second half, 'and in their insistence that the divine character be
reflected in the conduct of the people'.[26]

Turning to the Psalms, Davies admits that the imitation of God is
nowhere stated 'in clear and categorical terms' in them. He goes on to
plead, however, that it is 'perhaps implied in the way God's character
and deeds are presented as the basis on which the pious should model
their lives'.[27] The difficulties that we have found with this type of
argument recur here. What is demanded of the thesis is that the
imitation *should* be stated in 'clear and categorical terms'. Otherwise
what is being offered is a modern interpretation which may well be
distant from the intention of the psalmists – and almost certainly is.
To suggest that the frequent references to God's justice, mercy and
compassion 'were clearly designed to inculcate the same ethical
values in the worshipper' is a very modern reaction. Again 'walk in
my ways' in Psalm 81.14[13] is taken to mean imitating God, whereas
the previous line 'O that my people would listen to me' shows that it
refers to obeying God's commands.

The pairing of Psalms 111 and 112 is rather more suggestive of an
imitatio Dei. Divine attributes and human goodness are paralleled: the
righteousness of God and of the upright endures for ever (Pss. 111.3;
112.3), being 'gracious and merciful' applies to both (Pss. 111.4;
112.4[28]) and both act justly (Pss. 111.7; 112.5). God's giving food to
those who worship him can be set alongside the way the man who
fears Yahweh gives to the poor (Pss. 111.5; 112.9). Davies follows
Zimmerli in describing this as 'the characteristics of the pious mirror
those of God himself'.[29] The line between 'imitating' God and

---

[26] *Ibid.*, 106.

[27] *Ibid.*

[28] RSV refers the virtues in Ps 112.4 to Yahweh, following the LXX. NRSV, as most
EVV, rightly keeps to the MT.

[29] Davies, 'Walking', 107 (he refers to Zimmerli's 'Zwillingspsalmen'; see also
Walther Zimmerli, *Theology*, 142–143).

'mirroring' his actions is very fine. Nevertheless the distinction is important. Imitating is deliberate, mirroring means no more than that the actions of the worshipper are similar to those attributed to God. To imitate God is to attempt to recreate in the life of Israel and the activities of the individual the virtues and actions of God. To mirror means no more than that the two are parallel. This would be true whether those parallel actions were the result of obeying God's commands, part of 'natural law' or imitation.

The Old Testament narratives offer less still in support of the imitation of God as a basis for ethics, as Davies admits. Picking up Barton's point that some characters are described as having walked 'with' or 'before' God, Davies says: 'although such characters exhibit many admirable qualities, they are not portrayed as individuals who regularly reflected in their lives the divine attributes, nor are they regarded as normative models for the people to emulate'. As he rightly points out: 'the phrase [walked with God] was probably meant to imply only that they enjoyed a special relationship with God, not that they lived their lives in conscious imitation of his character', and 'nowhere are the people encouraged to imitate their behaviour, and nowhere are the characters themselves depicted as conscious imitators of God'.[30] This concession is of vital importance, for in the absence of anyone who is described as deliberately imitating God, the concept must be adjudged to be a scholarly wish. Davies seeks to secure support for his thesis, however, in the manner in which God is portrayed in the narratives, since only when God's character is known can it be imitated.[31] This fails to meet the point.

A similar criticism has to be made of Barton's reference to walking with God. To Davies's criticisms I would simply add that the verbal phrase 'to walk with' (hālak, hithp., + 'et) appears with reference to God only in Genesis 5.22, 24 (Enoch) and 6.9 (Noah), but in 1 Samuel 25.15 Nabal's servants tell Abigail that David's men protected them 'as long as we went with them'. Here the meaning is simply of 'intimate companionship',[32] or 'friendly everyday conduct with regard to one's neighbours'.[33] Certainly there is not the slightest suggestion that Nabal's men imitated the activities of David's band of outlaws who were running a protection racket. Even if we allow that the Priestly writer wished to single out Enoch and Noah as the only two truly righteous men, it is difficult to grant that more than

[30] *Ibid.*, 108.
[31] *Ibid.*, 107–109.
[32] John Skinner, *Genesis*, 131. Skinner adds that it implies 'a fellowship with God morally and religiously perfect'.
[33] Claus Westermann, *Genesis 1–11*, 358. The Commentaries I have consulted on 1 Samuel fail to discuss the phrase.

intimacy with God is implied,[34] and certainly nothing to suggest that either Enoch or Noah *imitated* God. I am not sure what is meant by 'a path, leading to the place where it will converge with the highway trodden by God';[35] in the context it is intended to support the claim that a teleological ethics can be found in the Old Testament.

Skinner questions whether walking 'with' God is greatly different from walking 'before' and 'after' him.[36] If this is so it brings a number of other passages into the debate, but none of these can plausibly be taken to express the sense of imitating God. Indeed, to walk 'after' God in Deuteronomy 15.4[5] and 1 Kings 14.8 is expressly linked with obeying God's commandments, obeying his voice, and doing only what is right in God's eyes. Even though God himself may be presumed to do what is right in his own eyes, what is intended is obeying him, not imitating him.[37]

Davies finds the origins of the concept of imitating God in the fact that Yahweh is often depicted in human form and that human beings are created in God's image. He follows this by the highly charged statement: 'The attraction of the concept of *imitatio Dei for the biblical writers* is not difficult to appreciate, for it implied a type of ethics that transcended the more mechanical "rule/obedience" model of morality.'[38] This should have read: 'The attraction of the concept of *imitatio Dei* for modern readers of the Old Testament', for Davies has singularly failed to show that the concept was attractive to the biblical writers themselves, as his subsequent elaboration of the reasons for its being attractive shows.

There is one final comment to be made on this question. Davies accepts that the idea of imitating Yahweh was not without its dangers: it might drift into an attempt to become 'like God', with individuals overstepping their creatureliness and seeking to arrogate to themselves the divine prerogatives, and 'it is clear that not all of God's attributes could be deemed worthy to serve as a model or paradigm for humans to emulate'.[39] Though pride is condemned by prophet and sage, it is only in Genesis 3 that humans find becoming like God attractive,

---

[34] Westermann distinguishes between the 'old tradition' and P, claiming that the old tradition 'understood the words in the sense that Enoch stood in direct and immediate relationship with God (F. Delitzsch refers correctly to 3.8), and so was entrusted with God's plans and intentions', though he concedes that P deliberately restricted the preposition 'with' to the two primaeval figures (*ibid.*).

[35] Barton, 'Basis', 20.

[36] Skinner refers to Gen. 17.1; 24.40 (before); Deut. 13.4[5], 1 Kgs. 14.8 (after). To these can be added 1 Sam. 2.30; 2 Kgs. 20.3 = Isa. 38.3; Pss. 56.14[13]; 116.9 (*Genesis*, 131).

[37] See Addendum (p. 330 below) for a fuller discussion of 'walking with God'.

[38] Davies, 'Walking', 111 (my italics).

[39] *Ibid.*, 113.

which is rather a narrow base on which to build this claim. Christian theology has distorted Old Testament exegesis, I fear.

The second point deserves deeper probing, and Davies's next sentence must be quoted. 'There was obviously no problem with the concept of *imitatio Dei* while it was confined to such exemplary characteristics as God's mercy, justice and compassion, but when God's behaviour appeared vindictive, tyrannical and capricious the command to imitate him would inevitably be seen as morally perverse.'[40] Nothing could better reveal the perspective from which Davies writes than this. We need to ask, to whom were the 'good' attributes of God 'no problem', while the unpleasant ones were? The answer clearly is the rabbis, Davies, and other modern interpreters of the Old Testament. The methods Davies applies to support the case for the imitation of God with regard to these 'good' attributes, can be applied equally well to such features as executing Yahweh's vengeance on the Midianites (Num. 31), or the actions of Yahweh in 'holy' or 'Yahweh' war. It is not the biblical writers who find the concept of the *imitatio Dei* more attractive than the 'rule/obedience' model of morality, and the way Davies writes, using the past tense to imply that what he is saying was their view, is highly misleading.

If this is the strongest case that can be made for finding the motive of the imitation of God in the Old Testament, the conclusion must be drawn that the attempt has failed and it remains true that the dominant conception of the basis of the kind of religious and moral life which the Israelites should live was obedience to God's commands. While there may be some evidence that a few writers within the Old Testament viewed human virtues as mirroring those of Yahweh, and possibly, but at most very occasionally, the idea of imitating God may be detected, the Old Testament writers did not normally think of either morality or purity as imitating God's actions or his character.[41] Naturally, of course, because Yahweh was holy and righteous, the holiness and righteousness which he demanded of his people would 'mirror' his own.[42]

---

[40] *Ibid.*, 113. In a footnote Davies observes that 'the rabbis were careful to emphasize that humans should not seek to emulate *all* the attributes of God'. The rabbis were more sensitive to ethical goodness than the Hebrew Bible.

[41] It is difficult to express this in English or in modern terms because, as I have argued throughout this study, to separate 'ethics' from purity and honour is to impose a concept which had not crystallized out in the thought of the writers of the Hebrew Bible.

[42] Bruce C. Birch devotes the middle part of his article in the *Semeia* collection to the character of God, and hence ethics as the imitation of God, but adds little to the argument. He stresses that ethics must be closely linked with theology and its basis must be found in the canon, with the result that it is the attractive features in the Old Testament picture of God which are brought into prominence ('Moral Agency', esp. 29–33).

The question must then be asked, why the idea of the imitation of God is so rare in the Old Testament. Partly, no doubt, it is because of the predominant emphasis upon obeying God's commands. Although many of these commands are supported by motive clauses, some of which refer to God's actions in the past, they remain teaching and commandments. But there is a deeper reason. Despite the extensive use of anthropomorphic language applied to God, throughout the Old Testament runs the conviction that God is other than human beings. His holiness is such that no one can look at his face and live. Even Moses saw only God's back – in a passage marked at once by extreme anthropomorphisms and a majestic sense of God's glory (Ex. 33.17–23). God is the hidden one. The strong prohibition against making any image of God found in the Decalogue and many other places tells against the whole idea of imitating him. Although it is the late prophet with his conception of the transcendence of the only God who declares:

> For my thoughts are not your thoughts,
>   neither are your ways my ways, says the LORD.
> For as the heavens are higher than the earth,
>   so are my ways higher than your ways
>   and my thoughts than your thoughts (Isa. 55.8–9)

this belief would be accepted by all the Old Testament writers. The idea of the imitation of God rests ultimately on the belief in a God who has been brought down to the human level, and this God is never found in the Old Testament.

This discussion shows most clearly yet again the importance of avoiding reading into the Old Testament modern ideas and virtues that are attractive to us. It is a foreign country on which we gaze.

8

THE TEN COMMANDMENTS

The Ten Commandments occupy a prominent position in the completed Pentateuch.

In Exodus they stand at the head of the collection of laws known as the Book of the Covenant (Ex. 20.21–23.19), slightly separated from them by an account of the fear of the people and their request that Moses should mediate between God and them and that God would not speak directly as he did with the Ten Commandments (Ex. 20.18–20). After the setting out of the laws in the Book of the Covenant, in what is probably a separate tradition but one which is now incorporated in the narrative, God tells Moses to come up to him on the Mountain so that he can give him the stones on which the commandments are written (Ex. 24.12–14). It is emphasized that they are 'written by the finger of God' (Ex. 31.18). The centrality of the Ten Commandments is reinforced by the narrative in Exodus 32.15–20 and 34.1–28, in which Moses breaks the first stone tablets when he discovers the people worshipping the golden calf, and receives a second set from God, although in the present narrative the laws of 34.11(17)–26 appear to be substituted for the original Decalogue, and whether it was God or Moses who wrote them down is ambiguous (Ex. 34.27–28).[1]

In Deuteronomy the Ten Commandments are distinguished from the main body of laws in chapters 12 to 28 and placed early in the speeches by Moses in which he recalls the events of the Exodus. They are linked firmly with the covenant which the Lord our God 'made with us' on Horeb, and are marked out, as in Exodus, by being written by God himself on the two tables of stone (Deut. 4.13; 5.22). As in Exodus the people express fear at hearing God speak and of being consumed by the great fire, and ask Moses to listen to God's words and pass them on (Deut. 5.1–27). And again as in Exodus, the account of the golden calf and the breaking of the original stones and their replacement is recounted (Deut. 9.9–17; 10.1–5), though here it is emphasized that it is the original Ten Commandments which are written by God on the second stones.

Thus the Ten Commandments are distinguished from the other laws in that they are the only laws spoken directly by God to the people

---

[1] See the commentaries, esp. Brevard S. Childs, *Exodus*, 615–617.

and written by God himself on the two stone tablets.[2] In their present form they reflect the theological and ethical interests of their final editors and take their meaning from the position within the narratives in which they are set.

For our immediate purpose two questions need to be considered: what is the earlier history of the Decalogue? and how extensive was its influence in later Israel?

The first is impossible to answer, given the present confusion in Pentateuchal criticism and the extent to which presuppositions control the conclusions of scholars. Whether the Decalogue interrupts the narrative sequence in Exodus is debated, it is commonly accepted that it does. That there was an earlier history is certain, for the existence of the two versions in Exodus and Deuteronomy, so remarkably similar and yet with striking differences, can hardly be explained in any other way. The most prominent differences are the motivation for keeping the Sabbath, where Exodus recalls God's resting on the seventh day of creation (Gen. 2.1–3), and Deuteronomy commends the sabbath as giving rest to slaves and domestic animals, backing this up with a reference to the time when the Israelites were slaves in Egypt (Ex. 20.10–11; Deut. 5.14–15). Many of the other differences are minor, the more obvious ones being the placing of 'wife' before 'house', the use of two different words for 'covet' and the addition of 'field' in the Deuteronomic version of the final commandment, with 'remember' instead of 'keep' and specifying 'ox' and 'donkey' in its version of the sabbath law.

There appears to be overlap between some of the commandments. If it is forbidden to 'covet' one's neighbour's wife and property, why is it necessary to prohibit adultery and theft? If taking God's name in vain was primarily concerned with giving evidence in a lawsuit, why is there also the prohibition of giving false witness?[3] This suggests that earlier laws (or possibly earlier short collections of laws) were grouped together to provide the 'Ten Words' in the narrative.[4] The

---

[2] James H. Watts, however, points out that for the later *readers* of the Pentateuch the mediation of Moses is 'tempered' because they read the law collections in Exodus and Leviticus (though not in Deuteronomy) as Yahweh's direct speech (*Reading Law*, 79).

[3] Attempts have been made to remove the overlap between theft and coveting by taking the Hebrew word *ḥāmaḏ* to include planning to obtain what is coveted and actually seizing it, and taking 'Thou shalt not steal' as referring to kidnapping. For details see the next chapter.

[4] If the belief that there must be *ten* laws is abandoned, such overlaps open up several possibilities. William Johnstone points out that a close analysis of the two versions suggests that the number might be reduced to six if adultery and coveting the wife, theft and coveting the neighbour's property, and taking God's name in vain and bearing false witness are rationalized, and worshipping other gods and making images are combined, while if all the distinct laws are separated the number is extended to twelve ('The "Ten Commandments"', 453–454). Perhaps this shows how artificial the number ten is.

different ways in which Catholics, Protestants and Jews number the Decalogue is perhaps a further indication of this.[5]

None of the attempts at tracing the earlier history inspires much confidence. It has been suggested that behind the two forms of the commandments in Exodus and Deuteronomy lies an earlier, simpler form, with all the commandments in the same, negative, form. Alternatively, there were small groups of laws which were combined by the editors of the two books. Or yet again, that there were at least three stages in the development, a Decalogue which underlies Exodus 20, a Deuteronomic revision of this in Deuteronomy 5, and the present form in Exodus, which comes from a priestly revision.[6]

For a study of Old Testament ethics it is unnecessary to follow these theories in detail. What they point to, however, is extremely important. Despite any hesitation in accepting particular theories, the fact that there was a prehistory shows that at least two levels of interpretation have to be taken into account. On the one hand are the theological and ethical ideas of the completed books, teaching set in an overarching framework of religious ideas. On the other hand there are the ethics within the social life of ancient Israel. In principle a further distinction can be made between what was generally regarded as 'right' and maintained purity and honour, and what was actually practised by the various groups within Israel. To what extent this can be discovered must remain extremely doubtful, though glimpses may be obtained, as was seen in the discussion of adultery.

---

[5] Reformed and Anglicans number them as the form in Exodus seems to suggests, taking vv. 3 and 4–6 as two commandments, and v. 17 as one. Catholics and Lutherans divide the coveting commandment into two, as seems to be indicated by the Deuteronomic version, separating the coveting of the neighbour's wife from desiring his goods, and retaining the number ten by taking the prohibition of other gods and making images as one commandment. Jewish tradition also treats this as one commandment, has only one commandment forbidding coveting, and takes Ex. 20.2/Deut. 5.6 as the first of the 'Ten Words'. Although it is clearly not a 'commandment', to include the 'introduction' with the laws points out what Jews have always stressed, that the translation of the Hebrew *tōrāh* by the Greek *nomos* gives a false emphasis, and the *tōrāh* is primarily 'teaching'. The Ten Commandments are taught as Israel's proper response to God's Exodus deliverance. Here references to the Commandments will follow the Anglican numbering.

[6] Besides the standard Old Testament Introductions, there are summaries in J. J. Stamm and M. E. Andrew, *The Ten Commandments*; E. Nielsen, *The Ten Commandments*; Walter Harrelson, *The Ten Commandments*; Dale Patrick, *Old Testament Law*; William Johnstone, 'The "Ten Commandments"'. Among the commentators Brevard S. Childs provides a useful short account in his *Exodus*, 391–401, while John I. Durham, *Exodus*, 278–283 and A. D. H. Mayes, *Deuteronomy*, 161–165, argue a case. I omit any reference to discussions of whether the Ten Commandments go back to Moses, since the early history of Israel is completely dark, and some scholars reject any attempt to derive Israel's history from biblical sources (see, e,g,, Niels Peter Lemche, *Ancient Israel*, and Philip R. Davies, *Ancient Israel*).

How far are the Ten Commandments central to Old Testament law?

Moshe Weinfeld regards the Decalogue as unique.[7] It is central to the covenant between God and Israel and occupied a primary place in the ceremony of covenant renewal. He begins by collecting parallels to the commandments, claiming that 'each of the Ten Commandments, except the last one, be it affirmative or negative, appears in a similar form somewhere else in the Pentateuch'. This unique position is not due to their antiquity nor to their later date, for neither can be proved. Rather emphasis must be placed on the role of the Decalogue in the cult. The Mishnah shows that the Ten Commandments were read daily in the Temple during the period of the Second Temple

Another scholar who traces their influence throughout the whole Old Testament is P. D. Miller.[8]

First, Miller finds summaries and allusions, which, he argues, show that they form the foundation of both the law and the whole ethos of ancient Israel. He sees the *shema'* (Deut. 6.4–5) as a clear effort to summarize the prologue and the first and second commandments, and thinks that these laws also appears in Psalm 81.9–11[8–10]. In Deuteronomy 6.13 and 10.20 the first three commandments are presented in a positive form. In Leviticus 19.3–4 the fifth, fourth, first and second commandments are gathered together. Indeed, he holds that this chapter 'brings the Commandments formally into the definition of what is meant by holiness as a way of characterizing the moral life'. The seventh, eighth and ninth commandments are referred to in Psalm 50.18–20. Prophetic indictments on the basis of the Ten Commandments are found in Hosea 4.2 and Jeremiah 7.9.

Secondly, he cites parallel laws, claiming that the 'force of the Commandments' is elaborated extensively in specific laws, though usually in a different form, with all the commandments 'spelled out' except the last. Here only a few of his examples can be noted: the Sabbath laws in Exodus 23.12; 31.12–17; 34.1–3; Numbers 15.32–36; honouring parents in the prohibitions of striking or cursing father or mother (Ex. 21.15, 17; Lev. 20.9; Deut. 21.18–21; 27.16); the prohibition of theft is set out with specific penalties related to the seriousness of the offence in Ex. 21.37–22.11[22.1–12], for example; and not bearing false witness in the detailed laws in Exodus 23.1–3, 6–9 and Deuteronomy 19.16–19. Miller also follows Kaufman's suggestion that the whole collection of laws in Deuteronomy 12–26 is structured on the Decalogue.[9]

---

[7] Moshe Weinfeld, 'The Decalogue'.
[8] P. D. Miller, 'The Decalogue'.
[9] S. A. Kaufman, 'Deuteronomic Law'.

Thirdly, Miller points to expansions of the scope of the commandments, using the currently fashionable term 'trajectory'. This, he suggests, enables them to 'function as direction for the conduct of individuals in the community'. Thus the fourth commandment is extended 'into a kind of "sabbatical principle"' in the year of 'release' (Deut. 15), the sabbatical fallow year (Ex. 23.10–14), the 'sabbath of solemn rest for the land' (Lev. 25.2–7) and the jubilee year, which is termed 'seven sabbaths of years' (Lev. 25.8–17). In a similar way, he maintains that honouring parents is enlarged into holding the right attitude towards authorities in general – judges, prophets, kings, priests (Deut. 16.18–18.22). An extreme example of such trajectories is the suggestion that there is a 'broadening' of the law against adultery in the laws against incest and sexual intercourse with animals. Finally, Miller urges that the commandment against coveting opens up the commandments as a whole to a broader understanding. It is 'a guard against an internal, private attitude or feeling that tends to erupt into public and violent acts against one's neighbour', of which David's lust for Bathsheba, Ahab's desire for Naboth's vineyard, Amnon's rape of Tamar, and Shechem's rape of Dinah are examples.

Much of this is questionable. Parallels to all the commandments apart from that against coveting can be found in the other collections of laws and elsewhere in the Old Testament, but this does not necessarily point to the centrality and primacy of the Decalogue. What would be required to secure this would be to show that the Ten Commandments were earlier than the other laws, and that the later writers consciously built upon this. This cannot be proved.

It should be observed first of all that the argument has now shifted from the position of the Ten Commandments within the *literature* of the Old Testament (their place within the completed Pentateuch) to their place in the *history* of Israel and the fabric of its social life. There is no question of the importance attached to the Decalogue in the books of Exodus and Deuteronomy as we now have them. The Ten Commandments stand apart. But today, with the disintegration of the classical source theory of JEDP, the Pentateuch is seen to be much more the creation of the authors than the deposit of historically datable sources. This removes the books from history, and opens up a gulf between the theological significance of the Ten Commandments within the completed Bible and their ethical importance in the life of ancient Israel.

Secondly, when the supposed derivation of the later laws is closely examined, Miller's claims appear distinctly shaky. His suggestion of their extension along trajectories carries little conviction. Does the law against bestiality really go back to the prohibition of adultery? Is subjection to various persons in authority derived from the command to honour parents? Only the development of the sabbatical principle carries any conviction, for here the actual term is used in some of the laws. But the most serious objection to Miller's theory is that there are so few *direct* references to the Ten Commandments elsewhere in the Old Testament.

It is strange, if Miller's view of the centrality of the decalogue were correct, that the term 'the ten words' occurs nowhere outside Exodus 34.28 and Deuteronomy 4.13 and 10.4 in the rest of the Old Testament. At most, therefore, all that has been shown is that similar types of wrong-doing to those forbidden in the Ten Commandments are legislated against, usually with penalties attached.

David Noel Freedman has attempted to show that violations of each of the first nine commandments are recorded in the books from Exodus to Kings, one each (apart from Exodus, which has two because it was impossible to include one in Genesis before the Ten Commandments had been given), and in correct sequence: apostasy and idolatry in Exodus 32; blasphemy in Leviticus 24.10–16; sabbath observance in Numbers 15.32–36; respect for parents in Deuteronomy 21.8–21; stealing in Joshua 7; murder in Judges 19; adultery in 2 Samuel 11–12 (the order of the last three commandments is that of Jeremiah 7.9!); and false testimony in 1 Kings 21. Freedman admits that this correlation requires 'a modicum of ingenuity and adjustment' and might be 'sheer coincidence', but suggests that it may be one theme introduced by the final redactor to show that Israel violated successive commandments until it ran out of options and was destroyed as a nation. This theory can hardly be taken seriously, since the incidents and laws picked out from the various books seem to be selected entirely to suit the theory. Moreover, the need to adopt the Jeremianic order of three of the commandments rather than that in which the redactor gives them is an illogicality that must throw grave doubts on the proposal.[10]

Both G. J. Wenham and Walter C. Kaiser see the Ten Commandments behind Leviticus 19.[11] Wenham finds the Decalogue as a 'unifying theme' in the chapter, claiming that 'all ten commandments are quoted or alluded to, and sometimes expounded or developed in a new way'. He gives the parallels as: Lev. 19.4 (Ex. 20.3–6); 19.12 (Ex. 20.7); 19.3, 30 (Ex. 20.8–12); 19.16 (Ex. 20.13); 19.20–22, 29 (Ex. 20.14); 19.11, 13 (Ex. 20.15); 19.15–16 (Ex.

---

[10] David Noel Freedman, 'The Nine Commandments'. Somewhat similarly Brevard S. Childs regards the narrative material as offering 'a major commentary within scripture as to how these commands now function within the canon', instancing the stories of Potiphar's wife and David and Uriah as going to the heart of the crime of murder (*OT Theology*, 64). This is equally questionable.

[11] G. J. Wenham, *Leviticus*, 264; Walter C. Kaiser, Jr., 'Leviticus', 1131.

20.16); 19.17–18: (Ex. 20.17). Kaiser draws attention to the same parallels and notes 'how foundational the Ten Commandments are to these laws'. Weinfeld sees Leviticus 19 as filling the lack of 'any reference to the Decalogue in the priestly legislation' by providing 'a "Decalogue" in a reworked and expanded form of its own'. While it is a variation of the Decalogue, it does not replace it.[12]

Even stronger criticisms must be made of these claims. None of the parallels are exact. Only two use the same verbs as Exodus or Deuteronomy (Lev. 19.3, 11, sabbath and stealing), though both are in the plural and in the sabbath law Leviticus has 'you shall keep' with Deuteronomy 5.12 against 'remember' in Exodus 20.8. Leviticus also has 'my sabbaths' instead of 'the sabbath day'. Martin Noth points out that outside Leviticus the plural 'sabbaths' occurs only in Ezekiel and late writings and, unlike the Decalogue, this law assumes that everyone knew what keeping sabbath comprised.[13] Even where the requirement is identical the wording is different. The Decalogue speaks of 'a graven image' and 'any likeness of anything': Leviticus speaks of 'idols' and 'molten gods'. Whereas the Decalogue has 'Honour (sing.) your father and your mother', Leviticus reads 'Every one of you shall reverence ('fear', plur.) his mother and his father.'

The other alleged parallels are so distant in language that it is impossible to suppose that the writer was consciously picking up laws in the Decalogue. Adultery is not mentioned; the laws in Leviticus 19.20–22, 29 refer to having sexual relations with a betrothed slave and devoting a daughter to cultic prostitution. Since adultery is specifically mentioned in Leviticus 20.10, had the Decalogue really been a basic theme of chapter 19 it might be expected that it would have been found there. There is no reference to murder in Leviticus 19. Instead we find, as an addition to the prohibition of slander, 'you shall not stand forth against the life (lit. blood) of your neighbour', which, as Wenham himself recognizes, refers to accusing one's neighbour falsely of crimes which bring the death penalty. Finally, it is quite impossible to suppose that Leviticus 19.17–18 is related to the law against coveting, or that it was inspired by it. Moreover, it is surely strange, if the Ten Commandments really functioned in the way that Wenham supposes, that the order is not followed and that the laws not derived from the Decalogue are interspersed among its commandments in a haphazard way.[14] It must be concluded that there

---

[12] Weinfeld, 'The Decalogue', 19–21.

[13] Martin Noth, *Leviticus*, 140.

[14] Weinfeld, however, with reference to rabbinic sources, argues that the order of the commandments in Leviticus 19.3–4 is chiastic. He also draws on rabbinic material to relate vv. 16, 25–29 and 35–36 to the Decalogue ('The Decalogue', 19–20).

is the most tenuous connection between the Decalogue and Leviticus 19, which was constructed on quite different principles.[15]

A similar lack of reference to the Ten Commandments is found in the historical books. It is often claimed that Nathan reprimanded David for breaking the commandments against adultery and murder, but, as we have seen,[16] this is far from certain. What is clear is that Nathan never mentions the Ten Commandments (2 Sam. 12.1–15). Similarly, Elijah does not refer to the Decalogue when he confronts Ahab over the killing of Naboth and the seizure of his vineyard (1 Kgs. 21). In fact there are no direct references to the Ten Commandments, either as the 'Ten Words' or as individual laws, anywhere in these books.

The attitude of the prophets is even more striking. The only passages where any immediate connections with the Ten Commandments can plausibly be made are Hosea 4.2: 'There is swearing, lying, killing, stealing, and committing adultery; they break all bounds and murder follows murder', and Jeremiah 7.9: 'Will you steal, murder, commit adultery, swear falsely, burn incense to Baal, and go after other gods that you have not known . . . ?' It is surely strange, if the Ten Commandments were so central to Israel's ethics, that the prophets should not go back to them in their announcement of God's coming punishment for Israel's sins. Various reasons can be supposed. The prophets did not know the Decalogue as a summary of the highest and most important of Yahweh's commands. Perhaps such brief summaries were being constructed at about the same time as these prophets were working.[17] If the Decalogue was already in existence, it may be that their own ethics was so different from that expressed in it that they did not find any support for their denunciation of their people's sin there. They may have assumed a knowledge of the Ten Commandments on the part of

---

[15] Philip J. Budd, *Leviticus*, 263–265, 267–268, 272–273, takes a somewhat similar view, though he regards the laws underlying Leviticus 19 as Deuteronomic. He regards vv. 3, 4, 11 and 12, and only these verses, as taking up key themes from the Decalogue or 'drawn from the Decalogue tradition'. The pattern in both 1–10 and 11–18 is to refer to some Decalogue laws and follow these with 'poor laws' in the first section and 'social justice' in the second. This is much more subdued and realistic. But how is the 'Decalogue tradition' to be understood?

[16] See p. 34 above.

[17] See R. P. Carroll, *Jeremiah*, 209. A. A. Macintosh, however, holds that Hosea's words are a 'free presentation of the substance of a number of Ten Commandments' and denies that his freedom in the choice of words and order of the laws shows that 'the Decalogue had not by his time reached a fixed form' (*Hosea*, 130–131). Francis I. Andersen and David Noel Freedman take a similar view (*Hosea*, 337). But there is nothing *distinctive* to link the verses in either Jeremiah or Hosea with the Decalogue as preserved in Exodus and Deuteronomy, while murder, theft and adultery are almost universally regarded as crimes.

their hearers, and therefore felt no need to refer to it directly; instead they set out their own ethics which went beyond it. Or again, the actions listed in the Decalogue are regarded as wrong in most societies and Hosea and Jeremiah may not have been referring to a written code at all. Certainly the ethics of the prophets is much wider than that of the Ten Commandments. For example, only a few verses before the one quoted, Jeremiah condemns oppression of resident aliens, orphans and widows (Jer. 7.6). Hosea stands out among the prophets for the number of local crimes that he mentions (e.g., Hos. 6.7–9), yet at the same time the main thrust of his message is against a false relationship with Yahweh, a baalized cult, and lack of steadfast love.

Some have seen the influence of the Decalogue in Ezekiel 18.5–9, 15–17 and even 22.6–12, but several of the good deeds listed here, such as giving bread and clothing to the hungry and needy do not occur in any of the laws in the Pentateuch. They may have been derived from the wisdom movement or from the cult. Other requirements (not eating upon the mountains, exacting a pledge, taking interest) are not found in the Decalogue. Even Weinfeld accepts that the lists in Ezekiel do not depend on the Ten Commandments. He finds additional evidence for this in that some of the demands apply only to particular groups within society (property owners and judges) and not to everyone, but this argument depends upon his belief that the Ten Commandments have universal application.[18]

As has already been noted, some have found connections between the Ten Commandments and prophetic-type accusations in Psalms 50 and 81, the 'entrance liturgies' in 15 and 24, and the 'royal' psalm, 72.[19] The parallels are not close. Rather these Psalms seem to proclaim a separate ethics, required of the people as they come to worship in the sanctuaries and upheld by the king.[20] Prominent in this ethics was a demand to give justice to the unprivileged members of society and to defend those likely to be oppressed by those in positions of power. Throughout the ancient Middle East kings claimed that they upheld these rights and offered this protection. The full content of this ethics is unclear. The psalmists, like the prophets, chiefly use general words like 'righteousness', 'steadfast love' and 'truth', the content of which has to be filled up, as has already been shown. All worship is better at moral uplift than practical policy.

---

[18] Weinfeld, 'The Decalogue', 23–24.

[19] S. Mowinckel, *Le décalogue* (Félix Alcan, 1927). Weinfeld rejects the connection both with the New Year Festival and the Decalogue, and links Psalms 50 and 81 with the Feast of Weeks and the giving of the law ('The Decalogue', 24–25, 26–32).

[20] On this see Chapter 19 below.

The Ten Commandments, then, cannot be regarded as the fount of the Pentateuchal laws, still less of Old Testament ethics. Neither can they be seen as a summary of the teaching of the prophets, or as a succinct expression of the central principles of a wider ethics. If this is accepted, the Decalogue needs to be examined on its own.[21]

Frank Crüsemann, in an important short study,[22] states that it is incontestable that the Decalogue applies only to adult men who are responsible for administering justice and are active in the cult. They are farmers who possess land and cattle, free citizens who own slaves. In short, they are individual members of the ʿam hāʾāreṣ 'the people of the land'. The Decalogue does not refer to children, women, slaves, or paid workers. With the introduction of the monarchy other groups appeared in Israel, notably court officials and members of the standing army, merchants and craftsmen, and these also did not come directly within its purview. He finds the social and historical occasion for the emergence of the Decalogue in the threat to the community of free farmers during the eighth century, and he dates its origin in the late pre-exilic period, the time between Hosea and Deuteronomy. The main principle of the Ten Commandments, in Crüsemann's view, is the securing of the freedom of the independent farmer. To break any single one commandment in this 'minimal list' would damage the freedom which they presuppose. This limitation is confirmed by the omission of a full expression of both what fulfilling the relationship with God involves and everything that belongs to social relations. It addresses the individual Israelite alone. It contains solely an ethics securing solidarity within the class or stratum of free Israelite farmers.

This explains why these laws and these alone are included. In his introduction Crüsemann notes that many of the central themes of Israelite ethics found in the other collections of laws are omitted. He fastens on four features of Old Testament laws and ethics which are

---

[21] Cf. Waldemar Janzen's assessment: 'It is my contention that the Decalogue, in spite of its unassailed centrality of position and function, neither qualifies as a comprehensive summary of the content of ethics, nor was intended and interpreted as such in the Old Testament' (*Ethics*, 91). He sees it as 'sampling several important aspects of the new life of obedience within the covenant' (*ibid.*, 92). Nevertheless, within his paradigm scheme, he holds that it presents a 'familial thrust' (*ibid.*, 99).

[22] Frank Crüsemann, *Bewahrung der Freiheit*; see esp. 8–11, 28–35, 79–86. William Johnstone discusses Crüsemann's book and provides a detailed summary in 'The "Ten Commandments"'. H. D. Preuss rejects Crüsemann's thesis on the ground that the Decalogue originated in Deuteronomy or the Deuteronomic movement and was formed through the redaction of older series of laws. It is 'a Deuteronomistic program for the form of new obedience that is demanded of "all Israel" during and after the exile and that is given its interpretation and amplification in the Book of Deuteronomy' (*Theology* I, 103). But note that he sees it as requiring 'interpretation and amplification'.

absent: (1) 'Taboo rules' (*Taburegeln*), concerning clean and unclean food, especially avoiding eating blood, and laws defining authorized sexual relations apart from adultery; (2) cultic matters, including sacrifice, firstlings, tithes, festivals and pilgrimage; (3) economic issues and matters concerning the state, for example payment of taxes, the conduct of the king and the officials, war and military service; and (4) most importantly of all, care of the powerless in society, widows and orphans, the deaf and blind, and resident aliens (only mentioned in connection with the sabbath rest). The moral demands of the prophets and the ethics of the wisdom writers give this last a large place.

The effect of all this, in the view of Crüsemann, is to make the ethics of the Ten Commandments highly individualistic and private. Throughout they are concerned with the individual Israelite owner of land. They do not apply to the people collectively or to society. I believe that this is entirely correct, and, with Crüsemann, I also believe that the failure to recognize it has had a severely detrimental effect on Christian ethics.

Independently of Crüsemann, David J. A. Clines asked whose interests the collection supports.[23] His answer – in sharp opposition to Westermann, who quotes the first commandment as applying 'to everyone and for all times',[24] Zimmerli, who holds that 'the law of Yahweh is addressed first and foremost to Israel as a nation',[25] Brevard Childs, who declares that 'the Decalogue is not addressed to a specific segment of the population, to a priestly class, or a prophetic office within Israel, but to every man',[26] and Weinfeld, who affirms that 'the commands of the Decalogue obligate everyone'[27] – is that the person envisaged is 'an individual, a male, an Israelite, employed, a house-owner, married, old enough to have working children but young enough to have living parents, living in a "city", wealthy enough to possess an ox and an ass and slaves, important enough to be

---

[23] David J. A. Clines, 'The Ten Commandments' and 'The Ten Commandments', rev. He became aware of Crüsemann only after he had published the first article; cf. the revised article, n.14, where he questions whether the 'ethic of freedom' can be extended beyond those who 'share that social standing'. Christiana van Houten, however, argues from the laws concerning resident aliens that it is inadequate to regard law as always the result of competing special interest groups, for the *gēr* possessed no power and yet is accorded fair treatment (*The Alien*, 177).

[24] Claus Westermann, *Elements*, 21.

[25] Walther Zimmerli, *Theology*, 138.

[26] Brevard S. Childs, *Exodus*, 399–400; see also Childs, *OT Theology*, 63, not quoted by Clines.

[27] Clines quotes from Moshe Weinfeld's 'The Uniqueness of the Decalogue', 4. The exact sentence does not appear in the other version of this paper, 'The Decalogue', but see p. 10. Weinfeld is referring to the shorter form of the Decalogue which he regards as the original (pp. 12–14).

called to give evidence in a lawsuit. It is a man who is capable of committing and probably tempted to commit, everything forbidden here – and likely to ignore everything enjoined here, if not commanded to observe it.' Only those equal to him are 'neighbours'. Other classes of people are not so much ignored as sidelined. Women, resident aliens, slaves, children, the dispossessed, perhaps also peasants and the urban poor, are present 'but not *addressed*'.[28] Clines argues that the group which benefits from the commandments consists of the 'fathers', the older men in the community. This is seen most plainly in the command to honour father and mother. The sabbath commandment is not in the interests of the poorer farmers, is directly against the interests of merchants and traders (cf. Amos 8.5), and, although other persons, such as slaves, benefit from the law, it is certainly not against the interests of the wealthy peasants. It forms a parallel with the commandments about worship, which would gain the support of the wealthy conservative leaders of society, who insist on maintaining traditional Israelite ways. The laws against theft, false witness, adultery, and blood revenge (so Clines interprets *rṣḥ*, 'kill') are plainly in the interest of the wealthy 'fathers'. Essentially these are directed against theft of his property, theft of his wife, damage to his good name, and instability in society. Clines concludes that the Ten Commandments serve a sectional interest.[29]

While some of these arguments (e.g., those concerning other gods, images and the sabbath) may be pushed beyond the natural interpretation of the laws, there seems no question that the Ten Commandments are directed to a narrow section of Israelite society. At the very least it has to be accepted that they apply only to men, a fact which NJB tries to obscure by rendering 'his wife' in the law concerning coveting as 'your neighbour's spouse'! Beyond this they assume that this male Israelite possesses considerable property, including slaves. Moreover, the law about honouring parents cannot be wrenched out from the group of laws that concern adults and be applied to small children. The whole point of having 'Ten Words' is that they cannot be fragmented.

If it is correct that the Ten Commandments serve the interests of the wealthy male Israelites, the failure of the prophets to refer to them, even if they had been formulated in their present form by that time, can be readily understood. It is impossible to condemn wrongs that are produced by the social structure on the basis of an individualistic

---

[28] Clines, 'The Ten Commandments', rev., 33–34.

[29] In the later version of his paper Clines recognizes that Frank Crüsemann anticipated his description of the person to whom the Ten Commandments are addressed, describing him as 'a middle-aged male householder, a member of the *'am ha'arets*' ('The Ten Commandments', rev., 34). Long before, Daube had pointed out that the person addressed was 'the male individual' (*Biblical Law*, 75).

ethics. The prohibition of murder, theft, adultery (in the Israelite sense) and coveting are essentially concerned with protecting property rather than caring for the oppressed.[30] How individualistic the Ten Commandments are has seldom been openly recognized, since their supposed centrality for ethics has had too firm a place within Christian tradition. As we have seen, Crüsemann almost alone draws attention to this. As he points out, it was probably the Deuteronomist who added the motive clause asserting that the sabbath provides rest for the overworked slaves and animals – and even that is subordinated to the reference to the Exodus and the demand for obedience to Yahweh's decree.

It might be argued that the omission of some important areas of ethics in the Ten Commandments is due to their brevity. But to fasten on their demands as of central importance leads to a very slanted interpretation of morality, and is in conflict with the richer ethics of prophets, sages, psalmists, and priests.

There remains one final issue. No penalties are attached to the commandments, apart from the threat of divine punishment for making images and taking the divine name in vain, together with the promise of long life for honouring parents. Despite this, as we have seen, Anthony Phillips argues that they all carried the death penalty, partly because such a penalty is specified in similar laws found elsewhere in the Old Testament (e.g., homicide or striking or cursing father or mother, Ex. 21.12–17), but mainly because he sees the Decalogue as established in order to maintain the covenant with Yahweh by removing from the community those whose offences would bring that covenant to an end. The offences are 'crimes' not 'torts', and the punishment inherent in them is carried out by the community and not by an individual whose redress for wrongs against him is by obtaining damages.[31] This has met with considerable criticism, on the grounds that it depends upon the theory that the idea of covenant was derived from Hittite vassal treaties, no punishments by human officials are stated, and not all the offences are subject to the death penalty elsewhere in the Old Testament. Moreover it also involves taking the commandment against coveting as planning to seize the desired objects and physically taking them, and this is subject to serious question.[32]

---

[30] On the face of it, Isaiah's oracle of woe against those 'who join house to house, who add field to field, until there is no more room' (Isa. 5.8) might seem to fit nicely with 'you shall not covet your neighbour's house'. It is true that covetous greed underlies the action of the dispossessors, but the prophet's complaint is probably grounded on a conservative view of the rights of the small peasant farmer, and it is the effect of the social system which is ultimately responsible for the conditions he condemns.

[31] Phillips, *Israel's Criminal Law*, 10–35.

[32] See the next chapter.

From the perspective of the completed Pentateuch, the lack of sanctions is significant. Jewish interpretation, fastening on the description of the commandments as the 'ten words', sees the Decalogue as an expression of the response which God expects from his grateful people. On this, the most probable interpretation, the commandments are not 'laws', breaking which is to be punished by the elders. Retribution is not their main characteristic. Rather they express God's will for his people, his teaching on how they should live. Instead of being Israel's criminal law, they should be seen as divine guidance concerning morality. Within the narratives of the books of Exodus and Deuteronomy, they are divine teaching.

It may be thought that to treat them in this way conflicts with the claim that they were formulated in the interests of the wealthy peasant farmer or other member of the élite, and it is important to distinguish at which level the commandments are being considered.

Crüsemann and Clines treat the Commandments in their present form but as separate from their context.

An earlier form, such as that proposed by Nielsen, with its stress upon the fellow Israelite ('thy neighbour' in commandments 6 to 10) carries a much more universal scope, albeit still within Israel.[33] Accepting Clines's criterion – in whose interests are the commandments? – the neighbour need only be adult, male, married, of the status to testify in a lawsuit, and possessing a house. However, on Nielsen's reconstruction of the eighth commandment, 'Thou shalt not steal any man from thy neighbour', the Israelite would be the head of the family.

Fohrer argued that the Decalogue derives from three shorter sets of commandments: (a) the present 1, 2, 3, 9, 10; (b) 6, 7, 8; and (c) 4 and 5; all in a shortened form, each of the three collections containing commandments with the same number of beats, four, two and three respectively.[34] If he is followed, it could be argued that (b) is of universal application (though adultery was almost certainly defined as having sexual intercourse with another man's wife), (c) could apply to all adult Israelites, and only (a) requires the adult to be male and of sufficient social status that his testimony would be accepted in law suits. As an independent collection of laws, collection (a) is best regarded as defending the rights of the head of the family.

But any earlier form of the Decalogue is hypothetical. In their present forms the Ten Commandments are embedded in Exodus and Deuteronomy, and the influence of the compilers of these two books is plain.[35] To attempt to get behind this is futile. To ask in whose

[33] Nielsen, *The Ten Commandments*, 84–85.
[34] Georg Fohrer, *Introduction*, 68–69.
[35] Note Johnstone's emphasis on the 'theological creativity of the Deuteronomic

interests the commandments were framed may assume a greater knowledge of the social conditions in ancient Israel than is warranted, and although from the wording those addressed can be hypothesized, this may involve too much emphasis on the form of the commandments. Within the completed Pentateuch, however, it was probably assumed that they applied to everyone, as was the case in later tradition, the specific references to 'wife', 'slaves' and so on being regarded as examples.

If this account of the Ten Commandments is correct, it raises important issues for Christians today. Has the church been mistaken in seeing the Decalogue as completely distinct from all the other laws in the Pentateuch and in consequence treating it as one of the main foundations upon which Christian ethics are built? For this is how it has normally been regarded.

In one sense, no. Murder, theft, and the corruption of justice strike at the heart of an ordered society. Adultery breaks the trust upon which marriage is built, and caring for elderly parents is part of stable family life. The teaching is sound. Yet concern must be felt at the prominence which has often been given to what is a very individualistic ethics, tailor-made, it might seem, for the rich. If the prophets knew the Ten Commandments, they appear to have been uneasy with the ethics they inculcated. If the list of commandments was formulated later than the eighth-century prophets, it is strange that some have argued that it is derived from their teaching, for, as we have seen, there are few oracles which are identical with any of the commandments, and the ethics of the prophets is very different from the narrow range of actions condemned. The sages look to international ideals instead of to the Decalogue. In worship the king seems to have been honoured primarily as the protector of the poor. In the Old Testament narratives men and women go about their business in the light of generally accepted norms which are in some ways similar to those of the Decalogue, but they show little awareness of the Commandments themselves as divine laws to be obeyed. Even within the law codes there is evidence of a much richer social ethics, as will be shown later.

Thus to make the ethical laws found within the Ten Commandments central to an ethics for the community is to replace the widely-ranging social ethics of law-givers, prophets, priests and wise men by an ethics which secures the property and social position of those who are well off but offers little to improve the lot of the poor. Is it not time to abandon the idea that in the Ten Commandments we possess a set of absolute laws which apply to all human beings in every society and in

---

school as it is evidenced in their edition of Exodus 19–40', with the Decalogue as 'the primary terms of the covenant' ('The "Ten Commandments"', 459).

every age? It may be granted that without sanctions against murder and theft, and without justice in the law courts, ordered life in community becomes impossible, but the Ten Commandments contain both more and less than this: more in that there are also religious and cultic commandments, and less because many norms which most people would regard as fundamental to the achievement of a fair and just society are missing. Alongside the ethical decrees are commands against worshipping other gods than Yahweh, making images, using God's name in vain, and a call to keep the sabbath. By contrast, vast areas of concern for social justice which are prominent in much of the rest of the Old Testament do not appear within the Decalogue.

The Ten Commandments, then, are no more than one strand of ethical teaching within the Old Testament. Their exalted position is due to the editors of the books of Exodus and Deuteronomy, a prominence which is not matched in the rest of the Old Testament. Why these editors should have given the Decalogue this prominence is less easy to determine.

The quick answer would be that they were formulated at a time when Israelite society was becoming more individualistic, as the gap between the rich and the poor widened (if we may trust inferences made on the basis of archaeological evidence in the towns). The other parts of the Old Testament, therefore, represent an earlier ethics. Even the wisdom writings, which, as books, are commonly regarded as late express an earlier, international ethics. A difficulty with this is that the Pentateuch as a whole does not seem to be slanted strongly towards the rich, even if it is controlled by the priests. Moreover, since the breakdown of the Wellhausen historical reconstruction, dating has become so problematical that we have to admit that we are in no position even to guess at datings of the literature.

An alternative answer might be to point to the way the laws are embedded in narrative in a way that is quite unique in the ancient Middle East. We need not go all the way with James W. Watts's rhetorical approach to grasp the significance of this.[36] At a fairly late stage in their history Exodus and covenant became central to the Jews' religion, and it was within this context that ethical norms were set. The tradition of lawgiving was strengthened by presenting the Ten Commandments as a set of laws sufficiently short to have been written by God himself and handed to Moses as the foundation documents of the covenant, but they were not conceived as the sum total of the ethical norms which were to control Jewish life. On this understanding they had symbolic value rather than being the most important laws.

[36] James W. Watts, *Reading Law*.

Subsequently both Jewish and Christian tradition built on this emphasis and to some extent distorted it by giving an even more central place to the Ten Commandments, although Judaism persisted in retaining an equal emphasis on the whole law. Weinfeld refers to the reading of the Decalogue daily in the Temple close to the time of offering the Daily Offering (*m. Tamid* 5.1). The Nash Papyrus 'reflects a liturgical form' by linking the Decalogue with the *shema*. Both *shema* and Decalogue are found together in phylacteries from Qumran.[37] Childs quotes Rashi's description of the Decalogue as 'the rare jewel of ten pearls', although Maimonides simply includes its commandments within the other 613 precepts. Within the New Testament, he points to Jesus's reference to the Ten Commandments in his discussion with the rich man (Mk. 10.17–22) and in the corban incident (Mk. 7.9–13). He notes 'the most detailed usage of the Decalogue' in Romans 13.8ff., and other references to the commandments in James 2.11, Hebrews 4.4, 10, and 1 Timothy 1.8ff. For later Christian teaching where the Decalogue is regarded as definitive for ethics he lists the *Didache*, Augustine, Aquinas, Luther, Calvin, and later systematic theology.[38] In England we are all familiar with the custom of writing the Ten Commandments and the Lord's Prayer on either side of the chancel arch in many Anglican churches.

The tenth commandment, however, can in no normal sense be taken as a 'law'. It stands apart, pointing to the intention behind overt actions. The next window provides a glimpse.

---

[37] Weinfeld, 'The Decalogue', 34. The words of the Mishnah are: 'The officer said to them, "Recite ye a Benediction!" They recited a Benediction, and recited the Ten Commandments, the *Shema*, and the *And it shall come to pass if ye shall hearken* [Deut 11.13–21], and the *And the Lord spake unto Moses* [Num 15.37–41].'

[38] Childs, *Exodus*, 431–435.

9

COVETING, HOMICIDE AND INTENTION

Thou shalt not covet

At the end of the last chapter it was pointed out how difficult it is to regard the tenth commandment in the Decalogue as a 'law' in the normal sense, since it appears to be concerned with inner desires and no law can legislate for mental attitudes or could be enforced in the courts. For this reason several attempts have been made to give it a different meaning, so that what is prohibited is an outward action.

One proposal claims that the Hebrew verb *ḥāmad* included both the plotting to obtain what was coveted and its actual seizure.[1] Two main arguments have been offered in support of this view. (1) The verb is often followed by verbs which mean 'take' or 'rob'. In Deuteronomy 7.25 the Israelites are told not to covet (*ḥāmad*) the silver or gold that is on the images of the Canaanite gods or take (*lāqaḥ*) it for themselves. Achan tells Joshua that he coveted (*ḥāmad*) a beautiful mantle, two hundred shekels of silver and a bar of gold and took (*lāqaḥ*) them (Josh. 7.21). Micah declares that the wicked 'covet (*ḥāmad*) fields and seize (*gāzal*) them' (Mic. 2.2). (2) In some places the context shows that the verb includes the seizing of what is coveted. In Psalm 68.17[16] the mountain of Bashan is asked why it looks in envy at the mountain which God desired (*ḥāmad*) for his abode, where God does not simply 'desire' to live in Mount Zion but actually took up his dwelling there. And in the laws concerning pilgrim festivals in Exodus 34, the promise is made that God will cast out the nations, enlarge Israel's borders, and no one will desire (*ḥāmad*) your land when you go to the sanctuary for the feast (v. 24), which is interpreted to mean that no enemy will actually seize the land while the men are away. In addition (3) support has been drawn from an Old Phoenician inscription from Karatepe which reads: 'or if he [the foreign king] covets this city and tears down this door . . .', where 'covet' is followed by action as in the first group of biblical passages.[2]

If this was the meaning of this commandment, however, it means that it has virtually the same meaning as the eighth. This difficulty seemed to have been overcome when Albrecht Alt reinterpreted the

---

[1] This was first proposed by J. Hermann, 'Das zehnte Gebot', 69–82.
[2] Quoted from Stamm and Andrew, *The Ten Commandments*, 103.

eighth commandment as referring to kidnapping, on the grounds that the verb requires an object, and that Exodus 21.16 and Deuteronomy 24.7 both refer to stealing a man who is a full member of the Israelite community, and the first of these is found in a small group of apodeictic laws.[3] Combining these two views, the eighth commandment applied to stealing persons while the tenth referred to theft of material goods. It is far from certain, however, that Alt's interpretation is correct. There is no proof that 'You shall not steal' was shortened from a longer form, and the laws in Exodus 21.15–17 are in the form of offence and penalty, not the pure apodeictic form in Exodus 20.

Phillips favours this interpretation because it chimes in with his claim that all the offences in the Decalogue were crimes that carried the death penalty, whereas in Israelite law theft of property was a tort and was not a capital offence.[4] Once the claim that the Ten Commandments constituted Israel's criminal law is rejected, the argument loses much of its force. There is no reason why theft should not have been included in the teaching given in the Decalogue.

If the Decalogue is considered as a unified collection of laws, and it is accepted that the eighth commandment deals with theft, little reason remains for including appropriation of the objects coveted in the tenth. Phillips, indeed, demolishes the arguments of Hermann and others very effectively. First, there is no indication of any other meaning than 'desire', 'delight' in the nouns derived from the root *ḥmd*, and the Karatepe inscription does not positively confirm that the word *must* include action. Secondly, an additional verb has to be added when property was actually seized (Deut. 7.25; Josh. 7.21; Mic. 2.2). This argument actually proves the reverse of what was alleged. If, therefore, seizure of property had been intended in the Decalogue words such as *lāqaḥ* or *gāzal* would have been used. Thirdly, Exodus 34.24 need not refer to invasion by those driven out but could indicate that no one would be left to desire the pilgrims' land when they attend the pilgrim feast. Fourthly, the Deuteronomist certainly understood the verb to mean desire alone, since he used *'āwāh* of coveting a man's possessions other than his wife.[5] Phillips does not specifically deal with Psalm 68 and Exodus 34, although he mentions them. Psalm 68 can hardly be brought as evidence, since there *ḥāmad*

---

[3] A. Alt, 'Das Verbot des Diebstahls im Dekalog', 333–340. The arguments are rehearsed in most of the main commentaries. Robert Gnuse collects seven arguments in favour of the reference being to kidnapping, but questions whether they prove the point, and concludes that the law referred to 'any act of theft' (*You Shall Not Steal*, 8–9).

[4] Phillips, *Israel's Criminal Law*, 130–141.

[5] Günter Mayer sees the change in Deuteronomy as the result of its 'preaching' and due to the influence of Wisdom (*TDOT* I, 136–137).

possesses a positive sense and is not a true parallel. He admits, however, that Proverbs 6.25 might indicate that *ḥāmaḏ* includes seizure in its meaning, since it has been qualified by 'in your heart' to show that no action was contemplated. These passages, however, show no more than that the initial movement towards seizing an object is desire for it, an interpretation of *ḥāmaḏ* which is confirmed by Proverbs 6.25, where being attracted by the woman's beauty leads to being captivated by her eyelashes and so to committing adultery with her.

Having rejected the attempt to include seizing in the meaning of *ḥāmaḏ*, Phillips offers an alternative suggestion for retaining the tenth commandment as a law concerning a crime that carried the death penalty. He suggests that originally a different verb was used (presumably *lāqaḥ* or *gāzal*), and the crime involved was seizing the house of the senior male member of the family and in this way depriving him of his status as an elder in the community. The law was later spiritualized by substituting *ḥāmaḏ* for this verb as a result of Jehoshaphat's reform, which replaced local elders by royal judges.[6]

Phillips's arguments for the meaning of *ḥāmaḏ* are to be accepted, but we need not follow his suggestion that originally a different verb was used in the tenth commandment, for this is pure hypothesis without any evidence in its support. Further positive arguments, however, have been proposed in support of the meaning of 'covet, desire'. The Deuteronomic substitution of *'āwāh* for *ḥāmaḏ* suggests that the writers regarded 'desire' as the sense. The LXX translated *both* verbs in Exodus and Deuteronomy by *epithumēseis*, which means 'long for', 'desire', 'lust after' as an inner disposition. Moreover, Hyatt and others have drawn attention to references to the condemnation of covetousness in Egyptian wisdom literature, where covetousness is 'a matter of the heart or mind, synonymous with greed or avarice'.[7]

One other discussion may be noted. In his *TDOT* article on *ḥāmaḏ* Gerhard Wallis declares that 'the semasiological range of *ḥmd* covers the entire human sequence from viewing through perception of pleasure or even delight and inward longing to the desire to possess and the act of possession', referring to Joshua 7.21 and Exodus 34.24. On the other hand he denies that the tenth commandment means

---

[6] Phillips, *Israel's Criminal Law*, 149–152. He gives a neat summary of his argument in *Deuteronomy*, 50–51. A somewhat similar position to that of Phillips, though based on the view that *ḥāmaḏ* includes seizing, is presented by Gunther Wittenberg in 'The Tenth Commandment'. He points to the emphasis on the neighbour's 'house', and traces the place of the commandment in the subsequent social and economic development in Israel.

[7] J. P. Hyatt quotes from the Instruction of Ptahhotep, the Instruction of Meri-ka-re, and the Tale of the Eloquent Peasant (*Exodus*, 216).

'desire for the wife or property of one's neighbor with the intention of stealing them, since theft has been dealt with in Ex. 20.15 = Dt. 5.19. Whether or not Alt is right that the prohibition refers exclusively to the theft of persons, it is probably impossible to interpret "desire" in the tenth commandment as meaning the wish to steal. The only remaining possibility, then, is to interpret *chāmadh* within the framework of an ethics of pure intention.' He resolves the apparent contradiction by claiming that 'it is not the desire for another man's wife or property and envy of his happiness and prosperity that are castigated as such, but rather the secret or open attempt to impugn the other property, to "steal the hearts" of his wife and servants (2 S. 15.6), selfishly to acquire the other's property by ignoble means, possibly not themselves demonstrably illegal.' He concludes that the commandment refers to a chain of actions: sight of a neighbour's prosperity, envy of his social position, leading to 'the development and realization of dark plots and intrigues'. In this it is not clear whether Wallis thinks that *ḥāmad* is simply desire which will lead to action, or whether the subsequent action is included in the verb.[8]

What seems to have come out of this debate is that, although the meanings 'to desire and to try to obtain'[9] and 'perh. take, appropriate (e.g. Ex. 20.17, 34.24)'[10] have entered the dictionaries, the traditional meaning of 'covet, desire' for *ḥāmad* is the right one.[11]

One way in which the meaning of *ḥāmad* as 'desire obsessively, covet or lust after for oneself' internally and emotionally can be integrated into the Decalogue has been proposed by John I. Durham.[12] He sees this reference to 'obsessive covetousness' as 'the gateway to the violation of every other principle in the Decalogue'. Thus in the same way that the first commandment provides the foundation of the covenantal relationship, the last 'functions as a kind of summary commandment, the violation of which is a first step that can lead to

---

[8] *TDOT* IV, 452–461, quotations on pp. 454, 457, 461. Brevard S. Childs adopts a somewhat similar mediating (or confused) position, accepting that 'the emphasis of *ḥāmad* falls on an emotion which often leads to a commensurate action', but then saying that the original commandment was directed to the desire, which included 'those intrigues which led to acquiring the coveted object'. The Deuteronomic recension 'simply made more explicit the subjective side of the prohibition which was already contained in the original command' (*Exodus*, 425–427).

[9] HALOT, 1, 325.

[10] DCH, III, 248.

[11] Walter Harrelson argues that desire and deed are closely related in Israelite thought, but are not identical or simultaneous (*The Ten Commandments*, 148). I leave till later in this chapter an account of the interpretations of Bernard S. Jackson and David Daube, both of whom limit the meaning of *ḥāmad* to inward desire. I pass over the suggestions by C. H. Gordon that the law was a reaction against Canaanite custom and that it has magical significance (for a discussion see Bernard S. Jackson, 'Liability', 204–205).

[12] John I. Durham, *Exodus*, 297–299.

the violation of any one or all the rest of the commandments'. This is correct in its interpretation of the tenth commandment as such, but reads too much into the final form and present position of the Decalogue. Such theological interpretations must be left till later. For the present the significance of 'You shall not covet' your neighbour's possessions needs to be considered on its own. And this leads to an examination of the place of intention in the legal and moral systems of ancient Israel.

Before taking this up, however, we turn to the laws concerning homicide, for this is almost the only crime which can be committed accidentally, and it brings out clearly some of the problems involved in any attempt to discover how the biblical writers understood intention and premeditation.[13]

Homicide

The Decalogue has simply: 'You shall not kill'.[14] No distinctions are made between different levels of culpability, and as with all the laws of the Decalogue no punishment is decreed. It is God's teaching that killing outside what is permitted by law or custom is wrong, or, expressed differently, is 'contrary to the will and best interests of the community'.[15] The qualification is necessary, for killing in war and judicial execution are clearly not within its scope. Whether the Decalogue limited the victim to members of the covenant community of Israel, as some have proposed, seems to go beyond what can be firmly determined.

In the Book of the Covenant an 'offence and penalty' law decrees that 'Whoever strikes a man so that he dies shall be put to death' (Ex. 21.12), but this is immediately qualified by case law: 'But if he did not lie in wait for him, but God let him fall into his hand, then I shall appoint for you a place to which he may flee. But if a man wilfully attacks another to kill him treacherously, you shall take him from my altar, that he may die' (Ex. 21.13–14). The initial apodeictic law, like the Decalogue, makes no distinction between murder and manslaughter, but the two casuistic additions define manslaughter as

---

[13] It is not my intention to deal with all the laws or incidents in the Old Testament involving killing human beings, nor do I plan to discuss the debate between Phillips, McKeating and others on the development of the laws on homicide. The subject is introduced purely for its relation to intention. On the larger issues see Phillips, *Israel's Criminal Law*, ch. 8; Henry McKeating, 'Homicide'; Anthony Phillips, 'Murder'; Peter Haas, 'Homicide'.

[14] The verb is *rāṣaḥ*, which is not used for killing animals, killing in war, or execution (with the exception of Num 35.30). It covers murder and manslaughter (see Deut. 4.41–42 for manslaughter), and there is no evidence to limit it to deliberate murder here (despite the modern translations). As Mayes succinctly puts it: 'The verb means simply to kill a man' (*Deuteronomy*, 170). Others have attempted to trace the development of its meaning (for a good account see Childs, *Exodus*, 419–421).

[15] So J. P. Hyatt, *Exodus*, 214.

accidental killing ('God let him fall (*'innāh*) into his hand'[16]), and mark off such killing by presenting three examples of deliberate murder – lying in wait (*ṣādāh*) for the victim, attacking him in hot anger (*yāzīd*), and killing treacherously (*l'hor'gō b'ʿormāh*). Two of these verbs are rare in the Old Testament and the precise meaning is uncertain. In the only other place where *ṣādāh* is found, 1 Samuel 24.12[11], the usual translation is 'hunt', although the dictionaries prefer 'lie in wait' (BDB) or 'waylay' (HALOT). The noun *ṣ'diyyāh* occurs in the laws on the cities of refuge in Numbers 35.20, 22, where the meaning is the same as here. The emphasis is clearly on deliberate intent. On the other hand *yāzīd* hardly means 'wilfully' (RSV, NRSV, REB; NEB has the rather old-fashioned 'has the presumption'). HALOT offers 'become hot with anger', and GNB has 'when anyone gets angry and deliberately kills someone else', and this seems to be more in accord with the other uses of the verb. The meaning of *b'ʿormāh* implies some kind of deceit or craftiness, but hardly includes the overtones of the English 'treachery', despite the almost unanimous agreement of the English versions. The commentaries offer little help, since they are more concerned to point out that the casuistic additions make a distinction between murder and accidental homicide, offer examples of sanctuary on the altar (1 Kgs. 1.50–53; 2.28–34), and declare that the law is probably an attempt to check the custom of blood vengeance.[17] Assuming that both casuistic additions belong together, the 'place' which God appoints to provide asylum to those who commit unintentional homicide is the altar at one of the local sanctuaries, and the law comes from the time before the centralization of worship in the Jerusalem temple. This, however, is not certain. Possibly the laws were originally separate and the first may have in mind the cities of refuge. They are remarkably reticent about the details. Moreover who decides whether a killing is to be treated as murder and what process is involved are unknown. The incidents in 1 Kings are of such a special character that little can be inferred from them.[18] Nevertheless we may conclude that, despite much that is

[16] John I. Durham rather oddly thinks of this as '*un crime de passion*' in *Exodus*, 322.

[17] For examples of blood vengeance see 2 Sam. 2.18–23; 3.27–30; 20.10; 1 Kgs. 2.5–6; and in a story 2 Sam. 14.4–11. See below for a discussion of the *gō'ēl haddām*, 'avenger of blood'.

[18] Phillips, on the basis of his understanding of Israel's criminal law, denies that murderers could ever seek asylum at the altar, because the community had an absolute duty to execute the criminal to propitiate Yahweh, and finds support for this in the fact that the only instances of persons seeking asylum at the altar were political refugees. In fact Joab was executed in the sanctuary itself as one who had committed intentional murder. Phillips thinks that the decision on

unclear, here was an attempt to give a place to intention within the law.

The situation is much plainer in the various laws concerning the 'cities of refuge' (Deut. 4.41–43; 19.1–13; Num. 35.9–34; Josh. 20.1–9).[19] The historical issues raised by the setting apart of these towns as places where those guilty of accidental homicide can seek asylum will not be considered here. Rather our interest is in the concept of intention that the laws reveal.

In Deuteronomy 4.41–43 the person who may flee to one of the three cities on the east of Jordan is described as having killed his neighbour 'unintentionally ($bib^e l\bar{\imath}$-$da'at$, lit. 'without knowledge, knowing'), without being at enmity with (lit. 'hating') him in time past'. REB boldly translates into modern legal parlance: 'without malice aforethought'. GNB offers the more colloquial: 'if he had accidentally killed someone who had not been his enemy'. Since there is no Hebrew word that exactly corresponds to 'intention' the meaning has to be expressed in other phrases.[20] Even today 'not deliberate', 'unintentional' and 'unpremeditated' are often used without any clear distinction between them being observed, and we often also use 'accidental' with much the same meaning. 'Without knowing' probably contains the sense which we would express by 'not deliberate', though comparison with the law of Hammurabi concerning the barber who removed a slave's mark at the instigation of a third person whom he supposed to have the authority to require it (see Appendix to this chapter) suggests that lack of knowledge is still in the background. The main criterion for determining the killer's intention in this passage seems to be whether there had been any bad feeling between the two men earlier, although this does not directly prove that the killing was intentional.

The account in Deuteronomy 19.1–13 is fuller. In it Mayes traces a pre-Deuteronomic casuistic law (vv. 4–5, 11–12) which has been embedded in a Deuteronomic framework (vv. 1–3, 7, 13), and has received post-Deuteronomic supplements (vv. 6, 8–10). Whether this is a correct account of the prehistory of the passage is of no great significance for our purposes, since the sections which concern intention are found in the (early?) casuistic laws, although verse 6 will

---

whether the asylum seeker was a murderer or not was entirely in the hands of the local community and was taken by the elders. He supposes that those who committed manslaughter, having committed a tort, would still be liable for damages to be paid to the victim's family (*Israel's Criminal Law*, 99–100). There is little firm evidence for much of this.

[19] The phrase itself is not used in Deuteronomy, where there is simply a reference to the 'cities'.

[20] What might have been thought the most obvious phrase, $'\bar{e}yn$ $b^e libb\bar{o}$ $l^e hor^e g\bar{o}$ ('it was not in his heart to kill him') does not seem to have been used.

need to be considered when the identity of the 'avenger of blood' is discussed. The provision for the person who has committed homicide is this:

> If any one kills his neighbour ($r\bar{e}^c\bar{e}h\bar{u}$, 'fellow-Israelite') unintentionally ($bib^el\bar{i}$-da^cat) without having been at enmity with him (lit. and he had not hated him) in time past – as when a man goes into the forest with his neighbour to cut wood and his hand swings the axe to cut down a tree, and the head slips from the handle and strikes his neighbour so that he dies – he may flee to one of these cities and save his life; [lest the avenger of blood ($g\bar{o}^{,}\bar{e}l$ $hadd\bar{a}m$) in hot anger pursue the manslayer and overtake him, because the way is long, and wound him mortally, though the man did not deserve to die, since he was not at enmity with his neighbour in time past.] . . . But if any man hates his neighbour, and lies in wait ($^,\bar{a}rab$) for him, and attacks him, and wounds him mortally so that he dies, and the man flees into one of these cities, then the elders of his city shall send and fetch him from there and hand him over to the avenger of blood, so that he may die.

This passage gives more details about the cities and the way those who have killed another person are to be treated. The fatal wounding in the example of the men felling trees appears to us entirely 'accidental', the man who happened to kill his friend being entirely innocent, even though the phrase used in Exodus 21.13, 'God let him fall ($^,inn\bar{a}h$) into his hand', is not used. Indications of deliberate intent to kill are previous bad feeling between the men and the murderer's lying in wait for his victim (the verb $^,\bar{a}rab$ is commonly used of military ambush and often has an evil connotation). It is the elders from the town where the man who killed his fellow-Israelite lived who determine whether it is a case of murder or unintentional manslaughter and if they decide it was murder hand him over to the 'avenger of blood', but by what process they arrive at their decision is not stated. Presumably it was through a judicial discussion 'in the gate'.

The identity of the 'avenger of blood' has been much discussed. The older view was that it was the victim's next of kin who was responsible for blood vengeance, and this is made explicit in several modern translations (NEB, REB, GNB). Phillips, however, has pointed out that it is only in the setting of the cities of refuge that the addition 'of blood' is made, and he argues that the phrase refers to an official who acted on behalf of the elders and who alone had the right to pursue and execute the killer. Certainly the unique phrase may distinguish this person from the nearest relative who had the duty of buying back land that had had to be sold and redeeming his kinsman from slavery (e.g., Lev. 25.25–34, 47–54; Jer. 32.6–8), but Phillips's arguments depend heavily upon his interpretation of the crime of murder and he has to explain the avenger's 'hot anger' (Deut. 19.6), which would be more easily understood if he were a relative, as being simply excessive zeal.[21]

To anticipate a little, it is striking that three of the five passages that deal with the cities of refuge assume that punishment of the murderer will be exacted by the 'avenger of blood'.[22] It is impossible to trace the development of the treatment of murder. Evolutionists suppose that blood vengeance by members of the family or clan was originally exacted on any member of the murderer's family. This was later modified and limited to the murderer himself. At a still later stage the elders in the community took the decision of guilt and the appropriate punishment. The wise woman's invented story in 2 Samuel 14 suggests that in the time of the monarchy the king could be appealed to although in this incident normal blood vengeance does not apply since the murderer was the dead man's brother. It is the family who demand the death of the murderer, however, and there is no reference to elders or any judicial process. One wonders, therefore, to whom the apodeictic (offence and penalty) law in Exodus 21.12 is addressed, and who takes the murderer from the altar if he seeks asylum according to the attached casuistic law. The apodeictic law in Genesis 9.5–6 is embedded in God's blessing to Noah. The Hebrew is ambiguous. In the traditional translation (AV, RV, RSV, NRSV) it decrees that it is 'by man' that the murderer is to be executed.[23] B. S. Jackson, however, has argued that the context shows that it is God who inflicts the punishment, agreeing with NEB (REB): 'for that man (human being) his blood shall be shed'.[24]

Numbers 35.9–34 provides an even fuller account of the functioning of the cities of refuge (*'ārē miqlāṭ*), here given this name (for the first time if P is later than Deuteronomy). The *six* cities (contrast Deut. 19.2, but cf. 4.41) are set apart 'that the manslayer who kills any person without intent (*biš'gāgāh*) may flee there'. Fuller examples of deliberate murder are provided: 'if he struck him down with an instrument of iron, so that he died' (v. 16), or 'with a stone' (v. 17), or 'with a weapon of wood' (v. 18); 'if he stabbed him[25] from hatred, or hurled at him, lying in wait (*biš'diyyāh*, cf. Ex. 21.13), so

---

[21] Phillips, *Israel's Criminal Law*, 102–106.

[22] Deut. 4.41–43 does not have the phrase but the implication that by fleeing to one of the three cities the man who killed someone unintentionally 'might save his life' has this as the background situation. The asylum law in Ex. 21.13–14 does not specify who executes the murderer.

[23] The NRSV's 'by a human' fails to recognize the patriarchal society of ancient Israel.

[24] B. S. Jackson, 'Reflections', 24–25. He compares the divine protection of Cain (Gen. 4.14–15).

[25] The verb means pushing or shoving, as the later English versions recognize, cf. 'if someone pushes another from hatred' (NRSV), 'sets upon a man openly and deliberately' (REB).

that he died, or in enmity (*b^e'ēyḇāh*) struck him down with his hand so that he died' (vv. 20–21). Instances of unintentional homicide are 'if he stabbed him suddenly without enmity, or hurled anything on him without lying in wait, or used a stone, by which a man may die, and without seeing him cast it upon him, so that he died, though he was not his enemy, and did not seek his harm' (vv. 22–23).

To our mind there are several different situations here rather than a simple distinction between deliberate and unintentional, with correspondingly different means of assessment. Casting a stone without seeing the man it hit is sheer accident.[26] Killing someone without enmity (presumably longstanding hatred is meant) may or may not be accidental, but as in Deuteronomy the emphasis lies in its being unpremeditated. On the other hand linking this with pushing suddenly and hurling anything (and this seems to refer to the various murder weapons that were listed earlier) seems to make the action rather less than unintentional, even though it may not be premeditated and is not 'of malice aforethought' – the significant feature seems to be that the consequences of the action were not foreseen.

The qualification *biš^egāgāh* is even more troubling. The word is elsewhere used of 'unwitting' sins (e.g., Num. 15.24–29; Lev. 4.2, 22, 27; 5.15, 18; 22.14), and is contrasted with sinning 'with a high hand'. The lists of ritual and ethical offences in Leviticus 5.1–16, 21–22[6.2–3], however, contain wrongs which cannot possibly have been committed without knowing that they were done. J. R. Porter suggests that sins for which it was possible to offer a sin or guilt offering were 'offences which were not so serious as to put a man outside the covenant relationship with God and so outside the nation'.[27] Gerstenberger, on the other hand, thinks that the variety of kinds of offences reveals an effort to determine whether knowledge, will, the unexpected element of accident, or the disposition of the perpetrator, or even the deed itself and the damage it inflicted on fellow human beings should be given most emphasis.[28] It is clear that 'unwitting' is an inadequate translation, and although the English versions favour the idea of 'accidentally' (NIV, JB, NJB, GNB), 'by accident' (NEB, though REB changes this to 'inadvertently') this does not seem to be entirely right.[29]

---

[26] It is difficult to imagine the scenario in each case. For example, was the stone thrown at a bird or an animal and accidentally hit a human being? Was it target practice for slingers (cf. Jdg. 20.16)?

[27] J. R. Porter, *Leviticus*, 37. Though noting this, Philip J. Budd interprets the meaning as 'inadvertence, arising from negligence or ignorance' (*Leviticus*, 81).

[28] Erhard S. Gerstenberger, *Leviticus*, 65. He regards the issue as important only to the priests, and then only in relation to atonement rites, not for passing judgment (p. 63).

[29] See below, pp. 105f., for Daube's suggestion that the term came to be used of acts that were purely accidental.

It is generally agreed that the account of the cities of refuge in
Joshua 20 is related to Numbers 35 as similarities of vocabulary show,
and most regard it as dependent upon that passage, though also
influenced by Deuteronomy 19. Verse 3 contains the two phrases
biš'gāgāh and *bib'lī-da'at*, which RSV translates as 'without intent'
and 'unwittingly', although the second is omitted by the LXX and
Vulgate and may be a later addition. As has been seen, it does not
occur in Numbers 35. The LXX (Vaticanus) also omits most of
vv. 4–6, where *bib'lī-da'at* also occurs, together with the
criterion of no previous hatred on the part of the man who committed
manslaughter. This passage, therefore, adds little to the present
discussion.[30]

Intention

We turn from this detailed study of intention as revealed in the laws
on murder to the broader perspective presented by Jackson and
Daube.

After arguing that 'the best that can be said of the interpretation of
the verb *hāmad* as "to take" is that there is the possibility that the
word can bear that meaning in some contexts', but that it is the regular
meaning 'completely fails of proof',[31] Jackson easily disposes of two
passages where it has been claimed that mere intention is condemned
as sin: Joseph and Potiphar (Gen. 39), where it is actual attempted
rape that is punished, not harbouring lustful desires, and the Israelites'
craving for food in the wilderness (Num. 11), where the divine
punishment follows only when 'the meat was yet between their teeth'.
On the other hand the divine judgment of the flood is because 'every
imagination of the thoughts of [the human being's] heart was only evil
continually' (Gen. 6.5, cf. 8.21), while David was blessed by God
because of his intention to build the temple (1 Kgs. 8.18). God says to
Samuel that 'man looks on the outward appearance, but the LORD
looks on the heart' (1 Sam. 16.7). From this Jackson draws the
conclusion that mere intention is under the judgment of God but
nowhere in any narrative does it come within the purview of human
punishment. This does not mean that Jackson regards the Decalogue
as simply ethics and not law. Rather punishment for infringement of
the commandments lies with God and not with human beings. This is
supported by the Deuteronomic call to obey the commandments 'that
you may live' (Deut. 5.33). In summary: 'there is no evidence that
liability for mere intention was ever applied in a human court', but,

---

[30] Trent C. Butler provides a useful table of comparisons between the five passages,
though he limits the 'conditions of eligibility' to four: 'not lie in wait', 'inadvertent',
'did not know' and 'not hate' (*Joshua*, 213).
[31] Jackson, 'Liability', 201.

equally important, 'the idea did exist that merely to intend a wrong was itself wrong'.[32]

In his fascinating lecture 'Error and Ignorance as Excuses in Crime',[33] which ranges from Assyrian law to nineteenth-century British law and modern American law by way of Greek tragedy, Roman law and rabbinic writings, Daube teases out some of the perplexing features of this whole question. There is no time to follow him down these many byways and I stick strictly to the Old Testament passages that he discusses.

He argues that there was no period in antiquity when error and ignorance were not comprehended as fully as today. The reason why the laws did not cater for them are: (1) 'submission to fate' (by which Daube refers to the fact that whether by error or accident the deed has been done and must be paid for), (2) 'the conundrum of delimitation' (the difficulty in exonerating those who performed crimes for reasons that were not fully culpable, as with the Amalekite who killed Saul and those who assassinated Ishbosheth in the mistaken belief that they were pleasing David (2 Sam. 1.1–16; 4.5–12)), and (3) most important of all, 'the difficulty of proof'. We have seen that holiness and morality are closely related. The good intention of Uzzah to save the ark from falling is not taken into account when the divine holiness strikes him dead, but David, with greater moral sensibility is angry with Yahweh for failing to take account of Uzzah's intention (2 Sam. 6.6–8).

In Genesis 20 Abimelech challenges God, when he is threatened with death for taking a married woman into his harem, giving as the alleviating circumstance that he had been misled. Even though God accepts this as mitigation, the deed has been done and payment of compensation together with Abraham's prayer is required in expiation. Here a mistake is due to deception (and Abimelech committed the offence genuinely 'unwittingly'). Jonathan is judged guilty when he eats the honey in breach of Saul's oath, and only escapes execution when the people plead his case (1 Sam. 14.24–46). They do not bring forward Jonathan's ignorance of his father's oath, however, but rather base their plea on the part he played in the victory. But God has already inflicted punishment by refusing to give an answer through the oracle.

This, Daube says, was developed by the priests in Numbers 35 to cover criminal law. This they did by applying *biš'gāgāh*, which

---

[32] *Ibid.*, 207. The rest of the article is devoted to tracing attitudes towards intention in post-biblical sources: LXX, the pseudepigrapha, Philo of Alexandria, and rabbinic teachers. An important feature that appears in these sources is that a failed attempt is treated as liable to judgment, quoting from Philo and R. Eliezer.

[33] David Daube, in *Biblical Law*, Lecture II, 49–70.

originated in the sacrificial laws, to homicide that was not committed from error or ignorance but was pure accident. He claims that 'henceforth, throughout the legal system, the word may denote any absence of evil intent as a basis for relief'. In the Old Testament narratives, however, Daube finds only one genuine instance of accidental killing – the prostitute who overlaid her baby (1 Kgs. 3.16–22). Yet Hosea condemns ignorance as culpable (Hos. 4.6), and it is only in the account of the suffering servant (Isa. 53.6) and at the end of Jonah that ignorance is a reason for pardon. Finally Daube is emphatic that ignorance is never accepted as a reason for mitigating human law or ethics. It is only 'a merciful deity' who takes it into account. Much in this lecture is a somewhat fanciful interweaving of law, ethics, legend, myth and poetry. Nevertheless he opens up ideas that a pedantic adherence to the letter of the Old Testament might miss.

Throughout the present chapter we have been chiefly concerned with laws, but we have learnt that law cannot be identified with ethics or practical morality. Even assuming that the laws on the cities of refuge represent the ways in which murder was treated in ancient Israel and the place of the elders in deciding whether an offence was manslaughter or not (and there are those who hold that the accounts in Numbers and Joshua are the invention of post-exilic priests), the phraseology used reveals the extreme difficulty that the writers had in defining intention. The evidence is insufficient to allow us to trace any development in ideas or legal practice, and those who propose such change largely rely on presuppositions about the stages in ethical and social evolution that are assumed to be universal. It appears plain that law could accommodate intention only with difficulty and even then relied upon outward evidence, such as the nature of the instrument which struck the fatal blow, whether the victim had been ambushed, or the existence of previous hostility between the two men. How 'pure accident' was determined, as when a man claimed that he did not see his victim when he threw the stone, is never explained. In Babylonian law an oath served this purpose, but unless some of the psalms represent such oaths, there is little evidence of such a practice in the Old Testament.[34] In the law concerning the jealous husband, where it is similarly impossible to provide evidence, resort is made to the ordeal (Num. 5.11–31), but this is the only explicit case of trial by

---

[34] J. P. Hyatt holds that 'only occasionally is it necessary for litigants to come to a sanctuary to take oaths "before God" in order to determine guilt', pointing to Ex. 21.6; 22.7, 8, 10 [8, 9, 11] (*Exodus* 219, 238–239, so also Brevard S. Childs, *Exodus*, 475–476). John I. Durham, however, makes a distinction between 22.7–8[8–9] and 22.10[11], rejecting the LXX addition of an oath in v. 7[8], and interpreting the purpose of drawing near to God in the former law as seeking a divine opinion through an oracle (*Exodus*, 326). Durham would seem to have more probability on his side.

ordeal in the Old Testament, although ordeals were not uncommon elsewhere in the ancient Middle East,[35] and it is not known whether guilt on other offences was so determined.

What is becoming still clearer is the essential difference between law and ethics, and Jackson is correct when he says that the presence of the law against coveting in the Decalogue shows that that collection of 'laws' does not belong to jurisprudence but declares the divine will. More generally we may conclude that Israelite law, like law in every culture, is unwilling, except in extreme circumstances, to go beyond actions. As Jackson expresses it: lawyers would say that 'the law . . . is concerned with the administration of a system of norms by which the orderly functioning of society may be ensured', and therefore 'regulates only those actions of mankind which have repercussions extending further than the mind, or even body of the offender, and which therefore affect the interests, directly or indirectly, of society at large. Thus the notion of liability for mere intention is a strange one.'[36] Ethics, however, concerns the whole person, and as David's anger against Yahweh revealed, here intention has to be taken into account.

We must accept this distinction, yet the Old Testament laws, despite their superficial resemblances to the law codes discovered in other societies of the ancient Middle East, have some marked differences from them. One of these is the widespread addition of 'motive clauses' to the individual laws, and we turn to this in the next chapter.

Appendix: Intention in Ancient Middle Eastern Law
A number of laws in the codes from the ancient Middle East give a place to intention, perhaps better described as 'ignorance of the circumstances' in some instances. Although they, like the Old Testament, refer mostly to homicide, other offences are occasionally mentioned.

In the laws of Hammurabi a free man who struck another of the same class in a brawl and inflicted injury is allowed to swear that he did not strike his victim 'deliberately' and is let off by simply paying for medical aid. Even if the victim dies he can swear the same oath and has only to pay a fine (CH 206–208). The literal phrase translated 'deliberately' by Theophile J. Meek and by Driver and Miles 'wittingly' is 'while I was aware of it' and is related to *biḇʾlī-daʿaṯ*.[37] Boecker, however, wonders how a blow inflicted during a fight could be 'unintentional' or 'unperceived', and suggests that the original law

---

[35] Eryl W. Davies gives a list of discussions of ordeals, *Numbers*, 51.
[36] Jackson, 'Liability', 197.
[37] *ANET*, 175; G. R. Driver and John C. Miles, *The Babylonian Laws*, I, 79, cf. II, 412–413, 423.

simply reduced the penalties for injuries received in a fight, and the later legal development introduced the participants' intentions.[38] Is it not perhaps that the accused man declares that he did not intend to wound his opponent so severely, still less to kill him? The same excuse is made by the barber who claims that he was prevailed upon by a third party to remove the identification mark on a slave, and on making this declaration he goes free (CH 227). In both instances the accused person takes an oath that he acted unwittingly. Such oaths of exculpation are found elsewhere in CH and seem to have been used where it was impossible to obtain evidence, and this is especially true of intention.

The Middle Assyrian laws recognize ignorance as a plea in the case of a free man who lies with the wife of another free man, but no indication is given of how he proves that he did not know that she was married, apart from the fact that he met her in a brothel or casually in the street (MAL A 13, 14).[39]

In the Sumerian laws we find: 'If (a man) deflowered the daughter of a free citizen in the street, her father and her mother having known (that she was in the street) but the man who deflowered her denied that he knew (her to be of the free-citizen class), and, standing at the temple gate, swore an oath (to this effect, he shall be freed).[40]

Finally we may note that the Hittite laws distinguish unintentional homicide by the phrase '(only) his hand doing wrong' (HL 3–4).[41]

---

[38] Hans Jochen Boecker, *Law*, 124.
[39] *ANET*, 181.
[40] *ANET*, 526.
[41] *ANET*, 189.

10

MOTIVATIONS

One feature which marks off Old Testament laws from laws found elsewhere in the ancient Middle East is the apodeictic form of many of the laws. Although this is not absolutely unique to Israel's laws, it is found much more commonly there, and when found elsewhere the form is not strictly identical, since the majority of such laws regulate prices or wages or other economic matters. The type of apodeictic laws which present ethical demands and which predominate among the apodeictic laws in Israel are totally lacking.[1] As we have already seen, the apodeictic form makes the laws much more the direct commands of God than human laws or customs, to which the casuistic form is suited. A second feature is the addition of reasons for keeping the laws and exhortations to obey them, and it is to these that the present chapter is directed, for they are one of the main ways in which law in ancient Israel veers towards ethics.

Reasons for keeping the laws are expressed in two ways. The first, found especially in Deuteronomy, are exhortations or advice which are separate from the laws. It is these exhortations which make that book look more like 'preaching' than a law code. We shall return to this later. More closely integrated with the laws are the 'motive clauses', which are usually linked to the laws by conjunctions or prepositions.[2]

---

[1] Albrecht Alt, usually credited with introducing the form-critical distinction between casuistic and apodeictic laws, is also often thought to have claimed its unique status in Israel. His actual words are rather more cautious: 'this form [casuistic law] is almost without exception the only one to be found in the legal codes of non-Israelite nations in the Ancient East' ('Origins', 92–93). He grouped three forms of law under the term 'apodeictic', but later scholars have distinguished true apodeictic commands or prohibitions, the participial form (action or offence and penalty), and curses; see Dale Patrick, *Old Testament Law*, 19–33, Hans Jochen Boecker, *Law*, 191–207, and Rifat Sonsino, *Motive Clauses*, 1–64 for valuable discussions. The only apodeictic laws that are at all similar to Israelite ones in form seem to be MAL A 40, which contains both apodeictic and casuistic laws on the veiling of women, and MAL A 59, which is close to the casuistic form. Laws fixing prices, wages and other economic matters are usually apodeictic (for examples see Laws of Eshnunna 1, 3, 7,16; Hittite Laws 48, 50–52, 56, 178, 181–184; Hammurabi 36, 38–40, 187), although so dominant is the casuistic form that even the setting of prices was sometimes expressed in this form.

[2] B. Gemser has identified twelve different forms of the clauses ('Motive Clause', 53–55). Sonsino distinguishes 'explicative notes' (which 'interpret or clarify specific

Motive Clauses

There has been some discussion as to whether these clauses were part of the original laws or are later additions.[3] This is impossible to determine, as is the original place the laws had in the social life of ancient Israel. On the other hand, it is possible to observe differences in ethical awareness between them. Tracing any ethical development lies beyond our grasp, because it is impossible to determine the dates of the various collections of laws.

Sonsino has calculated that 375 of the 1238 legal prescriptions found in the main collections of laws in the Old Testament have motive clauses attached to them, the majority (268) to apodeictic laws (or as Sonsino describes them 'formulated in unconditional form'). The highest percentage of laws with motivations is found in the Holiness Code (51 per cent of 214 laws), followed by Deuteronomy (50 per cent of 225 laws), the Decalogue (45 per cent of 11 laws), the Book of the Covenant (16 per cent of 104 laws) and the Cultic Decalogue (13 per cent out of 15 laws). The Priestly Code has 20 per cent of 669 laws. Broadly, then, it may be said that motive clauses are found more frequently as time went on. According to Sonsino, most of the laws with motive clauses deal with cultic or sacral matters, but he points out that this obscures the fact that, although on his classification humanitarian laws comprise only 8 per cent of all the laws in the Pentateuch, they have the highest percentage of motivations (53 per cent). He sees in this 'the special moral concern that animated the draftsmen who formulated biblical laws; they not only formulated moral instructions but, in order to ensure compliance to them, they also provided a great many of these instructions with motivations, stressing their importance for the welfare of the individual as well as society'.[4]

The motivations vary and it is not easy to classify them.

B. Gemser finds four types: (1) 'explanatory' (twenty-nine clauses), (2) 'ethical' (eleven or twelve), (3) 'religious' (some fifty in all), and

---

words or clauses within the law' or 'specify the scope of the particular legal prescription') and 'legal paraenesis', from true motive clauses (*Motive Clauses*, 66–69).

[3] The arguments for regarding them as secondary are: (1) the original laws were short; (2) the motive clauses are sometimes in a different grammatical form from the laws, e.g., switching from first to third persons or from singular to plural and vice versa; (3) stylistically they are judged to be akin to passages of late origin (see Sonsino, *Motive Clauses*, 193–218). Sonsino concludes that there is no proof that they are original, but that it is possible. Gemser points out that they are found in the early Book of the Covenant and Exodus 34, and this, together with their rhythmic form supports their originality ('Motive Clause', 63–64). Gerhard von Rad apparently regards some of them as original, even though he notes that they are more frequent in the later collections of laws (*Theology*, I, 197). Since different clauses are sometimes added to the same law (e.g., Ex. 20.11, Deut. 5.14–15), and the motive clauses tend to have characteristic forms in the various collections of laws, it seems more likely that most of them were added to the laws by the later editors or at some point during the transmission of the traditions.

[4] Sonsino, *Motive Clauses*, 98, 99–100.

(4) 'historico-religious' (about thirty, over half of them in Deuteronomy and ten in the Holiness Code).[5]

Von Rad draws upon Gemser's study. He calls the addition of 'I am Yahweh' (Lev. 19.13–18), 'for you are a people holy to Yahweh' (Deut. 14.21), and the statement that the offence is 'an abomination to Yahweh' (Deut. 17.1; 22.5; 23.19[18]; 25.16) 'theological tauto-logies', the law being reasserted as Yahweh's command, and he does not regard them as full motive clauses. His classification of what he terms 'substantiations' is (a) simple matter of fact interpretation, (b) ethical appeal, (c) theological motivation, and (d) references to salvation history.[6]

Sonsino divides the clauses into two main classes, (1) reiterating the law for emphasis, and (2) setting out the purpose behind the law by (a) stressing human dignity, (b) drawing attention to the special status of the actor, (c) expressing a value judgment, (d) stating the object of the action, (e) presenting a diagnosis (in the leprosy laws), (f) declaring God's authority, (g) recalling Israel's history, (h) awakening fear of punishment, and (i) promising well-being.[7] This has value in drawing attention to the different ways in which the purpose of the laws is grounded, but is perhaps too definite and seeks a precision which is not there in the text.

Donald E. Gowan classifies the clauses under the heads of references (a) to the past, intending to arouse emotions of gratitude for divine deliverance (or hatred of what the Ammonites, Moabites and Amalek had done to Israel, Deut. 23.5[4]; 25.17–19), (b) the present, referring to present conditions, or alluding to self-evident truth, appealing to self-interest, humanitarian instincts or religious commitment, and (c) the future, describing the result of keeping or disobeying the commandment.[8]

Greg Chirichigno analyses the clauses according to the topics to which they are attached and their themes. He claims, without giving statistics, that the topics are equally distributed among the law codes apart from war and kingship which are found only in Deuteronomy. On the matter of our present concern, the themes, he discerns three types: holiness, divided into four forms: 'separation toward' (e.g., Ex. 22.31; Lev. 20.7–8; Deut. 14.21), 'separation from' (e.g., Lev. 20.14; 22.22; Deut. 22.21), 'keeping holy' (e.g., Lev. 25.17, 18; Deut. 16.12; 17.13, 19), and the holiness of God (found exclusively in Leviticus); promise, in three categories: 'deliverance from and remembrance of Egypt' (e.g., Deut. 13.10; 24.22; Ex. 22.21), 'the giving of the land

---

[5] Gemser, 'Motive Clause', 55–61.
[6] Von Rad, *Theology*, I, 196–198.
[7] Sonsino, *Motive Clauses*, 106–117.
[8] Donald E. Gowan, 'Motive Clauses'.

and living in it' (e.g., Deut. 21.13; Lev. 18.28), and blessings (e.g., Deut. 15.4, 18; 19.13; Lev. 25.18); and a residual group of general motivations, divided between ethical (e.g., Ex. 22.27), and explanatory (e.g., Lev. 20.9; 25.55). He fails, however, to make a sharp distinction between motive clauses proper and paraenesis.[9]

Christiana van Houten attempts to trace a development in Israelite law by way of analysing the laws concerning the resident alien and through examining the motivations. In the Book of the Covenant she finds two types, which she characterizes as 'an appeal to the past' and 'goal-oriented'. The motivation of the sabbath law in the Decalogue in Exodus 20 is 'imitating God'. There are six reasons for keeping the laws in Deuteronomy: appeal to the past, appeal to humanitarian instincts, promise of divine blessing, appeal to principle, connection of the law to a goal, and threat of penalty for disobedience. In the Priestly laws van Houten also sees six types of motivation: appeal to the past, appeal to authority, explaining the purpose of the law, explaining the principle on which the law is based, describing the result of disobedience, and basing the law on the nature of creation.[10]

Instead of attempting yet another classification I shall examine the motive clauses in the Book of the Covenant, the Decalogue, the Deuteronomic laws, and the Holiness Code in turn. Before doing this, however, it should be noted that not only are motivations far rarer in collections of laws outside the Old Testament, occurring only in Hammurabi's law code and the Middle Assyrian laws, but they also differ from those in the Old Testament in four important respects.

First, they are expressed impersonally, whereas in the Old Testament most are directly addressed to the hearer or reader (though some impersonal and third-person clauses are found). The motivations in the Old Testament laws, therefore, are much more clearly exhortation, reinforcing the sense of direct address to the hearer that the narrative setting of the laws presents.

Second, in the Middle Eastern collections of laws the motive clauses do little more than reinforce the law, and do not give reasons for keeping it, in contrast to the Old Testament. Thus after various forms of theft or deceit it is stated: 'since the free man is a thief' or 'since he was a cheat and started a false report' (CH 7, 11, cf. 9, 10, 13, 194). In an elaborate account of adultery, a woman who claims that she committed the offence under pressure is let go free 'since she is guiltless' (MAL A 23, cf. 24). A woman whose husband has gone

[9] Greg Chirichigno, 'Motivation'.
[10] Christiana van Houten, *The Alien*, 166–172. David H. Engelhard considers the motivations which 'underlie concern for the underprivileged' in 'Motivated Concern', 17–23.

abroad and who did not wait the decreed five years for his return is sent back to her husband 'because she did not respect the marriage-contract but got married' (MAL A 36).

Third, a second main use of such clauses is to provide an explanation of the law, as when arrangements are made to enable a soldier's widow to bring up her young son 'in order that his mother may rear him' (CH 29). Similarly, the inheritance of the dowries of a deceased wife, or a wife whose father has died is explained by 'since her dowry belongs to her children', 'since her dowry belongs to her father's house', and 'since her patrimony belongs to her brothers' (CH 162, 163, 171, 178).

Fourth, the motive clauses outside the Old Testament never refer to historical events or to the religious myths, and they never promise well-being or declare the divine will.[11]

The biblical motivations, therefore, are quite distinctive, and as will be shown, this draws the laws strongly towards the teaching of ethics.[12]

The Book of the Covenant

Keeping in mind the question, Why do the Old Testament laws contain so many motive clauses and clauses of such distinctive kinds? we turn to the Book of the Covenant, which according to Sonsino's calculations has the lowest percentage of motive clauses and which contains a large number of casuistic laws, many of them similar in content as well as form to laws from elsewhere in the ancient Middle East, and especially to the Code of Hammurabi.[13] A kind of motive clause introduces the whole collection of laws in its present position in the book of Exodus. Moses is told to say to the people: 'You have seen for yourselves that I have talked with you from heaven' (Ex. 20.22). Some regard it as showing why images are forbidden, but its position suggests much more that it authenticates the complete collection of laws.[14] In the completed Old Testament, therefore, the

---

[11] See Sonsino, who rejects Gemser's claim that the biblical motive clauses were unique and discusses some twenty-five such clauses in CH and MAL. Importantly he also examines motive clauses in other types of text, especially wisdom instruction, where a large number of such clauses are found (*Motive Clauses*, 153–192).

[12] Von Rad makes this point, stressing that the commandments were not 'law' in a modern legal sense. Yahweh wants obedience, but he also wants human beings to understand his commands and 'assent inwardly as well' (*Theology*, I, 198–199).

[13] There is an immense literature on the Book of the Covenant. For a clear outline of the issues see J. P. Hyatt, *Exodus*, 217–224, or Brevard Childs, *Exodus*, 451–464.

[14] Among those limiting it to the law concerning images are M. Noth, *Exodus*, 175, Sonsino, *Motive Clauses*, 235, n.1, Clements, *Exodus*, 129; on the other hand Childs, *Exodus*, 465 takes v. 22 as redactional, probably from the Deuteronomist, 'subsuming the whole Book of the Covenant within the framework of the Sinai theophany', while John Durham, *Exodus*, 318, stresses that the verse emphasizes that Israel experienced

emphasis lies on the divine origin of the laws and gives this as the reason for keeping them.

The Book of the Covenant is commonly divided into two sections, 21.2–22.19[20] and 20.23–26 + 22.20[21]–23.19, the first consisting mainly of casuistic laws, similar to ancient Middle Eastern law,[15] while the second has a more ethical and religious stance and contains a number of apodeictic laws, in the 'true' form of commands or prohibitions (e.g., 20.23, 24, 26; 22.20[21], 21[22], 28[29]–29[30], 30[31]; 23.1, 6, 9a, 18, 19), and in the form of actor plus negative plus verb (22.17[18], 20[21], 27[28]; 23.8; cf. 23.3, 7b). By contrast in the first part of the Book of the Covenant the only laws that are not in casuistic form are six in the participial or offence and penalty form (21.12, 15, 16, 17; 22.18[19], 19[20]). In line with this, it is the second section which contains most of the motive clauses in the collection, the only ones in the first section being 21.8, 21, 26–27, and these, as will be shown, are not as strongly 'ethical' as those in the other parts of the collection of laws.

The history of the Book of the Covenant cannot be traced with certainty, although it is possible that underlying it was a collection of genuinely legal customs or traditions. Hyatt shows too much confidence in asserting that 'there can be little question' that the casuistic laws found in the first part of the Book were taken over from the Canaanites, and that some of them may have been adopted in the patriarchal period cannot be ruled out.[16] Since so little certainty exists about the early history of Israel before the time of the monarchy, this can be no more than unsupported hypothesis. All that can be shown are the close similarities with the other law codes and the lack of distinctively religious emphases.

In the present form of the laws, whether this is the result of extensive editing or, less probably, was an original feature of some of them, the motive clauses change their aspect between the two parts of the collection. The two (or possibly four) motive clauses in the section 21.2–22.19[20] set out the reason for the law. The woman who has been sold into slavery by her father and has been taken by her master as his concubine is not to be sold to a foreigner because 'he has dealt faithlessly with her' (21.8). The rather cynical reason why no action is to be taken against the master whose slave did not die immediately after being beaten – 'for the slave is his money' (21.21) – explains why the beating is treated as a severe punishment that

---

the theophany and thus the commandments are not those of Moses but Yahweh's. Hyatt, *Exodus*, 225, sees the verse as having both aims.
[15] Childs, *Exodus*, 462–463, gives a valuable table of parallels.
[16] Hyatt, *Exodus*, 219–221.

unfortunately resulted in death rather than as deliberate murder. The very brief 'for his eye', 'for his tooth', explains that the master who destroyed the eye or knocked out the tooth of his slave (male or female) is to let the slave go free because of the injury he has inflicted (21.26, 27).

The motive clauses in this section of the Book of the Covenant are similar to those found in Middle Eastern law codes, and it may be that they are original to the laws, though this lacks firm proof. Those in the other part of the collection are mostly of a different kind. Even those which are explanatory carry religious or ethical overtones. Thus the laws of the altar are concerned with purity (Ex. 20.25, 26). The explanation that the poor man's garment taken in pledge must be given back at night 'for that is his only covering, it is his mantle for his body; in what else shall he sleep?' (Ex. 22.26[27]) reaches beyond merely declaring the reason for the requirement and stresses the humanitarian purpose behind the law (the coat is the poor man's blanket as well as his coat, and he will be cold at night without it), an emphasis which is backed up by a second motive clause expressing God's support for the poor man: 'And if he cries to me, I will hear, for I am compassionate.' In a similar way the prohibition of taking bribes is supported both by the ethical demand to give justice to the poor and by God's declaration that he will not acquit the wicked (Ex. 23.7–8). Concern for the poor (and even for wild animals) is found in the motive clauses attached to the laws on the fallow year and the weekly sabbath (Ex. 23.11, 12), while the cause of widows and orphans is reinforced by the divine threat of death of the men in war, making their wives widows and their children orphans, if they are not cared for (Ex. 22.22–23[23–24]). Finally, and most importantly, the motive clauses attached to two of the laws refer to the time when the Israelites were resident aliens in Egypt (Ex. 22.20[21]; 23.9), the second of them emphasizing that this experience should make them understand what it is like to be an alien and therefore have sympathy with the resident aliens within their own society.[17]

We have seen earlier that law as such cannot be taken as evidence either of the actual practice of the Israelites or of the norms which they regarded as right and which they believed ought to be kept. This examination of the Book of the Covenant suggests that while this is true, editors have brought the laws closer to ethical instruction by adding special types of motive clauses. This is carried further in the Decalogue, Deuteronomy and the Holiness Code.

---

[17] A third clause referring to the exodus is linked to observing the feast of unleavened bread (Ex. 23.15).

The Ten Commandments

In the Decalogue motive clauses are added to four laws. Images are prohibited because 'I the LORD your God am a jealous God, visiting the iniquity of the fathers upon the children to the third and the fourth generation of those who hate me, but showing steadfast love to thousands of those who love me and keep my commandments' (Ex. 20.5–6/Deut. 5.9–10), and Yahweh's name is not to be taken in vain because 'the LORD will not hold him guiltless who takes his name in vain' (Ex. 20.7/Deut. 5.11). The Exodus form of the sabbath law relates the sabbath to creation (Ex. 20.11) while the Deuteronomist declares that it is the command of Yahweh and has the purpose of giving rest to slaves, calling the Israelites to remember that they were slaves in Egypt and Yahweh brought them out by exerting his power on their behalf (Deut. 5.12, 14–15). The motives for honouring parents are 'that your days may be long in the land which the LORD your God gives you' (Ex. 20.12/Deut. 5.16) with the addition 'as the LORD your God commanded you' and 'that it may go well with you' in Deuteronomy (5.16).

Although the Ten Commandments are introduced as the direct announcement by Yahweh, only the first of these motive clauses is in the first person. This, together with the fact that the main differences between the two versions are in the motive clauses, suggests that these clauses were added to the commandments by later editors. They stress that the laws are the direct commands of God, declare that he will punish the disobedient and reward those who keep his commandments, and offer reasons for keeping the sabbath (with a reference to the situation of the Israelites in Egypt as slaves, delivered by God). As we have seen, this last motive is explained elsewhere as having a twofold sense: the Israelites know what it feels like to be in a similar situation to those to whom they should show kindness, and they should be grateful to Yahweh for delivering them from Egypt (Ex. 22.20[21]; 23.9; Deut. 15.15; 24.18, 22). The motive clauses attached to the religious and ritual commandments in the Decalogue in their present form stress that what is being presented to Israel is God's own teaching, supported not by any human sanctions but by rewards and punishments given by God himself. The one place which goes beyond this, appeals to the fellow feeling that those who possess slaves should have towards those whom they own, and supports this by calling on them to remember God's deliverance in the Exodus. This is in line with the verse which Jews take as the first commandment and which Christians see as the introduction to them: 'I am the LORD your God, who brought you out of the land of Egypt, out of the house of bondage' (Ex. 20.2/Deut. 5.6), and which acts as a kind of motive clause sustaining the whole Decalogue. Too much, however, should not be made of this in a discussion of Old Testament ethics. The laws that are most clearly ethical lack motive clauses, and only the Deuteronomic motivations for keeping the sabbath show a concern for the unprivileged slave. From one aspect, Yahweh seems most deeply concerned with his own prestige and worship.

The Deuteronomic Laws (Deuteronomy 12–26)
The number of motive clauses in Deuteronomy is too large to make it possible to discuss all of them. We pass by the explanatory clauses, such as, 'for the blood is the life', giving the reason why the blood must be drained out before meat is eaten (Deut. 12.23), the giving of the third year's tithe to the Levite 'because he has no portion or inheritance with you' (Deut. 14.29), 'a bribe blinds the eyes of the wise and subverts the cause of the righteous' (Deut. 16.19), the husband who falsely accused his wife of not being a virgin at marriage is whipped and has to pay her father compensation 'because he has brought an evil name upon a virgin of Israel' (Deut. 22.18), or forbidding the taking of an upper millstone as a pledge 'for he would be taking a life in pledge' (Deut. 24.6). Many of these clauses introduce highly moral sentiments, and some are distinctive to Deuteronomy, but space demands that we concentrate on those motivations which are repeated several times and which therefore point to what is of special significance.

Two phrases which occur in the motive clauses have already been discussed in the account of purity: 'abomination' and 'purge the evil from the midst of you' (or 'from Israel').[18] The first is in a distinctive form applied either to the offender ('whoever does these things is an abomination to the LORD', Deut. 18.12; 22.5; 25.16)[19] or to the action ('for that is an abomination to (or before) the LORD', Deut. 17.1; 24.4).[20] The offences are frequently part of the Deuteronomist's anti-Canaanite polemic. Mayes accepts the view that it was originally a wisdom phrase, introduced into the laws by the Deuteronomist.[21] The second is found only in Deuteronomy apart from Judges 20.13, and with one exception (Deut. 19.19) gives the motivation for carrying out the death penalty.[22]

[18] See above pp. 10–14.
[19] Deut. 23.19[18], 'for both of these are an abomination to the LORD your God' is awkward, but probably refers to the male and female prostitutes.
[20] Cf. also Deut. 7.25 where taking images, gold and silver that should have been put to the ban has the same motive clause, and 20.18 'that they may not teach you to do according to all their abominable practices'.
[21] A. D. H. Mayes, *Deuteronomy*, 189.
[22] Mayes, as has been seen (p. 13 n. 26 above) denies that it is a legal formula or is derived from cultic practice. He suggests, probably correctly, that it may have been an ancient phrase which has been introduced by the Deuteronomist. The references are: Deut. 13.6[5]; 17.7; 19.19; 21.21; 22.21, 24; 24.7, with 'Israel' 17.12; 22.22, and in the form 'you shall purge the guilt of innocent blood from your midst' in the rite for

Similarly concerned with purity is the declaration that Israel must obey the laws because it is a holy people, chosen by Yahweh (Deut. 14.2, 21), a theme found most strongly in the Holiness Code.

Twice the motive for the action is 'that you may learn to fear the LORD your God always' (Deut. 14.23, referring to the eating of tithes in the place which Yahweh will choose; and Deut. 17.19, of the king who is to read the law in order to learn to reverence Yahweh his God by keeping his laws).

More significant for ethics is the motive of deterrence, a feature to which little attention has been given in the past. It is found in slightly varied forms after the imposition of penalties, each stressing that the report of the punishment will create fear among those who hear of it – stoning the close relative who suggested following other gods (Deut. 13.12[11]: 'and all Israel shall hear, and fear, and never again do any such wickedness as this among you'); failing to accept the legal ruling of the priests in difficult cases (Deut. 17.13: 'and all the people shall hear, and fear, and not act presumptuously again'); treating the malicious witness as he meant to do to his fellow Israelite (Deut. 19.20: 'And the rest shall hear, and fear, and shall never again commit any such evil among you'); stoning the rebellious son (Deut. 21.21: 'and all Israel shall hear, and fear'). It should be noted that the four offences to which these motive clauses are attached are all offences against authority – of God himself, of the priests, of the legal system, and parents. This is the mentality of the law-makers. To 'hear' of the penalty that has been imposed and to react with 'fear' is exactly the way they hope punishment will function within society.

Somewhat similar to these, and probably related to the general exhortations found in the book, are the clauses which express divine threats or promises. The threats differ from the penalties in that they are general and are imposed directly by God. Yahweh will require the fulfilment of vows (Deut. 23.22[21]). Sometimes an impersonal form is used, as in the law demanding the providing of parapets to the roof of a house, 'that you may not bring the guilt of blood (lit. simply 'bloods') upon your house, if any one fall from it' (Deut. 22.8). Far more commonly, however, Deuteronomy offers divine promises of long life (Deut. 17.20; 22.7; 25.15), 'blessing' (Deut. 14.29; 15.10; 16.15; 23.21[20]; 24.13; 24.19), or simply 'that it may go well with you' (Deut. 12.25; 22;7).[23] In 13.18–19[17–18] the Deuteronomist combines threat and promise, though with the emphasis upon the latter: the 'ban' is to be enforced 'that the LORD may turn from the fierceness of his anger, and show you mercy, and have compassion on you, and multiply you, as he swore to your fathers'.

---

cleansing after the discovery of a murder by unknown persons, 21.9.
[23] Cf. Sonsino, *Motive Clauses*, 115–116.

Deuteronomy is deeply conscious of God's deliverance in the past and the gift of the land of Canaan, and historical references are frequent. Prophets who call on Israel to worship other gods are to be put to death 'because he has taught rebellion against the LORD your God, who brought you out of the land of Egypt and redeemed you out of the house of bondage' (Deut. 13.6[5], cf. 13.11[10]).[24] A characteristic form of this motivation in Deuteronomy is a call to 'remember' the situation of the Israelites in the past and what God has done for them, e.g., 'You shall remember that you were a slave in the land of Egypt, and the LORD your God redeemed you; therefore I command you this today' (Deut. 15.15, cf. 24.18, 22).[25]

The Holiness Code (Leviticus 17–26)
As the name by which scholars have designated this collection of laws implies, the holiness both of God and of Israel his people, dominates this collection of laws, especially in the motive clauses and the paraenesis. 'You shall be holy; for I the LORD your God am holy' (Lev. 19.2).

Yahweh's authority is reiterated in the phrase that follows very many of the laws, 'I am the LORD', or 'I am the LORD your God' (e.g., Lev. 18.6, 21; 19.3, 4, 10, 16, 25, 30, 31, 34). Sometimes this is further defined by references to the Exodus (e.g., Lev. 19.36; 25.38, 55; 20.26 refers to Yahweh's separating Israel from the peoples, but is paraenesis rather than a motive clause attached to a law). Hence a further motivation is to avoid wrongdoing because this will be to 'profane the name of your God' (Lev. 18.21; 19.12; 22.2), a theme which is developed further in the idea of profaning God's sanctuary (Lev. 20.3; 21.12) and even meat which has become holy in the sacrifice of peace offering (Lev. 19.8).

The demand for holiness in the people of God underlies the clause which declares that homosexual practice is an 'abomination', while bestiality is 'to defile yourself' and 'perversion' (Lev. 18.22, 23; 20.13).[26] Priests, especially, have to maintain their holiness. They are not to marry a prostitute, a woman who has been 'defiled' (perhaps by being raped, unless the phrase is a further explication of being a prostitute), or has been divorced, 'for the priest is holy to his God'

---

[24] See also the motivation for prohibiting Ammonites and Moabites from the assembly, while permitting Edomites of the third generation (Deut. 23.5[4], 8[7]).

[25] The call to 'remember' is also found in the leprosy law recalling God's punishment of Miriam (Deut. 24.9). Remembrance is more widely important in Deuteronomy: it is the reason for keeping the Passover (Deut. 16.3).

[26] Sonsino describes Lev. 18.17, 23; 20.17, 21 as expressing a value judgment (*Motive Clauses*, 108–109), but the words used indicate the basic stress on holiness. Gemser ('Motive Clause', 61) includes Lev. 18.24. 27, 29, but these occur within paraenesis.

(Lev. 21.7).[27] Moreover, it is the requirement that the people are to be holy which lies behind the clause stating that those who have offended and so brought in pollution shall be 'cut off from [their] people' (Lev. 23.29).[28]

Holiness is so dominant that other motivations are rare. Most of the relatively few historical motivations are related to holiness, as has been seen. One exception is the reason for keeping the festival of booths: 'that your generations may know that I made the people of Israel dwell in booths when I brought them out of the land of Egypt' (Lev. 23.43). Another comes in the set of regulations about slavery, where it is forbidden to make a needy Israelite serve as a slave; instead he is to be treated as a hired servant and to be released in the year of jubilee. Fellow Israelites must not be sold as slaves, 'for they are my servants, whom I brought forth out of the land of Egypt' (Lev. 25.42).

Divine threats and promises, which played so large a part in Deuteronomy, are almost non-existent, the only obvious example being God's warning: 'whoever does any work on this same day [the day of atonement], that person I will destroy from among his people' (Lev. 23.30).[29]

The effect of the motivations in the Old Testament is striking. They stress that it is God who gives the laws. They are his direct commands. God speaks through his laws and the motivations. And they link the laws very firmly with God's past and present relations with Israel.

Exhortation
The other form of motivation, the exhortation (paraenesis), is found in Deuteronomy and the Holiness Code, but is rare in the Book of the Covenant.[30] Many scholars fail to distinguish between paraenesis and motive clauses, but Sonsino seems to be right in making a clear distinction between them.[31] (1) The purpose of paraenetic statements is to summon the hearers to obedience, whereas motive clauses give

---

[27] Sonsino classes this as referring to the special status of the actor (*Motive Clauses*, 108), but the underlying reason is to maintain holiness. See Budd, *Leviticus*, 301–302, for a discussion of the terms.

[28] The meaning of the phrase has been much discussed (for a brief summary see Budd, *Leviticus*, 122, 245). Usually in Leviticus it is the (human) punishment for offences. This is the only place where it forms a motivation.

[29] I do not discuss explanatory motive clauses (e.g., Lev. 17.14; 19.20; 20.9; 21.23; 22.7; 25.16, 33, 34), since similar clauses have been discussed earlier.

[30] The paraenesis in the Book of the Covenant may well be later additions to the original laws (Ex. 20.24b; 22.30a[31a]; 23.13a, and the conclusion to the collection, 23.20–22).

[31] Sonsino, *Motive Clauses*, 66–69, 224.

the reason for the law and the element of exhortation is secondary. (2) Formally, motive clauses are closely attached to individual laws as subordinate clauses or phrases, while paraenetic statements are independent, even when closely associated with a given law. (3) It follows that while motive clauses may be in first, second or third person form, paraenesis is usually addressed directly to the Israelites, either individually or as a group. N. Lohfink has pointed out that the exhortations in Deuteronomy often have a twofold structure: an appeal (usually with the imperatives 'observe', 'do', 'learn', or 'hear') and a blessing (of long life, inheritance of the land, or general well-being),[32] but other forms of paraenesis are found. While some of the motive clauses contain promises or threats, imperatives are notably absent from them.

So prominent is paraenesis in Deuteronomy that von Rad describes the book as 'law preached'.[33] The very form of the book is a speech by Moses to the people (cf. Deut. 1.1; 5.1, and other verses, e.g., 4.45; 6.1). Much of it consists of teaching which is very different from the apodeictic and casuistic laws that form the main part of the Book of the Covenant. In chapters 1–4 and 5–11 history is mingled with paraenesis. Within the main collection of laws (Deut. 12–26) small sections of paraenesis can be discovered,[34] and the laws themselves are incorporated within the overall structure so that the whole becomes, in the words of Mayes, 'a call to the service of one God by an elect people centered around one sanctuary, through obedience to the law in the land which God has given'.[35]

The main exhortations in Deuteronomy (and there are only minor differences between the section of laws (Deut. 12–26) and the rest of the book) can be classified under six heads. (1) The primary call is to obey the commands of Yahweh,[36] to fear him[37] and walk in his way.[38]

---

[32] N. Lohfink, *Das Hauptgebot*. I have not had access to this and draw from Sonsino's summary (*Motive Clauses*, 67).

[33] Gerhard von Rad, *Studies in Deuteronomy*, 16.

[34] Sonsino detects some twenty-eight paraenetic verses or groups of verses (see his analysis in *Motive Clauses*, 250–253).

[35] *Deuteronomy*, 57–58. Mayes traces an 'original' book, which was subjected to two Deuteronomistic editings. Even the original book, however, was presented as a speech of Moses giving the laws to Israel and contained a considerable amount of exhortation, both to encourage obedience to the law and to foster the view that Israel is Yahweh's own possession, to whom he has given the land (pp. 48–49).

[36] Examples are Deut. 4.39–40; 5.1, 29; 6.1–3; 8.6; 11.1, 8, 13; 13.1[12.32]; 23.24[23]; 26.16; 28.1; 30.16.

[37] Deut. 6.2; 10.12, 20; 13.5[4].

[38] Deut. 5.33; 8.6; 10.12; 11.22; 13.5[4]; 26.17; 28.9; 30.16; cf. 9.12, 16. Mayes distinguishes between the singular 'way' and the plural, holding that the former refers to the Decalogue (*Deuteronomy*, 199). I am not sure that this can be sustained. On walking in Yahweh's way see Chapter 7 above.

Such exhortations also warn against disobedience.[39] A characteristic of Deuteronomy is the call to 'lay up these words of mine in your heart and in your soul'.[40] (2) The promise of blessing for keeping Yahweh's commands is more frequent than warnings against disobedience, and is expressed in several stock phrases: 'that it may go well with you',[41] 'that you may live', 'that you may live long', and 'that you may prolong your days',[42] as well as 'he will bless you',[43] although the reverse of the blessing, the curse, is not absent.[44] This promise of blessing is complemented within the laws of 12–26 by a call to 'rejoice'.[45] (3) As with the motive clauses, there are frequent references to history, especially to the Exodus deliverance and the gift of the land, and the call to 'remember' is also repeated.[46] (4) There is a call to be a holy people and to keep the land undefiled.[47] (5) In the framework, but not within the laws, there are references to Yahweh as a jealous God, whose anger is kindled against his people if they are disobedient, who supports justice, and disciplines his people whom he loves.[48] (6) Through it all runs the idea of maintaining the covenant.[49]

Although paraenesis is less prominent in the Holiness Code, it is similar to that found in Deuteronomy, but sometimes goes beyond what is found there. The laws are presented as instructions given by Yahweh to Moses who is to transmit them to the people of Israel or to the priests (see the first verse of each chapter), and the call, somewhat 'Deuteronomic' in character, to keep Yahweh's statutes is repeated (Lev. 18.26; 19.19, 37; 20.8, 22; 22.31; cf. the demand following two of the individual laws that it shall become 'a statute for ever', Lev. 17.7; 23.31). Somewhat similar is the setting of chapter 18 within a paraenetic envelope (vv. 1–5, 24–30). The collection of laws receives its name from the call to Israel to be holy as Yahweh their God is holy (cf. Lev. 19.1; 20.7), and with this goes the call to Israel not to defile

[39] Deut. 4.15, 19; 8.11–20; 29.15–27[16–28].
[40] Deut. 4.39; 6.6; 11.18; cf. 4.29; 10.12; 11.13; 26.16; 30.2, 6, 10.
[41] Deut. 4.40; 5.29, 33; 6.3.
[42] Deut. 4.40; 5.33; 6.2; 8.1; 11.9.
[43] Deut. 7.13; 15.4, 6, 18; 30; cf. 11.27; 28.2.
[44] Cf. Deut. 11.26–28; 28.15–68; 30.17–18.
[45] Deut. 12.7, 12, 18; 14.26; 16.11; 26.11.
[46] Deut. 7.18; 8.2, 14–18; 10.20–22; 11.1–7; 16.20; 20.1; 21.23; 24.4; 25.19; 29.15[16]
[47] Deut. 7.6; 14.2; 21.23; 26.19; 28.9; cf. the call not to bring any 'abominable thing' into your house, 7.26.
[48] Deut. 7.4; 8.6; 10.15, 18; 11.16–17; but cf. 5.9.
[49] Deut. 4.23; 5.2; 7.6, 12; 8.18; 28.69[29.1]; 29.8[9] and extensively in the third speech of Moses in 29. Whether Deuteronomy is based on vassal treaties is debated; the earlier references to Hittite vassal treaties have now generally been abandoned, but the possible influence of Middle Eastern treaties is still maintained by some. How early the covenant idea appeared in Israel is also debated (see Ernest W. Nicholson, *God and His People*).

themselves, as the earlier inhabitants defiled themselves and the land (Lev. 18.24–25). Less frequently noticed is the exhortation to 'fear' Yahweh (Lev. 19.14, 32). Von Rad points out that the repeated 'I am Yahweh' helps to give the Holiness Code the sense of being direct speech by God.[50] The care for the resident alien is commonly seen as a distinctive feature of Deuteronomy, but the call, 'You shall have one law for the sojourner and for the native' (Lev. 24.22) must not be overlooked. Although it refers to punishments for offences, it draws the resident alien within the Israelite community (cf. also Lev. 19.33–34).

A further feature of the Code to which von Rad draws attention is the way 'the preacher . . . has sometimes on his own account given the prohibitions positive form and so intensified them'.[51] Added to the command to do no injustice in judgment is 'but in righteousness shall you judge your neighbour' (Lev. 19.15). 'You shall not hate your brother in your heart', itself a 'law' which could not be enforced by any law court and so is ethical rather than legal, continues: 'but you shall reason with your neighbour, lest you bear sin because of him' (Lev. 19.17). And the famous 'but you shall love your neighbour as yourself' follows the much more limited 'You shall not take vengeance or bear any grudge against the sons of your own people.' This positive paraenesis, von Rad thinks, shows that the laws were collected at a time when people were no longer satisfied with the negative style, having come to realize that it could not express the whole of God's will for human beings.

Motive Clauses, Paraenesis and Ethics

It is time to draw together the main implications of this survey of motive clauses and paraenesis for Old Testament ethics. Ethical features of the individual clauses have already been noted. Now their more general significance will be considered.

First, and most obviously, the clauses transform what might have been treated as bare legal enactments into divine commands and teaching. The laws become expressions of God's will for his people. They are 'my statutes'. The main exhortations in Deuteronomy call for obedience to Yahweh's commands and reverence, and there is the underlying theme of maintaining the covenant. The Holiness Code expresses much the same thought through the call to be holy as Yahweh is holy. How far this determines the character of the ethics will be considered after the other main features of the motivations have been listed.

---

[50] Von Rad, *Studies in Deuteronomy*, 26. The whole chapter is suggestive.
[51] *Ibid.*, 29.

Following directly from the divine origin of the laws come, secondly, those clauses which declare that God will reward those who keep his commands, and punish offenders. This divine sanction is to be distinguished from the human punishments that will be examined in the next chapter. What is striking about the present motivations is that they are attached to both apodeictic and casuistic laws, the promises are mostly general and the punishments often unspecified, and they are chiefly found where no human sanction is decreed. As has been noted already, divine punishment is sometimes expressed through impersonal forms. Often they do not function directly as a sanction but are rather a means of emphasizing the importance and gravity of what is decreed.[52]

Thirdly, many of the motivations set the laws within a theology. The dominant form of this is the Exodus deliverance and the gift of the promised land. We have already noted that these references draw upon several different motives: gratitude and remembrance being the chief ones, including remembering what it was like to be oppressed.

Fourthly, in contrast to the motive clauses that are found in other law codes from the ancient Middle East, the vast majority of such clauses in the biblical collections of laws give reasons for keeping the law or explain its purpose, rather than merely explicating the law itself.

The fact that much of the paraenesis and many of the motive clauses have the effect of presenting the laws as divine commands might seem to make the Old Testament ethics strongly heteronomous. To some extent this is true, despite the fact that it is 'teaching' rather than 'law'. The morality is what God desires for his people and will give them 'life', yet it cannot be denied that it is mainly presented as 'my statutes', which are to be 'for ever'. With the common denigration of heteronomous ethics since the time of Kant, it must be asked whether this places the Old Testament ethics on a lower plane than deontological or utilitarian or consequential ethics.

To discuss the relation between ethics and God would take us too far afield.[53] The common rebuttal of criticism fastens on the character of God. What God decrees is good because it is in accord with his nature. This, however, hardly solves the difficulty that an ethic which is obeyed because it is a command, albeit the command of a God who is perfect goodness and desires the highest well-being of his creatures, is lower than an ethic which is accepted by the actor

---

[52] For example, within the Decalogue the prohibition of making images is reinforced by the clause declaring that Yahweh is a jealous God (Ex. 20.5–6/Deut. 5.9–10), the motive for honouring parents is 'that your days may be long' (Ex. 20.12/Deut. 5.16), and the whole set of laws is expressed as Israel's response to the Exodus deliverance.

[53] See, e.g., W. G. MacLagan, *Frontier of Ethics*.

because he or she accepts that it is morally right. It is important, therefore, to consider whether the motive clauses point to any other ethical incentives.

Some of the clauses 'work' only because a prior ethic is assumed. For example, to say that 'a bribe blinds the eyes of the wise and subverts the cause of the righteous' (Deut. 16.19) implies that the eyes of the wise *ought not* to be blinded, and that the cause of the 'righteous' *should not* be subverted, as well as accepting that what is meant by 'the righteous' is known and understood. Similarly, the law that the husband who falsely accused his bride of not being a virgin at marriage is to be punished 'because he has brought an evil name upon a virgin of Israel' (Deut. 22.18) assumes that to disgrace a virgin is evil and ought not to be done. Sometimes the motive appears obvious, as with the explanation that taking an upper millstone as a pledge is 'taking a life in pledge', for it prevents the owner from grinding his corn for food. Yet even here, there is the implied ethic that there are limits in mutual dealings which it is *immoral* to pass. In all these cases the ethic is not derived from any divine command, and is akin to the instances of 'natural law' that were discussed in Chapter 6.

It should also be remembered that one effect of some motive clauses is to enable the hearers to understand the purpose behind the laws, as von Rad pointed out.[54] To explain a law is to pass responsibility to those receiving the command, and even if ultimately the law or teaching comes from God, by making it their own the hearers no longer obey simply because God decreed it.

Nevertheless, it must be accepted that the dominant force of the motive clauses, and even more of the paraenesis, is to present the ethics as the command of Yahweh. This, however, has to be understood in the light of the character of Yahweh and his actions in history, particularly through the Exodus deliverance and the gift of the land of Canaan, and with the recognition that the ethics are not presented as divine laws without remainder, but that beneath some at least of the motive clauses lies an ethics which is not heteronomous and which those responsible for the clauses took for granted.

[54] see above, p. 113.

11

SANCTIONS

Divine Rewards and Punishments
As we saw in Chapter 8, the laws in the Ten Commandments have no human sanctions attached to them. The second, third and fifth commandments (making images, taking Yahweh's name in vain, and keeping the sabbath), however, are reinforced by general statements promising God's blessing on those who keep them, and threatening divine punishment on those who break them, punishment which will extend to the fourth generation. This becomes a broad characterization of God, as can be seen in his words to Moses after the incident of the golden calf:

> The LORD, the LORD, a God merciful and gracious, slow to anger, and abounding in steadfast love and faithfulness, keeping steadfast love for thousands, forgiving iniquity and transgression and sin, but who will by no means clear the guilty, visiting the iniquity of the fathers upon the children and the children's children, to the third and the fourth generation (Ex. 34.6–7; cf. Num. 14.18; Ps. 79.8; 109.14; Isa. 65.6–7; Jer. 32.18).[1]

Even stronger warnings are found after other apodeictic laws, such as:

> If you do afflict them [resident aliens, widows and orphans], and they cry out to me, I will surely hear their cry; and my wrath will burn, and I will kill you with the sword and your wives shall become widows and your children fatherless (Ex. 22.22–23[23–24]; cf. 'for I will not acquit the wicked', Ex. 23.7).

The collections of laws in both Deuteronomy and the Holiness Code are followed by comprehensive sets of blessings and threats (Deut. 28; Lev. 26.3–45).

---

[1] At the time of Jeremiah and Ezekiel there was discontent with the idea that God punished the children of wrong-doers and both prophets quote the popular proverb, 'The fathers have eaten sour grapes, and the children's teeth are set on edge' (Jer. 31.29; Ezek. 18.2). Jeremiah says that in the good time coming the individual alone will suffer for his sin, while Ezekiel, who possibly quotes an earlier form of the proverb (the tense of the verb is imperfect, not perfect), teaches an atomistic individual responsibility in the present. For another reaction to the idea of inherited punishment see Lam. 5.7. See Robert P. Carroll, *Jeremiah*, 607–608, Walther Eichrodt, *Ezekiel*, 234–237; William H. Brownlee, *Ezekiel 1–19*, 282–283. In Deuteronomy 24.16 the execution of children for the sin of their fathers is forbidden.

126

A common phrase in the Holiness Code is, 'that man shall be cut off from among his people' (Lev. 17.4) or slight variations of the phrase (Lev. 17.9, 14; 18.29; 19.8; 20.18; 23.29; cf. 'that person shall be cut off from my presence', 22.3).What exactly is implied is not clear. It may mean that God was expected to intervene and punish the offender himself directly, as in the positive threat, 'I myself will set my face against that man, and will cut him off from among his people' (Lev. 20.3, 6; cf. the slight variations in 17.10; 20.5). Others have proposed that it refers to execution or that it is a form of forced exile (anachronistically referred to as 'excommunication').[2] If either of these were correct, the punishment would be a human sanction, but it seems unlikely, since where human beings are to carry out the punishment this is made clear in the law itself. The repeated, 'I am Yahweh' in the Holiness Code is probably to be taken as a warning of divine punishment if the law is disobeyed.

In Deuteronomy many promises of well-being as a reward for obedience are made. For example, every third year tithes are to be given to the Levites, resident aliens, the fatherless and widows 'that the LORD your God may bless you in all the work of your hands that you do' (Deut. 14.29; cf. 15.10; 16.15).

Such threats and promises are usually found with apodeictic laws, but they also occur in casuistic ones, such as in the motive clause attached to the law requiring the return of a neighbour's garment taken as a pledge: 'And if he cries to me, I will hear, for I am compassionate' with the implication of punishment (Ex. 22.26[27]), and the promise after the requirement to leave sheaves that were forgotten in the field for resident aliens, orphans and widows 'that the LORD your God may bless you in all the work of your hands' (Deut. 24.19).

How it was expected that God would carry out such punishments is rarely made explicit. The reward for obedience was through the granting of prosperity and long life, as in the promise attached to the command to honour parents in the Decalogue (Ex. 20.12/Deut. 5.16).[3] But the punishment is vaguer. Sometimes an impersonal or passive

---

[2] See the discussion in G. J. Wenham (*Leviticus*, 241–242), who retains the traditional interpretation, that it is a threat of direct punishment by God, usually in the form of premature death, and sees it as the main deterrent against offences that would not be easily detected. Philip J. Budd (*Leviticus*, 122) notes several proposals, and says that in many contexts 'some form of excommunication is possible'. J. P. Hyatt (*Exodus*, 135) says baldly: '[it] is the equivalent of "excommunication", accompanied by the expressed or implied threat of divine punishment'. The phrase is not limited to the Holiness Code, cf. Lev. 7.20, 21, 25, 27; Ex. 12.15, 19; 30.33, 38; 31.14, and elsewhere.

[3] See pp. 116–117 above. For the 'blessing' see Johs. Pedersen's seminal, *Israel I–II*, 182–212. 'Peace' often has similar connotations, as has often been shown.

threat indicates that God will carry this out. It appears that the punishment is the reverse of the blessing – poverty and distress, and sudden death, the kind of things that the psalmists often complain about because they do not believe they deserve to be treated in this way by God.[4] This is confirmed by the list of blessings and threats at the conclusion of laws in Deuteronomy (Deut. 28) and the Holiness Code (Lev. 26), where various national disasters are listed as punishment for failing to obey God and to keep his laws.

Human Punishments

In contrast to the apodeictic laws, which are most obviously divine commands (or teaching), and rarely have any punishment attached,[5] all the laws expressed with a participial clause by their very form (offence plus punishment) set out the precise penalty, as do most of the casuistic laws. Only once is there the bald, 'he shall be punished' (Ex. 21.20–21, *nāqōm yinnāqēm*, literally, 'he shall be avenged'[6]).

Death is a common punishment. There are groups of laws in the form: 'Whoever strikes his father or his mother shall be put to death' (Ex. 21.15, cf. 21.12, 16, 17; 22.18[19]; Lev. 24.16, 21). A slight variant of this is 'Whoever sacrifices to any god, save to the LORD only, shall be destroyed' (Ex. 22.19[20]).[7] A similar form in Leviticus, 'The man who . . . ' also demands the death penalty (Lev. 20.2, 9–16). The death penalty is also found in casuistic laws in all three main collections, though predominantly in Deuteronomy.[8]

How the execution is to be carried out is rarely stated. For some offences stoning is decreed (Deut. 13.10; 17.5; 21.21; 22.21, 24; Lev. 20.2, 27; 24.14, 16, 23; Num. 15.35–36; cf. the ox which gored a human being to death is also stoned, Ex. 21.28, 29, 32). The Holiness Code specifies burning as the punishment for the man who has sexual intercourse with a woman and her mother, and for the daughter of a priest who becomes a prostitute (Lev. 20.14; 21.9). Hanging is mentioned once, but without being linked to any particular offence,

---

[4] See, e.g., Pss. 6; 22.15–16, 18–19[14–15, 17–18]; 38; 88; cf. the certainty of retribution expressed, e.g., in Pss. 37; 52; 73.16–20.

[5] The only apodeictic law which expresses a penalty is 'You shall not permit a sorceress to live' (Ex. 22.17[18]). A casuistic law has been added to the bare 'You shall not afflict any widow or orphan' (Ex. 22.21–23[22–24]).

[6] None of the standard commentaries comment on this unique use of the verb, which elsewhere refers to revenge (e.g., Lev. 19.18, Qal; Jdg. 15.7; 16.28, Ni.). Childs comments: 'The formula "he will be punished" is strikingly vague and cannot be identified with the death penalty *per se*. Apparently the determination of the required penalty was left to the discretion of the judge' (*Exodus*, 471). *HALOT* renders 'to be avenged (vendetta ?)', BDB, 'suffer vengeance'.

[7] The Hebrew word is 'put to the ban' as with a defeated enemy in 'holy war'.

[8] Ex. 21.14, 29; Deut. 13.6[5], 10–11[9–10], 16–18[15–17] (again using 'the ban'); 17.5–7; 19.11–13; 21.21–22; 22.21–25; 24.7; Lev 21.9.

and it is generally agreed that what is meant is impaling the corpse after execution (Deut. 21.22–23).[9]

Other corporal punishments are flogging and mutilation. The first is found only twice in the laws, once in the requirement that no more than forty stripes are to be given (Deut. 25.2–3), the other the punishment of the husband who falsely accused his wife of not being a virgin on marriage (Deut. 22.18).[10] The only instance of mutilation is cutting off the hand of a woman who seizes the testicles of a man who is brawling with her husband (Deut. 25.11–12). If the law of *ius talionis* (Ex. 21.23–25; Deut. 19.21; Lev. 24.18–20) is taken literally, injuries to the person would be requited by mutilation, but this has been disputed.[11]

Strictly fines in the sense of money paid to the rulers or the community are not imposed as a penalty. In cases of damage to livestock or crops and of theft, restitution is paid to the owner. Where animals are killed by falling into a pit that was not covered there is simple restitution, and where an ox kills another ox the live ox is sold and the proceeds together with the dead ox are divided between the two owners (Ex. 21.33–36). Similarly crops which are damaged either by domestic animals or by fire are to be made good (Ex. 22.4–5[5–6]). Nevertheless, as De Vaux points out, since repayment for theft is from twofold to fivefold (Ex. 21.37[22.1]; 22.3[4], 6[7], 8[9], 9–14[10–15]) this has a penal aspect.[12] A money payment is to be made to the master of a slave killed by an ox, and in a number of injuries to the person (Ex. 21.32, 19, 22). In the case of the owner of an ox who has been warned that it is prone to goring, the death penalty if it kills a man or a woman can be commuted to a 'ransom laid on him'; who agreed to waive the death penalty, by whom the amount was determined, and to whom the money was paid are not

---

[9] The purpose of exposing the body in this way is uncertain. Craigie suggests that it served as a warning, and thinks the practice was 'very ancient', the Deuteronomist only imposing limitations upon it (*Deuteronomy*, 285). Mayes accepts the suggestion of Anthony Phillips that it was designed to appease the deity, but thinks that there may also be the idea that not to bury the body was an additional punishment (*Deuteronomy*, 305). The practice is seen in Josh. 8.29; 10.26–27; 2 Sam. 4.12; 21.8–9, but Craigie points out that these examples occur in war and are not judicial punishments.

[10] In Deut. 21.18 the parents of a disobedient son 'chastise' him, but this is not a punishment in a legal sense (cf. the many calls in Proverbs to discipline sons: 13.24; 19.18; 22.15; 23.13, 14; 29.15, 17; and Sir. 30.1).

[11] It should be noted that the law in Deut. 25.11–12 is not an example of the *talion*. Its significance has been disputed. Sophie Lafont compares MAL 8, and after pointing out that the Assyrian law was concerned to preserve the power of procreation, records that the motivation of the biblical law has been variously seen as condemning immodesty, safeguarding the ability to father children, preserving the sacred nature of the sex organs, and the survival of superstition (*Femmes, Droit et Justice*, 335). See pp. 135–136 below for a fuller discussion of the *talion*.

[12] Roland de Vaux, *Ancient Israel*, 159–160.

specified. Presumably it was to the family of the deceased, but whether the elders were involved in any way is quite unknown (Ex. 21.30).

The money payments made to the father for sexual offences against women are somewhat different. The man who seduces a virgin has to pay the 'marriage present' to her father, whether her father agrees to let him marry her or not (Ex. 22.15–16[16–17]). In the Deuteronomic version of this law the rapist has to pay a flat fifty shekels to the woman's father and marry her without the possibility of future divorce (Deut. 22.28–29).

The only example of compensation for loss in the laws of Deuteronomy and the Holiness Code, apart from the penalties for rape and making a false accusation of a bride's non-virginity in Deuteronomy 22.19, 29, is Leviticus 24.18, where the law of execution for murder is followed by the contrasting 'He who kills a beast shall make it good, life for life.'

Somewhat akin to the spirit of these laws is the freeing of slaves injured by their masters (Ex. 21.26–27). On the other hand, if a slave dies as the direct result of being beaten the master is to be punished, but the punishment is not defined, and somewhat inconsistently there is no penalty if the slave survives for more than a day. The reason, 'for the slave is his money', assumes that the master did not intend to kill his slave and that the loss of his slave is sufficient punishment (Ex. 21.20–21).[13]

We have noted in Chapter 3 that shaming was used by the widow to put pressure on her deceased husband's brother to carry out the levirate, but questioned whether shaming was a 'punishment' as such.

For completeness it should be added that imprisonment does not appear as a punishment in any of the collections of laws. In Leviticus 24.12 the son of the Israelite woman and an Egyptian who uttered blasphemy was held in custody pending Yahweh's judgment, and in Numbers 15.34 the man found gathering sticks on the sabbath is similarly held on remand awaiting a divine decision on his punishment. From the historical books and Jeremiah we learn that persons were shut up by the authorities (1 Kgs. 22.27; Jer. 37.15–18), and offenders were sometimes put in the stocks[14] (Jer. 20.2; 29.26; 2 Chron. 16.10).

[13] See Brevard S. Childs, *Exodus*, 471; J. P. Hyatt, *Exodus*, 232–233. This was one of the verses which raised doubts in the mind of Bishop J. W. Colenso, whose African helper was revolted at the thought that 'the Great and Blessed God, the Merciful Father of all mankind, would speak of a servant or maid as mere "money", and allow a horrible crime to go unpunished, because the victim of the brutal usage had survived a few hours' (*The Pentateuch and Joshua*, 50–51, quoted Mark D. Chapman, 'Colenso', 256).

[14] The meaning of the term is quite uncertain; either an instrument for restraining the offender or a prison chamber are suggested by the versions. It does not necessarily

Types of Offences Attracting Sanctions

More important than the listing of the kinds of punishment which are decreed is the type of offence to which a particular punishment is attached. Edwin M. Good has claimed that 'a society's values may be negatively exhibited in its punishments for the crimes it most detests'.[15] This is a valuable observation, although it needs to be qualified, as Good himself is well aware. I point to four features. (1) The laws do not provide a complete picture of the whole social system in ancient Israel, nor probably in any of the other ancient Middle Eastern societies. Many features of everyday life go unmentioned. (2) Further, as we have stressed earlier, many of the norms which control everyday behaviour are not expressed in laws, and this would be even more so in a relatively undeveloped society such as Israel's, where the village elders and the head of the family were probably more influential than the 'official' law-givers, and private actions, such as that of the 'avenger of blood' would have had an important place in the maintenance of morality. (3) Moreover the collections of laws come from interested groups, and we cannot be certain how far the values of these groups extended throughout Israelite society. This needs to be carefully watched when Deuteronomy and the Holiness Code are considered, for these may well be what the Deuteronomists and the priests wished should happen rather than reflecting actual practice. Frymer-Kensky's claim that the collections of laws represent legal philosophy may indicate that they reflect the current morality, but on the other hand it may point to their being idealistic and removed from the actions and moral convictions of the people.[16]

---

carry the overtones of shaming or the idea of torture (see McKane, *Jeremiah*, I, 460, Holladay, *Jeremiah*, I, 542–543, Carroll, *Jeremiah*, 390).

[15] E. M. Good has made a widely ranging study, and, after urging caution because of the nature of the extant evidence, concludes that in Babylon integrity was considered a prime virtue, and that some of the key values were maintenance of the family and its duties to its head, together with rights and duties owed to superiors by the head and his unfettered use of his possessions, his rights and duties towards superiors and duties and responsibilities to inferiors. In Assyria most capital offences appear to have to do with marriage, but the evidence is fragmentary and 'we cannot conclude from it that the Assyrians thought more about sex than about anything else'. Hittite law may represent a stage in the transition to a situation where the death penalty would be minimally applied — even murder was not a capital offence. Good holds that in the Bible 'the solidarity and integrity of the family was a quite central value'. The Israelites were far less stringent than the Babylonians about the inviolability of property, but were more severe on 'relatively peripheral sexual offences such as homosexuality or bestiality'. Purity of religion was far more important than for any of the other peoples of the ancient Middle East. In Israel there was a more explicit religious ethic, whereas in Babylon the ethic is 'based entirely on social or utilitarian considerations' ('Capital Punishment', 947, 975–977).

[16] Tikva Frymer-Kensky, 'Tit for Tat', 231, but note the qualification: 'Evidence for the practice of the times must be sought independently from letters, contracts, lawsuits, and other documents of daily life.' Cf. Christiana van Houten's forthright 'The laws

(4) Finally Dale Patrick has drawn attention to an important characteristic of Israelite law seen in what he has termed 'casuistic primary law', that is laws which decree not a penalty for infraction ('remedial' law), but the action that is to be followed in the particular case, or in his terminology, where 'the protasis describes a legal relationship and the apodosis prescribes the terms of the relationship (rights and duties before violation)'. This is an important insight, and becomes even more significant for ethics when Patrick's further observation, that primary law developed in the direction of 'personally addressed commandments', that is, laws like Exodus 22.24[25]: 'If you lend money to any of my people with you who is poor, you shall not be to him as a creditor, and you shall not exact interest from him', is taken into account.[17] On the one hand, this is a further instance of the way law in the Old Testament becomes primarily teaching, and on the other hand, it widens the scope of the law so that it has to be seen as more than largely negative and punitive, and thus is as much a presentation of society's values as the punitive sanctions.

Accepting these limitations, the following features may be extracted from a study of sanctions imposed in the laws.

First, the apodeictic laws have no sanctions.[18] This is of the greatest importance, since it undercuts the whole approach to the laws which views them as legal enactments. The apodeictic laws are an expression of what God commands. Indeed, they may be better seen as what God *desires* of his people, pointing to a very different understanding of Old Testament morality from that which is commonly held.

Secondly, the death penalty is applied more widely than is acceptable today, and more widely than in the Hittite laws, but even so it is limited to certain classes of offences. In the Book of the Covenant it is the penalty for six types of wrongdoing: sacrifice to other gods (Ex. 22.19[20]),[19] sorcery (Ex. 22.17[18]), murder (Ex. 21.12–14), kidnapping (Ex. 21.16), smiting or cursing parents (Ex. 21.15, 17),[20] and bestiality (Ex. 22.18[19]). Wenham, however,

---

. . . only indirectly reflect the status quo. They present the reader with what outht to be done. We cannot infer from these laws that the practices they describe were actually enforced.' She also argues that the laws were 'originally addressed to the people in a cultic setting with the aim of convincing them to live in a certain way', while the priestly laws had the additional purpose of creating a holy people whose purity would allow God to dwell in their midst (*The Alien*, 159).

[17] Dale Patrick, *Old Testament Law*, 23–24.

[18] Phillips's argument that the (unstated) penalty for breaking the commandments in the Decalogue was death has already been rejected.

[19] The use of *ḥērem* lifts this command from the scope of normal capital punishment.

[20] There is some debate as to whether 'smite' meant 'kill'. The verb *nākāh* certainly can mean 'to kill', but this would surely be murder and would be covered by the general law. Striking a parent probably represented total disrespect toward those who

questions how often the death penalty was actually carried out. He argues that since compensation is expressly forbidden in the case of murder (Num. 35.31), and, in his view, the Deuteronomic phrase, 'your eye shall not pity him' (Deut. 19.13; cf. 13.9[8]; 19.21; 25.12) has the same force, it would seem likely that compensation was permitted for other offences. He also holds that the penalties prescribed in the law were the maximum penalties, and where there were mitigating circumstances lesser penalties would have been imposed.[21]

In the laws in Deuteronomy the range of religious offences is widened and more closely defined to include the prophet who taught rebellion against Yahweh or did not speak words that Yahweh gave or spoke in the name of other gods (Deut. 13.2–6[1–5]; 18.20–22), the near relative who enticed members of the family to serve other gods (Deut. 13.7–12[6–11]), towns where there were those who encouraged worshipping other gods, which are to be put to the ban (Deut. 13.13–19[12–18]), individuals who broke the covenant and worshipped other gods or the heavenly bodies (Deut. 17.2–7), and failure to obey the priestly decision in serious cases (Deut. 17.8–13). Sexual offences have a larger place, and death is decreed for the woman who was not a virgin on marriage (Deut. 22.20–21), both the wife of another man and her partner who commit adultery (Deut. 22.22), the man who raped a betrothed virgin in a city together with the woman, and the rapist who carried out his attack in the open country but not the women in this case (Deut. 22.23–27). Murder (modified by the laws concerning the cities of refuge, so that it is differentiated from unintentional manslaughter) and kidnapping remain capital offences (Deut. 19.1–13; 24.7). The parents of a disobedient son may no longer act on their own initiative, but must bring him before the elders, who can impose death by stoning (Deut. 21.18–21).

The Holiness Code extends the offences more widely still. Death is now to await those who commit adultery, incest with their father's wife or their daughter-in-law, those who have intercourse with a woman and her mother, homosexuality and bestiality (Lev. 20.10–16), and the daughter of a priest who becomes a prostitute (Lev. 21.9). Cursing parents remains a capital offence (Lev. 20.9), as does killing a human being, without any distinction between manslaughter and deliberate murder (Lev. 24.17, 21). The religious offences for which the offender is to be executed are giving children to Molech (Lev. 20.2),[22] practising spiritualism or sorcery (Lev. 20.27, cf. v. 6, where

---

were owed complete obedience and seems to have been regarded as an extremely serious offence. Since the curse was expected to produce what was expressed in the words uttered, it too would be have been a most serious matter.

[21] Wenham, *Leviticus*, 285.

[22] A Canaanite god (see J. Day, *Molech*).

God inflicts the punishment by cutting off the offender from among his people), and blaspheming 'the Name' (Lev. 24.10–16, 23).

The utter rejection of worshipping gods other than Yahweh is to be expected in Deuteronomy, but the extension of the sex laws both in this collection and in the Holiness Code probably reveals the influence and interests of the priesthood. Execution by stoning or burning may indicate that the offences where this is prescribed were held to be serious infringements of purity rather than that they were particularly heinous moral wrongs (cf. Ex. 19.12–13).

Unlike the Code of Hammurabi and the Middle Assyrian Laws (and, it may be noted, English laws in the eighteenth and early nineteenth centuries), the death penalty is never imposed for offences against property. A sharp distinction seems to have been made between theft and damage to crops on the one hand, and certain religious and sexual offences, together with murder, kidnapping, and dishonouring parents on the other. Since this extends to all the biblical collections of laws it may be accepted as reflecting not merely the views of the law-makers but general Israelite values, although the stringency towards sexual offences may owe something to the priests.

Before leaving this discussion of sanctions, two phrases must be considered briefly, 'there shall be (no) bloodguilt for him' (Ex. 22.1–2[2–3]; Num. 35.27) and the 'eye for eye, tooth for tooth' of the *ius talionis* (Ex. 21.23–25; Deut. 19.21; Lev. 24.18–20).

Exodus 22.1–2[2–3] interrupts the set of laws concerning theft of oxen and sheep and several modern translations rearrange the text. It is clearly an interpolation, but Childs defends its position on the grounds that it was introduced to focus attention on the more important problem of loss of life as a result of the owner defending his property.[23] Its purpose, according to Childs, is to guard the lives of both parties involved. The householder is exonerated if he kills an intruder at night, but is responsible for manslaughter if he killed in daylight.[24] Childs adds: 'To my knowledge no other law code seems to have a similar concern for the life of the thief!' What precisely is

---

[23] Childs, *Exodus*, 474. John I. Durham (*Exodus*, 322, 325) finds this improbable, and prefers Daube's suggestion that such loose arrangements of laws are due to 'laziness, undeveloped legal technique, writing on stone or the like, oral transmission of the law, and regard for tradition' and the tacking on of supplementary laws to existing collections (he refers to David Daube, *Biblical Law*, 74–77, 85–89). As Hyatt (*Exodus*, 237) points out, the Laws of Eshnunna 12–13 distinguish between being caught in the field or house of a member of the social class connected with the palace or the temple in the day and at night, the penalty being a fine during daytime but at night 'he shall not get away alive' (*ANET*, 162).

[24] Göran Larsson (*Freedom*, 170–171) finds the basis of the law in self-defence, quoting the rabbinic 'If anyone comes to kill you, rise early and kill him first' (*b. Berakhoth* 58a; 62b; *b. Sanhedrin* 72a). At night it might be difficult to know whether the intruder poses a danger to life or is simply a burglar.

intended by the phrase 'there shall be bloodguilt for him' is uncertain. Childs suggests that the householder is vulnerable to blood vengeance. Despite the phrase occurring in Numbers 35.27, where the 'avenger of blood' appears, in the present context the more plausible interpretation is that the offender is subject to the death penalty, though by whom it is to be carried out is not specified. Presumably it would be by the same persons as other executions in the law.[25]

The *ius talionis* is equally ambiguous. In ancient Mesopotamia the principle first appears in the Hammurabi code, where it is set out in explicit detail: 'If a seignior has destroyed the eye of a member of the aristocracy, they shall destroy his eye. If he has broken a seignior's bone, they shall break his bone. If a seignior has knocked out a tooth of a seignior of his own rank, they shall knock out his tooth.'[26] Exact retribution is taken to the extreme of killing the daughter of a seignior if he caused the death of the daughter of a man of equal rank, and the son of a builder whose jerry-building caused the death of a seignior's son.[27] It has been claimed that the intention in the laws of Hammurabi marks the beginning of state protection of the person, since in an earlier period physical injury was treated as a tort, compensation by a monetary payment being made to the next of kin. The introduction of the *ius talionis* meant that the wealthy could no longer escape adequate punishment by paying what they could easily afford.[28] Göran Larsson regards it as 'a first step towards making violence a concern of the entire society'.[29] Whether it was ever implemented is quite another matter.

Later Jewish tradition interpreted the law to mean that the monetary value of a life or an eye had to be paid, and most recent commentators argue that the idea of compensation was included in the law itself from the outset. Larsson argues that the verb 'give' (*nātan*) in Exodus 21.23–24 'has precisely the meaning of paying compensation', that 'life for life' is used in Leviticus 24.18 for replacing an animal that has been killed, and the excluding of ransom for murder in Numbers 35.31 indicates that paying compensation for other forms of bodily injury was permitted. He quotes the rabbis, who

---

[25] Whether the phrase *['ēyn] lō dāmîm* should be distinguished from *dāmāyw bō* (Lev. 20.9) and *'āleykā dāmîm* (Deut. 19.10) is uncertain. All three refer to the guilt of shedding blood, and the last two imply liability to the death penalty, though it is not always inflicted by human hands. Edwin M. Good ('Capital Punishment', 954) holds that in the law requiring a new house to have a parapet round the roof (Deut. 22.8) '"blood-guilt" signifies liability to the actions of the *go'el*', and so presumably in every instance where the phrase occurs.

[26] Laws 196, 197, 200 (*ANET*, 175).

[27] Laws 210, 230, cf. 116 (*ANET*, 170, 175, 176); cf. MAL A 50 (*ANET*, 184).

[28] See Childs, *Exodus*, 472–473; Wenham, *Leviticus*, 283; A. D. H. Mayes, *Deuteronomy*, 290–291; Phillips, *Israel's Criminal Law*, 96–99.

[29] Larsson, *Freedom*, 164.

pointed out that it would be unjust and impossible to apply 'eye for eye, tooth for tooth' literally – to destroy an eye would be unfair if applied to a person who had only one eye, while the hand meant more to a craftsman than to a teacher. In the twelfth century Maimonides declared that all rabbinic authorities without exception understood the law as meaning the paying of an indemnity.[30] K. Luke argues that the codes of antiquity, biblical and other, represent theory rather than practice, and that many clauses (including the *ius talionis*) are 'simply ideal figments or fanciful creations of lawgivers', intended to secure fidelity to the cosmic order, though they are intended literally.[31] As has been noted, Tikva Frymer-Kensky also holds these codes to be legal philosophy rather than prescriptive laws, even though letters and other documents reveal that the *ius talionis* was a 'basic operating principle' in the Old Babylonian period. They were an attempt to provide appropriate penalties for misdeeds – 'to make the punishment fit the crime'. She argues that in Deuteronomy a literal meaning makes no sense, for Israel did not have a system of mutilation as punishment, except possibly for physical injury.[32] Although it is probable that none of the collections of laws was put into practice, they certainly reflect the desires of those who formulated them, and may also give some indication of the general ethos of the time when they were created. This, however, fails to provide any firm grounds for deciding whether the *ius talionis* was taken literally or as an abstract principle.

Principles of Punishment

Attention has often been drawn to the contrast between the importance the Old Testament laws give to offences against the person, as opposed to theft and other crimes involving property. Wenham expresses it in this way: 'In Israel, religious offenses and offenses against life and the structure of the family, tended to be punished more severely than elsewhere, whereas cuneiform law tended to rate financial loss as more serious than loss of life, or at least see loss of life in economic terms. For instance Babylonian law punished by death breaking and entering, looting at a fire, and theft; but in Israel no offenses against ordinary property attracted the death penalty. By contrast, in Israel the death penalty was mandatory for murder, because man is made in the image of God (Gen. 9.5–6), whereas other legal systems permitted monetary compensation.'[33]

---

[30] *Ibid.*, 164–167.

[31] K. Luke, 'Eye for Eye', 334–338.

[32] Frymer-Kensky, 'Tit for Tat'. Phillips sees the talion as a post-exilic insertion into Israel's law (*Israel's Criminal Law*, 96–99). Calum Carmichael, improbably, argues that the talion laws are responses to incidents in the historical books ('Talion').

[33] Wenham, *Leviticus*, 282; cf. de Vaux, *Ancient Israel*, 158.

While this is broadly true, it needs to be qualified. The almost unique place given to religious offences in the Old Testament not only shows that purity of religion was far more important in Israel than in any of the other cultures of the ancient Middle East, but, as Good points out, a religious ethic is sometimes explicitly given as the basis of the legislation, whereas Babylonian ethics appear to be based entirely on social or utilitarian considerations.[34] It is this, rather than a particular humanitarian outlook, which characterizes the Israelite laws.

Wenham singles out five principles underlying the biblical laws on punishment.[35] (1) The offender must receive his legal desert, which is not simply to be equated with revenge. This, he finds most clearly expressed in Genesis 9.6, 'Whoever sheds the blood of man, by man shall his blood be shed' and in the *ius talionis* formula (which, as we have seen, Wenham does not believe was taken literally). (2) Punishment is designed to 'purge the evil from the midst of you', which he (wrongly) interprets as referring to the 'guilt that rests upon the land and its inhabitants'. As has been argued earlier, the phrase belongs to the purity system. (3) Punishment is intended as a deterrent. (4) Punishment is expiation, in that it 'allows the offender to make atonement and be reconciled with society'. Subjecting the offender to degradation is explicitly rejected in Deuteronomy 25.3, and after he has paid the penalty, the offender suffers no loss of his civil rights.[36] (5) Since there is no system of fines, the punishment 'allows the offender to recompense the injured party' who, and not the state, benefits from the punishment.

Wenham claims, with some justification, that the Old Testament laws form basically a system of civil law to which various criminal law features have been grafted. He rightly adds that it is somewhat artificial to use the terms 'tort' and 'crime', since the whole of life is lived under God. He suggests that the type of penalty may provide a criterion, monetary compensation indicating a civil offence, the death penalty or corporal punishment showing that the offence was a crime.

---

[34] Good, 'Capital Punishment', 975–977. It should be noted that in Ex. 22.19[20] and Deut. 13.16[15] those who sacrifice to other gods are put to the ban, and Lev. 27.29 decrees that such persons are not to be ransomed, a law which, Good claims, suggests that those guilty of capital offences might be ransomed in other cases, although this is specified only in the law of the goring ox ('Capital Punishment', 971–972).

[35] Wenham, *Leviticus*, 282–284.

[36] Wenham adds: 'Mutilation is demanded only once in the Pentateuch, in an extreme case (Deut. 25.11–12), and there the penalty was mild compared with some of those in the Assyrian laws (e.g., MAL A 4–5, 8–9, 40)' (*ibid.*, 284). One does not need to be an ardent feminist to object to this assessment, although the punishment is readily understandable given the stress on the importance of male fertility and the religious significance of the male sex organs. The suggestion by M. Weinfeld that it was a matter of protecting female modesty must be rejected (M. Weinfeld, *Deuteronomic School*, 292–293, quoted by P. G. Craigie, *Deuteronomy*, 316).

Yet, he holds, even in the case of murder, which was clearly a crime since the payment of damages was prohibited, it was left to the family, through the avenger of blood, to execute the murderer.[37] This, however, allows little space for changing customs and legal development within the Old Testament. Moreover, whether it is quite correct to say that the laws in ancient Israel left it to the injured party 'to seek redress on his own initiative through the courts' may be questioned. In some cases the elders are clearly involved – the son whom his parents cannot control is taken by the parents before the elders (Deut. 21.18–21, but this is not a matter of tort), and the man who declares that his wife was not a virgin at marriage is brought to the elders by her father and mother and confronted with the 'tokens' of her virginity (Deut. 22.13–21). In many other cases no indication is given as to who initiates the suit; the laws simply set out the offence and the sentence. In fact the cultural setting was so different from anything that exists in modern society that comparisons are impossible. In a small-scale society offences would be widely known, and there would be no need for formal proceedings to be initiated either by the plaintiff or the elders, although probably in most cases the elders would act for the well-being of the community of which they were the leaders.[38]

Adopting a different and intriguing approach, Gershon Brin examines the formula 'If he shall not' that follows some regulations and signifies nonfulfilment or refusal to fulfil what is required by the law.[39] He first distinguishes between mandatory obligations and those undertaken voluntarily. As an example of the first he argues that in Exodus 13.13 and 34.20 the clause does not offer an alternative to redeeming the firstborn ass with a sheep, but, since the ass is more valuable than a sheep, it is threat: the monetary loss from his refusal will be greater than the cost of the proper fulfilment of the law. Among the voluntary obligations, his discussion of the law of the female slave (Ex. 21.7–11) and the law of the captive woman (Deut. 21.10–14) may be noted, in both of which failure to carry out the law brings a high cost to the violator. Brin concludes that the clause acts as a warning of a sanction threatened against those who do not fulfil their obligations, and suggests that where there is the potential for disobedience because detection is difficult the law-giver threatened heavier sanctions. Although in some of his examples, such as the refusal of the brother to carry out the obligations of the levirate (Deut. 25.5–10), the method of carrying out the threat is specified in the law,

---

[37] Wenham, *Leviticus*, 284.

[38] See the discussions in de Vaux, *Ancient Israel*, 150–158; Wenham, *Leviticus*, 286–288; the latter is particularly perceptive.

[39] Gershon Brin, "'If He Shall Not (Do)'".

in other cases no more than the requirement is stated, and even if Brin's interpretation of the formula is accepted it is not clear how it was expected to operate. Nevertheless, the discussion is valuable as pointing to possible sanctions that may have been imposed for the nonfulfilment of positive demands and not simply breaches of laws.

Mention should also be made of a monograph by J. A. Hoyles on punishment in the Bible, even though it adds little to what is found elsewhere.[40] Hoyles deals with the evidence from the narratives and the prophets together with the laws under the head of punishment as vengeance, the concept of justice, and punishment and reconciliation. He makes much of the theological basis of Old Testament ethics, and largely following Phillips, sees the aim of the penal provisions as being to propitiate Yahweh and prevent the calamity which would follow any breaking of the covenant.

It is natural in all discussions of punishment in the Old Testament to utilize the terms from modern ethical debate: retribution, expiation, compensation, deterrence. While this ensures that the account will not be a trivial rehearsal of the biblical punishments, it may give a distorted picture of the way in which the people of ancient Israel understood the matter. The stress on the theological basis of the Old Testament is therefore important. How the laws are to be understood is uncertain. Do they represent what actually happened in Israel, or are they idealistic reconstructions by interested groups, especially the priests? Were the punishments described in the laws actually carried out? Was the intention that the punishments should be imposed by the authorities, or was it expected that God would inflict them himself? Once we ask these questions it becomes obvious that a discussion in terms of retribution, expiation and deterrence is remote from the actual situation in Israel. Indeed, it is doubtful whether that culture can ever be recovered. And, as we have seen, the water is muddied by uncertainty as to whether the laws from other parts of the ancient Middle East were legal theory or prescriptions carried out in the courts.

The only secure way forward is to assume that the collections of laws were what those who assembled them desired. On this basis five conclusions may be drawn (with some repetition of what has been said earlier).

(1) The Book of the Covenant, the Deuteronomic laws, and the Holiness Code are all set within a narrative, are linked to the covenant, and are presented as God's directions for Israel. This does more than provide a religious foundation for the laws. Even if the

---

[40] J. Arthur Hoyles, *Punishment*. Hoyles, a retired prison chaplain, declares that his purpose is 'to discover how the concept of progressive revelation can be applied to the theory and practice of punishment as they are expounded in the Bible' (ix), and to show the relevance of biblical insights to the modern world.

laws in the other nations of the ancient Middle East set out ideals rather than positive law, the laws in Israel move towards ethics in a way that is unique. This is true, despite the hesitations which have to be maintained as to the propriety of reading off ethics directly from the legal commands.

(2) The presence of apodeictic laws which contain no sanctions, and casuistic primary laws which move towards addressed commandments confirms this. Here is divine teaching, an expression of what God desires for his people, and a declaration of what will be for their ultimate good.

(3) The sanctions, whether carried out literally or not, provide some indication of the main ethical stances of those who collected the laws. Care must be taken, however, not to fasten on those features which are more attractive to us today, or to interpret them in what to us is the most attractive light. Wenham is guilty of this to some extent in his assertion that the *ius talionis* expressed only a principle, and that the penalties were no more than the *maximum* permitted, while a large number of commentators draw too wide a conclusion from certain differences between the laws in the Old Testament and those in the other law codes from the ancient Middle East. In Israel, however, human life does seem to have been valued more highly, and offences against property to have been treated in different ways from those elsewhere.

(4) The importance of the religious commandments has not always been understood. The severe penalties decreed and the concern for purity which these laws reveal, combined with the fact that the religious commands are not distinguished in any way from the ethical laws, confirms what was said earlier about purity and ethics, and is more significant than the commonplace observation about the divine origin of the laws. It is not only the Holiness Code which stresses the purity which is demanded of Israel as God's people. We may find this strange, but unless we immerse ourselves in this way of thinking we shall fail to understand the nature and force of ethical ideas in the Old Testament.

(5) Thus, finally, this examination of the sanctions imposed in the Old Testament laws reinforces that interweaving of ethics, law and religion which makes Old Testament ethics so puzzling to modern readers of the Bible. It is not just that ethics has not been separated out as a distinct discipline or way of thinking. The whole approach to life is far removed from our modern secular society, where a major feature is the differentiation of the various social institutions. It is not just that religion has been excluded from much of present-day society. Rather the independence of family, economic, leisure, legal, political, and religious institutions has radically altered the meaning of each one of them. Old Testament ethics can only be understood within the

much wider context of the community within which the Israelite lived and died.

Several times in this chapter comparisons have been drawn with other laws from the ancient Middle East. It is time we faced up to the question of how unique Israelite law and ethics were. One demand which is found in law, prophecy, wisdom sayings, and the psalter, yet has not been discovered in any of the surrounding cultures appears to provide a test. Our next window looks out on this.

12

LENDING AT INTEREST

One of the ethical demands which is found throughout the Old Testament, and in several different types of literature – law, prophecy, psalms, and wisdom – is the unanimous and total rejection of lending at interest, whether money or goods. This is particularly striking because all the known law codes from the ancient Middle East accept the practice and regulate it.

The three main collections of laws are precise and definite:

The Book of the Covenant:

> If you lend money to any of my people with you who is poor, you shall not be to him as a creditor, and you shall not exact interest from him. (Ex. 22.24[25])

Deuteronomy:

> You shall not lend upon interest to your brother, interest on money, interest on victuals, interest on anything that is lent for interest. To a foreigner you may lend upon interest, but to your brother you shall not lend upon interest; that the LORD your God may bless you in all that you undertake in the land which you are entering to take possession of it. (Deut. 23.20–21[19–20])

The Holiness Code:

> And if your brother becomes poor, and cannot maintain himself with you, you shall maintain him; as a stranger and a sojourner he shall live with you. Take no interest from him, or increase, but fear your God; that your brother may live beside you. You shall not lend him your money at interest, nor give him your food for profit. I am the LORD your God, who brought you forth out of the land of Egypt to give you the land of Canaan, and to be your God. (Lev. 25.35–38)

Although there are references to lending in several of the prophets, only Ezekiel mentions interest specifically. It is significant, however, that he includes this in his characterization of the good and the wicked man in the chapter in which he declares that the individual will receive reward or punishment for his own sin:

142

If a man is righteous and does what is lawful and right – if he ... does not lend at interest or take any increase ... – he is righteous, he shall surely live, says the Lord GOD. (Ezek. 18.5–9, cf. 13, 17; 22.12)

In Psalm 15, a psalm often described as an 'entrance liturgy', because it sets out what is required of those who come to worship, there is the bald statement that the acceptable worshipper 'does not put out his money at interest', a sin set in parallel with taking bribes against the innocent (Ps. 15.5; cf. Ezek. 22.12).

Finally, one of the proverbs implies that the wise men did not approve of such activity:

> He who augments his wealth by interest and increase
> gathers it for him who is kind to the poor. (Prov. 28.8)

This raises important questions. Why was Israel alone in the ancient world in prohibiting interest on loans and in what ways was Israelite law distinctive? Were these laws carried out in practice, and hence how far do they reflect a living ethic in ancient Israel?

Interest in the Old Testament and the Ancient Middle East

Interest on loans was normal practice throughout the ancient Middle East. H. W. F. Saggs quotes a Babylonian proverb, which clearly refers to the interest which was received on repayment of a loan:

> The giving of a loan is like making love;
> The returning of a loan is like having a son born.

He comments, 'The religious feeling against usury, so prominent in Hebrew and Islamic law, was entirely absent from the Sumero-Babylonian world, where the payment of interest upon a loan was regarded as normal and respectable and was presupposed in laws and contracts.'[1] Driver and Miles point out that 'innumerable Babylonian and Assyrian documents prove that the Laws ... are dealing with a universal practice', adding that there is 'no trace of any attempt to prohibit this charging of interest in Accadian law as there is in Hebrew and Moslem law'.[2] Robert P. Maloney confirms this and extends its scope to the Assyrian, New-Babylonian and Persian periods, and also to the Saite, Persian and Hellenistic periods in Egypt.[3] Nevertheless, there is some slight evidence that special merit

---

[1] H. W. F. Saggs, *Babylon*, 247–248.
[2] G. R. Driver and John C. Miles, *The Babylonian Laws*, I, 174.
[3] Robert P. Maloney, 'Usury'. He quotes the legal maximum rates of interest, and observes that there are many examples of loans with and without interest in every period, and abundant examples of exorbitant interest-taking.

attached to lending without demanding interest. One of the assertions of innocence in the Egyptian *Book of the Dead* is: 'I have not *practised usury*.'[4]

An apparent exception to this universal practice is found in the Assyrian trading colony in Cappadocia in Asia Minor, where loans were granted without interest, security or witnesses, and with no fixed term. Saggs points out that this was a very specialized situation, where the loans were between members of the same merchant colony and presumably they could trust each other's credit.[5]

There were two methods of taking interest. In one the interest was deducted from the silver or grain when the loan was made. For example, a borrower would obtain a loan of 100 shekels, but would be given only 80, although he would have to pay back the full 100. In the other form the interest was added to the capital and both had to be repaid at the end of the term of the loan. Our borrower would receive his full 100 shekels, but would have to repay 120. The modern practice of regular monthly or yearly payments of the interest seems to have been unknown. In Babylon the period of the loan was often left vague, even though documents were exactly dated. Often it was from seedtime to harvest as the farmer needed to borrow grain to sow his field, but other terms are found, such as 'in the month of calling in for payment', or on the completion of a trading expedition, or even on demand.[6]

The laws set the rates of interest and attempted to protect debtors and curb fraudulent or rapacious lenders. One of Hammurabi's laws decrees that a creditor who charges more than the rate laid down by law shall lose his capital.[7] Another law protected the borrower whose crops were destroyed by flood or drought by decreeing that in the case of such disasters 'he shall not make any return of grain to his creditor in that year; he shall cancel his contract-tablet and he shall pay no interest for that year'.[8] Other laws deal with various offences by creditors and safeguard the borrower when he offers some of his goods in payment in place of grain or money.[9]

In the ancient Middle East generally, then, interest was regarded as normal, though abuses were recognized and the compilers of the collections of laws attempted to prevent both exorbitant rates and sharp practices by lenders and also to protect unfortunate borrowers

---

[4] B 14 (*ANET*, 35, where 'practised usury' is put in italic, suggesting some doubt about the translation).

[5] Saggs, *Babylon*, 249.

[6] *Ibid.*, 247–249, Driver and Miles, *The Babylonian Laws*, I, 174–177.

[7] Law 90 (*ANET*, 169).

[8] Law 48 (*ANET*, 168).

[9] Laws 93–96 (*ANET*, 169–170).

who had fallen on hard times. Why then was Israel out of step with the rest of the ancient world?

One possibility is that it was not. In Deuteronomy it is expressly stated that interest may be asked from the 'foreigner' (*nokrī*, i.e., the non-Israelite who is passing through the country, probably as a trader, not the 'resident alien', the *gēr*, the immigrant who had settled in Israel and is often mentioned in the laws as one to whom charity should be shown). While no mention of foreigners is made in the other two collections of laws, it is expressly stated that the person to whom loans are to be made without interest is poor. It may be, therefore, that the three laws on lending deal only with making loans to fellow Israelites who have fallen on hard times and need a loan to tide them over until the next harvest. On this interpretation a distinction is made between giving assistance to the poor and 'commercial' loans, and the only difference between the laws of the Old Testament and those in the other law codes would be that no legislation setting rates of interest is found in Israel. All the law-givers have a concern for the poor.[10]

Hyatt, however, denies that the law in Exodus applied only to 'loans to the very poor or poverty stricken – that is, on charity loans or distress loans'. In Israel, as in all other agricultural societies in the ancient Middle East, farmers must have needed loans at the beginning of planting, to be repaid at harvest time, and possibly loans were also needed in small business ventures. He holds that Deuteronomy 23.20–21[19–20] seems to forbid interest on *all* kinds of loans, even if that is not true of the Exodus form of the law, and suggests that one reason for the prohibition of interest was the high rates charged.[11] Hillel Gamoran also rejects the theory. He admits that the prohibition of lending at interest was written with the poor in mind, but holds that commercial loans were not explicitly banned because they were not

[10] This is argued by Driver and Miles: 'In Hebrew law, however, it is lending upon interest to a poor man which is forbidden, while it is expressly permitted if the borrower is a foreigner. A comparison between these prohibitions shows that lending upon interest is not *per se* regarded as wrongful or immoral, but that they refer to interest on money "lent for the relief of poverty brought about by misfortune or debt; it partakes thus of the nature of charity"' (*The Babylonian Laws*, 174–175, quoting S. R. Driver, *Exodus*, 232–233). R. E. Clements even goes so far as to say: 'money would normally be lent by professional money-lenders, at a reasonable rate of interest, to support commercial ventures'. With this he contrasts the present law, interpreted as meaning that 'no interest was to be taken from [the poor] in advance, and most interpreters have taken this to mean that no interest was to be taken in such a case' (*Exodus*, 146). Edward Neufeld also argued that the law against lending at interest in Exodus intended that the prohibition should be limited to the poor alone, and suggested that commercial loans were permissible ('Prohibition against Loans'). S. A. Kaufmann takes the same view ('Deuteronomic Law', 156).

[11] J. P. Hyatt, *Exodus*, 243–244.

considered. Not a single one of the biblical passages where lending is mentioned deals with a commercial loan. Such loans 'simply did not come under the biblical purview'.[12] Gamoran claims that the law in Deuteronomy 23 is a blanket prohibition of lending at interest, and rejects Neufeld's dismissal of this as a temporary expedient, on the grounds that it cannot be the intention of any biblical law that it should apply only for a limited period.

An alternative interpretation points to the Hebrew terms for 'interest', which, it is claimed, reflect the two types of lending elsewhere in the ancient Middle East. One, *nešek* ('biting off'), the word used in Exodus 22.24[25] and Deuteronomy 23.20–21[19–20], is held to refer to the deduction of interest at the time of giving the loan. The other, *tarbīt* ('increase'), denotes the adding of interest to the loan when it is repaid. It is then claimed that the second form of interest is nowhere prohibited.[13] But this is not correct. In Leviticus 25 both words are used in the law forbidding taking interest from the 'brother' who has become poor, as they are in Ezekiel 18 and Proverbs 28.8. It is doubtful whether the Israelites saw any difference between the two methods of reckoning interest.

If it is admitted that commercial loans were permitted and it was only loans to the poor and those who had suffered hardship which were prohibited, the laws of the Old Testament would be no more than an extension of the attempts in Babylon and elsewhere to protect the unfortunate members of society from rapacious lenders. It would be a very important and major extension, nonetheless, and would be in line with the general concern for the poor found elsewhere in the

---

[12] Hillel Gamoran, 'Loans on Interest', 131. He points out that in thirteen of these passages it is clear that the loan is intended for the relief of poverty (Deut. 15.1–11; 24.10–13; 28.12; 1 Sam. 22.2; 2 Kgs. 4.1; Isa. 50.1; Pss. 37.21–26; 109.11; 112.5; Prov. 19.17; 22.7; Neh. 5.4; 10.32). In the other three (Isa. 24.2; Jer. 15.16; Prov. 22.26) the recipient of the loan cannot be determined. It appears just possible, however, that Isa. 24.2, with its reference to 'buyer' and 'seller', implies commercial credit.

[13] This would seem to be the most probable interpretation of the term, and is accepted by NEB and REB in Leviticus (see R. De Vaux, *Ancient Israel*, 170). S. Loewenstamm, however, has argued that *nešek* is interest on a loan of money, and *tarbīt* on food ('Tarbit and Neshek'), and this is accepted by Gamoran ('Loans on Interest', 132), despite the fact that Deut. 23.20[19] uses *nešek* of both money and food. The main support for the distinction is Lev. 25.37, with the explicit 'do not deduct interest when advancing him money, or add interest to the payment due for food supplied on credit' (REB, the word in MT is *marbīt*, but the Samaritan text has *tarbīt*). Exodus 22.24[25] and Ps. 15.5 limit the restriction to money and use *nešek*. R. Gnuse notes a third interpretation by R. Stein and N. H. Snaith, that *nešek* referred to regularly paid interest and *tarbīt* to a lump sum (*You Shall Not Steal*, 20, 128). This seems the least probable of all, since there is no other evidence of the regular monthly or annual payment of interest.

Bible.[14] If, on the other hand, the laws are interpreted as the prohibition of any form of interest, this would be unique in the ancient Middle East. In either case it is still necessary to try to explain it.

One suggestion is that the Israelite economy was less advanced than that in Babylon, and loans would normally be required only by those who had fallen on hard times. The only commercial loans that were made or needed were to foreign traders, and legislation on such loans did not enter the collections of laws until the time of Deuteronomy (or if Deuteronomy is exilic or later, the addition might be due to contact with Babylonian society[15]). It was assumed that loans to fellow-Israelites who were in difficulties would be given freely without interest being charged.

This argument is usually linked to a second. The widespread concern for the poor in the Old Testament made it natural that the laws would seek to prevent a heartless attempt to obtain gain at the expense of an unfortunate fellow-Israelite. Some support for this may be found in the laws concerning pledges. Although interest was forbidden, it was not expected that unsecured loans would be made, but both the Book of the Covenant and Deuteronomy defend the poor against oppressive demands and discourtesy on the part of the lender.

> If ever you take your neighbour's garment in pledge, you shall restore it to him before the sun goes down; for that is his only covering, it is his mantle for his body; in what else shall he sleep? And if he cries to me, I will hear, for I am compassionate. (Ex. 22.25–26[26–27])

> No man shall take a mill or an upper millstone in pledge; for he would be taking a life in pledge. (Deut. 24.6)

> When you make your neighbour a loan of any sort, you shall not go into his house to fetch his pledge. You shall stand outside, and the man to whom you make the loan shall bring the pledge out to you. And if he is a poor man, you shall not sleep in his pledge; when the sun goes down, you shall restore to him the pledge that he may sleep in his cloak and bless you; and it shall be righteousness to you before the LORD your God. (Deut. 24.10–13)

---

[14] Lending to the poor was regarded as a good deed (Ps. 37.21, 26; 112.5). Ben Sira is realistic about lenders and borrowers (Sir. 29.1–7), and concern for the poor is not as universal as is often maintained (see Chapter 14 below).

[15] The questions about the historicity of the 'Exile' will now also have to be taken into account (cf. Lester L. Grabbe, ed., *Captivity*, and Richard J. Coggins, 'The Exile'). Gamoran thinks that Deuteronomy is the latest form of the law ('Loans on Interest', 132–133). He traces the development as: (1) Exodus refers to loans of money, Leviticus of both money and food, Deuteronomy of anything; (2) all three laws apply only to Israelites, but only Deuteronomy makes this explicit, possibly due to growing numbers of foreign traders; (3) all apply to poverty, only Deuteronomy making no specific mention of it; and (4) in Deuteronomy *nešek* has been expanded to refer to all types of interest. Yet despite differences in the phrasing the law is the same: an Israelite may not lend at interest to a fellow-Israelite.

The examples are extreme. What is the value of a pledge which has to be returned at night? And if a man was so poor that the only security he could offer was his cloak, what likelihood was there that the loan would be repaid?[16] Together with the laws requiring the annulling of loans at the end of a seven-year period[17] these regulations point up the problem of the relation between law and practice that we have already considered in the discussion of adultery.[18] For the present the laws can be taken simply as evidence that those legislating on loans had the welfare of the poor in mind.

Sometimes a historical basis is given to the theory. It is argued that the laws originated in earlier times when Israel was a nomadic people and felt a sense of close community. At that time lending was unnecessary, because the individual was a member of a larger family or clan and would be supported within that group. When the earliest laws were formulated, they were influenced by the sense that Israel was a single family – hence the use of the word 'brother'.[19]

Israel probably did have a simpler social structure and economy than the greater nation states, but this on its own hardly accounts for the presence of these laws. The difficulty with the emphasis on the concern for the poor is that it is not limited to Israel. We have seen that elsewhere in the ancient Middle East laws existed to protect borrowers who were in financial difficulties from unscrupulous lenders. Moreover, as will be shown later, the king at Ugarit and elsewhere was expected to protect the poor and defend those likely to be oppressed. Occasionally kings annulled debts in a way that is not totally dissimilar from the Levitical year of Jubilee. While the general care of the poor may have been one important motive behind the Israelite rejection of lending at interest, on its own it does not seem sufficient to account for the attitude.

Gamoran, writing before the present scepticism about the biblical traditions of Israel's history, combined the arguments. He argued that Israel's condemnation of interest was due to its 'unique historical experience. It was unique in the economic, the political, the religious,

---

[16] R. de Vaux distinguishes between movable pledges and the pledging of fields, vineyards and houses. Movable pledges, such as a garment, were not real pledges, equal to the value of the loan, but were symbolic – 'a probative pledge'. An ass or an ox (Job 24.3), however was a genuine pledge, and the creditor could even use the animal for profit (*Ancient Israel*, 171–172). Moreover to take an orphan's ass or a widow's ox would prevent them from tilling their land.

[17] See below, p. 170.

[18] See Chapter 4 above.

[19] Ferdinand E. Deist sets this within the context of a mixed economy of reciprocity and distribution (*Material Culture*, 178–179).

and the psychological sense.' Primarily early Israel in the desert was without land or government, and its earliest codes reflect a pastoral community, and had a sense that all the Israelites were brothers and the care for the poor rested on Israel's experience of slavery in Egypt.[20]

The Exodus *traditions* certainly exerted an influence upon the laws, as the motive clauses show, but as a *historical* explanation of the opposition to lending on interest the argument is less than satisfactory, since it is doubtful whether there is sufficient evidence to produce any credible reconstruction of that history. But what was believed to have happened is more important in the life of a people than the actual history.

Were the Laws Forbidding Interest Carried Out?

It is difficult to say whether the laws on interest were observed, as Gamoran admits.[21] Neufeld holds that they were often ignored, on the grounds that the prophets condemn money lenders who took interest and that the sympathy to debtors shown in the Bible implies that the lenders demanded interest.[22] But Gamoran is right in questioning both arguments. Only Ezekiel condemns lending at interest, and the other prophets do not mention it. Yet to conclude from this that the silence of the other prophets 'suggests some degree of compliance with the law' is to make too much of an argument from silence. Sympathy with those in debt could be felt even if no interest had been added to their burden, and the penalties for failing to repay a loan included losing their possessions and even having to sell themselves or members of their families into slavery.

Gamoran himself turns to the Egyptian papyri of the fifth to second centuries BC. Three contracts between Jews from the fifth and third centuries required interest, two from the second century included a penalty with interest for late payment, although only one of these last also required interest, but as it is a renewal of a loan it may be that the original loan was interest free. The number of contracts is too small to prove that at the earlier period Jews lent to each other at interest, but in the second century made interest free loans, though with a penalty for late repayment. Even if this is the correct interpretation, contracts from Egypt at a late date hardly provide adequate evidence for the practice in Israel and Judah.

Gamoran claims that while loans, foreclosing on mortgages, and selling oneself or one's children into slavery to pay a debt are mentioned in the Old Testament (2 Kgs. 4.1; Neh. 5.1–5), nowhere is

---

[20] Gamoran, 'Loans on Interest', 127–129.
[21] *Ibid.*, 133–134.
[22] Edward Neufeld, 'Rate of Interest', 196–197.

there any evidence which shows whether interest was levied or not,
Whether he is right depends on the interpretation of three difficult
sentences in Nehemiah's charge against the richer members of the
community in Judah, translated in RSV as: 'You are exacting interest,
each from his brother' (Neh. 5.7), 'Let us leave off this interest' (Neh.
5.10), and 'Return to them . . . the hundredth of money, grain, wine,
and oil which you have been exacting from them' (Neh. 5.11). As to
the first two, the verb *nāśā'* and the noun *maśśā'* are not used of
interest, and the people's complaint appears to be concerned with
seizing pledges (cf. REB, 'You are holding your fellow-Jews as
pledges for debt'[23]). Moreover *nāśā'* seems to mean simply to give a
loan, which could be a loan on pledge (cf. Ex. 22.24[25]; Deut.
24.10). In verse 11, the difficulty lies in *mᵉ'aṭ*. While even Williamson
takes it to mean 'percentage' (as interest), it would have this meaning
only here. It is commonly taken as 1 per cent, and if this is the
monthly interest it would work out at 12 per cent per annum, a low
rate compared with that in other countries of the ancient Middle East,
where 20 per cent on silver and 33 per cent on corn was common.[24]
Because this infringes the prohibition of interest in the laws, it has
sometimes been emended to *maśśa'ṭ* ('burden') or *maśśā'ṭ* ('loan'),[25]
but this is arbitrary. It would seem, therefore, that in the fifth
century Jews in Judah were possibly lending at interest, although
under pressure from Nehemiah they either returned the pledges or
cancelled the interest, or even cancelled the debts in the way that
Middle Eastern kings sometimes cancelled debts on special
occasions.

What is notable about this account in Nehemiah is that there is no
reference to any of the laws concerning loans or the cancelling of
debts. In common with the situation in Mesopotamia, life went on as
if the laws did not exist, even where the practice conformed either
closely or generally to the laws. It is further evidence that the laws,
both in Israel and in the rest of the ancient Middle East, were ideals or
legal theory.

[23] The NJB emends to *nāśā'* and *maśśā'* to produce 'Each of you is imposing a
burden on his brother', which has little to say for it, but keeps 'Let us cancel these
pledges' in v. 10. See the discussion in H. G. M. Williamson, *Ezra, Nehemiah*, 233. F.
Charles Fensham translates v. 10 'Let us absolve this loan', but he also accepts 'a
hundredth' in the next verse, explaining that the problem lay in the fact that the
farmers could not till their fields properly because of the time they had to spend
rebuilding the walls (*Ezra and Nehemiah*, 195). D. J. Clines rejects interest, taking the
lending to be against pledges (*Ezra, Nehemiah, Esther*, 168–169).
[24] Neufeld argues that only this verse reveals the rate of interest. Nehemiah asked for
two concessions: restoration of mortgaged property (v. 11a), and the remission of
interest (v.11b). He concludes that 12 per cent was a not unusual rate of interest ('Rate
of Interest', 194–204).
[25] So even HALOT II, 539.

A Unique Ethic?

The law prohibiting interest opens up the question of the extent to which Israelite law implies a unique ethic.

The prohibition of interest appears to be the only law which can be regarded as unique to Israel within the ancient Middle East, and even here it can be plausibly treated as the summit of a general concern to protect those who might be severely harmed by rapacious creditors. For the rest similarities run right across the ancient Middle East and include the non-Semitic Hittite laws.[26] Greengus suggests that some of these parallels 'may derive from societal norms that were held in common by both ancient Israel and her neighbors'.[27] He lists attitudes to sorcery, kidnapping and false witness, a demand for honesty in dealing with others, condemnation of judges who take bribes and merchants who use false weights and measures. There are common attitudes to property rights, the return of lost property, and responsibility for goods, also common customs, such as giving an extra share to the firstborn, a husband's obligations to his first wife if he took a second, and other family matters.

Despite these common norms and values, factors such as the stratification of society, religious and ritual presuppositions, assumptions about the nature of society and the relation between individuals affect the ways the laws were understood, so that, although Israel faced many of the same problems as troubled the lawmakers in other societies and often the response to wrongdoing was broadly similar, there are a number of special features in Israelite law.

We have already seen that the special type of apodeictic laws and the large number of distinctive motive clauses, together with the extensive paraenesis, distinguish the Old Testament from the other collections of laws found in the ancient Middle East. It is hardly satisfactory, however, to claim that the Old Testament ethics can be discovered by fastening on the laws in apodeictic form and those to which motive clauses are attached. Apart from the unlikelihood of the *form* of the laws being the criterion of a distinctive ethics, close examination shows that no absolute differences in content can be traced between the laws of different types. Laws changed between the collections, and some requirements are found in more than one form of law.

Another possible indication of the way Israel viewed social life is to observe the social areas which are omitted from the Old Testament

---

[26] S. Greengus, 'Law', 533–534, distinguishes three types of law: (1) identical laws, (2) laws which are similar but not identical, and (3) laws dealing with similar problems but treating them differently. It is not always clear why a particular offence is included in one category rather than another.

[27] Greengus, 'Biblical and ANE Law', 245.

laws. This, however, is not necessarily appropriate. Several of the law-codes are incomplete, some seriously so. Moreover, until the purpose of the various law-givers is determined, it will be impossible to decide why particular omissions were made. Yet some features may provide hints about the nature of Israelite law.

In none of the Old Testament collections of laws is there any parallel to the duties to the king or overlord that are found elsewhere. Israel was a monarchy, yet the only law concerning the king is hostile to him (Deut. 17.14–17). It has been suggested that the law is a reaction to the reign of Solomon. Certainly the compiler is intent to limit the power of the king, and is hardly a royal lawgiver. An ambiguous attitude towards the monarchy seems to run through many books of the Old Testament.

There are no laws regulating the leasing of land. The usual reason put forward for this is that the Israelites believed that the land belonged to Yahweh, who had given it to Israel. Therefore the individual Israelite did not own his land.[28] The reversion of land to the original owner in the jubilee year is expressly grounded on Yahweh's possession of the land: 'The land shall not be sold in perpetuity, for the land is mine; for you are strangers and sojourners with me' (Lev. 25.23).[29] Some scholars, however, see the chief purpose of the law to restrict growing inequality between members of the Israelite community and to prevent the utter ruin of debtors.[30] Since the jubilee is mentioned only in Leviticus 25, it seems likely that it is priestly idealism and had a purely religious basis.

Family legislation is more limited than elsewhere. There are no laws for adoption. Whether it ever took place is uncertain. The apparent references in Psalm 2.7 and 2 Samuel 7.14 are disputed. They may be purely metaphorical for the relation between Yahweh and the king, although even if this were so there must have been some human custom underlying the metaphor. The suggestion, on the basis of Nuzi documents, that Abraham adopted Eliezer has now been generally rejected, and whether Eliezer was adopted or not, customs in Genesis cannot be used as evidence for later Israelite practice. It has been

---

[28] Christopher J. H. Wright has emphasized the importance of the land in *God's People* and *People of God*.

[29] Wright discusses this verse in *God's People*, 58–65. Budd considers the non-observance and impracticality of the jubilee law, noting that it is not mentioned in Neh 5.1–13, but pointing out that some kind of jubilee seems to be implied in Jer 34.8–22, and that land releases similar to Israel's jubilee took place spasmodically elsewhere in the ancient Middle East at the command of the king (*Leviticus*, 341–342). G. J. Wenham, however, holds that the jubilee year 'remained an ideal, which was rarely, if ever, realized' (*Leviticus*, 318). He adds that rabbinic literature says that it was reckoned obsolete in post-exilic times. 2 Chronicles 36.21 implies that not even the sabbatical seventh year was observed in the pre-exilic period.

[30] See Wenham, *Leviticus*, 317–318.

suggested that in Babylon marriage was monogamous and therefore there was a greater likelihood of childlessness. Other explanations are that the levirate was an alternative to adoption, and that in Israel the emphasis was placed upon blood relationships. Yet another suggestion is that, since having children was a sign of God's blessing, to attempt to secure an heir by adoption would be an irreligious usurping of divine authority.

Divorce was accepted,[31] although it appears that a wife could not divorce her husband. The law does not regulate divorce except to decree that the husband may not remarry his wife if she has married again after he had divorced her (Deut. 24.1–4), and forbids divorce if a man falsely accused his wife of not being a virgin on marriage (Deut. 22.13–19), or had to marry a woman he had raped (Deut. 22.28–29). By contrast Hammurabi sets out detailed laws concerning divorce, with provisions for the treatment of the bride-price in various circumstances. The woman could also divorce her husband, providing she was not a 'gadabout' and did not neglect her house.[32] This provides another example of the difficulties involved in comparing the different laws. As we have seen, the Deuteronomic law is primarily concerned with purity. The grounds for divorce are mentioned incidentally and there is considerable uncertainty about the meaning of ' . . . if then she finds no favour in his eyes because he has found some indecency in her'. The reference to the divorce document which is given to the woman is also incidental to the law. Thus the basis on which the legislation is framed is completely different in the Old Testament from that in the laws of Hammurabi or the Middle Assyrian Law.

Rather than attempting to draw a sharp line between the biblical collections of laws and those of other peoples in the ancient Middle East, it is better to accept that Israel was part of the overall culture of the region, and its ethics has similarities with that of other nations. If that is accepted it then becomes easier to focus on the attitudes, presuppositions and values which control the ethos of the various societies.

The law of the goring ox (Ex. 21.28–32) has fascinated scholars and provides a good example of the problem.[33] Here is a situation which has to be dealt with in all agricultural communities. The Law in Eshnunna[34] is almost identical to the Israelite law, while the Code of

---

[31] See references to divorce in Hos. 2.4[2]; Isa. 50.1; Jer. 3.1–5.

[32] CH 137–149 (*ANET*, 172, commentary in Driver and Miles, *Babylonian Laws*, 1, 290–306), and cf. MAL A 37–38 (*ANET*, 183).

[33] It is discussed in most books on the laws. See in particular Dale Patrick, *Old Testament Law*, 77–79; S. M. Paul, *Book of the Covenant*, 78–84; J. J. Finkelstein, *The Ox That Gored*; R. Yaron, 'The Goring Ox'; Moshe Greenberg, 'Postulates'.

[34] Laws 54–55 (*ANET*, 163). The law follows the case of an ox goring another ox; the

Hammurabi[35] is not greatly different. The similarities extend to the distinction which is made between the ox who suddenly goes berserk and the habitual gorer, the fact that the owner has been warned but took no action, and that slaves are treated differently from free citizens.

Yet the Old Testament law stands apart in three respects: (1) the ox in each case is killed by stoning, and eating the flesh is not permitted; (2) the negligent owner is also executed, although it is possible for him to 'ransom' his life, presumably by a money payment; who gives the warning to the owner and who has the authority to commute the death penalty are not stated, but most probably the warning was given by the elders, and the family of the dead person could show mercy to the owner; (3) it is explicitly stated that the same procedure applies to a man's son or daughter, possibly to exclude the penalty being paid by the owner's children.

The biblical law treats loss of human life more seriously than the other codes do, both by killing the ox, which is treated as a 'murderer', and by imposing the death penalty on its owner. As we saw earlier, this is the only place in the Old Testament where the death penalty for killing a human being can be replaced by a money payment, but the way this is described – 'the redemption of his life' – has led some to argue that it is not a 'composition' or the indemnifying of the family, but that a religious motive lies behind it. The owner's life is forfeit, but he is permitted by God to 'ransom' it. The killing of the ox is also placed within the religious sphere, either because it is guilty of 'blood-guilt' or because its action breaks the established hierarchy by which human beings rule over animals. The slave is treated as property, for the loss of which the owner receives compensation, yet the ox is still stoned because it killed a human being.

In the Old Testament, therefore, the incident is not treated as a matter of property for which damages may be exacted as it is in the other law codes. Whether this means that it reflects a 'higher', even 'unique', valuing of human life is not so certain. This is possible, and even probable, at the theological level of the completed Pentateuch, though even there the influence of the purity system, seen clearly in the stoning of the offending ox, makes such a narrowly ethical interpretation less than certain. What is found here is not an ethic which is higher than that of the other law codes, but one which reveals thought at a different level altogether. The incident is not being treated merely as a matter of morality.

---

next four laws give similar penalties for failing to control a mad dog, and impose the death penalty for failing to strengthen a wall which causes the death of a free man.
[35] Laws 250–252 (*ANET*, 176].

We must fasten on this different foundation given by characteristic ways of thought in our attempt to discover the centre of Old Testament ethics. Superficially it is the difference between a religious and a secular legal principle. Even though the prologue to the laws of Lipit-Ishtar, Ur-Nammu, and Hammurabi declare a religious origin to the laws, and Hammurabi is depicted as receiving his collection of laws from the god, the gods appear rarely in the body of the laws. They are occasionally invoked to provide a sanction, often through an ordeal or the swearing of an oath.[36]

Yet even here the matter is not quite simple. It might be supposed that the ordeal and the demand for an oath provide clear examples of giving a place to divine judgment. Yet as we have seen,[37] the case of the jealous husband (Num. 5.11–31) is the only example of trial by ordeal in the Old Testament and the taking of oaths is not common.

The laws in Exodus 22.6–12[7–13] concerning animals or property entrusted to a neighbour that are stolen, lost, damaged, or that die are difficult to interpret. An oath is required if an animal so entrusted dies or is injured or has been driven away without any witnesses seeing, and simply taking the oath is held to be sufficient. The owner must accept the oath (v.10[11]). If, however, the animal had been stolen, this implies negligence and the householder must pay compensation to the owner (v. 11[12]). If it was killed by wild animals, evidence has to be presented and no divine intervention comes into play (v. 12[13]).

Where money or goods which have been entrusted to a neighbour are stolen and the thief is not found, the householder to whom they were entrusted 'shall come near to God, to show whether or not he has put his hand to his neighbour's goods' (vv. 6–7[7–8]). The LXX adds that he is to take an oath, and although some commentators accept this as the purpose of his coming near to God, this is not implied by the Hebrew phrase. Rather, as in the case when there are conflicting claims to animals or goods (v. 8[9]), the decision is made by God. How this is declared is not explained. Some form of ordeal, a sacred trial, the use of Urim and Thummim, or an oracle by a priest have all been suggested.[38]

---

[36] Cf. CH 2 [*ANET*, 166], where one accused of sorcery is thrown into the river, and (contrary to the practice elsewhere in the ancient Semitic world — and much later English practice), he is deemed guilty if he drowns (see Driver and Miles, *The Babylonian Laws*, I, 63). Theophile J. Meek notes that the word for 'river' has the determinative for deity and is regarded as a god (*ANET* 166, n. 41).

[37] See pp. 30–31 above.

[38] See p. 106 above. J. P. Hyatt, *Exodus*, 238, states without argument that in the one case the owner of the house to whom the deposit had been made, and in the other both parties, swear an oath, it being assumed that an oath in the presence of God is so serious that no one would dare to swear a false oath. But as Durham, *Exodus*, 326,

Thus the Old Testament laws are chary of invoking a direct divine judgment, although it has been suggested that it is presupposed by some of the psalms, where the psalmist declares his innocence (e.g. Pss. 5; 7; 17; 26). Even swearing an oath of innocence is rare, despite the frequent mention of oaths elsewhere in the Old Testament and in the other law codes from the ancient Middle East. If we are to find a theological perspective in the laws, it will have to be in the context of the completed Torah, the motivations and paraenesis. The content of the laws themselves is essentially at home within the culture of the whole area in the ancient world.

There is perhaps virtue in this. Ethics belongs to humanity as a whole, not to any particular group or cult. We have already seen the importance of 'natural law' in the Old Testament. Now we have seen that the laws themselves present an ethic which is not narrowly confined to Israel. It is always possible, of course, by careful selection to present the Old Testament as maintaining a 'higher' ethic than is found in the surrounding nations, but this distorts the overall ethos, and adopting similar methods a case could be made out in favour of some of the other law codes. The prohibition of lending at interest appears to be unique, although it can be understood as extending the concern which Hammurabi and other kings expressed for debtors who had fallen into the hands of unscrupulous creditors. What is not permissible is to present this prohibition as revealing a special concern for the poor that belongs to Israel alone.

The Law on Interest as Divine Revelation
The law forbidding interest raises a question which we shall consider more fully in the final chapter. Put simply it is this: the prohibition of lending at interest was apparently unique in the ancient Middle East, and therefore more than any other law deserves to be regarded as part of the divine revelation to Israel. Even when it is seen as a part of a wider caring for the poor and powerless, its specific demand has been found nowhere else. Yet later Judaism and Christianity have not obeyed it. There is rabbinic evidence that the Jerusalem temple exacted interest on loans, while in the parable of the talents placing money where it can attract interest is regarded as praiseworthy in a minor way (Mt. 25.27).[39]

---

points out, this does not fit the Hebrew text, where the phrase, as elsewhere, refers to drawing near to God in a sanctuary to receive a divine judgment. R. E. Clements, *Exodus*, 142–143, points to 1 Kings 8.31–32, but this includes swearing an oath before the altar of the temple, although it is followed by a reference to divine judgment. Although ultimately God is the witness and guarantor of the oath, the two practices are distinct.

[39] The Qur'an, however, prohibits the taking of interest and threatens hell-fire on those who disobey (2.275–276), and despite some attempts at casuistry, this was practised

Those commentaries which refer to the issue contrast loans to the poor with modern commercial credit. Hyatt, after pointing out that this law 'has been a source of embarrassment, and has led to casuistry, in both Judaism and Christianity', states categorically that 'it should never have been thought applicable to a highly developed, commercial society requiring large amounts of venture capital'.[40] Most would agree with this. The law belongs to a particular society and culture, and cannot be fitted into an entirely different one.

If this is accepted, however, it still remains to examine the implications of such a judgment. Does it imply that law is entirely relative to the society in which it functions? Can distinctions be made between laws which have a permanent validity in all human societies and those which are culture bound? If so, how can it be determined which fall into the class of universally relevant laws? Should we look for underlying principles which are always true, such as caring for the poor in the case of the law against lending at interest? And although there is no exact and immediate link between law and ethics, the two are related, and so the question of the relativity of ethics cannot be evaded. More broadly still, do the Old Testament laws and the Israelite ethic have any continuing force?

Most of these questions must be left until Chapter 20. Here it can be observed that although the prohibition of lending at interest was unique to Israel, it is possible to see it as simply one way of protecting the poor. Elsewhere in the ancient Middle East this concern was expressed in different ways, such as through the laws remitting interest in cases of natural disaster or by direct action of the king, who was held to have a duty to protect the poor. On the other hand, a more Marxist analysis might suggest that law is part of the superstructure and that inexorable economic changes are the cause of the failure to put the law against lending at interest into practice in the latter part of the biblical period and still more of its total rejection in the transition to a capitalist society. If that is so, however, it is difficult to see it in any way as divine revelation. Rather it is a relic from an earlier stage of society.

This discussion of lending at interest opens up the wider question of the attitude to the poor in ancient Israel, but before we turn to this it will be useful to stop and survey the way we have come so far.

---

for many centuries and is still held to be God's command.

[40] Hyatt, *Exodus*, 244.

13

INTERLUDE

The higher we have climbed our spiral staircase the more we have learned of the countryside, but still we cannot see the whole panorama. We can, however, begin to fit together those earlier glimpses through the narrow windows in the tower.

Perhaps what has struck us as most puzzling is how foreign the country looks. We are accustomed to separating out ethics as a philosophical discipline, distinguishing morality from religion and aesthetics. The pictures we have caught sight of seldom correspond to this. Much more fuzzily, ethics, purity and honour are intermingled, and although it is possible to impose modern distinctions upon the material, the fact that the ancient Israelites did not place them in separate compartments is a central feature of the Old Testament and gives it its peculiar quality. It means that its ethics takes on a completely different complexion. Since the interpretation we give to incidents and actions depends upon presuppositions and perspectives, a sharp divide opens up between ourselves and the ancient Israelites.

Another important discovery is the impossibility of reading Israelite morality from the prescriptions in the collections of laws. Who composed and collected the laws is largely unknown. Their date and background are obscure. And, as with all law, there are gaps between what the law-giver decrees and what the members of society regard as morally right. Custom plays a vital part in everyday life and is more important than law. This was illustrated by the study of adultery and the concept of what 'is not done in Israel'.

Nevertheless, the laws cannot be overlooked, Without them the evidence for Old Testament ethics would be scant indeed. What they offer, however, is determined, to a considerable extent, by their setting within the completed Pentateuch, where narrative and law are combined, and the whole is set within the story of the Exodus. An examination of the form and content of the Ten Commandments showed up the distinction between the sense which individual components of the Pentateuch present and the place and meaning they have within the completed narrative framework. Moreover, although many of the laws are closely similar to those in the collections of laws that have been discovered in the ancient Middle East, the way the Old Testament links ethics and religion closely together reveals important differences. As the Jews have always taught, law is more correctly teaching. Within their present context the laws declare what is the divine will.

This raises a further issue: is the Old Testament ethics heteronomic, in Kantian terms? Abraham's debate with God reveals that some among the ancient Israelites, whether consciously or not, held to a morality that was independent of God and by which he could be judged. It looks somewhat similar to what in Classical and Christian tradition has come to be known as 'natural law', but differences between the two make us wonder whether this is a satisfactory term to describe these features within Old Testament ethics. Moreover, the motive clauses which are attached to many of the laws in the Pentateuch offer further confirmation of the teaching aspect of the law, and because some of these motivations depend on the acceptance of a prior ethic, not derived from the divine command, the character of Old Testament ethics is further broadened.

Beyond these main aspects of the landscape, other features were also noted. The idea of liability for mere intention is strange and makes it impossible to understand the laws in a narrowly legalistic way. The sanctions against disobeying the law confirm that practice cannot be equated with command. In the Pentateuch ethics and theology are intertwined, and law is essentially divine teaching. A comparison of these sanctions with those decreed in the other law codes from the ancient Middle East makes it questionable whether the Israelite laws as a whole can be held to possess a 'higher' ethic. The only law that seems to be unique to Israel, the prohibition of lending at interest, increases this doubt.

Yet in certain aspects the Old Testament laws stand apart, and this leads on to two major questions that run through the present study: (1) to what extent do our contemporary interests distort our interpretation of Old Testament ethics? and (2) granted the wide range of ethical stances that appear within the Hebrew Bible, to what extent are we justified in fastening on the features which we judge to be 'higher' and then to declare that this is the 'true' Old Testament ethics?

The next five chapters will illustrate the difficulties which lie behind these questions. In the first place the topics are modern. As we shall see, to the Israelites the poor, war, the care of animals, dangers to the natural world, and the position of women in society were not problems. It is our current awareness of the two-thirds world and structural poverty within the developed countries which makes poverty as such a moral issue. It is the wars of the twentieth century, with the involvement of whole civilian populations, the development of weapons of mass destruction, and the vast numbers of people killed, which force us to treat war as perhaps the greatest evil of our time. Ecology became an issue only with the publication of Rachel Carson's *Silent Spring* in 1961 and the launching of the World Wide Fund for Nature. The fact that the churches followed rather than gave the lead indicates the paucity of biblical support for the protection of animals. And it was the feminist movement which pointed up the patriarchal character of the Bible. Just to select these topics, therefore, involves distorting Israelite values, but they can hardly be avoided in any discussion of ethics.

Secondly, modern ethical beliefs too readily determine both the evidence which is presented and the interpretations which are placed upon it. Details will be presented in the following chapters. Here one example will show how difficult it is to see clearly the Israelite ethical landscape. Broadly three attitudes towards the Old Testament treatment of women have been adopted in recent years. Some scholars, like Mary Daly and Daphne Hampson, regard the Bible as irredeemably patriarchal, and leave it at that, moving to a 'post-Christian' theological position. Others, such as Phyllis Trible, seek to bring biblical women out of the shadows, arguing that women have a larger place in the Bible than male interpreters in the past have recognized or admitted. To them the Old Testament is less patriarchal than has been supposed. A third group admit that Israelite society was patriarchal but seek a 'hermeneutic of liberation', whereby an overall ethic of justice and equality is discovered in the Bible which is then applied to the position of women in the church today. All three approaches are controlled by present-day ethical stances and all fail to appreciate how the situation in ancient Israel would have looked to those living at the time.[1]

After we have examined these five topics, it will be necessary to turn back to the more general question of whether the Old Testament writers were conscious of the distinct discipline or way of looking at things which we call ethics, and to assess the contribution of the wisdom writers, the prophets, and the narratives. Only then shall we have reached the top of the tower and be able to gaze round at the total landscape. Yet some parts will still remain hidden behind hills, trees and buildings, and we shall become very conscious not only that this study is incomplete but that completion is beyond the grasp of any modern student of the Old Testament. Too much about ancient Israel is unknown and can never be known, while postmodern philosophy forces us to take account of the way where we stand controls our perspective. Finally, returning to the ground and to our own century we shall have to ask what contribution the Old Testament can make to deciding on ethical dilemmas today.

---

[1] A fourth group, which includes women as well as men, accept both the patriarchal nature of the biblical records and its abiding validity.

14

THE POOR

Christian folklore holds that the biblical teaching about the poor is definite and consistent. The God of the Exodus is on the side of the poor, and the Bible teaches the 'option for the poor'. Emphasis is placed on Amos's condemnation of those who oppress the poor – 'who sell . . . the needy for a pair of shoes' and 'trample the head of the poor into the dust of the earth' (Amos 2.6–7), women who 'oppress the poor' and 'crush the needy' (Amos 4.1), people who 'turn aside the needy in the gate' (Amos 5.12), 'trample upon the needy' and 'bring the poor of the land to an end' (Amos 8.4), and 'buy the poor for silver and the needy for a pair of sandals' (Amos 8.6).

It is true that proper treatment of the poor is a major theme in the Old Testament, as many studies have shown,[1] but matters are not quite as simple or unambiguous as is commonly supposed.

Vocabulary
Many different words for 'poor' are found in the Old Testament.[2] Sometimes this springs from the demands of poetic parallelism, but it may also point to certain differences of attitude between the law, the prophets, and the wisdom writings.

In his article on *'eḇyōn* in *NIDOTTE* William R. Domeris surveys the semantic field of poverty and comments on eight terms (the translations are his). The most common, *'ānī* ('poor, humble, oppressed'), he holds, describes those without land who are therefore in need of economic protection. The related *'ānāw* ('oppressed, afflicted') indicates the frequent connection between poverty and oppression.[3] Both are socially dependent on someone who

---

[1] Among the more perceptive and sympathetic articles may be noted: Norman W. Porteous, 'Care of the Poor', Ronald Clements, 'Poverty'.

[2] *'eḇyōn, dal, 'ānāw/'ānī, rāš, mūḵ* ('become poor', only Lev. 25.25, 35, 39, 47; 27.8), *maḥsōr* ('poverty'), *miskēn* (only Qoh. 4.13; 9.15, 16, but cf. Isa. 40.20 and *misk'nūṯ*, Deut. 8.9). In his pioneering study 'Arm und reich', which includes a survey of pre-exilic society, A. Kuschke, examines most of these terms. He concludes that *rūš*, *ḥsr* and *miskēn* stand over against *'ānī, dal* and *'eḇyōn*, and reflect a different mentality and hence come from different social strata (p. 53).

[3] Thomas D. Hanks has made a comprehensive study of the vocabulary of oppression

possesses greater honour and power, and often the poor person has
been made poor so that someone else might gain wealth and power.
The third term, *dal* ('low, weak, poor, thin'), is used by Amos to
describe peasant farmers who have lost their lands to wealthy
landlords (Amos 2.7). The dominant stress of the word is placed on
their vulnerability and their loss of dignity. The fourth term, *'ebyōn*
('in want, needy, poor'), refers to people who are virtually destitute,
the day labourers who are completely dependent on other people for
their survival. Found chiefly in the wisdom literature, *rāš* ('in want,
poor') stands in contrast to the rich, referring to those belonging to
'the lower strata of the honor/shame table'. The sixth term which
Domeris lists is *miskēn* ('beggar, poor'), which also refers to 'the
poorest of the poor'. The last two terms are mentioned very briefly by
their roots, *mwk* ('poor') meaning temporary poverty, and *dk'*
('crush') 'often used for the crushing of oppression or poverty'.[4]
Although it may be questioned whether the distinctions are quite as
sharp as Domeris sets them out, since the variations between the
different types of literature need to be taken into account, his review is
a valuable introduction to the subject. In particular his emphasis upon
social distinctions and the importance of honour and shame provides a
necessary counter to the modern assessment of poverty almost entirely
in economic terms.

Milton Schwantes examines four of these terms, *rāš*, *dal*, *'ebyōn*,
'ānāw/'ānī, noting parallels and opposites and analysing the words in
the Pentateuch, the history books and the prophets (he leaves out the
Psalms).[5] He concludes that the four terms are always used
synonymously. They are often found in parallel, in close proximity, or
interchangeably. Yet they possess special nuances. The term *dal*
('weak') does not refer to socio-economic weakness in the narratives.
It is rarely linked with any protest in favour of the poor. Indeed, the
laws can even demand that judges must not be partial to the poor (Ex.
23.3; Lev. 19.15) and Jeremiah says that the poor do not know the law
(Jer. 5.4). By contrast *'ānī* and *'ebyōn* are almost always oppressed
and poverty-stricken in the laws and the prophets. The fourth term,
rāš, belongs completely within the wisdom writings, where it
connotes the exploited, although the *rāš* is sometimes himself
responsible for his condition. Schwantes holds that all four terms
belong to the same social-economic situation. They are impoverished,
dependent peasants, who still possess a house, cattle and fields. They

---

in *Vocabulary of Oppression*, 3–40.
[4] W. R. Domeris, *'ebyōn* (*NIDOTTE*, 1, 228–229). With this should be compared the
articles on the other terms: *dal* (M. Daniel Carroll R., *NIDOTTE*, 1, 951–952), *dk'* (W.
R. Domeris, *NIDOTTE*, 1, 943–945), *'ānāw/'ānī* (W. J. Dumbrell, *NIDOTTE*, 3,
454–464), *rwš* (W. R. Domeris, *NIDOTTE*, 3, 1085–1086).
[5] Milton Schwantes, *Das Recht der Armen*.

are never named with the *ʿebed*, the lowest strata in the population, but are frequently mentioned along with the *gēr*, whose poverty lies primarily not in economic impoverishment but derives from his position in society.

J. David Pleins[6] and R. N. Whybray[7] fasten on the poor in the wisdom writings.

Pleins compares the frequency of six terms (*ʾebyōn*, *dal*, *ʿānī*, *ʿānāw*, *rāš*, and *maḥsōr*), noting that *dal*, *rāš* and *maḥsōr* characterize the value system of the wise, which differed from that of the prophets. The background of the wisdom literature lies in the court, not in popular culture, and the wise men have little in common with the poorer peasants. Their values are those of the educated élite. They are ambivalent towards the poor, at times elevating them, at other times treating them with disdain. The terms *rāš* and *maḥsōr* are often connected with laziness. No attempt is made to improve the condition of the poor, and the sages show no awareness that the urban population was gaining by exploiting the poor, although opposition to mistreatment of the poor appears more strongly in the 'Sayings of the Wise' (e.g., Prov. 21.13; 22.9, 22). They certainly did not treat poverty as desirable, but they never move beyond charity towards poor individuals.

R. N. Whybray examines all the instances of the words for 'poor' in Proverbs. He concludes that, although elsewhere in the Old Testament the words may have had other connotations than simply 'poor',[8] 'no significant distinction between the words for "poor" and "poverty" was intended by these speakers' in Proverbs. He adds that the reason for their use of so many synonyms is not apparent.

The antonym of 'poor' is 'rich' (*ʿāšīr*). Whybray declares: 'In contrast with the plethora of words meaning "poor" it is remarkable that no other adjective or noun signifying "rich" occurs, although a number of other words and phrases denoting wealth and its acquisition are used quite frequently'.[9] Even *ʿāšīr* occurs rarely in

---

[6] J. David Pleins, 'Poverty'.

[7] R. N. Whybray, *Wealth and Poverty*.

[8] *Ibid.*, 22. He points out that *dal*, for example, is not conceived as being entirely impoverished in Ex. 30.15, where the *dal* is able to pay his half-shekel contribution or in Lev. 14.21, where he can contribute sacrificial offerings, though in Jer. 39.10 the *dallīm* are 'those who owned nothing', but Ex. 30 and Lev. 14 probably reflect different social and economic circumstances from Proverbs (p. 17).

[9] *Ibid.*, 22. He is referring to Proverbs 10.1–22.16 and 25–29, but adds in a footnote: 'This is true of the Old Testament as a whole.' Earlier, under the heading 'Wealth, power and high social status', he had listed with characteristic thoroughness seven abstract nouns denoting wealth, two verbs denoting the acquisition or possession of wealth, and four other expressions, together with a large number of references to such things as silver and gold, costly ornaments, commercial activities, inheritance of property, income and loss, lavish spending, generosity and meanness, bribery, and

the Old Testament writings, Proverbs alone being an exception.[10] Outside of this book the word is of uncertain meaning in Isaiah 53.9. Apart from this and the mention of 'the richest of the people' in the royal marriage song of Psalm 45, it is commonly contrasted with one or other of the words for poor, as in Exodus 30.15, 2 Samuel 12.1–4, Psalm 49.3[2], and Ruth 3.10. In the prophets it is found only in Jeremiah 9.22[23], set alongside 'wise' and 'mighty' (*gibbōr*), and Micah 6.12, where the prophet, after declaring God's condemnation of those who use biased scales, false weights and short measures, attacks rich men who are 'full of violence'. Job, in a speech which many think has been wrongly ascribed because it presents the conventional theory of retribution, declares that the wicked man goes to bed rich and when he opens his eyes his wealth has gone (Job 27.19).

The cynical Preacher gives his own slant on life. Qoheleth 5.9[10]–6.9, which Crenshaw subtitles 'The Disappointments of Wealth'[11] and which lists the factors which lead to disenchantment with riches, shows that it is important not to limit any discussion of the rich to the verses where *ʿāšîr* appears. In verse 11[12], where the word does occur, Crenshaw suggests that the ambiguity about the cause of sleeplessness (overeating or anxious worry about his possessions) may be intentional.[12] With the conservatism of the privileged sages, Qoheleth regards the humiliation of the rich as an evil (Qoh. 10.6) and recognizes that the power of the rich is on a level

---

warnings against going bail for others. Assuming that wealth, social status and power were closely associated in Proverbs, Whybray also includes ten words 'denoting persons of high social status and power', such as *melek*, *nādîb* and *mōšēl*. He notes that more than 120 verses out of the 513 in these chapters refer to wealth, while other words, such as 'proud', refer indirectly to the possession of riches (*ibid.*, 11–14). To this list might be added (outside of Proverbs) 'great' (*gādōl*), which sometimes carries the sense of 'rich'. In 1 Sam. 25.2 it is translated by RSV as 'rich', and in 2 Sam. 19.33[32] and 2 Kgs. 4.8 as 'wealthy'. Philip J. Budd notes that 'great' is 'commonly used of prominent, powerful and often wealthy people', listing Ex. 11.3; Lev. 19.15; 1 Sam. 25.2; 2 Sam. 3.38; 5.10; 19.33[32]; 2 Kgs. 4.8; 5.1; 10.6, 11; 18.19, 28; Est. 9.4; Job 1.3; Prov. 18.16; 25.6; Qoh. 9.14; Jer. 5.5; 27.7; Jonah 3.7; Mic. 7.3; Nah. 3.10 (*Leviticus*, 276). In most of these wealth is hardly the dominant feature, but the point is important and shows yet again the danger of assuming that word and concept coincide. Domeris sees the semantic field of wealth and riches as consisting primarily of three terms, *ʿāšîr*, *hōn* ('material possessions, including riches') and *nᵉkāsîm* ('possessions in general, including livestock') (*ʿšr*, *NIDOTTE* 3, 558).

[10] Whybray gives the total number of occurrences as twenty-three.

[11] Cf. Graham Ogden's subtitle: 'Is it Worth Being Wealthy?' (*Qoheleth*, 89).

[12] James L. Crenshaw, *Ecclesiastes*, 119, 121 (cf. Prov. 25.16; Sir. 31.1–4). Tremper Longman III, *Ecclesiastes*, 165, finds an even greater ambiguity: the rich man's insomnia may be due to indigestion, worry about losing his wealth, or thinking up ways of increasing it. Michael V. Fox suggests that the slave may also have eaten too much. The rich man worries about his wealth and frets that others will try to get hold of it (*A Time to Tear Down*, 236–237).

with that of the king, when he warns against cursing them (Qoh. 10.20).[13]

In Proverbs, on the other hand, are found sayings which describe the strong and enjoyable position of the rich, often contrasted with the miserable condition of the poor (see Prov. 10.15; 14.20; 18.11, 23; 22.7). Habel stresses that in Proverbs 1–9 wisdom was expected to bring wealth. The virtuous who pursue wisdom faithfully and honour Yahweh will have success. They will possess land (Prov. 2.21), live long (Prov. 4.10), and enjoy a rich harvest (Prov. 3.9–10). Wisdom offers long life, riches and honour in Proverbs 3.16. The comparison between wisdom and silver and gold in Proverbs 3.14–15 is not intended to belittle wealth. Rather 'if wealth is *bonum*, wisdom is the *summum bonum*'. In 8.12–21 there is no indication that wealth is a dubious blessing, and in 9.1–6 Wisdom is depicted as a 'woman of rank'. Among the proverbs collected in chapters 10–31, on the other hand, several different attitudes appear, and wealth is presented as an ambiguous blessing. Habel rejects the view of McKane that such proverbs as 15.16, 17; 17.1 are an expression of Yahwistic piety, 'a tendency to equate poverty and piety, conversely, wealth and impiety'.[14] Rather wealth is 'an ambivalent and precarious blessing'. The teaching of the sages in Proverbs 22.12–24.22 is different again. Although the rich are warned not to oppress the poor (Prov. 22.22–23, cf. 23.10–11), and riches are seen as impermanent (Prov. 23.4–5), the poor find their only help in Yahweh, and the overall perspective is that of the educated elite who see the folly of being obsessed with wealth and extol the virtue of moderation.[15]

Whybray, however, thinks that in Proverbs generally the portrait of the rich man is 'far from sympathetic' and points out that not a single virtue is attributed to the rich. Certainly there are a few proverbs which are distinctly hostile towards the rich and those who favour them. Thus 22.16 declares that those who oppress the poor to increase their wealth and give to the rich will come into poverty and 28.6 affirms: 'Better is a poor man who walks in his integrity than a rich man who is perverse in his ways.' Another sentence states that the intelligent poor will see through the rich who think they are wise (28.11). Since other proverbs make it clear that generosity to the poor is well attested, Whybray may be right in proposing that *ʿāšîr* may have a special connotation, and refer not simply to those who have achieved or inherited greater prosperity than others, but a particular type of person 'who represents the exact opposite of the truly

---

[13] Michael V. Fox regards this 'wry quip' as an afterthought; Qoheleth realizes that he has just insulted the king and the rich man in v. 16 (*A Time to Tear Down*, 310–311).
[14] William McKane, *Proverbs*, 486–487.
[15] Norman C. Habel, 'Wisdom, Wealth and Poverty' (quotations from pp. 30, 33, 42).

indigent. . . . There is no suggestion . . . that the speakers envied the *'āšîr* or wished to attain his status or the position of power that went with it.'[16] Finally Proverbs 22.2 needs to be considered. The speaker declares that Yahweh is the maker of both rich and poor, but the meaning is ambiguous. It hardly means that the rich and the poor are equal to one another, but need not necessarily imply that God deliberately 'made them high and lowly, and ordered their estate'. Some, possibly influenced by modern sentiments, suggest that it intends to teach the value of the poor.[17] Some commentators take Proverbs 29.13: 'The poor man and the oppressor meet together; the LORD gives light to the eyes of both' as saying virtually the same as Proverbs 22.2: poor people and those who exploit them have a common creator who gives them life.[18]

The upshot of all this is that while there are clear differences in their favoured vocabulary for 'poor' between the wisdom writers on the one hand and the prophets and laws on the other, the words themselves appear to be less distinctive in meaning.[19] The various attitudes to the poor cannot be determined from vocabulary alone, although this may alert us to features that might otherwise be overlooked. More importantly, the meanings of several of the words are so wide that a false impression of the teaching of the Old Testament writings can easily be obtained.

Before leaving this discussion of the vocabulary, mention must be made of the 'sojourner' or 'resident alien' (*gēr*),[20] widows and

---

[16] *Wealth and Poverty*, 22–23.

[17] Whybray notes that this proverb is susceptible of different interpretations, but thinks that it 'does not suggest either approval or disapproval of the economic and social system which regards [the rich] as innately superior to [the poor]' (*Wealth and Poverty*, 22, cf. 41–42). Kenneth T. Aitken denies that it implies that responsibility for this state of affairs lies with God, although he admits it 'strikes a rather conservative note' – it is a fact of life that some are rich and some poor (*Proverbs*, 180). William McKane holds that the Hebrew of Proverbs 22.2 means no more than that rich and poor are found side by side in every community and makes no attempt to explain how this is compatible with Yahweh's rule, though it does assert that both are contained within the order which he created and upholds (*Proverbs*, 569–570). On the other hand Richard J. Clifford declares that the saying 'relativizes such distinctions [those between rich and poor whose relationship is largely determined by wealth] by naming Yahweh the creator and sustainer of every human being' (*Proverbs*, 195).

[18] So Richard J. Clifford, who adds: 'Before God, judgments based on wealth are insignificant' (*Proverbs*, 252), and William McKane: 'it simply says that all social structures contain this polarity of wealth and poverty, power and weakness' (*Proverbs*, 640).

[19] T. Donald makes the valid point that the frequency of *'ānāw/'ānî* in the Psalms is more simply explained by the sociological sympathies of the Psalmists rather than an extension of the semantic range of these words ('Rich and Poor', 29).

[20] The translation of *gēr* presents difficulties. 'Sojourner' is archaic; 'resident alien' expresses the sense exactly, but alien has developed unfortunate nationalistic overtones and is understood by the young to refer to visitors from outer space.

orphans.[21] It is characteristic of the Old Testament that all three are frequently linked together as needing special protection, often being subject to oppression, and as being especially watched over by God (e.g., Deut. 14.29; 16.11, 14; 24.17, 19–21; 26.12–13; 27.19; Jer. 7.6; 22.3; Ezek. 22.7; Zech. 7.10; Ps. 94.6), and are sometimes placed alongside the poor.[22] As will be shown later, however, they are not necessarily poor, and the feature they have in common is their powerlessness and hence the fact that they are often denied their legal and social rights.[23]

Who, then, are the poor?

Who Are the Poor?

Richard Coggins has pointed out that the question is raised because of the religious overtones commonly possessed by 'ānī and 'ānāw primarily, but also by other words in the psalms (cf. Ps. 86.1–2).[24] References to being poor are frequently linked with a plea to be heard by God and are set in parallel with such terms as '[Yahweh's] servant' (Ps. 86.1–2). This can be expanded to include 'godly' (Pss. 12.1; 86.6), 'faithful' (Ps. 12.1), 'righteous' and 'upright' (Ps. 140.12–13). Moreover some of the individual laments are thought to have been spoken by the king, who calls himself poor and needy! Coggins draws attention to the similar use of 'poor' in Egypt.[25]

'Resident alien' is not used in normal speech, but I retain it for lack of a better. HALOT offers 'protected citizen, stranger', neither of which is satisfactory. Modern translations offer no help. The 'foreigner' of NJB and GNB fails to convey the sense of being resident and having certain rights, as does REB's and NIV's 'aliens'. 'Refugee' gives part of the sense, but will not do because of the connotation of fleeing from persecution. For the meaning Roland de Vaux, *Ancient Israel*, 74, can hardly be bettered: 'a foreigner who lives more or less permanently in the midst of another community, where he is accepted and enjoys certain rights'. On the *gēr* see Christiana van Houten, *The Alien*, and Christoph Bultmann, *Der Fremde*, as well as the dictionaries.

[21] As HALOT II, 451, points out, the word has a narrower meaning than our 'orphan' and refers to 'the boy that has been made fatherless'.

[22] Outside the Old Testament it is widows and orphans which are commonly mentioned together,

[23] Carolyn S. Leeb's study of the *na'ar* (*na'rāh*) might suggest that these should be added to the list of those without social rights and therefore 'poor'. She argues that while the term came later to mean 'young', originally it referred to those 'away from their father's house' and hence lacking his protection. Leeb finds it impossible to determine the relation between *na'ar* and *gēr*, but suggests that possibly 'the *gēr* is one who find himself outside the bounds of his ethnic group or nation for reasons similar to the ones which cast the *na'ar* outside the bounds of the household' (*Away from the Father's House*, esp. 41, 124, 190–192). They are not mentioned with the other three classes in the texts, however, and apart from references to vulnerable women, there appears to be no special concern to protect them. This may indicate how stereotyped a group widows, the fatherless and the resident alien are.

[24] Richard J. Coggins, 'The Poor'.

[25] Cf. 'I was needy in her city [the goddess Mut], a poor man, a beggar in her city. I

There has been considerable debate about the poor in the psalms. Hans-Joachim Kraus denies that the poor are a religious group or are the pious – they are just *poor*.[26] Sue Gillingham examines the vocabulary in the psalms and concludes that *dal* and *'ebyōn* predominantly describe material deprivation, but *'ānī* and *'ānāw* spiritual need.[27] The psalmists were convinced that God relieves both material poverty and religious need, and the two are linked together.

We might accept that references to poverty in the psalms are essentially religious language, the dominance of *'ānī* and *'ānāw* pointing to this, but Coggins goes further and asks whether 'poor' in the prophets may not carry the same overtones – for example *'ebyōn* is in parallel to *saddiq* in Amos 2.6. He seems to conclude that it does not, but it raises the important question: Does Amos assume that the destitute are also 'righteous' – in the right? Yet links between goodness and prosperity are so strong in Deuteronomy and the wisdom writings that one must question whether the Franciscan ideal of poverty is found anywhere in ancient Israel. Is not Amos defending the poor not because they are poor but because they are unable to obtain justice (hence the references to bribery, injustice 'in the gate', unequal weights, and 'refuse of wheat', all of which press on the poor)? Yet we may wonder what might be the significance of the fact that Amos does not include resident aliens, widows and the fatherless with the poor, although these are also vulnerable and are regularly linked with the poor in Deuteronomy.

Despite the description of the pious as poor, however, it might well be supposed that this would have little point if there were none who were really poor and to whom the various words for poor could be literally applied. Indeed, in many contexts, especially outside the Psalms, the poor, if not utterly destitute, are impoverished and oppressed.

Some support for this may be found in the widespread tradition throughout the ancient Middle East that the king should protect the needy, the widow and the orphan. This is expressed in Psalm 72.2–4, 12–14, and echoed in Jeremiah 22.2–3, 15–16 (cf. the condemnation of the 'princes' in Isa. 1.23; Ezek. 22.6–7). With this may be compared Yassib's complaint against his father Keret in a text from Ugarit:

> You do not judge the cause of the widow,
> you do not try the case of the importunate.
> You do not banish the extortioners of the poor,
> you do not feed the orphan before your face
> (nor) the widow behind your back.[28]

---

came into my possessions through her power' (Walter Beyerlin, *NERT*, 38).

[26] Hans-Joachim Kraus, *Psalms 1–59*, 92–95.

[27] Sue Gillingham, 'The Poor'.

[28] J. C. L. Gibson, ed., *Canaanite Myths*, 102. Cf. Daniel, who 'judged the cause of the

T. R. Hobbs, however, argues that when the king calls himself 'poor and needy' the words are to be understood in terms of status and honour, and this nuance needs to be taken into account.[29] With this interpretation of the meaning of poor we may compare W. R. Domeris's comment at the beginning of his discussion of *'ebyōn* in the Old Testament: 'Where Western thinking stresses the economic aspect of poverty, the ANE understood poverty in the context of shame and honor. So the possession of land, power, economic security, and social status made a person rich, and the absence of these factors made a person poor.'[30]

Different Attitudes to the Poor
Even if the words for poor are largely interchangeable, the attitudes towards the poor differ strikingly between the wisdom writings, the law, and the prophetic books.

(a) The Law
In the Book of the Covenant, three main types of caring for the poor are found: the prohibition against lending at interest is linked to the poor (Ex. 22.24[25]); in lawsuits the judges are not to pervert justice to the poor (Ex. 23.6), nor to be partial to the poor (Ex. 23.3);[31] and the sabbatical year is to provide food for the poor (and the wild animals, Ex. 23.11). With these laws may be linked the command not to wrong resident aliens, widows and orphans (Ex. 22.20–23[21–24]).

Deuteronomy moves beyond the Book of the Covenant in a more positive direction. The Deuteronomists place considerable emphasis on caring for these three last classes, including giving them gleanings and, every third year, tithes (Deut. 10.18–19; 24.17–18; 27.19;

---

widow, tried the case of the orphan' (*ibid.*, 107). Harry A. Hoffner quotes similar claims from Sumerian-Akkadian, Egyptian and Hittite sources showing officials providing justice and care of widows and others (*TDOT* I, 288–289). Hammurabi declares that Amun and Enlil named him 'to cause justice to prevail in the land . . . that the strong might not oppress the weak' (*ANET*, 164). E. Hammershaimb refers to this text to support his theory that the prophetic ethics, especially the defence of widows and orphans, largely derived from Canaanite ethics. He allowed, however, that some features were Israelite in origin ('Ethics of OT Prophets').

[29] T. R Hobbs, 'Reflections on "the poor"', 293.

[30] W. R. Domeris, *'ebyōn* (*NIDOTTE* 1, 228). The emphasis on honour and shame should be noted.

[31] BHS and some commentators (e.g., M. Noth, *Exodus*, 189) emend 'poor' (*dāl*) to 'great', 'powerful' (*gādōl*). John I. Durham comments: 'giving an unfair advantage in a legal proceeding to the poor, who had no advantage at all, is forbidden, an insight into human temptation so perceptive that some commentators . . . albeit wrongly, have felt compelled to emend *w^edāl* "and poor, weak," to *gādōl* "great, important"'. (*Exodus*, 330). Brevard S. Childs (*Exodus*, 481), and J. P. Hyatt (*Exodus*, 245) point to the similar command in Leviticus 19.15 in support of the masoretic text.

24.19–22; 14.28–29; 26.12–15). They urge lending to the poor even when the seventh year of 'release' of debts is near (Deut. 15.1–11). Moreover, hired servants who are poor are not to be oppressed and their wages are to be paid each day (Deut. 24.14–15). To this may be added the call to 'furnish [the released slave] liberally out of your flock, out of your threshing floor, and out of your wine press' (Deut. 15.14), and not to leave him destitute.[32]

Some of these commands recur in the Holiness Code. Gleanings are for the resident alien and the poor (Lev. 19.10; 23.22). The poor are not to suffer injustice in legal judgments, either by showing partiality to them or by deferring to the great (Lev. 19.15).[33] Using a unique verb (*mūk*)[34] the Holiness Code adds a number of laws concerning those who have become destitute: the brother who cannot maintain himself is to be supported, money is to be lent without interest, and food is to be given similarly. He is not be to bought as a slave, but if he sells himself he is to be as a hired servant or resident alien, and is to be released at the jubilee. Israelites who have had to sell themselves as slaves to foreigners or resident aliens are to be redeemed by their near relatives. As in Deuteronomy, motive clauses refer to the Exodus (Lev. 25.35–55).

(b) The Prophets

The defence of the poor by Amos has already been noted. Other prophets echo this, but there are fewer references than might be expected on the accepted view of the prophets as siding with the poor, and these are generally less vigorous than those of Amos.

In Isaiah, apart from general references to justice and oppression (e.g., Isa. 1.17, 23), there are four types of oracle: (a) the call to

---

[32] Norbert Lohfink points out that the words for poor are never used in connection with Levites, resident aliens, orphans and widows in Deuteronomy. He argues that the purpose was to change the structures of society so that these groups would no longer be poor. The laws which mention the poor (Deut. 15.1–11; 24.10–15) are concerned with situations where poverty may repeatedly recur even in the best societies. These laws demand that help should be given to the poor, even at the risk of financial loss, and add the sanction of God's hearing the cry of the poor. He thinks this was utopian, and sees the Holiness Code as 'trying to bring things back to reality' ('Poverty', 43–47).

[33] As noted above, this is similar to Ex. 23.3. Gerstenberger stresses the cleft between the social groupings in post-exilic Israel, referring to Pss. 9/10; 37; 49; 73 and Neh. 5, and wonders whether the proscription of showing partiality to the 'socially weak' (improbable in practice) represents the writer's attempt 'to establish the abstract, formal principle of equality', or possibly shows 'the danger that the representatives of the lower classes constitute a majority in the court' (*Leviticus*, 269–270).

[34] Apparently a by-form of *mākak*. BDB offers the meanings 'be low, depressed, grow poor' and HALOT 'become impoverished'. (*TDOT* does not include the word.) The emphasis seems to be placed on coming into reduced circumstances from a previous position of independence and moderate wealth.

'defend the fatherless, plead for the widow' (Isa. 1.17; cf. 1.23; and most notably, though perhaps not by Isaiah of Jerusalem, of the ideal king it is declared in 11.4: 'with righteousness he shall judge the poor (*dallīm*) and decide with equity for the meek (*'an'wēy*) of the earth);[35] (b) condemnation of taking spoil from the poor and oppressing them (Isa. 3.14–15); (c) a woe on those who turn the poor away from justice and their right (Isa. 10.2); (d) and finally, and strikingly, part of the punishment on Israel will be that God will no longer have compassion on the fatherless and widows (Isa. 9.16[17]).[36] Such concern for the poor is rarely found in chapters 40–55,[37] but one of the most powerful appeals to care for the poor is expressed in 58.6–7 (cf. v. 10):

> Is not this the fast that I choose:
>   to loose the bonds of wickedness,
>   to undo the thongs of the yoke,
> to let the oppressed go free,
>   and to break every yoke?
> Is it not to share your bread with the hungry,
>   and bring the homeless poor[38] into your house;
> when you see the naked, to cover him,
>   and not to hide yourself from your own flesh?

Jeremiah mentions the poor only four times. In poetic oracles (a) God condemns the Israelites because 'on your skirts is found the lifeblood of the guiltless poor' (*'ebyōnīm n'qiyyīm*, Jer 2.34), and (b) indicts the wicked because they 'judge not with justice the cause of the fatherless, to make it prosper, and they do not defend the rights of the needy (*'ebyōnīm*, Jer. 5.28). (c) In accord with the cultic descriptions of true kingship, Josiah is praised for judging the cause of the poor and needy (*'ānī* and *'ebyōn*, Jer. 22.16). (d) Finally, in the temple sermon Jeremiah declares that if the people amend their ways and do not 'oppress the alien, the fatherless or the widow, or shed innocent blood in this place' God will let them remain in the land (Jer. 7.6, cf. 22.3).

---

[35] Cf. Isa. 32.7: the wicked who 'ruin the poor with lying words, even when the plea of the needy is right' will be shown up in the coming age of justice.

[36] See now Andrew Davies, *Double Standards*, 131–136, esp. 133.

[37] But note Isa. 41.17:

> When the poor and needy seek water,
>   and there is none,
>   and their tongue is parched with thirst,
> I the LORD will answer them,
>   I the God of Israel will not forsake them.

What is not clear here, however, is whether this oracle is concerned with the literally poor. The poem is highly metaphorical.

[38] The word translated 'homeless' is rare and of uncertain meaning, while 'poor', which the Syriac omits, is regarded as a gloss by BHS (so also Whybray, *Isaiah*, 213).

In his allegory of the two sisters, Ezekiel condemns Judah for acting like Samaria in giving no help to the poor and needy (*'ānī* and *'ebyōn*, Ezek. 16.49, cf. 22.29, the people 'have oppressed the poor and needy, and have extorted from the sojourner without redress'). Oppressing the poor and needy (*'ānī* and *'ebyōn*) is part of the sin of the wicked, alongside robbery, murder, adultery, not restoring a pledge, 'eating upon the mountains', idolatry, committing 'abomination' and lending at interest (Ezek. 18.10–13, cf. vv. 5–9 and 15–18, where the oppression is extended to 'anyone' and giving bread to the hungry and clothing the naked, as well as executing true justice are added). Finally in his condemnation of the 'princes of Israel' Ezekiel includes 'the sojourner suffers extortion in your midst; the fatherless and the widow are wronged in you' among other sins (Ezek. 22.7).

The call of Yahweh which Zechariah declares the Israelites failed to follow, contains the commands 'do not oppress the widow, the fatherless, the sojourner, or the poor; and let none of you devise evil against his brother in your heart' (Zech. 7.10), while Malachi foretells punishment on those who 'oppress the hireling in his wages, the widow and the orphan' and 'thrust aside the sojourner' (Mal. 3.5).

There are no explicit references to the poor as destitute in the other prophets,[39] although Micah's attack on those who 'covet fields and seize them', 'oppress a man and his house' (Mic. 2.2), drive women out of their houses (Mic. 2.9), and 'eat the flesh of my people, and flay their skin from off them' (Mic. 3.3) are usually taken to refer to the oppression of the poor. This, as with so many of the commonly accepted references in the prophets, is more plausibly interpreted as an attack on injustice and the oppression of those without power or status in society rather than a defence of those who are poor in an economic sense.

This rapid survey of the poor in the prophets raises the question of the state of society in the eighth and seventh centuries. The danger of producing a circular argument by inferring the situation on the basis of the prophetic oracles and then interpreting the prophets against that social situation is very great, since other evidence is relatively sparse. Probably there were major social changes during the period of the monarchy, with the rich amassing land and the peasants becoming day labourers and being forced into poverty. Some evidence from archaeology suggests widening class divisions as reflected in two types of housing appearing in the towns at about this time.[40] Rainer

---

[39] In passages such as Zeph. 2.3 *'ānāw* seems to represent religious obedience to Yahweh rather than economic poverty.

[40] Cf. de Vaux, *Ancient Israel*, 72–74, treated with caution by Rainer Albertz, *History*, 160. Albertz, despite his reservations, ultimately draws much of his picture of the

Albertz suggests that the regulations in Ezekiel 46.16–18, while utopian, may have been intended to prevent the accumulation of land in the hands of officials or members of the royal family in the new beginning after the exile.[41] It was the creation of these large estates which 'made holes in the old Israelite order'. The main instrument of economic oppression was the harsh law of credit, which allowed a lender to seize the property, family members, and even the person of the defaulter. Albertz accepts that we must not allow 'the deliberately one-sided prophetic polemic' at the time of this social crisis to lead us into a false view of the upper classes, who after all were using largely legal means to secure their own interests. What was happening was mainly the result of 'a structural violence which had its basis in economic and social developments under the monarchy'. The members of the upper classes probably regarded the traditional self-sufficient farmers as being behind the times. Riches, after all, were a long-held proof of Yahweh's blessing.[42] In this period of social change the prophets put themselves on the side of the lower classes who were getting poorer. The criterion by which they judged the upper classes was 'justice and righteousness', which Albertz interprets as meaning 'a just balance of interests for the well-being of all, a social solidarity which secures basic rights for all Israelites'. The prophets pointed out that a social order which no longer gave protection to the rights of marginal groups in society is unjust, however legal the proceedings may be.[43]

With Albertz's account may be compared Norman K. Gottwald's sociological reconstruction. He speaks with bold assurance of the changing economic relations in the time of the monarchy. Many leading groups supported a 'native tributary political economy in which an Israelite elite would tax and indebt their own people . . . Surplus labor value was taken from the peasants in two cycles of extraction – a *tax* cycle and a *debt* cycle', through state taxation in kind and conscripted labour, and the introduction of 'credit in kind extended to peasants at onerous interest rates by state functionaries and their client landholders and merchants'. Within this tributary mode of production there was little or no private property, since the peasants have 'use-ownership' of the land they live on and till. Gottwald holds that it is this 'state-initiated and state-condoned double system of incapacitation of the peasantry' that the prophets attack. The prophets, however, 'stood within social sectors of the community who suffered from this massive shift in production and allocation of

---

changes in society from the prophets' denunciations. The interpretation of Deist has been noted earlier (p. 148, n. 19).

[41] Albertz, *History*, 112, cf. 286, n. 41.
[42] *Ibid.*, 160–162.
[43] *Ibid.*, 166.

goods necessary to life', even if some of them came from the advantaged classes. Gottwald also sees the reform measures found in the Book of the Covenant and the Deuteronomic laws as representing 'periodic attempts by coalitions of government leaders, wealthy landholders, lower priests, prophets, and groups of taxed and indebted peasants to correct abuses and close the spreading gulf between exploiters and exploited.'[44]

J. L. Mays paints a somewhat similar picture. He sees the main attack of the prophets as being against economic development – the accumulation of wealth achieved by means of the monarchy and the courts, where the rights of widows, the fatherless, and the weak were ignored. The main focus of the prophets' attack was land ownership, and they made the treatment of the poor and weak the criterion for a just society.[45] He relies on a relatively small number of passages, however, especially from Amos. The other prophets did have a concern for the poor, but it does not seem to have been as central or as dominant as is often supposed. Milton Schwantes points out that Amos and Hosea prophesied within a few years of each other, yet Hosea does not use any of the main words for poor, and in all the prophets those oppressed are not the totally impoverished, but rather peasants who have fallen on hard times.[46]

If this reconstruction is at all valid, it suggests that the prophets were not concerned with poverty as such, but rather with the situation in society which favoured the rich and pressed heavily on the peasant farmers. In a sense, it was the *changes* in society, and the *oppression of the powerless* which disturbed them, rather than the fact of absolute poverty. It is possible that they had as little time for the 'feckless poor' as the wisdom writers had.

(c) The Wisdom Writers

Job stands much closer to the care of the poor as revealed in the law codes than the other writers. Chapters 29–31 present Job's final appeal to God. As he looks back at the time when he was a prosperous and highly respected member of society, he sees a major feature of his goodness in the way he 'delivered the poor who cried, and the fatherless who had none to help him' (Job 29.12). His support of 'him who was about to perish' brought blessing, and he caused the widow's heart to 'sing for joy'. He was 'eyes to the blind', 'feet to the lame', and 'a father to the poor', and he defended the powerless against their oppressors (Job 29.13–17). Since he expected this to lead to lifelong prosperity he clearly holds his actions to be in accordance with God's

[44] Norman K. Gottwald, 'Sociology', 84–85. See also his earlier article 'Tribal Existence'.
[45] James Luther Mays, 'Justice'.
[46] Schwantes, *Das Recht der Armen*.

will, but equally he regards wealth and honour as rewards for goodness. In his great oath of clearance, he sets out in a negative way the things which he had done: listening to the complaint of his servants (or slaves), whom he accepted as equally created by God, not withholding anything from the poor that they needed or adding to the widow's grief ('making the widow's eye grow dim with tears', REB), sharing his food with the fatherless, providing clothing for the poor and destitute, not using his power against the fatherless, and welcoming resident aliens and travellers into his home (Job 31.13–21, 32). The reverse of this can be seen in some of the (false) accusations which Eliphaz makes against him as an explanation of his severe suffering. He exerted his power, stripping the naked of their clothing, refusing water to the weary and bread to the starving, sending widows away empty-handed, and giving no support to the fatherless (Job 22.6–7, 9). Among the sins of the wicked which Job lists are taking the orphan's donkey and the widow's ox, jostling the poor out of the way (with an extended account of their poverty and suffering, searching for food, without clothes at night, drenched by the rain without shelter, having to work with meagre pay and refused any of the wine they press out), and taking the children of the poor as pledges (Job 24.3–12).[47] In this the dominant theme is charity – a very enlightened and far-reaching charity, but charity none the less – rather than any realization that some of the poverty may be due to the structure of society. This is parallel to the words of the prophets in one way, but quite different in another. Job has a keen awareness of the plight of the poor as well as their powerlessness over against the rich and powerful members of society.

Although Proverbs has certain similarities to Job, it stands apart. J. David Pleins has argued that it never moves beyond giving charity to the poor, despite maintaining the traditional call for just weights and respecting land boundaries. There is no awareness that the wealth of the cities was amassed at the expense of the peasants. Rather it is assumed that poverty is inevitable, and the wise man seeks to avoid it. The motives for giving to the poor are: (1) you may suffer poverty yourself and not be helped (Prov. 21.13); (2) you will bring poverty upon yourself if you oppress the poor (22.16); and (3) charitable giving will reap a reward (Prov. 11.24). Pleins identifies the writers as the ruling élite who are ambivalent to the poor, give occasional charity, but believe that the poverty of the poor is their own fault and is due to laziness and profligacy.[48]

---

[47] Note also the conventional wisdom expressed by Elihu, that oppressors 'caused the cry of the poor (*dal*) to come to him [God], and he heard the cry of the afflicted (*ᶜᵃniyyīm*)' (Job 34.28).

[48] J. David Pleins, 'Poverty'. With this may be contrasted D. E. Gowan's view that the

R. N. Whybray, by fastening on the different collections of proverbs in the book provides a more sensitive analysis.[49] He distinguishes four types of sayings in Proverbs, behind which lie four social groups:

(a) The sentence literature (Prov. 10.1–22.16; 25–29, and the sentences in 5.15–23; 6.1–19; 24.23–24) was written or collected by persons of moderate means, mainly engaged in farming, whose attitude is conservative, and who take poverty and slavery as a normal feature of society. The poor, whatever term is used, are the destitute. They possess nothing at all, and are powerless and vulnerable. The speakers accept that life is precarious, but they regard laziness and extravagance as the main causes of poverty, which can be avoided by hard work.[50] It is a moral and religious duty to show generosity to the poor. Thus Whybray rejects the suggestions that the writers were learned scribes or belonged to schools and education. Rather the proverbs are a rich store of anonymous reflections based on experience.

(b) The instructions of Proverbs 22.17–24.22 and chapters 1–9 were written by members of the educated well-to-do, acquisitive society of the towns. They have little concern for the poor, and lack any sense of a caring community. Indeed, in chapters 1–9 there are no references to the poor at all.

(c) The words of Lemuel, King of Massa, which his mother taught him (Prov. 31.1–9), assume that the king is free to care for the welfare of the community for he is already at the top of the ladder, and he is expected to support the rights of those who cannot stand up for themselves, to judge fairly and maintain the rights of the poor and destitute.

(d) Finally, the background of the poem praising the diligent housewife (Prov. 31.10–31) is a well-to-do family, the members of which have made their way and do not need to be thrusting or ambitious. They do not forget to be generous to the poor.

Whybray concludes that the attitudes of the various writers of Proverbs are not entirely dependent on their economic status. Those striving to increase their wealth have little time for the poor, in contrast to the established wealthy members of society and the king. The small farmers do not despise wealth honestly acquired, and

---

proverbs explained why people are poor and were not claiming that poverty was deserved ('Wealth and Poverty', 348).

[49] Whybray, *Wealth and Poverty*; for a summary of his conclusions see pp. 113–118 and his earlier article 'Poverty'.

[50] Contrast Kenneth Aitken: 'Israel's sages were not so naive ... to think that poor people are mostly poor through their own fault. ... The poor people of this world are far more often the victims of the greed and folly of others than of their own folly' (*Proverbs*, 184). Whybray seems much closer to the implications of the text.

although they think that the poor deserve their fate they recognize their duty to help them.

These studies make it clear that Proverbs stands in marked contrast to the Law and the prophets. As Whybray says, it is plain that, while poverty is almost always taken for granted in the Old Testament and not regarded as an evil contrary to the will of God which can and must be abolished, in the sentence literature in Proverbs the point of view is 'static' to an exceptional degree. Although the speakers could experience a twinge of conscience, nowhere is there any thought that it can be eliminated by social action or changes in the structure of society. There is no call for social reform, and concern for the poor is limited to protecting them from exploitation and giving charity to prevent them from starving. In Whybray's words, 'What we see here is a self-portrait of a society on the whole uncritical of the *status quo*.'[51]

On the other hand, as has been noted earlier,[52] Whybray believes that the portrait of the rich (*'āšîr*) in Proverbs 10.1–22.16 and 25–29 is 'far from sympathetic'. The rich have security (Prov. 10.15; 18.11), their wealth brings them many 'friends' (who appear to love them only for their wealth, Prov. 14.20), they lord it over the poor (Prov. 22.7, cf. 18.23; 22.16), and may be dishonest (Prov. 28.6). But since wealth is regarded as desirable by the sages, the term 'rich man' (*'āšîr*) may possess overtones unknown to us. Perhaps we might infer that they belong to the groups which Whybray identifies as being behind the 'instruction' literature.[53]

Although there are these differences between Proverbs and most of the rest of the Old Testament, it is striking that it is only the wisdom literature which appears to take the poor *as poor* seriously.[54] While the

[51] Whybray, *Wealth and Poverty*, 10.

[52] See pp. 165–166 above.

[53] Whybray, *Wealth and Poverty*, 22–23. With this may be compared Habel's analysis. He detects six 'paradigms' in the Book of Proverbs: (1) in chs. 1–9 the goal of life is wisdom leading to wealth and honour, and is possible only for the élite; (2) chs. 10–15 see hard work as the way to success in life, but wealth is a dubious blessing, and the proverbs appeal to a wider audience including peasants and 'common folk'; (3) the third paradigm presents a realistic picture of a world in which injustice in society or the circumstances of life are the cause of riches or poverty; (4) chs. 28–29 portray the typically rich person who cheats and is self-centred and devious. The poor can see through him, and it is the fear of Yahweh which leads to prosperity; (5) the Thirty Sayings of the Sages 'serves as a rider' to the Prologue, warning the rich that Yahweh is on the side of the exploited poor, so that an obsession with wealth is folly; and (6) the Sayings of Agur teach that possessing great wealth and suffering great poverty are extremes to be avoided ('Wisdom, Wealth and Poverty', 47–48).

[54] T. P. Townsend's study, 'The Poor in Wisdom Literature', which includes Ben Sirach and the Wisdom of Solomon, attempts to show statistically the varied emphases upon poverty in these writings. This is questionable, but his analysis of seven topics related to the poor is suggestive and indicates further this treatment of the poor as poor.

poor are mentioned elsewhere, the emphasis there lies much more on oppression and injustice, and the singling out of resident aliens, widows and orphans is a symptom of this.

I wonder, however, whether the social divisions which Whybray traces behind the four sections of Proverbs can be determined quite as securely as he claims. After all, wisdom is part of an international movement and parallel teaching can be found in the writings from Egypt and Mesopotamia. More seriously, perhaps to move so immediately from the biblical text to the society in which that text was produced is dangerous. Moreover, it is difficult to avoid feeling that Whybray has discussed the book from a modern position which sees existence of the poor as a condemnation of society, and this issue must now be addressed.

Were the Poor a Problem?

The common view that ancient Israel reacted to poverty in ways that are very similar to our own can be documented in a large number of studies. I select six examples.

Norman W. Porteous is forthright in asserting that poverty was felt to be a real problem in the Old Testament.[55] He notes that the poor often appear in the narratives, the laws take account of them, the prophets are their champions, and the psalms contain the authentic words of the poor, even though he recognizes that in the wisdom literature poverty is sometimes regarded as culpable and indicative of laziness.

Ronald Clements, after describing the social conditions in ancient Israel, with the poor often standing very close to subsistence level and subject to many injustices, claims that 'welfare systems' operated in Israel for the relief of the poor – charitable giving, the opportunity to glean at harvest time, the levirate marriage, which he rather oddly sees as aimed at giving support and protection to the widow,[56] the introduction of a form of land tenure which enabled women to inherit land, the year of jubilee, and the tradition of permanent family inheritance. The king throughout the ancient Middle East was expected to protect the poor, especially widows and orphans. This leads up to the conclusion that 'it is as an aspect of his kingly rule that God himself fulfils the role of a compassionate fellow-citizen and looks after the cause of the poor'. There was, however, 'something of a conflict of ideologies': on the one hand it was believed that a charitable regard for the poor 'mirrored the concern of God', but against this was the

---

[55] Porteous, 'Care of the Poor'.

[56] This would be an incidental effect, but the *aim* is to provide a male heir to continue the dead brother's name (Deut. 25.6).

reality that kingship became the agency of exploitation and oppression.[57]

Lennart Boström, while admitting that poverty 'is not always treated with sympathy' in Proverbs, has a section on 'God and the weak', in which he paints a picture of God's concern for those who are defenceless, especially the poor, widows and orphans. He draws on selective texts, and compares them with a similar concern in the other writings of the Old Testament.[58]

Although Norbert F. Lohfink takes a somewhat similar line, he makes some valuable observations that suggest caution.[59] He points out that the expression 'the church of the poor' is not biblical. Rather God as creator desires and wills wealth and plenty for his creatures. What today would be called the 'option for the poor' is 'certainly' found in the societies surrounding ancient Israel, where the rich were brought up to care for the poor through the education reflected in the wisdom literature, the care for the poor was a special obligation of the king, and it was believed that the gods themselves had a special love for the poor. Most of the Old Testament statements about the poor belong within this ancient Middle Eastern culture. Thus the 'option for the poor' is not in any way specifically biblical or Christian but is a universal moral thrust. In common with much Liberation theology, however, Lohfink declares that what is distinctive to Israel is the Exodus story, which reveals God actively intervening and leading the poor into freedom. The aim of God's intervention is not to alleviate their suffering while leaving the system intact (as is usual elsewhere in the ancient Middle East); instead 'the poor are removed from the impoverishing situation'.[60]

Earlier Albert Gelin asserted categorically at the beginning of his study of *The Poor of Yahweh*: 'Poverty was obviously something that shocked thoughtful Israelites.'[61] He declares that poverty was regarded as 'a scandalous condition that should never have existed in Israel' since the people was properly a brotherhood where there was no poverty. Although he recognizes that what he terms 'the law of

---

[57] Clements, 'Poverty', quotations from pp. 22, 26.

[58] Lennart Boström, *God of the Sages*, 197–212. He also compares the teaching of Proverbs with writings from Egypt and Mesopotamia.

[59] Norbert Lohfink, *Option for the Poor*; see esp. 10–12, 17–25.

[60] *Ibid.*, 39. Note, however, Lohfink's further observation that although a lofty ethics of caring for the poor can be traced all over the ancient Middle East, the poor are not mentioned in any of the law codes, in contrast to the prologues and epilogues to those codes ('Poverty', 34–38). This seems to rely too much on vocabulary, although Lohfink admits that a few laws 'make a distant approach to the topic of the problems of the poor'. F. Charles Fensham argues that so widespread across the whole ancient Middle East is the policy of protection of the poor that rather than thinking of borrowing by Israel we should see it as inherited ('Widow').

[61] Albert Gelin, *The Poor of Yahweh*, 15.

temporal retribution' led to wealth being seen as a clear proof that the just were rewarded and hence the sages frequently declare that the poor are themselves to blame for their poverty, he holds that 'the confrontation of the poor just man and the wicked rich man' was a problem which had to be solved in the Day of Yahweh (Ps. 36) or the next world (Ps. 72).[62]

My final example is Leslie J. Hoppe, who claims he has examined every text where 'the poor' is found and draws two general conclusions. He accepts that there is diversity within the Hebrew Bible, but claims that 'the tradition is unanimous in asserting that material, economic poverty is a scandal, that it should not exist, that it is not in accord with the divine will'. Moreover, it is the result of human decisions, sometimes those of the poor themselves, but predominantly arising from the avarice and greed of the wealthy. 'There is no question that the biblical tradition recognizes the evil of economic oppression ... [and] affirms that God is the protector of those who are unjustly deprived of their access to the bounty of the earth and the fruits of their labor.' Secondly, he accepts that the tradition finds the experience of the poor an apt metaphor for the universal need of salvation, but adds that it never denies the evil of material poverty, and never suggests that poverty and oppression should be ignored in favour of 'spiritual poverty'.[63]

Hoppe may assert that this is beyond question, but T. R. Hobbs raises just these questions. He argues that our concern for the poor and our conviction that poverty is 'wrong' are due to our modern awareness of the 'Third World' (or the Two-Thirds World, as we are now taught to describe it), and of the existence of poverty in our own society.[64] Proverbs and Psalms come from the powerful centre of a society where riches were accepted as a matter of course. The proverb 'Riches and honour are with me, enduring wealth and prosperity' (Prov. 8.18) reveals this attitude very clearly. In a most important observation he says that since 'the poor' and 'the rich' are economic terms, dealing with value and exchange, it is important to understand what was valued in ancient Israelite society, and he thinks it was honour and social status, not primarily money or property or even political power.

This seems to be correct. In ancient Israel poverty was a misfortune not a problem. No one, not even the prophets, thought of it as due to

---

[62] *Ibid.*, 25. It is to be noted that Gelin's thesis is that there was a movement in the Old Testament towards 'poor' meaning 'poor in spirit'. He finds the turning point in Zephaniah.

[63] Leslie J. Hoppe, *Being Poor*, 175–176.

[64] T. R. Hobbs, 'Reflections on "the poor"'. He is highly critical of such studies as that of L. Hoppe, which he regards as an example of 'using the ancient world as a springboard for a larger political polemic' (quoting Moses Finley).

the 'structures of society' in any self-conscious way. The prophets were essentially conservatives, looking back to an older, stable society and condemning those who transgressed against the traditional norms of justice. In the same way that war, the position of women, and the treatment of animals were not 'problems' in ancient Israel, neither was the existence of the poor.

Alongside this assessment may be set Donald E. Gowan's study of wealth and poverty in the Old Testament. He fastens on Zechariah 7.9–10 as presenting 'an adequate, brief summary of the social message of the prophets' and providing 'the Old Testament's typical description of the nature of a healthy community', with its positive qualities (justice, loyalty and compassion) and four disadvantaged groups.[65] He points out that not all widows, orphans and resident aliens were poor. What all four groups had in common was their precarious social status, and in the Old Testament what is most often addressed is not hunger or lack of shelter but their inability to maintain their rights. Almost all Israelites were living at a subsistence level, and hard work was required to survive. Gowan asserts that the Old Testament writers held that there were ways of dealing with the problems of being hungry, ill-clothed and homeless, but they raged against the injustice which the members of these groups were powerless to prevent. The Old Testament does not present equality of wealth as an ideal. The aim of most of the motive clauses attached to the laws concerning the powerless, however, appears to be to remind and persuade those with power that the powerless are people like them, and are worthy of respect. Thus the Old Testament attitude towards the powerless is not that abundance should be shared with the needy, but rather it insists that in a sense every Israelite is among the needy, since they are all resident aliens in a land that belongs to God.[66]

We may conclude, then that the poor lacked power and honour, and were often subjected to oppression – and attempts were made to prevent them from starving and to secure justice for them. Both were seen to be important and in accord with obedience to God, but it is

---

[65] Donald E. Gowan, 'Wealth and Poverty', 341. He makes the interesting observation that a further disadvantaged group would be the disabled, but the Old Testament law shows little concern for these (cf. Lev. 19.14; Deut. 27.18; Job 29.15), and for the most part alleviation of their condition is reserved for eschatology (p. 344).

[66] With this assessment may be compared J. Emmette Weir, 'The Poor are Powerless'. David H. Engelhard usefully discusses concern for widows, orphans and resident aliens, but does not adequately distinguish between these groups and 'the poor' although he recognizes that they are distinct categories ('Motivated Concern', see p. 5). See also James Limburg, 'Human Rights', which, however, is a further example of a selective approach to the Old Testament, driven by a desire to show that it supports modern 'human rights' and 'option for the poor' attitudes.

quite false to suppose that the Israelites thought that God was 'on the side of' the poor and was hostile to the rich. Wealth and honour were the signs of his favour, and the rich had a duty towards the poor. It was the task of the king to protect widows, orphans, resident aliens and the poor, particularly by ensuring that they obtained justice. Most of the biblical writers held that God protected the poor, though he protected them from injustice rather than by putting an end to their poverty by reordering society. Job, however, stands apart in questioning this. Against two references to God's concern for the poor in the speeches of Eliphaz and Elihu (Job 5.15–16 and 34.28), are to be set Job's account of injustices in chapter 24 and his description of the way the powerful oppress the poor, ending with his bitter: 'yet God pays no attention to their prayer' (v. 12).

I pointed out at the beginning of this chapter that one strand of modern Christian theology singles out the Exodus as the paradigm of God's protection and deliverance of the poor. This also needs to be questioned. No one can doubt the dominance of the Exodus theme throughout the Old Testament (apart from the wisdom writings). In word and worship it recurs again and again. But the extent to which it relates to the poor is limited.

We turn first to references to the Exodus in the motive clauses. This is commonly (and rightly) regarded as a unique feature of the biblical laws. But such clauses are never attached to laws concerning the poor in general. In the Book of the Covenant they follow calls to protect resident aliens, 'for you were strangers ($g\bar{e}r\bar{\imath}m$) in the land of Egypt' (Ex. 22.20[21]; 23.9), to the second of which is added 'you know the heart of a stranger ($g\bar{e}r$)'. In Deuteronomy the exhortation to supply a freed slave with the means of a livelihood is supported with 'you shall remember that you were a slave in the land of Egypt, and the LORD your God redeemed you' (Deut. 15.15). The law against perverting the justice due to the resident alien is extended to the fatherless and the widow and is supported by the statement 'you shall remember that you were a slave in Egypt and the LORD your God redeemed you from there' (Deut. 24.18), repeated later in relation to leaving gleanings of olives and grapes for the same three groups (Deut. 24.22). All three of these Deuteronomic motive clauses are followed by the comprehensive 'therefore I command you to do this' (cf. Deut. 16.12). In the paraenetic introduction to the Deuteronomic laws we find: 'He (Yahweh) executes justice for the fatherless and the widow, and loves the sojourner, giving him food and clothing. Love the sojourner, therefore; for you were sojourners in the land of Egypt' (Deut. 10.18–19).[67] The connection with the resident alien recurs in the

---

[67] A further attractive reference is Deut. 23.8[7], where the Egyptians are not to be regarded as an 'abomination' because the Israelites were resident aliens in Egypt.

Holiness Code: he must not be wronged, he is to be treated in the same way as native Israelites, and 'you shall love him as yourself; for you were strangers in the land of Egypt' (Lev. 19.34). At the end of this chapter RSV links 'I am the LORD your God, who brought you out of the land of Egypt' to the demand for correct weights and measures, but the clause is more naturally regarded as forming a conclusion to this collection of laws, joined more closely to the following demand to keep all of Yahweh's statutes and commandments (as NJB). Finally within the law of the jubilee, the commands concerning debt slaves conclude with a rather different application of the Exodus theme: 'For to me the people of Israel are servants (REB 'slaves'), they are my servants whom I brought forth out of the land of Egypt: I am the LORD your God' (Lev. 25.55).

The point is obvious. The references to Egypt are invoked because they are linked with laws concerning resident aliens and slaves. The oppressed groups are then extended to include other persons who were liable to be oppressed and to suffer injustice, such as widows and the fatherless. All these groups were often also economically poor (though resident aliens were not always so), but this is not the significant fact about them which is highlighted by the Exodus motive clauses. The Exodus is *never* introduced as a motive for caring for the poor as such.

This is supported by a second observation. None of the words for poor is ever used of the Israelites in Egypt. They enter the country with their flocks and herds. They are well treated by the Egyptians at first and flourish. The later oppression by the Egyptians is because they are 'too many and too mighty for us' (Ex. 1.9), and they then force them into slavery. They are very much the typical *gērīm*, subject to the whim of the host people, and their experience is very similar to that of the foreigners who have settled in Israel and whose plight the law attempts to alleviate.

Those who see in the Exodus the central Old Testament teaching about God's 'option for the poor' make two unjustified moves. First they interpret the condition of the Israelites in Egypt as economic poverty, and secondly they treat the Exodus deliverance as the ending of that poverty by overturning the structural features of society which they claim are its cause. Neither of these is valid.[68]

While the link between the Exodus and God's care for the poor is to be rejected, this does not mean that that care is absent from the Old Testament. It is there, and this has already been clearly seen. But it is not a care which has as its main object the lifting of the poor out of their poverty. Chiefly it comprises a demand not to oppress those who

---

[68] Compare the carefully nuanced discussion by Walter Vogels ('"Haves" and "Have-nots"').

are powerless (hence the frequent mention of resident aliens, widows and orphans as well as simple references to 'the poor'). Alongside this is a call for charity to be given to the poor and help to those who have fallen on hard times, and in this are included such features as the release of debts and the freeing of debt slaves in the seventh year, and the more idealistic jubilee.

Deuteronomy is ambivalent about the continued existence of the poor within Israel. On the one hand there is the promise 'there will be no poor among you . . . if only you will obey the voice of the LORD your God' and keep his commandments (Deut. 15.4–5), and on the other (and implied for most of the time) 'the poor will never cease out of the land' (Deut. 15.11). There is a similar ambivalence running through the rest of the Old Testament. It is expected that goodness will be rewarded, and that the righteous poor will rise from their poverty. Indeed, the poor may be destitute because of their own failure to work hard, or more harshly, because their poverty is the punishment for their wickedness. On the other hand, there is a continual call to treat them with compassion and give them charity, because God himself is compassionate towards all his children. It is recognized in the law that means have to be found for making food and financial provision for those who are destitute through such means as the right of gleaning (Deut. 24.19–21; Lev. 19.9–10), the spontaneous harvest of the fallow year (Ex. 23.11), the tithe of the third year (Deut. 14.29), and readiness to lend to the poor without interest (Ex. 22.24[25]; Lev 25.35–37).[69] What is *not* found is a belief that the presence of the poor in society is somehow 'wrong', and that society itself must be changed to remove poverty from its midst. It is accepted that there will be rich and poor, powerful and weak, those who possess prestige and those lacking in honour. The main concern is to see that those who are vulnerable are protected.

In one sense, therefore, the ethics of poverty is subsumed under that of oppression. To treat that subject adequately, however, would require another chapter at least as long as the present one, and this is clearly impossible to accommodate in the present work.[70] It can simply be noted that it is not only the destitute who are liable to be oppressed and concern for those who suffer oppression is found in all the types of biblical literature, law, prophets, wisdom, psalms, and narrative.

---

[69] David H. Engelhard holds that the welcoming of the resident aliens, orphans, widows and slaves to the Feasts of Weeks and Tabernacles was a further indication that those financially poor were not to be excluded because they could not make expensive gifts and therefore a further indication of caring for the poor. It is doubtful whether economic issues entered here ('Motivated Concern', 16).

[70] See Jacques Pons, *L'Oppression*; Thomas D. Hanks, *Vocabulary of Oppression*.

15

WAR

As we have seen, T. R. Hobbs warns us against assuming that ancient Israel regarded the existence of the poor as a problem. He had earlier made the same point about war: 'It is clear from a reading of the Old Testament itself that the act of war was *not* a problem for the ancient Israelites . . . there is no evidence to suggest that warfare *per se* is regarded as even a necessary evil. It is taken for granted as a part of life.'[1]

Two broad views about war have emerged. One emphasizes the extent of war throughout the Old Testament and its brutality. What, we are asked, is to be made of a book which advocates genocide and ethnic cleansing? It is a question that is difficult to meet, and it leads very easily to a Marcionite view of the Bible. The other approach admits the prevalence of war in the Old Testament, but seeks to explain and justify it, and even to find a peace message in it. The differences spring from differing exegesis, differing emphases, and some picking and choosing among the biblical texts.[2] Yet as Hobbs emphasizes, both approaches are controlled by the writers' own presuppositions. We look first at the evidence from the historical books.[3]

The Evidence from the Histories
The Old Testament can easily appear to be the most bloodthirsty of all the sacred scriptures within the great religious traditions. Only Ruth and the Song of Songs are completely free from battles, and even in the Song war imagery seems to be used. Somewhat grotesquely in our eyes, the neck of the beloved is likened to 'the tower of David, built

---

[1] T. R. Hobbs, *War*, 17.
[2] For an account of a wider spread of views see P. D. Hanson who lists (a) 'the Bible is simply consigned to the category of primitive, violent literature without value for the morally sensitive modern individual'; (b) 'the Bible admonishes the righteous nation today to be sure that God is on its side in its preparations to destroy godless adversaries'; (c) 'God the warrior leading the faithful into conflict is to be understood in spiritual terms as a call to personal piety'; (d) Israel's wars were defensive; (e) the biblical accounts express 'the model of the miraculous war in which the deity fights without human participation' ('War', 32–45).
[3] For a classic survey of war in ancient Israel see Roland de Vaux, *Ancient Israel*, Part III, Military Institutions.

for an arsenal,[4] whereon hang a thousand bucklers, all of them shields of warriors' (Song 4.4). Her beauty is 'terrible as an army with banners' (6.4, 10),[5] while the 'little sister' is a wall, upon which the lovers will build 'a battlement of silver' (8.9–10). It is a curious fact that more is known about weapons, military campaigns, and the ideology of war than about almost any other topic, so dominant is warfare.

A rapid survey of the outline story contained in the Old Testament will illustrate this. The Exodus liberation may not quite accurately be termed a conflict between Yahweh and the pharaoh, but the destruction of the Egyptian armies in the Red Sea is depicted as Yahweh's victory. In the Song of Moses Yahweh is praised as 'a man of war' (Ex. 15.3), and this remains his character throughout the Old Testament.

The Exodus is followed by the conquest of Canaan in a series of highly aggressive military campaigns. The capture and total destruction of Jericho and Ai, with all their inhabitants, is followed by victories over the Amorites in the south of the country and the Canaanites in the north (Josh. 6–8; 10–11). Current scholarship is divided in its reconstructions of the course of historical events between theories of conquest,[6] gradual infiltration by nomadic or semi-nomadic peoples,[7] and a peasant revolt.[8] Many scholars now doubt whether any firm history can be reconstructed on the basis of the biblical narratives.[9] Thomas L. Thompson comments: 'One of the things the Bible almost never is, however, is intentionally historical . . . The Bible's language is not an historical language. It is a language of high literature, of story, of sermon and of song.'[10] For our present purposes it is sufficient to recall the way in which the narratives present the history, for this is how those who wrote and edited them pictured God's plan for his chosen people.

The book of Judges is equally a book of wars, although now they are mainly defensive – against Eglon of Moab (Jdg. 3), Sisera (Jdg. 4–5), the Midianites (Jdg. 6–8), and the Ammonites (Jdg. 10.6–12.7). By contrast to these actions the attack on Laish is the saddest and most

---

[4] Or 'built in courses' (NRSV, similarly REB). Marvin H. Pope gives a full discussion (*Song*, 465–469).

[5] This is a renowned crux, with two rare words. REB renders it 'majestic as the starry heavens' while Marvin H. Pope, adopts 'awesome with trophies', with an extensive note (*Song*, 551 and 560–563), and HALOT offers 'terrifying' and 'row of flags'.

[6] Championed by W. F. Albright and his school.

[7] Associated with Albrecht Alt and Martin Noth.

[8] So George E. Mendenhall and Norman K. Gottwald.

[9] See, e.g., Philip R. Davies, *In Search of 'Ancient Israel'*, 60–70; Niels Peter Lemche, *Ancient Israel*, 104–117; Gösta W. Ahlström, *History*, 28, 286, 343–349. For a critique see Ferdinand E. Deist, *Material Culture*, 57–77.

[10] Thomas L. Thompson, *Bible in History*, 99.

horrifying of all. Its inhabitants were living quietly and in peace, troubling no one and expecting no attacks, and they were therefore easily overpowered and annihilated by the Danites, and the writer sees this as divine providence (Jdg. 18.7–10, 27–29).

Wars against the Philistines follow and persist throughout the reign of Saul. Not until the time of David were they finally defeated (see 1 Sam. 4–7; 11; 13–15; 31; 2 Sam. 8.1; 21.15–22; 23.9–17). David then carries out a series of conquests of the surrounding peoples, often with great cruelty and ruthlessness. Two thirds of the captured Moabites were killed, horses were hamstrung, twenty-two thousand Syrians and eighty thousand Edomites were slain. Later there is an account of the slaughter of seven hundred charioteers and forty thousand horsemen (2 Sam. 5.6-10; 8.2–14; 10.1–11.1; for the present purpose the question of possible exaggeration of the numbers is irrelevant. The writer glories in the large number of the enemy who are killed.). There is no hint of any criticism of David's military zeal, apart from the explanation of his failure to build the temple, although the implication here may be that he had no time until God had subdued all his enemies (1 Kgs. 5.3, but contrast 1 Chron. 22.7–10; 28.3). Wars still dominate the narratives in the books of Kings, though defeats are now more prominent than victories, and the destruction of Northern Israel and Judah and Jerusalem occupies much of the story.

Here is one of the greatest difficulties for the modern reader of the Bible. Before all this is dismissed out of hand three issues need to be addressed.

(a) The Way the Israelites Thought of War
The Old Testament refers to 'the wars of Yahweh' (Num. 21.14), and right from the time of the Exodus Yahweh is depicted as fighting on the side of the Israelites. It is he who gives them victory, not the prowess of the warriors, so that the number of men on the field of battle does not affect the outcome. Gideon is told deliberately to reduce the army he has collected (Jdg. 7.4–7). If the support of Yahweh was crucial for victory, we may ask, Did this mean that war itself was regarded as a religious activity?[11] It leads us directly to the question of 'holy war'. Von Rad presented a schematized reconstruction,[12] its main features being:

1. Before hostilities began Yahweh was consulted, often by means of the sacred lot, sometimes through a prophet (Jdg. 20.18, 23, 28; 1 Sam. 14.36–37; 23.2, 4; 30.7–8; 1 Kgs. 22.5).

---

[11] Cf. Robert P. Carroll: 'War was not only politics continued by other means, it was also religion in practice' ('War', 163).
[12] Gerhard von Rad, *Holy War*. He sets out the theory in a rather different way from that which I have adopted (pp. 40–51).

2. Sacrifices might be offered (1 Sam. 13.8–9).

3. The warriors were 'consecrated', in particular they had to avoid contact with women (1 Sam. 21.6[5]; 2 Sam. 11.11; Isa. 13.3).

4. A trumpet was sounded and the cry went up, 'Yahweh has delivered the enemy into our hands' (Jdg. 3.27–28; 6.34; 7.15; 1 Sam. 13.3).

5. It was believed that Yahweh marched ahead of the army and gave the victory. The symbol of his presence was the ark, which was sometimes taken on the battlefield (Josh. 10.11; Jdg. 4.14; 5.20–21; 2 Sam. 5.24; Josh. 3.6, 11; 6.6–7; 1 Sam. 4).

6. Yahweh threw the enemy into a panic (Josh. 10.10; 1 Sam. 5.11; 7.10; 14.15).

7. After victory the spoil was regarded as belonging to Yahweh. It could not be seized by the Israelites and was totally destroyed, though valuable goods were sometimes placed in the sanctuary. There was a special word for this (*ḥērem*, 'the ban'), and the practice played an important part in the conquest of Canaan (cf. Josh. 6.17–24; 7.10–26; 1 Sam. 15.1–33). It is not to be interpreted as sheer bloodlust, even though all war involves indiscriminate and wholesale killing, but reflects devotion to Yahweh. The practice was not unique to Israel, however, and is found in the inscription of Mesha, the King of Moab, who 'devoted' (the same word) seven thousand men and women to Chemosh, his god.

Despite considerable debate and criticism,[13] largely on the grounds that the term 'holy war' does not occur in the Old Testament and von Rad's construction is abstracted from different sources from various dates, it represents some of the main features of war as idealized in the Old Testament, especially in Deuteronomy, where it accords with a determination to eliminate everything which was Canaanite (cf. Deut. 2.33–35; 7.1–5, 16; 13.16–18[15–17]; 20.10–18).[14] Whether the practice was actually carried out or not (and the Mesha inscription suggests that it probably was, at least on some occasions, although Deuteronomy and the Deuteronomistic histories are aware that Israel often failed to practise it), the ban is an important feature in the way ancient Israel thought about war.

(b) Yahweh as a Warrior

It has already been observed that Yahweh is described as a 'man of war' in the hymn of praise at the Red Sea (Ex. 15.3; the title occurs

---

[13] Among the immense literature may be mentioned Norman K. Gottwald, '"Holy War"'; id., 'War, Holy'; Gwilym H. Jones, '"Holy War"'; and Ollenburger's Introduction to the English translation of von Rad's study. For Gottwald's sociological discussion of *ḥērem* see *Tribes of Yahweh*, 543–550.

[14] Gottwald, '"Holy War"' provides a good survey of the legal material in Deuteronomy and especially the ban. On the ban see also Charles Sherlock, *HRM* .

also in Isa. 42.13). In Ps. 24, a psalm which appears to have been part of an elaborate liturgy at the Jerusalem temple, Yahweh is acclaimed as 'mighty in battle'. In the Song of Moses, Yahweh is depicted as setting himself up as a warrior (Deut. 32.41–42), while a similar image lies behind the grim picture of the destruction of Israel's enemies in Isa. 34, where Yahweh presides over a sacrifice:

> The LORD has a sword; it is sated with blood,
>   it is gorged with fat,
>   with the blood of lambs and goats,
>   with the fat of the kidneys of rams.
> For the LORD has a sacrifice in Bozrah
>   a great slaughter in the land of Edom. (v. 6)

In a later section of Isaiah there is an even more terrible account of Yahweh wading in the blood of his enemies as if treading grapes in a wine-press (Isa. 63.1–6). The language may be metaphorical, but it is a real victory which is given to Israel.[15]

Scholars debate the precise meaning of the title 'Yahweh of hosts', or, in fuller form, 'Yahweh, God of hosts'.[16] Some suggest that it refers to the stars, the hosts of heaven, but since it occurs in passages linked with the ark is seems more likely that the reference is to the armies of Israel (1 Sam. 1.3, 11; 4.4; 15.2; 2 Sam. 6.2), and in one passage (1 Sam. 17.45, possibly late) the actual phrase, 'God of the armies of Israel' is found. Yet the majority of occurrences are in the writings of the prophets,[17] and it has been argued that it is unlikely that they would have favoured a highly nationalistic title for God. The main difficulty with the alternative view is that 'hosts' in the plural is never used of the stars, and the prophets seem to have had no special problems with the depiction of Yahweh as a warrior.[18] Seow would seem to be correct: 'the name YHWH Seba'ot denotes God as a victorious warrior enthroned as king of the divine council. He is ever ready to fight battles with the forces of chaos. As YHWH Seba'ot fought and won the cosmogonic battle, so he fights the battles of his people in the historical realm and will fight the ultimate battle in the end time.'[19]

---

[15] See Patrick D. Miller, 'God the Warrior', 39–40 for a succinct account of the theme.

[16] C. L. Seow provides a good survey in his article 'Hosts, Lord of'. The variation in frequency across the books of the Old Testament and the syntax of the phrase should be noted.

[17] The most frequent occurrences are in Isaiah 1–39, Jeremiah (but far fewer in the LXX text), Haggai, Zechariah, Malachi, and the Psalms. It does not appear in the Torah or Ezekiel. Seow suggests that this points to links with the Zion tradition.

[18] Walther Eichrodt finds the only possibility, if the attempt to find a meaning is not abandoned altogether, is to follow the hint of the LXX, and take it as referring not to any particular 'hosts' but to 'all bodies, multitudes, masses in general, the content of all that exists in heaven and in earth' (*Theology*, I, 192–193).

[19] Seow, 'Hosts, Lord of' (*ABD* III, 307).

(c) Did Individual Groups View War Differently?

It might be expected that those at the royal court would support the waging of war. This seems to be so. None of the kings or their advisors shows any hesitation about it. Indeed, war was such a normal activity that the time of David's sin with Bathsheba is described as 'the spring of the year, the time when kings go forth to battle' (2 Sam. 11.1).

The Jerusalem cult appears to have been dominated by ideas of the defeat of the king's enemies, who are at the same time the enemies of Yahweh (cf. Pss. 2; 18; 20; 21; 82; 89; 144). National laments plead with God after defeat (cf. Pss. 44; 74; 79; 80; 83). Some scholars have proposed that many of the laments of the individual are really prayers by the king,[20] but this has been questioned. A similar division of opinion exists as to whether some or all of these psalms refer to actual war or to a ritual combat in which the king may have played a central part. It has been pointed out that in all wars the enemy is commonly derided and depicted as sub-human, and in several of the psalms the enemies are described as liars and corrupt, and as dangerous animals (cf. Pss. 144.8, 11; 22.12–13).

We might expect the common people to be opposed to wars that ravage their land and destroy their homes and their crops, for they are the ones who chiefly suffer from war, but we must be careful not to impose modern ideas upon ancient Israel. Certainly there are grim scenes of the suffering of ordinary people, with women resorting to cannibalism (2 Kgs. 6.26–29; Jer. 14.16; 19.9). Nevertheless, there seems to have been little opposition to the wars which the kings wage. Indeed, the morale among the inhabitants of Jerusalem at the time of Sennacherib's siege is depicted as very high (2 Kgs. 18.36).

How far it is possible to recover the prophets as historical individuals from the material recorded in the books of the 'latter prophets' is currently questioned. This is part of the larger problem of the relation between the biblical writings and 'ancient Israel', and cannot be pursued here. The following paragraphs should be taken as expressing the views of those who compiled the prophetic books.

The prophets are presented as standing apart from the court and are closer to the sufferings of the people. It is important, therefore, to examine carefully what their attitude is. Occasionally they oppose foreign alliances – but on the ground that the king should trust in Yahweh rather than because of the evils of war (Isa. 30.1–7; 31.1–3). Samuel is depicted as supporting the war against the Philistines (1 Sam. 7.5–14). Elisha aided the Israelite armies against Syria and

---

[20] See especially J. H. Eaton, *Kingship*, who sees the enemies of the king as God's enemies, for the king is the unique representative of God and God's people, a view akin to that of the Assyrian kings (*Kingship*, 137–141).

Moab (2 Kgs. 3.13–20; 6.8–23). Within the later part of the book of Isaiah the prophet looks for the defeat of Babylon (Isa. 47, cf. 42.13; 51.9–10).

Several of the prophets see foreign enemies as the means by which God punishes Israel. Isaiah points to the Assyrians, and his later condemnation of them is for their arrogance rather than their cruelty (Isa. 10.5–19). Jeremiah regards the Babylonians as the agents of God's punishment. His letter to the exiles urging them to pray for the welfare of Babylon (Jer. 29.7) must be interpreted in the light of this, rather than as a prophecy in support of peace in our sense. Many of the collections of oracles contain prophecies against the nations (Amos 1.1–2.3; Isa. 13–19; 21–23; Jer. 46–51; Ezek. 25–32; cf. Nahum and Obadiah). The main scholarly discussions centre on questions of date and authenticity, and few examine their ethical significance.[21] Whether they originate in war situations, where the prophet is called upon to curse Israel's enemies (cf. Num. 22–24), or in the cult, where the enemies of God are identified as the enemies of Israel (cf. Ps. 60.8–11[6–9]), is disputed. From the perspective of the ethics of war, it must be noted that these oracles find no problem with war and generally seek the downfall of the enemy nations.

It is true that Amos condemns atrocities in war, and seems to assume that everyone will agree on this, even those outside of Israel, but his main message is of a national disaster as punishment for Israel's sins, which may come through military defeat as well as other means. It is difficult to find any texts where war itself is condemned, even if some of the prophets oppose 'expansionist' policies. War is a fact of life. Some, however, find a 'critique of war' in writings of the prophets and elsewhere in the Old Testament and to this we turn before examining the 'oracles of peace'.

A Critique of War?

The sub-heading is taken from Susan Niditch's impressive study, *War in the Hebrew Bible*.[22] Hosea's declaration that Yahweh instructed him to name his eldest son Jezreel, 'for yet a little while, and I will punish the house of Jehu for the blood of Jezreel, and I will put an end to the kingdom of the house of Israel' (Hos. 1.4), is seen as 'a criticism of ban-like activities', though the RSV translation is not the only meaning that may be found in Hosea's highly allusive oracle and it may well be that Hosea is not to be seen as adopting a higher ethics than that of the earlier support for Jehu's revolt (e.g., 2 Kgs. 10.30).[23]

---

[21] Apart from the commentaries see John H. Hayes, 'Oracles against Foreign Nations' and John Barton, *Amos's Oracles*.

[22] Susan Niditch, *War*, 136. See the whole discussion 136–149, and cf. 132–133.

[23] See the very full discussion in Francis I. Andersen and David Noel Freedman,

The oracles of Amos 1–2, according to Niditch, are 'a powerful critique of the ideology of expediency': seeking territorial gain does not justify terror, treaties should be honoured, war against kin is improper, excessive fury in fighting and atrocities are wrong. Amos sought to limit war. Further, Chronicles presents a more extended critique and provides 'an ideology of non-participation'. Niditch points to such features as the omission of some of David's cruelties, the elimination of the attempt of the Israelites to put the Canaanites to the ban (2 Chron. 8.7–8, cf. 1 Kgs. 9.20–21), the depiction of Solomon as a leader of peace. Moreover the Chronicler stresses that God helps the weak Israelites and miraculously wins them victory. Even she has to admit, however, that peace is often victory in war, and the result of 'great slaughter' (2 Chron. 13.12–17). It is 'a late biblical tradition groping toward peace'.[24]

More generally Niditch finds threads of opposition to war and its evils running through the ideologies of war that she has traced in the Old Testament writings. The ban, with its concept of God's portion, sacrificed to him, was an attempt to distance human beings from the responsibility for the killing, and its ideology, which seeks to justify killing by emphasizing the sin of the enemy, 'shouts of self-doubt', but this overlooks the fact that demonizing of the enemy has been a feature of all wars down to the present. In any case to see the ban as in some way absolving the warriors from the killing is most improbable. Niditch thinks that the ritual cleansing required of those engaged in war in Numbers 31 'may well admit of guilt concerning killing in war', but this fails to recognize that the issue here is ritual purity not guilt. She claims that the bardic tradition, seen in such phrases as 'man of valour', the combat between David and Goliath and war as sport in 2 Samuel 2.12–16, reveals 'a code of fair play, limitation, and reciprocity', and provides 'a model for a more secular just-war tradition', but even if these are features of the tradition (which is doubtful) war as it was actually waged, and indeed as it is described in some of these bardic passages, does not accord with these high ideals. Niditch concludes that only the ideology of expediency lacks any critique of killing in war.

How far this is special pleading will doubtless be judged differently by each reader. Niditch herself points to contrasting attitudes. Alongside recording that during the recital of the plagues in the Passover *seder* her grandfather shed tears for the Egyptians, she quotes Rabbinic commentaries which gloat over their sufferings. The

---

Hosea, 176–182. Notably they find the sin of the kings of Hosea's own day as precisely the sin of the Omrides, so that the oracle means that 'what God did to Ahab and his brood by means of Jehu is exactly what he will now do to Jeroboam and his family, *and for similar reasons*' (p. 181, their italics).

[24] Niditch, *War*, 132–133, 139–149; quotation, p. 149.

concessions which she is forced to admit largely undercut her arguments. The main value of her study (apart from the suggestive identification of seven ideologies of war and its comprehensive examination of the relevant texts) lies in its underlining of the many different strands within the Old Testament, often contradictory and impossible to harmonize into a single 'Old Testament teaching on war'. And while some opposition to the excesses of war may be found, it is doubtful whether the possible critiques are anything like as strong or as obvious as Niditch claims. The dominant view is surely that which she terms 'the ideology of expediency', which, in her own words, 'treats war as business as usual'.[25] And if this is true, then Hobbs is closer to the truth than Niditch will allow.

Prophecies of Peace
Against this background the well-known prophecies of peace need to be examined carefully, since they are the main evidence for finding teaching that accords with modern ethical ideas.

In Isaiah 9.2–7 one title of the future king is 'prince of peace'. As we shall see, 'peace' (*šālōm*) has very different connotations from our English word, and while it may include absence of war, its dominant meaning is represented much better by 'prosperity'. It is probable that there are links between this prophecy and the Jerusalem cult, and there are close resemblances to Ps. 72. Even if the prosperity is linked with 'peace' in our sense, it is achieved by the defeat of Israel's enemies. The joy is akin to the delight of the victors as they divide the spoil taken in war (cf. Ps. 119.162; 1 Sam. 30.16; 31.8; 2 Chron. 20.25).

Isaiah 11.1–9 looks rather more hopeful as a peace programme: the messiah will inaugurate an age of universal peace. Even here, however, caution signs must be set up. The leader will 'smite the earth with the rod of his mouth' and 'slay the wicked'. Since he is a Davidic messiah and cultic themes are present, it is not improbable that the 'wicked' are Israel's enemies. Certainly they are conceived as the enemies of Yahweh. This is not a prophecy of reconciliation but of the annihilation of the opponents. Moreover, as we shall see,[26] the paradisal age in which there is peace between the animals is achieved by turning the wild beasts of prey into domestic animals, no longer carnivorous.

The prophecy in Isaiah 2.2–4 and Micah 4.1–4 is probably the only prophecy which genuinely looks beyond the present age of warfare and hostility to a time when all peoples will live in peace and no longer feel the need to defend themselves. The house of the LORD is

[25] Niditch, *War*, 154.
[26] Chapter 16 below.

established on the highest mountain and all the nations come to it in order to receive his teaching.

> For out of Zion shall go forth the law,
>   and the word of the LORD from Jerusalem.
> He shall judge between many peoples,
>   and shall decide for strong nations afar off;
> and they shall beat their swords into ploughshares,
>   and their spears into pruning hooks;
> nation shall not lift up sword against nation,
>   neither shall they learn war any more;
> but they shall sit every man under his vine
>   and under his fig tree,
>   and none shall make them afraid.

Here is the vision of true peace, when weapons will no longer be needed and the only use of bronze or iron will be for making agricultural tools. The nations will not learn war any more. The additional verse in Micah (quoted above) confirms this picture: the fear of enemies ravaging the land, of which the peasant always went in dread, is finally to be banished.

Although 'in the latter days' clearly shows that this is a hope for the future, the additions in both Isaiah and Micah seem to direct the readers to the present. What is a vision is to be acted upon according to the exhortation in Isaiah 2.5:

> O house of Jacob,
>   come, let us walk
>   in the light of the LORD.

Micah 4.5 draws a contrast between the nations, who still follow the ways of their own gods, and the Israelites, who declare their determination to live in the present in accordance with the vision.

Zechariah is the only prophet to look beyond war to a new era of peace in the land of Judah, a time when old men and women will sit in Jerusalem watching children play. Yet even this comes ultimately because Israel's enemies have been quelled (Zech. 8.1–13). There is a glimmer of a better age. Foreigners will seek Yahweh and will therefore come in peace to Jerusalem. In the additions to Zechariah's words (chs. 9–14), there is the famous prophecy of the king who rides on a donkey rather than a war horse (Zech. 9.9–10), but it still has to be noted that the peace comes because the king has been 'triumphant and victorious'[27] and his 'dominion' will extend worldwide. Even this peace is 'commanded' by Yahweh. Other prophecies in this section of the book speak of war in the terms with which we have become

---

[27] Cf. REB: 'his cause is won, his victory gained'. The Hebrew is ṣaddīq wᵉnōšaʿ hūʾ.

familiar: Yahweh will sound his trumpet and march out as a warrior, and in this way will 'save' his people (Zech. 9.14–15, cf. 9.1–8; 10.5–12; 14.1–5, 12–15). Much of the imagery is akin to that of 'holy war'.

Finally from the prophets, Isaiah 19.18–25 appears to point to reconciliation between Israel, Egypt and Assyria, an almost unique hope.

Laws Regulating War

Among the law codes only Deuteronomy contains regulations for war. This is striking in view of the fact that the Deuteronomists may have been responsible for reviving the idea of 'holy war' or 'Yahweh war' and their fierce determination to destroy everything Canaanite and put people and animals to the ban.[28] Three sets of laws need to be considered.

First there are the laws which excuse certain classes of Israelite men from war service: those who have built a house and not dedicated it, who have planted a vineyard and not enjoyed the fruit, who are betrothed but have not yet taken their wives, and even those who are afraid (Deut. 20.5–8; cf. the rationalizing in 24.5). The reference to the last group should alert us to the possibility that they may not be humanitarian laws after all. We are reminded of the command to Gideon to reduce his force of warriors so that it would be clear that the victory was God's alone (Jdg. 7.2). It is likely, therefore, that the whole batch of laws belongs with the view that war is a religious activity and the real concern is to maintain the holiness of the army. Most of the groups which are singled out are those who have begun tasks but have not completed them. In a sense, therefore, they are not full warriors. To us it might seem that they will have only half their mind on the war and will lower the morale of the fighting force. To the Israelite, however, what is at stake is holiness and dedication to Yahweh's war.

That Deuteronomy is setting up an ideal is obvious from the distinction which is made between cities in Canaan and those more distant. This difference was made in the application of the ban (Deut. 20.10–18). In 20.19–20 the laws concerning the protection of fruit trees seem to be equally idealistic, since they are disregarded in some of the historical narratives, and Elisha even encouraged the kings of Israel and Judah to cut down every good tree, stop up all the wells, and ruin every piece of land with stones in their war against Moab (2 Kgs. 3.19, 25).

Similarly the law about women captives is probably also part of the Deuteronomists' idealism. Any conflict with the earlier prohibition of

---

[28] See von Rad, *Holy War*, 115–127; *Studies in Deuteronomy*, 45–59.

marriage with Canaanite women is removed by restricting this legislation to occasions 'when you go for to war against your enemies', in other words to distant wars (Deut. 21.10–14, cf. 7.3; women were normally part of the spoils of war, cf. Jdg. 5.30; Num. 31.18). Even if these regulations did not form part of holy war, they must not be interpreted in terms of the later Christian doctrine of the 'just war'. At most they are minimal alleviations of the horrors of war. The main thrust of Deuteronomy is the exhortation to annihilate the Canaanites, seeing defeat as divine punishment. In any case, the law in Numbers 31.17–18, with its distinction between virgins and women who had had sexual experience (with non-Israelite men) adds to the likelihood that the Deuteronomic law was primarily concerned with purity. The captive who is to marry an Israelite has to shave her hair, cut her nails, and live in seclusion for a month before being married, which again belongs primarily to the realm of purity.

Shalom

A great deal is commonly made of the Hebrew word *šālōm*. Its rich connotations are extolled and it has entered into our own language through sermons and pop music.[29] Very great care, therefore, is needed in attempting to relate it to war. As an initial warning, David's question to Uriah concerning the *šālōm* of Joab, the *šālōm* of the people, and the *šālōm* of the war (!) should be noted (2 Sam. 11.7). What is meant is 'How is the war progressing? Are we winning?'[30]

The heart of the meaning of *šālōm* is 'welfare', 'prosperity'. It lies behind the questions about the 'peace' of someone (e.g. Gen. 43.27; Ex. 18.7), and in such passages as 2 Kgs. 5.21 it means something like, 'Is everything all right?'.[31] The natural way to translate David's anxious question about Absalom would be, 'Is the lad safe?' (2 Sam. 18.29, cf. GNB). This is also the basis of the use of *šālōm* as a greeting (e.g., 1 Sam. 17.22; 25.5–6; 30.21). Occasionally it may mean, 'Come to no harm' (as clearly in 1 Sam. 20.13; 2 Sam. 3.21–23), but normally it is simply a wish that the journey may be prosperous (as in Ex. 4.18; 1 Sam. 1.17; 2 Sam. 15.9), which can degenerate, as with our 'good-bye', into little more than a conventional phrase at parting (perhaps in 2 Kgs. 5.19, and similar places). To go to one's fathers in *šālōm* is an euphemism for dying a quiet death (Gen. 15.15; 1 Kgs. 2.6; 2 Kgs. 22.20; Jer. 34.5).

[29] How easily even a good scholar can be misled by modern attitudes is shown by A. E. Harvey's discussion in *Demanding Peace*, 1–13. It is striking that he complains that the REB 'fails to reproduce the sense of the Hebrew word *shalom*' in 1 Sam. 25.6 ('Prosperity to yourself, your household, and all that is yours!'), when it does precisely this (p. 129, n. 2).

[30] Cf. REB: 'How the campaign was going'.

[31] Cf. REB: 'Is something wrong?' and GNB: 'Is anything wrong?'

We turn to those instances when *šālōm* stands in some relation to war. To return 'in *šālōm*' means to come back 'victorious', as when Gideon threatens the men of Penuel with retribution after he has defeated the Midianites, and both the King of Israel and Micaiah mean the same (Jdg. 8.9, 2 Sam. 19.25[24], 31[30]; 1 Kgs. 22.27–28; 1 Chron. 12.18; similar overtones are probably found in such passages as Isa. 41.3; Jer. 38.4; 43.12). When peace is secured after war it is because the conqueror has succeeded in crushing his enemies. Subjugation of the foe is what is desired (cf. Jdg. 21.13; Mic. 5.5). The Deuteronomists say that *šālōm* must be offered to the city that is attacked, but unconditional surrender is what is demanded (Deut. 20.10–11). A 'covenant of *šālōm*' is rarely peace and reconciliation between hostile states. Rather it means that Israel will have totally subjugated its enemies (cf. Lev. 26.3, 6–8).[32] In Ezekiel 34.25 *šālōm* involves freedom from the attacks of wild animals who are 'made to cease' from the land. Shalom may on occasion be contrasted with war (cf. Josh. 9.15), but this is not its main connotation.

'Rest' (*nūaḥ*) and 'quietness' (verb *šāqaṭ*) are rather closer to our ideas of peace, but even here is it usually peace after Israel's enemies have been quelled. In Joshua the land had rest from war after the conquest, and in Judges the land was quiet, undisturbed by war, during the lifetime of each deliverer, but only after Israel had defeated the enemy (Josh. 11.23; 14.15; Jdg. 3.11, 30; 5.31; 8.28, cf. Deut. 3.20; 12.10; 25.19). Zechariah says that the whole world is again at rest, probably after Darius had put down the rebellions after the death of Cambyses (Zech. 1.11).

There is, then, no true parallel in the Old Testament to the modern yearning for peaceable relationships based on mutual trust and respect. Always Israel looks for the defeat of its enemies and security through conquest and subjection. Even the covenant of peace is *imposed* upon the weaker nation, its citizens effectively reduced to vassals or slaves.

Attempts to Explain the Old Testament Attitude to War
The attitude to war in the Old Testament offends many twentieth-century Christians, the more so because they are aware of the malign influence it has had upon the European nations down through history, with the crusades and the churches' support for their

---

[32] Johs. Pedersen emphasizes this (*Israel I–II*, 312). He distinguishes between peace between friends and peace between enemies. Susan Niditch finds this 'insistence that peace is virtually equivalent to domination' 'too sweeping', though she admits that all her counter-examples are between fellow-Israelites (*War*, 135–136).

governments in both world wars as terrible examples.[33] Perhaps only in time of war has this unease abated.

The best known treatment of the issue is Peter C. Craigie's *The Problem of War in the Old Testament*. He writes from a conservative position, intent to retain the whole Hebrew Bible as Christian scripture. Three features are singled out: the characterization of God as a warrior, the question of the Old Testament as revelation, and the problem of ethics. In fact all are ethical problems, since for us the central problem about war in the Old Testament is that war was *not* a problem to ancient Israel.

Craigie first acknowledges the limitations of human language, and claims that to speak of God as warrior points to some important truths about him: that he is involved in human history and both judges and redeems. This, however, raises philosophical questions about God's action in the world, and is misleading if it is held to defend a belief in his support of military action today.

Secondly, to meet the problem that God revealed himself to his chosen people through warfare, he emphasizes that the whole Old Testament must be taken into account, defeats as well as victories, and that, with brutal honesty, it accepts that violence is inevitable and shows up the horror of war. Moreover, the first revelation of the Kingdom of God was the state of Israel; its failure led to the Kingdom of God in the teaching of Jesus. While the old Kingdom was established by the *use* of violence, the new Kingdom was established through the *receipt* of violence. But this is inadequate. Even if the destruction of the Canaanites did not happen as it is described in the book of Joshua, this only increases the problem, since the ban is the ideal that is supported by the theology of the writers and the theology increased the ruthlessness. Nowhere in the Old Testament is there anything approaching the Jewish legend of God's response to the angels who joined in Miriam's song at the Red Sea: 'My children are drowning and you would sing!' The nearest to this is God's rebuke to Jonah (Jonah 4.11), but this is not in the context of war. Craigie, however, will not resort to the escape of supposing that ancient Israel misunderstood God's will.

Thirdly, Craigie takes the hardest way by asking, 'In what way, if any, can the Old Testament be used as a resource for the formulation of ethics? . . . does the Old Testament provide the data for formulating

---

[33] Niditch, *War*, 3–4 refers to a sermon by Cotton Mather in 1689 as an example of the use of scripture to encourage the soldiers in their war against the native inhabitants of New England. Roland Bainton, *War and Peace*, gives other examples, and the support given by the churches to their governments in the First World War, often drawing on the Bible, has been well documented, see Alan Wilkinson, *First World War* and *Dissent or Conform?* The 'Fall' of the church is often associated with the conversion of Constantine, see, e.g., John Driver, *Peace with War*.

a Christian view of war?'[34] He then partly sidesteps the real problem by pointing out that Jesus drew the love commandment from the Torah, but his main answer is that many of the laws applied to the state of Israel and cannot be transferred to the Kingdom of God as revealed by Jesus. Whatever the truth of this, the principle of violence between states remains. This is unacceptable to the pacifist, and it is doubtful whether it should be acceptable to the non-pacifist either, for no account is taken of the different situation today.

The basic weakness of Craigie's position lies in his unwillingness to recognize the extent to which the Old Testament *glories* in war. We have seen that there is no criticism of war as such in any part of it. The main problem for the Israelites arises when they suffer defeat, and texts which are sometimes cited as attempting to alleviate the worst excesses of war are of doubtful meaning.

Walter C. Kaiser, Jr., an extreme conservative, accepts that war is 'God's ultimate, but reluctant, method of treating gross evil that resists every other patient and loving rebuke of God'.[35] He holds that, because of their flagrant sins, the destruction of the Canaanites was just. They had been given forty years to repent after receiving God's warning, and had they not been destroyed, Israel and the world would have been in danger of being corrupted. The sins which Kaiser singles out are burning children in honour of their god, and the practising of 'sodomy, bestiality and all sorts of loathsome vices'. The destruction of the Canaanites was on the same principle as that on which the whole world was judged in the Flood, or the cities of the plain, or Pharaoh's army.[36] I find it difficult to take this seriously, or rather, I find it so ethically flawed that I am amazed that it should be proposed today. Certainly it is a position which is possible only on a fundamentalist view of the Bible, which is prepared to accept scripture as true even if it goes against our moral sensitivity and against what is now known about Canaanite religion. If reverence for scripture leads to such an attitude it is little wonder that humanists find it easy to condemn religion as having a malign influence.[37]

With this may be compared the study by another conservative Christian scholar, F. Derek Kidner.[38] He finds three kinds of war in the Old Testament, aggression, defence, and war of divine judgment.

---

[34] Peter C. Craigie, *War*, 100.

[35] Walter C. Kaiser, Jr., *Ethics*, 178.

[36] *Ibid.*, 266–269. This is part of his discussion of 'Moral Difficulties in the Old Testament', pp. 247–304.

[37] See also his discussion of war on pp. 172–180, in which he is rather more cautious, denying that sanctions can be carried over directly into the present (p. 175), pointing out that the ethics of war are never given blanket approval in the Old Testament, and many wars and the methods of carrying them out receive a stern rebuke (p. 177).

[38] F. Derek Kidner, 'War'.

Each causes him some disquiet. The *ḥērem* was a matter of holiness, and Kidner picks up Norman H. Snaith's statement that 'one god's *qōdeš* is another god's *ḥērem*'. Further 'war as a holy exercise had its set-piece rituals'. The monarchy substituted a professional army and the latest weaponry for holy war, and these lapses from faith attracted the protests of the prophets. At every stage of Israel's history, however, faith and secularism can be found. He stresses that in ancient Israel 'church and state were one', and Israel stood in a unique relation to God, so that its wars were 'the wars of the LORD'. The equivalent to these wars for us are spiritual conflicts, and show that God's war now and his future judgment are 'total'. Nevertheless lessons about earthly war can be drawn. Contrasts and similarities can be seen between the Old Testament and the 'just war' doctrine. No war is now 'holy war', but the ideas of the 'just cause', war as the only means for securing justice, and employing the right means, have parallels, especially the last in the attempts to limit the cruelties of war. Kidner proceeds to draw attention to three further 'features and principles' of war: the ubiquity of war, which is so much a fact of life that Israel's history is largely military history and the ruler's chief preoccupation is with defence; victory is viewed as 'salvation' and 'rest' from one's enemies is a gift from God; and although security comes from God alone this 'is not an invitation to a people to drop its guard'. Rather obscurely, despite the distinction he makes between the Israelite nation and the Christian church, Kidner seems to regard prayers for the nation in times of trouble as justified. Finally, he sets out his view of the Old Testament vision of peace: primarily it is peace between God and human beings secured by atonement; secondly it is secured 'by divine onslaught'; and thirdly the peace of Isaiah 2.2–4 and Micah 4.1–4 which is the result of justice and God's reign is contrasted with our attempts to secure peace by seeking disarmament. Even granted that Kidner's main emphasis is on the theological rather than the ethical 'lessons for the present era' that can be drawn from the Old Testament, this is driven by a preconceived dogmatic position and shows little awareness of the serious moral issues that are involved.[39]

The proposal of Henning Graf Reventlow, runs on much the same lines.[40] He argues that 'the texts we have may give an exaggerated view of the importance of the warlike character'. The wars recorded within them have to be understood as an idealization coming from the

---

[39] Somewhat similar to Kidner is the study *God is a Warrior* by Tremper Longman III and Daniel G. Reid, who trace 'God's Cosmological Battle' through five stages: God fights Israel's enemies; God fights Israel; the hope of the future divine deliverer; Jesus fights the principalities and powers; and the final battle (p. 17).

[40] Henning Graf Reventlow, 'Just War', 171–172.

small Jewish community at the end of the Exile, who experienced political and economic difficulties and look back on their glorious past. The Old Testament does not legitimate aggression, and the hope of future peace is grounded on the eschatological action of God. This characterization of the biblical texts may be true, but does not remove the difficulty that, even if the descriptions are not historically accurate, war is glorified in sacred scripture.

By contrast Norman K. Gottwald singles out Isa. 2.1–4 and 19.18–25 as showing 'the mature view of Israel's representatives' who reject holy war. He points out that the Deuteronomists believed that Canaanite civilians 'either *were* or *should have been* exterminated in the name of God' and that 'one people had the religious right to dispossess another people'. Setting this in its context may 'illuminate and even palliate' it, but ultimately it is a dangerous tradition and the Old Testament has to be judged by the ethics of Jesus who put an end to the idea that war can ever be the instrument of God.[41]

H. Eberhard von Waldow adopts an even more extreme position.[42] He criticizes Craigie and others for limiting their discussion to passages which treat of war, and instead finds the early chapters of Genesis normative for the Old Testament. War is a violation of God's order of creation and thus is sinful. There can be no such thing as a just war. Fastening on the threat of 'sword, hunger and pestilence', he sees war always as divine punishment. Although von Waldow mentions some of the more difficult practices, such as the *ḥērem*, he evades the ethical issues by asserting that they reflect 'an ancient and very common speech-form honoring the deity as the giver of victory'.

Patrick D. Miller[43] offers what has become the stock defence of the concept of Yahweh as warrior: it shows God actively at work within human history; at the centre of the institution of Holy War lies Israel's faith in the rule and sovereignty of God, universal, on a historical plane and with a cosmic dimension; and when God is at work for his people their proper response is to have faith and trust without fear. This is remythologizing to a high degree, and while some may accept its place in preaching (which after all is Miller's

---

[41] Gottwald, '"Holy War"', 307–309. Lest this should be condemned as anti-Semitic Gottwald declares that the church has a heavy responsibility in the way it uses Holy War texts: 'By the way the church has used the Passion story it has often conveyed anti-Semitism consciously or unconsciously. By the way it has used holy war texts it has often conveyed consciously or unconsciously, the nobility and religious grandeur of war' (p. 310).

[42] H. Eberhard von Waldow, 'War'.

[43] Patrick D. Miller, 'God the Warrior', 42–46.

main theme in this article),[44] it almost totally fails to address the moral issues.[45]

A mediating position between these extremes is presented by Walter Houston.[46] He rejects any attempt to set the Old Testament against the New, for the New Testament took the Old for granted. The use of the ban against the Canaanites was in order to preserve Israel's holiness and may have been a necessary stage in salvation history, but God's command to us is entirely different. Houston accepts passages such as Deuteronomy 20.10–20 and Amos 1–2 as attempts to limit the evil of war, and points to Isaiah's warning to Israel to wait and trust in God, a restraint against engaging in hasty war. This is a brave attempt to retain the authority of the Old Testament, but hardly deals with the seriousness of the problem.

T. R. Hobbs describes his study as an approach from a 'military history' angle. It is not a treatise on the 'theology of war' nor a summary of the 'teaching' of the Old Testament on war, although, because he believes that theories based on lack of knowledge are less than useful, he hopes it will contribute to the 'struggle of Christians to come to terms with the issues of violence, peace and Gospel'.[47] In it he presents the main features of war in the Old Testament period – the warriors, the matériel, and the art of war. He then singles out three attitudes to war reflected in the literature of the Old Testament, all of which accept the reality and justice of war. (a) At the time of the judges warfare was necessary to the survival of the covenant community. (b) During the reign of David war became an instrument of state policy. (c) The prophets reacted to the monarchical use of warfare by transforming the conventional war poems, but nevertheless were not against war as such – indeed they accepted it as a part of life. Hobbs's own answer to the problem is that policy must be related to the social conditions in which it is pursued, and the question has to be put, what options were possible to ancient Israel? He concludes that the options were severely limited. What conclusions are to be drawn from this are not clear, beyond an acceptance of the natural aggressiveness of human beings. As we have seen, Hobbs is highly critical of most discussions of war in the Old Testament, on the grounds that they explain away those elements in the Bible which disagree with their own position and presuppositions, read back into the past the concerns of the present, and engage in a

[44] Cf. 'Still a third way in which the wars of Yahweh may be appropriated for theology and preaching . . .' (*ibid.*, 45).
[45] To these may be added the pacifist studies by Millard Lind, *Yahweh is a Warrior*, and Lois Barrett, *The Way God Fights*, who seek to reinterpret the Old Testament, stressing that we do not need to fight because God fights for us.
[46] Walter Houston, 'War'.
[47] Hobbs, *War*, 10, 9.

highly selective reading of the Old Testament.[48] The main conclusion which seems to be drawn is that at heart the Old Testament has little to say to today, so embedded is it in the social conditions of its time.[49]

As we have seen, Susan Niditch is severely critical of Hobbs, especially his assertion that 'these primitive Israelites simply are not like us, their culture is not our culture, their ethics not ours'.[50] This appears to push aside too easily the massive differences of culture that exist between different societies and historical periods which Dennis Nineham pointed up most strongly.[51] Nineham has been criticized for creating a past which is so different from the modern world that, even if it ever existed, it would be totally incomprehensible to us, and this is clearly not the case. We can understand, if only in part and perhaps sometimes mistakenly, ancient Israel and classical Greece (and mediaeval Christianity). Nevertheless, no one who has read Nineham can any longer suppose that it is sufficient to assert that 'human nature does not change'. We may grant that the ancient Israelites felt the anguish of pain, grieved over their dead, and longed for security, yet this does not mean that they even glimpsed the reaction to war which two world wars and countless conflicts since then have evoked in many today. The truth seems to be more on the side of Hobbs than of those who find a basic opposition to war and a vision of peace as the essential message of the prophets and some other Old Testament writers.[52]

Before leaving this question the strikingly different approach of Robert M. Good must be considered.[53] On the basis of Amos 1.3–5; Joel 4.1–3, 9–13; 2 Chronicles 20.6–12; Judges 5.9–11, 13; 11.15–27; and Exodus 15, he argues that in ancient Israel war was a judicial activity, 'the expression of a *legal* judgment of Yahweh made for the purpose of resolving a dispute between Israel and neighboring states'.[54] Several features of a legal action (coercion, recourse to authority, application to all like cases, and reciprocal rights and obligations of disputants) are found in the texts discussed. It is emphasized that although Yahweh is Israel's God, this does not prevent him from playing the part of arbitrator between his people and

---

[48] Among others, one of the most strikingly slanted (not discussed by Hobbs) is Bruce C. Birch, 'Peacemaking'.

[49] Hobbs, *War*, see esp. 19–20 and ch. 7. See also T. R. Hobbs, 'Militarism'.

[50] Niditch, *War*, 8–9.

[51] Dennis Nineham, *Use and Abuse*. See also his later study *Christianity Medieval and Modern*.

[52] The literature on war in the Bible is now immense. Among other studies of the 'problem' may be mentioned J. Andrew Dearman, 'Problem of War', who questions some attempts to remove the difficulties, but says that warrior language cannot be rejected because it is 'an indispensable element of Christology'.

[53] Robert M. Good, 'Just War'.

[54] *Ibid.*, 387.

their adversaries, since this could happen in lawsuits within Israel, and Psalm 82 reveals that Israel both accepted the existence of other gods and assigned sovereignty to Yahweh. Good has certainly identified significant references to judgment in connection with war, but it is doubtful whether this is sufficient to support the move to regarding war itself as a judicial process. Indeed, there is a certain ambiguity in his article. Is the war the legal dispute or the carrying out of the sentence? To suggest that it is a kind of ordeal muddies the water, for while Yahweh was seen to be the one who gives the 'verdict' in the ordeal, this is distinct from a legal action, and was recognized as such by ancient Israel. Good concludes his article with the suggestion that the judicial aspect of war has implications for the concept of the just war. The image of Yahweh as divine warrior must be subordinated to that of judge. 'In matters of war, Yahweh seems not to have been conceived as a might-makes-right sovereign' but as judge he has the duty to act according to the standards of justice.[55] When Jephthah argues the case for his war against Ammon in Judges 11 and Jehoshaphat pleads his case against his enemies in 2 Chronicles 20, appeal is made to historical events as a legal plea rather than to Yahweh's special care of Israel. This opens up the possibility of marshalling a moral critique of war. Even if this is true for the very small number of texts which Good uses, it does not seem to have been widely held in ancient Israel or to have influenced many of the wars recounted in the Old Testament.[56]

Concluding Observations

The purpose of these concluding comments is primarily to examine the relation of this study of war to the general issue of Old Testament ethics.

1. It is unsatisfactory to single out passages which appear to accord with our own ethical stance and declare them to be the *true* teaching

---

[55] Good seems not to be aware of the implications of speaking of God having to function 'in accordance with standards of justice' (p. 399). And his claim that in the phrase *ṣidᵉqōṯ* Yahweh in Jdg. 5.11 'we find war denoted as something just' is questionable. Here *ṣidᵉqōṯ* means 'victories' (though cf. John Gray, 'acts which vindicate God's purpose and his people', or if an abstract noun 'vindication' (*Joshua, Judges, Ruth*, 270) and HALOT 3, 1006, which surprisingly renders 'deeds of justice, deeds of loyalty to the community, or covenant'). Even if this were right it would not show that the waging of war was itself 'something just'. In the whole argument 'just' seems to be used in a variety of senses.

[56] P. D. Hanson offers a somewhat similar interpretation, stressing the unique emphasis on impartial and universal justice found in Ps. 82 and underlying the Exodus narrative, and what he terms the 'order of *shalom*' ('War', 40–41). Joshua 6–11 is explained away as being an expression of 'a triumphant royal ideology', whereas the Song of Deborah is a 'celebration of *shalom*', war being inflicted on them by the forces of chaos (pp. 44–45).

of the Old Testament. The whole Old Testament must be taken into account – and this does not mean constructing, usually on the basis of one's own moral position, what is deemed its 'central' message or 'main thrust'. Moreover, it has been shown that even the 'golden' texts cannot bear the interpretation which has been commonly imposed upon them. In particular, the preservation of purity was probably more important than any ethical judgment, while peace was usually founded on the subjugation of Israel's enemies.

2. Still less satisfactory is the bypassing of ethical issues by fastening on what is deemed the theological teaching of the Old Testament on war. In the first place, theology cannot be divorced from ethics in this way. Secondly, most of those who take this path end by offering a spiritualizing solution to the problem, which is alien to the plain meaning of the Old Testament texts. Thirdly, such an approach often has a hidden agenda, depending on the presuppositions of the writer, whether supporting pacifism or adopting what is usually described as a 'realist' position.

3. It follows from this that modern war and modern attitudes to war are widely different from the attitudes found in the Old Testament. War was not the problem to the ancient Israelites that it is to us, and it was taken for granted.[57] An activity does not enter the realm of ethics, however, until it is thought about and questioned. This means that there is little teaching about the ethics of war as such. Israel practised war much as the other nations of the ancient Middle East did, and while there is evidence of a longing for the peace that springs from security against enemies, and the prophet Amos assumed that everyone accepted that some of the actions that occurred during war were wrong (cf. Amos 1–2), there was no attempt to banish war itself. It has been argued that most of the passages which are commonly adduced as either opposing the worst excesses of war or presenting the hope of peace in the future need to be interpreted more narrowly.

4. More attention needs to be given to the problems which this raises for the authority of the Old Testament as divine revelation. None of the attempts which have been made to come to terms with the presence of war and the attitudes towards it can be regarded as satisfactory. In the Old Testament war was not only accepted but

---

[57] Sadly, of course, the actual attitudes of twentieth-century nations and governments have differed little from those of ancient Israel. Divine support has often been claimed for one's own side, if not always as blatantly as in the First World War at least through assertions that 'ethical' principles, such as 'freedom' or 'democracy' are being defended. Ideology replaces religion as the motor driving hostility. Moreover, once war is embarked upon, it rapidly degenerates into acceptance of what were regarded earlier as atrocities that civilized human beings could not commit. It is, then, not a matter of adjusting the ethic of the Old Testament to the modern world, for the Israelite view of war cannot be so adjusted.

religion commonly both justified it and intensified its evil. This view of war is irredeemable. While it is possible to understand the attitudes of the Israelites, given their political situation among the nations of the ancient world, their practice is not to be followed and an ethics of war which can meet the modern situation has to be derived from some other source than the Old Testament.[58] One consequence of this is that Christians and others who seek a scriptural basis for their ethical decisions are driven to re-examine the source of their moral philosophy. And if this is so with regard to war, how far does it also apply to other aspects of Old Testament ethics? This larger question must be left to a later chapter.[59]

---

[58] The ethics of the 'just war' shows the way some Christian moralists have sought to discover the grounds for such an ethic. Despite its distinguished pedigree and high prestige, current attempts to restate it in terms that cover modern warfare and bring it under control must be adjudged to have failed.

[59] Again to avoid misunderstanding, I should like to make it plain that my own position is that of a troubled pacifist, who is well aware that massive evils have to be opposed, but is highly cynical of the actions of governments claiming to be defending 'freedom', 'democracy' and 'human rights'. I should also stress again that my interpretation of Old Testament attitudes to war must not be taken as any form of anti-Semitism. Christianity has proved to be one of the most militaristic religions in human history (see n. 33 above).

16

ANIMALS

Nowhere have modern attitudes affected the interpretation of the Old Testament more than with the treatment of animals. Anxiety about the environment has forced the whole question of the relation of human beings to nature to the forefront of ethical discussion. Theologies of nature are being developed, and the Bible is mined for texts which support current ecological concern. This is, however, a very late development, and it has been pointed out that far from being in the van of caring for the natural world, the reality is that the Christian church has at last almost caught up with the secular world.[1] Few preceded or followed St Francis in preaching and practising kindness to animals. Aquinas asserted human dominance over the animals and Pius IX forbade the opening of an animal protection office in Rome on the grounds that human beings had no duties to animals.[2] St Paul asks whether God has any concern for oxen (1 Cor. 9.9–10). Finding support in the Bible for a more enlightened ethics of animal welfare has demanded a highly selective approach.[3] The history of the attitude

---

[1] For a fierce attack on the failure of the churches to produce a single document or official statement on the environment before the 1980s, despite the work of individual Christians, see Martin Palmer, 'Ecology'. He comments: 'The churches are late comers in the world of conservation. They have had to be pushed, shoved and cajoled into noticing that "God's creation" was going down the plughole. . . . They have had to be argued with and debated with to allow a shift away from an almost totally human centred understanding of God in creation' (p. 174).

[2] An Anglican clergyman, Arthur Broom, took a leading part in the founding of the British RSPCA (as the SPCA) in 1824. For a historical account of attitudes see Andrew Linzey, *Rights of Animals;* Keith Thomas, *Natural World.* Vegetarianism also has a long pedigree. On Aquinas see Andrew Linzey, *Animal Theology,* 12–15. Whether the Celtic church had a different ethic is disputed (see Gilbert Márkus, 'Celtic Christianity', 52–53). Other writers, including Colm Ó Baoill and Donald E. Meek have also heavily criticized romantic views, see Meek, *Celtic Christianity* (on attitudes to the natural world, 82–86). Judaism seems to have been marked by a more generous and caring attitude, though even here opposing interpretations are found: contrast Lewis G. Regenstein: 'The teachings and laws of Judaism strongly emphasize kindness to animals and reverence for nature' (*Replenish the Earth,* 183 and the whole section 183–217) with Elijah Judah Schochet: 'The quest for "perfection of soul and intellect" which characterized rabbinic scholars and medieval philosophers clearly had no place for the animal' (*Animal Life,* 5).

[3] Andrew Linzey, who has written extensively on animal welfare, tends to use the Bible selectively in this way, although in his treatment of later writers he is fair in

towards animals within the church should alert us to the fact that the teaching of the Bible is highly ambiguous. In this chapter I shall attempt to take into account attitudes towards animals across the whole of the Old Testament, and consider wider questions of nature and the environment in the next.[4]

A major problem concerns the extent and nature of the evidence. Animals appear throughout the Old Testament. It has been calculated that some 120 species are mentioned,[5] although some are found only in lists of clean and unclean animals. The identification of many of the Hebrew names of animals and birds is uncertain.[6] Some, like Leviathan and Behemoth, are almost certainly mythological,[7] while some names may refer to different stages in the life cycle, as with the various words for locust.

Simile and Personification

It is difficult to know how to approach the evidence. Should the many metaphorical references be passed over?[8] But if we read metaphor and simile backward they can throw important light on the ways the Israelites thought about the animals. The psalmist describes his enemies as coming back every evening, 'howling like dogs and prowling about the city', and adds, 'They roam about for food, and growl if they do not get any' (Ps. 59.15–16[14–15]). This displays an attitude towards dogs that is very different from the modern view that is reflected in the television adverts. Dogs are scavengers in the Old Testament and are viewed with hostility. The only pet dog belongs to Tobias in the Apocrypha (Tobit 5.16; 11.4).

---

representing opposing viewpoints. For a more extreme example of biased selection and interpretation see Regenstein, *Replenish the Earth*, 19–56, even though he fully recognizes and documents the failure of the later church to defend animals.

[4] Franz-Elmar Wilms has provided a splendid overview in *Das Tier*. See also Bernd Janowski, Ute Neumann-Gorsolke and Uwe Gleßmer, eds. *Gefährten und Feinde*. An attractive little book which presents a rather different perspective from that which I am arguing is John Eaton's *Circle of Creation*, in which he sets out 'the ideal of a loving community of all the species', which he believes is fundamental to God's eternal purpose.

[5] Schochet, *Animal Life*, 9. Cf. Y. Aharoni, 'Animals'. Schochet has relied on F. S. Bodenheimer's *HaHai*, and *Animals*, and J. Feliks's *Animal World*.

[6] To give just one example out of many: the *hapax legomenon qippōz* in Isa. 34.15 has been variously taken as owl, sand-partridge, and arrow-snake. The LXX has 'hedgehog', apparently reading as *qippōd*, which itself has been identified as hedgehog, short-eared owl and ruffed bustard. G. R. Driver is famous for his attempts to make proper identifications, especially of birds ('Birds'). Walter Houston provides a table of translations and interpretations of twenty terms in *Purity and Monotheism*, 44–45.

[7] Some scholars, however, identify Behemoth as the crocodile and Leviathan as the whale (so NEB and REB). Others think that Behemoth is the hippopotamus.

[8] Robert Murray analyses animal themes under those with 'little or no metaphor', 'personification' and 'metaphor in full sense' (*Cosmic Covenant*, 95–96).

Human characteristics are transferred to the animal, and what it is compared with reflects the Israelite's attitude. To say that Yahweh is like a mother eagle (Deut. 32.11) shows the countryman's close observation of nature, and also how the behaviour of the mother eagle is interpreted. To compare Israel with a camel or wild ass in heat (Jer. 2.23–24) applies ethical ideas to the animals, in the same way that Isaiah can speak of the ox and donkey *knowing* their master and their home, unlike Israel (Isa. 1.3). When the wise man presents the ants as examples of industry (Prov. 6.6–11) he interprets the behaviour of ants in human terms as gathering in the harvest. These metaphors, therefore, are double sided: they reveal both the writer's views on human behaviour and the way he thinks about animals.

Somewhat akin to this is the personification of wild animals. When God gives food to the young ravens in response to their cry (Ps. 147.9), this seems to mean that they pray to him. In a similar way, the young lions seek their prey from God (Ps. 104.21) – and in this psalm they are not vegetarian! This personification extends to what we regard as inanimate objects. In Psalm 148.7–10 'all deeps', fire, hail, snow, storm wind, mountains, cultivated and forest trees are called upon to praise God, alongside sea monsters, wild and domestic animals, creeping things and birds. It seems to be highly unlikely, given the close relation between animals and human beings which the similes and personifications imply, that the Israelites believed with Descartes that animals are simply machines.[9]

Sacrifice

Moving on from metaphor, we might ask what is to be made of the fact that the majority of references to animals outside of the wisdom writings are related either to sacrifice or to purity. How many animals were sacrificed each year is uncertain. Diets across the ancient world were predominantly vegetarian.[10] Meat was eaten only on special occasions, and before the Deuteronomic reform it could be eaten only as part of a sacrifice. The *'ōlāh*, the 'whole burnt offering', where the animal was totally burnt on the altar, was probably relatively rare. After the exile, when the priests gained a greater control over the cult, regular daily sacrifices, together with those offered by individuals and at the great annual festivals, may have increased the numbers of animals killed in this way. The laws of sacrifice prescribe the kinds of

[9] Descartes held that animals do not possess souls and are unable to think. It is not clear that he believed that they could not feel pain, although this has often been seen as a consequence of their being similar to clocks (see selections from *Discourse on Method* and letters to the Marquess of Newcastle and to Henry More in Andrew Linzey and Tom Regan, *Animals and Christianity*, 45–52).

[10] Of course, not in the modern sense of a conscious rejection of meat. Meat was outside the normal food that was available to subsistence farmers.

animals that may be offered, their sex, and the demand for victims without blemish.[11]

To us, killing of animals in sacrifice hardly seems to show a great concern for their welfare, and since the method of slaughter by slitting the throat may have caused some suffering, it also appears to reflect a callous disregard of their pain. Even if the pain was limited (and there is some dispute about the suffering that slitting an animal's throat causes), to take animals and compel them to die as part of the worship of God and to expiate human sin seems to imply a low view of their intrinsic worth – they are little more than disposable, though valuable, property. But is this a correct understanding?

Some have fastened on the Israelite belief that the blood was the life of the animal. Whenever an animal was eaten it had to be sacrificed (or after the Deuteronomic reform 'secularized' slaughter, its blood poured out). Donald E. Gowan, for example, avers that because the Israelites believed that 'the life of every creature is the blood of it' (Lev. 17.14), and all life belongs to God, the killing of animals had to be done in the presence of God and the blood given back to him. The sacrifice was a reminder that in order for human beings to enjoy meat an animal has had to surrender its life.[12] The implication drawn from the treatment of the blood in sacrifice appears to reflect modern attitudes, and is almost certainly alien to ancient Israel.

That all life belongs to God is clearly part of Israelite thought. He alone gives it and sustains it. The blood is the life, and that is why human beings have no right to consume it.[13] Thus when human beings take the life of an animal they have to 'return' the life to God, otherwise they are 'stealing' from him. Only then are they free to eat the flesh. This reflects a higher regard for animals as God's creation. Yet this must not be taken in a purely ethical way. The pouring out of the life-blood is better interpreted as revealing ideas of avoiding potentially powerful forces and is related to ideas of purity. To speak of *mana* is out of fashion, but the term expresses the sense of mysterious power that resides in the blood and threatens danger to the human beings who drink it.

In ancient Israel little thought appears to have been given to the feelings and rights of the animals offered in sacrifice, in contrast, it

---

[11] Meir Bar-Ilan makes the curious comment that only male animals were sacrificed 'so as not to decrease the population of animals in the future' (*Some Jewish Women*, 130, n. 49). Mary Douglas makes an equally curious suggestion that 'the sacrifice of young animals at multiple sanctuaries was the breeder's alternative to castration for keeping the population of males and females under control' (*Leviticus*, 95). She holds that only Deuteronomy demanded a single central sanctuary.

[12] Donald E. Gowan, *Reclaiming the OT*, 98.

[13] See, for example, Roland de Vaux, *Sacrifice*, 42.

has been claimed, to the Greeks, who were concerned with the compliance of the animal.[14] When the psalmist disparages sacrifice he puts satirical questions in the mouth of God, but shows no concern for the well-being of the animals themselves:

> I will accept no bull from your house,
>   nor he-goat from your folds.
> For every beast of the forest is mine,
>   the cattle on a thousand hills.
> I know all the birds of the air,
>   and all that moves in the field is mine.
> If I were hungry, I would not tell you,
>   for the world and all that is in it is mine.
> Do I eat the flesh of bulls,
>   or drink the blood of goats? (Ps. 50.9–13)

The underlying assumption is that animals exist to be eaten.[15]

Similarly when the prophets demand justice they sometimes appear to reject sacrifice, or at least say that, unless it is accompanied by a moral life and a just society, God will not accept it. Yet the passion with which they condemn wrongs done to human beings is not echoed in any condemnation of possible wrongs done to the animals. A concern for the welfare of the animals involved in sacrifice is entirely absent from such passages as Amos 5.21–24 and Isaiah 1.11–17. Jeremiah (or the author or compiler of the book which takes his name), who reveals sympathy with the animals that are caught up in the punishment of Israel (cf. Jer. 14.5–6), makes no comment about the fate of the animals offered in sacrifice (Jer. 6.20; 7.21–23). Even if Isaiah 66.3 asserts that sacrifice of every kind is wrong, and this is far from certain, many scholars holding that what it opposes is syncretism, it clearly does not adopt this position out of any concern for the welfare of the animals which are killed.[16]

The fact seems to be that sacrifice was simply accepted. It was the means God had established for maintaining the covenant, dealing with sin, and fostering the welfare of the community. The suffering of the animals did not come within the orbit of thought of the Israelites. Their attention was turned to other matters – worship, sin, expiation, relations with God.

---

[14] So B. Hudson McLean, *The Cursed Christ*, 57, n.111.

[15] Whether the following line calls for replacing sacrifice by thanksgiving is disputed.

[16] The Hebrew is highly condensed ('slaughtering of an ox, killing (smiting) of a man, sacrificing of a sheep, breaking the neck of a dog . . .'), and the insertion of 'is like' is far from probable. The participial clauses are simply juxtaposed and the prophet's complaint may be against practising foreign cults, though the verb used for killing a human being is not a sacrificial term.

It is significant that hardly any of the studies of Old Testament sacrifice before the 1970s discuss the ethical issue of the actual killing of animals in sacrifice, despite their detailed discussions of its origins, history, and purpose.[17] Claims that in pastoral and agrarian societies killing animals evoked guilt appear only with the emergence of a heightened environmental concern. Blood-spilling is then claimed to be an offence against nature, and animal sacrifice 'serves therefore to sanctify the act of meat consumption'.[18] Naturally those supporting animal rights are keenly aware of the need to counter the Old Testament sacrificial system which seems to subject animals to the welfare of human beings. Regenstein claims that compared with surrounding countries, sacrifice in Israel was carried out humanely, and makes great play of condemnations of sacrifice in 1 Samuel 15.22, Isaiah 1.11–13, Psalms 40.7[6] and 50.8–15, 23, Amos 5.21–22, Hosea 6.6, Jeremiah 6.20, 7.21–22, which he interprets as the total rejection of sacrifice.[19] Linzey admits that animal sacrifices are found throughout the Old Testament apart from the time of Adam and Eve in Eden and responds by asking how a God who created animals out of love could delight in their 'gratuitous destruction'. He follows Mascall in arguing that sacrifice is the freeing of the animal's life to be with God, and like Regenstein, stresses the 'question and protest' of the prophets.[20] This applies twentieth-century ethics to the Old Testament and fails to appreciate the culture of ancient Israel.

It is a mark of the way recent viewpoints have influenced Old Testament study that Professor John Rogerson contributes an article on animal sacrifice in a book which seeks to address fundamental theological questions about animals.[21] He begins by arguing that there would probably have been many different views about animal sacrifices among the ancient Israelites, and singles out five: condemnation of unworthy priests (1 Sam. 2.12–17), conformist

---

[17] See the main Theologies. Linzey draws attention to Robert Dobbie's 'Sacrifice and Morality' as 'a rare discussion of animal sacrifice from an ethical perspective' (*Animal Theology*, 180), but the issue is not referred to in this article which is a critique of H. H. Rowley's view in *The Unity of the Bible* and is primarily concerned with the need for sacrifice in human relations with God. Rowley replied in 'A Rejoinder'.

[18] W. W. Hallo, 'Sacrificial Cult', summarized by Philip J. Budd, *Leviticus*, 32. Budd also notes that Nancy Jay observes that blood sacrifice is typical of agrarian and pastoral societies, but not hunter-gatherer or industrial ones, and is also linked with patrilineal descent groups. She therefore sees it as the means by which men overcome their dependence on women's reproductive powers and maintain male inheritance (p. 33; Nancy Jay, 'Sacrifice'). Whether this is a correct interpretation or not, it further supports my contention that ethical issues about the killing of animals were not prominent in the thought of those who practised sacrifice.

[19] Regenstein, *Replenish the Earth*, 45–53.

[20] Linzey, *Animal Theology*, 103–105.

[21] John Rogerson, 'Animal Sacrifice'.

acceptance of sacrifice as a religious duty, the utter sincerity of Job (Job 1.5), 'spiritualizing' sacrifice (Ps. 51.19[17]), and outright hostility to sacrifice (Isa. 66.3). After surveying several theories of sacrifice, Rogerson seeks to reconcile the priestly system of animal sacrifices with the priestly account of creation that was vegetarian (Gen. 1.30). After the Flood the world of our experience is no longer as God intended it to be (cf. Gen. 9.2–4). He argues that the importance of the paradisal violence-free world is that it witnesses to a possible form of existence that offers a radical criticism of the actual world of human experience. Inspired by Lohfink's argument that the historical part of the priestly source deliberately tried to present a violence-free account of Israel's history and hence that the source envisaged a community in which war between animals and humans had taken the place of violence between human beings,[22] Rogerson claims that Genesis 9.2 expresses the actual relationship between human beings and wild animals. But it was domestic animals which were used in sacrifice, and domestic animals were rarely eaten (cf. Prov. 27.25–27). To sacrifice large numbers of animals would have led to economic disaster, and probably few animals were available for the temple offerings in post-exilic Judah. Rogerson concludes that 'it is probably wrong to say that animal sacrifice constituted the institutionalization of violence against animals'. The priestly legislation is no more than an ideal, and was but one viewpoint in the Old Testament. For some priests animal sacrifice symbolized the failure of humanity to live in the world as God intended.

Several comments can be made about this. In the first place, it is almost entirely restricted to the priestly source, and within that source it fastens on the overall ideology proclaimed in Genesis 1. It may well be true that the priestly legislation sets out an unrealized ideal, but it is doubtful whether so much stress can be placed upon a few verses at the beginning of that history. Secondly, although anthropology may offer insights by supplying possible theories of sacrifice, we must be cautious of allowing theory to control interpretation of the texts, and still more of the beliefs of the ancient Israelites. Thirdly, granted the existence of animal sacrifice throughout the biblical writings, and equally throughout the ancient world, the priestly source, even if it does present the view which Rogerson champions, can hardly be held up as the Israelite understanding of sacrifice. Much more probably, as with the poor and war, the Israelites saw no problem in killing animals in sacrifice. It was not merely that they were 'conformist'. It never occurred to them that animals had any rights or that there was anything morally wrong in killing them as highly valuable offerings to God. This does not condemn them for cruelty to animals, or criticize

---

[22] Norbert Lohfink, 'Die Schichten'.

them as insensitive to ethical demands. In the face of universal animal sacrifice it would have been a quite exceptional individual who reacted to it as we do. One thing is clear, nowhere in the whole Old Testament is any criticism of sacrifice based on the welfare of animals.

Clean and Unclean Animals
The lists of clean and unclean animals in Leviticus 11 and Deuteronomy 14 are part of the concern for purity that controlled much of the life of ancient Israel.[23] They may also reflect an interest in classifying animals and other natural objects. Many different theories to explain why some animals were regarded as unclean have been proposed.[24] The suggestion that the distinction between clean and unclean animals originated from motives of hygiene,[25] the pig especially often being the carrier of trichinosis, has now been abandoned, as has the claim that the unclean animals were associated with non-Israelite worship.[26] The proposal that the restrictions were intended to limit the consumption of meat and thus teach respect for life is ruled out because it is foreign to ancient culture, and in any case did not restrict the eating of the clean animals.[27] There must have been some rationale behind the distinctions, so that the view of some rabbis that it was a meaningless divine requirement intended simply to teach obedience must be rejected.[28] The proposal that the prohibitions had an economic ground, ensuring that food preferences did not lead to economic insecurity (pigs requiring more food resources than sheep,

[23] Walter Houston notes that outside these two chapters references to the distinction between clean and unclean animals are sparse, the main ones being Gen. 7.2–3; Jdg. 13.7; Hos. 9.3 (*Purity and Monotheism*, 145–147).
[24] Mary Douglas and Walter Houston give excellent surveys (*Purity and Danger*, 43–49; *Purity and Monotheism*, 68–123).
[25] So Maimonides, Naḥmanides, and W. F. Albright (references in Houston, *Purity and Monotheism*, 69–70, who decisively rejects the theory).
[26] So Origen, Martin Noth, W. Kornfeld (see Houston, *Purity and Monotheism*, 72–74, who does not deny that cultic considerations must play a part in the interpretation of the system, but faults this view as a complete explanation on the grounds that it seizes on 'a single narrow point not explicit in the text').
[27] Walter Houston groups these types of explanation under the head 'Moral-Symbolic', and refers to Philo, Maimonides, S. R. Hirsch, J. Milgrom, and L. E. Goodman. He accepts that in their present context there is a moral purpose in the dietary laws but denies that this is directly visible in the particularities of the laws on unclean flesh. He also makes the important point that such theories contain a large element of 'cultural subjectivity' (*Purity and Monotheism*, 74–78).
[28] Philo combined this with the idea that since among the unclean animals were those whose flesh was the finest the laws sought to restrain gluttony. With this may be linked the allegorical exegesis of the *Epistle of Aristeas* and Philo (and others including the Christian *Epistle of Barnabas*), whereby the unclean animals were explained as various vices. (See Mary Douglas, *Purity and Danger*, 43–48.)

goats and cattle), even if true, which is unlikely, is no more than a possible unintended result of the laws and was certainly not their purpose.[29] Mary Douglas's well-known theory, that only 'proper' animals, that is those that possessed all the attributes of their 'kind' or were similar to the familiar farm animals, were clean, has received less support recently.[30] An alternative suggestion, proposed by Walter Houston, starts from a conviction that any adequate explanation of the food rules must take into account the limits of geography and food production in the whole eastern Mediterranean region and social and cultural constraints. He holds that the distinction between clean and unclean animals was rooted in a pastoral economy in which pigs played a very small part. The fact that the stated purpose of the law was to keep Yahweh's people holy (Lev. 11.44) lies at the base of the laws, and Houston argues that this was achieved by making Israel's diet conform to Yahweh's, i.e. the animals that were acceptable for sacrifice. This was then extended by a process of classifying the non-sacrificial animals by the rule that clean ones had to be ruminants and have cloven hooves. He accepts that this explanation fails for fish and insects, however, since these were never offered on the altar. It also suffers from our inability to know whether the reason certain animals could be sacrificed was because they were 'clean' or because these were the ones that Yahweh wished to eat. It was noted as early as the *Letter of Aristeas* that the excluded birds were predators or eaters of carrion, and the motives may have varied between quadrupeds and other kinds of living creatures. Importantly Houston finds a moral purpose in the dietary laws in their present context. He accepts that 'the triple pattern of vegetarianism followed by unrestricted meat-eating followed by restricted meat-eating is a typical example of the pattern of two extremes and a mediating position that is found again and again in the myth and ritual of many peoples'. Vegetarianism is the ideal, but sin corrupts it. The solution is God's election of Israel to be holy to him and observe the restraints on meat eating. This, of course, is myth, as Houston recognizes, but he holds that it enables the priestly solution to be presented in narrative form.[31]

As was noted earlier,[32] Mary Douglas interprets the use of *šeqeṣ* in Leviticus 11 as a demand 'completely to shun' the various kinds of animals listed, and hence a call to 'keep out of their way, not harm, still less eat, them'.[33] This forms part of a lengthy argument claiming

[29] Walter Houston discusses the theories of F. J. Somoons, Marvin Harris and others (*Purity and Monotheism*, 81–93).

[30] Mary Douglas, *Purity and Danger*, 49–57. Walter Houston examines the theory in *Purity and Monotheism*, 93–107.

[31] Houston, *Purity and Monotheism*, 256–257.

[32] See p. 12, n. 24, above.

[33] Mary Douglas, *Leviticus*, 167.

that the priestly writer was concerned to protect these creatures. The 'swarming' animals exemplify fertility, since 'teeming' is to fulfil God's command to multiply (Gen. 1.22). The law is 'a mark of respect for these creatures'. Mary Douglas extends this to the story of the quails in Numbers 11. God is angry with the Israelites for eating the quails not because it exhibited gluttony (the explanation of the rabbis) but because quails as 'teeming' birds were 'a well-known protected form of life'. The arrival of the quails may have been 'a trap or a curse in response to their continual murmurings'.[34]

Regarding the unclean animals, Mary Douglas claims that, because all animals can be touched while alive without incurring uncleanness, the rule against touching unclean dead animals protects them during their lifetime.[35]

As she says right at the beginning of her book: 'Leviticus has to be read in line with Psalm 145.8–9: the God of Israel has compassion for all that he made. His love for his animal creation lies behind his laws against eating and touching their corpses. The flocks and herds of the people of Israel are brought under the covenant that God made with their owners, and the other animals benefit from the promises he made in Genesis after the flood, that he would guarantee the regularity of the seasons and the fertility of the ground. The more closely the text is studied, the more clearly Leviticus reveals itself as a modern religion, legislating for justice between persons and persons, between God and his people, and between people and animals.'[36]

I find it impossible to believe that this was the intention of the writers of Leviticus and Numbers. It appears much more to be a reading of the biblical texts with the ethical sensitivities of the modern environmentalist, even if in the event to be classified as an unclean animal 'ought to be an advantage for the survival of the species'.[37]

The only convincing approaches are those which set the distinction between clean and unclean animals firmly within the culture of ancient Israel and the wider ancient Middle East, and give due place to the importance of maintaining purity within Israel. This erects a warning sign before a too ready application of moral and ethical interpretations to some of the laws concerning the treatment of

---

[34] Ibid., 163, 168, 170–171, following Jacob Milgrom, Numbers, 92.

[35] Ibid., 142. Rather incongruously, in view of her concern for the welfare of animals, she writes: 'While they are alive camels and asses can be harnessed, loaded, ridden, dogs can be beaten, cats can be kicked, mice can be trapped, without incurring impurity, but once they are dead they convey uncleanness' (p. 141).

[36] Ibid., 1–2.

[37] Ibid., 142. Was the protection of animal life through the laws of clean and unclean animals and the shunning of teeming animals really an attempt to upstage the forbidding of killing in Egyptian religion, Hinduism, Buddhism and Jainism? 'You are forbidden to kill cows. We are forbidden to kill insects!' (pp. 171–172, her italics).

animals. We have seen that ideas of purity are far more important in the Old Testament than is commonly appreciated, and reach out far beyond the question of which animals can be eaten and sacrificed.

The Laws

The difficulty of knowing to what extent the laws were obeyed and whether they represent the viewpoint of the main body of Israelites has already been discussed. Are the requirements of the various collections no more than the idealism of the priestly law-givers, or would most Israelites accept that this is how they ought to treat their livestock? And what relation was there between the behaviour which the Israelite peasants thought they ought to practise and what actually took place on the farms? Since all we possess are the religious texts contained within the Hebrew Bible, some inscriptions, non-epigraphic archaeological material, and a number of later writings, it is unlikely that any satisfactory answer can be given to these questions. Nevertheless, to keep them in mind will prevent making assumptions that are too facile.

Despite our lack of fully satisfactory evidence, it seems fairly certain that the peasant farmers who were seeking to make a living in the fields would have felt threatened by poor soil, drought, and wild animals, and this will have a close bearing upon their attitudes towards animals. David as a shepherd had to protect his flock from lions and bears (1 Sam. 17.34–37). A lion killed a disobedient prophet (1 Kgs. 13.24), and two she-bears mauled the rude boys who mocked another holy man (2 Kgs. 2.24). The Israelites would have had a very different attitude from the World Wildlife Fund. The threat of wild animals was regarded as a divine punishment: 'I will let loose the wild beasts among you, which shall rob you of your children, and destroy your cattle, and make you few in number, so that your ways shall become desolate' (Lev. 26.22, cf. Jer. 15.3 where God appoints four kinds of 'destroyers': the sword, dogs to tear, and birds and wild animals to devour and destroy, and 5.6 where those who punish are a lion, a wolf, and a leopard).

Dogs are scavengers – we have seen that the only pet dog is Tobias's companion (Tobit 5.16; 11.4). Did people keep pet lambs? Apparently, for Nathan's parable would only 'work' if it reflected what actually happened in Israelite society (2 Sam. 12.1–6). In general, however, the Israelites seem to have had a different attitude to animals from that of the Egyptians. A famous Egyptian relief shows a cow being milked and shedding a tear because its calf is tethered and cannot reach its udder. Eugen Stronhal draws an attractive picture of the Egyptians surrounded by animals in their daily life and in their homes and feeling kindly disposed towards them. Shepherds pick up lambs when crossing a river (cf. Isa. 40.11) and stroke a pig when feeding it.[38]

It may be wrong to maintain that the Israelites had little sympathy with animals, but it would be even less correct to suppose that they were governed by modern urban sentimental feelings towards them.

A further issue is even more fundamental. It can best be approached through the comment by St Paul in 1 Cor. 9.9–10. He quotes 'You shall not muzzle an ox while it is treading out the grain' (Deut. 25.4), and then says: 'Is it for oxen that God is concerned? Does he not speak entirely for our sake? It was indeed written for our sake.' The Torah for Paul was sacred scripture, and Paul could not believe that scripture could be concerned with anything as trivial as muzzling an ox. We need to ask why he regarded the literal sense as so far beneath the dignity of scripture that it could not have been what God intended. It would seem that he had very little interest in animals or concern for their welfare. To him, therefore, God must have been using an allegory to teach that those who preached the gospel had a right to be supported by their converts. What appears to us as one of the relatively few laws which deal with cruelty to animals meant something completely different to Paul. Presumably he would not have allowed the muzzling of an ox, since this was what was written in the sacred scriptures, but the law did not evoke any sense of the rights of animals. Still less did he see it as an example which should be extended more widely to other acts of cruelty.[39]

The intention of the law-makers and the way the laws were understood may well have been vastly different from the interpretations which we put upon them.

The law codes will be examined individually.

(a) The Decalogue

In the Decalogue domestic animals ('your cattle', Ex. 20.10; 'your ox or your ass, or any of your cattle', Deut. 5.14), like the slaves, are included in the sabbath rest from work. The Exodus form of the sabbath law links it with God's rest at the end of creation. This made the day holy, but does not necessarily imply that its purpose is to give rest to the animals. Deuteronomy, which has this motive, adds that no work is to be done so that the slaves 'may rest as well as you', but

---

[38] Eugen Stronhal, *Ancient Egypt*, 117–118, 128.

[39] Christopher J. H. Wright is unable to accept what is the obvious meaning of Paul's rhetorical question, and says that Paul did not deny the original meaning of the law (God's concern for cattle) but redirected it to the new human situation (*Deuteronomy*, 265). John Barton makes the important observation that to Paul the text looked trivial, but since it was part of scripture he could not accept this and had to find a non-trivial meaning. To us, on the other hand, it is not trivial because we see it as an early recognition of animal rights (*Spirit and Letter*, 135).

does not include the animals in this motive clause. It seems to be going beyond the evidence to suggest that any concern for the well-being of the animals lies behind this sabbath law in either version, even though we today may interpret it in this way.

(b) The Book of the Covenant (Ex. 20.22–23.19)
The Book of the Covenant contains a number of laws about animals.

Attention may be drawn first to its version of the sabbath law (Ex. 23.12), where the seventh day's rest is explicitly stated to be for the benefit of animals, slaves, and resident aliens. Indeed, ox and donkey are mentioned before the homeborn slave. In contrast to the Deuteronomic decalogue, this appears to reflect a genuine concern for the draught animals. It goes too far, however, to claim that the sabbath was introduced originally for the benefit of the animals.

Whether the laws about returning an ox or ass that has strayed to its owner, even if he is a personal 'enemy' (Ex. 23.4) and giving help to lift up the donkey belonging to a man who hates you when it has fallen under its load (Ex. 23.5) are motivated by a concern for the animals is doubtful. Despite the interpretations of supporters of animal rights,[40] it seems much more likely that the emphasis lies upon the value of the animal to its owner, and that this is a property law rather than one based on humane motives.[41] Certainly there is no suggestion that it was morally wrong to overload the donkey in the first place.

This is supported by the law about animals which fall into a pit that has been left open (Ex. 21.33–34). The man who dug the pit makes restitution to the owner of the animal by paying him its price, and then

---

[40] The extreme instance is probably Regenstein, who claims that this and similar laws make it clear that 'these injunctions to help animals were intended for the sake of these creatures, and not that of the owner . . . one could not "pass by" an animal in distress' (*Replenish the Earth*, 21). Andrew Linzey, however, is more cautious: 'While it would be foolish to look to the Old Testament for a charter of animal rights, what can be clearly gleaned from these examples [Ex. 20.8–11; 23.5, 12; Jonah 4.11; Prov. 12.10] is that the human use of power must be subject to certain constraints for the sake of the animals themselves' (*Rights of Animals*, 32). Robert Murray finds that while many laws concern animals as property, some genuinely express care for them (*Cosmic Covenant*, 118–119).

[41] The commentators are fairly agreed that the law deals with the property of a man with whom one has a legal dispute, and has no concern for the animals themselves. Thus J. P. Hyatt, 'the return of a lost ox or ass may not have been motivated by purely humanitarian reasons; there would have been good reason to return the animal of an enemy who might be disposed to bring a charge of theft' (*Exodus*, 246), and even more forcefully John I. Durham, 'The point at issue in these two verses is not so much a humane attitude towards a lost or improperly laden animal as it is a refusal to take advantage of another's misfortunes because he happens to be an enemy.' Durham suggests that the loose animal would be enjoying itself and the donkey protecting itself under 'a poorly placed load'. The one at risk is the owner (*Exodus*, 331).

keeps the dead animal. It is a purely commercial transaction. In much the same way (in a slightly complex law), if an animal which has been lent to another Israelite is injured or dies, the man who borrowed it must pay full restitution, though only if its owner was not present when the accident occurred (Ex. 22.13–14[14–15]). That the animals are simply property is even more obvious in the laws concerning disputed ownership and the loss of animals left with another person for safe keeping (Ex. 22.8–13[9–14]).

The much discussed law about the goring ox, a law which has parallels in law codes across the ancient Middle East, presents a further complication. When an ox causes the death of another ox the live ox is sold and the proceeds divided between the two owners, and the dead ox is also divided between them. If it was known that the ox was accustomed to gore, the owner has to pay the full price of the dead ox. In both cases it is a purely commercial transaction (Ex. 21.35–36). If, however, it is a human being who has been killed the ox is to be stoned – it is treated as a murderer (Ex. 21.28). But this is not all. Its flesh must not be eaten. This probably means that it is regarded as unclean – ethics and purity have become intertwined. Further, in common with the prescriptions in other law codes, the owner of the goring ox is responsible if the ox was known to be a gorer: he is to suffer the death penalty when the victim is human (Ex. 21.29–30) though the statement that his life can be ransomed suggests that this was the normal practice and execution was rarely carried out.

So far the animals seem to have been treated as valuable property and even as 'delicate tools'[42] which can prove dangerous if not carefully controlled. Three other laws carry rather different connotations. During the 'sabbath' year grain which springs up in the fallow fields is for the poor, and, after they have taken what they need, for the wild animals (Ex. 23.10–11). The implication seems to be that the fallow fields revert to Yahweh, to whose care the wild animals belong.[43] There is no suggestion, however, that the Israelite is

---

[42] So Elijah Judah Schochet describes the Israelite view of animals in the title of one of his chapters. He writes: 'The animal is essentially a piece of property, little more, akin more to a tool than to a slave' (*Animal Life*, 76), and 'The religion of Israel, viewing the world as a product of God's artisanship, saw the animal as an intricately shaped and valuable tool loaned out to man for his use.' He adds that this use is limited. Human beings must not misuse the tools, and it is 'forbidden to destroy such tools without the craftsman's permission, and he is obligated to care for them' (*ibid.*, 78).

[43] Most commentators are concerned with the origins of the sabbath year and whether it was put into practice, and say little about the wild animals. Martin Noth comments that the concern is not because the animals 'were the object of a love which we can hardly presuppose in the ancient world, but because they are an integral part of the creation which from time to time is to return to its "rest"' (*Exodus*, 190). On the other hand Brevard S. Childs believes that the practice stems from 'a genuine humanitarian

under any obligation to care for the wild animals. They did not put out food for the birds!

The law of sacrificing the firstborn of oxen and sheep declares that the calf or lamb is to remain for seven days with its mother (Ex. 22.29[30]). Philo of Alexandria in the first century CE believed that this is due to kindly consideration for the mother animal. He suggested that to kill the young animal immediately after birth would show a 'cruel soul' by inflicting the pain of immediate separation on the mother so soon after her birth pains, and would cause the mother to suffer still more through the unrelieved pressure of her milk (*Virt.* 125–130). It seems more likely that the restriction was related to the ritual impurity associated with birth, and may be compared with the delaying of circumcision until the eighth day (Gen. 17.12; Lev. 12.2–3). Philo, living long after the formation of the Book of the Covenant and in a different culture, may not be a trustworthy guide. It is doubtful whether much can be drawn from the surrounding laws in Exodus 22, which refer to firstfruits, the offering of firstborn sons, and the impurity involved in eating meat from animals that have been injured or killed by the attacks of wild animals, but the whole setting is within the ideas of purity and what is owed to God.

The Book of the Covenant ends with the curious law: 'You shall not boil a kid in its mother's milk' (Ex. 23.19; cf. 34.26; Deut. 14.21). The suggestions that this reflects a somewhat sentimental attitude towards the animals, or because it is improper to use milk, which should support life, for purposes of death[44] are hardly right, although Murray accepts that the true reasons for all three 'mother and young' laws (Ex. 22.29[30]; Lev. 22.28 and this one) are that they 'offend against *proper order* by bringing death into shocking contact with the source of life in such a way as to desecrate the due "piety" of relationships'. It is a sin against compassion and against nature.[45] It is possible that the law is opposing a Canaanite practice, but no clear example of such a rite has been found so far.[46] From the time of the

---

feeling of sympathy for the underling and creature alike' (*Exodus*, 482).

[44] Cf. Philo, who regards it as improper to use milk which should feed the living animal to flavour it after it has been killed. It also offends against the bond between mother and child. Philo permits the cooking of meat in milk, but not that of the animal's mother. Those who do so show themselves to be cruelly brutal and lacking in compassion (*Virt.*, 143–144). Philo is a good example of the way his Hellenism affected his interpretation of scripture, here akin to much modern reading of the Old Testament.

[45] Murray, *Cosmic Covenant*, 116–118, his italics.

[46] So Ronald E. Clements in 1972 without any hesitation (*Exodus*, 153), and Brevard S. Childs in 1974 (*Exodus*, 485–486). The suggestion goes back as far as Maimonides (*Guide to the Perplexed*, iii.48). Support was found in Virolleaud's suggestion that a Ugaritic text should be translated '[let them cook] a kid in butter', but it is now

Mishnah (*m. Hul.* 8.4) the law has been interpreted within the requirement to keep meat and milk separate in cooking and eating, but this does not seem to have reached back into biblical times. Drawing from iconography, Othmar Keel proposes that maternity in animals symbolized divine care for life and the blessings of fertility, and the practice would offend against God's love for his creatures.[47] While it is possible that the practice is condemned because it offends against natural 'family' relations, the origins and purpose of this law are totally obscure. While the law is somewhat isolated in all its contexts, it seems to be more closely related to cultic requirements than ethical ones.

(c) Deuteronomy

Two laws in Deuteronomy have been met already in the Book of the Covenant, the straying ox or sheep, and the ox or donkey fallen under its load (Deut. 22.1–4), but here they are extended to the animals of fellow Israelites rather than one's enemy. The straying animal, however, is to be kept by the finder until its owner can be discovered, which may indicate some concern for its welfare.[48] And boiling a kid in its mother's milk crops up again (Deut. 14.21).

Three laws which are found only in this book, however, are frequently appealed to as revealing a more humanitarian aspect. Two concern domestic animals. Despite Paul in 1 Corinthians 9.9, 'You shall not muzzle an ox when it treads out the grain' (Deut. 25.4) can hardly have any other force than to oppose the cruelty of preventing the ox from eating any of the corn that is at its feet. This, however, may well be a unique example of sympathy for animals, for although many have claimed that the purpose behind the law, 'You shall not plough with an ox and an ass together' (Deut. 22.10), is to safeguard the weaker donkey, this is unlikely.[49] It is placed among a group of laws against 'mixtures' (not sowing fields with two kinds of seeds, and not wearing clothes of mixed wool and linen), and it is because it

---

recognized that this translation is improbable (J. C. L. Gibson gives, 'coriander in milk', *Canaanite Myths*, 123). Peter C. Craigie points out that even if the reference is to a kid and milk, it does not specify its *mother's* milk (*Deuteronomy*, 233, n. 19). Robert Murray also rejects the suggestion, holding that 'the text is neither near enough in time nor sure enough in reading and sense to provide a solution' (*Cosmic Covenant*, 117).

[47] Othmar Keel, *Das Böcklein*.

[48] Robert Murray sees this as certainly implying relief of suffering. In Judaism it was the basis of the Talmudic principle called the duty of relieving 'suffering of living beings' (*Cosmic Covenant*, 118).

[49] So Regenstein: 'pairing animals of different sizes and strengths would cause a conflict and would place a strain on the weaker of them, or perhaps on both' (*Replenish the Earth*, 21). It should be noted that even Schochet accepts this interpretation (*Animal Life*, 59).

would mean ploughing with 'mixed' animals that it is forbidden. It is an offence against purity.[50]

'If you chance to come upon a bird's nest, in any tree or on the ground, with young ones or eggs and the mother sitting upon the young or upon the eggs, you shall not take the mother with the young; you shall let the mother go, but the young you may take to yourself; that it may go well with you, and that you may live long' (Deut. 22.6–7). A remarkably varied number of interpretations have been offered for this law, which initially might seem also to be humane – 'the first recorded legislation in history for the protection of birds!' Schochet declares.[51] It would, of course, assist the maintenance of the species,[52] but this is hardly an idea current in the time of the collector of the laws. Some of the rabbis said that it was singled out for reward because it was *unimportant*, and simply called for obedience to God's command.[53] Maimonides could discover no reason for the law. Should it not be linked with the laws concerning the sacrificing of the firstborn and boiling a kid in its mother's milk, and a ritual or purity meaning be sought? After all, little concern seems to be shown for the grief of the mother bird. Murray notes that the promise of prosperity and long life is found elsewhere only in the Decalogue in this form, where it is linked with honouring father and mother, and thinks that

[50] Presumably peasants who were not wealthy enough to own a pair of oxen would yoke their ox with a donkey. S. R. Driver notes that ploughs were still (1895) harnessed to this combination of animals in Palestine. A. D. H. Mayes, however, thinks that the proposal of C. M. Carmichael that the law should be interpreted in the light of the prohibition of mixed breeding in Lev. 19.19, giving 'plough' the sense of sexual relations suits the context better. If this is rejected he thinks the motive is humanitarian (*Deuteronomy*, 308). How an ox and a donkey could be persuaded to mate is not explained. Christopher J. H. Wright thinks the rationale behind the law lies in the fact that donkeys were unclean and should not be 'mixed' with the clean oxen, which he sees as a 'badge' of Israel's distinctiveness from the nations, a most improbable interpretation (*Deuteronomy*, 242).

[51] Schochet, *Animal Life*, 58, referring to *Encyclopaedia Britannica*, 1955, 3.636. Gerhard von Rad thinks the law can be attributed only to humane motives (*Deuteronomy*, 141).

[52] A. D. H. Mayes believes that it is 'basically concerned with the continuity of life in general and with the source of food in particular; when only the young are taken the continuance of the life of the species is assured' (*Deuteronomy*, 307). This is most improbable. The Deuteronomists were concerned with religion and cult rather than ecology. A good example of the way modern environmental concerns intrude upon biblical exegesis is provided by Christopher J. H. Wright's comment on this verse: 'Perhaps the most likely rationale . . . is the conservationist principle of preserving a source of food supply for the future by not consuming it all in the present. Long term prudence should set limits to short term greed. . . . Sadly, this is so ignored today that environmentalists warn us that our current ecological destruction . . . is putting the possibility of any "long term" in question' (*Deuteronomy*, 241).

[53] Discussed by Schochet, *Animal Life*, 179–184.

the concept of filial piety extends beyond the merely human sphere,[54] and it is possible that the concern of the Deuteronomist is with respect for parents.

(d) The Holiness Code (Lev. 17–26)
In this collection only four laws are of immediate interest.

The law requiring that the firstborn be left for seven days with its mother (Ex. 22.29[30]) is extended to cover the sacrifice of all young animals (Lev. 22.27), and to it is added a prohibition against killing an animal and its young on the same day (Lev. 22.28). The same questions apply to the first as to the law in Exodus. The second is more difficult. Philo declared that 'it is the height of savagery to slay on the same day the generating cause and the living creatures generated' and regards it as 'the worst possible breach of sacred bonds'.[55] To suggest that it is a matter of economics ('herds must be spared if the family is to survive') would seem most improbable, even though Gerstenberger can quote Evans-Pritchard in support of this.[56] Gordon J. Wenham's observation, 'Every Israelite was expected to do his part in conservation by avoiding wanton destruction of the God-given creation',[57] imports modern concerns into the Old Testament world. Martin Noth thinks, without giving any evidence, that the regulation may forbid a practice found in foreign cults as a fertility rite.[58] Gerstenberger may be on the right lines when he observes that 'For some mysterious, magical reason, a mixing taboo obtains here.'[59] He suggests that it is probably a matter of the sexual distinction between the male calf and its mother. Whatever lies behind the prohibition, it is hardly sympathy with the animals.

In a group of laws concerning murder has been placed one which requires restitution for an animal: 'He who kills a man shall be put to death. He who kills a beast shall make it good, life for life' (Lev. 24.17–18). Attention is drawn to the distinction between killing animals and human beings in v. 21: 'He who kills a beast shall make it good; and he who kills a man shall be put to death.' It fits the hierarchy of value which controls most of the Old Testament.[60] This

---

[54] Murray, *Cosmic Covenant*, 119. He adds, however, that the context 'does not lend itself to simple analysis'. The view has rabbinic precursors.

[55] Robert Murray holds the rhetoric flowery but the exegesis good (*Cosmic Covenant*, 115).

[56] Erhard S. Gerstenberger, *Leviticus*, 331. The reference is to Edward E. Evans-Pritchard, *Nuer Religion*.

[57] Gordon J. Wenham, *Leviticus*, 296.

[58] Martin Noth, *Leviticus*, 163. So also J. R. Porter, *Leviticus*, 177.

[59] Gerstenberger, *Leviticus*, 331.

[60] Elijah Jacob Schochet posits a hierarchy with God at the apex. Beneath him are his

entails that the penalties for injury to slaves are less than those for committing the same offences against full members of the Israelite community, and animals are of less value than slaves. Nevertheless, the fact that killing animals is placed next to laws dealing with murder may show an awareness that animals are not being treated *merely* as property.

The Wisdom Literature

To move to the wisdom writings is to enter another world. Apart from the different forms, two features stand out: animals are mentioned far more often, and yet there are only two verses in Proverbs which can be seen as possessing any clear ethical thrust. The first: 'A righteous man has regard for the life of his beast, but the mercy of the wicked is cruel' (Prov. 12.10), is generally taken to teach caring for one's animals. The word translated 'life' is *nepeš* ('soul'), and translations vary: 'know the needs of their animals' (NRSV), 'cares for his beast' (REB), 'has compassion on his animals' (NJB), 'Good people take care of their animals' (GNB). Robert Murray proposes 'A just person feels for the nature of his animals.' Drawing attention to the highly charged words within the proverb, *ṣaddīq* ('righteous') and *raḥ^amīm* (compassion), words used of the attitudes of God towards human beings and of human beings towards each other, he argues that this brings animals within the sphere of human ethics. There is not the same directness, however, as appears in the protestations of innocence in the Egyptian *Book of the Dead* which Robert Murray quotes: 'I have not committed evil against men. I have not mistreated cattle.'[61] Richard J. Clifford notes that the phrase 'to know the soul' is found in Exodus 23.9, where it means that the Israelites know what it feels like to be a resident alien. Nevertheless, he rejects this here in favour of the more general meaning: 'to be sympathetically aware of an animal's condition, especially whether it has enough to eat' both because the animal can feel pain and because it provides its owners with food and clothing.[62] As early as 1899 Toy found kindness to animals in this proverb, and went so far as to say that the good man shows more care of the animals than of human beings.[63] It seems

---

servants, the human beings, who till the soil and herd cattle. At the lowest level are domestic animals. Wild animals, however, stand outside human care. Human beings have no obligations towards their well-being (*Animal Life*, 5).

[61] Murray, *Cosmic Covenant*, 113. The quotation from the *Book of the Dead* can be found in *ANET*, 34 (A1 and A2).

[62] Richard J. Clifford, *Proverbs*, 131. Cf. William McKane: 'The *ṣaddīq* is the humane person who has regard for the well-being of his animals', in contrast to the wicked who are 'as hard as flint' (*Proverbs*, 452).

[63] Crawford H. Toy, *Proverbs*, 247–248.

probable that a genuine concern for domestic animals is expressed here.

The second, 'Know well the condition of your flocks, and give attention to your herds' is less certainly ethical, since the sentence continues, 'for riches do not last for ever' (Prov. 27.23–24), suggesting that the reason for caring for the animals is because this will lead to increased wealth. Possibly agricultural wealth is contrasted with that of trade and commerce, as McKane suggests.[64]

A more fruitful approach to the attitude of the wise men towards animals is to observe the way they refer to them. Although proverbs are passed on across the generations, and they become stock examples, many of them reveal a close observation of animals, and throughout the wisdom writings a greater appreciation of nature than is found in most of the rest of the Old Testament may be discerned. The large number of references to animals is striking. As we have already seen human beings can learn from the animals (Prov. 6.6–11; 30.24–28). There is a sense of wonder at some of the animals, such as eagles, snakes, ants, badgers, locusts, the lizard, lions, cockerels, and goats (Prov. 30.19, 24–28, 30–31). Similes express the characteristics that are commonly attributed to animals: the wife of a man's youth is a lovely doe (Prov. 5.19), the king's wrath is like the growling of a lion (Prov. 19.12), riches vanish suddenly like the flight of an eagle (Prov. 23.5), and wine bites like a serpent (Prov. 23.32). Yet despite deep wonder at the natural world, the primary interest of the sages is in human society. They ask what lessons nature can teach us. It is a modern writer who adds: 'That we human beings can learn wisdom from observing how animals behave is a sobering thought.'[65]

Despite this apparent appreciation of animals, the wise men accept with a conservative compliance the ways they are usually treated. Domestic animals are used for ploughing and as food (Prov. 7.22; 9.2; 14.4; 15.17), and horses in war (Prov. 21.31). The use of bridle and whip are mentioned without comment (Prov. 26.3), wild animals are hunted and snared (Prov. 1.17; 6.5; 7.22–23), although they are also feared (Prov. 17.12; 22.13; 26.13, 17).

Qoheleth stands out from most of the other writers in denying that there is any distinction between human beings and animals: both die, both suffer the same fate, and there is no knowing whether the human spirit goes upward and the spirit of animals goes downward to the earth (Qoh. 3.18–21). In view of Qoheleth's philosophy of life, this should probably be taken to mean that there is no life after death for

---

[64] McKane, *Proverbs*, 618, so also Richard J. Clifford, who finds a double meaning in the verbs: take care of your flocks and attend to the kind of wealth they provide (*Proverbs*, 241).

[65] Kenneth T. Aitken, *Proverbs*, 121.

either animals or human beings, and puts in question the superiority of human beings over the animals. Tremper Longman III opposes Whybray's assertion that the thought of the whole Old Testament is in complete agreement with Qoheleth, since these verses in effect reject a special relationship with God and rule over the animals.[66] But Graham Ogden thinks that Qoheleth believes that human beings *ought* to be superior animals, but death negates any distinction.[67]

Apart from this his views are similar to the rest of the Old Testament. Animals are wealth (Qoh. 2.7). Snakes are dangerous (Qoh. 10.8, 11). It is accepted without question that fish are netted and birds snared (Qoh. 9.12). And dead flies make perfume stink (Qoh. 10.1).

The Yahweh speeches in the book of Job (Job 38–41) present the most striking view of nature in the whole Bible. By displaying the wonders of both the inanimate world and the world of the animals, God points out to Job his insignificance and his own majesty and power.[68] Job is excluded from nature, ignorant of the breeding cycle of the mountain goats, scorned by the wild ass, unable to tame the wild ox, and powerless to command either hawk or eagle. Even if it is an addition to the original poem, and despite the reference possibly being to a mythological monster, the question, 'Can you draw out Leviathan with a fishhook?' expresses the feebleness of Job's power over nature. God alone understands his creatures.[69]

---

[66] *Ecclesiastes*, 129–130.

[67] Graham Ogden, *Qoheleth*, 61.

[68] In contrast to this, in the poem on wisdom (Job 28), the fact that miners go where no 'bird of prey' or 'proud beasts' have been (vv. 7–8) perhaps implies that human beings possess a certain superiority to the animals, if only in technology.

[69] So Murray: 'The theme of God's knowledge of and care for all creatures is strongly represented in the Bible' (*Cosmic Covenant*, 120). He also points to God's benevolent care for all creatures hymned in Ps. 104, and other psalms, and at the end of the book of Jonah. Robert Gordis sees the significance of the Yahweh speeches in the fact that the elements of the natural world are 'expressions of God's creative will and have been called into being *without any reference to man's desires or needs, or even his existence*' ('Job and Ecology', 195, his italics; Gordis believes that Behemoth and Leviathan are natural creatures, not mythological monsters). The speeches, in his view, make the point that 'man is not the center of the universe nor the goal of creation' (p. 196). From this he draws three conclusions: (1) 'the universe is not anthropocentric, but theocentric, with purposes known only to God, and which man cannot fathom'; (2) since the universe was not created with man as its center, neither the Creator nor the cosmos can be judged from man's vantage point'; (3) 'Man takes his place among the other living crreatures, all of whom are the handiwork of God and have an equal right to live on His earth. Man, therefore, surely has no inherent right to abuse or exploit the living creatures or the natural resources to be found in a world not of his making, nor intended for his exclusive habitation' (pp. 198–199). Gordis accepts that Genesis presents a different view, although he sees in the vegetarian diet of human beings a limit placed on their absolute power over nature. He also, very properly, notes that the poet did not intend to present a religio-ethical basis for ecology.

Regenstein gives the title 'Job, the Naturalist' to his account of the book. He sees as a 'primary thesis' the view that human beings must live in harmony with nature and learn from its 'wise and mysterious' ways. Elihu gives Job a 'lesson in ecology'. He draws from Job 30.1 the teaching that 'some animals are better than some people'.[70] This again is to import modern presuppositions into the interpretation of the Old Testament text. In stark contrast Habel sees Job's statement as stressing the degraded character of his tormentors by comparing them to animals. Dogs were symbols of filth and baseness (cf. 1 Kgs. 14.11; 21.19, 23–24; Prov. 26.11).[71] On the other hand it may well be that Job is not placing those who mock him alongside dogs but suggesting that he would not have employed them to take charge of the dogs (so Hartley, who describes this as 'a very low job').[72]

Whether ethical questions concerning animals came within the purview of the author of Job is doubtful. What is certain is that he had a vision of the majesty of nature that is matched only by some of the psalms. Moreover, the descriptions reveal its independence of human beings, who are never seen as rulers over any part of it or stewards of it. This rightly puts them in their place, but it has little to teach on kindness to animals.

The Prophets

A striking feature of many of the prophets' words is the abundance of animal metaphors and similes. Lion is a common image for Yahweh (Hos. 5.14; 13.7; Jer. 25.36–38); Yahweh roars like a lion (Amos 1.2; Hos. 11.10; Isa. 31.4), as do Israel's enemies (Isa. 5.29–30; Jer. 2.15). The distress of the Moabite women is likened to the fluttering of birds (Isa. 16.2); the Babylonians will be like a hunted gazelle (Isa. 13.14). The King of Assyria boasts that he has brought down his enemies 'like a bull' (Isa. 10.13). In his psalm-like prayer, Hezekiah declares that God breaks his bones like a lion, while he moans like a swallow, a crane, or a dove (Isa. 38.13–14, cf. 59.11; Ezek. 7.16; Nahum 2.7). In God's sight the inhabitants of the world are like grasshoppers (Isa. 40.22), and will die like gnats (Isa. 51.6), while those who wait on Yahweh will mount up with wings like eagles (Isa. 40.31). The watchmen are 'dumb dogs' and cannot bark (Isa. 56.10). Sinners hatch adders' eggs and weave a spider's web (Isa. 59.5). As we saw earlier, Jeremiah depicts Israel as a restive young camel, a wild ass in heat (Jer. 2.23–24), well-fed lusty stallions, each neighing for his neighbour's wife (Jer. 5.8). A proverbial saying likens those who

---

[70] Regenstein, *Replenish the Earth*, 31–33.
[71] Norman Habel, *Job*, 418.
[72] John E. Hartley, *Job*, 397.

amass unjust riches to a partridge gathering a brood she did not hatch (Jer. 17.11). The oracles against the nations at the end of Jeremiah yield a clutch of metaphors: Egypt as a beautiful heifer attacked by a gadfly, her hired soldiers like fatted calves, her enemies more numerous than locusts, while she makes a sound like a serpent gliding away (Jer. 46.20-23); even though Edom makes its nest as high as the eagle's Yahweh will bring it down (Jer. 49.16; cf. Obad. 4); its enemy will fly swiftly like an eagle (Jer. 49.22); Babylon's enemies will bring up horses like bristling locusts (Jer. 51.27). Besides his elaborate allegories of the eagle and the lioness (Ezek. 17; 19), Ezekiel likens the princes to lions and wolves (Ezek. 22.25, 27), and refers obscenely to Oholibah's lovers (Ezek. 23.20). Hosea likens Israel to a stubborn heifer (Hos. 4.16; cf. 10.11), Yahweh to a moth (or perhaps 'festering sore' REB, Hos. 5.12); Ephraim is like a dove (Hos. 7.11), and its glory will fly away like a bird (Hos. 9.11). Micah says he will make lamentation like jackals and mourn like ostriches (Mic. 1.8), and calls on the Israelites to make themselves bald as eagles (Mic. 1.16). Habakkuk says that the horses of the Chaldeans are swifter than leopards, fiercer than evening wolves, and their horsemen fly as swiftly as eagles (Hab. 1.8).

Amid this wealth of imagery, the repetition of a few stock images is notable – lions, eagles, birds, locusts. It suggests that the prophets picked up common characterizations of a relatively few animals rather than actively noting the animals themselves, although the background was that of a peasant society where the farmers knew the dangers to their flocks and the way some of their livestock acted. They seem to be at one with the Israelite peasants in taking animals for granted. Flocks and herds are a sign of wealth, as in the patriarchal stories, and to live without fear of attack is a symbol of security under divine protection (e.g., Isa. 32.18, 20). Descriptions of the way God will 'shepherd' his people must reflect the way shepherds looked after their flocks, gathering the lambs in their arms and gently leading those with young (Isa. 40.11), looking for those who had wandered away, gathering those which had been scattered (Jer. 23.3) and protecting them like a shepherd (Jer. 31.10). In one of the rare places in Ezekiel where metaphor comes alive, Yahweh condemns the 'shepherds' who have failed to care for the flock and declares that he himself will be Israel's shepherd, rescuing them, feeding them on good pasture, seeking the lost, binding up the crippled, strengthening the weak, and saving them from wild animals, so that they can live in safety in abundant pasture. This security is increased by banishing the wild animals which prey upon the domestic animals and the crops, and even kill human beings (Ezek. 34). Comparisons with shepherds perhaps are the places where more concern for animals and care for them are found.

Trapping animals, netting fish, setting snares for birds and taking their eggs appear in the writings of the prophets without any sense of these activities being out of the normal, still less wrong (Amos 3.5; Hos. 5.1; 7.12; 9.8; Isa. 8.14; 10.14; Jer. 5.26–27; 16.16; 48.44; Ezek. 12.13; 19.8–9; 26.14; 47.9–10; Hab. 1.15–17). Although there are no descriptions of a hunt, hunting is a metaphor for hostile attacks (e.g., Isa. 13.14), and must reflect what was a fairly common practice, especially in view of the laws concerning the eating of game (Deut. 12.15–16; 14.5; 15.22–23; Lev. 17.13–14). It is against this atmosphere of normality that the way the prophets refer to the treatment of animals must be set.

It has already been noted that the prophets make no comment on the possible suffering of animals when they are sacrificed, although the phrase 'like a lamb for the slaughter' is found more than once (Isa. 53.7; Jer. 11.19; 12.3), and silence is likened to the way sheep are silent when they are being shorn (Isa. 53.7). Even those prophets who question the validity of sacrifice, whether outright or because the sacrifice is not backed up with social justice, say nothing about the animals which are being killed. Yahweh's vengeance and victory are depicted as a sacrificial feast (Isa. 34.6–8). This lack of interest in the treatment of animals is general. Justice is between human beings only, and there is little recognition that animals possess rights, a modern conception that does not go unchallenged even today.

Jeremiah and Joel show a greater sensitivity to the plight of animals when they describe the famine and drought with which God is going to punish Israel (Jer. 14.5–6; Joel 1.18), and 'Second Isaiah' notes that the fish die of thirst when God brings drought (Isa. 50.2), but they are unusual in the Old Testament.

Wild animals are one of the traditional means by which Yahweh punishes Israel's sin, alongside the attack of a foreign enemy, plague, and drought: locusts (Amos 7.1; Joel 1.4), lions, wolves and leopards (Jer. 5.6), dogs, birds of prey, wild animals (Jer. 15.3). Often animals become metaphors for the enemy (Isa. 5.29–30; 7.18; 46.11; 56.9; and sometimes it is not certain whether the threat is real or metaphorical, e.g., the serpents in Jer. 8.17; 12.9). The power and terror of the avenging enemy is emphasized by describing the might of their horses, riders and chariots (the hoofs of the enemy's horses are like flint (Isa. 5.28; cf. Jer. 4.13; Hab. 1.8 for the speed and fierceness of horses)).

A conventional way of emphasizing the utter devastation that is coming upon Israel or its enemies is to portray cities being destroyed so completely that they become the haunt of jackals and other wild animals (Isa. 13.21–22; 14.23; 32.14; 34.11,13–15; Jer. 10.22). They may even turn back to pasture (Isa. 5.17; 17.2; 27.10), or to total desolation (Hos. 4.3; Jer. 9.9–10[10–11]; 12.4; 32.43; 33.10;

Ezek. 25.5; Joel 1.18, 20; Zeph. 1.3; 2.14–15). The horror of war is increased by pictures of vultures descending on the corpses and wild animals devouring them (Isa. 18.6; Jer. 7.33; 16.4; 19.7; 34.20 (a Deuteronomic theme, Deut. 28.26); Ezek. 29.5).

This makes the passages which look to a future time when there will be peace between animals and human beings appear strikingly isolated, but a few passages lead gently towards them.

Isaiah contrasts the obedience of the farm animals with the wilful rebellion of Israel: the ox knows its owner, the ass its master's crib, but the people of Israel, though God's children, neither know God nor understand him (Isa. 1.2–3). The later prophet describes the weary labour of the animals which are forced to drag the Babylonian images away (Isa. 46.1). Jeremiah, more strikingly, turns to the wild birds rather than the domesticated animals. By a hidden knowledge of God's will for them, stork, turtle dove, swallow and crane migrate at the appropriate times, but God's people does not know and obey his law (Jer. 8.7). We remember that it was Jeremiah who expressed sympathy with the animals who were caught up in God's punishment of Israel (14.5–6), but 'Second Isaiah' declares that when God provides water in the desert as he prepares for the homecoming of his exiled people, it is the wild animals, jackals and ostriches, who honour him (Isa. 43.20).

Wild animals are always a threat to the peasant farmer and his livestock, however, and one feature of the happy future, as depicted by Ezekiel, when Yahweh himself is king, is that they will be banished from the land and the Israelites will be secure (Ezek. 34.25, 28). It is not clear whether they are to be annihilated or simply will be prevented from coming into Israel's land. The verb, wᵉhišbattî ('and I will cause to cease'), is ambiguous and the English translations equally so: 'banish' (RSV, NRSV), 'rid the land of wild beasts' (NEB, REB, NIV), 'rid the country of wild animals' (JB, NJB), 'I will get rid of all the dangerous animals' (GNB). Few commentators on this passage consider what happens to the wild animals, Zimmerli, for example, simply saying that Ezekiel speaks of their 'removal', in contrast to Hosea 2.18[20] which understands the covenant with the animals as a 'covenant of reconciliation'.[73] Eichrodt, however, after stressing the contrast with Hosea, where the animals are full partners in the covenant, points out that the animals benefit little from the covenant that Ezekiel envisages, for they are driven from the land by Yahweh's power.[74] Pedersen similarly finds two versions of the covenant: 'either the beasts of the field are to be exterminated or they are to be entirely transformed.' In Ezekiel they are exterminated. He

[73] Walther Zimmerli, *Ezekiel*, 2, 220.
[74] Walther Eichrodt, *Ezekiel*, 479–480.

points out the significance of this. 'The security of Israel, its prosperity and undisturbed joy at its growth and fertility is the centre of life. Round this centre everything else must be arranged. Beasts of prey must disappear or be transformed.' He links this with the similar desire that human foreign enemies must be exterminated or subordinate themselves to Israel.[75] It seems to me that whether the wild animals are simply driven out of the land (presumably into the desert) or are exterminated, the effect is much the same. Everything is for the benefit of human beings. Leviticus 26.6 has the same phrase as Ezekiel,[76] while Isaiah 35.9 says that no ravenous beast will come up to the highway across the desert for the Israelite return, both apparently intending that the land and the highway will be kept free of predators.[77]

Hosea may possibly go further. In the happy future, when Israel abandons Baal worship and responds once again to Yahweh as she had done in the wilderness period, God promises that he will make a covenant with the wild animals, the birds, and the creeping things, as well as making an end of war (Hos. 2.20[18]). Most think that the animals are not driven out of the land, still less exterminated. The Israelites will live at peace with the wild animals. Yet some doubts must still be felt. Although this appears to be a genuine covenant with the animals, nature is reordered for the sake of Israel. The covenant is 'for them' (i.e., for the Israelites' benefit) and its aim is not to *produce* a peaceful coexistence between human beings and wild animals, but to ensure the harvest of 'the grain, the wine, and the oil'.[78]

In the face of these doubts, the prophecy in Isaiah 11.6–9 appears almost unique. Not only do the animals live at peace with human beings, they are at peace with one another, wolves and lambs, leopards and kids, lions and fatlings. The prophecies at the end of the book echo this, but add that the serpent's food will be dust (Isa. 65.25[79]). As in the creation story in Genesis, the carnivorous animals become vegetarian, and the curse after the 'Fall' is reversed. In sum,

[75] Johs. Pedersen, *Israel I–II*, 325–326.

[76] Apart from Mary Douglas, the commentators on Leviticus are equally uninterested in the fate of the wild animals. Mary Douglas, however, does not discuss 26.6, although she notes that wild animals are part of God's curse in 26.22 (*Leviticus*, 161–162).

[77] Otto Kaiser, however, interprets Ezek. 34.25, Isa. 35.9 and Lev. 26.6 as the *destruction* of the wild animals in the time of salvation (*Isaiah 1–12*, 2nd edn., 259).

[78] A. A. Macintosh points out the contrast with v. 14[12], where the wild animals lay waste Israel's vines and fig trees, and sees the covenant as imposed by Yahweh. The 'balance of nature is ordered for Israel's benefit' (*Hosea*, 81–82).

[79] Since the reference to the snake is not found in Isa. 11.7 Claus Westermann (*Isaiah 40–66*, 407) and R. N. Whybray (*Isaiah 40–66*, 278–279) regard it as a gloss. It is almost certainly a reference to Gen. 3.14, and it is difficult to see how it can refer to paradise restored (but cf. John N. Oswalt, *Isaiah 40–66*, 662).

'they will not hurt or destroy on all my holy mountain' – but at the cost of changing the nature of the beasts of prey. John N. Oswalt, aware that 'the lion's carnivorousness is fundamental to what a lion is' and a literal fulfilment of the prophecy would mean 'a basic alteration of the lion's nature', believes that the passage is an extended figure of speech, making a single point, that 'in the Messiah's reign the fears associated with insecurity, danger, and evil will be removed, not only for the individual but for the world as well'.[80] His interpretation is wrong. The creation myth described all the animals as vegetarian, and this is a vision of paradise restored. Otto Kaiser regards a lion which eats straw as 'an unnatural, sick phenomenon', while the child playing safely with the most poisonous snakes means that the old enmity between the offspring of the woman and the snake has been removed. He thinks that the passage must have had a wider original context, beyond our hope of discovering,[81] and finds the expectation of the return of primal peace, embracing both men and animals, limited to Isaiah 11.6–9 and Isaiah 65.25 (with perhaps Hosea 2.20[18] also). R. E. Clements is aware of the essential role predatory behaviour plays in securing the survival of many animals, and sees that a literal fulfilment of the prophecy would mean 'the abolition of "the wild" in the form in which we have come to know it'.[82] After a careful exegesis of the passage within the unit Isaiah 10.5–12.6, which finds several layers of text and at its heart royal promises in the exilic and post-exilic period, he contrasts the implicit assumption of the passage that there is something seriously wrong with the present order of the world with the general view throughout the Old Testament that killing by predatory animals is normal. He suggests that the hyperbole in the passage (and Hos. 2.20[18]) 'appears to have arisen out of a concern to outlaw human warfare', and it is human violence which is the primary target. Animal aggression is not to be used as an excuse for human aggression.[83]

It begins to look as though the Old Testament is thoroughly anthropocentric, one of the worst vices in the eyes of those championing the rights of animals. This raises the wider question of the Israelite attitude to nature, a subject which demands a chapter to itself.[84]

[80] Oswalt, *Isaiah 1–39*, 283.
[81] Kaiser, *Isaiah 1–12*, 2nd edn., 260.
[82] Clements, 'The Wolf', 83–84.
[83] *Ibid.*, 97, 99. The examples of the normal activity of predators which he offers are Ps. 104.21; Job 38.39–41; 1 Sam. 17.34–37; 1 Kgs. 13.24–25; 2 Kgs. 17.25–28; sometimes in divinely willed retribution.
[84] Katharine J. Dell's 'Animal Imagery' appeared when this book was in proof. She usefully collects the evidence in Psalms, Proverbs, Job and Qoheleth, but shows little appreciation of the gap between ourselves and ancient Israelite society and culture.

17

NATURE

The Debate over the Old Testament and the Environment

It is usual to begin discussions of the relation between Christianity and the modern concern for the environment with Lynn White's famous article, 'The Historical Roots of Our Ecological Crisis', and indeed we shall come to that shortly. But the debate began earlier than that. One important contribution was the study originally with the title *The Intellectual Adventure of Ancient Man*, which was transmuted into *Before Philosophy* when it crossed the Atlantic. In this the Frankforts present a glowing account of science as an 'instrument for the interpretation of experience, one that has achieved marvels and retains its full fascination'. It is science which 'progressively reduces the individual phenomena to typical events subject to universal laws' through the postulate of causality. With a confidence in science, which today seems absurd, they laud the way it has reduced the phenomenal world to an 'it', introduced the distinction between subject and object, and analysed causality. And this they claim was made possible because Hebrew thought began to break away from myth. The transcendence of God reduced nature to his creation and hence 'all concrete phenomena are devaluated'.[1] (They see the final emancipation from myth achieved by Greek philosophy, but that does not concern us here.) Thus in the period when few dared to question the ability of science to achieve lasting blessing for humankind, credit for the rise of science was given to the Judaic–Christian biblical tradition.[2]

---

[1] Henri Frankfort, *et al.*, *Before Philosophy*, 11–14, 19–20, 23–24, 237, 242.

[2] In his Inaugural Lecture as Lady Margaret Professor of Divinity in the University of Oxford, John Macquarrie pointed to Harvey Cox's *The Secular City* and Johannes Metz's *Theology of the World* as further examples of this theme ('Creation and Environment', 4). He criticizes them, yet he describes the Old Testament view as 'monarchical', with God a self-sufficient, transcendent being, although he also finds traces of a view in which 'God and the world are not sharply separated'. It is of interest to note, in view of more recent criticisms, that Macquarrie questions the suggestion that human beings are 'stewards' of the natural world, on the grounds that it still treats the world as a piece of property (p. 8). James Barr adds several other scholars to these, including John Macmurray and Alan Richardson ('Man and Nature', 13–14). In his commentary on Genesis 1–11, however, Richardson sets alongside his suggestion that we may see 'in the marvels of modern science, and in the astounding dominion over

Lynn White, on the other hand, wrote at a time when an awareness of the ecological crisis and possible disaster for the whole planet was beginning to be felt widely, when, in his own words, science and technology, 'to judge by many of the ecologic effects, are out of control'. His article is often summarized as if he were simply saying that the responsibility for this situation lies in Genesis 1.26–28. In fact it is much more far-reaching in its scope, surveying most of Christian history, especially the Middle Ages, and judging that: 'Christianity bears a huge burden of guilt.'[3] The critical passage for our purposes, however, is this:

> In sharp contrast [to Graeco-Roman mythology], Christianity inherited from Judaism not only a concept of time as nonrepetitive and linear but also a striking story of creation. By gradual stages a loving and all-powerful God had created light and darkness, the heavenly bodies, the earth and all its plants, animals, birds, and fishes. Finally, God had created Adam and, as an afterthought, Eve to keep man from being lonely. Man named all the animals, thus establishing his dominance over them. God planned all of this explicitly for man's benefit and rule: no item in the physical creation had any purpose save to serve man's purposes. And, although man's body is made of clay, he is not simply part of nature: he is made in God's image.
>
> Especially in its Western form, Christianity is the most anthropocentric religion the world has seen.[4]

White recognizes that there is 'an alternative Christian view', seen in St Francis, whom he proposes as a patron saint for ecologists, but he does not appear to think this alternative has much chance of influencing either the church or society. His gloomy conclusion is that 'we shall continue to have a worsening ecologic crisis until we reject the Christian axiom that nature has no reason for existence save to serve man'.[5]

White's article provoked a large number of ripostes from Christians generally, although as James Barr has pointed out, both White and

---

the world of nature which man has achieved thereby, a partial fulfilment of the divine intention in the creation that man should "subdue" the earth' the warning that human beings are responsible to God for their stewardship, pointing to the dust-bowl and Hiroshima as the consequences if they do not (*Genesis 1–11*, 55). Hans Walter Wolff sees the nature of the 'universal human stewardship' as 'absolute dominance', but qualifies this by affirming that the dominion must not lead to pollution of the environment or to 'man's being dominated by a myth of technology' (*Anthropology*, 163–164).

[3] White, 'Historical Roots', 1206. I find the obsession with Lynn White in many recent studies somewhat perplexing, since his reference to Genesis 1 forms only a minor part of his argument.

[4] *Ibid.*, 1205.

[5] *Ibid.*, 1207.

those who had a favourable view of science accepted the same thesis.[6] Here I fasten only on Old Testament studies.

James Barr was not only one of the first to examine carefully the biblical evidence[7] but also presents one of the clearest arguments. He denies that the image of God in man was his position of dominion over nature, rejects the idea that human domination in Genesis 1 consisted of power and exploitation, and points out that whatever interpretation is given to *rādāh* ('have dominion over') and *kābaš* ('subdue'), it does not include eating animals, for Genesis 1.30 states explicitly that both human beings and animals were vegetarian. It is only after the Flood that authority to eat animal flesh is granted, and only then that there is any suggestion that dominion included terrifying consequences for the animal world (Gen. 9.2–3). As for the two verbs, while *rādāh* is used of treading the wine-press in Joel 4.13, this is a different semantic department of it, and it is used generally of kings ruling over regions, masters controlling servants, and God ruling his land. The verb *kābaš* can suggest violence, but in the Genesis context it is applied to the earth and what is meant is tilling the land. Thus exploitation is not intended, and Barr compares Isaiah 11, where there is peace between the animals and human beings. He questions whether the Genesis passage had as great an effect in encouraging technological exploitation as is claimed. Moreover, the stories in Genesis show little interest in the development of tools and weapons.[8] After examining the later section of White's article, Barr ends with four biblical 'insights' that may be relevant to ecological concerns: (1) in the creation story everything was 'good', which seems to be a motive against exploitation and pollution of the world; (2) the world is an ordered world, something held in common by science; (3) the 'dominion' given to the first human beings is not narrowly defined but appears to be leadership rather than exploitation, and this is in accord with the task of conserving and caring for the natural resources; and (4) such insights into incipient science and technology are found primarily in the wisdom literature, but, although the Israelites recognized the world of techniques, they did not claim it for their own, and did not justify it from their own religious tradition.

Walter Houston, in an immensely learned article which ranges far beyond the Old Testament, openly takes as his starting point modern exploitation of the natural world and the value system which has

[6] Barr, 'Man and Nature', 15–16.

[7] Walter Houston, however, notes that C. F. D. Moule considered the question as early as 1964 ('"And let them have dominion . . ."', 168; the reference is to *Man and Nature*).

[8] Barr contrasts Genesis with *Jubilees* 11.23–24, where Abraham instructs skilled carpenters to make a seed drill to prevent the birds from eating the seed ('Man and Nature', 25).

economic growth as the one universally recognized standard of value that is permitted to affect our economic activity.[9] He interprets the terminology of Genesis 1 and 9 and Psalm 8 as derived from the ideology of kingship, and emphasizes that the king was accountable to God and responsible for preserving the covenant, maintaining justice, and defending the weak (cf. Ps. 72). Hence the 'dominion' was not intended for man's own benefit. He was given permission to exploit plants for food, and later animals, and Houston argues that if explicit permission were required, then man's dominion did not provide sufficient grounds for it. Thus 'in the intention of creation man's dominion over the earth and its creatures is directed entirely to *God's* kingdom and glory and *not at all* to his own welfare'. Thus 'man is made God's *responsible representatives* (*sic*) *on earth*'.[10] Nevertheless, the priestly writer is realistic. Genesis 1 is a vision of an ideal past, in the same way that Isaiah 11 is a vision into an ideal future. Man's present state is sinful, and the language of military conquest is used in Genesis 9.1–7 of his relation to the animals. Hence God will appoint institutions to contain sin and limit its destructive effects.[11] Inter-testamental Judaism was fully aware of these effects of human sin.[12]

Despite the passion with which these scholars write, I wonder whether the debate is beside the point so far as Old Testament ethics is concerned, since it begins from the present concern about the environment. As I suggested in the last chapter, the Israelite peasant

---

[9] Houston, '"And let them have dominion . . ."'.

[10] *Ibid.*, 165–167, quotations 167, 165 (his italics). Houston refers to Gerhard von Rad, *Genesis*, 58, and Walther Eichrodt, *Theology* II, 127. He regards Barr's attempt to minimize the harshness of the expressions in Gen. 1.26–28 as irrelevant, since they do not grant the right to exploitation (*ibid.*, 182, n. 26).

[11] *Ibid.*, 168–169.

[12] Among other studies which stress the responsibility of human beings in their exercise of the dominion over nature, we may note J. A Loader's 'Image and order', and Jonathan Helfand's 'The Earth is the Lord's', writing from a Christian and Jewish standpoint respectively. Claus Westermann concentrates on the image of God, providing an excursus on the history of exegesis (*Genesis 1–11*, 147–158). He regards the dominion over the animals as kingly; it 'certainly does not mean their exploitation by humans' (*ibid.*, 159). In his valuable discussion of a Theology of Nature Richard Bauckham makes, *inter alia*, the following points: (1) Gen. 1.26–27 does not state in what the divine image consists, but the idea enables the writer to declare man to be God's representative, sharing God's rule over the world, starting from an empirical observation of human beings as the dominant species; (2) Genesis has been held to teach that the rest of nature was created *for* humanity (cf. 2 Bar. 14.18, 'And you said that you would make a man for this world as a guardian over your works that it should be known that he was not created for the world, but the world for him'); Gen. 2.18–20 comes nearest to this, but if we draw this conclusion it implies that Eve was created for man's benefit too; (3) the Noahic covenant (Gen. 9.8–17), Job 39 and Ps. 104 make it impossible to suppose that the authors thought the animals existed only for human benefit ('Theology of Nature', 232–235).

farmers, who waged a continuous war against the animals that attacked their flocks and crops, would not have been averse to the promise of dominion over the wild animals. Their main regret would surely have been that this was not more complete! Perhaps we should begin with the biblical understanding of nature.

Nature

John W. Rogerson has drawn attention to some of the most important issues and his 1977 paper is the obvious place to start.

He first criticizes the claim of such scholars as H. Wheeler Robinson, Gerhard von Rad, Walther Zimmerli, and Th. C. Vriezen that the writers of the Old Testament had no concept of nature corresponding to our modern idea.[13] He distinguishes between the way the Old Testament writers experienced the natural world and the way they talked about it, arguing that their experience was similar to ours, though their talk was different, and rejecting the view that they experienced it differently as well. One main reason for the scholars' erroneous judgment is their faulty definition of nature, although Wheeler Robinson is the only one to provide a definition. Instead of adopting the definition, 'the creative and regulative physical power which is conceived of as operating in the material world and as the immediate cause of all the phenomena', which Robinson quotes, Rogerson prefers an alternative offered by *SOED*, 'the material world, or its collective objects and phenomena, especially those with which man is most directly in contact'.[14] This is surely right, and is in fact the way most people would think of 'nature'. And it is the way the Old Testament thinks of it.

The other points which Rogerson makes can be summarized very briefly. The Israelites clearly knew the difference between 'ordinary' events that belong to the order and regularity of the natural world and 'miracle' which is abnormal and supernatural, even though they probably would not have made the abstract distinction. It is the very abnormality of 'miracle' which is an essential part of the claim that they are signs and wonders and reveal the divine activity.[15] Further,

---

[13] John W. Rogerson, 'View of Nature', 67–68. The references are to H. Wheeler Robinson *Inspiration*, 1; von Rad, *Wisdom*, 71, and 'Natur- und Welterkenntnis', 120; Zimmerli, *Die Weltlichkeit*, 24; Vriezen, *Theology*, 220.

[14] *Ibid.*, 69–70, 72. Cf. Richard Bauckham's analysis of six theological meanings: (1) the essence of something, (2) the whole of the created world distinguished from God the creator, (3) the whole of the observable world as distinguished from 'the supernatural', (4) the world, including human beings, in its created state prior to God's redemption, (5) nature as opposed to grace, (6) the observable, non-human world, not excluding any part of the universe, but tending to focus on the natural environment of human life ('Theology of Nature', 229).

[15] Rogerson, 'View of Nature', 74–77.

writings such as Proverbs 16.7–12 and Psalm 104 are 'religious texts, containing a religious interpretation of the natural world' and do not show that the ordinary Israelite understood the natural processes in a different way from that of modern men and women, as von Rad and H.-J. Kraus claim.[16] A distinction, therefore, should not be made between the way for us nature is a third 'thing' interposed between God and human beings, independent and autonomous, and the Old Testament view of natural happenings as the direct working of God. Again such views are religious interpretation.[17] Rogerson concludes: 'the attempt of the Old Testament writers to claim the sovereignty of God over nature and its working was not something easily attained with the help of thought processes or an "outlook" that readily saw the divine in everything. It was rather a courageous act of faith, persisted in when there was often much in personal experience and competing religions and outlooks, that suggested that such a conviction was false.'[18]

The whole of this debate, of course, is concerned with understanding and revelation, and does not impinge immediately upon ethics. It has an important bearing on the subject, nevertheless. For if Rogerson is right, and I judge him to be so, then although there is no Hebrew word for nature, and despite the Old Testament writings being religious texts, it is possible to sift out from those texts hints of the way the Israelites reacted to the natural world.[19]

We and the ancient Israelites are essentially at one in what we see and experience as we gaze out at the world around us. We have only to read Wheeler Robinson's eloquent description of the way the biblical writers depict the beauties and mysteries of the natural world to gain something of the appreciation of that world which they possessed.[20] The Old Testament goes far beyond the New in this, and while I judge it still to be true that the writers' main concern was with human beings and the activity of God in relation to Israel, the wealth of imagery drawn from the natural world must not be overlooked.[21]

The problem for those who wish to read the Old Testament as an environmentalist tract, however, is that there is hardly any evidence that the Israelites saw themselves as protectors of the natural world, and to this we now turn.

---

[16] *Ibid.*, 77–79.

[17] *Ibid.*, 79–80.

[18] *Ibid.*, 84.

[19] 'The natural world' is a better term to use than 'nature', since this is what environmentalists are talking about and also what the biblical writers are referring to.

[20] See *Inspiration*, 4–7.

[21] Martin LaBar adopts these values from Holmes Rolston III's analysis and applies these to the Old Testament, some more successfully than others, but the validity of such an approach must be questioned ('Biblical Perspective').

Did the Israelites Protect the Environment?

I begin with one of the best discussions of the attitude of the Old Testament towards the natural world, Robert Murray's *The Cosmic Covenant*. The work is massively wide-ranging and springs from the conviction that the standard Christian theology of creation is fatally flawed and has failed to present the scope and power of biblical teaching. Christians have fastened too narrowly upon the Mosaic covenant, and have failed to appreciate that alongside Sinai stands God's covenant with the whole of nature. Ancient Israel shared with other peoples of the Middle East 'the belief in a divinely willed order harmoniously linking heaven and earth'. In Israelite tradition this harmony was established at creation and 'broken and permanently threatened by disorderly supernatural beings and forces, hostile to God and to humankind', but at the re-creation after the Flood God promised his 'eternal covenant' with all creatures, placing on human beings the duty to maintain justice and mercy. The theme was enacted in rituals in which the king played a leading part, and these rituals secured the control of the hostile forces. Within it all is the idea of peace between human beings and the animals.[22] It will take us too far afield to trace this theme through hints and metaphors across the Bible and beyond as Murray does in his fascinating work.[23] I begin with his references to animals, for although this repeats some of the themes of the last chapter, they cannot be overlooked if a complete view of Murray's thesis is to be obtained.

Drawing on the passage which he describes as 'formally establishing the covenant' (Gen. 9.8–17), paying attention to the preceding seven verses, and comparing it with Genesis 1 and 2, Murray finds two models for thinking about human beings and animals, the first, 'peace *with and between* wild animals as a metaphor for cosmic and social peace', paradisal, the second, 'peace *from* them as a practical aspect of desired *šalom*', this-worldly and realistic.[24] This distinction has rarely been noticed and is of central importance. Examples of the covenant of peace, but peace *from* animals, are Leviticus 26.6 and Ezekiel 34.25.[25]

Although Murray tends to fasten on passages which support animal welfare, he recognizes that there are certain limitations. For example, despite expressions of admiration and sympathy for animals, nowhere are they seen as 'covenant-partners'. The nearest to this is Job 5.22–23, where Eliphaz pictures the blessing given to those who humbly accept God's discipline:

[22] Robert Murray, *Cosmic Covenant*, xx–xxi.
[23] See my review in *ET* 103, 1991–92, 321–323.
[24] Murray, *Cosmic Covenant*, 34.
[25] *Ibid.*, 38–39.

> At destruction and famine you shall laugh,
>   and shall not fear the beasts of the earth.
> For you shall be in league with the stones of the field,
>   and the beasts of the field shall be at peace with you.

Despite the odd mention of 'stones', Murray finds here a belief that 'a religious person will live at peace with all other creatures, as if he were on terms of a solemn treaty or pact with them'.[26]

This brings him to Isaiah 11, which he interprets as blessings desired for a Davidic prince, born or soon expected, and thus fits his overall theme of the relation of the covenant to kingship. Stressing that it is a poem, he finds it difficult to decide whether it promises peace *with* or peace *from* wild animals, but is clear that underlying it is the idea of paradise restored, with references to Genesis 1–2.[27]

Next Murray considers human duties towards animals, laws about killing young animals, and care for living animals, much of which has already been noted when the various passages were discussed earlier. Beyond this he refers to several passages where expressions of feeling for animals are found, such as the 'humour and affection' in the Balaam story (Num. 22.22–30) and the care of shepherds for their sheep (Ps. 23; Isa. 40.11; Ezek. 34.15–16). Moreover, animals frequently are depicted as responding to God better than human beings do (Isa. 1.3; Jer. 8.7; Prov. 6.6–8, all already considered). Above all they praise God (Pss. 96.10–12; 98.7–9; 148; Isa. 44.23; 55.12–13, and later the *Benedicite*).[28]

The book is both immensely learned and also extremely attractive, not least in the message which Murray gives to his readers at the end: 'When the Bible's teaching on God's creation and our place in it is duly digested, I believe that it cries out to us "you are brothers and sisters of every other human being, and fellow-creatures of everything else in the cosmos; you have no *right* to exploit or destroy, but you have *duties* to all, under God to whom you are responsible".'[29]

It is of considerable significance, therefore, that Murray finds only two passages in the laws dealing with care of plants. They deserve to be quoted in full.

> When you come into the land and plant all kinds of trees for food, then you shall count their fruit as forbidden; three years it shall be forbidden to you, it must not be eaten. And in the fourth year all their fruit shall be holy, an offering of praise to the LORD. But in the fifth year you may eat of their fruit, that they may yield more richly for you. (Lev. 19.23–25)

---

[26] *Ibid.*, 102, referring to Qimhi and Rashi.
[27] *Ibid.,* 103–110.
[28] *Ibid.*, 112–121.
[29] *Ibid.*, 174.

Murray describes the requirement as 'young fruit trees are to be nursed', and again refers to Philo, who praises the law as another example of the lawgiver's 'kindness and graciousness' (*Virt.* 156–160). This is a further example of Murray's desire to interpret the Old Testament in ways that fit his environmentalist position. Most commentators see pre-Yahwistic customs beneath this law, in which the fruits belong to the tree deities or to the spirit of the ground.[30] It is questionable whether such ideas would have been tolerated by the priestly writer, and the only way that anything can be salvaged from this theory would be to suppose that the practice of not taking the fruit for four years had become a traditional custom by his time, with its original meaning long lost. The Hebrew phrase translated 'you shall count their fruit as forbidden' is the strange 'you shall treat its fruit as its uncircumcised foreskin' (NJB actually translates 'you will regard its fruit as uncircumcised'), which clearly shows that we are dealing with ritual and purity, not ethics here.[31] The promise that if they leave the fruit for three years and give the fourth year's fruit as an offering of praise to Yahweh, the trees will yield more richly is hardly a sufficient foundation for taking the law as either showing kindliness to the tree, or a matter of efficient husbandry.

The other passage to which Murray draws attention is Deuteronomy 20.19–20:

> When you besiege a city for a long time, making war against it in order to take it, you shall not destroy its trees by wielding an axe against them; for you may eat of them, but you shall not cut them down. Are the trees in the field men[32] that they should be besieged by you? Only the trees which you know are not trees for food you may destroy and cut down that you may build siegeworks against the city that makes war with you, until it falls.

Murray again refers to Philo, who emphasizes the innocence and friendliness of trees, and notes that this law became the basis for the rabbinic principle of care for created nature and has been developed to form the main foundation of Jewish teaching about use of the environment.[33] It was a common practice among Egyptians, Assyrians and Greeks to devastate the land they conquered, and Elisha prophesies that when Yahweh gives Israel victory over the Moabites

---

[30] So J. R. Porter, *Leviticus*, 157–158, Philip J. Budd, *Leviticus*, 282, Erhard S. Gerstenberger, *Leviticus*, 274–275. G. J. Wenham rationalizes (*Leviticus*, 271).

[31] While it is true that the root *'rl* is used in metaphorical ways (of heart (Lev. 26.41; Deut. 10.16; Jer. 4.4; 9.25[26]; Ezek. 44.7), lips (Ex. 6.12, 30), flesh (Ezek. 44.7, 9) and ear (Jer. 6.10)), the link with the rite is closer here.

[32] Almost everyone emends the definite article of the MT pointing to the interrogative, certainly rightly.

[33] Murray, *Cosmic Covenant*, 119–120.

and they conquer every fortified city, they will 'fell every good tree, and stop up all springs of water, and ruin every good piece of land with stones', a prophecy which was fulfilled to the letter (2 Kgs. 3.19, 25). Many commentators agree with von Rad and Mayes that the law is attempting, 'to restrain the vandalism of war',[34] and 'is a deuteronomic protest against a practice considered unnecessarily destructive'.[35] Some, however, emphasize utilitarian motives: 'not only would [the fruit trees] provide food for the besieging army, but after the victory they would become part of Israel's new possessions';[36] 'the law ensured that after the siege there should still be a regular supply of food';[37] while Hobbs says that the law in Deuteronomy did not apply in the campaign against Moab, since it was designed 'to ensure that the army's food supply would not be cut off'.[38] These last do not seem entirely right. The rhetorical question which distinguishes between human beings and trees implies that more than mere pragmatic motives lie behind the law, although the fact that other trees may be felled without limit does not suggest that the concern is with the environment as such. Fruit trees serve human beings, but are not active participants in war, and so should be spared destruction.

Alongside Robert Murray's study should be set that of Ronald A. Simkins,[39] a study which is fully aware of the dangers of ethnocentrism ('the judging of all persons in the whole world in terms of one's own culture on the presupposition that, since "we" are by nature human, so if anyone else is human then they should and must be just as we are') and anachronism ('the judging of persons in the past according to standards only relevant to the present') in interpreting the Old Testament writings. Recognizing the difficulty of discovering the impact of the Israelites on their environment, and noting some studies which examine the effect their environment had upon Israelite religion and culture, Simkins sets out to provide a systematic account of the ancient Israelites' worldview and values toward nature, using anthropological models and fastening on the biblical creation myths and metaphors. He identifies three attitudes towards nature: (a) subjugation-to-nature ('Humans have no control over nature and are subject to the inevitable effects of nature'); (b) harmony-with-nature ('Humans are united with nature in a precarious balance so that their actions affect nature and themselves in turn');

---

[34] Gerhard von Rad, *Deuteronomy*, 133.

[35] A. D. H. Mayes, *Deuteronomy*, 296.

[36] Peter C. Craigie, *Deuteronomy*, 277.

[37] Anthony Phillips, *Deuteronomy*, 137.

[38] T. R. Hobbs, *2 Kings*, 37.

[39] Ronald A. Simkins, *Creator and Creation*, quotations pp. 34–35 (with reference to Bruce J. Malina, *Christian Origins*, 29, and T. R. Hobbs, *War*, 210–214).

and (c) mastery-over-nature ('Nature is made up of impersonal objects and forces that humans can/should manipulate for their own purposes').[40] In each culture one of these is preferred, although all are present. The ancient Israelites maintained an unalterable distinction between God as Creator and the creation, but also accepted that human beings and the rest of nature are closely linked as two separate but related parts of the created world.

Simkins claims that the texts which reflect the royal ideology of Jerusalem present a mastery-over-nature orientation when the king is seen as God's earthly vicegerent, especially when defeating his enemies (the outgroup), but a harmony-with-nature orientation in so far as by administering justice he secures the blessing of nature upon his people. The Yahwist and the priestly writer, the prophets, and texts expressing the covenant theology prefer the harmony-with-nature value-system, but because of his innocent suffering, Job experiences nature as hostile and falls back on a subjugation-to-nature orientation, which is also found in some of the exilic prophets as a result of oppression by foreign nations. These prophets, however, look beyond the distress to God's new creation, when Judah will become a new Eden.[41]

Other points which Simkins makes are also important. Thus he rejects the common view, exemplified in von Rad's claim that 'in genuinely Yahwistic belief the doctrine of creation never attained to the stature of a relevant, independent doctrine' but was always subordinated to the doctrine of salvation.[42] Some of his detailed comments on biblical passages have been noted earlier.

Simkins just manages to escape the criticisms which I made about those writers on Old Testament ethics who develop grand, overarching theories, but his own scheme is on a high level of abstraction, and despite his efforts to avoid anachronism, his exegesis of Genesis 2 is largely controlled by feminist thinking, which can hardly be right, given that Israelite society and culture was firmly patriarchal.[43]

In his Epilogue, Simkins argues that the view that the Bible is irrelevant and dangerous to environmental concern is due to scholarly misinterpretation, and he attempts an approach which allows Israel's worldview and values towards nature to make a positive contribution. I shall discuss this later.[44] For the present I simply note that Simkins correctly accepts that the biblical writers 'did not envision our current

[40] *Ibid.*, 33.
[41] Taken mainly from Simkins's own summary, *ibid.*, 252–255.
[42] *Ibid.*, 8–10; referring to von Rad, 'Doctrine of Creation', 142. He notes that von Rad slightly modified this in 'Some Aspects'.
[43] *Ibid.*, 178–193, see, e.g., 183.
[44] See Chapter 19 below.

environmental crisis, nor should we expect them to have addressed it'.[45]

Before looking at other studies, the laws on the sabbatical year (Ex. 23.10–12; Lev. 25.2–7, 18–22) may be briefly noted, since these are sometimes evoked in support of ecology. In their present form the laws offer two main reasons: the natural growth in the seventh year is for the poor and the wild animals (Ex. 23.11); it is a 'sabbath', a time of complete 'rest' for the land, when nothing from it is eaten (Lev. 25.5, but this is complicated by vv. 6–7, which say that the 'sabbath of the land' (a unique phrase) will provide food for everyone, farmer, slaves, resident aliens, animals, both domestic and wild, and Lev. 25.18–22 appears to think of the manna of the Exodus and states that the sixth year will yield sufficient to last over the fallow period). The Leviticus laws are clearly idealistic, and there has been debate as to whether the practice was ever carried out (there is some post-exilic evidence that the attempt was made: Neh. 10.31; 1 Macc. 6.49, 53; Josephus, *Ant*. XIII.viii.1 (234), XIV.x.6 (206)), and whether it was feasible (Gerstenberger suggests that it was possible in the older form when isolated fields were left fallow, but not in the priestly extension to the whole land in the same year[46]). The motive, whatever it was originally,[47] is religious and not utilitarian (to preserve the fertility of the soil), and while it is possible to find an environmental 'message' in the idea that the land belongs to God and is held only on lease,[48] such a concern with ecology is alien from the biblical texts.[49]

Some Environmental Studies

I end this chapter by looking briefly at some studies which find such environmental teaching in the Old Testament.[50]

Regenstein is perhaps the most extreme example of a writer who misreads the Old Testament in order to press 'the Bible's Message of

[45] Simkins, *Creator and Creation*, 263.

[46] Erhard S. Gerstenberger, *Leviticus*, 375.

[47] Among the various suggestions may be noted: the fallow year customary in many cultures, restoration of the land to the original state in which God had given it (Martin Noth, *Exodus*, 189, Ronald E. Clements, *Exodus*, 151), to leave the produce for the spirits of the soil (J. R. Porter, *Leviticus*, 198, who interprets Lev. 19.9 in the same way).

[48] So Brevard S. Childs, *Exodus*, 482: 'to preserve the thought of Yahweh's ownership of the land which he simply lent to Israel for use'.

[49] Cf. Lewis G. Regenstein 'the scriptures impart a strong conservation message, warning against overutilizing and wearing out natural resources' (*Replenish the Earth*, 19). Sean McDonagh is more circumspect: 'Many ecologists insist that modern agriculture should attempt to recapture this sensitivity to the land' (*Greening*, 129).

[50] I do not discuss Ian Barbour's short account of the biblical material in volume 2 of his Gifford Lectures, since he is largely concerned with Lynn White's criticisms (*Ethics*, 74–77).

Conservation'. I pick out the worst cases. He describes Leviticus 19.23–25 as 'strict and detailed rules . . . on caring for trees'.[51] He neglects the context and appears to give a modern sense to 'pollute' in his (partial) quotation of Numbers 35.33–34 to show that the 'land itself is sacred and should not be polluted or defiled'. Isaiah's prophesy in 5.8 is described as 'a word of admonition to real estate developers . . . who build homes and fields too close together and leave no room for nature and the solitude people so often need', while the law of the Levitical cities in Number 35.2–5 is described as a requirement that 'cities in Israel be surrounded by a natural area, or greenbelt'.[52] He treats the AV translation of Genesis 1.28, to 'replenish' the earth in the modern sense of restocking with plants and animals.[53] Qoheleth 3.19 is given the strange interpretation that 'our own fate depends on protecting and preserving the earth's life support systems' since 'if the wildlife perishes, humans will not long survive'.[54]

Ian Bradley seeks to meet the criticisms of Lynn White and others by showing that they rest on 'a total distortion of the original meaning of the biblical texts' as well as a reversal of the teachings of the early church.[55] Much of what he says is sound and fully in line with the best biblical scholarship, but running through it all is the attempt to relate Old Testament texts directly to the modern situation. Sometimes he recognizes this by writing: 'these verses could be interpreted as having a very Green message'.[56] This actual sentence refers to Jeremiah 14.4–6, on which he comments: 'Living where he did in a place where fertile land merged into desert, Jeremiah must have been well aware of how easy it was to destroy the thin layer of top soil and create dust bowls', and he suggests that the prophet may have had this in mind as he described the drought. Again, he finds 'powerful endorsement' from scripture for the campaign to move away from intensive farming towards organic husbandry, pointing to the fact that the Old Testament contains 'a good deal of advice on the subject of good agricultural practice', such as the sabbath rest for the land every seventh year and the awareness of how precious water is.[57] It is a pity that he spoils a good case by treating the Old Testament as if its

---

[51] *Replenish the Earth*, 19. By a slip he ascribes the law to Genesis.

[52] *Ibid.*, 20.

[53] *Ibid.*, 27. It is perhaps strange that most of the discussions of Genesis 1.26–28 fasten on 'dominion' and fail to take account of the problem of over-population, despite this command to 'fill the earth' (but see Norbert Lohfink, *Great Themes*, 173–176).

[54] *Ibid.*, 24.

[55] Ian Bradley, *God is Green*, 3.

[56] *Ibid.*, 61.

[57] *Ibid.*, 26–28.

writers worked from the same view of the environment as environmentalists have today.

Lawrence Osborn presents an equally persuasive case for the religious basis of environmental concern, is extremely fair in his treatment of Lynn White, and generally treats the Old Testament correctly. Nevertheless, despite his criticism of scholars who have allowed their own anthropocentric assumptions to influence their exegesis,[58] a few of his own interpretations reveal the opposite bias. For example the laws in Leviticus 19.19, 23–25 and Exodus 23.10–11 are said to amount to 'a ban on exploitative agricultural methods' (he presents the prohibition of mixed crops as 'intercropping to increase yields is forbidden'!).[59] Another slightly different instance of importing modern ideas into Old Testament texts is the description of the picture of desolation in several of the prophets as divine judgment 'in terms of ecological catastrophe'.[60] The error here is the failure to identify the sin of which this is the judgment. Osborn seems to assume, or wishes his readers to assume, that it is mistreatment of the environment, when in fact it has nothing to do with this in the cases he instances (Isa. 24.1–13; Hos. 4.3). This is very clear in Hosea, where the sins condemned are lack of faithfulness, kindness, knowledge of God, and swearing, lying, killing, stealing, committing adultery. Moreover, since this is divine judgment it is Yahweh who has caused the desolation of the earth,[61] not the effect of human exploitation. So while we may accept all that Osborn says about creation and God's delight in the natural world, he has failed to show that the Old Testament writers shared the modern environmental concerns – as he was bound to do.

Far more sensitive to the situation of ancient Israel – and therefore far more convincing – is Sean McDonagh's *The Greening of the Church*. Coming from his experience as a missionary in the Philippines, and presenting a passionate appeal to the church to respond to the ecological crisis facing the earth today, he gives considerable prominence to the fact that 'Israel came to birth in a harsh and hostile land'. Following Frederick Turner,[62] he accepts that the environment in which the Israelites lived has to be taken into account in any attempt to understand the natural world. Human beings in order to survive 'had to channel all their efforts into dominating, controlling and taming the natural world', for much of the land is barren, difficult to work, and not very fruitful. Moreover they had a

---

[58] Lawrence Osborne, *Guardians*, 81–82.
[59] *Ibid.*, 91.
[60] *Ibid.*, 94.
[61] This might be seen as an extension of Andrew Davies's claim that Yahweh is depicted as doing evil things in the book of Isaiah (*Double Standards*, see ch. 6).
[62] Frederick Turner, *Beyond Geography*.

constant battle against the elements. This is reflected in Genesis 3.17–19, where 'the world takes the role of an adversary', and 'almost military tactics' had to be adopted in order to make the earth fruitful and responsive to human needs.[63] In his discussion of Lynn White's thesis, McDonagh points out that Genesis 1.26–28 and Psalm 8.4–9[3–8] 'make sense' in the light of the struggle within many Middle Eastern cultures to control chaos and wilderness. Yet because he is concerned with the modern environmental crisis he links these passages with others such as Psalm 72, with its expectations of the righteous king, and Genesis 1.29, where the first human beings were expected to be vegetarians, and so moves to ideas of stewardship. Despite the strong consensus among Old Testament scholars that the first couple were thought of in royal terms, and the consequent utilization of kingship motifs in determining their role in the natural world, I am not convinced that this is correct. As I said earlier, in face of the hardships of farming in ancient Israel, it seems to me that the whole argument which McDonagh has set out should have led to the conclusion that 'dominion' over the other creatures would have been welcome to the Israelite peasants, and that even the more ruthless control of Genesis 9.2–7 would have been accepted as a positive blessing in the harsh reality of existence in Palestine.

Throughout the three chapters devoted to creation, the covenant tradition, and the prophets, psalms and wisdom literature, McDonagh approaches the biblical material with understanding and sensitivity, which makes this by far the best of these studies. He is aware of the dangers of moving too quickly from the Bible to the present day and of reading more into the texts than they contain. Thus, after he has quoted the stock set of laws that are commonly presented as showing that the Israelites were concerned for the environment (Ex. 23.10–12; Lev. 25.4–7; 25.18–22; 26.32–35; Deut. 20.19; 22.6–7; 25.4), he says that the 'covenant tradition', which is primarily concerned with Israel's relation to God and fellow human beings and stands on the side of life and justice 'would have little difficulty incorporating modern prescriptions which respect ecological laws'.[64] This is exactly the point. The tradition did not contain any ecological concern because it did not occur to those who developed and passed on the tradition that the environment needed to be cared for. Again, absolutely correctly, he does not argue that the prophets, psalmists and wisdom writers *presented* an ecological ethics, but rather that the way the psalmists and Job in particular speak of the natural world leads away from 'the narrow anthropocentric cul-de-sac on which much of

---

[63] McDonagh, *Greening*, 113–114.
[64] *Ibid.*, 130.

our economic, educational, social, political, technological and even religious activities are based'.[65]

Because of his keen awareness of the geographical and cultural setting of the ancient Israelites, it is rare for McDonagh to commit the kind of errors which have been noted in the previous three studies that have been examined. Very occasional lapses contrast strongly with his central argument. Thus he finds in the Noah story 'a profound message for the modern world' since God commanded Noah 'to conserve nature', without taking into account the fact that it was God who instigated the destruction of all the living creatures in the first place.[66]

This is a remarkably fine study, which has not received the attention it deserves. Not least of its virtues is its documentation of the failure of the church to show any awareness of the environmental crisis until very late in the day.

Nearly all these studies, however, have attempted to turn the Old Testament writers into late twentieth-century environmentalists.[67] They were not. It needs to be asserted as forcefully as possible that *the question of safeguarding the environment did not enter into their thinking*. To say this is not to deny that there is a keen appreciation of the beauty and wonder of the natural world in the Old Testament or that it was seen as God's world or that the fertility of the Promised Land was seen as directly due to God's goodness, idealistic though this is. What I am claiming is that there is no *explicit* demand to *care for* the environment, because it did not occur to anyone in ancient Israel to make such a plea. Such a demand may be implicit in the creation narratives and the 'cosmic covenant', but hardly ever (if at all) in the Old Testament are human beings urged to take active measures to conserve nature.[68] Whether this is regarded as showing that the Old Testament writers spoke more than they knew, or whether the opposite view is taken, that it contains no true environmental teaching, probably depends on the temperament of the reader.[69]

---

[65] *Ibid.*, 153.

[66] *Ibid.*, 123. Holmes Rolston III commits the same error – 'Noah and his ark is the first "endangered species project"', despite stressing the fact that the Old Testament cannot be expected to contain modern scientific ecology ('Bible and Ecology', 23; he makes similar false interpretations regarding the sabbatical year and the parting of Abram and Lot).

[67] See note on The Earth Bible Series on p. xi above.

[68] This sparsity of direct references to the activity of human beings in conservation and caring for the earth may be the reason for the excessive concentration on the myths of Genesis 1–9 in the literature.

[69] Perhaps yet again I should make it clear that although I believe the second to be true, I personally accept fully the case which environmentalists make. To question whether the Old Testament actively teaches care of the environment does not mean that I reject the importance of such care.

18

WOMEN

Israelite society was patriarchal.[1] As a result the Old Testament is also patriarchal.[2] This is an embarrassment to modern readers, and has resulted in various attempts to reinterpret it so that it fits into the values which we esteem today.

In the Interlude I referred to the three main ways in which modern feminist scholars have reacted to the patriarchal character of the Old Testament, some holding it to be irredeemable and rejecting it, others claiming that women play a larger part than has been recognized in the past, others again seeking a 'hermeneutic of liberation', with a fourth group which accepts both the patriarchal nature of the biblical record and its abiding truth. It is now necessary to elaborate on this.

H. M. Conn finds three models: (1) rejectionist or post-Christian: the Bible promotes an oppressive patriarchal structure, and must be rejected; (2) the loyalist or evangelical model, which has two forms: (a) order through hierarchy is accepted, women's place is to accept a role of submission to male leadership, but this does not diminish the true freedom and dignity of women; (b) the full biblical data call for equality between men and women; (3) the reformist or liberal model, also in two forms, both of which see patriarchal chauvinism in the Bible and desire to overcome it: (a) one looks for a positive role of women in scripture; (b) the other seeks a 'usable' hermeneutics in the prophetic tradition, fastening on the prophets' demand to create a just society free from oppression, or calls for a feminist 'hermeneutic of suspicion'.[3]

A. Brown finds three groupings of feminists: (1) post-Christian feminists; (2) revisionists; (3) biblical feminists who challenge the way the Bible has been interpreted.[4]

Elisabeth Schüssler Fiorenza discusses four main 'hermeneutical strategies' developed by feminists: (1) the first seeks texts about

---

[1] Carol Meyers suggests that 'androcentrism' is to be preferred to 'patriarchy', both with Israelite society and biblical literature, since calling early Israel 'patriarchal' masks other kinds of power distinctions ('The Family', 34–35).
[2] Cf. Phyllis Trible: 'Born and bred in a land of patriarchy, the Bible abounds in male imagery and language' ('Feminist Hermeneutics', 23).
[3] *NDT*, 255–256.
[4] *NDCEPT*, 380–381.

women in the Bible, separating the positive tradition from stories of women as victims; (2) the second focuses on the women characters in the Bible, retelling their stories so as to 'break the marginalizing tendencies in the androcentric text'; (3) the third seeks to recover works written by women to discover woman's voice; (4) the fourth applies a 'hermeneutics of suspicion', seeing androcentric texts as '"windows" or "mirrors" of women's reality in antiquity'.[5] She identifies three strategies: loyalist, revisionist and compensatory.[6]

Phyllis Trible singles out three stages in feminist approaches to the Bible: (1) at first feminists documented the case against women, which led to five conclusions: (a) some, failing to appreciate Israelite culture, condemned biblical faith as hopelessly misogynous; (b) some used the evidence to support anti-semitism; (c) some treated the Bible as a historical document devoid of continuing authority; (d) some despaired over the male power that the Bible and its commentators hold over women; (e) some demanded a new approach to the Bible; (2) in the second stage discerning a critique of patriarchy within scripture led to attempts to discover traditions which challenge the culture by: (a) highlighting neglected texts; (b) accenting neglected females in the Bible; (c) reinterpreting familiar women, such as Eve; (3) feminists in the third stage offered sympathetic readings of abused women, such as the Levite's concubine in Judges 19.[7]

Katharine Doob Sakenfeld finds three options for feminists: (1) looking to texts about women as a counter against texts used 'against' women; (2) looking for a theological perspective offering a critique of patriarchy; (3) looking for texts which reveal to women their true position. She regards none of these immune from the risk of finding the Bible 'hurtful, unhelpful, not revealing of God, and not worth the effort of coming to grips with it'.[8]

Finally notice should be taken of Danna Nolan Fewell's observation that each position adopted by feminists involves emphasizing some features of the Hebrew Bible and sliding over others. The text does not have a thematic unity, and what is needed is to deconstruct the patriarchal texts.[9]

All these approaches (even that accepting a patriarchal Bible as divine truth!) are controlled by present-day ethical stances and all fail to appreciate how the situation in ancient Israel would have looked to those living at the time.

[5] *ABD* II.786–787.
[6] *Ibid.*, 789–790.
[7] Trible, 'Feminist Hermeneutics'.
[8] Katharine Doob Sakenfeld, 'Feminist Uses', quotation p. 64. Alice Ogden Bellis offers a more nuanced analysis in *Helpmates*, 16–20.
[9] Danna Nolan Fewell, 'Feminist Reading', note p. 82..

A Patriarchal Culture

There is little need to repeat yet again the evidence for the patriarchal culture of the Old Testament. Many studies have set it out.[10] The main actors in the Old Testament are men. The language, largely because it has masculine and feminine forms of both second and third persons of the verb, is strongly masculine. The laws are mainly addressed to men. The term for the family is the 'father's house' (*bēt 'āḇ*). Genealogies follow the male line. The authority of the male head of the family is extensive, and even where the law sets limits to his power it is transferred to the (male) elders of the village. And Yahweh is spoken of almost entirely in male terms. He has no consort and his priests are solely men. There is no word in classical Hebrew for priestess, no feminine form of Levite. While a few women prophets are found, the only positions within the official cult occupied by women are minor ones, sometimes with uncertain functions (cf. Ex. 38.8).

In such a society the women are naturally subordinated to the men. Mothers desired sons rather than daughters. The expectation of daughters was that they would marry and have sons, for it was marriage which gave them security and sons which brought them honour. It was required that they should remain virgin until marriage. Indeed, their value to their father was greatly diminished if they were raped, and the law was severe on those who lost their virginity voluntarily. The husband is called the *baʿal* ('master') of his wife, and the verb is used of marrying a woman. In a few places a wife addresses her husband as *'āḏōn* ('lord'). Whether the wife was regarded as the possession of her husband is disputed, but certainly a woman's sexuality was under the control first of her father, then of her husband. Adultery was an offence against a woman's husband, while married men suffered no penalty for having sexual relations with unmarried women. While men could divorce their wives, women were permanently bound to their husbands. The wife was not a slave, however, and could not be sold, as slaves or daughters could be. Women could not own property, the only exception being where there were no sons, but even this concession was circumscribed by limiting their marriage within their father's tribe. Whether wives retained the *mōhar*, the payment made by the bridegroom's family to the bride's father which may not have been strictly a 'bride-price', is uncertain. Even though women were permitted to make vows, the vow could be

---

[10] Thus Johs. Pedersen, *Israel I–II*, 46--96; Roland de Vaux, *Ancient Israel*, 19–55; Phyllis Trible, 'Woman in the OT'; Phyllis A. Bird, 'Women (OT)'. Useful studies of the family are found in Leo Perdue, Joseph Blenkinsopp, John J. Collins and Carol Meyers, *Families.* Blenkinsopp himself stresses that there is no 'Old Testament view of Women', but rather a plurality of views determined by such variables as epoch, literary genre, and social class (*ibid.*, 75). See also John Rogerson, 'Family'.

repudiated by their father or husband. It has been frequently noted that the position of wives in Israel was inferior to that in other countries of the ancient Middle East,[11] and among the Jews at Elephantine wives could own property, enter into contracts, and obtain a divorce. It has to be remembered, however, that the evidence from Mesopotamia and Egypt is richer than that provided by the Old Testament, in that alongside literary texts, archaeology has provided many contemporary documents. The extra-biblical evidence in Palestine consists of little more than some seals possibly belonging to women.

Such was the overall position of women within the patriarchal Israelite culture. Where uncertainty, and hence dispute, arises is at the fringes. The main reason for disagreement lies in the position from which interpretation is made, and few scholars today appear able to divest themselves of the very proper belief in the full equality of men and women. This inevitably distorts their understanding of ancient Israelite thought. It becomes particularly misleading when it is combined with a conviction that because the Bible is sacred scripture, it must contain an ethics which supports the position which we all accept today. The only satisfactory way forward is to approach the disputed passages from the presuppositions of the underlying patriarchal society and its institutions and values.[12] Where there is doubt about the meaning of any narrative, law or wisdom saying, the presumption must be that the Israelites understood it within the context of a patriarchal culture.[13] On the other hand allowance has to be made for the fact that the Hebrew Bible is the work of male authors and editors, so that the picture of women which it contains is presented through the eyes of men. How different our understanding might have been did we only possess a few letters written by women.

Genesis 1–3
So extensive is the literature and the range of viewpoints which are presented by modern scholars that it is necessary to confine the present discussion to those few issues which impinge directly upon

---

[11] A useful short survey of the position of women in ancient Mesopotamia is provided by Rivkah Harris, 'Women (Mesopotamia)'. See also, more briefly, R. Harris, 'Woman in ANE' and H. W. F. Saggs, *Babylon*, 155–159.

[12] Carolyn Pressler's study, *The View of Women*, is a model of such an approach. Phyllis Bird also recognizes this ('Women (OT)', 951).

[13] At the risk of being deemed neurotic, I must yet again emphasize that my interpretation of the position of women in the Old Testament is not anti-Semitic and that I fully accept the complete equality of men and women. At the time when my own church refused to accept the ordination of women lest it might harm relations with the Anglican church, I strongly supported their ordination. Jesus appears to have treated the women he met with courtesy and as equals, although even he was sufficiently inhibited by the culture of the time to restrict his choice of the Twelve to men (with disastrous results for the Christian church).

ethics. I begin with Genesis 1–3, which, as we have seen earlier, holds a curious fascination for biblical scholars although it appears to have had little influence on the rest of the Old Testament, and only became important for theology and ethics in the inter-testamental period and in certain New Testament writings.[14]

Most scholars nowadays accept that Genesis 1.26–27 places men and women on a complete equality. Mary Hayter's forthright 'An unbiased exegesis of Genesis 1.26f. and 5.1f. provides no grounds for holding that woman participates in the image of God in a different way from man' is plainly correct.[15] Nevertheless, note should be taken of the comment by Phyllis A. Bird, that although the formulation implies an essential equality of the two sexes, the priestly writer did not fully perceive this, as his male genealogies and exclusively male priesthood show.[16] Clines, indeed, claims that the text does not mean that women every bit as much as men have dominion over the animals. Men and women are equal in being created by God and being human, but 'most of the time the distinction between the sexes is not in view', so that the most that can be said is that Genesis 1 on its own 'does not exclude the idea of the equality of the sexes'. Taking Bird's

[14] The connection between Ezek. 28.11–23 and Gen. 3 is uncertain, but most commentators think the prophet was recalling the story. It, however, contains no reference to the woman. Hos. 6.7 is of doubtful interpretation, but Adam is almost certainly a place name and the verse contains no reminiscence of Genesis (see A. A. Mackintosh, *Hosea*, 236). Pamela J. Milne thinks the only texts which might reflect the story are Deut. 4.32; 1 Chron. 1.1 and Job 31.33 ('Patriarchal Stamp'. 149. n. 2), while Norman C. Habel finds references in Job 5.6–7 and 31.38–40 as well as 31.33 (*Job*, 426). Even if these two scholars are right, however, the references to Genesis 1–3 do not show that the stories had any theological or ethical influence on the attitudes towards women or to a 'fall', unless the argument of Ronald A. Simkins is accepted, that the myth in Gen. 2–3 'symbolizes, and thereby constructs and reinforces, the ancient Israelites' most fundamental cultural values, especially their understanding of gender' ('Gender Construction', 34). The idea of the 'fall' appears in 4 Ezra 7.118: 'O Adam, what have you done? For though it was you who sinned, the fall was not yours alone, but ours also who are your descendants' (but contrast 2 Bar. 54.19). Ben Sirach seems to be the first writer to put the blame on Eve: 'From a woman sin had its beginning, and because of her we all die' (Sir. 25.24), and this reappears in the New Testament in 1 Tim. 2.11–14. The subjection of women to men is found in 1 Cor. 11.8–9; 14.33–35; 2 Cor. 11.3; 1 Pet. 3.1, while the idea of the 'Fall' underlies Paul's doctrine of salvation (Rom. 5.12–21). There is a good discussion in Mary Hayter, *New Eve*, 118–145. Hayter also quotes some later Christian interpreters of Gen. 2–3 who stress the subjection of women to men (*ibid.*, 84–85, 95–117; they include Tertullian, Diodore of Tarsus, Chrysostom, Augustine, Aquinas and Gratian, as well as modern scholars such as E. L. Mascall and J. I. Packer; note especially her criticism of Barth for finding evidence that 'God himself exists in relationship' in the text). I find it impossible to follow Phyllis Trible in seeing the Song of Songs as a response to Genesis 2–3, redeeming the story of 'love gone awry' (*Rhetoric*, 144 165).

[15] Hayter, *New Eve*, 88. For a literary analysis of the verses see Phyllis Trible, *Rhetoric*, 12–21.

[16] Phyllis A. Bird, 'Images of Women', 287, n. 87.

point, however, he argues that when set in the contexts of Genesis 2–3 and the priestly writer generally, Genesis 1 is 'indefeasibly androcentric' and cannot be redeemed from its patriarchal stance.[17] We shall look at the extent to which the priestly writings are patriarchal later.

The chief problem arises with Genesis 2–3.[18] It is quite impossible to deal with this fully in the space available here and I pick three issues which are of central relevance to the present discussion.[19]

(a) How is the creation of woman as a 'helper corresponding to him' ('$\bar{e}zer$ $k^e neg\bar{d}\bar{o}$) to be understood? Clines dismisses the argument that since the word 'helper' in the Old Testament is used predominantly of God, it cannot imply subordination, on the grounds that 'helping' is always an inferior role, whatever the status of the helper.[20] He argues that the help which Eve gives to Adam is the only work which he is unable to do, bear children and thus fulfil the divine command to 'be fruitful and multiply'. There is no evidence in the text that she helped him in the tasks which were assigned to him, tilling the garden and keeping it, and she was not yet created when he named the animals.[21] When God said that it is not good for man to be alone, he did not mean 'good *for Adam*' but not good at all, and Clines infers from this that God himself regards Eve as 'primarily a child-bearing creature'. Augustine and Aquinas were right after all! I am not sure about all of this. The man's ecstatic cry, when God brings the woman to him: 'This at last is bone of my bones and flesh of my flesh', coupled with the unpatriarchal saying, 'Therefore a man leaves his father and his mother and cleaves to his wife' suggests a closer

[17] David J. A. Clines, 'Eve', 41–45. He claims that his footnote removes any ground for supposing that the text 'implies' equality.
[18] Among the multitude of studies the following may be noted: Mary Hayter, *New Eve*, 95–117; Phyllis Trible, 'Depatriarchalizing') and *Rhetoric*, 72–143; David J. A. Clines, 'Eve', 26–41; Lyn M. Bechtel, 'Rethinking Genesis 2.4b–3.24' and 'Human Maturation'; Carol L. Meyers, *Discovering Eve* and 'Gender Roles'. Alice Ogden Bellis provides a survey of interpretations (*Helpmates*, 45–66).
[19] Phyllis Trible lists eleven features which have been adduced as evidence for the subordination of women to men (*Rhetoric*, 73). In the following discussion I dismiss the argument of Phyllis Trible and others that the '$\bar{a}d\bar{a}m$ which God initially created, an 'earth creature' was either androgynous or sexless (*Rhetoric*, 79–81; Lyn M. Bechtel, 'Rethinking Genesis 2.4b–3.24', 85; Mary Hayter, *New Eve*, 96–98, who accepts not everyone may be convinced by this interpretation), since the story assumes that he is male (so Ronald A. Simkins, 'Gender Construction', 40 n. 30, and Phyllis A. Bird, 'Images of Women', 287, n. 88, who points out that the man's loneliness reveals that he is conceived of as a man).
[20] Clines, 'Eve', 27–32. Phyllis Trible argued first that 'helper' cannot connote an inferior role ('Depatriarchalizing', 36), and later that being a 'helper' is a superior role, since God is a helper, though '"corresponding to" tempers this connotation' (*Rhetoric*, 89–90). Mary Hayter reproduces many of the arguments (*New Eve*, 101–102).
[21] Clines, 'Eve', 32–37.

companionship than simply impregnation in order to produce children, and is hardly evidence that he is setting up another patriarchal unit.[22] Nevertheless, if the story is read from the context of Israel's patriarchal culture, it is difficult to avoid a sense of androcentricity in it.[23]

(b) Does the naming of woman by the man in Genesis 2.23 endorse subordination? Phyllis Trible finds a clear distinction between God's bringing the animals to the man to see what he would name them and bringing the woman, where no purpose is stated. The first gives the man dominion over the animals. Dominion is excluded from the second as is shown by the absence of the noun 'name', and the fact that *'iššāh* ('woman') is not a name but a common noun, designating gender not specifying a person. This seems to be special pleading, since what we may infer the man 'called' the animals was 'cow', 'sheep', 'goat', 'lion' and so on. Rather emphasis should be placed on the delight that the words express: 'At last, Lord, you've got it right!' The naming declares the essential unity of man and woman who do not exist alongside each other as partners in work, but seek to belong to each other.

(c) Is the subordination of women to men the result of the 'fall'? This is a frequent assertion in modern interpretations of the story. 'Sexuality has splintered into strife; human oppression prevails' as Phyllis Trible has famously described it.[24] As we have seen, it is not certain that Genesis 2 expresses full equality between men and women, so that this attempt to show that the Old Testament does not teach the subordination of women is somewhat uncertain. Lyn M. Bechtel argues that the traditional understanding of Genesis 2.4b–3.24 as 'sin and fall' is false. Rather the myth is about 'human maturation', whereby the originally innocent 'children' become mature adults, knowing good and bad. On this interpretation Genesis 3.16 expresses 'the reality of adult female life'. The woman learns that her role contains the potential of procreative power accompanied by sexual desire for her husband and her contribution of physical labour to support the family, though it is subject to limitation. What the man controls, however, is woman's sexual desire, not her entire life. The

---

[22] Phyllis Trible declares that the man's words 'speak unity, solidarity, mutuality, and equality', and points out that in the following statement no procreative purpose is to be found (*Rhetoric*, 99, 104).

[23] Phyllis A. Bird points out that the story is told from the man's point of view exclusively ('Images of Women', 277). The distinction which was made earlier between the status of women in Israelite society and within the Old Testament and the oppression of women needs to be kept in mind here.

[24] Trible, *Rhetoric*, 132. She sees the other outcomes of human guilt as plants giving way to thorns, fulfilling work becoming alienated labour, power over the animals deteriorating into enmity with the serpent.

purpose of this control is to channel the woman's desire and procreative power within the boundaries of the family, and may also have to do with monitoring her sexual desire and hence reducing the risk-prone activity of childbirth. Bechtel sees the story as a reflection of the demands for an increased population and the winning of a livelihood in the period before the monarchy, where the man has the task of food production and protection, subject to the limitation of the tremendous physical effort that a large household requires, especially when the ground produces thorns and thistles, and ultimately of death.[25] Although Bechtel's argument is attractive, and to some extent solves the problem of the lack of any reference to a 'fall' in the rest of the Old Testament, I wonder whether it introduces twentieth-century values, in spite of her explicit aim of interpreting the myth within the 'group-oriented culture' of ancient Israel. Was the husband's control over his wife's fecundity really in order to reduce the risk of frequent childbirth? Yet even if the story in Genesis 3 is not a myth of a 'fall' from an original state of goodness and innocence, but is more akin to similar myths from the ancient Middle East which are focused on the loss of immortality, the modern obsession with the relation between the man and the woman is foreign to the culture in which it was written and recited.

It appears, then, that Genesis 2–3 is exactly the kind of story which might have been expected to arise in the patriarchal culture of ancient Israel. The surprising thing is that it does not put women in subjection to men more openly. The question which Alice Ogden Bellis asks remains: 'The story is certainly androcentric. Is it intrinsically sexist?'[26]

Social Position and Treatment

A distinction needs to be made between the position of women in Israelite society and the way they were treated.[27] The first concerns status and roles and is a feature of the culture. The second is obviously dependent to a large extent upon this, but is more directly a matter of the *mores* and ethics. The first is reflected in such features of the biblical writings as the absence of inclusive language and the form of many of the laws, and is the basis of the way many narratives are

[25] Lyn M. Bechtel, 'Human Maturation', 23–25. She regards the myth as 'unquestionably patriarchal in its orientation', though subsequent traditional interpretation has exaggerated this to teach that women are 'secondary, inferior, and should be subordinated to men as their punishment from God' ('Rethinking Genesis 2.4b–3.24', 77–78, 111–116).

[26] Alice Ogden Bellis, *Helpmates*, 63.

[27] See now Ferdinand E. Deist, *Material Culture*, 263–265, distinguishing legal position and status.

told.[28] The second is revealed most clearly in the narratives in which women play a part, but is also reflected in some of the punishments imposed by the laws,[29] and in the way women are referred to in the wisdom writings.[30] Most importantly for an understanding of Old Testament ethics, the first would have been accepted by all the members of Israelite society not simply without question but also without realizing that any different social organization was possible, while the second may provoke complaint, comment, and even censure by some within that society. Because of the culture in which it arose, the Old Testament is bound to be androcentric, and to this extent equality between men and women is foreign to it. One can, therefore, understand and respect those feminists who regard it as irredeemable. Indeed, their position is more consistent than that of those who seek to read it in a less sexist way, importing modern attitudes into the texts. In this they are often motivated by a deep and entirely proper resentment at the way the Old Testament has been used by men in later societies to justify the subjugation and oppression of women right up to the present. But later use of the Bible must be separated from the meaning which it possessed within its own society and the culture in which it was written. The culture of ancient Israel cannot measure up to advanced feminist thought, or indeed to the position which men as well as women ought to demand in our society today.

One approach adopted by many feminist and other scholars is to fasten on all the women mentioned in the Old Testament. In this at least four types of interpretation are presented: (1) emphasis is given to the active roles which are assigned to many of them;[31] (2) different

---

[28] Keren Engelken approaches an analysis of the different statuses of women by examining the use of five terms: ʿalmāh, bᵉtūlāh, pīlegeš, šiphāh, and ʾāmāh. She concludes that there was a hierarchy of women: the ʿalmāh was the term for the wives of aristocracy, women connected with the palace and those having duties as musicians; bᵉtūlāh represented the free Israelite women who have the potential to be wives and mothers: pīlegeš was the free woman with lesser rights in a marriage, but not a slave; the šiphāh was half-free, while the ʾāmāh was a slave – the 'unfree' who are the property of others. Oddly Engelken omits ʾiššāh on the grounds that it would have unduly lengthened the book, but says that it would have added nuances to her study (Frauen). Esther Fuchs has suggested that the frequent depiction of women as deceivers· is due to their inferior social position and political powerlessness in a patriarchal society. Recording the deceptiveness of women in the Old Testament perpetuates the distrust of women and validates their subordination ('Who is Hiding the Truth?').

[29] The only instance of mutilation as a punishment is imposed on women (Deut. 25.11–12), while in the ordeal demanded by the jealous husband, while an attempt is made to clear the innocent wife, the husband is not punished if his accusation is false, in contrast to other laws of false accusation (Num. 5.11–31; contrast Deut. 19.16–19).

[30] Cf. the warnings to young men in Proverbs (e.g., 5; 6.24–35; 7) The misogyny of Ben Sira is well-known and is documented by Warren C. Trenchard, Ben Sira's View of Women. How far Ben Sira reflected the views common to his culture is disputed.

[31] It is found in very many studies, either by suggesting that the women discussed

types of women, such as prophets and prostitutes, are analysed to reveal the way women were regarded;[32] (3) it is pointed out that many of the women are unnamed and are often described in relation to men, such as fathers, brothers, and sons, and stress is placed upon 'patriarchy';[33] (4) the precarious position of women is expounded through the stories of the ill-treatment of women who are victims.[34] Attention is chiefly given to narratives.[35] All this can be documented in many studies and there is no need to traverse the ground yet again. At most they show that many roles, while normally restricted to men, could be taken by women, either because they were institutionalized in this way (e.g., the queen-mother and female prophets), or through the forceful personality of dominant women (such figures as Abigail spring to mind). It has to be borne in mind that while there are such prominent figures, women achieved their status in society through marriage, and above all by becoming mothers, especially mothers of sons. The linking of mother and father, as in the Ten Commandments (Ex. 20.12/Deut. 5.16), other laws (Ex. 21.15, 17; Deut. 21.13, 18-19; 22.15; 27.16; Lev. 20.9; 21.11) and in several places in Proverbs (Prov. 1.8; 4.3; 6.20; 10.1; 15.20; 19.26; 20.20; 23.22, 25; 30.11, 17), as well as other places in the historical books (e.g., Jdg. 14.2 etc.; 1 Sam. 22.3; 2 Sam. 19.38[37]; 1 Kgs. 19.20), the prophets (e.g., Jer. 16.7; Mic. 7.6; Zech. 13.3) and Psalm 27.10, is sometimes presented as evidence of the equality of men and women, but the basis of this lies in the honour that is accorded to mothers and does not imply equality in the modern sense. The roles of women were essentially

---

played a larger part than the present (androcentric) text allows, or by fastening on those women such as Ruth, Esther, Susanna, Judith, Jael, the four women prophetesses, Miriam, Deborah, Huldah and Noadiah, and the like. Of the first Phyllis Trible's 'Miriam' is the most famous. André LaCocque, *Feminine Unconventional* is an example of the second. Both approaches are found in such studies as Grace I. Emmerson's 'Women' and Alice Ogden Bellis's *Helpmates*. Some figures, such as Delilah and Jezebel, present problems for feminists since their actions appear to be ambivalent (see Carol Smith, 'Delilah').

[32] This is the approach in the first part of Athalya Brenner's *Israelite Woman*, where she discusses in turn queens, wise women, women poets and authors, prophetesses, magicians, sorcerers and witches, and female prostitution.

[33] This runs through many of the studies.

[34] Phyllis Trible's *Texts of Terror* is outstanding, but attention should also be given to treatments of the 'pornographic' treatment of women in such prophecies as Ezek. 16 and 23 (cf. Athalya Brenner and Fokkelien van Dijk-Hemmes, *On Gendering Texts*, 167–193; T. Drorah Setel on Hosea, 'Prophets and Pornography').

[35] An indication of this is provided by the series of Feminist Companions, edited by Athalya Brenner, in which Exodus to Deuteronomy, and the Latter Prophets are allocated only a single book each, as against the volumes on Genesis, Judges, Ruth, Samuel–Kings, Esther/Judith/Susanna, the Song of Songs, and the Wisdom Literature in the first series, and Genesis, Judges, and Ruth/Esther so far in the second. Even in the volume on Exodus to Deuteronomy more interest is shown in the narratives than the legal sections.

those of wives and mothers, and it was in these that they attained honour (and brought honour to their fathers and husbands). Thus de Vaux, who was well aware of the position of women in the modern Arab society where he lived for so many years, rightly presents the main part of his discussion of the place of women in Israel under the heads of the family and marriage, with only a short chapter on the position of women and widows.[36]

Instead of pursuing this line of inquiry any further, I intend to fasten on the extent to which women were oppressed by the prevailing culture and institutions within Israelite society.[37]

In a single chapter it is impossible to do more than consider a somewhat arbitrary selection of texts and set out a few broad sweeps of interpretation. I take up two issues: (a) the reasons which have been proposed to explain the exclusion of women from the priesthood; (b) rape, which reveals the way status and treatment are linked.

(a) Priests

The priesthood was the only office in ancient Israelite society from which women were totally debarred, and various reasons for this have been proposed.[38]

(1) Women are too weak physically to undertake the work of priests, which required a man's strength. Even if women are unable to slaughter animals (questionable), it was normally the worshipper who carried out the killing, while the other activities in the sacrifice – manipulating the blood and placing the pieces of the animal on the altar – could obviously be performed by women. And the teaching and mantic functions of the priest could certainly be carried out by women.

---

[36] Roland de Vaux, *Ancient Israel*, Part I, chs. 1–3. Note should be taken, however, of Frank Crüsemann, who adopts as a 'working hypothesis' that 'where men are discussed [in the laws] women are not necessarily excluded'. He holds that 'the weighty language of Deuteronomy which addresses free, landowning males as representatives of the entire nation – "you" – does not consider women to be part of the groups excluded from this (like Levites, priests, aliens, slaves) but rather includes them in "you"' (*Torah*, 252, see pp. 249–260).

[37] I recognize that in this I am swimming against the tide of current Old Testament, and particularly feminist, scholarship, with its emphasis upon the text and its reader-response approach. Carol Smith observes that feminist biblical criticism could not have happened without the advent of literary criticism and reader response methods — and, in her opinion, canonical criticism and structuralism ('Delilah', 101). Does this mean that an approach which rejects the 'authorial fallacy' and attempts to recover Israelite society is either doomed or bound to be sexist?

[38] These are usefully listed and assessed by Mary Hayter (*New Eve*, ch. 4). She deals effectively with attempts to show, largely on the grounds that women could take part in the cult, that women could be priests (pp. 60–63; the references are to I. J. Peritz, 'Women' and J. H. Otwell, *And Sarah Laughed*).

(2) Women married young and their work within the family, especially having to care for children, left no time for the work of the priesthood. It has even been suggested that women's 'priestly' work was to perpetuate God's people! The latter is absurd and bears no relation to biblical conceptions of either motherhood or priesthood. The former is clearly false, since it did not prevent women performing other time-consuming roles. These two arguments are on a par with the suggestion sometimes made that circumcision was introduced for hygienic purposes.

(3) More to the point is the proposal that the low social status of women would have affected their theological standing in the community, but it too reads too many modern ideas into ancient Israelite society as well as failing to explain how women were able to be leaders (e.g., Deborah, Huldah, and others). Hayter questions how solid is the evidence of the social status of women in ancient Israel, but even if we grant that Israel was a patriarchal society (and I personally think this is unquestionable), this is insufficient in itself to explain why it was from the priesthood alone that women appear to be excluded among all the cultic offices. Nevertheless she thinks that this was a contributory factor. 'The priesthood was a profession – one lived by it and supported a family by it (Lev. 7.8ff.; Deut. 18.3–8) – and such professions were not open to Hebrew women.'[39]

(4) Women were disqualified from performing priestly functions because the priesthood was a symbol of the priestly community of Israel (cf. Ex. 19.6) and women were not full citizens of Israel, and since they were not directly subject to the law they had no direct awareness of sin and so could not have performed the priestly expiatory rites.[40] Hayter assesses this as being weak in its claim that women were never full citizens, referring to Phillips, who argues that the Deuteronomic law brought women fully within the covenant community, but it has greater strength within later Judaism. The way this argument is expressed makes it weaker than it need be. As by nature uncircumcised, women inevitably had a lower place within Israelite religion.

(5) J. and G. Muddiman have pointed out that most men were also debarred from being priests, who had to be the descendants of Aaron and to have no physical deformity (Lev. 21). Ritual holiness was the *sine qua non* of the Old Testament priesthood, but menstruation and childbirth made women regularly unclean.[41] This would seem to be the main reason for the priestly writer's rejection of women as priests. Indeed, rejection is too strong a word. It did not

---

[39] Hayter, *New Eve*, 67.
[40] Referring to Margaret E. Thrall, *Ordination of Women*.
[41] J. and G. Muddiman, *Women*, 3–4 (see Hayter, *New Eve*, 69–70.

occur to most Israelites that women could be priests. It was not a deliberate exclusion but a matter of course, given the importance of purity.

(6) Whether the existence of priestesses in non-Israelite cults played any part in the refusal of Israel to have them in Yahweh worship is uncertain. Hayter believes such priestesses were usually linked with fertility rites and that Israel 'deliberately avoided a female priesthood in order to distinguish the worship of Yahweh from that of fertility cult deities'. How far sacred marriage and sexual fertility rites were practised outside of Israel is uncertain, and recent study of Canaanite religion has suggested that it was less distinct from that of ancient Israel than had once been held, so that the strength of this argument is probably weaker than Hayter believes.

Some scholars have attempted to widen the issue by showing that women were not excluded from the cult. Mayer I. Gruber has surveyed some of these activities and proceeds to show that despite his firm patriarchal stance, the priestly writer expects women to take an active part in the worship.[42] Exodus 38.8 'may actually speak of women functionaries in the cult whose activity was similar to that of the Levites in the book of Numbers', though Qimhi, commenting on the similar phrase in 1 Samuel 2.22, suggested that the women may have been coming to offer sacrifices.[43] Women present sacrifices in Leviticus 12.6 and 15.29. Numbers 6.2 explicitly states that a woman may undertake a Nazirite vow.[44] Gruber goes further in proposing that where P uses the 'neutral nonsexist expressions' *nepeš* and *'ādām* , as in Leviticus 2.1; 4.2, 27; 5.1, 17, 21, women are included (cf. Num. 5.5–7). Even the slaughter of the animal could be carried out by a woman. This hardly affects the question of women priests, however, since Gruber admits that women were 'less than equal partners in the cult'.[45]

Given that the priesthood had the nature of a closed guild, it is only to be expected that a traditionally male order of priests within a patriarchal society would succeed in keeping it that way. And no one in Israel would have thought for one moment that there was anything odd in this, or indeed, demeaning of women. The problem again is

---

[42] Mayer I. Gruber, 'Women in the Cult'. The article is essentially a riposte to the claim that the subordination of women increased in the later parts of the Old Testament and in Judaism. For a strong presentation of the case for the increasing subjugation of women after the Exile (wrong in many respects) see Samuel Terrien, *Till the Heart Sings.*

[43] *Ibid.*, 36.

[44] Gruber wrongly gives the reference as 7.22. See also George Buchanan Gray, *Numbers*, 61, who, in addition to Gruber's reference to *m.Naz.* iv.1–2, adds Bernice's vow (Josephus, *War* II.xv.1, 313).

[45] *Ibid.*, 39.

that in our egalitarian society we find it extremely difficult to imagine what it was like to live in such a society as that of ancient Israel.

(b) Rape.
On any showing rape is the ultimate degradation of women. It occurs in every society, and what is important to discover is how it is regarded and what protection is provided to women.

> If there is a betrothed virgin, and a man meets her in the city and lies with her, then you shall bring them both out to the gate of that city, and you shall stone them to death with stones, the young woman because she did not cry for help though she was in the city, and the man because he violated his neighbour's wife . . .
>
> But if in the open country a man meets a young woman who is betrothed, and the man seizes her and lies with her, then only the man who lay with her shall die. But to the young woman you shall do nothing; in the young woman there is no offence punishable by death, for this case is like that of a man attacking and murdering his neighbour; because he came upon her in the open country, and though the betrothed young woman cried for help there was no one to rescue her.
>
> If a man meets a virgin who is not betrothed, and seizes her and lies with her, and they are found, then the man who lay with her shall give to the father of the young woman fifty shekels of silver, and she shall be his wife, because he has violated her; he may not put her away all his days. (Deut. 22.23–29)

These are commonly described as rape laws,[46] but Carolyn Pressler correctly points out that although they deal with forcible sexual intercourse, they are not concerned with 'rape' in the modern sense, since the offence is not regarded as against the woman at all but rather against the woman's father or husband. It is true that force is implied (the man 'seizes' or 'takes hold of' the woman and 'violates' her), and an attempt is made to protect the innocence of the woman (by distinguishing between rape in the city and in the open country). Nevertheless, as Pressler shows, the laws, like those in Deut. 22.13–22, revolve around the woman's marital status and lack of consent, but they do not treat the man's action as sexual assault against her.[47] Since the laws regard female sexuality as the possession of her father or husband, she has no claims over her own sexuality, and hence cannot be assaulted. Pressler argues that in contrast to these laws, the woman who seizes the genitals of her husband's opponent in

---

[46] So, e.g., Raymond Westbrook, 'Punishments', *ABD* 5, 552; Tikva Frymer-Kensky, 'Sex', *ABD* 5.1145, translating *ʿānâh* Pi. as 'rape'.
[47] Blenkinsopp suggests that the reason may have been financial, to secure the return of the *mōhar* or to avoid having to return the dowry ('The Family', 65).

a brawl is apparently held to be guilty of sexual assault (Deut. 25.11–12), thus emphasizing the difference between the attitudes to men and women.[48]

So far the law, but what is told about incidents of rape? Genesis 34 is difficult to determine, since the story is told for purposes quite other than the fate of Dinah and it is part of the patriarchal sagas the relation of which to Israelite ethics during the period of the monarchy and after is uncertain. The events are certainly not viewed through the eyes of Dinah, and while it is perfectly legitimate for feminists to attempt this, they are in effect reading the story with modern presuppositions and values. Several issues need to be considered. First is the question of whether Dinah was in fact raped. This has been the view of most commentators, but Lyn M. Bechtel has argued that this is not how the Israelites regarded it.[49] She contrasts the modern 'individual-oriented' perspective with the 'group-oriented dynamics' of the time. Dinah and Jacob are interested in interacting with outsiders, whom Simeon and Levi regard as impure. The two brothers want to maintain strict group purity and separation. In support of this she draws attention to the verbs used: ʿānāh Pi. in a sexual context indicates the 'humiliation' or 'shaming' of a woman, not always through rape. 'To lie with' is a euphemism for sexual intercourse, but has no inherent suggestion of rape. Shechem and Hamor are depicted as honourable men, and their aim is to unite and cooperate with the Israelites. Bechtel also claims that Shechem's continuing love for Dinah is contrary to the reaction of rapists, and, rather less convincingly, that since the brothers say that Dinah has been treated as a prostitute, this shows that they did not regard the act as rape – 'harlots are not raped'. More to the point, she notes that the act is called pollution in verses 5 and 13: Dinah has been tainted by engaging in sexual intercourse with uncircumcised outsiders.

Against this Susanne Scholz demands that the incident should be read from a feminist perspective (the only 'right' one) siding with Dinah.[50] She argues that the three verbs describing Shechem's action are a hendiadys and mean simply 'rape' ('And-he-took her, then-he laid-her,[51] and-he-raped-her'), while his subsequent action is that he remained with Dinah, 'lusted' after her (not 'loved'), and 'attempted to soothe' her (rather than wooing her). Scholz concludes: '[This] interpretation confirms the notion of feminist scholarship that rape is sexual violence. When rape is accentuated, love talk is not involved.'

---

[48] Carolyn Pressler, 'Sexual Violence'.

[49] Lyn M. Bechtel, 'Dinah'.

[50] Susanne Scholz, 'Through Whose Eyes?'. See also 'Rape' in which she offers a critique of several studies, including that of Bechtel.

[51] The verb šākaḇ is used with ʾeṯ pointed in the MT as the sign of the object, not as the preposition 'with'.

In her other article Scholz finds in many of the interpretations of the story 'numerous assumptions complicit with contemporary belittlement of rape' – that the rapist 'really' loved Dinah, that rape was less harmful in ancient Israel, that in Israel marriage could redeem the rape, that the story reflects tribal conflict, or that the original was a love story, now overlaid by the theme of rape.[52]

These two studies illustrate very clearly the difficulty in understanding the import of the narrative within ancient Israel. The story was told from a male perspective, and it could be told in no other way in Israel's patriarchal society. In that society there appears to have been no verb that corresponds exactly to the English 'rape'. The Hebrew *'ānāh* Pi. covers a much wider semantic field. What significance should be given to *šākab* with the sign of the object is uncertain, since this is only a matter of the (late) pointing and the LXX translates 'he lay with (*meta*) her' both in Genesis 34.2 and 2 Samuel 13.14, which is without question a matter of rape.[53] The reference to pollution suggests that the main thrust of the story is not rape, and while the description of Shechem's action as 'folly' (again as in 2 Samuel 13.12) may suggest that the brothers describe it as rape, we cannot be certain that this was not for their own purposes. Male bias can be seen in some of the commentaries, of course, where it has been suggested that Dinah was largely to blame for going unaccompanied in Canaanite territory, but this does not seem to have been present in the thought of the narrator.

If, then, we return to our initial questions of how rape was regarded and what protection was offered to women, the answer appears to be that in the Dinah story the feelings of the woman did not come into consideration, that the main concern was over her having been impregnated by an uncircumcised 'Hivite' (Horite) and thus 'polluted', and that the rape (and probably in modern terms of forcible

[52] Scholz, 'Rape', 195. Carolyn S. Leeb points out that whether rape or consensual extramarital intercourse is indicated is beside the point, since 'the consent required is her father's, not her own' (*Away from the Father's House*, 136, n. 33).

[53] Some have suggested that *šākab* has replaced *šāgal*, which the masoretes seem to have regarded as obscene, since they substitute *šākab* as the Qere in the four places where it occurs (Deut. 28.30 (Qal); Isa. 13.16; Zech. 14.2 (Ni.); Jer. 3.2 (Pu.)). Perhaps the equivalent of vulgar English words for sexual intercourse, the verb itself does not seem to have meant 'to rape' in the modern sense, although each of the four instances are of rape. It is possible that where *šākab* is followed by a direct object or a suffix (Deut. 28.30 Q) it had acquired some of the overtones of *šāgal*. What is significant for the present discussion is that in Isa. 13.16 and Zech. 14.2 the raping of the women is part of the punishment through war, and Jer. 3.2 is metaphorical for Judah's apostasy. The context of Deut. 28.30 suggests that rape may be implied. In no case is any sympathy shown towards the women. We may compare Job 31.9–10 where the enslavement and rape of his wife is presented as punishment on him if he had committed adultery.

sexual intercourse with an unwilling woman it should be regarded as such) provided an opportunity for the two brothers to kill those they regarded as enemies (many more men are 'punished' than just Shechem). It is striking that the desire of Shechem and Hamor to enter into a proper marriage with the payment of a 'bride-price' is emphasized. This is the 'protection' given to women in the society of the time rather than retribution and punishment of the offender. We are within a totally different culture here.

On the other hand the story of Tamar in 2 Samuel 13 is without question a matter of rape in our sense. Amnon's lust for his half-sister, the plot devised by Jonadab, the urgent plea by Tamar and the reaction of Absalom all show this, without any need to stress the verbs describing Amnon's actions: 'being stronger than she, he forced her, and lay her' (with the sign of the direct object, 2 Sam. 13.14). This may possibly be reinforced by his immediate hatred of Tamar. Nevertheless her anguished, 'this wrong in sending me away is greater than the other which you did to me', and her subsequent tearing of her special robe and putting ashes on her head immediately shows us that the Israelite culture was not the same as our own. What is of concern to Tamar is that she was not to be married and had lost her virginity, rather than the violence to which she had been subjected in itself. Amnon's action may be contrary to the moral norms of society and *nᵉbālāh* (which Phillips claims is 'a general expression for serious disorderly and unruly action resulting in the breakup of an existing relationship', and McCarter, following Roth, translates as 'sacrilege' and *HALOT* renders 'wilful sin'),[54] yet its consequences fall on Tamar. She remains 'desolate' for the rest of her life. She it is who is 'shamed'. Moreover, the overall context of the incident shows that the narrator is primarily concerned with the political conflicts within David's family, and even Absalom's 'revenge' for his sister's rape may be equally well read as part of his own schemes to become David's successor as king. Trible, through her elegant literary analysis of the story, draws out our sympathy with the woman and links it with modern failures adequately to protect women from rape.[55] Clearly we must agree with her plea, but I remain unconvinced that this was the reaction of either the narrator or the Israelite readers.

The other horrendous story of rape is the account of the Levite's concubine in Judges 19. Although there are some ambiguities in the story (Did the men of Gibeah want to rape the Levite (v. 22)? Was the

---

[54] Anthony Phillips, '*NEBALAH*', W. M. W. Roth, '*NBL*', P. Kyle McCarter, *II Samuel*, 322–323; note A. A. Anderson, who regards 'sacrilege' as taking 'too much for granted'; his view is that the term denotes 'a serious breach of customary law' (*2 Samuel*, 174–175).
[55] Phyllis Trible, *Texts of Terror*, 37–63.

concubine actually dead when the Levite found her lying at the door as he was leaving (v. 27)? What is signified by the dismembering of the concubine's body and sending the pieces throughout Israel (v. 29)? Why did the Levite present the offence as wanting to kill him as well as actually 'humbling' (*'ānāh* Pi.) his concubine (20.5)? And is the punishment inflicted because of the rape, or the murder, or both together?), to us today the rape lies at the centre. The narrator of the final chapters of Judges sees the entire incident with its sequel as an example of the anarchy that prevailed in Israel before the monarchy (Jdg. 19.1; 21.25).

Phyllis Trible's famous discussion stresses that it 'depicts the atrocities of male power, brutality, and triumphalism; of female helplessness, abuse, and annihilation',[56] and she draws attention to the subservient place that the women have in a male world: the inferior status of a concubine, the *men* eat and drink together in her father's house, the concubine is never asked for her preferences, the offer of the old man's virgin daughter and the Levite's concubine to the men of Gibeah: 'ravish (*'ānāh* Pi.) them and do with them what seems good to you' ('if done to a man, such an act is a vile thing; if done to women, it is "the good" in the eyes of men'[57]), the Levite thrusts his concubine out to the men to save himself, apparently he intended to depart alone without regard to his concubine, he does not mourn for her but cuts her body up,[58] and in the sequel the Israelites turn over four hundred young virgins to the six hundred remaining Benjamites, and when this is not enough they sanction the abduction of two hundred young women as they come out to dance in the yearly festival to Yahweh,[59] finally the editor of Judges uses the horrors of

---

[56] *Ibid.*, 65.

[57] *Ibid.*, 74. Phyllis Trible compares the similar Gen. 19.1–29. She comments: 'rules of hospitality in Israel protect only males.' Cf. Lyn M. Bechtel's very different attempt to see the narrative 'through group-oriented eyes', rather than with an 'individual-oriented' approach, refusing to impose the assumptions of homophobia and the devaluation of women on the text. She claims that the intended crime may not be male rape, but even if it was its intention was to diminish the status of the messengers and protect their own group. Lot does not offer his daughters as an act of self-preservation, or the heroic deed of a perfect host, or the desperate act of a wicked man, or as a father doing what he has a right to do, but to defuse the situation, confident that its inappropriateness will prevent further aggression ('Genesis 19.1–11'). While Bechtel is to be commended for attempting to set the story within Israelite culture, I find it difficult to believe that its function was '[to challenge] . . . xenophobic and isolationist tendencies' in the Israelite community, and do not believe that the main thrust concerns group relations. (Bechtel finds radical differences between Gen. 19 and Jdg. 19: in Judges the genuine rape is carried out by 'insiders'.)

[58] Phyllis Trible draws attention to Saul's action in 1 Sam. 11.7 –'in the end, she is no more than the oxen that Saul will later cut up', using the same verb (*nāṭaḥ*, *Texts of Terror*, 80–81).

[59] 'In total, the rape of one has become the rape of six hundred' (*ibid.*, 83).

the story to promote monarchy, but the reign of David 'brings its own horrors. David pollutes Bathsheba; Amnon rapes Tamar; and Absalom violates the concubines of his father'.[60] Some of Trible's exegesis is forced, and her application of Isaiah 53 and references to Jesus from the Gospels shows a lack of taste, but her article shows up very clearly the position of women in this narrative and the attitudes to rape which prevailed in ancient Israel. On the other hand, to say with Terrien that the stories of Tamar and the Levite's concubine reveal 'ethical revulsion' against sexual violence is hardly correct.[61] There are too many features in the narrative that have a very different thrust.[62]

The sexual violation of women in the Old Testament has to be understood within an androcentric and patriarchal culture which viewed women from the perspective of their relation to their fathers and husbands. This means that there was no true 'rape' in our sense, since the harm done to the woman was viewed in terms of the way she had been shamed, the honour of her male relatives had been damaged, and the fact that the possibility of her marriage to anyone but her rapist was negligible. The law, the narratives, the prophets,[63] and Job are at one in this. Thus women are largely powerless in a male world, and any sexual violence they suffer is not viewed in terms of the harm done to them.[64] Little protection is given to them, apart from the defence which a male relative, especially the head of the family and the husband, could offer.[65] They were not subject to any kind of *purdah* restrictions. Whether they were veiled in public is uncertain: in Isaiah's taunt song over Babylon a mark of humiliation is the removal of the veil.[66]

Evidence for the incidence of rape in ancient Israel is lacking, but it may be questioned whether it was very common.[67] Although the

---

[60] *Ibid.*, 84.

[61] Samuel Terrien, *Till the Heart Sings*, 197.

[62] Two recent studies emphasize that rape is violence rather than a sexual matter, Ilse Müllner, 'Lethal Differences' and Alice Bach, 'The Body Politic', the latter comparing the actions of Serb men against Muslim women in Bosnia.

[63] Isa. 13.16. and Zech 14.2 have already been noted. Amos does not mention rape in his list of war crimes (Amos 1–2), only assaults on pregnant women. But cf. Lam. 5.11 on the consequences of war, where the relation of the women to their male relatives is not made explicit.

[64] Irmgard Fischer claims that in Israel sexual violence against women was institutionalized and that 'androcentric law legitimates violence against women' ('"Go and Suffer Oppression!"', 75, 76).

[65] Hence the ease with which widows were oppressed. Isaiah 4.1 shows that women were desperate to secure the protection of being married and the status which this gave.

[66] In Gen. 24 Rebekah is unveiled throughout until she meets Isaac, perhaps because lifting the veil was part of the marriage ceremony (de Vaux, *Ancient Israel*, 33–34, noting Song 4.1, 3; 6.7).

[67] While even a single instance of violence against women is to be condemned, is it

dangers which an unaccompanied woman faced are obvious,[68] it seems likely that rape was far less common than in modern society. The control which men maintained over women makes it inherently probable that women were more secure. The accounts of rape in the Old Testament are told as if they were exceptional, although the limitations of the narratives which mainly deal with the court make it impossible to know what the life of the peasants was like. It is difficult to believe, however, that in village communities widespread raping of women would have been tolerated. The way the prophets mention rape suggests that it chiefly occurred in war. This does not make it less serious, but it should force us to attempt to understand rape within the wider setting of Israelite society.

While the stories of rape that we have considered show how the status of women within the culture of ancient Israel is linked both with the way they were sometimes treated and with the way women themselves regarded rape, the stories of active and forceful women show that it was possible for some of them to 'work the system' and achieve influence and even power.

The Significance of this for Ethics

The ancient Israelites would not have considered the position of women in society an ethical matter at all. Women derived their status primarily as members of the family and it was the family which protected them and saw that wrongs committed against them were avenged. This, however, does not necessarily imply a low view of women. There were, of course, those who held such an opinion – Ben Sira stands out – but as mothers women were held in high regard by everyone.[69]

What has to be avoided is to import modern ideas about the position of women into the Old Testament. This results in distorting the evidence either by isolating prominent women (and those less prominent who are elevated into prominence by modern feminist scholars) from their social and cultural environment, or by 'reinterpreting' the texts in a way which makes them accord with

---

not significant that Fischer collects only eleven examples including Susanna from the Apocrypha?

[68] The assault by the watchmen in Song 5.7 shows what could happen to an unaccompanied woman. This would be true, even if a mythological interpretation is adopted. We may note also the instructions which Boaz gives to his young men in Ruth 2.9, which also hints at the dangers facing a woman on her own, a danger of which Naomi fails to warn Ruth (cf. Danna Nolan Fewell, 'Feminist Reading', 82).

[69] One can sympathize with the many feminists who recoil in horror at this, since it fails to value the woman for herself. Esther Fuchs argues that the patriarchal framework of the biblical stories prevents the mother-figure from becoming 'a full-fledged *human* role model' ('Mothers', 136).

modern beliefs.[70] Naturally great care must be taken not to misrepresent the Hebrew writings in an exaggerated patriarchal way in a reaction to this, which is why it is important here to recognize that, while women were subordinated to men in positions of authority (as indeed were men of lower status), they were held in high regard within the positions where they were placed. Even within this patriarchal society it was possible for women to attain positions of power, but this was through their own personality, intelligence and skill, coupled with the chance of the circumstances in which they happened to find themselves. They attain their power in spite of the system: that they have come into prominence does not destroy or weaken the influence of the overall culture. Above all, as has already been emphasized, this patriarchal culture was accepted as natural, normal, and right and proper by everyone.[71]

Where it became an ethical matter was when women were wronged. This also, however, is not easy to disentangle. As we have seen women were often treated in ways which we would regard as morally evil. Even when attempts were made to right the wrongs, these were inevitably confined within the patriarchal pattern of society and the procedures differ markedly from those of which we would approve. Moreover the wrongs themselves were viewed in different ways from the way we would see them. Less attention was paid to the feelings and person of the woman (some would say, no attention at all). The harm done to them was primarily thought of in terms of the damage which had been done to the near relative (father or husband). A strong element in the way rape was perceived belongs to the purity system rather than the ethical one. Finally some would claim that in the telling of the stories the women were simply effaced and forgotten.

What must not be done is to judge Israelite cultural and ethical norms by those of feminists in the modern world.[72] It is of first importance to recognize that Israelite culture differed massively from ours in respect of hierarchy, patriarchy, and the way women were perceived and valued.

---

[70] Had there been space I would have considered the question of 'inclusive' translations of the Bible. Basic to such exercises as NRSV is the conviction that the church's sriptures must be allowed to address all believers equally and in current English usage. The NIV Committee were more cautious, but even they say: 'it was recognized that it was often appropriate to mute the patriarchalism of the culture of the biblical writers' ('Preface', v).

[71] I believe this to be true both of ancient Israel and the writers of the Hebrew Bible. There is, however, no way to prove it. The problem of reconstructing the life of ancient Israel is insoluble. All we can claim is that this is the picture which the biblical writings present.

[72] This is not to forget that we should probably have not been aware of the position in which women were placed in ancient Israel without the writings of the many feminists who have opened our (male) eyes.

19

HOW DID THE OLD TESTAMENT VIEW WHAT WE CALL ETHICS?

It will be recalled that in Chapter 13 we noted that the country which we glimpsed from the slit windows in the tower appeared puzzlingly foreign. The Old Testament does not distinguish sharply between ethics, purity and honour, and indeed to speak of these three topics in the abstract in this way is alien to its way of thought. When we fastened on five ethical issues which are of great importance to us, we discovered not merely that they were treated differently from the way we would approach them, but that they were hardly regarded as moral problems at all. Indeed, situations which greatly trouble us were accepted as normal and matter of course. The Old Testament picture of the world and of human society is very different from ours.

This is commonly forgotten. The bold acceptance of the gap between the biblical world and our own by Dennis Nineham has been pushed aside, the more easily because of the influence of canonical approaches to the Bible on the one hand and the too ready openness to postmodernist relativism on the other.[1] The water has been muddied by literary approaches, which have severed the link between history and text and by treating the text as a human artefact have permitted it to be read as if it were written today rather than at least 2,200 years ago. Modern translations sustain this error. The point has now been reached when we must face the question of how far it is possible to recover the way in which what we term ethics appeared to the ancient Israelites. How can this be done?

It is highly probable that the laws reflect the ideas of the priestly circles within which they were compiled and transmitted. The influence of the scribal redactors on the other parts of the Old Testament is as great. Yet without those scribes we should have no Hebrew Bible at all. We only possess this collection of writings because they were regarded as religiously important and later as 'Holy Scripture'. In the end it is impossible to move beyond the theology and ethics which those who wrote, edited, transcribed and reverenced the texts permit us to see. And our dependence on the biblical texts is

---

[1] The points which Nineham made so forcefully in *Use and Abuse* need to be given full weight, especially his emphasis upon the different worlds of thought.

the greater because of the paucity of contemporary epigraphical material. The contrast between Israel and Mesopotamia has already been noted. This is the given situation and while the recent studies of physical changes in Palestine have filled in the background to some extent, religion and ethics belong so exclusively within the culture that the recovery of climatic changes, types of settlement, farming practices, and the like can offer no more than a setting, within which a wide variety of religious and ethical institutions and norms becomes possible.[2]

In the last five chapters we found ourselves constantly being made aware that situations which are ethically highly charged in our eyes were accepted as a matter of course by the Israelites. Poverty as such was not an issue, although it was accepted that weaker members of society ought not to be oppressed. War was a normal fact of life: why Yahweh permitted Israel to be defeated was the problem. Domestic animals were treated as superior and delicate tools, while wild animals were a continuous threat: rare indeed is any awareness that kindness should be shown to them, and isolated is the vision of peace with the animals and between them. Ecology and the equality of men and women hardly feature in the Old Testament at all, although there was an awareness of the wonders of nature and within their various social statuses women were honoured. All this was taken for granted, and it would have been astonishing if any major features of the culture had been challenged. The very fact that so much was regarded as self-evident by the Israelites has enabled us to sift out some features of the ethics. Is it possible to go any further?

So far in this study the narratives, the wisdom writings, and the psalms have been introduced chiefly as a means of testing the laws or providing illustrations. May it not be that the glimpses of them that we obtain from higher windows in our tower will further our quest?

Immediately further problems arise. Beyond the fact – far from insignificant – that all that we possess are religious texts, is the cultural level from which our texts derive. That they are written means that they derive from those classes which are literate. The main actors

---

[2] Walter Houston has brilliantly shown how much archaeological discovery can contribute to our interpretation of the Old Testament laws on clean and unclean animals, but his study also reveals the limitations of both written and material evidence (see *Purity and Monotheism*, 124–129). A good account of the use of archaeology in the reconstruction of Israelite society is provided by Paula M. McNutt, *Ancient Israel*. The impossibility of discovering religious beliefs from material remains, however, is shown strikingly at Stonehenge, where the configuration of the stones clearly relates them to the sun, but the beliefs of those who moved the stones to the site and erected them can only be conjectured. Written religious texts are difficult enough to interpret: the ideas behind material artefacts without contemporary epigraphic remains are almost entirely obscure.

within the narratives are kings, members of the court, and prophets. The wisdom writings are part of a wider international movement, and how far proverbs which were popular among the peasants and others of low status have been preserved is impossible to know.[3] And our knowledge of the background to the psalms is minimal: their date, authorship, relation to the king, place in the cult, and position within the literature of the Hebrew Bible are all alike matters of conjecture and theory – we simply do not know.[4]

The Book of Proverbs

The wisdom writings have often been castigated as being 'conservative', in contrast to the supposedly innovatory and radical teaching of the prophets. This is quite wrong. It is true that in some ways the wise men exhibited the biases of their class. As we have seen, they sometimes taught that the poor were themselves to blame for their poverty, yet at the same time, it is only the wisdom writings which show any concern for the poor as *poor*.[5] Naturally those who are living a comfortable life will not be revolutionaries, but it is questionable whether revolution figures in any of the biblical writings. Indeed, the idea is alien not only to earlier societies but to much of the Christian era. It needed rapid change, whether through natural disaster or technological innovation to spark off radical movements and ideas.

The book of Proverbs is important for the study of ethics because the wise men accepted the *status quo*, and it is the *status quo* which reveals most clearly how the Israelites viewed the society in which they lived and the ethics which sustained it. Gerhard von Rad has pointed out that if the book is regarded as containing 'a concentrated deposit of ancient Israelite morality', this assertion is only correct provided that 'morality' is used as referring to Israelite ideas and not as in philosophical or theological ethics. The proverbs are rooted in the very specific world of values that belongs to ancient Israel, and that world is unfamiliar to us. In Israelite society the individual conformed unthinkingly to the norms and values that derive from the communities in which he or she lived. 'The community life has its ethical atmosphere; it compels the individual to live up to specific expectations which people have of him, it provides him with long

---

[3] Even if there were an 'old wisdom', largely free from a Yahwistic religious colouring (so William McKane, *Prophets and Wise Men* and *Proverbs*), the writings we possess are those preserved by the wisdom scribes. But the theory has not been widely accepted (see, e.g., James L. Crenshaw, *Wisdom*, 77, 87 n. 58). On the other hand the arguments, using proverbial material from Africa, of Friedemann W. Golka, *Leopard's Spots*, are not to be brushed aside too hastily.

[4] I emphasized the extent of our ignorance in my commentary on the psalms in *OBC*.

[5] See above pp. 163–166, 174–178.

established examples and values. As a rule, the individual conforms unthinkingly to these community-determined factors.'[6]

It is not easy to determine what the ideas of the wise men and the society they represent actually were. I have already pointed out that 'righteousness' is an empty cell, waiting to be filled with whatever values and actions are viewed favourably by the speaker. This is shown strikingly in Proverbs, where 'the righteous' and 'the wicked' are frequently used (commonly juxtaposed) but never explained. Kenneth T. Aitken collects sixty-three proverbs which deal with the righteous and the wicked.[7] Even though some of these contain synonyms of ṣaddīq and rāšāʿ, they form no more than a sample. There are, for example, no less than fourteen proverbs containing ṣaddīq or ṣᵉḏāqāh in Proverbs 10 alone, though Aitken's list contains only nine. Always, however, the one who composed or transcribed the proverb assumed that what is meant by righteous and wicked is known by his readers or listeners. Still taking Proverbs 10 as an example, the 'reward' (in various forms) of being righteous is mentioned seven times (vv. 2, 3, 6, 16, 25, 28, 30), their memory is a blessing (v. 7), their mouth (= teaching) is a fountain of life (v. 11) and choice silver (v. 20), and speaks wisdom (v. 31) and what is acceptable (v. 32), their lips feed many (v. 21), and what they desire will be granted (v. 24). David J. Reimer notes that Proverbs prefers the adjective ṣaddīq to the noun ṣᵉḏāqāh, and finds in this an interest in the nature of the one who is righteous rather than in abstract conceptions of righteousness. Nevertheless, his subsequent discussion shows that it is the consequences of being righteous which are his main interest (and perhaps the main interest of the writers of the proverbs). He lists, however, some of the characteristics of the righteous man: he is honest, generous, steadfast, bold, loyal, merciful and just, several of which are equally in need of filling out before their ethical sense is certain.[8] Moreover, the pair of terms 'wise' and 'fool'[9] refer not to intellectual knowledge and learning but to practical understanding of right and wrong,

How, then, does Proverbs present what we might term ethics? Most of the older scholars were interested in matters of date, provenance,

---

[6] Gerhard von Rad, *Wisdom*, 74–75. Sociology and hermeneutics alike today show that even in modern society with its wide range of choices, individuals are more determined by the society of which they are a part than most of us like to think.

[7] Kenneth T. Aitken, *Proverbs*, 138–141.

[8] David J. Reimer, *ṣdq* , *NIDOTTE*, 3.756–758.

[9] Although no less than eight different terms are used for the fool, and attempts have been made to distinguish between them, apart perhaps from the *pᵉtî* ('simple' and 'naïve' person) it is uncertain whether there are very great differences in meaning in the way they are used in Proverbs (cf. James L. Crenshaw, *Wisdom*, 67–68 for the list with suggested nuances).

relation to international wisdom, and theological factors such as the absence of the Exodus deliverance, the Torah, and the covenant, and the question of reward and punishment. Where they consider the substantial ethics it is to criticize it for the absence of such virtues as courage, beauty, and self-sacrifice, its emphasis on outward actions, the rigid division of human beings into good and bad, wise and simpletons, and its appeal to common-sense or the command of God rather than presenting an inward morality.[10] By contrast, Kenneth T. Aitken treats the proverbs under 'Types of Character' (e.g. the hothead, the scoffer, the sluggard, the drunkard, the mischief-maker), 'Wisdom in Various Settings' (the home, the community, the market, the law court, the palace, the school of wisdom), and 'Ways of Man and the Ways of God' (which include observations on nature, wise ways with words, and prayer, sacrifice and vows).[11] We shall return to this shortly.

Von Rad asks how we can progress in our question as to what Israel and her teachers understood by 'ethical' and returns to the point that 'under the teachers there could be absolutely no discussion as to what good and evil were'.[12] In ancient Israel life was understood as lived within a universe in which goodness led to blessing and evil to weakness and disaster. This meant that 'the good man is the one who knows about the constructive quality of good and the destructive quality of evil and who submits to this pattern which can be discerned in the world'. Further the 'righteous' man was the one who 'fulfilled the claims made upon him by a community', who 'lived up to what the community expected of him'.[13] This is of the greatest importance for properly understanding Old Testament ethics. Put in another way we might say that goodness is a matter of living in such a way that it brings blessing to the community.[14] It also provides the basis for the emphasis upon honour which we have already discussed, for honour is essentially a community matter, concerning as it does the status of the individual within the community of which he is a part and without which he has no existence as a person.

[10] So Crawford H. Toy, *Proverbs*, xi–xiv. Toy goes on to discuss the 'Religious' and 'Philosophical' features in the book.
[11] Kenneth T. Aitken, *Proverbs*, see Contents, viii–ix. It should be noted that much recent writing has been concerned with feminist issues, fastening in particular on the figure of wisdom (see, e.g., Athalya Brenner, ed., *Wisdom Literature*; the articles by Gerlinde Baumann, Alice Ogden Bellis and Christl Maier in Athalya Brenner and Carole Fontaine, *Wisdom and Psalms*, and Claudia V. Camp, *Wisdom and the Feminine*).
[12] Von Rad, *Wisdom*, 77.
[13] *Ibid.*, 78.
[14] The emphasis which Johs. Pedersen places upon the 'blessing' should be remembered (*Israel I–II*, 182–212).

Given the centrality of the community, von Rad is able to discuss the actions and attitudes which are commended by the writers of the proverbs, such as the condemnation of pride and hot-temper. He stresses that the sages did not base their teaching on laws, certainly not the Decalogue, but simply accepted the standards found within the social order and made no attempt to change or replace them. This I believe to be correct, and would repeat that it is wrong to describe it as conservatism. It provides the key to the Old Testament way of understanding morality.

Many scholars have drawn attention to the fact that the wise men make experience the primary ground of their teaching about life. Von Rad, for example, fastens on the motive clauses attached to some of the proverbs as a main part of the evidence. He finds the authority which the sages claim for their teaching in the experiences which their ancestors had and passed on, the blessings which goodness brings according to that experience, and above all in their experience of the 'specific, highly stable, social order'.[15] With this may be compared the detailed analysis of the motive clauses in Proverbs by P. J. Nel, who finds only eleven 'religious' motivations. In contrast to von Rad, however, he claims that the social order rarely acts as a motivation. Seventy-seven per cent of motivations refer to experience and logic, showing the truth and validity of the admonitions. This leads Nel to conclude that the writers of Proverbs based their ethics on their experience of inherent natural laws. Further, he claims that it is the motive clauses which give the admonitions their authority by declaring their truth. He argues that the ethos of the wisdom writers is based on the created order. By grasping the true nature of that order they attain to knowledge of the Creator.[16] Accepting that this conclusion is founded on a very narrow base (the admonitions in Proverbs), and that to extend the claims made to the whole wisdom movement goes well beyond what the evidence can sustain, this is a valuable observation and needs to be set alongside the limiting of experience to life within society. Nevertheless, the sentence literature is much closer to von Rad's view. Primarily the proverbs present an ethics which is essentially an attempt to maintain the well-being of society.

It is hardly possible to place too much emphasis upon this. Our modern understanding of ethics is strongly influenced by Kant's categorical imperative and Bentham and Mill's utilitarianism, even if we do not follow the theories developed in the twentieth-century, such as intuitionism, emotivism, prescriptivism, and the like. To us the individual conscience and the consequences of our actions are of

[15] Von Rad, *Wisdom*, 88–93, 94.
[16] P. J. Nel, *Structure*, 18–67.

primary ethical importance. There is also an emphasis upon happiness and the evil of cruelty, which are often assumed to be a major ground for determining right or wrong actions.[17] It was not so among the Israelites. The Greek concern for virtue, which seems to be receiving renewed interest among moral philosophers, is closer to the Old Testament ethics.[18]

Proverbs, then, has much to teach about the way the Israelites understood ethics, once we cease to be deflected by its supposed conservative élitism. Aitken sets us on the right track, but his analysis needs to be modified slightly. The primary setting is the community. The types of character attain their significance through the effect which these persons have upon the community, while the market and law court can be subsumed under it. The family is the more immediate setting of the individual Israelite, but the family itself is part of a larger network of families within the society of the village or the small town, so that once again the community is central.[19] What, then, was important in the life of those who lived in this community?

Primarily, what Proverbs seeks is a *satisfactory* style of life which contributes to the well-being and stability of that society. If it is not a heroic ethics, it is none the worse for that. We today who have seen the breakdown of ordered society in Kosovo and elsewhere should not be the first to condemn those who looked for a community at ease with itself. The issues that we have been considering in the last five chapters were either unrecognized or were met in simple and kindly ways. The poor may be suffering the result of their own folly and laziness, but they are none the less to be helped. It is an advance on

---

[17] The contrast between modern and Old Testament ethics is strikingly seen by comparing the biblical approach to that of Anne Thomson. In her textbook, *Critical Reasoning in Ethics*, she declares that ethical decisions are made on the basis of certain unassailable values, such as 'the prevention of harm', 'justice' and 'respect for autonomy'. These she appears to accept on intuitionist grounds (p. 97, cf. 109).

[18] See *ibid.*, 79. Notable modern studies are Peter Geach, *The Virtues* and Alasdair MacIntyre, *After Virtue*. See also the discussion of MacIntyre in Peter Vardy and Paul Grosch, *The Puzzle of Ethics*. Von Rad instances Hesiod. Possibly Plato and Aristotle should also be considered, though differences between them, and with the Old Testament, must not be overlooked. It should be noted that von Rad stresses that to suggest that the 'success thinking' of the wise men was utilitarianism or eudemonism is a complete misunderstanding (*Wisdom*, 80, 'one could hardly misunderstand it more'). Peter J. Paris suggests that some basic questions drawn from Aristotle might usefully provide guiding principles for the study of Old Testament ethics ('Ethicist's Concerns', 176–177).

[19] I pass over, perhaps too hastily, the questions of whether the wisdom writings originated in scribal schools or the court, and whether the international aspect of the wisdom movement means that the writings contain an international rather than an Israelite ethics. These are large and complex matters which are unresolved. My personal view is that, while the wisdom *books* come from scribal circles of some kind (as indeed all the books of the Old Testament must, for they were written and copied), the scene depicted in them is not too distant from the life of the small communities in Israel.

what is found in the Torah and the prophets to consider the needs of the poor simply as poor, but we cannot expect the sages to consider whether it is the structure of society itself which makes them so. War, curiously, does not come within the purview of the sages, possibly because it is so much at odds with all that they hold dear that they have nothing to say on the matter. Animals are hardly regarded as posing any ethical questions, even within the scope of the ethics which the makers of proverbs accept,[20] and although the sages are aware of the mysteries of the natural world,[21] it would be highly anachronistic to suppose that they even glimpsed the need to protect nature. Women play a larger part, mainly because of the importance of the family. It would again be false to the patriarchal attitudes of the time to suppose that their status was any different from that of other parts of the Old Testament. The family is viewed through male eyes, even when mother is placed alongside of father and wisdom is personified as a woman. It is always the young *man* who is being given instruction. What must not be overlooked is the fact that it is the traditional family which the sages sought to preserve, and their teaching is aimed at securing its stability.

In contrast to the issues which concern those living in the twenty-first century, what the writers of proverbs and the givers of instruction are worried about are those who threaten the stability and easy functioning of the community. This can be seen from various angles.

Within the family, the son who is rebellious and disobeys his father and mother is a danger. Hence the calls for obedience and the castigation of sons who flout the authority of their parents (e.g., Prov. 10.1; 13.1; 15.5, 20; 19.26; 20.20; 28.7, 24; 30.17).[22] Honouring parents (mothers as well as fathers, since it is by becoming a mother that a woman gains honour, cf. Prov. 15.20; 23.22, 25) is an important feature of the patriarchal society. Since the sages believe that instruction will lead to right living, i.e., living according to the norms of the society, they urge parents to instruct and discipline their sons (Prov. 13.24;19.18; 22.6, 15; 23.13, 14; 29.15, 17).

Adultery destroys marriage, bringing shame upon the husband, endangering the adulterer, and posing a threat to comfortable relations between the men within the community. This, then, becomes an important theme in Proverbs, and as with Ben Sirach, though in a less misogynous spirit, the blame is placed upon the woman. This is seen particularly in the instructions in chapters 1–9, where the wiles of the adulteress and 'strange woman' are set out in great detail

---

[20] Prov. 6.6–8; 12.10; 27.23–27.

[21] Prov. 30.18–19, 24–31. The sages lack the poetic sense of wonder of some of the psalmists and the writer of Job.

[22] In contrast to Ben Sirach, there are no parallel accusations against daughters.

(Prov. 5.1–23; 6.20–35; 7.1–27;[23] for the warnings in the later sections of the book see 22.14; 23.26–28; 30.20).

It is not only adultery which harms marriage. The sages are hard upon the nagging wife, and are also aware that fathers are not always perfect. The proverbs describing a quarrelsome wife as like continual dripping of rain (Prov. 19.13; 27.15) are well known and the sages have been accused of male chauvinism. They were written by men and present a male point of view, as is natural in a patriarchal society. It is no use to rail against the type of society that is found in the Old Testament simply because if offends our modern susceptibilities. It is there and the concern of modern readers, both scholars and Christian believers, has to be to understand and explain it. The home in which there was continual strife was the opposite of the ideal which was desired, a happy, contented and quiet marriage relationship, and normally the sages expected that the wife was responsible if things did not measure up to this ideal. Only two proverbs admit that husbands and fathers can destroy that peace within the home by their irresponsible actions (Prov. 11.29), and by not remaining at home (Prov. 27.8).[24] The criticism of the nagging wife, however, should be set against the ideal as the sages saw her. The acrostic in Proverbs 31.10–31 is justly famous. Again it belongs to a patriarchal society. The wife works long and hard in order that her husband may attain a position of high honour and have the time to sit with the elders in the gate. Yet she has considerable authority and clearly possesses skills beyond that of docile home-maker.[25] Beyond this poem, both Aitken and Fontaine collect up two sets of proverbs, those describing the nagging wife, the seductress and the prostitute on the one hand, and those expressing the great blessing which a good wife brings to her husband.[26] Behind all of them is ultimately the desire for a home which provides security for the husband and children.

Home and the wider society cannot be separated. Stability within the community is of central importance to the sages, and they are

---

[23] It is sometimes suggested that within these chapters the 'strange woman' represents foreign cults. There are no firm grounds for holding this, and the language, especially in 7.10–20, which is surely a picture of literal seduction, is more easily taken as offering warnings to the young men.

[24] William McKane thinks this includes the thought that the wanderer cuts himself off from his family (*Proverbs*, 612). Might not the wandering include associating with other women?

[25] It must not be overlooked that it is a well-to-do family which is depicted. Feminist writers on the whole are favourably disposed to the poem, acknowledging that it is patriarchal but emphasizing the intelligence, sound business sense, and energy of this industrious housewife (see Alice L. Laffey, *Introduction*, 212–213; Claudia V. Camp, *Wisdom*, 90–93; Carole R. Fontaine, '"Many Devices"', 148).

[26] Aitken, *Proverbs*, 128–129, 152–153 contrasted with 153–158, and Fontaine '"Many Devices"', 149, contrasted with 147–148.

swift to condemn those who disturb it. Aitken has collected a group of seven proverbs under the heading 'Righteousness and Wickedness in High Places', pointing out that the words and actions of the righteous man contribute to the well-being of the community.[27] As is usual when the terms 'righteous', 'upright', and 'wicked' are used, it is assumed that what these imply is known and does not need to be explained. It is all the more significant, therefore, that these proverbs stress the benefits and evils which will fall upon the community. They are not concerned with the goodness or wickedness of the individual as such. Through such persons a town is 'exalted' or 'overthrown' (Prov. 11.11). When the rulers are righteous there is great rejoicing (Prov. 29.2, cf. 11.10), while when they are evil, not only does their evil filter down among all the members of society but good men have to go into hiding (Prov. 29.16; 28.12). Several proverbs express the common theme from the ancient Middle East, that the good king dispenses justice to the poor and punishes the wicked (Prov. 29.14; 20.8, 26). Such a king gives stability ($ya^{ca}m\bar{\imath}d$) to the land (Prov. 29.4).

At the extreme of those who destroy this stability are robbers and murderers (Prov. 1.11–19), but the makers of proverbs are aware of the insidious danger posed by mischief makers (Prov. 24.8), those who act shamefully (Prov. 13.5), and cover up their evil schemes with false words (Prov. 10.6, 11). Since justice depends on the honesty of witnesses, there is special condemnation of those who utter lies and a recognition of the immense evil that they can cause (Prov. 14.25; 19.28; 25.18). Corrupt judges are even more a threat to the stability of the community, which depends upon equal justice (Prov. 17.15; 18.5; 24.23–25), and bribery is condemned (Prov. 17.23).[28] The two proverbs which mention the use of casting lots in settling disputes puzzle the commentators, who tend to limit their discussions to questions of the way the lot may have worked and references to lots outside the book of Proverbs. Proverbs 16.33 sees the decision as Yahweh's, putting a religious gloss on the practice. More significant is 18.18. The welfare of the community is threatened when two powerful members within it are locked in a dispute. The proverb hopes that by resorting to the lot the potentially disruptive conflict may be brought to a satisfactory end.

Beyond the law court, other types of false and deceptive words and conduct disturb the ease of the community. Lies may be spoken more

---

[27] Aitken, *Proverbs*, 200.

[28] Yet, as Aitken points out, although there are these unequivocal condemnations of bribery, other proverbs suggest that it has its uses (e.g. Prov. 17.8; 18.16; 19.6; 21.14), perhaps simply recording reality and what was accepted social custom (*Proverbs*, 199). If the latter is the correct reading, it illustrates yet more strongly the way custom and social norms control the ethics of the wise men.

widely than when the elders are judging a case and are no less
disruptive (Prov. 26.28). It is no wonder that Yahweh abhors them
(Prov. 12.22). Flattery is a cloak for hidden evil (Prov. 29.5; cf.
28.23). Even more insidious is the spreading of rumour, which leads
so easily to quarrelling and strife (Prov. 16.28; 26.20).[29]

The prophets and the laws condemn false weights and measures,[30]
and the sages do the same (Prov. 11.1; 16.11; 20.10, 23). Two
proverbs may, however, look a little deeper. '"It is bad, it is bad", says
the buyer; but when he goes away, then he boasts' (Prov. 20.14) and
'The people curse him who holds back grain, but a blessing is on the
head of him who sells it' (Prov. 11.26). The commentators see the
first as simply a vivid picture of normal eastern haggling and the
second as drawing a contrast between the merchant who holds out for
a higher price regardless of the common good and the one who has a
sense of social responsibility and sells without concern for maximum
financial gain.[31] This may well be so, but perhaps the sages are
pointing to something more serious. Such practices may be
commonplace, but at heart they strike at the welfare of the
community. This would be true even if everyone accepted haggling as
the customary method of buying and selling, and recognized the
merchant who put profit first.[32]

Despite this emphasis upon conduct which maintains the stability of
society and secures the welfare of all its members, it has to be
recognized that a certain individualism is found running throughout
the book of Proverbs. The sages believe that the righteous will prosper
and the wicked suffer disaster. Proverb after proverb speak of the
many different kinds of 'reward' and 'punishment' which come upon
those who walk in one or other of the 'two ways'.[33] How far this is to
be described as 'retribution' has been disputed.[34] In Proverbs it
appears that sometimes the results of righteousness and wickedness
come directly from Yahweh, but more commonly they are the result

---

[29] The disapproval of whisperers, slanderers and tale bearers is seen in the relatively
large number of proverbs in which such practices are mentioned (cf. Prov. 10.18;
11.12, 13; 12.19; 17.4; 18.8; 20.19; 25.23; 26.22, 23; 29.5).

[30] Cf. Lev. 19.36; Deut. 25.13–16; Amos 8.5; Mic. 6.11; Ezek. 45.10–12. Aitken
gives some rabbinic rules which indicate how concerned the rabbis were for absolute
honesty.

[31] See, e.g., Toy, *Proverbs*, 388, 235; McKane, *Proverbs*, 542 ('mirrors with
wonderful accuracy and humour the climate and devices associated with the striking of
a bargain in a commercial context where fixed prices have no place'), 434; Richard J.
Clifford, *Proverbs*, 184, 126.

[32] 'Perhaps we are meant to reflect that dishonesty can be found on either side of the
counter. Perhaps we are simply meant to smile' (Aitken, *Proverbs*, 203).

[33] Kenneth T. Aitken has conveniently collected together some of the proverbs which
declare this (*Proverbs*, 138–141).

[34] See Klaus Koch, 'Retribution'.

of what has been built into an orderly world. The sages seem unaware that things do not always work out neatly and it needed the writer of Job and Qoheleth to point this out.

Even though there are many proverbs which appear to be concerned simply to enable the individual to get on in the world, enough evidence has been offered, I trust, to indicate the importance of a stable society to the writers of Proverbs. Advice is given so that the young man may succeed *within the existing society*. Never is there any suggestion that society might be altered – or need be. Here is one of the greatest contrasts between our modern world and that of the sages (and of ancient Israel generally). In the latter part of the twentieth century rapid change became one of the most desired features. The means of amassing ever increasing knowledge and disseminating it widely is inbuilt into our educational and industrial systems. Research and development, advertising and marketing are given high priority. Greater productivity is the driving force in society and is accorded the highest value. Stability is regarded as stagnation. The future dominates over the past. The young and the innovator receive the acclaim. In ancient Israel the old are revered and their wisdom is sought. Life as it always was is accepted and efforts are made to retain it unchanged. Stability is the highest value. It is within this stable society, where right and wrong are sustained by the natural order of the world, that morality has to be practised. Old Testament ethics has to be understood in this context.

The Narratives
The central problem with the narratives is to determine their relation to the history they retell. For those concerned with Old Testament ethics the question appears differently from the way it presents itself to those interested in reconstructing the history of Israel. As is well known, many scholars today question how far the biblical record can form the basis of such a reconstruction, some denying its value outright and turning instead to archaeology. For those studying the ethics, only texts can yield useful information, and it is impossible to turn away from the Bible in favour of the secular history of the ancient Middle East. Are the narratives, therefore, to be treated as quasi-historical, enabling us to obtain an insight into the way the Israelites acted and the ethical ideas which they held, or are they simply 'stories', the ethics of which can certainly be discussed but cannot be claimed to be that of the historical characters, for the characters may not have been accurately portrayed – or even existed at all. Because of the current uncertainty, and perhaps guided by my own inherent scepticism, I am tempted to treat

the narratives as stories and look simply at the ethics which they display.[35]

The only writer on Old Testament ethics to fasten on the narratives as the basis for his entire exposition is Waldemar Janzen. He selects five stories 'each of which claims in its own way to model right ethical behavior': Genesis 13 (familial), Numbers 25 (priestly), 1 Samuel 25 (wisdom), 1 Samuel 24 (royal), and 1 Kings 21 (prophetic).[36] Immediately we are faced with two difficulties: Do the stories themselves actually make these claims or are they imposed upon them by Janzen? and how far is the selection of passages and models the result of Janzen's prior decision about the way his ethics is to be structured? One can sympathize with Janzen's need to be selective – there are simply too many narratives to deal with in a single book. He defends his use of the selected texts by saying that the intended reader is 'primarily the Christian who confronts the Old Testament in its entirety as part of the Christian canon'. 'Nowhere', he adds in a footnote, does he 'intend to suggest that historical Israel consciously accepted and lived by this pattern.' Nevertheless, he believes that the paradigms derive from Israel's historical experience and that they guided the nation, groups, or individuals in 'living out God's revealed will'.[37] While, therefore, much that is valuable can be drawn from Janzen's work, it is less than satisfactory for our present purpose, which is to move away from the position of the modern Christian who is in possession of the canon, in order to try to enter into the world of ancient Israel – or at least that of the ancient writers. To illustrate his method I select his discussion of the priestly model story, Numbers 25.[38]

Into the account of the plague sent by Yahweh as punishment for idol worship while the Israelites were at Shittim, is set the story of the man who brazenly brought a Midianite woman into his family, and took her into the 'inner room', presumably to engage in sexual intercourse, which was possibly part of the fertility cult of Baal.[39] Outraged, Phinehas follows them and thrusts his spear through both of them. The narrative stresses that Phinehas belongs to the Aaronic priestly line, and Janzen thinks that his motivation is to preserve the holiness of the sanctuary. Phinehas's action has two consequences: the

---

[35] Since I deny that the 'intentional fallacy' is fallacious, however, and think that it is legitimate to try to discover something about the writers' intentions, I take this to represent the ethics of the writers.

[36] Waldemar Janzen, *Ethics*, 2.

[37] *Ibid.*, 3, 5–6.

[38] *Ibid.*, 12–14.

[39] Whether the 'inner room' is within the sanctuary or the man's tent is debated by the commentaries. Janzen admits that the precise details and meaning are uncertain (*Ethics*, 12–13, 21).

plague ceased because he turned back Yahweh's wrath from the people of Israel, and he himself is highly praised and rewarded. Janzen finds the modelling clear: 'Phinehas has acted as an exemplary priest. Therefore the office of priesthood is assured to him and his descendants.'

Janzen points out that the story repels the Christian reader because of the violence of Phinehas's action, but he claims that it is not told to put Phinehas forward as a model because of his spear wielding. Rather his exemplary qualities are his zeal for Yahweh and his making atonement for the people of Israel, qualities which mark the ideal priest.

Later in the book Janzen enlarges on the priestly paradigm, linking it with other narrative and legal passages and relating it to the 'familial paradigm' which he holds to be basic for Old Testament ethics.[40] His discussion is largely controlled by his overall theory concerning the ethics. He argues that living a life of constant and zealous attention to Yahweh's holy presence constitutes the first great ethical imperative within the priestly paradigm, with the consequence that the Israelites, as God's holy people, are to do God's will. He concludes that if ethics is defined narrowly as 'right neighbor-related behavior' the priestly paradigm adds nothing to what can be found in the familial one. If, however, ethics is 'a concern for right behavior not limited to a human target', the priestly acknowledgement of God's holiness provides an important constituent part.

Janzen's paradigm approach does not convince. It is too much an attempt to extract features which have an abiding value for ethics, and imposes an external pattern upon the narratives and other material. One may grant that Phinehas's zeal controls the story, yet the expression of that zeal is in the thrust of the spear, and since the activity of the man and the Midianite women is apostasy even if it was not 'sacred marriage', it was entirely appropriate that they should have been speared to death together. The ethics and the action cannot be separated. Moreover, Janzen does not follow up sufficiently the implications of the important point which he makes about the extension of the meaning of ethics. The concern of the writer of the story fastens on the religious offence and the ethics cannot be separated out. This is very similar to the activity of the prophets, who are as concerned with the rejection of foreign gods as they are with justice – perhaps even more. The great merit of Janzen's approach,

---

[40] *Ibid.*, 106–118. The main passages he includes are Jdg. 6, in which Gideon is depicted as a man who responds rightly to a theophany, Lev. 19, a 'sampling' like the Decalogue and all the Old Testament law codes, in which the familial ideal is given cultic focus, and Lev. 25, which he sees as expressing the identity between the priestly and familial paradigms. (The earlier quotation about Phinehas is on p. 13.)

however, lies in its avoidance of placing the emphasis upon the character of individuals, which is usually the way the narratives are mined for ethical themes. We can see examples of this in the 'Succession Narrative' or 'Court History' (2 Sam. 9–20; 1 Kgs. 1–2), to which I turn next.

Most commentaries and monographs limit their interest to the extent, origin, purpose and date of the narrative, and its relation to other genres within the Old Testament, especially wisdom,[41] though there have been notable studies of individual incidents, such as David and Bathsheba and the two parables in chapters 12 and 14.[42]

Although Whybray has failed to prove links between the Succession Narrative and Proverbs, following Rost he has pointed out how rich is the depiction of character in these chapters. Few persons are presented in black and white terms, and an ambiguity runs through much of the narrative.[43] Even very minor characters in the drama are skilfully presented, and most are also open to widely differing interpretations.[44] In this the Succession Narrative is almost unique, and it is necessary to ask to what extent character was recognized as an ethical issue.

It will be useful to outline the points which Whybray makes. He begins with David, the most fully delineated of the characters in the Old Testament, yet remaining elusive because he has the complexity of a real person. In incident after incident more than one possible explanation of his conduct is possible. Was he magnanimous to Meribaal or simply anxious to keep him under his eye (2 Sam. 9.1–13)? Was he genuinely pious or were his actions a calculated attempt to impress his followers?[45] The narrator comes closest to giving an unambiguous picture when portraying his faults: the tragedies of Amnon, Absalom and Adonijah were due to David's own weaknesses, which the author suggests by showing that the sons inherited their father's vices and by describing in detail and

---

[41] The two most accessible studies linking the Succession Narrative with wisdom, and especially Proverbs, are Gerhard von Rad, 'Historical Writing' (cf. *Theology*, 1, 311–317), and R. N. Whybray, *Succession Narrative*, esp. ch. 3. David M. Gunn has presented a severe critique, which is largely convincing (*King David*, 26–29).

[42] I accept as a working hypothesis that the heart of the narrative consists of the chapters indicated. Leonhard Rost (*The Succession*) attached some earlier passages, David M. Gunn (*King David*), argues for an even longer narrative, while P. Kyle McCarter (*II Samuel*, 9–16) splits it into several stories, notably claiming that only 1 Kgs 1–2 is an apologetic for the Solomonic succession.

[43] R. N. Whybray, *Succession Narrative*, 35–45. He refers to earlier recognition of this by Rost and von Rad.

[44] Thus while Whybray describes Bathsheba as 'a rather negative person', good-natured but rather stupid, some see her as a scheming seductress, while others stress that she is a victim in a patriarchal society (cf. Alice L. Laffey, *Introduction*, 118–122; Trevor Dennis, *Sarah Laughed*, 140–175; Alice Ogden Bellis, *Helpmates*, 161–162).

[45] Whybray points to 2 Sam. 12.23; 15.26; and 16.10 (*Succession Narrative*, 36).

objectively David's relations with Absalom. David had been guilty of lust, treachery and murder, and his sons repeat these crimes. Far from taking a firm line with Amnon and Absalom, he is merely 'very angry' at the rape of Tamar, while Absalom 'hated' Amnon (2 Sam. 13.21–22), suggesting that it was David's weakness which led to Absalom taking the law into his own hands. He showed a 'maudlin sentimentality' when driven from Jerusalem by his son, and his grief at his death shows that he cares for no one else (2 Sam. 19.2–8[1–7]).

I wonder about all this, especially as Whybray ends by saying that 'the picture of obsessive love which brings death to its own objects and misery to the one who loves as well as to others can seldom have been surpassed *even by modern novelists*'.[46] How much of Whybray's interpretation springs from European romanticism? It is, of course, impossible to know how the first listeners to the stories would have reacted to them. My hesitation comes from an account which I read years ago of the showing of a Japanese film in America in which the mother of a man whose wife had deserted him said to her son, 'But you still have me.' This was met with peals of laughter in the American cinema. In Japan it would have been accepted with full seriousness as reminding the man of where his true allegiance lay. It is so difficult to know what the feelings, ideas and values of a people brought up in a culture which is foreign to us will be.[47]

Janzen barely touches on this narrative except for discussing the contest between Hushai and Ahithophel, which he interprets as indicating the limits of wisdom.[48] He thinks it unclear whether Ahithophel's fall is due to his exercise of his wisdom in an unrighteous cause or to the fact that 'even the highest human competence must yield to the inexorable plans of God'. That Ahithophel hanged himself when his advice was rejected contains an implied criticism of his equating his counsel with the oracle of God.[49]

The treachery of Ahithophel is complete when he advises Absalom to take his father's concubines openly (2 Sam. 16.20–22), for this not only made any retraction impossible but declared his claim to the

---

[46] *Ibid.*, 38, my italics. Cf. his description of Joab's blunt rebuke of David in 2 Sam. 19.2–8[1–7] as 'one of the high points of tragedy in the book' (*ibid.*, 43). Is this how the Israelites saw it?

[47] Another example of differences in the culture leading to different interpretations is the story of David and Jonathan, which is now sometimes taken to be a case of homosexuality. This would never have occurred to earlier Christian readers of the Old Testament, and in view of the hostility to homosexuality in ancient Israel it seems highly unlikely. I am, of course, aware of the impressive work of scholars such as Robert Alter (see, e.g., Robert Alter and Frank Kermode, eds., *Literary Guide*).

[48] Janzen, *Ethics*, 130–131

[49] Janzen adds that it is only within the wisdom paradigm that any warning of limitations is given (*ibid.*, 131). William McKane, of course, based a major theory on the character of Ahithophel (*Prophets and Wise Men*; see esp. 13, 55–62).

throne. Ahithophel's further advice to pursue David immediately is equally treacherous and sensible from the point of view of bringing success to the rebellion, and his willingness to kill David marks the depth of his duplicity (2 Sam. 17.1–4). For a son to rebel against his father was a heinous offence throughout the ancient Middle East,[50] and Ahithophel abets Absalom in this. Over against Ahithophel is Hushai, who seeks to frustrate this good advice by offering contrary advice that is bad from the point of view of Absalom's prospects (2 Sam. 17.5–13). Faced with this conflicting counsel, Absalom and those with him choose Hushai's, because, says the narrator in a rare instance of direct intervention by God, 'the LORD had ordained to defeat the good counsel of Ahithophel, so that the LORD might bring evil upon Absalom' (2 Sam. 17.14). The narrative continues with accounts of secret agents and the suicide of Ahithophel. Did he despair because his advice was not adopted, or was it rather that he preferred death to the ignominy of probable execution by David, who he now realized would defeat Absalom in the end? Whybray thinks that the suicide reveals his character as that of 'a professional counsellor whose devotion to logical calculation is so much the dominating force in his life that he can apply it ruthlessly even to choosing the moment of his own death: he will not seek to prolong for a little while longer a life which he knows to be already forfeit; yet he will not die without setting his house in order. He is the "new man", who is determined to be master of his own fate.'[51] 'New man'! This is dependent both on von Rad's interpretation of the time of David and particularly Solomon as the Israelite 'Enlightenment', and on the importing of modern conceptions into the Old Testament.

Because the whole action lies in the realm of the politics of the court and of war, it is impossible to determine how the actions of these two advisers are to be understood ethically. Lying and deceit belong to the trade of diplomacy and war. Today we would not attribute the success of Hushai to God's intervention, and, indeed, the narrator's comment makes God an accomplice in the subterfuge.[52] It is doubtful, therefore, whether Janzen's attempt to extract ethics out of the incident is successful.

The extent of deceit within the Succession Narrative as a whole is quite large. Alongside Hushai who practised deceit on Absalom are the wise woman of Tekoa who misled David (2 Sam. 14.1–20), Joab who sent her to David, Ziba, whose report about Mephibosheth's remaining in Jerusalem looking for the return of the kingdom to him cannot be verified or refuted (2 Sam. 16.3–4; 19.25–31[24–30]), and

---

[50] Cf. the action of Yassib (Keret 16. vi, 25–53).
[51] Whybray, *Succession Narrative*, 43–44.
[52] Again cf. Andrew Davies, *Double Standards.*

running through the whole account the dubious actions and words of Absalom. Only on Absalom does the narrator pass any kind of censure. Desperate remedies are required by desperate situations.

Or take Jonadab. The writer describes him as 'wise' (*ḥākām*). Whybray describes 'wisdom' as 'a purely intellectual and morally neutral quality',[53] and von Rad emphasizes that wisdom 'describes men who, in some sense and in some sphere, are "competent", "skilled"'. It can be used even of manual workers and sailors, and (in the present passage) 'describes a man who is an expert in the shady tricks and dodges which at court lead one to the desired goal'.[54] Despite what these scholars say, it is only in this verse that 'wisdom' has a derogatory connotation, hence the difficulties which translators have in deciding upon an English term which carries the right overtones.[55] Even if Jonadab intended his advice only to secure a way in which Amnon could meet Tamar, who otherwise was kept in seclusion (a highly doubtful suggestion) and did not plan the rape,[56] it was hardly commendable, and the conclusion must be drawn, either that the Hebrew term possesses a very much wider semantic range than the English 'wise', or that the writer of the narrative felt some hidden admiration for his scheme. Certainly on the only other occasion we meet Jonadab he offers correct information and sensible advice to David (2 Sam. 13.32–33). So to shrug him off as 'the clever but irresponsible crony who shows Amnon how to achieve his criminal purpose but omits to point out the probable consequences if he succeeds in achieving it', as Whybray does,[57] hardly seems adequate. It is impossible to determine whether the narrator approved of Jonadab's actions or not, since he does not divulge whether he regarded his advice to Amnon as an encouragement to rape Tamar or not.

---

[53] Whybray, *Succession Narrative*, 58, supported by P. Kyle McCarter, *II Samuel*, 321.

[54] Von Rad, *Wisdom*, 20.

[55] Thus: 'crafty' (RSV, NRSV), 'shrewd' (NEB, REB, JB, NJB, NIV, GNB). Moffatt gets over the favourable overtones of 'shrewd' with his 'a shrewd fellow'. CEV paraphrases: 'Jonadab always knew how to get what he wanted'. Only CEV at all adequately conveys the sense. McCarter's 'wise' was foreshadowed by Tyndale, but McCarter notes Freedman's complaint that it is misleading because of the connotation in English (*II Samuel*, 321). Stuart Weeks finds a similar sense of 'shrewd calculation, with no ethical or professional implication' in Ex. 1.10 and, probably, 1 Kgs. 2.6, 9 (*Wisdom*, 74), but the first is not strictly parallel, since there is nothing shady in the activity of the Egyptians from their own point of view — indeed it might be seen as wise political advice – while the second is more political acumen, evil in intention though it may be, than craftiness. Modern politicians deal as ruthlessly with their rivals, though not so drastically.

[56] So Stuart Weeks, *Wisdom*, 77. Only Jonadab and David (2 Sam. 14.20) are called wise, apart from the wise woman of Tekoa and the wise woman in Abel of Bethmaacah (2 Sam. 14.2; 20.16).

[57] Whybray, *Succession Narrative*, 45.

So much for character. What can be learned from the overall intention of the writer? David M. Gunn surveys the various theories which have been proposed: history writing, political propaganda, wisdom literature pointing a moral. His own view is that it was intended as 'serious entertainment'. For our purposes it is important to note that Gunn accepts that Whybray has shown that situations arise in the narrative which raise 'serious problems of moral evaluation' for the reader, but he argues that one thing that the author never does is explicitly to draw a moral.[58] What he finds in the work is 'a picture of the rich variety of life that is often comic and ironic in its contrasting perspectives and conflicting norms'. Even Yahweh's involvement in human affairs has an element of mystery, and whether his activity is related to the moral order at all is far from clear.[59]

This last point deserves following up. A distinction needs to be made between the way the narrator speaks of Yahweh and the way the characters speak of him. There are also quite a large number of places where Yahweh and God occur in descriptions (the heritage of the LORD, 2 Sam. 20.19; the ark of God, 2 Sam. 15.24, 25, 29; the LORD's anointed, 2 Sam. 19.22[21]), oaths (2 Sam. 12.5; 14.11; 15.21; 19.8[7]; 1 Kgs. 1.17, 29, 30) and vows (2 Sam. 15.7). The narrator ascribes actions to Yahweh, however, in only two places: in his reaction to David's adultery with Bathsheba and the death of Uriah, where David's action 'displeased' him, he sent Nathan to David, killed Bathsheba's child, and loved Solomon (2 Sam. 11.27; 12.1, 15, 24, together with several references in the speech of Nathan), and in countering the advice of Ahithophel (2 Sam. 17.14). On the other hand, the actors often refer to the intervention of Yahweh (2 Sam. 18.19, 28, 31), offer prayers to him or are asked to do so (2 Sam. 10.12; 14.11, 17; 1 Kgs. 1.36, 37, 48), and worship him (2 Sam. 15.8), while David confesses that he has sinned against him (2 Sam. 12.13). In David's last instructions to Solomon the narrator makes him tell Solomon to walk in Yahweh's ways and keep his commandments written in the law, so that God will fulfil what he has promised concerning the dynasty (1 Kgs. 2.2–4) and in the following speech Yahweh is frequently mentioned. The instructions, however, are hardly moral and in several respects directly flout previous promises made with the support of an oath or a vow. In a theological discussion of the activity of God, this would need to be subjected to careful analysis, but from the perspective of ethics only three comments need be made. First, although Nathan specifies the evil which David has done as killing Uriah and taking his wife, and describes this as despising the word of Yahweh it is not linked to any laws, as we saw

[58] David M. Gunn, *King David*, 28–28, 61.
[59] *Ibid.*, 110–111.

earlier, and there is some doubt as to the nature of the wrongdoing. Second, the narrator describes the death of Bathsheba's child as punishment directly inflicted by Yahweh, so that God is depicted as providing sanctions against those who go against what is pleasing to him. Third, while the narrator declares that Yahweh took an active part in frustrating Ahithophel's support for Absalom, he gives no reason for this. Presumably it is part of God's support of David and opposition to a rebellious son. How far it is a moral decision is doubtful. With regard to the actors, although they live much more closely with a personal God, the extent to which they picture him as commanding an ethics or sustaining it with sanctions is less clear. Gunn appears to be correct in his assessment.

I have, therefore, much sympathy with Gunn's approach, although I think he has not given sufficient place to the distance between Israelite culture and our own.[60]

I turn rather more briefly to the book of Judges.

As is well known, much of the work is structured on the basis of Israel's sin, Yahweh's sending of an oppressor as punishment, Israel's repentance and cry for help, and Yahweh's raising up of a deliverer. While the sages saw this built into the structure of the world and effective for the individual, Judges declares it to be the direct action of Yahweh and applies it to the nation. In contrast to the teaching of the sages, however, the sin of the nation is worshipping the baals (Jdg. 2.11–13, 17, 19; 3.6, 7; 6.8–10 (cf. 25–32); 8.33–34; 10.6, 10–16). Doing what was evil in the sight of Yahweh (Jdg. 2.11; 3.7, 12; 4.1; 6.1; 13.1) and failing to obey his commandments or keep his covenant (Jdg. 2:17, 20; 3.4) are also mentioned, but no content is given to the terms. These verses, of course, are all part of the framework in Judges and represent the view of the editor of the book. Actions which would have been regarded as serious wrongs in normal times, such as the treachery of Jael against the duties of hospitality, are praised, although the conventional view of honour is expressed when Barak's enemy is killed by a woman (Jdg. 4.9, 17–22). The general disorder at the time of Abimelech is condemned (Jdg. 9.56–57). In times of oppression the son of a prostitute and his band of outlaws ('worthless fellows', '"nāšîm rēqîm) are called upon to deliver Israel (Jdg. 11.1–11).

Feminists have fastened on the account of Jephthah's daughter as evidence of the evils found in patriarchal society.[61] While sympathizing with their concerns, I wonder what is to be made of the story in terms of ethics. The narrator gives no hint as to whether the

---

[60] See his comments, *ibid.*, 87.

[61] E.g., Phyllis Trible, *Texts of Terror*, 93–116; Esther Fuchs, 'Marginalization'. Shulamit Valler ('Jephthah's Daughter') and Phyllis Silverman Kramer ('Jephthah's Daughter') point out the changing attitudes of the rabbis.

outcome would have been any different if it had been a son who came to meet Jephthah as he returned from the victory – the absolute demands of the vow are paramount.[62] The daughter's weeping for her virginity is probably an aetiological legend explaining a local custom, possibly a fertility cult, and may well have originally been separate from the Jephthah story.[63] What we seem to have here is a story belonging to a very early period of Israel's history, which strangely has been preserved in the tradition. It accords with the overall emphasis on total obedience to God which is found elsewhere in Judges.

The evils recounted in the concluding chapters of Judges are explained by the narrator as being due to the absence of a king in Israel (Jdg. 17.6; 18.1; 19.1; 21.25), revealing both his condemnation of the actions and his support for the monarchy.[64] Since they concern war, the treatment of women and the use of the terms 'abomination' and 'wantonness' (Jdg. 19.23, 24; 20.6), these aspects have already been discussed.[65]

The period covered by the book of Judges is depicted as one of unrest and disorder, when Israel was guilty of worshipping the baals and was disobedient to Yahweh. It was a time of emergency when even human sacrifice could be condoned. The extreme evils of failure to perform the established duties of hospitality and the committing of rape within that setting bring condemnation. The seizing of the women dancing at Shiloh also appears to be condemned in the final verse of the book.

Attention needs to be drawn to the phrase 'every man did what was right in his own eyes' (Jdg 17.6; 21.25). The commentators give little more by way of explanation than that it comes from a pro-monarchy editor and has links with Deuteronomy 12.8–12 (note v. 8). But with what is the contrast made by the writer? Is it simply that a king was expected to exert his authority over the whole land and maintain law and order? Or is there more? Is not the contrast between a rampant individualism and a concern for the common good? If so, it appears that the writer places the emphasis upon a stable community which

---

[62] Within the story, of course, a son is impossible, since Jephthah has only one child.

[63] So John Gray, *Joshua, Judges, Ruth*, 319–320. J. Alberto Soggin has a valuable discussion, in which he emphasizes that this is the only human sacrifice recorded in the Old Testament which is not censured in any way (*Judges*, 215–219).

[64] W. J. Dumbrell sees Jdg. 21.25 as setting before us a dilemma: 'If it endorses kingship with enthusiasm, then it contradicts earlier accounts which damn the institution.' He suggests that Judges is not an apology for the monarchy but sees the Exile as a time when Israel could begin again, united in peace. God had preserved Israel whatever its political organization, and would continue to do so ('No King in Israel', see esp. pp. 27–30)..

[65] Above pp.11–12, 44–47, 186–187, 266–268.

was also the aim of many of the proverbs? Certainly the expectation that the king would maintain morality is found here.[66] Yet this seems to be only part of the editor's concern. Although he has fastened on the worship of other gods as the explanation of the repeated oppression of Israel by foreign states in the earlier part of the book, in these final chapters he directs the attention to the general breakdown of ordered society. The description of the horrors as 'folly' (n'ḇālāh) confirms this. It is what ought not to happen within Israel.

It may well be that other passages would have more to offer Old Testament ethics than those I have concentrated on, but I am not convinced that this is so. I conclude that the purpose of the narrators was not primarily ethical. None of the passages effectively raise moral dilemmas, and through them neither God nor the writers offer moral teaching to the reader. Of course, the modern reader can discover ethics in them, but this is achieved by applying modern distinctions and modern moral ideas to them. Can more help be obtained from the books of the prophets?

The Prophets
Most students of the Old Testament see the prophets as at the heart of Old Testament ethics. This is strange. As I hope to show, ethics in our sense does not form a major part of their message. Moreover, their approach to their preaching is in many ways utterly foreign to our views of the way ethics should be determined.

I begin with the controversial question of the basis of their ethical teaching.

One suggestion is that it was Yahweh's covenant with Israel. This founders on the fact that Amos, Isaiah and Micah do not mention the term, and Hosea uses it only twice (Hos. 6.7; 8.1). Various explanations have been offered. Eichrodt argued that it was due to the covenant being treated mechanically at the time, so that for the prophets to base their condemnations on the importance of the covenant would not have achieved their purpose.[67] Clements argues that the originality of Amos lies not in the introduction of a new ethical standard or a new doctrine of God, but in his announcement of what God was about to do.[68] Nicholson follows Kraetzschmar in arguing that the prophets before Jeremiah know nothing of the covenant relationship, because it was a theological innovation in the time of the late monarchy, not an ancient institution.[69]

[66] See below, pp. 296–300, for place of the king in Israelite ethics.
[67] Walther Eichrodt, *Theology*, I, 51–52.
[68] R. E. Clements, *Prophecy and Covenant*, 43. He modifies his views in his later *Prophecy and Tradition*.
[69] Ernest W. Nicholson, *God and His People*. But the historicity of Jeremiah is fiercely debated; see, e.g., Robert P. Carroll, *Jeremiah* and William L. Holladay, *Jeremiah*.

A second view finds the law behind the prophets' polemic. Thus Clements, who accepts the antiquity of the Decalogue and holds that the law codes presuppose the fact of the covenant, argues that before the prophets there was a long tradition of morality and ethics. The eighth-century prophets were not the first to introduce ethics into religion. Phillips argues that two distinct traditions can be discerned in the prophetic books,[70] the first, found in Amos, Micah and Isaiah, is firmly grounded in the law, the other is seen in Hosea, who nowhere (apart from 12.7) mentions the exploitation of the defenceless and whose whole emphasis is upon apostasy, denounced as harlotry. In Jeremiah the two traditions come together.[71]

Thirdly, there is another suggestion put forward by Clements that the 'entrance liturgies' (Pss. 15; 24.3–6) influenced the prophets. He draws attention to Isa. 33.14–16 and Mic. 6.6–8,[72] but is sceptical about the actual influence of the 'cultic torah-liturgy' upon Israel during the period of the monarchy.[73]

Fourthly, there has been considerable interest in the question of the influence of wisdom on the prophets, but the relation between wisdom and prophecy is not clear. R. N. Whybray, who has traced the history of the discussion, denies that there was a distinct class of 'wise men' in the period of the monarchy and doubts whether any direct literary connections between the prophetic and wisdom books can be found earlier than Ben Sirach.[74]

Finally, the prophetic 'Thus says the LORD' (perhaps it is closer to the Hebrew to translate, 'Thus said the LORD') suggests that the prophets claimed to derive their ethical teaching directly from Yahweh. This, however, it not quite as simple as it seems. I limit my examples to the eighth-century prophets and take them in turn.

The majority of Amos's oracles are straight threats (e.g., 2.6; 3.2, 11, 13–15). The phrase 'you did not return to me' (Amos 4.6–11)

---

[70] Anthony Phillips, 'Prophecy and Law'.

[71] Note also Eryl W. Davies's study of Isaiah. He concludes that 'the prophet's concern with social justice did not primarily involve such duties as are laid down in any extant law code' (*Prophecy and Ethics*, 115), and comments: 'there is often ground for scepticism regarding the effectiveness of the law to combat social abuses and to correct injustice and oppression' (*ibid.*, 116).

[72] R. E. Clements, *Prophecy and Covenant*, 82–84, 93–97.

[73] Alongside this may be set Robert Murray's attempt to trace out the way the oracles of the prophets 'echo, but often transform, liturgical language and themes', taking Isa. 33 as an example ('Prophecy and Cult', quotation p. 200). He, however, moves far beyond the entrance liturgies and ethics. E. Hammershaimb suggests that the ethics was taken over from the Canaanites ('Ethics of OT Prophets').

[74] R. N. Whybray, 'Prophecy and Wisdom'. For a summary and assessment of the main arguments see Eryl W. Davies, *Prophecy and Ethics*, 116–118. His conclusion is that prophecy and wisdom are 'parallel forms of spiritual and literary activity' and that no question of the dependence of one on the other need arise.

implies that the people had abandoned Yahweh. When to this is added the fact that Amos uses general ethical terms, such as 'righteousness' (Amos 5.7, 24; 6.12), 'justice' (Amos 5.7, 15, 24; 6.12), 'right' (Amos 3.10), 'good'/'evil' (Amos 5.14–15), and 'sin' (Amos 5.12; 9.8, 10, as well as many times in chs. 1–2), while details of specific ethical demands or wrongs by the Israelites are relatively few (Amos 2.6–8, 12; 3.10; 4.1; 5.10–12, 15; 8.4–6), and some of these involve justice in the law courts, it is clear that even Amos expresses very little of a new ethics. What is new is the threat of punishment.

Hosea is notable for the large number of metaphors he uses, which places some distance between the moral demand or lapse and the oracle. Like Amos, he makes a large number of threats of punishment (e.g., 1.4–5; 4.9–10;7.12–13). Hosea's main complaint is against Baal religion. Like Amos, there is a general indictment of sin, especially that Israel has forgotten Yahweh (Hos. 2.15[13]; 13.6), and lacks knowledge of Yahweh (Hos. 4.1, 6; 5.4; 6.6), truth (Hos. 4.1), and steadfast love (Hos 4.1; 6.4, 6). Like Amos he uses general terms such as 'righteousness' (Hos 10.12), and 'justice' (Hos. 12.7[6]). There are some references to specific crimes (Hos. 6.8–9; 7.1; 12.8–9[7–8]), and as we have already seen, there are references to the covenant (Hos. 6.7; 8.1) and laws (Hos 4.2, 6; 8.1, 12). There are complaints about kings (Hos. 8.4) and foreign policy (Hos 5.13; 7.8, 11; 8.9; 12.2[1]). But again there is little evidence of a new ethics. Like Amos, the main emphasis is upon the threat of punishment, though alongside this is the promise of Yahweh's continuing love (Hos. 2.16–25[14–23]; 11.8–9).

The situation is similar in Isaiah, with general references to sin (e.g., Isa. 1.4, 21; 3.8, 9–11; 5.18) and calls for 'righteousness' (e.g., Isa. 5.7). There are quite a large number of demands for specific acts of goodness, such as 'defend the fatherless, plead for the widow' (Isa. 1.17, cf. 1.23; 3.14–15; 10.1–2), and condemnation of specific sins, such as amassing large estates (Isa. 5.8), drunkenness (Isa 5.11–12; 28.1–4, 7–8), bribery (5.23, cf. 29.20–21), luxury (Isa 3.16–4.1), pride (Isa. 22.15–25), and foreign alliances (Isa. 31.1–3). And there are similar threats of punishment.

Much the same is found in Micah: threats (1.3–7; 3.4, 12; 6.13–16), general words for sin (Mic. 1.5; 2.1; 3.8; 6.10), a call for righteousness, lovingkindness and walking with God (Mic. 6.8), together with some specific sins: coveting fields (Mic. 2.2), driving women from their homes (Mic. 2.9), bribery (Mic 3.11), false weights (Mic. 6.11), violence (Mic. 6.12), and (in a metaphor) tearing the flesh off God's people (Mic. 3.3).

What is striking about this rapid survey of four prophets is the minority of verses which contain references to specific virtues or sins, in contrast to many generalizations and the even greater number of threats. It is as though the prophets expected their hearers to know the difference between right and wrong, and which actions fell into each class, and they needed to do no more than warn those who committed wrong that God would certainly punish them, and that the punishment would fall soon. Certainly there is little evidence that they were presenting a novel ethics to the people which they had obtained directly from God.

This conclusion would be confirmed if it is right that the prophets assumed that their listeners would know and accept what John Barton has termed 'natural law', and what the prophets declare is that the work of Yahweh is to maintain this by imposing punishments for breaches of what is acknowledged to be right conduct.[75]

Thus the prophets appear to have largely accepted what Eichrodt has termed 'popular morality', though how far they moved beyond this, as he claims they did, seems doubtful.[76] J. L. Mays offers a somewhat similar interpretation. The prophets use the term 'justice' as if it were self-evident what it means, and never analyse or explain it. I draw attention to Mays's conclusion: 'For those who intend to recognize some authority in them in a purely moral sense or to recognize the authority behind them in a religious sense, they create a predicament. They do not fit any of the roles we usually play. The prophets were not ethicists or theologians or interpreters and did not go about their task in the way we pursue ours. . . . They were not social reformers or political activists or revolutionaries, certainly not conservatives or reactionaries.'[77] They were men of their time.

Two further features in the work of the prophets need to be noted which make them foreign to our ways of thinking and acting: the way they receive their messages, and the form in which they expect the divine punishment to come.

How far the prophets received visionary experiences is debated. Did, for example, Amos see a basket of summer fruit in a vision (Amos 8.1–2) and was Jeremiah's almond branch also visionary (Jer. 1.11–12), or was it a physical basket and a living branch which led the prophets by means of pun to claim they had a message from Yahweh? Whichever they were, the fact that it was through such experiences that they obtained their messages should alert us to the distance that separates them from us. At the end of his valuable discussion of Jeremiah's vision and auditions, Zimmerli asks whether the visionary element diminishes in importance in the course of Jeremiah's prophetic proclamation, and notes that no visions are recorded by Second-Isaiah, where the word of God is in control, but

---

[75] See above Chapter 6.
[76] Eichrodt, *Theology*, II, 316–337.
[77] James Luther Mays, 'Justice', quotation p. 17.

occur frequently in Ezekiel, and are developed in Zechariah and Daniel.[78] I am not sure what implications Zimmerli would draw from this. Is he suggesting that the message has a firmer foundation when it is not received through visions? If this is so, his conclusion is likely to be due to modern susceptibilities. We would give no credence at all to a political speaker who declared that his criticism of some economic or social scandal came from God through a vision. We demand research before we take any action, and politicians often use this universal demand as an excuse to avoid implementing measures which they know will be unpopular or which entail a heavy cost financially.

The notion of divine punishment is equally alien. The prevalence of consequentialist ethics, coupled with the emphasis upon research into the causes of social evils and the possible consequences of actions that might be taken to relieve them, means that we retain the idea that what is done will have beneficial or harmful results. But this is not what the prophets are saying. They hold that Yahweh will intervene personally with direct action, and this we no longer believe.[79]

The King
Throughout the ancient Middle East the king was regarded as the defender of the poor and the oppressed. Reference has already been made to the complaint of Yassib against his father:

> You have been brought down by your failing power.
> You do not judge the cause of the widow,
> you do not try the case of the importunate.
> You do not banish the extortioners of the poor,
> you do not feed the orphan before your face
> (nor) the widow behind your back.[80]

Hammurabi declares that Anum and Enlil named him 'to promote the welfare of the people' and 'to cause justice to prevail in the land, to destroy the wicked and the evil, that the strong might not oppress the weak', although the rest of the prologue to his collection of laws is taken up with a declaration of the way he has honoured the gods. The theme is reverted to in the epilogue, in which Hammurabi speaks of the 'laws of justice' which he has set up making an end of war, promoting the welfare of the land, so that the people have prospered.

---

[78] Walther Zimmerli, 'Visionary Experience', 115.

[79] The Lisbon earthquake in the eighteenth century put an end to this way of thinking, and the failure of God to intervene when the Nazis exterminated six million Jews confirms it in our own time.

[80] Keret 16. vi, 45–50, quoted from J. C. L. Gibson, *Canaanite Myths*, 102. Aubrey R. Johnson places considerable emphasis upon this and other texts from Ugarit (*Sacral Kingship*, 4–7, n. 4).

In particular he declares:

> In order that the strong might not oppress the weak,
> that justice might be dealt the orphan (and) the widow,
> in Babylon, the city whose head Anum and Enlil raised aloft,
> in Esagila, the temple whose foundations stand firm like heaven and earth,
> I wrote my precious words on my stela,
> and in the presence of my statue as the king of justice
> I set (it) up in order to administer the law of the land,
> to prescribe the ordinances of the land,
> to give justice to the oppressed.[81]

The other law-codes contained similar claims, but most are fragmentary. Lipit-Istar declared that when Anu and Enlil called him to be king it was in order to 'establish justice in the land, to banish complaints, to turn back enmity and rebellion by force of arms, (and) to bring well-being to the Sumerians and Akkadians'.[82] The Laws of Ur-Nammu claim that the king has established equity in the land, banished violence and strife, and it has become a time when 'the orphan was not delivered up to the rich man; the widow was not delivered up to the mighty man; the man of one shekel was not delivered up to the man of one mina'.[83] Saggs points out that Hammurabi's second regnal year was known as 'the year in which he set forth justice in the land', and he holds that the 'justice' which the kings maintained was primarily economic justice.[84]

Within the Old Testament attention is usually drawn to Psalm 72, with its plea to God:

> Give the king thy justice, O God,
>> and thy righteousness to the royal son!
> May he judge thy people with righteousness,
>> and thy poor with justice! . . .
> May he defend the cause of the poor of the people,
>> give deliverance to the needy,
>> and crush the oppressor!

and later there is the declaration:

> For he delivers the needy when he calls,
>> the poor and him who has no helper.
> He has pity on the weak and the needy,
>> and saves the lives of the needy.
> From oppression and violence he redeems their life;
>> and precious is their blood in his sight.

---

[81] Prologue, i, and Epilogue, reverse xxiv, 59ff., quoted from *ANET*, 164, 178.

[82] Prologue, quoted from *ANET*, 159.

[83] Laws of Ur-Nammu, lines 114–116, 162–168, quoted from *ANET*, 523–524.

[84] H. W. F. Saggs, *Babylon*, 177–190, reference on 177.

This ideal may be traced in Jeremiah 21.11–12; 22.3, 15–16, where again it is executing justice for the poor, delivering the oppressed and seeing that no wrong is done to resident aliens, orphans and widows which are picked out as peculiarly the duty of the king. Similarly the ideal future king in Isaiah 9.6[7] will maintain justice and righteousness, while in the other 'messianic' prophecy in Isaiah 11 he will judge the poor with righteousness and decide the case of the 'meek' with equity (v. 4).[85]

As with the teachings coming from other groups, the ideal is limited in scope. The 'empty cell' words 'justice' and 'righteousness' are frequent, and when particular ethical practices are mentioned they go little further than the protection of the poor and the oppressed, and especially the groups which are likely to suffer in this way, widows, the fatherless, and resident aliens. Similarities with the demands made by the prophets are striking, as in their condemnation of the 'princes' in Isaiah 1.23 and Ezekiel 22.6–7. I am not suggesting that protecting the helpless is unimportant. Rather, that this is the especial duty of the king across the ancient world. Presumably other groups are deemed sufficiently powerful to protect their own interests, and overall the customary morality is accepted as controlling behaviour within society.

Is it possible to determine whether this ideal was given concrete form in the Israelite monarchy? Keith W. Whitelam has attempted to differentiate between this ideal portrayal of the king and its practical understanding and functioning in Israelite society.[86]

From the historical books he seeks examples of the working out of the ideal in such narratives as the fictitious legal cases presented to David by Nathan and the wise woman of Tekoah (2 Sam. 12.1–15; 14.1–24), the fact that Absalom could obtain a following by condemning David's failure to decide lawsuits (2 Sam. 15.1–6), the incident of Naboth's vineyard (1 Kgs. 21.1–20) – the last two showing that there were 'vast differences' between theory and practice of royal judicial authority – and the condemnation of Ahab by an unknown prophet who comes to the king on the pretext of seeking a judicial decision (1 Kgs. 20.35–43), as well as other accounts of the king exercising quasi-judicial authority, such as the case of cannibalism in 2 Kings 6.24–31 and the Shunamite woman in 2 Kings 8.1–6. Also Solomon's judgment must not be forgotten (1 Kgs. 3.16–28).[87]

---

[85] I do not consider the date and authenticity of any of these passages since the present purpose is simply to set out the ideal.

[86] Keith W. Whitelam, *Just King*.

[87] *Ibid.*, 136. The discussions of passages are on pp. 123–135, 137–142, 170–181, 167–170, 181–184, 162–164. Aubrey R. Johnson had already noted several of these (*Sacral Kingship*, 4, n. 4).

Beyond these examples Whitelam attempts to trace historical development and change in the activity of the king, distinguishing the actual from the ideal. He fastens chiefly on the extent of the king's *judicial* functions and authority, and argues that there is no evidence to show that the king acted as the highest court of appeal in Israel. On the other hand, he believes that the king possessed the same authority to create or promulgate law in Israel as in other parts of the ancient Middle East.[88] He also holds that the ideal influenced the historical working out of kingship in Israel. Whitelam's emphasis on the administration of justice means that ethical judgments of the king receive less attention. In any case, for ethics the ideal and the fictitious have an equal importance with what can be credited as historically true, for they reveal what was regarded as proper and right. It should not be overlooked that the narratives depict the kings as frequently using their power and even their judicial authority to achieve their own ends and oppress their subjects, a state of affairs predicted by Samuel (1 Sam. 8.10–18). Moreover the main criticism of the kings by Deuteronomists responsible for the framework of the books of Kings is that they committed apostasy and permitted the worship of idols and other gods, and most famously set up the rival shrines in the Northern Kingdom, rather than failures in ethics. Only of Manasseh is it said that he 'shed very much innocent blood' (2 Kgs. 21.16).

Finally, we recall that one of Janzen's five models was the royal paradigm. Despite his initial presentation of the paradigm through the incident of David's cutting off a strip from Saul's robe in the cave (1 Sam. 24),[89] the way Janzen uses the idea of model makes his account appear idealistic. Even though he asserts that the paradigm is presented through characters, Janzen singles out the chief characteristics: the king's accountability to God and the demand that he use his power to secure justice. He notes the tensions between the ideal and the form of monarchies in the surrounding nations, and between the 'seminomadic tribal structure' and the monarchy, quoting Millard C. Lind, Frank Moore Cross and Walter Brueggemann who see a falling away from the 'Mosaic alternative community' in David or Solomon.[90]

---

[88] Hans Jochen Boecker holds that the king's judicial activities were much more restricted, being limited to the army, the court, and the city of Jerusalem (*Law*, 40–49). Waldemar Janzen argues for a wider influence (*Ethics*, 150).

[89] Janzen wrongly centres on the exemplary character of David's action, but is right in rejecting the view that the principle behind this is 'repaying good for evil'. He points out that the motive of the sparing of Saul is that he is 'the LORD's anointed', but in his desire to relate biblical ethics to our own, he fails to see that this belongs to a world that is utterly foreign to us.

[90] Janzen, *Ethics*, 15–17, 140–154, quotation, 142. The references are to Millard C. Lind, *Yahweh is a Warrior*, 114–144, Frank Moore Cross, *Canaanite Myth*, 237–241,

Janzen finds an ethical difficulty in this, in that the paradigm might lead away from the will of God into some compromise or even idolatry. This he counters by claiming, first, that once introduced the monarchy was there to stay and concern rested on securing the proper nature of kingship under Yahweh, and, secondly, that from a canonical perspective both Israel and the church retained the story of the monarchy and ascribed large parts of the wisdom writings and the psalms to the king. Further, he stresses that the Old Testament 'in its canonical balance does not attribute inherent ethical value, whether positive or negative, to any one social structure'.[91] His conclusion is that the Old Testament paradigm of the king is of one who 'subjects himself to God, upholds justice, and thereby creates shalom. The content of royal justice is provided by Torah, Israel's narrative and legal tradition whose ethic we have earlier characterized as the familial paradigm. The king upholds it not only by his executive power, but also through his own stature as the representative Israelite or First Worshipper and Citizen.'[92] Here his religious assumptions control his exposition, which I find muddled.

The king as Yahweh's representative clearly is an important figure in Old Testament ethics, yet the tensions between the ideal and the actual, the lofty place the king holds in the cult[93] and the criticisms made of the king by prophet and Deuteronomist, make it difficult to know how to relate the monarchy to ethics. The divine demand in such texts as 2 Samuel 7 and Psalm 89 shows that even within the cult the king is only assured of Yahweh's support if he keeps his commands. Criticism exceeds praise. Power tends to corrupt. It seems that the ideal failed.

In this chapter we have tried, not very successfully, to enter into the minds of the Old Testament writers, and through them to the ancient Israelites. What has come out most strongly is the way most scholars have been unable to rid themselves of the assumptions and interests of the modern world, and this is almost certainly also a defect of the present study. We have tried, nonetheless, to make our eyes *see* what we glimpsed through the windows of our tower, and not to impose upon it our own construction of reality. The country *is* foreign. Yet, as we shall see in the final chapter, the Old Testament can only provide help with modern ethical problems if its strangeness is taken fully into account.

---

and Walter Brueggemann, *Imagination*, 31. See also Brueggemann's exposition of the king as mediator in his *Theology*, 600–621, in which he recognizes the tensions within the Old Testament, stresses attempts to subject the king to the Torah, but turns finally to the messianic vision and its adoption by Christians.

[91] Janzen, *Ethics*, 146.

[92] *Ibid.*, 154.

[93] This has been examined so many times that I simply refer to such studies as Aubrey R. Johnson, *Sacral Kingship* and John H. Eaton, *Kingship*.

20

THE OLD TESTAMENT AND ETHICS TODAY

Studies of Two Issues

I begin with an article which Immanuel Jakobowits, the former Chief Rabbi, wrote in *The Times* on the implications of AIDS.[1] His first three paragraphs are worth quoting in full:

> I have delayed publicly expressing a view on the awesome menace of Aids now hanging like a monstrous medieval plague over mankind, despite pressures from within my community and beyond to make some authentic Jewish pronouncement. This is due not merely to the fact that most authoritative Jewish statements on the moral issues were made thousands of years ago.
>
> The earliest sources of Jewish law and morality are quite unambiguous. The Bible brands homosexual relationships as a capital offence (Lev. 20:13), and execrates any sexual licentiousness as an abomination, whether in the form of premarital 'harlotry' (Deut. 23:18) or of extra-marital adultery (Lev. 20:10). Equally stern are the warnings of national doom consequent on any defiance of these principles: the land itself will 'vomit out' peoples violating these injunctions (Lev. 18:28–29).
>
> My hesitation in adding a Jewish voice to the many religious and moral statements already widely publicized, and worthy of endorsement, has been accentuated by the uncompromising nature of these biblical strictures. The difficulties go beyond the dilemma of choosing between soothing platitudes and unpalatable truths.

The article is to be admired for the cautious, careful, and eminently humane and sensitive way in which Rabbi Jakobowits wrote about the AIDS epidemic as long ago as 1986, at a time, it should be remembered, when some were declaring that it was divine punishment for homosexuality. Sir Immanuel Jakobowits, as he was then, admits that there are questions, some 'practical', some 'purely human', to which there are no categorical answers. But he goes on to say that 'we are never entitled to declare a particular form of suffering as a punishment for a particular manifestation of wrongdoing. We can no

---

[1] Immanuel Jakobowits, 'Moral Revolution', 20.

more divine why some people endure terrible ills without any apparent cause than we can comprehend why others prosper though they clearly do not deserve their good fortune.' Further we are even less justified in being selective: 'subjecting some scourges to this moral analysis while exempting others (Aids, yes; but earthquakes or floods or droughts, no)'.

He then makes a most important distinction. 'There is all the difference – even if the distinction is a fine one – between ascribing massive suffering to personal or social depravity as a divine visitation, and warning that such depravity may *lead* to terrible consequences. . . . If people recklessly indulge in infidelity and end up in the agony of a broken marriage, they suffer no vengeance; they simply pay the inevitable price for moral negligence or turpitude.' Thus he judges that AIDS is the price we pay for the 'benefits' of the permissive society which has demolished 'the last defences of sexual restraint and self-discipline, leading to the collapse of nature's self-defence against degeneracy'. He judges that what is crucial is the cultivation of new attitudes to sexuality: 'nothing short of a moral revolution will in time contain the scourge'. At the same time there is a need 'to promote the utmost compassion for those struck by a hideous killer as the result of failings which may not be theirs but the society's into which they were born, and which to ennoble is the charge of us all'.

What is interesting, and morally important, about this article is that the Chief Rabbi is faced by several facts which he is in no position to alter. In the first place there is the Torah, 'uncompromising' in its teaching as he points out. But then there is the fact of AIDS, and his recognition that, as he declared in a later article, 'under no circumstances would we be justified in branding the incidence of this disease, individual or collectively, as punishment that singles out individuals or groups for wrongdoing and lets them suffer as a consequence. We are not inspired enough, prophetic enough, we have not the vision that would enable us to link, as an assertion of certainty, any form of human travail, grief and bereavement or suffering in general with shortcomings of a moral nature.'[2] Although this reaction is probably influenced by centuries of Jewish and European thought, it has its roots in the Hebrew Bible, where Job, Qoheleth and some of the Psalmists are fully aware of the unfairness of human life. Thirdly, Jakobowits's observation that the authoritative Jewish statements on moral issues were made 'thousands of years ago' should be noted. He does not develop this, but had he done so he might well have drawn attention to the vast increases in our knowledge of human biology and the causes of disease. If sexual orientation is a matter of our genes rather than an acquired characteristic, it makes a huge difference to

---

[2] Gad Freudenthal, *AIDS*, p. 14.

our reaction to homosexuality. Moreover – and again he made no reference to this in his 1986 article – he would certainly not advocate that those who practise homosexuality should be put to death as the law in Leviticus 20 required. Finally he emphasizes the distinction between 'divine visitation' and the 'consequence' of particular actions. This would appear to draw back from the biblical belief that everything is the result of God's actions, even to the hardening of Pharaoh's heart or the thwarting of Ahithophel's good advice. Nevertheless it goes beyond what would be accepted by many in modern European society. While they might accept in principle that if no sexual intercourse ever took place outside of marriage, sexually transmitted diseases would be greatly reduced and would not have spread as rapidly as they have done, they would balance this against the 'pleasures' of the permissive society and look for solutions through medical discoveries.

I take Rabbi Jakobowits's article as a starting point in this discussion because he is not permitted the escape which is often taken by Christians, that the Old Testament has been superseded by the New and that in Christ an end has been made to the Law. If this were a book on New Testament ethics, or even more widely 'biblical ethics' in the Christian sense, then questions as difficult as that which this article has opened up would have to be addressed.

What can be deduced from what Jakobowits says?

First, he describes the laws he quotes as 'authoritative Jewish statements' that are 'quite unambiguous'. Yet he has modified them to some extent. He would not permit the execution of practising homosexuals, preferring to stress that the forbidden sexual relationships are 'an abomination' which will lead to a doom on societies which permit them. This in turn, as we have observed, removes the immediacy of God's action within the world. And they were made 'thousands of year ago', which opens up a space for modern knowledge, and in the modern Western climate suggests that they may be 'out of date'. The 'authority' of the statements, therefore, has been reduced. Even the most 'unambiguous' Jewish statements are not taken at face value and acted upon. Rather their implications and the principles which underlie them are what is primarily fastened upon.

Secondly, even though he is writing for a mixed, and largely secular readership, he quotes various later Jewish scholars and interpretations of the law. Jewish tradition and the experience of Jews play an important part in his understanding of the moral issues involved in the appearance of AIDS. To trace this is beyond the scope of the present study, and in any case I do not possess the necessary knowledge of Judaism. From a Christian point of view, however, it suggests that the scriptures cannot be taken as a once-for-all revelation, fixed in stone.

Nor can the approach to them be that of seeking to return to the society and morality of the times in which they were written. Nor again can they be separated from the ways in which they have been interpreted and used down the centuries within Christian tradition, a tradition in which they came to be seen as authoritative and yet were not adhered to strictly to the letter, since that would have proved impossible with the changes in society and culture.

Thirdly, and much more tentatively, we might seek to discover where actually Rabbi Jakobowits derived his views of the current situation. It seems to me that, despite his firm acceptance of 'the earliest sources of Jewish law and morality', he could not avoid being influenced by modern Western thought, as we all are. It is impossible to leap out of the culture in which we were brought up. Jakobowits is fortunate, in that his Jewish culture insulated him to some extent from the extreme secularism of today, and thus gave him some purchase by which to resist the large-scale acceptance of modern values that seems to characterize much church thinking at the present time.[3] Yet one wonders how far it is modern culture which leads him to select out of Jewish tradition the features to which he draws attention. And once this is stated, it poses the important question which has never been far away throughout this study, how far is our reading of the Old Testament influenced by ideas derived from the culture from which we have derived our ethical norms and values, emphasizing those parts which accord with them, and passing lightly over other features which we find unacceptable. One reason why the emphasis has been placed on those other features in this whole study has been to try to redress the balance.

Alongside the short article by Rabbi Jakobowits on AIDS, I set one by John Rogerson on abortion. The second paragraph begins: 'Fortunately, in the case of the debate about abortion, there are no texts that can be simply applied to the matters. The Bible does not directly mention abortion anywhere.'[4] The situation, therefore, is the opposite of that to which Rabbi Jakobowits addressed himself, even though AIDS did not exist in the biblical period. After explaining what was known about pregnancy and birth practices in biblical times, and providing evidence that abortion was known, practised and punished in the Middle Assyrian laws, Rogerson thinks that abortion was not prohibited in the Bible because it was not commonly practised, if at all, in ancient Israel. To support this he draws on the

---

[3] I am not saying that these values are necessarily false, only that they are often unthinkingly accepted and even made the basis of ethical judgments, without any questioning of whether they are in line with Christian tradition. Indeed, they are often regarded as 'Christian', revealing a degrading of that term to mean little more than 'morally acceptable'.

[4] John Rogerson, 'Abortion', 77.

fact that female children were exposed and this was regarded as a serious crime (Ezek. 16.4–5), but since male children were desired, it is unlikely that pregnancies were interfered with lest a male child should be lost. He suggests that few situations existed where abortion would be necessary. Thus the social and cultural situation presupposed by the Bible was totally different from ours today. In the one children were desired: in the other the world is over-populated and abortions are numbered in millions. Turning to arguments commonly put forward in support of the pro-life position, Rogerson has little difficulty in showing that the laws against killing do not apply to killing an unborn child and passages alleged to show that human life begins in conception fail because the Israelites knew nothing about conception in the modern medical sense, although the writers of Job and Psalm 139 believed that God was *directly* involved in the growth of the unborn child, a belief which is not easily accepted today.[5]

Rogerson then turns to ways in which the Bible might be used to support the pro-life position.[6] He singles out three. (1) The main purpose of the Bible is to help us to respond to God, and its proper use in social and moral questions is 'to discover the imperatives which arise from the proclamation of God's redemption, and to apply those imperatives to the situations in which we find ourselves'. This is the way forward in the abortion debate, rather than trying to discover texts that can be applied to it literally. (2) At the heart of the Christian proclamation is the belief that it is the love of God which makes possible the Christian life. This means that 'any degradation of the life of any human being' must be resisted, and since the 'programming' of a human being is present from the moment of fertilization, this suggests that its life should be protected. (3) The Bible has much to say about the protection of the weak and defenceless (e.g., Pss. 72.4; 82.2–4; Ezek. 34.4) and the unborn child is among the defenceless. Rogerson concludes that the use of the Bible in ethics 'is not a matter of selecting texts and of trying to apply them as though they were legislation for modern situations'. Rather, 'the Bible's primary function is to bring us to faith and to keep us in faith'. The moral

---

[5] With this may be compared Joseph Blenkinsopp's reservations about appealing to the Bible to support the traditional Jewish or Christian view of marriage: (1) the theological statements about 'one flesh' must not be mistaken for or confused with social realities; (2) the physical, psychological, and emotional environment of the household was quite different in biblical times; (3) more than one form of marriage is found in the Old Testament, including polygyny; (4) economic aspects of marriage are always present in the Old Testament ('The Family', 58).

[6] It should be noted that Rogerson is dealing with the whole Christian Bible, and his discussion is not limited to the Old Testament. This affects some of his arguments, especially his second point.

imperatives are derived from a faith in a God who responds to human need, and our task is to work out those imperatives in the situation in which we find ourselves.

This is a coherent and in many ways attractive approach. Whether it is satisfactory, however, is questionable. We may pick up first of all Rogerson's comment about the absence of any direct teaching on abortion being 'fortunate'. Presumably, therefore, it is *unfortunate* that there is explicit and unambiguous teaching on other issues. The problem here is not simply that teaching and laws which we cannot accept are found in the Bible (and to show that this does not spring from any hostility to the Old Testament, some of the statements about the position of women in the New Testament can be instanced), but that if we refuse to accept such teaching we are admitting a conflict between the 'proclamation' and the way this proclamation was interpreted within the biblical societies. Two conclusions must inevitably be drawn from this: either (1) it must be claimed that, while parts of the ethics are unacceptable (i.e., false, wrong, and evil) today, they were a true expression of the proclamation within a society that was vastly different from our own, or (2) it must be held that the proclamation is eternally true but was misunderstood in biblical times. Both strain credibility: the first because it can hardly be maintained that every single law, teaching, and action of the Israelites and the first Christians was a right working out of the proclamation for the times, while the distinction between the proclamation and its moral application in the second must surely raise questions about the value of a proclamation, the implications of which were misunderstood or went unrecognized. In fact the plausibility of arguments such as those of Rogerson resides in the ambiguity of the way the proclamation is expressed.[7] We have seen several times during this study that terms like 'righteous' and 'love' are empty cells which have to be filled with concrete ethical actions. This is the reason why the ethics can be constantly adapted to fit the prevailing situation, and also why conflicting ethics can be ascribed to the underlying faith. If incorrigible heresy results in eternal torment in hell, it is a loving action to torture the unfortunate heretic to save him or her from that fate (and to dissuade others from adopting the heresy). Augustine's 'love and do what you will' is a most dangerous doctrine. If 'authority' is sought in the Bible, Rabbi Jakobowits is on firmer ground, although the examples he quotes reveal the impossibility of transferring explicit commands to different cultures.

---

[7] Take, for example, 'At the heart of the Christian proclamation is the belief that it is the love of God which makes possible the Christian life' ('Abortion', 88). While Rogerson goes on to give examples of this love, several of these are open to alternative interpretations.

John Rogerson dealt with the question of the use of the Old Testament in Christian ethics more generally in two other articles. In the first[8] he rejects the assumption that 'the starting point for using the Old Testament in social and moral questions is that it is there to provide laws that should be enforced in modern society or church discipline, provided that the difference between the Old Testament and modern attitudes on the issues concerned is not insuperable'. He deprecates the 'legalistic' use of the Old Testament, which he thinks is becoming prominent in recent discussions of moral issues in theologically conservative circles. He himself bases his approach upon two key ideas, 'natural morality' and the 'imperative of redemption'.

By 'natural morality', a term he derives from N. H. G. Robinson, he means 'a moral consensus common to sensitive and thoughtful people, religious and non-religious alike'. The concept enables him to take into account the ethics found in the writings of the other peoples of the ancient Middle East. He claims that the advantages of approaching the laws and moral attitudes of the Old Testament in this way are: (1) it makes it easier to distinguish between what is culturally no longer acceptable (e.g., executing the owner of the ox known to be a gorer, Ex. 21.28–32) and the underlying morality (that lives should not be put at risk by dangerous animals); (2) those who believe in God should observe natural morality because 'God commands it because it is good'; and (3) 'as natural morality changes in accordance with deepening sensitivity in moral matters, so the obligation upon believers changes', so that the Old Testament is seen not to lay down timeless laws but as teaching that 'God approves what moral sensitivity at its best holds to be right'.

Yet humanity has not progressed uniformly in moral sensitivity, so that the need for redemption remains. This forms the second moral imperative. One motive for obeying the commandments in the Old Testament is God's deliverance of Israel from slavery in Egypt, which leads to a demand for generous behaviour towards the weak and the poor 'in a sort of *imitatio dei*'. This imperative can be seen 'forcing [natural morality] into deeper sensitivity'.

All this is valuable, and I imagine that many readers will be able to go along happily with it. Nevertheless I am left with the feeling that what it amounts to in practice is taking values and norms arrived at in a variety of ways, but largely from the dominant 'liberal' or 'tender-minded' ethics of those aware of social problems and the sufferings of the disadvantaged in society, and adjusting (for want of a better word)

---

[8] J. W. Rogerson, 'Social and Moral Questions'. In some of what follows I draw upon my article 'Use of the OT', in which I discuss the whole issue from a slightly different perspective.

the biblical texts to fit these moral attitudes. To pick up Rogerson's illustration of the goring ox. His method of distilling out the central ethical teaching is fine and can hardly be faulted, but we do not accept that dangerous animals must be restrained *because* the Old Testament teaches it. At most the Old Testament law focuses our attention on the matter. How many Christians, I wonder, based their decision that pit bull terriers needed to be legally controlled on the Old Testament law, or even thought of that law when they watched on their television screens children who had been savaged by dogs?

There is one further question which the increasing scepticism of biblical scholars about the possibility of deriving the history of Israel from the biblical record forces upon us. Rogerson finds one motive for protecting the weak and oppressed in the Exodus deliverance and the call to imitate God. But what if the deliverance never happened? Or what if we think it likely that a small group escaped from Egypt, but no longer find it possible to believe that God directly intervened in their escape?[9] Either view undermines Rogerson's claim, which can only be salvaged by adopting a literary approach to the Bible, seeing the *idea* that God saved his people as the ground for developing an ethics. This, however, is to deprive it of its original virility, and brings us close to the non-realist position of scholars such as Don Cupitt. The Exodus deliverance is one of the motivations found in the collections of biblical laws, and the Israelites naturally accepted it as historical fact. Thus it is important within Old Testament ethics. It is very doubtful, however, whether it can function in this way as a method of applying that ethics to the modern world.

In the second article[10] Rogerson begins by pointing out that in Colossians 3.22–4.1 and Ephesians 6.5–9 the writer or writers wrote about slavery without any reference to the Old Testament laws, and that by sending Onesimus back to Philemon Paul flies in the face of the explicit command in Deuteronomy 23.15–16. After commenting on the three strategies the early church adopted to cope with the application of the Old Testament to moral problems, allegorization, dispensationalism, and classification, in order to discourage the attempt to select an Old Testament passage and apply it directly to today's problems, he offers his own suggestions. He argues (drawing on E. Otto's work) that Old Testament ethics have been driven by

[9] Cf. the related question of 'salvation history'. Not only have questions been raised about its validity within Old Testament theology (see D. G. Spriggs, *Two Theologies*), but H. W. F. Saggs has shown that no significant differences exist between the view of history in Israel and in Mesopotamia (*Encounter with the Divine*, 64–92). At which point in the biblical account 'solid' history can be traced is a question now so well known as hardly needing documenting.

[10] John W. Rogerson, 'Christian Morality'.

theology, especially the idea of God's graciousness, so that the bringing together of secular laws and theological principles makes 'the laws as a whole a practical expression of the implications of the compassion of God'.[11] He holds that the collections of laws in the Old Testament were never intended to regulate the whole of Israel's life, but are a selection, the intention of which was to 'make a theological statement about the character of God and the divine requirements for Israelite society', though he does not deny that it was expected that they should be obeyed, even if some are idealistic.[12]

This leads him to suggest four points about the use of the Old Testament in contemporary Christian morality. (1) There are some imperatives in the Old Testament which remain valid across time and culture – not to murder, commit adultery, lie, steal. Yet even these may be affected by special circumstances and we may be forced into a choice between two evils. (2) Many moral teachings cannot be so immediately applied. Some laws are offensive to modern readers, with others the situation no longer holds.[13] (3) Some laws may be read at the level of the spirit rather than the letter, such as the Jubilee laws or the laws about slavery. (4) The main contribution of the Old Testament laws is by way of example rather than precept. We should ask what claims the imperatives of redemption make upon us today.

It is difficult to find fault with any of this. Two problems, however, remain. The theme of redemption may be prominent in the Old Testament, but it is not all-pervasive, and to fasten on the idea of compassion reads too much like modern liberal morality. More seriously, the theme is so general that it is open to a wide range of interpretations when the attempt is made to apply it to a concrete modern situation. Or if we fasten on the spirit rather than the letter, the spirit in the Old Testament may be a matter of purity or some other motive rather than the ethical one which we impose upon the text. Or we might ask on what grounds we find some laws 'offensive'? It might be that we aver that they are inconsistent with the overall theme of redemption, but the Israelite writers rarely recognized this. And among the imperatives which Rogerson quotes as valid across time and culture is not committing adultery, yet adultery in the Old Testament was an offence against the husband, not what it means in the Christian view. In the end, it is difficult not to say, 'Why bother? We have the New Testament and modern moral sensitivities.'

[11] *Ibid.*, 426, referring to E. Otto, *Theologische Ethik.*
[12] *Ibid.*, 427.
[13] Rogerson instances Ex. 21.15, the slavery laws, and leaving a sheaf for the poor (Deut. 24.19).

Five Proposals

I turn to five other attempts to retain Old Testament ethics for the present day.

The first is a remarkably thorough study by Richard Bauckham, in which he makes a determined effort to avoid many of the pitfalls that endanger attempts to provide a place for the Bible in Christian ethics.[14] In particular he criticizes the way Christians select elements from the teaching of the Old Testament and simplistically assume that it needs only a little adjustment to apply them to our own society. Against this he stresses the importance of three separate contexts, the original historical setting, the place in the canon, and our own situation, and asserts: 'If a biblical text is not to mean whatever we want it to mean, we must pay disciplined attention to its original and canonical contexts. But if it is to mean something for us, we must pay equally disciplined attention to the contemporary context in which we interpret it.'[15] For him it is the canonical context which is authoritative for its meaning. He recognizes how difficult it is to allow the Bible to challenge and change our attitudes, and admits that no set of principles will automatically lead to a correct understanding of the meaning. There is also a need for insight, imagination, critical judgment, expert knowledge of our contemporary world, and the guidance of the Holy Spirit. If we do this we discover that while nothing in the Old Testament provides *instructions* for us today, reading the Old Testament can be highly *instructive*.

His study is illuminating because he selects six examples from the Old Testament to expound in the light of these principles: Leviticus 19, Proverbs 31.1–9, Psalms 10 and 126, Exodus, Esther, and the Flood story in Genesis. All deserve careful reading, but space limits a discussion to one of these and I select his exposition of Leviticus 19.

On the chapter as a whole Bauckham notes the curious mixture of commands in it, but finds the key to its meaning in the introduction: 'You shall be holy; for I the LORD your God am holy.' Thus the theme of the chapter is 'the holiness of the people of God in the whole of their life as a people belonging to him', and this consists of both cultic and moral holiness.[16] Further he claims that the fact that 'most of the ten commandments appear in some form' in the chapter shows that the law works on general principles, which include the love commandment. The Pentateuch does not provide exhaustive rules for all specific cases, any more than Jesus does. What are offered are

---

[14] Richard Bauckham, *Bible In Politics*. See esp. pp. 3–19 for a discussion of the general issues. The problem, however, permeates the entire book, which is so wide-ranging that it cannot be discussed adequately in the space available here. See also my review in *ET* 100, 1988–89, 401–403.

[15] *Ibid.*, 16.

[16] *Ibid.*, 23.

'exercises' in legal thinking, 'examples' of laws rather than an exhaustive collection.

Yet the problems of how the Old Testament laws can be applied to modern society are not solved by looking for general principles. Taking the law protecting the right of the poor to glean in the fields, Bauckham identifies two underlying principles: the need to provide for those who lack economic resources, ultimately going back to the call to love one's neighbour as oneself, and the belief that Israelite landowners were only tenants on the land which belongs to God, and they held it in trust from him (Lev. 25.23). Thus the law is rooted in Israel's relation to her God. Because Israel was envisaged as a theocratic society, the model it provides for the church must be qualified by the fact that the church is a voluntary community, and the model it provides for the state must equally be qualified by the fact that the modern, secular, pluralistic state lacks the wholehearted commitment to God which the law demanded of Israel.

Bauckham has little difficulty in showing the modern relevance of verse 32, 'You shall rise up before the hoary head, and honour the face of an old man, and you shall fear your God.' After pointing out that the New Testament says nothing about this, revealing that it presupposes the Old Testament rather than superseding it, he draws attention to the social function which parents and the old generally had in ancient Israel as part of the respect due to the agents of law and government. But he claims that the form of the commandment shows it included those too frail in body or mind to exercise authority, and then declares that it hardly needs to be said that respect for the old is much needed in our own society. He suggests that the strategy of Leviticus 19 is needed alongside legal and institutional measures, nurturing values that hold the aged in respect.[17]

By contrast the law concerning the man who sleeps with a slave-girl who is betrothed might seem to be far removed from today's society. Bauckham's treatment of this law illustrates his approach very well.[18] After pointing out that the action would have been adultery if the woman had not been a slave, he makes the correct observation that the fact that the couple are spared the death penalty for adultery may seem merciful to us, 'but the *reason* for this is not mercy, but the fact that the law considers the girl a chattel not a legal person'. Yet because the case hovers between slavery (when compensation to the owner would be the proper penalty) and adultery (where the law imposed the death penalty), the man has to offer compensation to God in the form of a 'reparation offering' ('guilt offering'). Again, this is misunderstood if the grounds are thought to be because *any* slave is a

[17] *Ibid.*, 31–33.
[18] *Ibid.*, 33–37.

person in the sight of God. Rather it is because *this* slave is betrothed and 'this anomalous legal status makes the case neither clearly one of adultery nor clearly not one of adultery.' From this Bauckham draws the conclusion that although the law is based on the *principle* of slavery, a principle which we reject, there is also the principle that the law must treat adultery as a violation of Israel's covenant with her God. After noting that there are aspects of Israelite law on slavery which might be interpreted as not just mitigating the institution of slavery but undermining it, he points out that by accepting the principle of slavery the law has to start where the Israelites are. From our vantage point we can see that some practices are inconsistent with the fundamental will of the biblical God. Thus while Israelite law had 'to start where its own people are' and 'adopts many of the principles and practices of its environment', Bauckham concludes that 'we have to measure the laws of the Old Testament against the whole thrust of the biblical revelation of God's will'. And our warrant for doing this is Jesus's treatment of the law on divorce (Mk. 10.4–6; Mt. 19.7–8).

Several comments need to be made on Bauckham's approach. First, the problem that ethical laws are mixed with cultic and purity ones in Leviticus 19 cannot be solved by what Bauckham terms the 'correct' Christian recognition that the law's distinction between the holy, the clean and the unclean 'has been rendered obsolete for Christians by the New Testament, which consistently translates such notions into matters of moral holiness'.[19] If it in fact does this (which I doubt), it has misunderstood the significance of purity. As we saw earlier the idea of purity is not only pervasive throughout much of the Old Testament but has an importance in its own right. The existence of the purity system, in fact, has important implications for Old Testament ethics, as I have tried to show.[20]

Secondly, it may well be that the singling out of principles may superficially make it easier to relate the ethics of the Old Testament to the modern world. They are easier to transfer because they are more abstract than specific laws and teaching. This carries the danger that during their voyage to our own society they lose some of their Old Testament ethical values and attract to themselves some modern ones. Moreover, the example of the slave-girl shows that even Old Testament principles are adjudged to be wrong or false today, so that even these cannot be regarded as 'fundament moral principles'.[21]

---

[19] Bauckham, *Bible In Politics*, 27.

[20] Cf. Tom Deidun, 'The view that the purity laws have nothing to do with ethics mystifies me. They may have nothing to do with *our* ethics, but that is because we have, for one reason or another, chosen to exclude them' ('The Bible and Christian Ethics', 41, n.16, his italics).

[21] It should be noted that Bauckham uses 'principle' in two distinct senses: (1) as a social norm (the 'principle' that a slave does not have the same legal status as a free

The question then has to asked, on what basis is this judgment made? In the present passage, Bauckham seems to take the teaching of Jesus as this ground, but this leaves us with enormous critical and historical problems. Later in his book he considers slavery directly, arguing that the Old Testament 'fully recognizes the inconsistency of the enslavement of Israelites with the fundamental freedom and equality of all God's people, whom he redeemed from slavery in Egypt'. The laws accept the fact of slavery, but they treat it as an 'abnormality to be minimized as far as possible'. Job 31.13–15 shows that the wisdom literature reached the same conclusion by declaring that the same God created both master and slave. 'In the end both kinds of argument require the abolition of slavery, and it is perfectly proper that we should follow the *direction* of these Old Testament principles as far as they point, even beyond Old Testament practice and, for that matter, even beyond New Testament practice.'[22] Attractive as this may seem, it is difficult to maintain, since (1) 'direction' suggests that a developing and progressively higher ethics can be found in the Old Testament, which founders on our ignorance of the dating of the literature, and (2) the 'direction' is in fact determined from our present perspective and acceptance of what that higher ethics is. If the position of women deteriorated in the post-exilic period, as many scholars believe, this suggests a 'direction' which we find totally unacceptable.

Thirdly, there is the idea of the 'whole thrust' of the biblical revelation of God's will. Since, on Bauckham's own showing, there are considerable inconsistencies within the Old Testament, what this boils down to is that some ethical stances which appeal to us are declared to be that main thrust, even though they may not have been recognized as such in the Old Testament itself, or their implications may not have been followed out. If one thing has become clear as the result of the present study, it is that there is *no* 'whole thrust'. As in all societies, inconsistencies and compromises abound. It is this which allows the selectivity which marks almost all studies of Old Testament ethics. Thus when the Exodus is seized upon as at the heart of the Old Testament and therefore the key to its ethics, the conquest of Canaan and the annihilation of the previous inhabitants is forgotten.[23]

---

person, and hence the acceptance of the institution of slavery); and (2) a moral norm (that adultery is a violation of the covenant). It is sometimes difficult to decide which is dominant in any particular context.

[22] Bauckham, *Bible In Politics*, 107–109, his italics.

[23] *Ibid.*, 5. As part of his discussion of whether the New Testament makes the Old Testament ethic obsolete Bauckham mentions 'holy war', and notes two attempts to deny that it applies any longer: some declare it has been replaced by Jesus's ethic of non-violence, and others that modern wars do not have the divine sanction of Israel's wars. The problem is not considered in chapter 7 on the Exodus and freedom except in

Much that Bauckham says is extremely valuable and no one should fail to think carefully about the issues he raises and the solutions he offers, but in the end it fails to provide an overall answer to the problem of the Christian use of the Old Testament in ethics, simply because the modern enlightened ethics comes first and the Old Testament is read in its light.

I turn secondly to John Goldingay. His ultimate concern is to answer the question asked by H. W. Wolff, 'What does the Old Testament text in its historical meaning say to mankind living in the eschaton of Jesus Christ'? and he considers five approaches to the Old Testament: as 'faith', as 'a way of life' (the chapter on ethics), as 'the story of salvation', as 'a witness to Christ', and as 'scripture'. He begins his discussion of the Old Testament as 'a way of life' by listing five ways in which scripture may be regarded as shaping our life: (1) with explicit commands, (2) in narratives which may provide potential examples of behaviour, (3) as a source of values or principles, (4) by influencing our overall view of reality, and (5) by shaping our character.[24] He admits that each of these presents problems, but the main part of his discussion is limited to commands, and he deals very summarily with the other four. The main function of the narratives is to relate how God has acted, and they do not mean to offer us models of behaviour. Moreover their specificness makes it impossible directly to transfer them to a different situation. There is even a difficulty about identifying the meaning of the biblical narrative itself (and Goldingay points to Dennis Nineham's stress on the cultural gap). The chief ethical values which he discerns in the Old Testament are holiness, justice, faithfulness, mercy, steadfast love, *shalom*, brotherhood, and stewardship. No criticism of this is offered apart from noting the diversity of the Old Testament and the lack of any one key value. Why the latter should be a weakness is not clear,[25] while the generality of all the values provides little guidance for today and makes it easy to find biblical support for actions and decisions which happen to appeal to us. Goldingay explains the approach of finding the key in 'the overall view of reality' as viewing Old Testament ethics as 'a response to the activity of the redeemer God' (and the creator God), but this has the same weaknesses. Finally he admits that allowing the Bible to shape character is 'a subtle affair', and declares that it ought not to obscure the prominence in the Bible of explicit commands, to which he then turns.

---

a footnote (p. 159, n. 17).

[24] John Goldingay, *Approaches*, 38–43.

[25] He notes, however, G. C. Stead's point that once you have more than one prescription there is the possibility of a context in which they clash (*ibid.*, 50–51).

He accepts that many commandments are not binding today (he instances 'much in Dt. 12; 13; 20'), and asks how we can say that others are. Can they be universalized? How can they be related to the New Testament and modern insights? How can they be applied to the modern world, so different from that of the biblical writers?[26] To answer these questions he concentrates on the way Christians can appropriate these laws. The main problems are the 'specificness' of the commands, the 'diversity of Old Testament standards', and the 'limitations' of these standards.

The historical context does not prevent the commands being 'the concrete expression of some principle', there is some ordering and suggesting of priorities, and the wider canon offers further guidance on interrelating them. Looking for the principles is 'a useful means to discover what are the equivalent statements for today'. This is parallel to the idea of 'middle axioms', championed by R. H. Preston and others, notably William Temple.[27] Despite his apparent support of this approach, he expresses the criticism that it is not these 'hypothetical principles' which are normative or canonical. The Bible itself remains the norm, and the principles we find in it are limited because they are part of our own interpretation. And in any case what we need are specific contemporary statements, the equivalent of the biblical commands. So we should take the laws as a paradigm for our own ethical construction.[28]

Besides the ethical diversity in the Old Testament, some of the commands conflict with the teaching of Jesus and express sub-Christian moral standards. Goldingay rejects development as a solution, since it suggests that early material can be ignored and later standards are not always closer to God's ideal. All legislation is a compromise between what is ethically desirable and what is feasible. What he terms the 'condescending standard' is not to be dismissed, for it is part of God's condescension to the hardness of human hearts. He admits that God may appear to encourage a lowering of standards, but attention to the entire canon will correct this.[29]

Yet are there not some issues where the Bible is 'simply wrong'? (1) The Bible often fails to make explicit the implications of its own theology. Moreover (2) the Torah 'mixes up . . . custom (which can conceal, hinder, or develop morality), law (which draws boundaries, but related only to what can be controlled), and religion (which relates

---

[26] *Ibid.*, 39.

[27] Goldingay refers to R. H. Preston's 'Bible to the Modern World' (*Approaches*, 55). See now the discussion by R. John Elford, who points out that the concept originated in the Oxford Conference of 1937, and that Preston now dislikes the term (*Middle Way*, 9–11, cf. Preston's own comment, *Middle Way*, 267–269).

[28] Goldingay, *Approaches*, 51–55.

[29] *Ibid.*, 56–61.

morality to a worldview and to God, but can confuse the ethical with the merely cultic)'. Further (3) some Old Testament commands are specifically expressive of the religion of Israel and are not binding on Christians (such as circumcision, tithing, sabbath observance). Goldingay's response is to argue that the tension between the ideal and the present remains. He admits that much material in the Old Testament is at best of only indirect value for ethics, but ends by asserting that all have to be seen in the light of Christ and all may be instructive 'in the light of the principles they embody'.

This seems to me less than coherent, and I suspect that the reason is that Goldingay starts from the belief that the whole Bible is authoritative in a sense not too far removed from a fundamentalist one, and then has to find ways of explaining those features which are blatantly unacceptable to a Christian today. This prevents him boldly making the New Testament, or the teaching of Jesus, the yardstick by which the Old Testament can be judged, though he is clearly tempted to do this. It also prevents him from boldly rejecting a large part of the law as not binding on the Christian, although he can assert this of circumcision.[30] His attitude towards a policy of discovering the principles behind the laws is ambivalent: sometimes he appears to regard this as the way the Old Testament ethics can be applied to present-day issues, sometimes he sees it to be flawed because the principles derived from the specific laws are 'hypothetical' and the result of our own interpretation. And while he suggests five ways in which the Bible can shape the Christian's way of life, his concentration on laws (often approached in a legalistic way rather than as teaching) gives an undue prominence to the commandments.

Christopher Wright has published extensively on Old Testament ethics, and like Bauckham and Goldingay writes from a conservative position. In *Living as the People of God*, which was considered in Chapter 1 in terms of the pattern which he imposes upon Old Testament ethics, he proposes treating the ethical demands as a 'paradigm', using the word in the grammatical sense of a model on which to form other verbs or nouns, or in this case, ethics for the modern world.[31] He points out that a paradigm is 'not so much imitated as applied'. He later incorporates into the idea two further connotations: 'the overall set of assumptions, theories, beliefs and standards in any given field', and 'a concrete example of experimental research' (when the parallel is Israel as a society). His most succinct account of his method comprises four steps: (1) 'Distinguish the general categories of Old Testament law', such as criminal, civil, family, cultic, and compassionate; (2) 'Analyse the functions of

---

[30] But there were those among the first Christians who thought that it was!

[31] Christopher J. H. Wright, *People of God*, 43–45.

particular laws and instructions', asking how they function within the overall system; (3) 'Define the objective(s) of particular laws', noting such things as whose interests each law is trying to protect, whose power it restricts, what behaviour it encourages or discourages; and (4) 'Preserve the objective but change the context', which is different from extracting highly generalized principles from the law. He claims that this procedure 'bridges the gap between an authoritative text which cannot be directly applied and applied principles which have no intrinsic authority'. Put in other words, it avoids thinking in terms of a literal imitation of Israel – for we cannot simply transpose the social laws of an ancient people into the modern world – but on the other hand does not dismiss the social system of Israel as relevant only to historical Israel and totally inapplicable to the Christian church or the rest of humanity. Despite his criticism of principles, which he wishes to distinguish sharply from paradigms, he uses the term approvingly in a number of places in his study. To take one example, on appropriating the laws, he rejects the idea that Christians must try to impose by law in a secular state provisions lifted directly from the laws of Moses and proposes that Christians will work 'to bring their society nearer to conformity with the principles underlying the concrete laws of Old Testament society'.[32] He even declares: 'We need to see how any particular law functioned in its own Israelite context and what moral principles underlie it. It is those principles (or "middle axioms") which then feed our ethical thought and action in our own environment.'[33]

At the end of a masterly survey of approaches to the problem of the ethical authority of the Old Testament,[34] Wright summarizes the theological assumptions and hermeneutical methods on which he is working. His assumptions are: (1) the authority and relevance of the Old Testament for Christians – 'the question, therefore, is not *whether* the Old Testament has authority and relevance for us as Christians, but *how* that given authority is to be earthed and that relevance applied'; (2) the unity of scripture – 'what God said and did in Old Testament Israel therefore matters to me as a Christian because it is part of the way I have been saved . . . what God required of Israel ethically must speak to me also, because of the moral consistency of God and the continuity of the people of God to whom I belong with them'; (3) the priority of grace – 'the foundation of biblical faith and ethics in *both* testaments is God's grace and redemptive initiative'; (4) the mission and purpose of Israel – 'God created and called Israel to fulfil his purpose of blessing to the nations'; (5) the function of law in

---

[32] *Ibid.*, 162.
[33] *Ibid.*, 158.
[34] Christopher J. H. Wright, 'Ethical Authority'. See also 'Ethical Decisions'.

relation to the mission of Israel – 'the law was not explicitly and consciously applied to the nations . . . [it] was given to Israel to enable Israel to live as a model, as a light to the nations'; (6) Israel and its law as paradigmatic – 'the law was designed (along with many other aspects of Israel's historical experience) to mould and shape Israel in certain clearly defined directions, within its own historico-cultural context' and thus to be a paradigm. A paradigm can be used in two further ways: as 'the overall set of assumptions, theories, beliefs and standards in any given field' (Old Testament theology corresponds to this) and as 'a concrete example of experimental research which provides a model problem-solving in other areas' (to which Israel as a society corresponds).[35] He then sets out his method as in his earlier book.

Although the idea of a paradigm is extremely suggestive, it is doubtful whether it actually takes us much further than Bauckham. The problem lies in what is involved in *applying* the paradigm. To return to the grammatical example. *Within a single language* the paradigm of a verb enables us to form the parts of other verbs *of the same conjugation.* It is useless with other conjugations and when it is transferred to another language all that it can offer is a systematization of the number, person, tense, mood, and voice. The further apart the two languages are the less these will coincide. The question, therefore, is how close modern society and culture is to that of ancient Israel – if Dennis Nineham is right, not close at all, certainly not sufficiently close to regard them as within the same language. But there is more. It is relatively simple to replicate a paradigm in a verb of similar form. It is much more difficult to decide *how* the ethical paradigm is to be applied to a different situation in a distant society with an alien culture. I suspect that Wright in fact is reducing the paradigm law to a principle, which is then reactivated in modern society. If this is so, then this is no different from Bauckham's proposal.

This can be seen in his treatment of the jubilee. He first analyses its purpose: 'to prevent the accumulation of the bulk of the land in the hands of a few. It protected a system of land tenure that was intended to be broadly equitable, with the ownership of land widely spread throughout the population. It was an attempt to impede, and indeed periodically to reverse, the relentless economic forces that lead to a downward spiral of debt, poverty, dispossession and bondage. Its major focus of concern was for the economic viability of the smallest economic units, namely the household with its land: it was a "family-orientated" economic law. Within the limits of primitive agriculture, its sabbatical fallow embodied a concern for the "health" of the soil

---

[35] Wright, 'Ethical Authority', 225–229.

itself.'[36] Almost the whole of this may be questioned. We have already rejected the view that the fallow year had an ecological purpose. But even if everything were accepted, the way Wright transfers the paradigm to the modern world is by suggesting ethical aims and the means by which these purposes are carried out. So immediately there is a shift from the concrete paradigm to a much more abstract level of intention. To give him his due, Wright recognizes that the stage of applying the paradigm to modern economic institutions is extremely complex – so complex, I would suggest, as to make it impossible.[37] Further, since Wright has produced a highly schematic account of Old Testament ethics, which is also selective in what is included, the paradigms are not the actual laws, actions, teaching, ideas of ancient Israel, but his own account of what these are within the triangle of God, Israel and land. This is one reason why the book lacks the vitality and vivid action of the Old Testament itself.

The way Waldemar Janzen approaches Old Testament ethics by way of narratives has already been considered in some detail. Here it is necessary only to set out his proposal for moving from the world of the Old Testament to today. He adopts from Wright the idea of 'paradigm', but departs from Wright in seeing the paradigm as the whole story, 'a personally and holistically conceived image of a model' such as, in the Old Testament, a 'wise person' or a 'good king', and for North America a 'good driver'.[38] He develops five paradigms from the main stories which he examines[39] and others which he samples: familial, priestly, wisdom, royal and prophetic, of which the familial is dominant as 'the primary ideal of the Old Testament's ethic', 'the center and goal of the Old Testament ethos'.[40] We are never far from the liveliness of the Old Testament, and the paradigms appear genuinely to arise out of the narratives. In particular Janzen rejects Wright's attempt to find basic principles which remain unchanged over time, seeing this as reductionist, although principles and laws possess their own legitimate function.[41] Much of this is sound, but it is difficult to see how the model narratives are to be

[36] Wright, *People of God*, 101.
[37] Earlier Wright suggests that the application of a paradigm to the present day is like what we do with the life of Jesus, using 'the example of Jesus paradigmatically in our ethical decisions, seeking to move from what we know Jesus *did* do to what we might reasonably presume he *would* do in our changed situation' (*ibid.*, 44). This is an impossible move, since (a) we know too little about the life of Jesus to be certain of what he did do, (b) our situation is so different from his that no answer is possible to the question of what he would do. Moreover, it is doubtful whether what *Jesus* would have done in our situation is the same as what *we* ought to do in that situation.
[38] Janzen, *Ethics*, 26–28.
[39] Gen. 13; Num. 25; 1 Sam. 25; 1 Sam. 24; and 1 Kgs. 21.
[40] Janzen, *Ethics*, 3, 178.
[41] *Ibid.*, 27–29.

transferred to the present, without either singling out the virtue which is being presented, or fastening on some basic principle. Janzen, however, is mainly concerned with presenting the ethics of the Old Testament rather than attempting to apply them specifically to the present day.

An extremely fine article by Tom Deidun, written from a Roman Catholic perspective and with frequent references to the magisterium and Vatican II, contains much sound observation and sensible comment, even though for our purposes it suffers from the drawback that it is largely concerned with the New Testament.[42] Unfashionably, and to my mind absolutely correctly, he holds that it is essential to explain the text in its historical and literary context, and strongly defends historical-critical analysis. 'Experience surely teaches us (if common sense failed to do so) that interpreters who turn to biblical texts in search of "relevance" will surely find what they are looking for, but only after imposing on the texts their own notions of what counts as relevant.'[43] Deidun effectively demolishes what he calls 'some standard approaches' to the use of the Bible in Christian ethics.[44] Those who treat it as a repository of divine commands cannot avoid selecting among its prescriptions, yet there is no acceptable criterion for distinguishing those that are still 'valid' from the rest. Those who choose a 'master theme' (love, justice, freedom, the imitation of Jesus) to provide a divinely authoritative framework for Christian ethics end up by ignoring the diversity of the biblical writings in favour of what they deem relevant. In any case these master themes are too general to be useful. Those who use the biblical writers' moral assessments of the situations which confronted them as the basis for judging analogous situations today tend to select analogues which suit their own prior stance (he notes that Exodus and Conquest are both judged positively by the biblical writers). The proposal that the Bible contains the revelation of the character of God rather than a morality might be fruitful, but suffers serious difficulties. Does it make sense to speak of God 'doing' anything? What side of God's character is to be selected – the 'jihad' God of some Old Testament passages or the God who looks approvingly on all of creation? For the Bible does not give us a uniform portrayal of God. The weakness of the suggestion that the role of the Bible is to nurture particular attitudes and intentions is seen in some of the appalling attitudes that have been fostered by it when unimpeded by critical scholarship. Deidun finds Gustafson's approach the most honest and circumspect. Gustafson favoured a 'loose' approach, taking account

---

[42] Deidun, 'The Bible and Christian Ethics'.
[43] *Ibid.*, 4.
[44] *Ibid.*, 21–28.

of the great variety of moral values, norms and principles in the Bible and concluding that 'scripture is one of the informing sources for moral judgments, but it is not sufficient in itself to make any particular judgment authoritative'.[45] A serious problem with this, however, is that the ethics tend to arise 'in any humane and Christian conscience' and there is no necessity to assume that the Bible *must* have something authoritative to say about every moral issue that has to be faced today.

This leads Deidun to consider the authority of the Bible. Although there are some views of biblical authority which are less unsatisfactory than others, he judges that so long as it is held to be normative no approach is problem-free. Indeed, he sees the whole problem of the relation between the Bible and Christian ethics as deriving from a preoccupation with the Bible's authority. The value of the Bible should be compared with the value of imbibing a great foreign culture. The approach which he favours, therefore, is 'free and unpredictable', 'inventive', 'versatile and imaginative'. 'It will be disdainful of biblical one-liners, and suspicious of "favourite" biblical texts or "themes".' It will take the Bible seriously but not woodenly. 'It might on occasion put forward the opinion that the ethical insight of this or that biblical writer is wonderfully intuitive, while accepting with perfect equanimity that this or that other biblical writer's stance is irrelevant or distasteful.' It might decide that the Bible has nothing to say about some modern ethical issues, or nothing beyond the broadest generalizations. One of its values will be 'to stimulate unfamiliar reflections', even turning its very foreignness to advantage – to expand our ethical horizons by posing strange questions.[46]

With almost all of this I am in complete agreement. It seems to me that the windows through which we have looked at Old Testament ethics have made it impossible to accept any authoritative view of the Bible. But more than this, I am certain that no one adopts an ethical viewpoint by first of all finding out what 'the Bible says' and then applying this to the present day. The ethical decision is taken on a large number of different grounds, not least those found in the culture in which the individual has been brought up, the 'professional' ethics of his working environment, and the norms and values which have been unconsciously internalized. The Bible may well have played a part in this as one of the grounds on which the decision has been taken. More often, I suspect, the decision has already been taken in

---

[45] *Ibid.*, 28, quoting Gustafson's article in Charles E. Curran and Richard A. McCormick, *Use of Scripture*, 165, to which I have not had access.

[46] *Ibid.*, 28–35, quotations on 31. The whole section deserves careful attention for the wisdom expressed in it.

substance before the Bible is searched to discover corroboration and 'authority' for it.[47]

Using the Old Testament

All the scholars whose works we have discussed are aware of the dangerous power exerted by our own prejudices and values, and strive in various ways to minimize this distorting influence. Whether they have succeeded is uncertain. The history of interpretation and application of biblical ethics is not reassuring. Certainly it is clear that attempts to discover the 'main thrust' of the Old Testament ethics and its 'underlying principles' which can then be transferred to the present day have largely produced broad generalizations or vague ethical virtues which can be filled out with almost any moral or political programme which happens to be popular at the moment. This can be seen in the vogue which the Exodus had in liberation theology and the claim that the Bible proclaimed the 'option for the poor'. We have seen that the first conveniently omitted the conquest of Canaan which is an integral part of the Old Testament Exodus theme while the second runs up against the questions we have raised about the Old Testament attitude towards the poor and the fact that before sociology began to influence biblical studies concern for the poor would have been interpreted in terms of individual charity rather than as a demand for a just society, a view which is much more in accord with Old Testament attitudes than most are willing to admit today. The same point can be made with regard to the position of women in ancient Israel, and the Old Testament attitude to war. Neither presented any sort of 'problem' to the biblical writers. How then can it be claimed that the 'main thrust' of the Old Testament runs in support of modern attitudes towards freedom, the poor, women and war? Only, I suggest, by being highly selective and holding that the relatively few texts which support modern sensitivities represent the 'real' message of the Old Testament. The 'thrust' is as much that of the reader as of the writings. Similar criticisms can be made of attempts to find middle axioms or underlying principles in the specific laws. The fact that the

---

[47] Four other studies which consider the issues may be simply noted: Michael Keeling, *Foundations*, J. Philip Wogaman, *Christian Ethics*, Thomas W. Ogeltree, *Use of the Bible*, and J. I. H. McDonald, *Biblical Interpretation*. In addition Stephen C. Barton offers a useful survey on a narrower front in 'Biblical Hermeneutics'. Of special interest is Peter J. Paris's 'Ethicist's Concerns', a response to the previous articles in *Semeia* 66, in which he notes the way that the scholars 'render themselves vulnerable to anachronistic judgements' by using modern ethical classifications such as natural law, deontology and teleology, and stresses the need to treat the scriptures in their own setting. He also questions whether such topics as the bias in favour of the poor 'inhere in the scriptures as a whole or merely reflect selected traditions therein' (see pp. 173, 178).

principles discovered are always such as are acceptable today should immediately suggest that something is wrong.

The moral of this review of attempts to show how the Old Testament relates to modern ethical problems is that if you start with revelation there is no way in which a coherent and plausible method can be devised. Direct application of the Old Testament laws to our present situation is impossible and can be exceedingly dangerous, as Frank Cross has shown.[48] Yet most, if not all, of the scholars whom we have considered work with a conception of revelation as the imparting of information and the giving of commands.[49] Philosophers generally regard this as the least satisfactory theory of revelation,[50] but it is doubtful whether any view of revelation can avoid the problem. So long as some divine influence on the moral teaching of the Old Testament is retained it is impossible to explain how the Old Testament can offer authoritative guidance to those faced by very different ethical dilemmas today.[51] If the divine influence was decisive, the inconsistencies within the Old Testament itself become inexplicable; if it was partially or wholly misunderstood, no unimpeachable way can be devised to distinguish those ethical values and norms which were truly the divine requirement; if God accommodated his influence to the historical situation, we are left with uncertainty as to how far what the Old Testament presents is distant from the ideal and in which situations within the scriptures such accommodations occur. This is compounded when strong emphasis is placed upon the canon, for this presents the Bible in a way which is essentially static and takes no account either of the

---

[48] Frank Moore Cross, 'Redemption', 103. He points out that for most of human history it was necessary for men and women to 'be fruitful and multiply and fill the earth'. Today, however, the ancient command is no longer valid. Indeed, 'frozen in time, as an eternal imperative of nature, it has become at once murderous and suicidal', and those who cling to it are guilty of the rape of nature. He adds, however, that the biblical view of 'the unity and wholeness of human and natural history' can be the basis of modern theology if used with great caution. This might be the place to point out that rabbinic interpretation of the Torah was not 'legalistic' in the pejorative Christian sense. Rather it was an attempt to apply it to the current situation. Often, indeed, the rabbis show great moral sensitivity. Jonathan Helfand has provided an interesting discussion of this in his article 'The Earth is the Lord's'.

[49] This is true, even where other aspects of the life of ancient Israel are taken into account. The fascination with commands is almost universal. Only Deidun avoids most of the pitfalls.

[50] This is not the place to enter into a discussion of the philosophy of revelation. For a clear account see David Pailin, *Groundwork*, 109–115. Earlier works which still repay reading are Ninian Smart, *Philosophy of Religion*, 99–137; H. D. Lewis, *Philosophy of Religion*, 227–253.

[51] I use the term 'influence' to avoid the connotations which 'inspiration' has attracted to itself in the course of Christian history, and also to try to escape from the emotional overtones which the word possesses.

'movement', the change across time, which is found in the biblical writings or the vibrant and varied activity to which they bear witness.[52]

Whatever theory is proposed, whatever position is adopted, it is impossible to avoid the fact that we the readers pass judgment on the biblical writings. Were this not so, we should not be speaking of moral 'problems' at all,[53] and the only problems that we should recognize would be those created by the inconsistent ethical stances within the canon. It is precisely because most of us reject without hesitation the death penalty for homosexual offences, rebellious sons, kidnappers and witches, and condemn the practice of the ban after victory in war, that we are forced to find some means of denying that they still apply and also compelled to explain why the laws given by God to Moses impose these punishments and command these practices.

It is necessary to underline the point. It is not that we find anything in the New Testament which *explicitly* declares that these laws have been superseded and hence are null and void. Indeed, while Paul does not demand the death penalty on those guilty of homosexual practices, he condemns them as the result of sin (Rom. 1.27). It is not even that we have adopted a Marcionite position and deny that the Old Testament has any continuing place in the Christian religion. It is simply because the ethical position which we hold itself condemns these laws – and many other features, some found in the New Testament.[54] As I have said several times during this study, what needs to be teased out is how Christians today arrive at ethical decisions.[55] Regardless of the answer we give to that question, what appears quite certain to me is that when we reject the death penalty for homosexual practice or are disturbed by the subjection of women to

[52] See C. F. Evans, 'Difficulties', 27–30. He prefers 'movement' to 'development' as avoiding the idea that the writings of the Bible can be 'plotted on a single graph in some sort of generic relationship to one another' (p. 30).

[53] It is highly significant that the ultra-conservative Walter C. Kaiser finds it necessary to devote three chapters of his book to 'Moral Difficulties in the Old Testament', even though he himself finds no difficulties at all, and ascribes the difficulties to writers whom he would doubtless regard as 'liberal' (*Ethics*, 247–304). The apologetic which he presents varies in plausibility, and often he appears to be forced to defend positions which I would regard as immoral, even positively evil.

[54] On homosexuality see Walter Moberly, 'Use of Scripture'. He makes several useful points, such as that the same name may apply to a different reality (as we have seen with 'adultery'). But once he admits that 'not all within Scripture is of equal enduring significance' he opens up the question of who makes the decision. His article is more concerned with how to live with different interpretations of scripture than how to discover a right attitude to homosexuality.

[55] Richard G. Jones sought to do this in his article, 'Ethical Decisions' and in his book *What To Do?* He makes some interesting points, but to my mind does not dig deeply enough.

men in almost all of the Bible, it is not because we have found some law, incident or teaching which brings us to this decision, or even that we have come to regard these ideas as in conflict with the 'general thrust' of the Bible or the theology of redemption. We reject the biblical demands *out of hand*. It is only after we have done that that we begin to look for justification of our action.[56]

If, then, we choose to accept that the Old Testament is divine revelation and its ethics possesses authority given by God, we find ourselves up against insuperable problems. This in itself convinces me that to begin with revelation, and to look for authority, constitutes the problem, which can only be solved when this is abandoned.[57] To attempt to discuss revelation will lead us too far astray, but I believe that a brief comment on authority will advance my argument.

It is my firm conviction that no external authority is possible for thoughtful human beings. However much they may assert, and believe, that they are subject to such an authority, ultimately the decision to accept it as an authority has been made by them. They *choose* – even if the internalized norms and values which come from the culture in which they were nurtured greatly influenced their decision. In the final analysis, my own decision has to be decisive for me. Once the decision has been taken, of course, the authority functions as an external control, but it does this only because I have made the initial commitment. There can be no authority external to me, only power which imposes itself upon me. And even then the martyrs have shown that external power has limits beyond which it is unable to go in forcing another person to do its will.

---

[56] Inconsistencies within the Bible, contrasts between the Testaments, and the gap between ancient Israel and the totally different society in which we live, of course, make it impossible to apply the ethical teaching directly to today, but I am not concerned here with the social and cultural differences between the world of ancient Israel and our own. My point is that we are judging the Bible by a standard which we regard as right.

[57] A very large number of books and dictionary articles have been written on revelation and the authority of the Bible. The following may be noted: William J. Abraham, *Inspiration*; William J. Abraham, *Revelation*; James Barr, *Holy Scripture*; David L. Bartlett, *Scriptural Authority*; John Barton, *People of the Book?*; Raymond E. Brown, *Critical Meaning*; Avery Dulles, *Revelation*; Robert Gnuse, *Authority*; Donald K. McKim, ed., *Authoritative Word*; Robert Gnuse, 'Authority'; John Barton, 'Authority'; F. Gerald Downing, 'Revelation'; James Barr, 'Revelation'. An alternative approach, more directly linked to ethics, is found in Kevin Giles's discussion of slavery. He points out that only three positions are possible, once it is accepted that slavery is morally wrong: (1) those evangelicals who supported slavery in the nineteenth century were mistaken in their interpretation of scripture; (2) those evangelicals were right – the Bible does endorse slavery, simply regulating its worse excesses; (3) they were right in their biblical exegesis, but wrong in viewing the Bible as timeless oracles, not conditioned by history ('Slavery', 14–15). Giles then applies this to the subordination of women. Cf. Willard M. Swartley, *Slavery*.

Alongside this, however, needs to be set the query which David Clines raised about the validity of authority as a Christian concept. He asks whether the very concept of 'authority' comes from a world we have left behind. 'To imagine that the Bible could be "authoritative" sounds as if we still are wanting to plunder it for prooftexts for theological warfare. As if one sentence from the immense unsystematic collection of literature that is the Bible could *prove* anything.' He goes on:

> So why not say, Authority is not the point. The authority of a text has to do with its nature; we want to be saying things about the Bible that have to do with its *function*. We want to be saying, not so much that the Bible is right, not even that the Bible is wrong, but that it impacts for good upon people. Despite everything, we might want to add, despite its handicaps, despite the fact that it has misled people and promoted patriarchy, it has an unquenchable capacity – when taken in conjunction with a commitment to personal integrity – to inspire people, bring out the best in them and suggest a vision they could never have dreamed of for themselves.[58]

He adds that he finds it strange that feminists have not seen that 'authority' is a concept from the male world of power-relations. What is needed is 'the more inclusive human language of influence, encouragement and inspiration'.

To many this will appear unacceptably vague and appallingly open to the danger of being misled by scripture. The way the Bible has had a malign influence through history cannot be pushed aside.[59] Yet, as Clines says, it has also had an immense impact for good. Whether the good outweighs the bad can be debated. And perhaps Clines is still hankering after some kind of special position for the Bible among the whole of world literature. These are vast issues and we must return to Old Testament ethics.

If the laws cannot be applied directly to the modern world, if to distil principles to transfer to the society of the twenty-first century is too fraught with risk and uncertainty, if the paradigms and models will not fit readily into another culture, then it is difficult to see how the ethics can influence, encourage and inspire, however much the great religious scenes from the Old Testament, its hymns and the words of the prophets may do so. We are still too close to the attempt to take some ethical 'thing' from the Old Testament and bring it into our own situation.

---

[58] David J. A. Clines, 'Eve', 47–48.
[59] See Robert P. Carroll, *Wolf*. After a lecture I asked Professor Carroll why, if the Bible had such a malign effect, we should continue to read and study it. His reply was essentially that we could not thrust it aside because it exists, it is *there*.

To look to the Old Testament as an authority, or even as a source of influence, encouragement and inspiration, will inevitably lead to imposing our own prejudices upon it. The tender-hearted turn gladly to passages which look forward to a time of universal peace, and delight in the familiar words of Isaiah about beating swords into ploughshares and spears into pruning hooks (Isa. 2.4), neglecting Joel's reversal of this prophecy (Joel 3.9–10), and passing rapidly by the demand of the Deuteronomist to annihilate the Canaanites, even though this is proclaimed as the direct will of God (Deut. 7.1–2; 20.16–18). They interpret *šālōm* as if it corresponded exactly to modern ideas of reconciliation between nations, and overlook the fact that most often in the Old Testament 'peace' comes as a result of the total defeat or even annihilation of Israel's enemies.

The tough-minded call for the reintroduction of capital punishment for murder by quoting Genesis 9.6, 'Whoever sheds the blood of man, by man shall his blood be shed', but overlook other laws which impose the death penalty on those who strike or curse their parents (Ex. 21.15, 17; Lev. 20.9), commit adultery (Lev. 20.10; Deut. 22.22), or engage in kidnapping (Ex. 21.16), which would be totally unacceptable in modern society, and they would never dream of burning witches, despite the command, 'You shall not permit a sorceress to live' (Ex. 22.18).

All the methods of applying the Old Testament ethics to modern society that have been considered contain the danger of introducing our own ethical values and ideas upon the 'principles', 'paradigms', 'models', 'main thrust', 'ethical direction', and even the nurturing of attitudes that are proposed as the means of moving from the biblical culture to our own. All are too vague and indefinite to avoid this. And where any law happens to be completely unambiguous, but at the same time totally unacceptable today, that law is rejected out of hand, as indeed it has to be unless those who retain that law are to be condemned as dangerous fanatics. No modern government would permit the open promoting of the execution of those engaging in homosexual acts.

What is needed is something completely different. As I have argued, the first requirement is to abandon the propositional view of revelation, and with it the belief in the Bible as an external authority. We need to leave the Old Testament where it is, in its own world – or rather worlds, for it stretches across different periods of history and contains the ethics of many different human groups. Then we can go to visit it. Our visits need to be prolonged and we need to travel into many different parts of the country. As far as possible we shall follow the advice that Henry St John Hart gave half a century ago: 'By a willing suspension of disbelief I will join myself for a little while to the sons and daughters of Jerusalem, their people shall be my people, and their God my God.'[60] As we discover that purity and honour have an equal place with ethics, and religion rules over all, we shall begin to understand how the ancient Israelite lived his life, and how the Israelite women accepted their place within that society.

It is, indeed, a strange land that we have glimpsed as we have climbed our tower.[61] Yet many things conspire to hide its strangeness from us. Modern translations of the Bible iron out differences. Indeed, the attempt to provide 'dynamic equivalence' leads to the modernizing of the Bible and rests ultimately on a belief that the Bible fits neatly into our modern culture and speaks directly to the twenty-first century. Such translations are the equivalent of package holidays: they ensure that we are provided with a full English breakfast and see only the pleasanter and more picturesque features of the country we are visiting. Another, and even more insidious obstacle, is the fact that we give false meanings to words and concepts in texts from a different age and culture without realizing it. When we come across a word in Chaucer or Shakespeare the meaning of which we do not know, we simply look it up in the glossary. That is no problem. The difficulty comes with words that we regularly use today, but which had a widely different meaning in the time of Chaucer or Shakespeare. We have met this several times in this study. One of the clearest examples is 'adultery'. We read it as meaning disloyalty to a marriage partner of either sex through having sexual intercourse with a third person. In the Old Testament, as we have seen, it is an offence against the rights of a husband over his wife. By giving our meaning to 'You shall not commit adultery' we blind ourselves to the fact that we are in an alien country. Again, the praiseworthy efforts of feminists and modern translators to foster the equality of women has had the effect of making the Old Testament appear less foreign than it is. The all-pervasive patriarchal culture must not be glossed over. These, of course, are all features where we would judge the biblical culture to have a lower ethics than our own, but even so these norms and values make us look afresh at our own ideas and practices. Where the biblical culture has a higher ethics will be more difficult to discern, largely because we have so internalized the norms and values of our own culture that we shrug aside those of the Bible as quaint and old-fashioned, impossible to accept and live by today.

But it is in the very strangeness of the land that its virtue lies. The value of the Old Testament for our own ethical quest resides in the

[60] H. St J. Hart, *Foreword*, 178. The whole of this Postscript is fascinating.
[61] Robert Carroll has emphasized this strangeness, though with regard to the religion of the Old Testament rather than its ethics: 'How the reader's adventures in that weird world will affect their lives or minds cannot be predicted. ... Whatever you may imagine the gods are like, what you encounter in the Bible will be different' (*Wolf*, 146).

fact that it does *not* provide rules which can be applied directly to the modern world to tell us what we are to do. It is able to render help in that quest only through opening our eyes to completely different assumptions and presuppositions, motives and aims. If it chimed in exactly with the dominant norms and standards of the Western world – democracy, equality, tolerance, free-market economics, hedonism and individualism – it would have nothing to offer that we could not buy elsewhere. And if we attempt to make it support these values we twist it into shapes that it never held. Only by moving between that land and our own, or to retain the metaphor which has controlled most of this book, only by gazing out again and again through the different windows of the tower which we climbed with so much labour, will the Bible be able to offer assistance in our attempt to solve the many puzzling moral issues which face us today.

ADDENDUM

Walking with God

The evidence may be displayed as follows:

hālak (qal) + *'et*: (God) Mal. 2.6.

hālak (hithp.) + *'et*: (God) Gen. 5.22, 24; 6.9; (David's men) 1 Sam. 25.15.

hālak (qal) + *'im*: (God) Mic. 6.8; cf. Lev. 26.21, 23, 27, 40 where it is walking contrary to God's will.

hālak (qal) + *lip'nēy*: 1 Kgs. 2.4; 3.6; 8.23, 25 (= 2 Chron. 6.14,16); 9.4 (= 2 Chron. 7.17); Job 3.5; Ps. 97.3. In addition there are references to God's walking before Israel (e.g., Ex. 13.21) and Cyrus (Isa. 45.2), as well as other human agents.

hālak (hithp.) + *lip'nēy*: (God) Gen 17.1; 24.40; 48.15; 1 Sam. 2.30; 2 Kgs. 20.3 (= Isa. 38.3); Ps. 56.14[13]; 116.9; (anointed one) 1 Sam. 2.35; ('you', sc. the people) 1 Sam. 12.2.

hālak (qal) + *'aḥªrēy*: (God) Deut. 13.4[5]; 1 Kgs. 14.8; 18.21; Jer. 2.2; 2 Chron. 34.31; and Hos. 11.10 (with a somewhat different sense). The phrase is frequently found in Deuteronomistic writings referring to walking after other gods (Deut. 6.14; 8.19; 11.28; 13.5; 28.14; Jdg. 2.12, 19; 1 Kgs. 11.5, 10; Jer. 7.6, 9; 11.10; 13.10; 16.11; 25.6; 35.15; cf. also following after Baal, 1 Kgs. 18.18, 21; Jer. 2.35; 9.13) as well as idols, the host of heaven, and abominations.

hālak (qal) + preposition *beth*. A wide range of terms is found, including law (*tōrāh*, Ex. 16.4; 2 Kgs. 10.31; Jer. 9.12; 26.4; 32.23; 44.10, 23; Ps. 78.16; Dan. 9.10; Neh. 10.30; 2 Chron. 6.16), statute (*ḥuqqāh*, Lev. 18.2, 4; 20. 23; 26.3; 1 Kgs. 3.6; 6.12; 2 Kgs. 17.8, 19; Jer. 44.10, 23; Ezek. 5.6, 7; 11.12; 11.20; 18.9, 17; 20.13, 16; 20.18, 19, 21; *ḥōq*, Ezek. 33.15), commandment (*miṣwāh*, 1 Kgs. 6.12), judgment (*mišpāṭ*, Ezek. 37.24; Ps. 89.31; Job 34.23), testimony (*'ēdūt*, Jer. 44.24), counsel (*mō'ēṣāh*, Jer. 7.24; Mic. 6.16; Ps. 81.13; *'ēṣāh*, Ps. 1.1; 2 Chron. 22.5), as well as virtues such as faithfulness, righteousness, uprightness.[1]

hālak (qal) + 'in the way' is very frequent, especially in the Deuteronomistic writings (cf. Deut. 1.33; 5.33; 8.6; 10.12; 11.22;

---

[1] See DCH II, 550.

13.6[5]; 19.9; 26.17; 28.9; 30.16; Josh. 22.5; Jdg. 2.22; 1 Kgs. 2.3; 3.14; 8.36, 58; 11.33, 38; 2 Kgs. 21.22; in other writings cf. Isa. 30.21; 42.24; Jer. 7.23; 42.3; Hos. 14.10[9]; Zech. 3.7; Pss. 119.3; 128.1).

Whether any distinction can be made between the qal and hithpaʿel forms of the verb in the phrases listed is doubtful. If any is to be found, it seems that the hithpaʿel expresses more general walking as companionship, as the example of Nabal's servants and David's men shows (1 Sam. 25.15). This appears when followed by both 'with' and 'before'. According to DCH the hithpaʿel is not followed by 'after' in any of the biblical or non-biblical texts, which perhaps is natural if the sense is wandering rather than walking with a sense of purpose. This would appear to confirm what was claimed earlier, that the instances of Enoch and Noah do not imply imitation of God. The fact that God 'took' Enoch, and that Noah was the sole righteous man at the time of the flood, has perhaps distorted the view of some scholars.

In the qal, walking 'with' God is equally rare, and again no suggestion of imitating God can be discerned. In Malachi 2.6 the emphasis is upon the merits of Levi, who not only gave true instruction and turned the wicked from their evil ways, but was himself upright. The walking with God seems to mean no more than that Levi lived in peace and uprightness. The subordination of the infinitive construct to $w^e haṣnēaʿ$ in Micah 6.8 suggests that the emphasis lies on the humility (or however the verb is to be translated[2]) before God, rather than the walking, and the *sense* would seem to be placed on obedience rather than imitation. Some confirmation of this connotation may be seen in Leviticus 26.21, 23, 27, 40, where punishment is threatened for disobeying God. Indeed, the punishment takes the form of Yahweh's reflecting Israel's 'contrariness' ($q^e rî$, 'hostile encounter', HALOT, Lev. 26.24, 28, 41).

The view of Skinner and others that walking 'before' God (with both qal and hithpaʿel) is little different from walking 'with' him has been noted above. Yet some change of emphasis can be traced, most notably where the phrase seems to have the sense of 'living, being alive' in Psalms 56.14[13] and 116.9, without any particular ethical stress. A similar sense is found in 1 Samuel 2.20. Westermann interprets Genesis 17.1 as 'God orders Abraham (now representing Israel) to live his life before God in such a way that every single step is made with reference to God and every day experiences him close at hand',[3] in other words the emphasis seems to be placed on fellowship

---

[2] HALOT 3.1039 has a full note with references, preferring 'carefully', 'wisely', or 'attentively'.

[3] Claus Westermann, *Genesis 12–36*, 259. His translation is 'live always in my presence' (p. 253).

with God and obedience to him. Hezekiah's prayer stresses the king's faithful obedience to God, and when it is remembered that the redactor praised Hezekiah's single-minded loyalty to Yahweh in removing the pagan cults (2 Kgs. 18.1–6), this was probably what was intended. In the Solomon narratives (1 Kgs. 2.4; 3.6; 8.23, 25; 9.4), blessing is promised to the kings who follow David in walking before Yahweh, again with the emphasis on faithfulness and obedience, and the mention of God's commands.

A predominant number of instances of walking 'after' refer to worshipping alien gods (generally, e.g., Deut. 6.14; 8.19; Baal, e.g., 1 Kgs. 18.18, 21; Ashtoreth, 1 Kgs. 11.5; the host of heaven, Jer. 8.2), and are chiefly Deuteronomistic. The only texts which link 'walking after' with Yahweh stress keeping his commandments. Deuteronomy 13.5[4] is a good example. 'You shall walk after the LORD your God and fear him, and keep his commandments and obey his voice, and you shall serve him and cleave to him.' Similar is 1 Kings 14.8, in which the prophet Ahijah tells the mother of Abijah that her son will die because Jeroboam has not been like David, 'who kept my commandments and followed me with all his heart, doing only that which was right in my eyes'. Elijah on Mount Carmel contrasts walking after Yahweh and walking after Baal (1 Kgs. 18.21). In 2 Kings 23.3 (= 2 Chron. 34.31) Josiah's covenant with Yahweh is 'to walk after the LORD and keep his commandments and his testimonies and his statutes, with all his heart and all his soul, to perform the words of this covenant that were written in this book'. That walking after Yahweh meant obeying his commandments could hardly be plainer.[4]

This leaves the considerable number of instances where the walking is 'in the way of Yahweh'. Again, almost all of these explain the meaning of the metaphor as keeping Yahweh's laws. Deuteronomy 5.33 has already been quoted as making it plain that what is meant is obeying God's commands. In many places a similar link between walking in Yahweh's ways and obeying his laws can be found.[5] Those who argue that walking in God's ways means imitating him might find some support in 1 Samuel 8.3, 5, where the elders complain to Samuel that his sons 'do not walk in your ways'. Here the meaning is that the sons are not behaving as Samuel did, and the narrator tells the readers that they 'turned aside after gain', taking bribes and perverting

[4] The only other references are Jer. 2.2 and Hos 11.10. It should be noted that 'to walk' is commonly followed by the preposition *beth* with one of the many words for law or commandment (see DCH, 550).
[5] Deut. 8.6; 13.6[5]; 1 Kgs. 2.3; 8.36; 11.33; Isa. 30.21; Jer. 7.23 may be singled out, but there are others where keeping the law is set alongside walking in God's way, such as Deut. 11.22; 26.17; 30.16; Josh. 22.5; 1 Kgs. 3.14; 8.58; 11.38; Isa. 42.24; Zech. 3.7.

justice.[6] Initially Judges 2.22 appears parallel to this: God declares that he is leaving some Canaanites in the land 'that by them I may test Israel, whether they will take care to walk in the way of the LORD as their fathers did', but the similarity is not quite exact, since what is being compared is the obedience of the ancestors and the present generation to God's commands. Although Josiah 'walked in all the way of David his father, and he did not turn aside to the right hand or to the left', this is explained as '[doing] what was right in the eyes of the LORD' (2 Kgs. 22.2). It appears that sons can imitate fathers (or perhaps more accurately, act in the same way as their fathers acted), but not even the king, still less ordinary human beings, can imitate God.

The analysis of *derek* offered by DCH is no more authoritative, of course, than the scholar who compiled that part of the dictionary, but it is suggestive that 'the way of Yahweh' is presented as: (a) 'commandments of Y.' and (b) 'activity of Y.', with far more texts listed under the first.[7] HALOT offers only a selection of references, but in much the same way gives the translations: 'God's behaviour, action (Deut. 32.4; Ezek. 18.25, 29; Hos. 14.10[9]; Job 26.14; 40.19), activity' (Prov. 8.22) and 'the conduct required by God' (Gen. 18.19; Jer. 5.4; Deut. 9.16; Ps. 18.22[21]; 25.4; 1 Kgs. 2.3).[8] Singling out the last set of passages is important as showing that the way or ways are commanded by God, without any hint that human beings are to imitate his character or actions.

There is no question about *derek* meaning 'manner, custom, behaviour', to quote the translations offered by HALOT, and it might be a useful exercise to trace all the passages where the word has this sense to discover what actions were regarded as important for ethics. What seems clear from this discussion, however, is that no support for the idea of the imitation of God can be drawn from the idea of walking with God or in his ways.

---

[6] Cf. the frequent complaint that kings of the Northern Kingdom walked in the way of the kings of Israel (2 Kgs. 8.18; 16.3; cf. 1 Kgs. 15.26, 34; 16.2, 19, 26) or of the house of Ahab (2 Kgs. 8.27).

[7] DCH II, 466.

[8] HALOT, 1, 232. The relevant entries in DOTTE for all the words and phrases are disappointingly meagre and conventional.

BOOKS AND ARTICLES REFERRED TO IN THE TEXT

ABRAHAM, William J., *The Divine Inspiration of Holy Scripture* (OUP, 1981) [*Inspiration*].

Abraham, William J., *Divine Revelation and the Limits of Historical Criticism* (OUP, 1982) [*Revelation*].

Aharoni, Y., 'Animals mentioned in the Bible' (*Osiris* 5, 1938, 461–478) ['Animals'].

Ahlström, Gösta W., *A History of Ancient Palestine from the Palaeolithic Period to Alexander's Conquest* (JSOTSup 146, Sheffield Academic Press, 1993) [*History*].

Aitken, Kenneth T., *Proverbs* (DSB, Saint Andrew Press/Westminster Press, 1986).

Albertz, Rainer, *A History of Israelite Religion in the Old Testament Period*. Vol. 1, *From the Beginnings to the End of the Exile*, Vol. II, *From the Exile to the Maccabees* (SCM Press, 1994) [*History*].

Albright, W. F., *Yahweh and the Gods of Canaan* (Doubleday, 1968).

Alt, Albrecht, 'The Origins of Israelite Law', Eng. trans. in *Essays on Old Testament History and Religion* (Basil Blackwell, 1966, reprint Sheffield Academic Press, 1989) ['Origins'].

Alt, Albrecht, 'Das Verbot des Diebstahls im Dekalog' in *Kleine Schriften zur Geschichte des Volkes Israel* I (Munich, 1953, 333–340).

Alter, Robert and Kermode, Frank, eds., *The Literary Guide to the Bible* (Collins, 1987) [*Literary Guide*].

Andersen, Francis I. and Freedman, David Noel, *Hosea* (AB, Doubleday, 1986).

Andersen, Francis I. and Freedman, David Noel, *Amos* (AB, Doubleday, 1989).

Anderson, Arnold A., 'Law in the Old Testament: Laws Concerning Adultery' in Barnabas Lindars, ed., *Law and Religion* (James Clarke, 1988, 13–19) ['Law'].

Anderson, Arnold A., *2 Samuel* (WBC 11, Word Books, 1989).

André, G., *ṭāmē'* (*TDOT* V, 330–331, 332–342).

Atkinson, David J. and Field, David H., eds., *New Dictionary of Christian Ethics and Pastoral Theology* (IVP, 1995) [*NDCEPT*].

Averbeck, Richard E., *'āšām* (*NIDOTTE* 1, 557–566).

Averbeck, Richard E., *ḥaṭṭā't* (*NIDOTTE* 2, 93–103).

BACH, Alice, 'Rereading the Body Politic: Women, Violence and Judges 21' in Brenner, Athalya, ed., *The Feminist Companion to the Bible (Second Series) 4. Judges* (Sheffield Academic Press, 1999), 143–159 ['The Body Politic'].

Bainton, Roland, *Christian Attitudes Toward War and Peace* (Abingdon, 1960) [*War and Peace*].

Ball, Edward, ed., *In Search of True Wisdom: Essays in Old Testament Interpretation in Honour of Ronald E. Clements* (JSOTSup 300, Sheffield Academic Press, 1999) [*True Wisdom*].

Bar-Ilan, Meir, *Some Jewish Women in Antiquity* (Brown Judaic Studies 317, Scholars Press, 1998) [*Some Jewish Women*].

Barbour, Ian, *Ethics in an Age of Technology: The Gifford Lectures 1989–1991*, Vol. II (SCM Press, 1992) [*Ethics*].

Barbour, R. S., ed., *The Kingdom of God and Human Society* (T&T Clark, 1993, 13–27).

Barr, James, *The Bible in the Modern World* (SCM, 1973) [*Bible in Modern World*].

Barr, James, *Holy Scripture: Canon, Authority, Criticism* (Clarendon Press, 1983) [*Holy Scripture*].

Barr, James, 'Man and Nature – The Ecological Controversy and the Old Testament' (*BJRULM* 55, 1972, 9–32).

Barr, James, 'Revelation' (*HDB*, 1963, 847–849).

Barrett, Lois, *The Way God Fights* (Herald Press, 1987).

Bartlett, David L. *The Shape of Scriptural Authority* (Fortress Press, 1983) [*Scriptural Authority*].

Barton, John, *Amos's Oracles against the Nations* (SOTS Monograph Series 6, CUP, 1980) [*Amos's Oracles*].

Barton, John, 'Approaches to Ethics in the Old Testament' in John Rogerson, ed., *Beginning Old Testament Study* (SPCK, 1983, 113–130) ['Approaches to Ethics'].

Barton, John, 'Authority of Scripture' (*DBI*, 69–72).

Barton, John, 'The Basis of Ethics in the Hebrew Bible' in Knight, D. A., ed., *Ethics and Politics in the Hebrew Bible* (*Semeia* 66, Scholars Press, 1995, 17–20) ['Basis'].

Barton, John, ed., *The Cambridge Companion to Biblical Interpretation* (CUP, 1998).

Barton, John, *Ethics and the Old Testament* (SCM Press, 1998) [*Ethics*]

Barton, John, 'Ethics in Isaiah of Jerusalem' (*JTS* NS 32, 1981, 1–18) ['Ethics in Isaiah'].

Barton, John, 'Natural Law and Poetic Justice in the Old Testament' (*JTS* NS 30, 1979, 1–14) ['Natural Law'].

Barton, John and Muddiman, John, eds., *The Oxford Bible Commentary* (OUP, forthcoming) [*OBC*].

Barton, John, *People of the Book? The Authority of the Bible in Christianity* (SPCK, 1988).

Barton, John, *The Spirit and the Letter: Studies in the Biblical Canon* (SPCK, 1997) [*Spirit and Letter*].

Barton, John, 'Understanding Old Testament Ethics' (*JSOT* 9, 1978, 44–64) ['Understanding'].

Barton, Stephen C., 'Biblical Hermeneutics and the Family' in Barton, Stephen C., ed., *The Family In Theological Perspective* (T&T Clark, 1996, 3–23) ['Biblical Hermeneutics'].

Barton, Stephen C., ed., *The Family In Theological Perspective* (T&T Clark, 1996) [*The Family*].

Bauckham, Richard, *The Bible In Politics: How to Read the Bible Politically* (SPCK, 1989) [*Bible In Politics*].

Bauckham, Richard, 'First Steps to a Theology of Nature' (*EvQ* 58, 1986, 229–244) ['Theology of Nature'].

Bechtel, Lyn M., 'A Feminist Reading of Genesis 19.1–11' in Brenner, Athalya, ed., *A Feminist Companion to the Bible (Second Series) 1. Genesis* (Sheffield Academic Press, 1998, 108–128) ['Genesis 19.1–11'].

Bechtel, Lyn M., 'Genesis 2.4b–3.24: A Myth about Human Maturation' (*JSOT* 67, 1995, 3–26) ['Human Maturation'].

Bechtel, Lyn M., 'Rethinking the Interpretation of Genesis 2.4b–3.24' in Brenner, Athalya, ed., *The Feminist Companion to the Bible 2. Genesis* (Sheffield Academic Press, 1993, 77–117) ['Rethinking Genesis 2.4b–3.24'].

Bechtel, Lyn M., 'Shame as a Sanction of Social Control in Biblical Israel: Judicial, Political and Social Shaming' (*JSOT* 49, 1991, 47–76) ['Shame as a Sanction'].

Bechtel, Lyn M., 'What if Dinah is not Raped? (Genesis 34)' (*JSOT* 62, 1994, 19–36) ['Dinah'].

Bellis, Alice Ogden, *Helpmates, Harlots, and Heroes: Women's Stories in the Hebrew Bible* (Westminster John Knox Press, 1994) [*Helpmates*].

Beyerlin, Walter, ed., *Near Eastern Religious Texts Relating to the Old Testament* (SCM Press, 1978) [*NERT*].

Birch, Bruce C., 'Moral Agency, Community, and the Character of God in the Hebrew Bible' (*Semeia* 66, Scholars Press, 1995, 23–41) ['Moral Agency'].

Birch, Bruce C., 'Old Testament Foundations for Peacemaking in the Nuclear Era' (*The Christian Century* 102, 1985, 1115–1119) ['Peacemaking'].

Bird, Phyllis A., 'Images of Woman in the Old Testament' in Gottwald, Norman K., ed., *The Bible and Liberation: Political and Social Hermeneutics* (Orbis Books, 1983, 252–288) ['Images of Woman'].

Bird, Phyllis, 'The Place of Women in the Israelite Cultus' in Miller, P. D., Hanson, P. D. and McBride, S. D., eds., *Ancient Israelite Religion: Essays in Honor of Frank Moore Cross* (Fortress Press, 1987, 397–419) ['Women in the Cultus'].

Bird, Phyllis, 'Women: Old Testament' in *ABD* 6.951–957 ['Women (OT)'].

Blenkinsopp, Joseph, 'The Family in First Temple Israel' in Perdue, Leo G., Blenkinsopp, Joseph, Collins, John J. and Meyers, Carol, *Families in Ancient Israel* (Westminster John Knox Press, 1997) ['The Family'].

Bodenheimer, F. S., *Animals and Man in Bible Lands* (E. J. Brill, 1960) [*Animals*].

Bodenheimer, F. S., *HaHai be-Artsot ha-Mikrah* (2 vols., 1951, 1956) [*HaHai*].

Boecker, Hans Jochen, *Law and the Administration of Justice in the Old Testament and the Ancient East* (Augsburg Publishing House, 1980) [*Law*].

Boström, Lennart, *The God of the Sages: The Portrayal of God in the Book of Proverbs* (*CB*, OT Series 29, Almqvist & Wiksell, 1990) [*God of the Sages*].

Botterweck, G. Johannes and Ringgren, Helmer, eds., *Theological Dictionary of the Old Testament* (Eerdmans, 1974–) [*TDOT*]

Bourdillon, M. F. C. and Fortes, Meyer, eds., *Sacrifice* (Academic Press, 1980)

Bourke, V. J., 'Natural Law' in Macquarrie, John, ed., *Dictionary of Christian Ethics* (SCM Press, 1967).

Bradley, Ian, *God is Green: Christianity and the Environment* (Darton, Longman & Todd, 1990) [*God is Green*].

Brenner, Athalya, ed., *A Feminist Companion to the Bible 1. The Song of Songs* (Sheffield Academic Press, 1993).

Brenner, Athalya, ed., *A Feminist Companion to the Bible 2. Genesis* (Sheffield Academic Press, 1993).

Brenner, Athalya, ed., *A Feminist Companion to the Bible 3. Ruth* (Sheffield Academic Press, 1993).

Brenner, Athalya, ed., *A Feminist Companion to the Bible 4. Judges* (Sheffield Academic Press, 1993).

Brenner, Athalya, ed., *A Feminist Companion to the Bible 5. Samuel and Kings* (Sheffield Academic Press, 1994) [*Samuel and Kings*].

Brenner, Athalya, ed., *A Feminist Companion to the Bible 6. Exodus to Deuteronomy* (Sheffield Academic Press, 1994).

Brenner, Athalya, ed., *A Feminist Companion to the Bible 7. Esther, Judith and Susanna* (Sheffield Academic Press, 1995).

Brenner, Athalya, ed., *A Feminist Companion to the Bible 8. The Latter Prophets* (Sheffield Academic Press, 1995).

Brenner, Athalya, ed., *A Feminist Companion to the Bible 9. Wisdom Literature* (Sheffield Academic Press, 1995).

Brenner, Athalya, ed., *A Feminist Companion to the Bible (Second Series) 1. Genesis* (Sheffield Academic Press, 1998).

Brenner, Athalya and Fontaine, Carole, eds., *A Feminist Companion to the Bible (Second Series) 2. Wisdom and Psalms* (Sheffield Academic Press, 1998).

Brenner, Athalya, ed., *A Feminist Companion to the Bible (Second Series) 3. Ruth and Esther* (Sheffield Academic Press, 1999).

Brenner, Athalya, ed., *A Feminist Companion to the Bible (Second Series) 4. Judges* (Sheffield Academic Press, 1999)

Brenner, Athalya and Van Dijk-Hemmes, Fokkelien, *On Gendering Texts: Female and Male Voices in the Hebrew Bible* (E. J. Brill, 1993).

Bright, John, *Jeremiah* (AB, Doubleday, 1965).

Brin, Gershon, 'The Formula "If He Shall Not (Do)" and the Problem of Sanctions in Biblical Law' in Wright, David P., Freedman, David Noel and Hurvitz, Avi, *Pomegranates and Golden Bells* (Eisenbrauns, 1995, 341–362) ['"If He Shall Not (Do)"'].

Brown, A., 'Feminism' (*NDCEPT*, 380–382).

Brown, Francis, Driver, S. R. and Briggs, Charles A., eds. *A Hebrew and English Lexicon of the Old Testament with an Appendix Containing the Biblical Aramaic* (Clarendon Press, corrected impression 1952) [BDB].

Brown, Raymond E., *The Critical Meaning of the Bible* (Paulist Press, 1981) [*Critical Meaning*].

Brownlee, William H., *Ezekiel 1–19* (WBC 28, Word Books, 1986).

Brueggemann, Walter, *The Prophetic Imagination* (Fortress Press, 1978) [*Imagination*].

Brueggemann, Walter, *Theology of the Old Testament: Testimony, Dispute, Advocacy* (Fortress Press, 1997) [*Theology*].

Budd, Philip J., *Leviticus* (NCBC, Marshall Pickering/Eerdmans, 1996).

Bultmann, Christoph, *Der Fremde in antiken Juda: Eine Untersuchung zum sozialen Typenbegriff <ger> und seinem Bedeutungswander in der alttestamentlichen Gesetzgebung* (Vandenhoeck & Ruprecht, 1992) [*Der Fremde*].

Butler, Trent C., *Joshua* (WBC 7, Word Books, 1983).

CAMP, Claudia V., *Wisdom and the Feminine in the Book of Proverbs* (Bible and Literature 11, Almond [JSOT Press], 1985) [*Wisdom and the Feminine*].

Carley, Keith, 'Psalm 8: An Apology for Domination' in Habel, Norman C., ed., *Readings from the Perspective of Earth*, 111–124 ['Psalm 8'].

Carmichael, Calum, 'Biblical Laws of Talion', *Hebrew Annual Review* 9, 1985, 107–126) ['Talion'].

Carroll R., M. Daniel, *dal* (*NIDOTTE* 1, 950–954).

Carroll, Robert P., *Jeremiah* (SCM Press, 1986).

Carroll, Robert P., 'War', in Smith, Morton and Hoffmann, R. Joseph, *What the Bible Really Says* (Prometheus Books, 1989) ['War'].

Carroll, Robert P., *Wolf in the Sheepfold: The Bible as a Problem for Christianity* (SPCK, 1991) [*Wolf*].

Channing, J. H., ed., *Abortion and the Sanctity of Human Life* (Paternoster Press, 1985) [*Abortion*].

Chapman, Mark D.,'"In Honesty of Preaching" 2. Colenso and the Bible' (*ET* 111, 1999–2000, 256–259) ['Colenso'].

Childs, Brevard S. *Exodus* (SCM Press, 1974).

Childs, Brevard S., *Old Testament Theology in a Canonical Context* (SCM Press, 1985) [*OT Theology*].

Chirichigno, Greg, 'A Theological Investigation of Motivation in Old Testament Law' (*JETS* 24, 1981, 303–313) ['Motivation'].

Clements, Ronald E., 'Christian Ethics and the Old Testament' (*Modern Churchman* NS 26, 1984, 13–26) ['Christian Ethics'].

Clements, Ronald E., *Exodus* (CBC, CUP, 1972).

Clements, Ronald E., 'Poverty and the Kingdom of God – an Old Testament View' in Barbour, R. S., ed., *The Kingdom of God and Human Society* (T&T Clark, 1993, 13–27) ['Poverty'].

Clements, Ronald E., *Prophecy and Covenant* (SBT 43, SCM Press, 1965).

Clements, Ronald E., *Prophecy and Tradition* (Growing Points in Theology, Basil Blackwell, 1978).

Clements, Ronald E., 'The Wolf Shall Live with the Lamb: Reading Isaiah 11:6–9 Today' in Harland, Peter J. and Robert Hayward, eds., *New Heaven and New Earth: Prophecy and the Millennium* (E. J. Brill, 1999) ['The Wolf'].

Clifford, Richard J., *Proverbs: A Commentary* (OTL, Westminster John Knox Press, 1999).

Clines, David J. A., ed., Elwolde, John, exec. ed., *The Dictionary of Classical Hebrew* (8 vols., Sheffield Academic Press, 1993–) [*DCH*].

Clines, David J. A., 'The Ten Commandments, Reading from Left to Right', in Davies, Jon, Harvey, Graham, and Watson, Wilfred G. E., *Words Remembered, Texts Renewed. Essays in Honour of John F. A. Sawyer* (JSOTSup 195, Sheffield Academic Press, 1995, 96–112) ['The Ten Commandments'], also, revised, in *Interested Parties: The Ideology of Writers and Readers of the Hebrew Bible* (JSOTSup 205, Sheffield Academic Press, 1995, 26–45) ['The Ten Commandments', rev.].

Clines, David J. A., 'What Does Eve Do to Help?' in David J. A. Clines, *What Does Eve Do to Help? and Other Readerly Questions to the Old Testament* (JSOTSup 94, Sheffield Academic Press, 1990, 25–48) ['Eve'].

Clines, David J. A., *What Does Eve Do to Help? and Other Readerly Questions to the Old Testament* (JSOTSup 94, Sheffield Academic Press, 1990).

Coggins, Richard J. and Houlden, J. Leslie, eds., *A Dictionary of Biblical Interpretation* (SCM Press, 1990) [*DBI*].

Coggins, Richard J., 'The Exile: History and Ideology' (*ET*, 110, 1998–99, 389–393) ['The Exile'].

Coggins, Richard J., Phillips, Anthony and Knibb, Michael, eds. *Israel's Prophetic Tradition: Essays in Honour of Peter Ackroyd* (CUP, 1982).

Coggins, Richard J., 'The Old Testament and the Poor' (*ET* 99, 1987–88, 11–14) ['The Poor'].

Colenso, J. W., *The Pentateuch and the Book of Joshua Critically Examined* (Longmans, 1962).

Collins, Adela Yarbro, ed., *Feminist Perspectives on Biblical Scholarship* (Scholars Press, 1985).

Collins, John J., *Jewish Wisdom in the Hellenistic Age* (T&T Clark, 1998) [*Jewish Wisdom*].

Committee on Bible Translating, *The New Testament, Psalms and Proverbs, New International Version: Inclusive Language Edition* (Hodder & Stoughton, 1995) ['Preface'].

Conn, H. M., 'Feminist Theology' (*NDT*, 255–258).

Countryman, L. William, *Dirt, Greed and Sex: Sexual Ethics in the New Testament* (SCM Press, 1988) [*Dirt*].

Cox, Harvey, *The Secular City* (Macmillan, 1965).

Craigie, Peter C., *The Book of Deuteronomy* (NICOT, Eerdmans, 1976) [*Deuteronomy*].

Craigie, Peter C., *The Problem of War in the Old Testament* (Eerdmans, 1978) [*War*].

Crenshaw, James L., *Ecclesiastes: A Commentary* (OTL, SCM Press, 1988).

Crenshaw, James L., *Old Testament Wisdom: An Introduction* (revised and enlarged edn., Westminister John Knox Press, 1998) [*Wisdom*].

Crim, Keith, ed., *The Interpreter's Dictionary of the Bible*, Supplementary Volume (Abingdon Press, 1976) [*IDBSup*].

Cross, Frank Moore, *Canaanite Myth and Hebrew Epic: Essays in the History of the Religion of Israel* (Harvard University Press, 1973) [*Canaanite Myth*].

Cross, Frank Moore, 'The Redemption of Nature' (*The Princeton Seminary Bulletin* 10, 1988, 94–104) ['Redemption'].

Crüseman, Frank, *Bewahrung der Freiheit: Das Thema des Dekalogs in socialgeschichtlicher Perspektive* (Chr. Kaiser, 1983) [*Bewahrung der Freiheit*].

Crüsemann, Frank, *The Torah: Theology and Social History of Old Testament Law* (Fortress Press/T&T Clark, 1996) [*Torah*].

Curran, Charles E. and McCormick, Richard A., *The Use of Scripture in Moral Theology* (Paulist Press, 1984) [*Use of Scripture*].

DAUBE, David, 'The Culture of Deuteronomy' (*Orita* 3, 1969, 27–52).

Daube, David, *Studies in Biblical Law* (CUP, 1947, reprint Ktav, 1969) [*Biblical Law*].

Daube, David, 'To Be Found Doing Wrong' (in *Studi in onore de Volterra*, Rome, 1969, 1–13).

Davies, Andrew, *Double Standards in Isaiah: Re-evaluating Prophetic Ethics and Divine Justice* (E. J. Brill, 2000) [*Double Standards*].

Davies, Douglas, 'An Interpretation of Sacrifice in Leviticus' (*ZAW* 98, 1977, 388–398, reprinted in Lang, Bernhard, ed., *Anthropological Approaches to the Old Testament*, Fortress Press/SPCK, 1985, 151–162) ['Sacrifice in Leviticus'].

Davies, Eryl W., 'Ethics of the Hebrew Bible: The Problem of Methodology' (*Semeia* 66, Scholars Press, 1995, 43–53) ['Ethics'].

Davies, Eryl W., *Numbers* (NCBC, Eerdmans, 1995).

Davies, Eryl W., *Prophecy and Ethics: Isaiah and the Ethical Traditions of Israel* (JSOTSup 16, Sheffield Academic Press, 1981).

Davies, Eryl W., 'Walking in God's Ways: The Concept of *Imitatio Dei* in the Old Testament' in Ball, Edward, ed., *True Wisdom* (JSOTSup 300, Sheffield Academic Press, 1999, 99–115) ['Walking'].

Davies, Philip R., *In Search of 'Ancient Israel'* (JSOTSup 148, Sheffield Academic Press, 1992) [*Ancient Israel*].

Day, J., *Psalms* (Old Testament Guides, Sheffield Academic Press, 1990).

Day, J., *Molech: A God of Human Sacrifice in the Old Testament* (CUP, 1989).

De Vaux, Roland, *Ancient Israel: Its Life and Institutions*, trans. McHugh, John (Darton, Longman & Todd, 1961) [*Ancient Israel*].

De Vaux, Roland, *Studies in Old Testament Sacrifice* (University of Wales Press, 1964) [*Sacrifice*].

Dearman, J. Andrew, 'The Problem of War in the Old Testament: War, Peace, and Justice' (*Austin Seminary Bulletin* 99, 1983, 5–14) ['Problem of War'].

Deidun, Tom, 'The Bible and Christian Ethics' in Hoose, Bernard, ed., *Christian Ethics: An Introduction* (Cassell, 1998, 3–46).

Deist, Ferdinand E., Edited with a Preface by Robert P. Carroll, *The Material Culture of the Bible: An Introduction* (The Biblical Seminar 70, Sheffield Academic Press, 2000).

Dell, Katharine J., 'The Use of Animal Imagery in the Psalms and Wisdom Literature of Ancient Israel' (*SJTh* 53, 2000, 275–291) ['Animal Imagery'].

Dennis, Trevor, *Sarah Laughed: Women's Voices in the Old Testament* (SPCK, 1994) [*Sarah Laughed*].

Dobbie, Robert, 'Sacrifice and Morality in the Old Testament' (*ET* 70, 1958–59, 297–300) ['Sacrifice and Morality'].

Domeris, W. R., 'ebyōn (NIDOTTE 1, 228–232).

Domeris, W. R., dk' (NIDOTTE 1, 943–946).

Domeris, W. R., 'ānāw/'ānī (NIDOTTE 3, 454–464).

Domeris, W. R., 'šr (NIDOTTE 3, 558–561).

Domeris, W. R., rwš (NIDOTTE 3, 1085–1087).

Donald, T., 'The Semantic Field of Rich and Poor in the Wisdom Literature of Hebrew and Accadian' (Oriens Antiquus 3, 1964, 27–41) ['Rich and Poor'].

Douglas, Mary, Leviticus as Literature (OUP, 1999) [Leviticus].

Douglas, Mary, Purity and Danger: An Analysis of the Concepts of Pollution and Taboo (Routledge & Kegan Paul, 1966) [Purity and Danger].

Downing, F. Gerald, 'Revelation' (DBI, 591–593).

Driver, G. R. and Miles, John C., The Babylonian Laws (2 vols., Clarendon Press, 1952, 1955).

Driver, G. R., 'Birds in the Old Testament' (PEQ 87, 1955, 5–20, 129–140) ['Birds'].

Driver, John, How Christians Made Peace with War (Herald Press, 1988) [Peace with War].

Driver, S. R., Deuteronomy (ICC, T&T Clark, 1895).

Dulles, Avery, Models of Revelation (Doubleday, 1983) [Revelation].

Dumbrell, W. J., '"In those Days there Was No King in Israel; Every Man Did what Was Right in his Own Eyes." The Purpose of the Book of Judges Reconsidered' (JSOT 25, 1983, 23–33).

Dumbrell, W. J., 'ānāw/'ānī (NIDOTTE, 3, 454–464).

Durham, John I., Exodus (WBC 3, Word Books, 1987).

Eaton, J. H., The Circle of Creation: Animals in the Light of the Bible (SCM Press, 1995) [Circle of Creation].

Eaton, J. H., Kingship and the Psalms (SCM Press, 1976, 2nd edn. Sheffield Academic Press, 1986) [Kingship].

Eichrodt, Walther, Ezekiel: A Commentary (OTL, SCM Press, 1970).

Eichrodt, Walther, Theology of the Old Testament, Vol. I (SCM Press, 1961), Vol. II (SCM Press, 1967) [Theology].

Elford, R. John and Markham, Ian S., eds., The Middle Way: Theology, Politics and Economics in the Later Thought of R. H. Preston (SCM Press, 2000) [Middle Way].

Emmerson, Grace I., 'Women in Ancient Israel' in Clements, R. E., ed., The World of Ancient Israel: Sociological, Anthropological and Political Perspectives: Essays by Members of the Society for Old Testament Study (CUP, 1989, pp. 371–394).

Engelhard, David H., 'The Lord's Motivated Concern for the Underprivileged' (Calvin Theological Journal 15, 1980, 5–26) ['Motivated Concern'].

Engelken, Karen, *Frauen im Alten Israel: Eine begriffsgeschichtliche und sozialrechtliche Studie zur Stellung der Frau im Alten Testament* (BWANT, Seventh Series, 10, Kohlhammer, 1990) [*Frauen*].

Eslinger, Lyle and Taylor, Glen, eds., *Ascribe to the Lord: Biblical and other studies in memory of Peter C. Craigie* (JSOTSup 67, Sheffield Academic Press, 1988).

Evans, C. F., 'Difficulties in Using the Bible for Christian Ethics' (*Modern Churchman* NS 26, 1984, 27–34) ['Difficulties'].

Evans-Pritchard, Edward E., *Nuer Religion* (Clarendon Press, 1956).

FELIKS, J., *The Animal World of the Bible* (1962) [*Animal World*].

Fensham, F. Charles, *The Books of Ezra and Nehemiah* (NICOT, Eerdmans, 1982) [*Ezra and Nehemiah*].

Fensham, F. Charles, 'Widow, Orphan, and the Poor in Ancient Near Eastern Legal and Wisdom Literature' (*JNES* 21, 1962, 129–139) ['Widow'].

Ferguson, Sinclair B. and Wright, David F., eds., *New Dictionary of Theology* (IVP, 1988) [*NDT*].

Fewell, Danna Nolan, 'Feminist Reading of the Hebrew Bible: Affirmation, Resistance and Transformation' (*JSOT* 39, 1987, 77–87) ['Feminist Reading'].

Finkelstein, J. J., *The Ox That Gored* (*Transactions of the American Philosophical Society*, 71, pt. 2, The American Philosophical Society, 1981).

Fiorenza, Elisabeth Schüssler, 'Feminist Hermeneutics' in *ABD* 2.783–791.

Fiorenza, Elisabeth Schüssler and Copeland, Mary Shawn, eds., *Violence Against Women* (*Concilium*, 1994/1, SCM Press/Orbis Books).

Firmage, Edwin B., Weiss, Bernard G. and Welch, John W., eds., *Religion and Law: Biblical-Judaic and Islamic Perspectives* (Eisenbrauns, 1990).

Fischer, Irmgard, '"Go and Suffer Oppression!" said God's Messenger to Hagar: Repression of Women in Biblical Texts' in Fiorenza, Elisabeth Schüssler and Copeland, Mary Shawn, eds., *Violence Against Women* (*Concilium*, 1994/1, SCM Press/Orbis Books, 75–82) ['"Go and Suffer Oppression!"'].

Fohrer, Georg, *Introduction to the Old Testament* (Abingdon Press/SPCK, 1968) [*Introduction*].

Fontaine, Carole R., '"Many Devices" (Qoheleth 7.23–8.1): Qoheleth, Misogyny and the *Malleus Maleficarum*' in Brenner, Athalya and Fontaine, Carole, eds., *A Feminist Companion to the Bible (Second Series) 2. Wisdom and Psalms* (Sheffield Academic Press, 1998, 136–168) ['"Many Devices"'].

Fowler, H. W., *A Dictionary of Modern English Usage* (2nd edn., revised by Ernest Gowers, Clarendon Press, 1965) [*Modern English Usage*].

Fox, Michael V., *A Time to Tear Down and A Time to Build Up: A Reading of Ecclesiastes* (Eerdmans, 1999) [*A Time to Tear Down*].

Frankfort, Henri, Frankfort, H. A., Wilson, John A. and Jacobsen, Thorkild, *Before Philosophy: An Essay on Speculative Thought in the Ancient Near East* (Penguin, 1949), original edition *The Intellectual Adventure of Ancient Man* (University of Chicago Press, 1946).

Freedman, David Noel, Herion, Gary A., Graf, David F. and Pleins, John David, eds., *The Anchor Bible Dictionary* (6 vols., Doubleday, 1992) [*ABD*].

Freedman, David Noel, 'The Nine Commandments: The Secret Progress of Israel's Sins' (*Bible Review* 5, 1989, 28–37, 42) ['The Nine Commandments'].

Freudenthal, Gad, ed., *AIDS in Jewish Thought and Law* (Ktav, 1998) [*AIDS*].

Frymer-Kensky, Tikva, 'Sex and Sexuality' in *ABD* 5. 1144–1146 ['Sex'].

Frymer-Kensky, Tikva, 'Tit for Tat: The Principle of Equal Retribution in Near Eastern Law' (*BA* 43, 1980, 230–234) ['Tit for Tat'].

Fuchs, Esther, 'The Literary Characterization of Mothers and Sexual Politics in the Hebrew Bible' in Collins, Adela Yarbro, ed., *Feminist Perspectives on Biblical Scholarship* (Scholars Press, 1985, 117–136) ['Mothers'].

Fuchs, Esther, 'Marginalization, Ambiguity, Silencing: The Story of Jephthah's Daughter' in Brenner, Athalya, ed., *The Feminist Companion to the Bible 4. Judges* (Sheffield Academic Press, 1993, 116–130) ['Marginalization'].

Fuchs, Esther, 'Who is Hiding the Truth? Deceptive Women and Biblical Androcentricism' in Collins, Adela Yarbro, ed., *Feminist Perspectives on Biblical Scholarship* (Scholars Press, 1985, 137–144).

GAMMIE, John G., *Holiness in Israel* (Fortress Press, 1989) [*Holiness*].

Gamoran, Hillel, 'The Biblical Law against Loans on Interest' (*JNES* 30, 1971, 127–134) ['Loans on Interest'].

Geach, Peter, *The Virtues* (CUP, 1977).

Gelin, Albert, *The Poor of Yahweh* (The Liturgical Press, 1964).

Gemser, B., 'The Importance of the Motive Clause in Old Testament Law' (*VTSup* 1, 1953, 50–66) ['Motive Clause'].

Gerlemann, G., 'Der Nicht-Mensch. Erwägungen zur hebräischen Wurzel *NBL*' (*VT* 24, 1974, 147–158).

Gerstenberger, Erhard S., *Leviticus: A Commentary* (OTL, Westminster John Knox Press, 1996) [*Leviticus*].

Gerstenberger, Erhard S. *Psalms: Part 1 with an Introduction to Cultic Poetry* (FOTL XIV, Eerdmans, 1988) [*Pslams: Part 1*].

Gibson, J. C. L., ed., *Canaanite Myths and Legends* (T&T Clark, 1978) [*Canaanite Myths*].

Giles, Kevin, 'The Biblical Argument for Slavery: Can the Bible Mislead? A Case Study in Hermeneutics' (*EvQ* LXVI, 1994, 3–17) ['Slavery'].

Gillingham, Sue 'The Poor in the Psalms' (*ET* 100, 1988–89, 15–19) ['The Poor'].

Gilmer, Harry W., *The If-You Form in Israelite Law* (SBLDiss 15, Scholars Press, 1975) [*If-You Form*].

Gnuse, Robert, *The Authority of the Bible: Theories of Inspiration, Revelation and the Canon of Scripture* (Paulist Press, 1985) [*Authority*].

Gnuse, Robert, 'Authority of the Bible' (*DBI, A–J*, 87–91).

Gnuse, Robert, *You Shall Not Steal: Community and Property in Biblical Tradition* (Orbis Books, 1985).

Goldingay, John, *Approaches to Old Testament Interpretation* (IVP, 1981, rev. edn. 1990) [*Approaches*].

Goldingay, John, *Theological Diversity and the Authority of the Old Testament* (Eerdmans, 1987) [*Theological Diversity*].

Golka, Friedemann W., *The Leopard's Spots: Biblical and African Wisdom in Proverbs* (T&T Clark, 1993) [*Leopard's Spots*].

Good, Edwin M., 'Capital Punishment and Its Alternatives in Ancient Near Eastern Law' (*Stanford Law Review* 19, 1967, 947–977) ['Capital Punishment'].

Good, Robert M., 'The Just War in Ancient Israel' (*JBL* 104, 1985, 385–400) ['Just War'].

Gordis, Robert, 'Job and Ecology (and the Significance of Job 40:15)' (*Harvard Annual Revue* 9, 1985, 189–202) ['Job and Ecology'].

Gottwald, Norman K., ed., *The Bible and Liberation: Political and Social Hermeneutics* (Orbis Books, 1983, revised edn. SPCK, 1993).

Gottwald, Norman, 'From Tribal Existence to Empire: The Socio-Historical Context for the Rise of the Hebrew Prophets' in Thomas, J. Mark and Visik, Vernon, eds., *God and Capitalism: A Prophetic Critique of Market Economy* (A-R Editions, 1991, 11–29) ['Tribal Existence'].

Gottwald, Norman K., '"Holy War" in Deuteronomy: Analysis and Critique' (*RevExp* 61, 1964, 296–310) ['"Holy War"'].

Gottwald, Norman K., 'Sociology (Ancient Israel)' in *ABD* 6.79–89 ['Sociology'].

Gottwald, Norman K., *The Tribes of Yahweh: A Sociology of Religion of Liberated Israel 1250–1050 B.C.E.* (SCM Press, 1980) [*Tribes of Yahweh*].

Gottwald, Norman K., 'War, Holy' in *IDBSup*, 942–944.

Gowan, Donald E., *Reclaiming the Old Testament for the Christian Pulpit* (John Knox Press, 1980) [*Reclaiming the OT*].

Gowan, Donald E., 'Reflections on the Motive Clauses in Old Testament Law' in Hadidian, Dikran Y., ed., *Intergerim Parietis Septum (Eph. 2:14)* (Pickwick Press, 1981, 111–127) ['Motive Clauses'].

Gowan, Donald E. 'Wealth and Poverty in the Old Testament: The Case of the Widow, the Orphan, and the Sojourner' (*Interpretation* 41, 1987, 341–353) ['Wealth and Poverty'].

Grabbe, Lester L., *Judaic Religion in the Second Temple Period: Belief and Practice from the Exile to Yavneh* (Routledge, 2000) [*Judaic Religion*].

Grabbe, Lester L., ed., *Can A 'History of Israel' Be Written?* (JSOTSup 245, Sheffield Academic Press, 1997).

Grabbe, Lester L., ed., *Leading Captivity Captive: 'The Exile' as History and Ideology* (JSOTSup 278, Sheffield Academic Press, 1998) [*Captivity*].

Gray, George Buchanan, *Numbers* (ICC, T&T Clark, 1903).

Gray, John, *Joshua, Judges, Ruth* (NCBC, Marshall, Morgan & Scott, 1986).

Greenberg, Moshe, *Ezekiel, 1–20* (AB 22, Doubleday, 1983).

Greenberg, Moshe, 'Some Postulates of Biblical Criminal Law' in Haran, M., ed., *Yehezkel Kaufmann Jubilee Volume* (Jerusalem, 1960, 5–28) ['Postulates'].

Greengus, Samuel, 'Law: Biblical and ANE Law' in *ABD* 4.242–252 ['Biblical and ANE Law'].

Greengus, Samuel, 'Law in the Old Testament' in *IDBSup* 532–537 ['Law'].

Gruber, Mayer I., 'Women in the Cult According to the Priestly Code' in Neusner, Jacob, Levine, Baruch and Frerichs, Ernest, eds., *Judaic Perspectives on Ancient Israel* (Fortress Press, 1987), 35–48 ['Women in the Cult'].

Gunn, David M., *The Story of King David: Genre and Interpretation* (JSOTSup 6, JSOT Press, 1978, reprint 1982) [*King David*].

HAAS, Peter J., '"Die he shall surely die". The Structure of Homicide in Biblical Law' (*Semeia* 45, Scholars Press, 1989, 67–87) ['Homicide'].

Haas, Peter J., 'The Quest for Hebrew Bible Ethics: A Jewish Response' (*Semeia* 66, Scholars Press, 1995, 151–159).

Habel, Norman C., *The Book of Job: A Commentary* (OTL, SCM Press, 1985) [*Job*].

Habel, Norman C., ed., *Readings from the Perspective of Earth* (The Earth Bible 1, Sheffield Academic Press, 2000) [*Readings*].

Habel, Norman C., 'Wisdom, Wealth and Poverty: Paradigms in the Book of Proverbs' (*Bible Bhashyam* 14, 1988, 26–49) ['Wisdom, Wealth and Poverty'].

Habel, Norman C., and Wurst, Shirley, eds., *The Earth Story in Genesis* (The Earth Bible 2, Sheffield Academic Press, 2000) [*Earth Story*].

Hallo, W. W., 'The Origins of the Sacrificial Cult: New Evidence from Mesopotamia and Israel' in Miller, P. D., Hanson, P. D. and McBride, S. D., eds., *Ancient Israelite Religion: Essays in Honor of Frank Moore Cross* (Fortress Press, 1987, 3–13) ['Sacrificial Cult'].

Hammershaimb, E., 'On the Ethics of the Old Testament Prophets (*VTS* 7, 1960, 75–101) ['Ethics of OT Prophets'].

Hanks, Thomas D., *God So Loved the Third World: The Biblical Vocabulary of Oppression* (Orbis Books, 1983) [*Vocabulary of Oppression*].

Hanson, P. D., 'War, Peace and Justice in Early Israel' (*BRev* 3, 1987, 32–45) ['War'].

Harland, Peter J. and Hayward, Robert, eds., *New Heaven and New Earth: Prophecy and the Millennium* (E. J. Brill, 1999).

Harrelson, Walter, *The Ten Commandments and Human Rights* (OBT, Fortress Press, 1980) [*The Ten Commandments*].

Harris, Rivkah, 'Women in the Ancient Near East' in *IDBSup*, 960–963 ['Women in ANE'].

Harris, Rivkah, 'Women: Mesopotamia' in *ABD* 6.947–951 ['Women (Mesopotamia)'].

Hart, H. St J., *A Foreword to the Old Testament: An Essay in Elementary Introduction* (A. & C. Black, 1951) [*Foreword*].

Hartley, John E., *The Book of Job* (NICOT, Eerdmans, 1988) [*Job*].

Harvey, A. E., *Demanding Peace: Christian Responses to War and Violence* (SCM Press, 1999).

Hastings, James, ed., rev. edn. Grant, Frederick C. and Rowley, H. H., eds. *Dictionary of the Bible* (T&T Clark, 1963) [*HDB*, 1963].

Hayes, John H., ed., *Dictionary of Biblical Interpretation* (2 vols. A–J, K–Z, Abingdon Press, 1999) [*DBI, A–J*; *DBI, K–Z*].

Hayes, John H., 'The Usage of Oracles against Foreign Nations in Ancient Israel' (*JBL* 87, 1968, 81–92) ['Oracles against Foreign Nations'].

Hayter, Mary, *The New Eve In Christ: The Use and Abuse of the Bible in the Debate about Women in the Church* (SPCK, 1987) [*New Eve*].

Helfand, Jonathan, 'The Earth Is the Lord's': Judaism and Environmental Ethics', in Hargrove, E. G., ed., *Religion and Environmental Crisis* (University of Georgia Press, 1986, 38–51).

Hermann, J., 'Das zehnte Gebot' in *Sellin-Festschrift* (Leipzig, 1927).

Hertzberg, H. W., *1 & 2 Samuel* (OTL, SCM Press, 1964).

Herzfeld, Michael, 'Honour and Shame: Problems and Comparative Analysis of Moral Systems' (*Man* 15, 1980, 339–351).

Hobbs, T. R., 'An Experiment in Militarism' in Eslinger, Lyle and Taylor, Glen, eds., *Ascribe to the Lord: Biblical and other studies in memory of Peter C. Craigie* (JSOTSup 67, Sheffield Academic Press, 1988, 457–480) ['Militarism'].

Hobbs, T. R., *2 Kings* (WBC 13, Word Books, 1983).

Hobbs, T. R., 'Reflections on "the poor" and the Old Testament' (*ET* 100, 1988–89, 291–293) ['Reflections on "the poor"'].

Hobbs, T. R., *A Time for War: A Study of Warfare in the Old Testament* (Michael Glazier, 1989) [*War*].

Hoffner, Harry A., *'almānāh* (*TDOT* I, 287–291).

Holladay, William L., *Jeremiah* (2 vols., Hermeneia, Fortress Press, 1986, 1989).

Hoose, Bernard, ed., *Christian Ethics: An Introduction* (Cassell, 1998) [*Christian Ethics*].

Hoppe, Leslie J., *Being Poor: A Biblical Study* (Glazier, 1987).

Houston, Walter, '"And let them have dominion. . . " Biblical Views of Man in Relation to the Environmental Crisis' (*Studia Biblica* 1978: I, 161–184).

Houston, Walter, *Purity and Monotheism: Clean and Unclean Animals in Biblical Law* (JSOTSup 140, Sheffield Academic Press, 1993) [*Purity and Monotheism*].

Houston, Walter, 'War and the Old Testament' (*Modern Churchman* 28, 1985, 14–21) ['War'].

Hoyles, J. Arthur, *Punishment in the Bible* (Epworth Press, 1986) [*Punishment*].

Hughes, Gerard J, 'Natural Law' in Macquarrie, John and Childress, James, eds., *A New Dictionary of Christian Ethics* (SCM Press, 1986).

Hyatt, J. P., *Exodus* (NCBC, Eerdmans/Marshall, Morgan & Scott, 1971, rev. edn. 1980).

JACKSON, Bernard S., 'Liability for Mere Intention in Early Jewish Law' (*HUCA* 42, 1971, 197–225) ['Liability'].

Jackson, Bernard S., 'Reflections on Biblical Criminal Law' (*JJS* 18, 1973, 8–38) ['Reflections'].

Jakobowits, Immanuel, 'Only a moral revolution can contain this scourge' (*The Times*, 27 December 1986, 20) ['Moral Revolution'].

Janowski, Bernd, Neumann-Gorsolke, Ute and Gleßmer, Uwe, eds., *Gefährten und Feinde des Menschen: Das Tier in der Lebenswelt des alten Israel* (Neukirchener Verlag, 1993) [*Gefährten und Feinde*].

Janzen, Waldemar, *Old Testament Ethics: A Paradigmatic Approach* (Westminster John Knox Press, 1994) [*Ethics*].

Jay, N., 'Sacrifice, Descent and the Patriarchs' (*VT* 38, 1988, 52–70).

Johnson, Aubrey R., *The Cultic Prophet in Ancient Israel* (University of Wales Press, 1944, rev. edn. 1962) [*Cultic Prophet*].

Johnson, Aubrey R., *The Cultic Prophet and Israel's Psalmody* (University of Wales Press, 1979) [*Cultic Prophet and Psalmody*].

Johnson, Aubrey R., *Sacral Kingship in Ancient Israel* (University of Wales Press, 1967) [*Sacral Kingship*].

Johnstone, William, 'The "Ten Commandments": Some Recent Interpretations' (*ET*, 100, 1988–89, 453–461) ['The "Ten Commandments"'].

Jones, Gwilym H., '"Holy War" and "Yahweh War"?' (*VT* 25, 1975, 642–658) ['"Holy War"'].

Jones, Richard G., 'New Occasions Teach New Duties?: 7. How Christians Actually Arrive at Ethical Decisions' (*ET* 105, 1993–94, 292–296, repr. in *New Occasions*, 85–96) ['Ethical Decisions'].

Jones, Richard G., *What To Do? Christians and Ethics* (Thinking Things Through 7, Epworth Press, 1999) [*What To Do?*].

KAISER, Otto, *Isaiah 1–12: A Commentary* (OTL, SCM Press, 1972; 2nd edn., completely rewritten, 1983).

Kaiser, Walter C., Jr., 'The Book of Leviticus' in *NIB* I.983–1191 ['Leviticus'].

Kaiser, Walter C., Jr., *Toward Old Testament Ethics* (Academie Books, 1983) [*Ethics*].

Kaufman, S. A., 'The Structure of the Deuteronomic Law' (*MAARAV* 1, 1979, 105–158) ['Deuteronomic Law'].

Keck, Leander E. *et al.*, eds., *The New Interpreter's Bible* (12 vols., Abingdon Press, 1994–) [*NIB*].

Keel, Othmar, *Das Böcklein in der Milch seiner Mutter und Verwandtes im Lichte eines altorientalischen Bildmotives* (OBO 33, Vandenhoeck & Ruprecht, 1980) [*Das Böcklein*].

Keeling, Michael, *The Foundations of Christian Ethics* (T&T Clark, 1990) [*Foundations*].

Kellermann, D., *'āshām* (*TDOT* I, rev. edn. 429–437).

Kidner, F. Derek, 'Old Testament Perspectives on War' (*EvQ* LVII, 1985, 99–112) ['War'].

Klein, Ralph W., *1 Samuel* (WBC 10, Word Books, 1983).

Knight, D. A., ed., *Ethics and Politics in the Hebrew Bible* (*Semeia* 66, Scholars Press, 1995) [*Ethics and Politics*].

Koch, Klaus, *chāṭā'* (*TDOT* IV, 309–319).

Koch, Klaus, 'Is There a Doctrine of Retribution in the Old Testament?' in Crenshaw, James L., ed., *Theodicy in the Old Testament* (Issues in Religion and Theology 4, SPCK/Fortress Press, 1983, 57–87) (German original 1955) ['Retribution'].

Koehler, Ludwig and Baumgartner, Walter, eds., revised by Baumgartner, Walter and Stamm, Johann Jakob, trans. and ed. under the supervision of Richardson, M. E. J., *The Hebrew and Aramaic Lexicon of the Old Testament* (4 vols., E. J. Brill, 1994–) [*HALOT*].

Koehler, Ludwig, *Old Testament Theology* (Lutterworth Press, 1957) [*Theology*].

Kornfeld, W., 'Reine und unreine Tiere im AT' (*Kairos* 7, 1965, 134–147).

Kramer, Phyllis Silverman, 'Jephthah's Daughter: A Thematic Approach to the Narrative as Seen in Selected Rabbinic Exegesis and in Artwork' in Brenner, Athalya, ed., *The Feminist Companion to the Bible (Second Series) 4. Judges* (Sheffield Academic Press, 1999, 67–89) ['Jephthah's Daughter'].

Kraus, Hans-Joachim, *Psalms 1–59* (Augsburg, 1988).

Kuschke, A., 'Arm und reich im Alten Testament mit besonderer Brücksichtigung der nachexilischen Zeit' (*ZAW* 57, 1939, 31–57) ['Arm und reich'].

LaBar, Martin, 'A Biblical Perspective on Nonhuman Organisms: Values, Moral Considerability, and Moral Agency' in Hargrove, Eugene C., ed., *Religion and Environmental Crisis* (University of Georgia Press, 1986) ['Biblical Perspective'].

LaCocque, André, *The Feminine Unconventional: Four Subversive Figures in Israel's Tradition* (OBT, Fortress Press, 1990) [*Feminine Unconventional*].

Laffey, Alice L., *An Introduction to the Old Testamment: A Feminist Perspective* (Fortress Press, 1988) [*Introduction*].

Lafont, Sophie, *Femmes, Droit et Justice dans l'Antiquité orientale: Contribution à l'étude du droit pénal au Proche-Orient ancien* (OBO 165, Editions Universitaires Fribourg Suisse/Vanderhoeck & Ruprecht, 1999) [*Femmes, Droit et Justice*].

Lapsley, Jacqueline E., *Can These Bones Live? The Problem of the Moral Self in the Book of Ezekiel* (BZAW 301, Walter de Gruyter, 2000) [*Moral Self*].

Larsson, Göran, *Bound for Freedom: The Book of Exodus in Jewish and Christian Traditions* (Hendrickson, 1999) [*Freedom*].

Leeb, Carolyn S., *Away from the Father's House: The Social Location of na'ar and na'arah in Ancient Israel* (JSOTSup 301, Sheffield Academic Press, 2000) [*Away from the Father's House*].

Lemche, Niels Peter, *Ancient Israel: A New History of Israelite Society* (Sheffield Academic Press, 1988) [*Ancient Israel*].

Lewis, H. D., *Philosophy of Religion* (Teach Yourself Books, English Universities Press, 1965).

Limburg, James, 'Human Rights in the Old Testament' in Müller, Alois and Greinacher, Norbert, eds., *The Church and the Rights of Man* (*Concilium* 124, Seabury Press/T&T Clark, 1979, 20–26) ['Human Rights'].

Lind, Millard, *Yahweh is a Warrior: The Theology of Warfare in Ancient Israel* (Herald Press, 1980).

Lindars, Barnabas, 'Imitation of God and Imitation of Christ' (*Theology* 76, 1973, 394–402) ['Imitation'].

Linzey, Andrew and Reagan, Tom, eds., *Animals and Christianity: A Book of Readings* (SPCK, 1989).

Linzey, Andrew and Yamamoto, Dorothy, eds., *Animals on the Agenda: Questions about Animals for Theology and Ethics* (SCM Press, 1998).

Linzey, Andrew, *Animal Theology* (SCM Press, 1994).

Linzey, Andrew, *Christianity and the Rights of Animals* (SPCK, 1987) [*Rights of Animals*].

Loader, J. A., 'Image and order: Old Testament perspectives on the ecological crisis' in the *11th Symposium of the Institute of Theological Research* (University of South Africa, 1987, 6–28).

Loades, Ann, ed., *Feminist Theology: A Reader* (SPCK/Westminster John Knox Press, 1990).

Loades, Ann, 'Feminist Interpretation' in Barton, John, ed., *The Cambridge Companion to Biblical Interpretation* (CUP, 1998, 81–94).

Loewenstamm, S., 'Tarbit and Neshek' (*JBL* 88, 1969, 78–80).

Lohfink, Norbert, *Das Hauptgebot. Eine Untersuchung literarischer Einleitungsfragen zu Dtn 5–11* (Analecta Biblica 20, Rome, 1963) [*Das Hauptgebot*].

Lohfink, Norbert, ed., *Gewalt und Gewaltloskeit im Alten Testament*, (Herder Verlag, 1983).

Lohfink, Norbert, *Great Themes from the Old Testament* (T&T Clark, 1982) [*Great Themes*].

Lohfink, Norbert, *Option for the Poor: The Basic Principles of Liberation Theology in the Light of the Bible* (Bibal Press, 1987).

Lohfink, Norbert, 'Poverty in the Laws of the Ancient Near East and of the Bible' (*TS* 52, 1991, 34–50) ['Poverty'].

Lohfink, Norbert, 'Die Schichten des Pentateuch und der Krieg' in Lohfink, Norbert, ed., *Gewalt und Gewaltloskeit im Alten Testament* (Herder Verlag, 1983, 51–110) ['Die Schichten'].

Longman III, Tremper, *The Book of Ecclesiastes* (NICOT, Eerdmans, 1998) [*Ecclesiastes*].

Longman III, Tremper and Reid, Daniel G., *God is a Warrior* (Zondervan/Paternoster Press, 1995).

Luke, K., 'Eye for Eye, Tooth for Tooth' (*Indian Theological Studies* 16, 1979) ['Eye for Eye'].

MCCARTER, P. Kyle, 'The River Ordeal in Israelite Literature' (*HTR*, 66, 1973, 403–412) ['River Ordeal'].

McCarter, P. Kyle, *I Samuel* (AB, Doubleday, 1980).

McCarter, P. Kyle, *II Samuel* (AB, Doubleday, 1984).

McDonagh, Sean, *The Greening of the Church* (Geoffrey Chapman, 1990) [*Greening*].

McDonald, J. I. H., *Biblical Interpretation and Christian Ethics* (CUP, 1993) [*Biblical Interpretation*].

Macintosh, A. A., *Hosea* (ICC, T&T Clark, 1997).

MacIntyre, Alasdair, *After Virtue: A Study of Moral Theory* (University of Notre Dame Press, 1981).

McKane, William, *Prophets and Wise Men* (SBT 44, SCM Press, 1965).

McKane, William, *Proverbs* (SCM Press, 1970).

McKeating, Henry, *Amos, Hosea, Micah* (CBC, CUP, 1971) [*Amos*].

McKeating, Henry, 'The Development of the Law on Homicide in Ancient Israel' (*VT* 25, 1975, 46–68) ['Homicide'].

McKeating, Henry, 'A Response to Dr Phillips by Henry McKeating' (*JSOT* 20, 1981, 25–26) ['Response'].

McKeating, Henry, 'Sanctions against Adultery in Ancient Israelite Society, with some Reflections on Methodology in the Study of Old Testament Ethics' (*JSOT* 11, 1979, 57–72) ['Sanctions against Adultery'].

McKim, Donald K., ed., *The Authoritative Word: Essays on The Nature of Scripture* (Eerdmans, 1983) [*Authoritative Word*].

Maclagan, W. G., *The Theological Frontier of Ethics* (Allen & Unwin, 1961) [*Frontier of Ethics*].

McLean, B. Hudson, *The Cursed Christ* (JSNTSup 126, Sheffield Academic Press, 1996).

McNutt, Paula M., *Reconstructing the Society of Ancient Israel* (SPCK/Westminster John Knox Press, 1999) [*Ancient Israel*].

Macquarrie, John, 'Creation and Environment. The Inaugural Lecture at Oxford University' (*ET* 83, 1971–72, 4–9).

Macquarrie, John, ed., *Dictionary of Christian Ethics* (SCM Press, 1967) [*DCE*].

Macquarrie, John and Childress, James, eds., *A New Dictionary of Christian Ethics* (SCM Press, 1986) [*NDCE*].

MALINA, Bruce J., *Christian Origins and Cultural Anthropology: Practical Models for Biblical Interpretation* (John Knox Press, 1986) [*Christian Origins*].

Malina, Bruce J. and Neyrey, Jerome H., *Honor and Shame in Luke-Acts: Models for Interpretation* (Hendrickson, 1991) [*Honor and Shame*].

Maloney, Robert P., 'Usury and Restrictions on Interest-Taking in the Ancient Near East' (*CBQ* 36, 1974, 1–20) ['Usury'].

Márkus, Gilbert, 'The End of Celtic Christianity' (*Epworth Review*, 24, 1997, 45–55) ['Celtic Christianity']

Mauchline, John, *1 and 2 Samuel* (NCBC, Oliphants, 1971).

Mayer, G., *ydh* (*TDOT* V, 431–443).

Mayes, A. D. H., *Deuteronomy* (NCBC, Oliphants, 1979).

Mays, James Luther, 'Justice: Perspectives from the Prophetic Tradition' (*Interpretation* 37, 1983, 5–17) ['Justice'].

Mays, James L., *Amos* (OTL, SCM Press, 1969).

Meek, Donald E., *The Quest for Celtic Christianity* (Handsel Press, 2000) [*Celtic Christianity*].

Metz, Johannes, *Theology of the World* (Herder & Herder, 1969).

Meyers, Carol L., 'Gender Roles and Genesis 3.16 Revisited' in Brenner, Athalya, ed., *The Feminist Companion to the Bible 2. Genesis* (Sheffield Academic Press, 1993, 118–145) ['Gender Roles'].

Meyers, Carol L., *Discovering Eve: Ancient Israelite Women in Context* (OUP, 1988).

Meyers, Carol, 'The Family in Early Israel' in Perdue, Leo G., Blenkinsopp, Joseph, Collins, John J. and Meyers, Carol, *Families in Ancient Israel* (Westminster John Knox Press, 1997, 1–47) ['The Family'].

Meyers, Carol, 'Hannah and her Sacrifice: Reclaiming Female Agency' in Brenner, Athalya, ed., *The Feminist Companion to the Bible 5. Samuel and Kings* (Sheffield Academic Press, 1994, 93–104) ['Hannah'].

Meyers, Carol L., 'The Roots of Restriction: Women in Early Israel' in Gottwald, Norman K., ed., *The Bible and Liberation: Political and Social Hermeneutics* (Orbis Books, 1983, 289–306) ['Roots of Restriction'].

Milgrom, Jacob, 'The Biblical Diet Laws as an Ethical System' (*Interpretation* 17, 1963, 288–301).

Milgrom, Jacob, *Numbers* (JPS Commentary, Jewish Publication Society, 1990).

Miller, Patrick D., Hanson, P. D. and McBride, S. D., eds., *Ancient Israelite Religion: Essays in Honor of Frank Moore Cross* (Fortress Press, 1987).

Miller, Patrick D., 'God the Warrior: A Problem in Biblical Interpretation and Apologetics' (*Interpretation* 19, 1965, 39–46).

Miller, Patrick D., 'The Place of the Decalogue in the Old Testament and Its Law' (*Interpretation* 43, 1989, 229–242) ['The Decalogue'].

Milne, Pamela J., 'The Patriarchal Stamp of Scripture: The Implications of Structuralist Analyses for Feminist Hermeneutics' in Brenner, Athalya, ed., *The Feminist Companion to the Bible 2. Genesis* (Sheffield Academic Press, 1993, 147–172) ['Patriarchal Stamp'].

Moberly, Walter, 'The Use of Scripture in Contemporary Debate about Homosexuality' (*Theology* CIII, No. 814, 2000, 251–258) ['Use of Scripture'].

Morgan, D. F., *Wisdom in the Old Testament Tradition* (Basil Blackwell, 1981) [*Wisdom*].

Moule, C. F. D., *Man and Nature in the New Testament: some reflections on Biblical Ecology* (1964 Ethel M. Wood lecture, Athlone Press, 1964) [*Man and Nature*].

Mowinckel, Sigmund, *Psalmenstudien III: Kultprophetie und prophetische Psalmen* (S.N.V.A.O. II, 1922).

Mowinckel, Sigmund, *The Psalms in Israel's Worship* (2 vols., Basil Blackwell, 1962) [*Psalms*].

Muddiman, J. and G., *Women, The Bible and the Priesthood* (MOW paper, 1984) [*Women*].

Müllner, Ilse, 'Lethal Differences: Sexual Violence and Violence against Others in Judges 19' in Brenner, Athalya, ed., *The Feminist Companion to the Bible (Second Series) 4. Judges* (Sheffield Academic Press, 1999), 126–142 ['Lethal Differences'].

Murray, Robert, *The Cosmic Covenant: Biblical Themes of Justice, Peace and the Integrity of Creation* (Heythrop Monographs 7, Sheed & Ward, 1992) [*Cosmic Covenant*].

Murray, Robert, 'Prophecy and Cult' in Coggins, Richard J., Phillips, Anthony and Knibb, Michael, eds. *Israel's Prophetic Tradition*, 200–216.

NEL, P. J., *The Structure and Ethos of the Wisdom Admonitions in Proverbs* (*BZAW* 158, de Gruyter, 1982) [*Structure*].

Neufeld, Edward, 'The Prohibition against Loans and Interest in the Ancient Hebrew Laws' (*HUCA* 26, 1955, 398–399) ['Prohibition against Loans'].

Neufeld, Edward, 'The Rate of Interest and the Text of Nehemiah 5.11' (*JQR* 44, 1953–54, 194–204) ['Rate of Interest'].

Neusner, Jacob, Levine, Baruch and Frerichs, Ernest, eds., *Judaic Perspectives on Ancient Israel* (Fortress Press, 1987).

Neyrey, Jerome H., *Honor and Shame in the Gospel of Matthew* (Westminster John Knox Press, 1998) [*Honor and Shame*].

Nicholson Ernest W., *God and His People: Covenant and Theology in the Old Testament* (Clarendon Press, 1986) [*God and His People*].

Niditch, Susan, *War in the Hebrew Bible: A Study in the Ethics of Violence* (OUP, 1993) [*War*].

Nielsen, Eduard, *The Ten Commandments in New Perspective* (SCM Press, 1968) [*The Ten Commandments*].

Nineham, Dennis, *Christianity Medieval and Modern* (SCM Press, 1993).

Nineham, Dennis, *The Use and Abuse of the Bible: A Study of the Bible in an Age of Rapid Cultural Change* (Macmillan, 1976) [*Use and Abuse*].

Noth, Martin, *Exodus: A Commentary* (OTL, SCM Press, 1962).

Noth, Martin, *The History of Israel* (SCM Press, 1958) [*History*].

Noth, Martin, *Leviticus* (OTL, SCM Press, 1965, rev. edn. 1977).

OGDEN, Graham, *Qoheleth* (Readings – A New Biblical Commentary, Sheffield Academic Press, 1987).

Ogletree, Thomas W., *The Use of the Bible in Christian Ethics* (Fortress Press, 1983) [*Use of the Bible*].

Olyan, Saul M., 'Honor, Shame, and Covenant Relations in Ancient Israel and Its Environment' (*JBL* 115, 1996, 201–218) ['Honor, Shame'].

Osborn, Lawrence, *Guardians of Creation: Nature in Theology and the Christian Life* (Apollos, 1993) [*Guardians*].

Oswalt, John N., *The Book of Isaiah: Chapters 1–39* (NICOT, Eerdmans, 1986) [*Isaiah 1–39*].

Oswalt, John N., *The Book of Isaiah: Chapters 40–66* (NICOT, Eerdmans, 1998) [*Isaiah 40–66*].

Otto, Eckart, 'Forschungsgeschichte der Entwürfe einer Ethik im Alten Testament' (*VF* 36/1, 1991, 3–37) ['Entwürfe'].

Otto, Eckart, 'Of Aims and Methods in Hebrew Bible Ethics' (*Semeia* 66, Scholars Press, 1995), 161–172 ['Aims and Methods'].

Otto, Eckart, *Theologische Ethik des Alten Testaments* (Kohlhammer Verlag, 1994) [*Theologische Ethik*].

Otto, Rudolf, *The Idea of the Holy* (OUP, 1924) [*The Holy*].

Otwell, J. H., *And Sarah Laughed: The Status of Women in the Old Testament* (Fortress Press, 1977) [*And Sarah Laughed*].

PAILIN, David, *Groundwork of Philosophy of Religion* (Epworth Press, 1986) [*Groundwork*].

Palmer, Martin, 'Ecology – Prophetic or Pathetic?' (*ET* 106, 1994–95, 100–104), reprinted in Rodd, Cyril S., ed., *New Occasions Teach New Duties?* (T&T Clark, 1995, 173–185) ['Ecology'].

Paris, Peter J., 'An Ethicist's Concerns about Biblical Ethics' (*Semeia* 66, Scholars Press, 1995, 173–179) ['Ethicist's Concerns'].

Patrick, Dale, *Old Testament Law* (John Knox Press, 1985/SCM Press, 1986).

Paul, S. M., *Studies in the Book of the Covenant in the Light of Cuneiform and Biblical Law* (E. J. Brill, 1970) [*Book of the Covenant*].

Pedersen, Johs., *Israel: Its Life and Culture I-II* (OUP/Povl Branner, 1926), *III-IV* (OUP/Povl Branner, 1940).

Perdue, Leo G., Blenkinsopp, Joseph, Collins, John J. and Meyers, Carol, *Families in Ancient Israel* (Westminster John Knox Press, 1997) [*Families*].

Peritz, I. J., 'Women in the Ancient Hebrew Cult' (*JBL* 17, 1898, 111–148) ['Women'].

Phillips, Anthony, *Ancient Israel's Criminal Law: A New Approach to the Decalogue* (Basil Blackwell, 1970) [*Israel's Criminal Law*].

Phillips, Anthony, 'Another Look at Adultery' (*JSOT* 20, 1981, 3–25).

Phillips, Anthony, 'Another Look at Murder' (*JJS* 28, 1977, 105–126) ['Murder'].

Phillips, Anthony, *Deuteronomy* (CBC, CUP, 1973).

Phillips, Anthony, 'NEBALAH – a term for serious disorderly and unruly conduct' (*VT* 25, 1975, 237–242).

Phillips, Anthony, 'Prophecy and Law' in Coggins, Richard J., Phillips, Anthony and Knibb, Michael, eds., *Israel's Prophetic Tradition*, (CUP, 1982, 217–232).

Philo, *On the Virtues* (trans. F. H. Colson, *Philo*, Loeb Classical Library, Harvard University Press, Vol. VIII, 1939, 158–305) [*Virt.* (refs. to the sections)]

Pleins, J. David, 'Poverty in the Social World of the Wise' (*JSOT* 37, 1987, 61–78) ['Poverty'].

Pons, Jacques, *L'Oppression dans l'Ancien Testament* (Letouzey et Ané, 1981) [*L'Oppression*].

Pope, Marvin H., *Song of Songs* (AB, Doubleday, 1977) [*Song*].

Porteous, Norman W., 'Care of the Poor in the Old Testament' in Porteous, Norman W., *Living the Mystery* (OUP, 1967, 143–155) ['Care of the Poor'].

Porteous, Norman W., *Living the Mystery* (OUP, 1967).

Porter, J. R., *Leviticus* (CBC, CUP, 1976).

Pressler, Carolyn, *The View of Women Found in the Deuteronomic Family Laws* (BZAW 216, de Gruyter, 1993) [*The View of Women*].

Pressler, Carolyn, 'Sexual Violence and Deuteronomic Law' in Brenner, Athalya, ed., *A Feminist Companion to the Bible 6. Exodus to Deuteronomy* (Sheffield Academic Press, 1994, 102–112) ['Sexual Violence'].

Preston, R. H., 'From the Bible to the Modern World: A Problem for Ecumenical Ethics' (*BJRL* 59, 1976–77, 164–187) ['Bible to Modern World').

Preuss, Horst Dietrich, *Old Testament Theology*, Vol. I (Westminster John Knox Press/T&T Clark, 1995), Vol. II (Westminster John Knox Press/T&T Clark, 1996) [*Theology*].

Pritchard, James B., ed., *Ancient Near Eastern Texts Relating to the Old Testament* (Princeton University Press, 1950, 1969) [*ANET*].

REGENSTEIN, Lewis G., *Replenish the Earth: A History of Organized Religion's Treatment of Animals and Nature – Including the Bible's Message of Conservation and Kindness to Animals* (SCM Press, 1991) [*Replenish the Earth*].

Reimer, David J., *ṣdq* (*NIDOTTE* 3, 744–769).

Reventlow, Henning Graf, 'The Biblical and Classical Traditions of "Just War"' in Reventlow, Henning Graf, Hoffman, Yair and Uffenheimer, Benjamin, eds., *Politics and Theopolitics in the Bible and Postbiblical Literature* (JSOTSup 171, Sheffield Academic Press, 1994, 160–175) ['Just War'].

Reventlow, Henning Graf, Hoffman, Yair and Uffenheimer, Benjamin, eds., *Politics and Theopolitics in the Bible and Postbiblical Literature* (JSOTSup 171, Sheffield Academic Press, 1994).

Richardson, Alan, *Genesis 1–11* (TBC, SCM Press, 1953).

Ringgren, Helmer, *Israelite Religion* (SPCK, 1966).

Ringgren, Helmer, *bʿr* (*TDOT* II, 201–205).

Ringgren, Helmer, *ṭāmēʾ* (*TDOT* V, 331–332).

Robinson, H. Wheeler, *The Old Testament Doctrine of Man* (T&T Clark, 4th edn. 1958) [*Doctrine of Man*].

Robinson, H. Wheeler, *Inspiration and Revelation in the Old Testament* (Clarendon Press, 1946) [*Inspiration*].

Rodd, C. S., ed., *New Occasions Teach New Duties? Christian Ethics for Today* (T&T Clark, 1995) [*New Occasions*].

Rodd, C. S., 'New Occasions Teach New Duties? 1. The Use of the Old Testament in Christian Ethics' (*ET* 105, 1993–94, 100–106, reprinted in Rodd, Cyril S., ed., *New Occasions*, 5–19) ['Use of the OT'].

Rodd, C. S., 'Shall not the judge of all the earth do what is just? (Gen 18^{25})' (*ET* 83, 1971–72, 137–139) ['(Gen 18^{25})'].

Rogerson, John W., *Anthropology and the Old Testament* (Basil Blackwell, 1978, repr. Sheffield Academic Press, 1984) [*Anthropology*].

Rogerson, John W., ed., *Beginning Old Testament Study* (SPCK, 1983, rev. edn. 1998).

Rogerson, John W., 'Christian Morality and the Old Testament' (*HeyJ* 36, 1995, 422–430) ['Christian Morality'].

Rogerson, John W., 'The Family and Structures of Grace in the Old Testament' in Barton, Stephen C., ed., *The Family In Theological Perspective* (T&T Clark, 1996, 25–42) ['Family'].

Rogerson, John W., 'The Old Testament and Social and Moral Questions' (*The Modern Churchman* 25, 1982, 28–35) ['Social and Moral Questions'].

Rogerson, John W., 'The Old Testament View of Nature: Some Preliminary Questions' (*OTS* 20, 1977, 67–84) ['View of Nature'].

Rogerson, John W., 'Sacrifice in the Old Testament: Problems of Method and Approach' in Bourdillon, M. F. C. and Fortes, Meyer, eds., *Sacrifice* (Academic Press, 1980) ['Sacrifice'].

Rogerson, John W., 'Using the Bible in the Debate about Abortion' in Channing, J. H., ed., *Abortion and the Sanctity of Human Life* (Paternoster Press, 1985, 77–92) ['Abortion'].

Rogerson, John W., 'What was the Meaning of Animal Sacrifice?' in Linzey, Andrew and Yamamoto, Dorothy, eds., *Animals on the Agenda*, SCM Press, 1998, 8–12) ['Animal Sacrifice'].

Rolston III, Holmes, 'The Bible and Ecology' (*Interpretation* 50, 1996, 16–26) ['Bible and Ecology'].

Rost, Leonhard, *The Succession to the Throne of David* (trans. Rutter, Michael D. and Gunn, David M., Introduction by Ball, Edward (Almond Press, 1982).

Roth, Wolfgang M. W., *NBL* (*VT* 10, 1960, 394–409).

Rowley, H. H., 'Sacrifice and Morality: A Rejoinder' (*ET* 70, 1958–59, 341–342) ['A Rejoinder'].

Rowley, H. H., *The Unity of the Bible* (1953).

Russell, Letty M., ed., *Feminist Interpretation of the Bible* (Basil Blackwell, 1985).

SAGGS, H. W. F., *The Encounter with the Divine in Mesopotamia and Israel* (Athlone Press, 1978) [*Encounter with the Divine*].

Saggs, H. W. F., *The Greatness that was Babylon: A Survey of the Ancient Civiliization of the Tigris-Euphrates Valley* (Great Civilizations Series, Sidgwick & Jackson, 1962, fully revised and updated, 1988) [*Babylon*].

Sakenfeld, Katharine Doob, 'Feminist Uses of Biblical Materials' in Russell, Letty M., *Feminist Interpretation of the Bible* (Basil Blackwell, 1985, 55–64) ['Feminist Uses'].

Sanders, E. P., *Paul and Palestinian Judaism* (SCM Press, 1977).

Schmidt, Hans, *Das Gebet der Angeklagten im Alten Testament* (Töpelmann, 1928) [*Gebet*].

Schmidt, Hans, *Die Psalmen* (HAT 15, J. C. B. Mohr [Paul Siebeck], 1934).

Schochet, Elijah Judah, *Animal Life in Jewish Tradition: Attitudes and Relationships* (Ktav, 1984) [*Animal Life*].

Scholz, Susanne, 'Through Whose Eyes? A "Right" Reading of Genesis 34' in Brenner, Athalya, ed., *A Feminist Companion to the Bible (Second Series) 1. Genesis* (Sheffield Academic Press, 1998, 150–171).

Scholz, Susanne, 'Was it Really Rape in Genesis 34? Biblical Scholarship as a Reflection of Cultural Assumptions' in Washington, Harold C., Graham, Susan Lochrie and Thimmes, Pamela, eds., *Escaping Eden: New Feminist Perspectives on the Bible* (Sheffield Academic Press, 1998) ['Rape'].

Schreiner, J., ed., W*ort, Lied und Gottesspruch: Beiträge zu Psalmen und Propheten. Festschrift für Joseph Ziegler* (2 vols., Echter Verlag, 1972) [*Wort*].

Schwantes, Milton, *Das Recht der Armen* (Lang, 1977).

Seebass, Horst, *bôsh* (*TDOT* II, 50–60).

Segal, Ben-Zion, ed., *The Ten Commandments in History and Tradition* (The Magnes Press, 1990).

Seow, C. L., 'Hosts, Lord of' in *ABD* 3.304–307 ['Lord of Hosts'].

Setel, T. Drorah, 'Prophets and Pornography: Female Sexual Imagery in Hosea' in Russell, Letty M., *Feminist Interpretation of the Bible* (Basil Blackwell, 1985, 86–93).

Sherlock, Charles, 'The Meaning of *HRM* in the Old Testament' (*Colloquium* 14, 1982, 13–24) [*HRM*].

Simkins, Ronald A., *Creator and Creation: Nature in the Worldview of Ancient Israel* (Hendrickson, 1994).

Simkins, Ronald A., 'Gender Construction in the Yahwist Creation Myth' in Brenner, Athalya, ed., *A Feminist Companion to the Bible (Second Series) 1. Genesis* (Sheffield Academic Press, 1998, 32–51) ['Gender Construction'].

Skinner, John, *Genesis* (ICC, T&T Clark, 1910).

Smart, Ninian, *The Philosophy of Religion* (Random House, 1970) [*Philosophy of Religion*].

Smith, Carol, 'Delilah: A Suitable Case for (Feminist) Treatment?' in Brenner, Athalya, ed., *The Feminist Companion to the Bible (Second Series) 4. Judges* (Sheffield Academic Press, 1999, 93–116) ['Delilah'].

Smith, Gary V., 'Job IV 12–21: Is it Eliphaz's Vision?' (*VT* 40, 1990, 453–463) ['Eliphaz's Vision?'].

Smith, Morton and Hoffmann, R. Joseph, *What the Bible Really Says* (Prometheus Books, 1989).

Snaith, Norman H., *Leviticus and Numbers* (NCBC, Nelson, 1967).

Snaith, Norman H., *The Distinctive Ideas of the Old Testament* (Epworth Press, 1944) [*Distinctive Ideas*].

Soggin, J. Alberto, *Judges*, (OTL, SCM Press, 1981).

Sonsino, Rifat, *Motive Clauses in Hebrew Law* (SBLDiss 45, Scholars Press, 1980) [*Motive Clauses*].

Speiser, E. A., *Genesis* (AB, Doubleday, 1964).

Spriggs, D. G., *Two Old Testament Theologies* (SBT, Second Series, 30, SCM Press, 1974) [*Two Theologies*].

Stamm, Johann Jakob and Andrew, Maurice Edward, *The Ten Commandments in Recent Research* (SBT, Second Series 2, SCM Press, 1967) [*The Ten Commandments*].

Steingrimsson, S., *zmm* etc. (*TDOT* IV, 89–90).

Stronhal, Eugen, *Life in Ancient Egypt* (CUP, 1992) [*Ancient Egypt*].

Swartley, Willard M., *Slavery, Sabbath, War, and Women* (Herald Press, 1983) [*Slavery*].

TERRIEN, Samuel, *Till the Heart Sings: A Biblical Theology of Manhood and Womanhood* (Fortress Press, 1985).

Thomas, Keith, *Man and the Natural World: Changing Attitudes in England 1500–1800* (Penguin Books, 1984) [*Natural World*].

Thompson, Thomas L., *The Bible in History: How Writers Create a Past* (Jonathan Cape, 1999) [*Bible in History*].

Thomson, Anne, *Critical Reasoning in Ethics: A Practical Introduction* (Routledge, 1999).

Thrall, Margaret E., *The Ordination of Women to the Priesthood: A Study of the Biblical Evidence* (London, 1958) [*Ordination of Women*].

Townsend, T. P., 'The Poor in Wisdom Literature' (*Bible Bhashyan* 14, 1988, 5–25).

Toy, Crawford H., *The Book of Proverbs* (ICC, T&T Clark, 1899) [*Proverbs*].

Trenchard, Warren C., *Ben Sira's View of Women: A Literary Analysis* (Brown Judaic Studies 38, Scholars Press, 1982).

Trible, Phyllis, 'Bringing Miriam out of the Shadows' (*Bible Review* 5, 1989, 170–190), reprinted in Brenner, Athalya, *A Feminist Companion to Exodus and Deuteronomy* (Sheffield Academic Press, 1994, 166–186).

Trible, Phyllis, 'Depatriarchalizing in Biblical Interpretation' (*JAAR* 41, 1973, 30–48) ['Depatriarchalizing'].

Trible, Phyllis, 'Feminist Hermeneutics and Biblical Studies' in Loades, Ann, ed., *Feminist Theology: A Reader* (SPCK/ Westminster John Knox Press, 1990) ['Feminist Hermeneutics'].

Trible, Phyllis, *God and the Rhetoric of Sexuality* (OBT, Fortress Press, 1987) [*Rhetoric*].

Trible, Phyllis, *Texts of Terror: Literary-Feminist Readings of Biblical Narratives* (OBT, Fortress Press, 1984).

Trible, Phyllis, 'Woman in the OT' in *IDBSup*, 963–966.

Turner, Frederick, *Beyond Geography: The Western Spirit against the Wilderness* (Viking, 1980).

VALLER, Shulamit, 'The Story of Jephthah's Daughter in the Midrash' in Brenner, Athalya, ed., *The Feminist Companion to the Bible (Second Series) 4. Judges* (Sheffield Academic Press, 1999, 48–66) ['Jephthah's Daughter'].

Van der Toorn, K., *Sin and Sanction in Israel and Mesopotamia: A Comparative Study* (Van Gorcum, 1985) [*Sin and Sanction*].

Van Houten, Christiana, *The Alien in Israelite Law* (JSOTSup 107, Sheffield Academic Press, 1991) [*The Alien*].

VanGemeren, Willem A., ed., *New International Dictionary of Old Testament Theology and Exegesis* (5 vols., Zondervan/Paternoster Press, 1996/1997) [*NIDOTTE*].

Vardy, Peter and Grosch, Paul, *The Puzzle of Ethics* (Fount, 1994).

Vogels, Walter, 'Biblical Theology for the "Haves" and the "Have-nots"' (*Science et Esprit* XXXIX, 1987, 193–210) ['"Haves" and "Have-nots"'].

Von Rad, Gerhard, 'The Beginnings of Historical Writing in Ancient Israel' in *The Problem of the Hexateuch and Other Essays* (trans. Dicken, E. W. Trueman, Introduction by Porteous, Norman W., (Oliver & Boyd, 1966, 166–204) ['Historical Writing'].

Von Rad, Gerhard, *Genesis* (OTL, SCM Press, 1961).

Von Rad, Gerhard, *Deuteronomy* (OTL, SCM Press, 1966).

Von Rad, Gerhard, *Holy War in Ancient Israel* (trans. and ed. Dawn, Marva J., Introduction by Ollenburger, Ben C., Bibliography by Sanderson, Judith E., Eerdmans, 1991) [*Holy War*].

Von Rad, Gerhard, 'The Joseph Narrative and Ancient Wisdom' in *The Problem of the Hexateuch and Other Essays*, 292–300 ['Joseph Narrative'].

Von Rad, Gerhard, *Old Testament Theology*, Vol. I (Oliver & Boyd, 1962), Vol. II (Oliver & Boyd, 1965) [*Theology*].

Von Rad, Gerhard, *The Problem of the Hexateuch and Other Essays* (trans. Dicken, E. W. Trueman, Introduction by Porteous, Norman W., Oliver & Boyd, 1966).

Von Rad, Gerhard, 'Some Aspects of the Old Testament World-View' in *The Problem of the Hexateuch and Other Essays*, 144–165 ['Some Aspects'].

Von Rad, Gerhard, *Studies in Deuteronomy* (SBT 9, SCM Press, 1953).

Von Rad, Gerhard, 'The Theological Problem of the Old Testament Doctrine of Creation' in *The Problem of the Hexateuch and Other Essays*, 131–143 ['Doctrine of Creation'].

Von Rad, Gerhard, *Wisdom in Israel* (SCM Press, 1972) [*Wisdom*].

Von Waldow, H. Eberhard, 'The Concept of War in the Old Testament' (*HBT* 6, 1984, 27–48) ['War'].

Vriezen, Th.C., *An Outline of Old Testament Theology* (Basil Blackwell, 1958) [*Theology*].

WALLIS, G., *chāmadh* (*TDOT* IV, 452–461).

Washington, Harold C., Graham, Susan Lochrie and Thimmes, Pamela, eds., *Escaping Eden: New Feminist Perspectives on the Bible* (Sheffield Academic Press, 1998).

Watts, James H., *Reading Law: The Rhetorical Shaping of the Pentateuch* (The Biblical Seminar 59, Sheffield Academic Press, 1999).

Watts, John D. W., *Isaiah 34–66* (WBC 25, Word Books, 1987).

Weeks, Stuart, *Early Israelite Wisdom* (Clarendon Press, 1994) [*Wisdom*].

Weinfeld, Moshe, 'The Decalogue: Its Significance, Uniqueness, and Place in Israel's Tradition' in Firmage, Edwin B., Weiss, Bernard G., Welch, John W., eds., *Religion and Law: Biblical-Judaic and Islamic Perspectives* (Eisenbrauns, 1990, 3–47) ['The Decalogue'].

Weinfeld, Moshe, *Deuteronomy and the Deuteronomic School* (Oxford, 1972) [*Deuteronomic School*].

Weinfeld, Moshe, 'The Uniqueness of the Decalogue' in Ben-Zion Segal, ed., *The Ten Commandments in History and Tradition* (The Magnes Press, 1990).

Weir, J. Emmette, 'The Poor are Powerless' (*ET* 100, 1988–89, 13–15).

Wenham, G. J., *The Book of Leviticus* (NICOT, Eerdmans, 1979).

Wenham, G. J., 'The Gap between Law and Ethics in the Bible' (*JJS* 48, 1997, 17–29) ['Law and Ethics'].

Westbrook, Raymond, 'Adultery in Ancient Near Eastern Law' (*RB* 97, 1990, 542–580) ['Adultery'].

Westbrook, Raymond, 'Punishments and Crimes' in *ABD* 5.546–556 ['Punishments'].

Westermann, Claus, *Elements of Old Testament Theology* (John Knox Press, 1982) [*Elements*].

Westermann, Claus, *Genesis 1–11* (trans. Scullion, John J., Augsburg/ SPCK, 1984).

Westermann, Claus, *Genesis 12–36* (trans. John J. Scullion, Augsburg, 1985/SPCK, 1986).

Westermann, Claus, *Isaiah 40–66* (OTL, SCM Press, 1969).

Westermann, Claus, *The Structure of the Book of Job: A Form-critical Analysis* (Fortress Press, 1981) [*Structure of Job*].

White, Jr., Lynn, 'The Historical Roots of Our Ecological Crisis' (*Science*, 155, No. 3767, 1967, 1203–1207) ['Historical Roots'].

Whitelam, Keith W., *The Just King: Monarchical Judicial Authority in Ancient Israel* (JSOTSup 12, Sheffield Academic Press, 1979) [*Just King*].

Whybray, R. N., *The Intellectual Tradition in the Old Testament* (BZAW 135, de Gruyter, 1974) [*Intellectual Tradition*].

Whybray, R. N., *Isaiah 40–66* (NCBC, Oliphants, 1975).

Whybray, R. N., 'Poverty, Wealth, and Point of View in Proverbs' (*ET* 100, 1988–89, 332–336) ['Poverty'].

Whybray, R. N., 'Prophecy and Wisdom' in Coggins, Richard J., Phillips, Anthony and Knibb, Michael, eds., *Israel's Prophetic Tradition* (CUP, 1983, 181–199).

Whybray, R. N., *The Succession Narrative: A Study of II Sam. 9–20 and I Kings 1 and 2* (SBT, 2nd series, 9, SCM Press, 1968) [*Succession Narrative*].

Whybray, R. N., *Wealth and Poverty in the Book of Proverbs* (JSOTSup 99, Sheffield Academic Press, 1990) [*Wealth and Poverty*].

Wilkinson, Alan, *The Church of England and the First World War* (SPCK, 1979) [*First World War*].

Wilkinson, Alan, *Dissent or Conform? Peace and the English Churches 1900–1945* (SCM Press, 1986) [*Dissent or Conform?*].

Williamson, H. G. M., *Ezra, Nehemiah* (WBC 16, Word Books, 1985).

Wilms, Franz-Elmar, *Das Tier: Mitgeschöpf, Gott oder Dämon* (EHS.T 306, Lang, 1987) [*Das Tier*].

Wilson, Robert R., 'Sources and Methods in the Study of Ancient Israelite Ethics' (*Semeia* 66, Scholars Press, 1995, 55–63) ['Sources and Methods'].

Wittenberg, Gunther, 'The Tenth Commandment in the Old Testament' (*JTSoA*, 22, 1978, 3–17) ['The Tenth Commandment'].

Wogaman, J. Philip, *Christian Ethics: A Historical Introduction* (Westminster John Knox Press, 1993).

Wolff, Hans Walter, *Anthropology of the Old Testament* (SCM Press, 1974) [*Anthropology*].

Wolff, Hans Walter, 'Erkenntnis Gottes im Alten Testament' (*EvTh* 15, 1955, 426–431) ['Erkenntnis'].

Wolff, Hans Walter, '"Wissen um Gott" bei Hosea als Urform von Theologie' (*EvTh* 12, 1952–53, 533–554).

Wright, Christopher J. H., *Deuteronomy* (NIBC, Hendrickson, 1996).

Wright, Christopher J. H., 'The Ethical Authority of the Old Testament: A Survey of Approaches' (*TynB* 43, 1992, 101–120, 203–231) ['Ethical Authority'].

Wright, Christopher J. H., 'Ethical Decisions in the Old Testament' (*EuroJTh* 12, 1992, 123–140) ['Ethical Decisions'].

Wright, Christopher J. H., *God's People in God's Land: Family, Land and Property in the Old Testament* (Eerdmans, 1990) [*God's People*].

Wright, Christopher J. H., *Living as the People of God: The Relevance of Old Testament Ethics* (IVP, 1983) [*People of God*].

Wright, David P., *The Disposal of Impurity* (SBLDiss 101, Scholars Press, 1987) [*Disposal*].

Wright, David P., Freedman, David Noel and Hurvitz, Avi, *Pomegranates and Golden Bells* (Eisenbrauns, 1995, 341–362).

YARON, R., 'The Goring Ox in Near Eastern Laws' (*Israel Law Review* 1, 1966, 396–406) ['The Goring Ox'].

ZIMMERLI, Walther, *Ezekiel*, 2 vols. (Hermeneia, Fortress Press, 1979, 1983).

Zimmerli, Walther, *Old Testament Theology in Outline* (T&T Clark, 1978) [*Theology*].

Zimmerli, Walther, 'Visionary Experience in Jeremiah', in Coggins, Richard J., Phillips, Anthony and Knibb, Michael, eds. *Israel's Prophetic Tradition* (CUP, 1982, 95–118).

Zimmerli, Walther, *Die Weltlichkeit des Alten Testaments* (Vandenhoeck & Ruprecht, 1971) [*Die Weltlichkeit*].

Zimmerli Walther, 'Zwillingspsalmen' in Schreiner, J., ed., *Wort*, II (Echter Verlag, 1972, 105–113).

INDEX OF SUBJECTS

INDEX OF MODERN AUTHORS

References only in footnotes in italic.

INDEX OF BIBLICAL REFERENCES

Hebrew verse numbering

Apocrypha and Pseudepigapha

New Testament